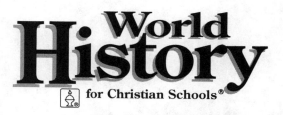

for Christian Schools®

Second Edition

World History
for Christian Schools®
Second Edition

David A. Fisher

Bob Jones University Press
Greenville, South Carolina 29614

WORLD HISTORY for Christian Schools®
Second Edition

David A. Fisher, Ph.D.

Produced in cooperation with the Bob Jones University Department of History of the College of Arts and Science, the School of Religion, and Bob Jones Academy.

for Christian Schools is a registered
trademark of Bob Jones University Press.

© 1994, 1999 Bob Jones University Press
Greenville, South Carolina 29614
First Edition © 1984 Bob Jones University Press

Printed in the United States of America
All rights reserved

ISBN 1-59166-650-3

15 14 13 12 11 10 9 8 7 6 5 4 3 2 1

Contents

List of Maps

To the Student: How to Use This Book

Units and Chapters

WORLD HISTORY for Christian Schools is divided into seven units. The main theme of each unit is presented in a brief summary and illustrated by a two-page color picture. Each unit in turn contains from two to five chapters. These begin with a brief introduction to the period to be studied. The chapters are divided into main sections and subsections. For instance, one of the main sections in Chapter 1 is **Eden: The Place of Beginnings.** The first subsection under this is **Creation.** Often subsections are further divided to help you quickly identify the major topics of discussion.

Section Reviews

At the end of each major section of a chapter is a set of section review questions. These are primarily recall questions designed to test your understanding of the material you have just read. There are normally three to four sets of section review questions in each chapter.

Chapter Reviews

Each chapter ends with a review section. These sections should help you study the chapter. The Chapter Review is divided into three parts: terms, recall questions, and thought questions.

1. Key terms are listed in the order in which they appear in the text. They are grouped under three headings: **Can You Explain? Can You Identify?** and **Can You Locate?** You should be able to define the words in the first list, identify the terms or dates in the second list (answering the questions Who? Why? Where? When? How?), and locate on a map and state the importance of the places in the third list. With the exception of dates, all terms found in **Can You Explain?** and **Can You Identify?** are in **boldface** type in the text.
2. The purpose of the questions from **How Much Do You Remember?** is to help you recall what you have read in the chapter. Try to answer these questions without looking back

into the chapter. This will help you to see what you know and what you need to review.
3. The questions under **What Do You Think?** require you to formulate your own opinions. Be sure that these opinions are based on facts and are not just ideas that you think up. Some questions ask you to examine what the Bible has to say on a particular subject. Remember that it is important for a Christian always to use the Bible as his guide when formulating ethical and moral standards.

Illustrations, Charts, and Maps

Each illustration and chart in the book has been included to aid you in your understanding of world history. Take time to look at these and read the captions associated with them. The maps will help you visualize the size and location of various countries or the region in which a particular people live.

Highlights

Each chapter has a number of interesting articles contained in color-shaded boxes. These will not only help broaden your knowledge of history but also make your reading of WORLD HISTORY for Christian Schools more exciting. If you are curious, for instance, about how we got our calendar, who wrote ''Joy to the World,'' or how during World War II the United States knew ahead of time that the Japanese were going to attack Midway, you will be able to read all about it in these boxes.

Dates

In your reading of WORLD HISTORY for Christian Schools you will find many dates. We do not intend for you to memorize all of these. Dates are given so that you will be able to fit people and events into a time frame. In addition, there are some facts you need to know about dates.

1. *How to use B.C. and A.D.*
   Today it is customary to label events that happened before the birth of Christ B.C. (meaning ''before Christ'') and events that happened

after His birth A.D. ("Anno Domini"; Latin, meaning "in the year of our Lord"). B.C. is written after every date before the birth of Christ. We do not write A.D. next to a date, however, unless it might be confused with a B.C. date. Therefore, when you see a date in the book without B.C. after it or A.D. before it, you may assume it is A.D. When A.D. is used, it is proper to write it before the date (e.g., A.D. 70).

2. *How to count in B.C.*

The dates of events before the birth of Christ are much like the countdown of a rocket launch (10, 9, 8, . . . 3, 2, 1). Ancient civilizations, of course, did not count backwards like this. But because of the historical significance of the birth of Christ, we today date ancient events from the number of years they occurred before His birth.

3. *How to recognize an approximate date*

Because of incomplete historical records, it is sometimes impossible to establish an exact date for a historical event. When this is the case, we express an approximate date by placing the abbreviated form of *circa* (Latin for "around") before the date (e.g., ca. 1446).

4. *How to understand dates printed after a person's name*

The dates in parentheses after a person's name indicate his life span. Dates for monarchs or popes are the dates they held office. If a question mark appears after a date, it means we are uncertain about the time of a person's birth or death, for example, John Wycliffe (1320?-84).

5. *How to determine in what century an event took place*

The first century includes the years 1 to 100; the second, 101 to 200; the third, 201 to 300; and so on. The twenty-first century will therefore be from 2001 to 2100. The same procedure is used for establishing centuries B.C. Can you determine the centuries for the following dates? 586 B.C., ca. 1446, 1900.

Pronunciation Guide

The pronunciation key used in this text is designed to give the reader a self-evident, acceptable pronunciation for a word as he reads it from the page. For more nearly accurate pronunciations, the reader should consult a good dictionary.

Stress

Syllables with primary stress appear in LARGE CAPITAL letters. Syllables with secondary stress and one-syllable words appear in SMALL CAPITAL letters. Unstressed syllables appear in lowercase letters. Where two or more words appear together, hyphens separate the syllables within each word. For example, the pronunciation of *Omar Khayyam* appears as (OH-mar kie-YAHM).

Consonant Sounds

Most consonants and consonantal combinations in the key have only their one visual sound. There are a few exceptions:

Symbol	Example	Symbol	Example
c	cat = KAT	th	thin = THIN
g	get = GET	*th*	then = *TH*EN
j	gentle = JEN tul	zh	fusion = FYOO zhun

Vowel Sounds

Symbol	Example	Symbol	Example
a	cat = KAT	ar	car = KAR
a-e	cape = KAPE	aw	all = AWL
ay	paint = PAYNT	o	bone = BOHN
e	jet = JET	oa	don't = DOANT
eh	spend = SPEHND	o-e	groan = GRONE
ee	fiend = FEEND	oh	own = OHN
i	swim = SWIM	u	some = SUM
ih	pity = PIH tee	uh	abet = uh BET
eye	icy = EYE see	oo	crew = CROO
i-e	might = MITE	*oo*	push = P*OO*SH
ye	Levi = LEE vye	ou	loud = LOUD
ah	cot = KAHT	oy	toil = TOYL

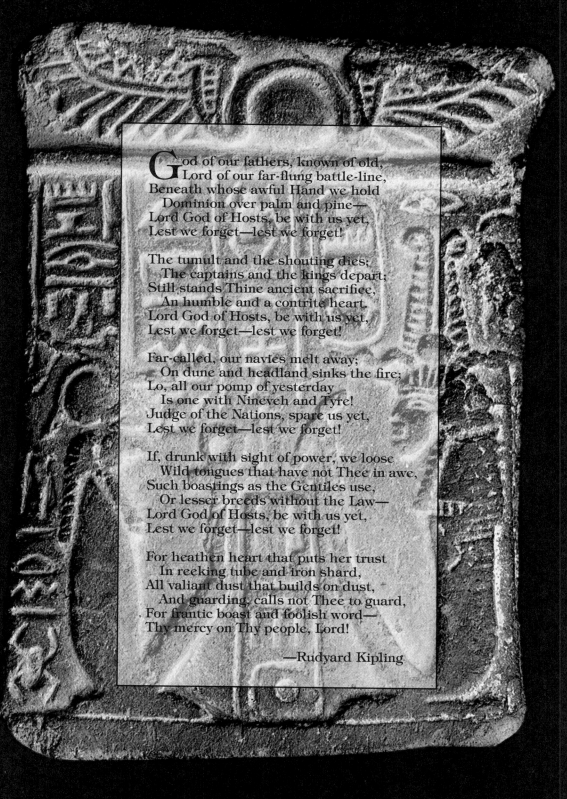

God of our fathers, known of old,
  Lord of our far-flung battle-line,
Beneath whose awful Hand we hold
  Dominion over palm and pine—
Lord God of Hosts, be with us yet,
Lest we forget—lest we forget!

The tumult and the shouting dies;
  The captains and the kings depart;
Still stands Thine ancient sacrifice,
  An humble and a contrite heart.
Lord God of Hosts, be with us yet,
Lest we forget—lest we forget!

Far-called, our navies melt away;
  On dune and headland sinks the fire;
Lo, all our pomp of yesterday
  Is one with Nineveh and Tyre!
Judge of the Nations, spare us yet,
Lest we forget—lest we forget!

If, drunk with sight of power, we loose
  Wild tongues that have not Thee in awe,
Such boastings as the Gentiles use,
  Or lesser breeds without the Law—
Lord God of Hosts, be with us yet,
Lest we forget—lest we forget!

For heathen heart that puts her trust
  In reeking tube and iron shard,
All valiant dust that builds on dust,
  And guarding, calls not Thee to guard,
For frantic boast and foolish word—
Thy mercy on Thy people, Lord!

                    —Rudyard Kipling

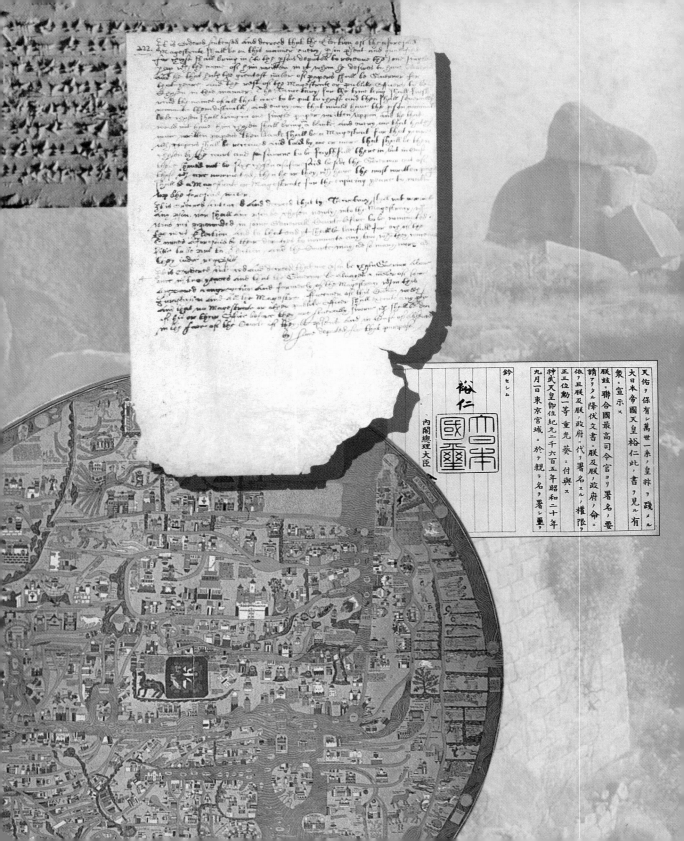

"In the beginning God created the heaven and the earth."

Christoforo Scacco, God the Father, *Bob Jones University Collection of Sacred Art*

Through the years, opinions on the definition of history and on the value of its study have varied widely. Here are a few examples:

- "There is much profit in a knowledge of the past. Every kind of experience is there for all to see. Historical documents contain examples for our instruction: models for a person or a nation to imitate and shameful things for all to avoid."

—Livy
(Roman historian, 59 B.C.–A.D. 17)

Introduction

Remember the former things of old: for I am God, and there is none else; I am God, and there is none like me, declaring the end from the beginning, and from ancient times the things that are not yet done, saying, My counsel shall stand, and I will do all my pleasure: calling a ravenous bird from the east, the man that executeth my counsel from a far country: yea, I have spoken it, I will also bring it to pass; I have purposed it, I will also do it.

—Isaiah 46:9-11

History and Historians

- "History is a pack of lies agreed upon."

  —Napoleon
  (French emperor, 1769-1821)

- "History is indeed, little more than the register of the crime, follies, and misfortunes of mankind."

  —Edward Gibbon
  (English historian, 1737-94)

- "History is the witness of the times, the light of truth, the life of memory, the teacher of life, the messenger of antiquity."

  —Cicero
  (Roman statesman and orator, 106-43 B.C.)

- "History is a nightmare from which I am trying to awake."

  —James Joyce
  (Irish author, 1882-1941)

- History is "the arena wherein [God's] will expresses itself as action."

  —J. S. Whale
  (British educator and theologian, 1896-)

- "The present is the past rolled up for action, and the past is the present unrolled for understanding."

  —Will Durant
  (American historian, 1885-1981)

- "History is the record of facts which one age finds remarkable in another."

  —Jakob Burckhard
  (Swiss historian, 1818-97)

- "History is a memorial of the mercies of God, so that posterity may know them, remember them, and [sing] His praises."

  —Perry Miller
  (American historian and critic, 1905-63)
  [writing about the Puritans' view of history]

- "History is bunk!"

  —Henry Ford
  (American auto manufacturer, 1863-1947)

- **"History is the record of the past from creation to the present, revealing the actions of God and man."**
  —*WORLD HISTORY for Christian Schools*

The Historian and His Resources

Our word *history* comes from a Greek word meaning "inquiry." History is the inquiry into what has happened in the past and why it has happened. But how do we discover what has happened in earlier days? Historical researchers act much like detectives. They search for clues that will unlock the secrets of the past. Historians find evidence from three basic resources: artifacts, tradition, and written records. These resources provide the raw material of historical study. By collecting, analyzing, and interpreting this material, the historian can arrive at a knowledge of the past.

Artifacts

The historian studies artifacts to learn about the background and culture of a people. Artifacts are objects made by man. They may be small relics, towering monuments, or priceless works of art. Most artifacts are simple, everyday items. Pottery, tools, weapons, furniture, clothing, coins, and jewelry unearthed by archaeologists (men who search for and study the artifacts of the past) give us valuable information about everyday life in past centuries.

Resources of History

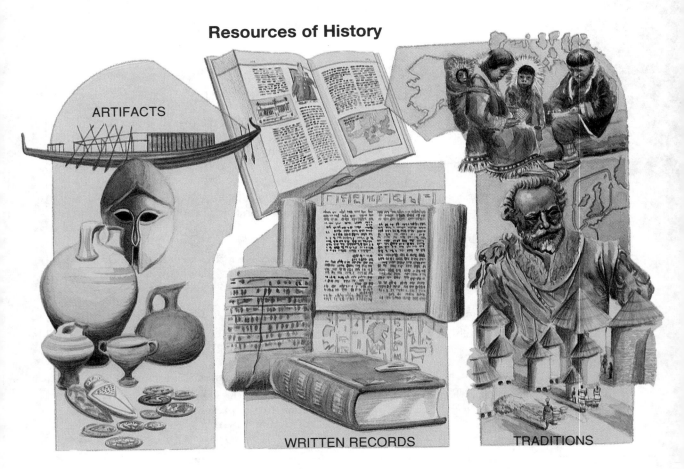

ARTIFACTS

WRITTEN RECORDS

TRADITIONS

An archway from ancient Tyre

Even works of art aid the historian in understanding the past. Statues, drawings, paintings, and tapestries—"pictures of the past"—depict the customs, beliefs, hobbies, fashions, and way of life of past generations.

Tradition

Think of your own family's history. You may be able to trace your heritage back many generations. How did you learn about your family's past? Most likely this information was passed down by parents or grandparents who talked of the "good old days." Such oral communication was the earliest method of transmitting historical information. It is called tradition, which is simply the handing down of information by word of mouth from generation to generation. Over the centuries tradition has taken many forms. Legends, ballads, folk songs, and tales are but a few of these forms. But tradition is more than just the mere reciting of songs and stories about the past. It includes the imparting of religious beliefs, family heritage, and social customs.

Written Records

Because word-of-mouth information can easily be forgotten or distorted, men have written down the traditions of the past to preserve a more accurate record for future generations. In the past, men have left behind writings chiseled in stone, carved in wood, impressed on clay, penned on papyrus, or printed on paper. These written remains are abundant and diverse. Historians gather knowledge about an age from private letters, inventory lists, inscriptions, coins, diaries, and journals. They rely on information preserved in family and church records, in lists of kings and dynasties, and in political and legal documents. They gain insight into the thoughts, attitudes, and feelings of past generations by examining their works of literature. Earlier historical works—detailed accounts of people, places, and events—are also valuable tools in understanding the past.

The historian also derives information from architecture. He considers, for example, the pyramids in Egypt, the Acropolis in Athens, the Colosseum in Rome, the Great Wall in China, the Mayan temples in Central America, the soaring cathedrals in Europe, the Taj Mahal in India, or the towering skyscrapers of New York City. These impressive structures reflect the creative skill that God has given to men as well as the character of the people who built them.

The Bible and History

Ruins of Belshazzar's banquet hall, Babylon

For the Christian, the proper study of history begins with a firm belief in the Bible as the authoritative Word of God. While artifacts, traditions, and written records are excellent resources, the Bible is the primary source of truth and certainty. It is historically accurate and trustworthy in its presentation of historical facts. It reveals the purpose and character of God and displays the true nature of man. It provides eternal principles that help us discern the importance and relevance of historical events. It also gives answers to man's basic questions about life: Where did I come from? Why am I here? Where am I going? Artifacts can be mis-interpreted, traditions may reflect human error, and written records often show the bias of sinful men, but the Word of God stands forever. Only as we view the record of the past in the light of biblical teaching can we fully understand the true meaning of history.

Ungodly men have often questioned the historical accuracy of the Bible. They refuse to acknowledge that the Bible is the inspired Word of God—that "all scripture is given by inspiration of God, and is profitable for doctrine, for reproof, for correction, for instruction in righteousness" (II Tim. 3:16). Instead, these men attempt to find errors in the biblical record. They take delight in pointing out supposed contradictions between Scripture and the resources of history. Unless they have evidence to support the truth of events mentioned in the Bible, they usually reject the events as though they never happened. But no matter how hard these critics try, they have not and will not prove that the Bible contains any error. So-called contradictions are not the fault of the biblical account. They result when men ignore the Bible and base their conclusions solely on the incomplete historical record.

Let us look, for example, at the apparent contradiction between the book of Daniel and historical records of ancient Babylon. Daniel says that Belshazzar was the king of Babylon at the time of its fall. In Daniel 5 we read that King Belshazzar gave a great feast. He and his guests drank wine out of the vessels taken from the temple in Jerusalem. They "praised the gods of gold, and of silver, of brass, of iron, of wood, and of stone" (Dan. 5:4). Suddenly fingers appeared and wrote a message on the palace wall. The troubled king promised to make the person who could interpret the message the third ruler in the kingdom. Only Daniel was able to interpret the writing on the wall; he told the king of God's impending judgment on the king and the city. That very night the seemingly invincible city of Babylon fell to the Medes and Persians, and Belshazzar was slain.

Other historical records have similar accounts of the fall of Babylon. However, only the book of Daniel records the name Belshazzar. During the early nineteenth century, scholars said that Nabonidus, not Belshazzar, was the last king of the great city of Babylon. They relied on old Babylonian lists of kings and the testimony of ancient historians. These accounts made no mention of Belshazzar. Scoffers said that the biblical writers simply invented the name, that Belshazzar never existed, and that the Bible was wrong.

But in the mid-nineteenth century, archaeologists unearthed a great number of clay tablets near Babylon. These tablets not only mentioned the name of Belshazzar but also referred to him as Nabonidus's son. Most interesting were the tablets that indicated that Nabonidus made his son coruler of the kingdom. Subsequent studies have revealed that Nabonidus spent the last years of reign in Arabia, leaving Belshazzar as the ruling monarch in Babylon. These tablets help us understand why Belshazzar would offer to make Daniel the *third* ruler in the kingdom instead of the second (Dan. 5:29). As coruler, Belshazzar was second to his father; third place was the next rank available.

Time and again, archaeological findings have silenced the critics' objections to historical events mentioned in the Bible. But whether or not there is evidence to confirm events recorded in the Bible, those events happened just as the Bible says they did. The Bible does not need to be proved correct; it is true no matter what men may believe.

Biblical Principles and History

The Bible is our guide to history. It provides principles that help us to better understand and interpret historical events.

Concerning God

1. God controls history. He is omniscient and omnipresent: He knows everything and His watchful eye oversees all His creation. He is omnipotent: His powerful hand directs the course of history. He moves the hearts of men (Prov. 21:1) and establishes the bounds of nations (Acts 17:26). The forces of nature do His bidding (Nahum 1:3).

2. God's dealing with people and nations reveals His character—His holiness, justice, love, mercy, and longsuffering. Though God may deal with people and nations in different ways, God does not change in His character and purpose. He is "the same yesterday, and to day, and for ever" (Heb. 13:8).

3. God blesses all people and nations who choose to obey and honor Him (Deut. 11:26-28; Ps. 33:12).

4. God brings judgment upon people and nations who choose to disobey, ignore, or dishonor Him (Ps. 9:17; Rom. 1:18-32).

Concerning Man

1. Man is a created being. For this reason, man is dependent upon and responsible to his Creator (Gen. 1:26-28, 2:7). God created man to glorify Himself (Pss. 86:8-10; 139:14).
2. Man fell from his original state (Rom. 5:12). Sin broke his fellowship with God. Man in his sinful state cannot please God (Rom. 3:10-18). He is in need of a Savior.
3. Man is free to choose his own way. If he chooses to glorify his Creator through faith and obedience, he will enjoy Him forever. If he chooses to dishonor Him through disbelief and disobedience, he will suffer everlasting punishment. Though man has a free will, he is never free from God's sovereign control (Eph. 1:11).
4. Man was made in the image of God. Though this image has been marred by sin, man possesses God-given talents and abilities through which he can accomplish remarkable things. But man's achievements, no matter how remarkable they may be, do not change the sinfulness of the human heart.

Concerning the Plan of History

1. God has a plan for history. History is not accidental; it is providential: "Known unto God are all his works from the beginning of the world" (Acts 15:18). History demonstrates God's desire to rescue men from their fallen state and restore them unto Himself.
2. Christ is the center of God's plan. "For God so loved the world, that he gave his only begotten Son, that whosoever believeth in him should not perish, but have everlasting life" (John 3:16).
3. The Bible reveals God's perfect plan and will for men and nations.
4. Satan opposes God's plan. History reveals the conflict between God and Satan, between righteousness and unrighteousness, between the godly and the ungodly.

"Known unto God are all his works from the beginning of the world" (Acts 15:18); the earth as viewed above the lunar horizon by the astronauts of Apollo 11

History and You

As you study history, you will quickly see that God has a perfect plan for everything. He has a plan for your life as well. That plan can be understood only if you first accept Jesus Christ as your Savior. Jesus Christ died on Calvary's cross for your sin. By repenting of your sin and by accepting through faith God's free gift of salvation, you can have eternal life. True happiness and success come only as you seek to become more like Jesus Christ and follow His plan for your life.

The study of world history has additional meaning and value.

1. It displays the greatness and goodness of God. The more you know of God, the more you should seek to glorify Him. "Oh that men would praise the Lord for his goodness, and for his wonderful works to the children of men!" (Ps. 107:8).

2. It sharpens your ability to discern good and evil, truth and error. By observing the successes and failures of previous generations, you can recognize the different ways that men have perverted the truth and avoid doing the same.

3. It illustrates the consequences of sin and the necessity of a righteous life. Historical examples verify the biblical truth that "whatsoever a man soweth, that shall he also reap. For he that soweth to his flesh shall of the flesh reap corruption; but he that soweth to the Spirit shall of the Spirit reap life everlasting" (Gal. 6:7-8).

4. It fosters a sense of gratitude for the contribution of previous generations. It will show you that much of what you have today you inherited from the peoples of the past.

5. It instills an appreciation for your heritage and the responsibilities that you have as a citizen of your country.

6. It imparts a general education in art, music, literature, and science, and in related disciplines such as politics, economics, and geography. This exposure to the wide range of human experience will be a helpful tool in your service and witness for the Lord Jesus Christ.

7. It gives a sense of mission and ministry as you learn of the world around you. It will acquaint you with different lands and peoples who are in need of the gospel. "Go ye into all the world, and preach the gospel to every creature." (Mark 16:15).

Cicero, the famed orator of the Roman Republic, once said, "He who knows only his own generations remains forever a child." History abounds with valuable lessons from which you can profit. You can gain inspiration and encouragement; you can find warning and instruction. God expects you to learn from the past; "For whatsoever things were written aforetime were written for our learning, that we through patience and comfort of the scriptures might have hope" (Rom. 15:4).

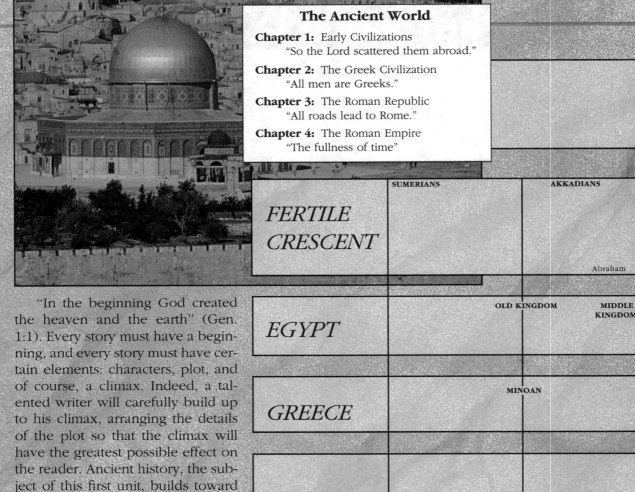

The Ancient World

FERTILE CRESCENT	SUMERIANS		AKKADIANS	
				Abraham
EGYPT			OLD KINGDOM	MIDDLE KINGDOM
GREECE		MINOAN		
ROME				
		★BATTLES		
	3000	2500		2000

"In the beginning God created the heaven and the earth" (Gen. 1:1). Every story must have a beginning, and every story must have certain elements: characters, plot, and of course, a climax. Indeed, a talented writer will carefully build up to his climax, arranging the details of the plot so that the climax will have the greatest possible effect on the reader. Ancient history, the subject of this first unit, builds toward such a climax. In steady succession, empires rise and fall, each new empire appearing even greater and more extensive than the last. Finally, with the Roman Empire, ancient history reached its climax—but not with the empire itself. The Roman Empire merely provided the setting for the real climax, the birth of Jesus Christ. "But when the fulness of the time was come, God sent forth his Son, made of a woman, made under the law, to redeem them that were under the law, that we might receive the adoption of sons" (Gal. 4:4-5).

THE ANCIENT WORLD

AMORITES   HITTITES   ARAMEANS   ASSYRIANS   CHALDEANS

                                                          LYDIANS   PERSIANS   **•BIRTH OF CHRIST (ca. 4 B.C.)**

          PHOENICIANS   Sennacherib   **•CRUCIFIXION OF CHRIST (ca. 30)**

ammurabi   **•DESTRUCTION OF JERUSALEM (586)**

                              Nebuchadnezzar   Cyrus   **•DESTRUCTION OF JERUSALEM (70)**

    Moses   David   Solomon   Belshazzar   Darius III (336-330)

NEW KINGDOM

HYKSOS   **•EXODUS (ca. 1446)**

  Thutmose III   Rameses II
      Amenhotep II

MYCENAEAN   ★**MARATHON (490)**
                                   Philip (ca. 382-336)

    DORIANS   **PERICLEAN AGE (460-429)**
                                    Alexander the Great (ca. 336-323)
                          Socrates (ca. 470-399)

                         ROMAN REPUBLIC (509-30 B.C.)
                                Mark Antony (83?-30 B.C.)
                       PUNIC WARS   **•COUNCIL OF NICAEA (325)**
                       (264-146) Julius Caesar (100-44 B.C.)

                                Augustus Caesar   Theodosius I
             •FOUNDING OF   (27 B.C.–A.D. 14)   (379-95)
             ROME (753)   **PAX ROMANA (31 B.C.–A.D. 180)**
                         Sulla (138-78)   Nero (54-68)   Constantine
                                               (306-37)
                       Gracchi (133-121)
                                            •EDICT OF MILAN (313)
                          Pompey (106-48)

                                         Diocletian (284-305)
            ETRUSCAN PERIOD   Marcus Aurelius (161-80)
                             CIVIL WARS   **FALL OF THE**
                        Hannibal   **ROMAN EMPIRE**
                      (247-183)   ★**ACTIUM (31 B.C.)**   **(476)**

| 1500 | 1000 | 500 | B.C. † A.D. | 500 |

CHAPTER 1

"So the Lord scattered them abroad."

Evolutionists believe that man descended from lower forms of life—that he developed from the simple to the complex. They contend that man was on the earth for millions of years before he was capable of building a civilization. Their conception of man's origin and nature is entirely false. The Bible tells us that God created man as a mature, intelligent being; man did not evolve over millions of years as some would have us believe. God placed him in a "fully grown" world, rich in vegetation, fertile soil, and mineral resources. Using the intelligence and abilities that God had given him, man established the first civilization shortly after his expulsion from the Garden of Eden. This chapter is the story of God's creative work and man's early civilizations.

Eden: The Place of Beginnings

Creation

For he spake, and it was done; he commanded, and it stood fast.

—Psalm 33:9

History begins with creation. God brought the universe into existence by the word of His mouth. By divine decree He established the earth and spread out the planets and stars across the far reaches of the heavens. Into this glorious creation He placed man; God formed him of the dust of the ground and breathed into him the breath of life. God made man in His own image. The first man, Adam, was perfect and sinless, as was Eve, his wife, whom God made from a rib from Adam's side. They were created to enjoy God's blessings and to walk in fellowship with Him eternally.

God placed Adam and Eve in the Garden of Eden—a blissful paradise on earth. Imagine a garden without thorns, or nettles, or choking weeds; a forest without vicious beasts or birds of prey; a life without pain, disease, or death. All was complete harmony and peace. God gave man dominion over this wondrous world—"over the fish of the sea, . . . the fowl of the air, . . . the cattle, and . . . every creeping thing" (Gen. 1:26). He told man to "be fruitful, and multiply, and replenish the earth, and

subdue it" (Gen. 1:28). God told Adam that he could eat the fruit of every tree in the garden except for the fruit of the tree of the knowledge of good and evil. He warned him: "Thou shalt not eat of it: for in the day that thou eatest thereof thou shalt surely die" (Gen. 2:17).

The Fall

Though blessed with the full measure of God's goodness, man chose to disobey his Creator. Satan, the enemy of God, tempted Eve to doubt God's word and to eat of the forbidden fruit. Deceived by the wiles of the serpent, she took a bite of the fruit and then gave some to her husband to eat. Adam's disobedience brought physical and spiritual death upon the whole human race. "By one man sin entered into the world, and death by sin; and so death passed upon all men, for that all have sinned" (Rom. 5:12).

Man's condition after the fall was hopeless. Because of his sin, he was separated from God and sentenced to an eternity apart from Him. He could do nothing to save himself. But God in His infinite love had provided a means of restoring man to Himself. As a holy God, He could not look upon sin, but in His boundless mercy He was "not willing that any should perish, but that all should come to repentance" (II Pet. 3:9). His plan for redeeming

Opposite Page: A shepherd watches over his sheep near Shiloh in Israel.

man was accomplished through the death of His Son, Jesus Christ. "But God commendeth his love toward us, in that, while we were yet sinners, Christ died for us" (Rom. 5:8).

From the time of the first sin in the garden to the present, all men have followed one of two courses in life: the way of God or the way of Satan. Like Adam and Eve, they have decided either to accept or to reject the will of their Creator. The children of Adam and Eve—Cain and Abel—illustrate the con-trast between these two ways. Cain brought a sac-rifice to God that represented natural man's attempt to please God apart from faith. Abel "by faith . . . offered unto God a more excellent sacrifice" (Heb. 11:4). Sin, rebellion, and death characterize the way of Cain. Faith, obedience, and trust in God mark the way of Abel. "Without faith it is impos-sible to please [God]: for he that cometh to God must believe that he is, and that he is a rewarder of them that diligently seek him" (Heb. 11:6).

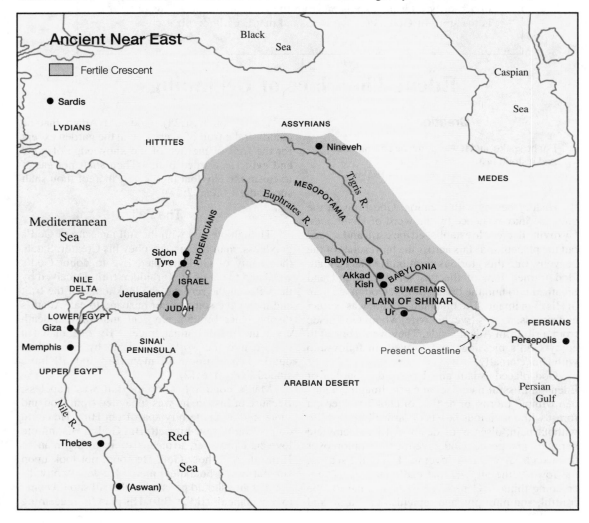

Peter Paul Rubens, The Dead Abel, *Bob Jones University Collection of Sacred Art*

Civilization

Civilization is human society characterized by cities, specialized labor, government, arts and science, religious beliefs, and written language. In the early chapters of Genesis we read that Adam's son Cain built a city. Within a few generations, men became involved in specialized labor: some kept cattle; others worked with bronze and iron; still others became skilled musicians, masters of string and wind instruments (Gen. 4:17-22). People before the Flood also had long life spans and spoke the same language. The pre-Flood civilization undoubtedly was one of great accomplishment.

This high level of achievement, however, did not—and could not—change the sinfulness of man. People continued in their rebellion against God. "God saw that the wickedness of man was great in the earth, and that every imagination of the thoughts of his heart was only evil continually" (Gen. 6:5). He decided to destroy man; His holiness and justice demanded, and still demands, punishment for sin.

Godly Noah did not follow the wicked ways of the world. God showed mercy to him by warning him of the coming destruction. During the 120 years before the Flood, Noah, the "preacher of righteousness," undoubtedly warned his generation of God's coming judgment. They ignored him. God sent the Flood, which covered the entire earth and destroyed every living creature. But Noah, who obeyed God and built the ark, found safety for himself, his family, and at least two of every kind of animal (Gen. 7:1-3, 6-9).

After the waters had receded, God placed a rainbow in the sky as a reminder of His promise that He would never again destroy the world by flood. Nevertheless, man continued in his evil ways. The descendants of Noah gathered in the land of Shinar between the Tigris and Euphrates rivers to build a city and a tower. This tower—the Tower of Babel—was symbolic of man's rebellion against God. At Babel, God confused man's language and scattered him throughout the earth. From these scattered peoples come the distinctive cultures of past and present that we will examine in this book.

Section Review

1. With what event does the history of this world begin?
2. What are the two ways of life that men have followed since the first sin in the garden?
3. Define *civilization*.
4. What ancient structure was symbolic of man's rebellion against God?

Mesopotamia: The Restoration of Civilization

Blessed is the man that walketh not in the counsel of the ungodly, nor standeth in the way of sinners, nor sitteth in the seat of the scornful. But his delight is in the law of the Lord; and in his law doth he meditate day and night. And he shall be like a tree planted by the rivers of water, that bringeth forth his fruit in his season; his leaf also shall not wither; and whatsoever he doeth shall prosper.

—Psalm 1:1-3

It is no coincidence that the psalmist compares the life of a godly man to a tree planted on a riverbank. To the people of the ancient world, rivers were the source of life. It was along riverbanks that civilization began anew after the Flood.

After God scattered the nations at the tower of Babel, some people remained and settled in the fertile region of the Tigris and Euphrates rivers. Later the Greeks described this region with the word *Mesopotamia* (MES uh puh TAY mee uh), meaning the "land between the rivers." By about 3000 B.C. the people in the southern part of this area had established the Sumerian civilization.

Sumerian Civilization

Sumer consisted of about a dozen independent city-states that had no political unity but possessed a similar culture. The cities fought constantly among themselves, each trying to gain dominance over the others. The Sumerians believed that their cities belonged to the gods. For this reason the temple was not only a place of worship but also the center of education, government, and trade. Each city had its own ruler, usually a priest, who acted as the representative of the gods.

The Sumerians were a **polytheistic** people (that is, they worshiped many gods). They believed that their gods influenced everything that they did. The most popular of their gods were those of water, agriculture, and the sky. To these gods they gave human characteristics. Although God created man in *His* own spiritual and personal image, the Sumerians rejected God and made gods in *their* own physical image. "Professing themselves to be wise,

Statue of a Sumerian worshiper (ca. 2600 B.C.)

they became fools, and changed the glory of the uncorruptible God into an image made like to corruptible man" (Rom. 1:22-23).

Cuneiform

Much of what we know about Sumer has come from the discovery of thousands of clay tablets bearing **cuneiform** (KYOO nee uh FORM), the earliest known form of writing. Using a wedge-shaped stylus (a split reed), the Sumerians made impressions on tablets of wet clay, which they later baked until hard. They could express ideas by the manner in which they arranged these wedge-shaped impressions. Young men learned this complex writing in a formal educational system. Professors were called "school-fathers," and the students were called "school-sons." Sumerian boys also studied the Sumerian numerical system—a system based not upon ten like ours today, but on the number sixty.

An Account of a Sumerian Schoolboy

I recited my tablet, ate my lunch, prepared my (new) tablet, wrote it, finished it. . . . When school was dismissed, I went home, entered the house, and found my father sitting there. I told my father of my written work, then recited my tablet to him, and my father was delighted. . . . When I awoke early in the morning, I faced my mother and said to her: "Give me my lunch, I want to go to school." My mother gave me two "rolls" and I set out. . . . In school the monitor in charge said to me, "Why are you late?" Afraid and with pounding heart, I entered before my teacher and made a respectful curtsy.[1]

Farming and Architecture

The major occupation of the Sumerians was farming. They built an elaborate network of canals and dikes to provide irrigation for their crops. Although agriculture was the basis of their economy, the people lived in fortified cities. They built their homes and public buildings with baked clay bricks. The most outstanding examples of Sumerian architecture are the temple towers called **ziggurats** (ZIG uh RATS). These impressive pyramidlike structures had terraces at different levels along their exterior. The bricks used in these buildings were often glazed in different colors.

Sargon

During the period of Sumerian dominance, a new people migrated into the northern Sumerian cities. They adopted much of the Sumerian culture. At the same time, they began to assert their own influence upon the cities in which they settled. Around 2350 B.C. the ruler **Sargon** came to power in the city-state of Kish. Sargon conquered other city-states and established the first known **empire**—the rule of one people over another. Making the city of Akkad his capital, he created a united kingdom—the Akkadian (uh KAY dee un) Empire—which stretched from the Persian Gulf to northern Mesopotamia. Under Sargon, the king's authority surpassed that of the priests. Many people began viewing the kings as gods.

About a century after Sargon's death, the city of Ur rose to prominence. This powerful city-state was the home of Abraham, the "father" of the Hebrew people. Although Abraham lived among a polytheistic and idolatrous people, he served the one true God. "The God of glory appeared unto . . . Abraham, when he was in Mesopotamia . . . and said unto him, Get thee out of thy country"

A reconstructed ziggurat at Ur

(Acts 7:2-3; see also Gen. 12:1-3). Abraham left Ur and traveled to the land of Canaan, where God blessed him with many descendants. From him came the great nation of Israel.

Sumerian Contributions

By 2000 B.C. the Sumerian civilization had died out. However, aspects of her culture continued in later civilizations. The Amorites, Hittites, Assyrians, and Persians used cuneiform. Roman architects adopted Sumerian building techniques such as the arch. Even today we use Sumerian inventions: the wheel, the division of a circle into 360 degrees, and the division of hours and minutes into sixty units. These influences testify of Sumerian knowledge and technological skill. Yet the Sumerians were pagans, having departed from the knowledge of God to exalt man and images of beasts. As a consequence their civilization faded from history.

Amorite Civilization

Weakened by a series of wars with her neighbors, the Sumerian civilization, centered at Ur, fell to Amorite invaders. The Amorites established the "Old Babylonian" Empire. Its capital was the city of Babylon (BAB uh lun), one of the greatest cities of the ancient world. The history of this city began shortly after the Flood, when Nimrod established a kingdom that included Babylon (Gen. 10:10). It was in or near this city that the tower of Babel was built.

Hammurabi

The sixth king of the Amorites, **Hammurabi** (HAH moo RAH bee), united the land of Mesopotamia under his rule. He was a successful military leader and an able administrator. His large staff assisted in the building and maintenance of the canals for irrigation, in the collection of taxes, and in the regulation of the administrative and business matters of the kingdom.

Hammurabi is best remembered for his code of laws. He did not write these laws but compiled, organized, and simplified existing laws. Hammurabi's code became the standard of judgment in moral, social, domestic, and commercial matters throughout the empire.

"To cause justice to prevail in the land, to destroy the wicked and the evil, that the strong might not oppress the weak"[2]—this inscription introduced the 282 laws set forth in this code. Hammurabi's law was one of retaliation—"an eye for an eye and a tooth for a tooth." The penalty for a particular offense varied with the social class of the offender. For example, if a man of the wealthy class broke a bone of a member of his own social class, his own bone was to be broken. If, however, such a man broke the bone of a commoner, he had only to pay a fine. Hammurabi had the code engraved in stone pillars and placed throughout the kingdom so that everyone would know the law.

The Laws of Hammurabi and Moses

The law of Moses is not derived from Hammurabi's law code, but there are several similarities between the two systems.

Hammurabi	Moses
Kidnapping—If a citizen steals the child of a citizen, he shall die. (14)	He that stealeth a man . . . shall surely be put to death. (Exod. 21:16; see also Deut. 24:7)
Lying—If a citizen in a [court] case has borne false witness. . . [and] if that case is one warranting the death penalty, that citizen shall be put to death. (3)	If a false witness rise up against any man . . . then shall ye do unto him, as he had thought to have done unto his brother. (Deut. 19:16, 19)

There are also many important differences between Hammurabi's and Moses' (God's) law codes.

Theft—If a citizen has committed a robbery and is caught, that man shall die. (22)	[The one who stole] shall restore that which he took. (Lev. 6:4; see also Lev. 6:2ff. and Exod. 22:1ff.)
If a son has struck his father, they shall cut off his hand. (195)[3]	And he that smiteth his father, or his mother, shall be surely put to death. (Exod. 21:15)

The stele containing Hammurabi's law code; the carving portrays the Babylonian god Shamash presenting the law to Hammurabi.

Hammurabi's laws governed man's conduct, but Moses said that the most important thing was man's heart (Lev. 19:17-18; Deut. 6:1-6). Second, Moses' law was more fair; for any crime it decreed the same punishment to all men, regardless of their social status (Lev. 19:15). In Hammurabi's view a crime was not as serious if it was committed by a "superior" against an "inferior." Most important, Moses' law was God-centered. Crime was not merely a sin against man; it was a sin against God. Hammurabi's law code was a great improvement over the capricious decrees of other ancient kings, but Moses' law, because it was given by God, is far superior to any law code of man.

The *Epic of Gilgamesh* and the Universal Flood

A noted example of Babylonian literature is the *Epic of Gilgamesh.* This epic poem (a long narrative poem dealing with the deeds of a heroic figure) describes the adventures of the legendary hero Gilgamesh (GIL guh MESH) and his search for eternal life. In his travels Gilgamesh meets Utnapishtim (OOT nah PEESH teem), the only man to have attained immortality.

One of the most interesting sections of the poem is its account of a universal flood. Utnapishtim is given the following instructions:

> Tear down (this) house, build a ship!
> Give up possessions, seek thou life.
> Despise property and keep the soul alive!
> Aboard the ship take thou the seed of all
> living things.[4]

Having built a ship, Utnapishtim gathers aboard his family, the craftsmen who helped him, and the animals of the field. The rains and flood rage for six days and nights and subside on the seventh.

Most ancient civilizations had similar legends. In all of these stories a great flood destroys the human race except for a Noah-like figure through whom the human race is preserved. The similarities of these accounts attest to the truth of the biblical account of Noah and the universal Flood (Gen. 6-8). The difference between these legends and the biblical record—the only trustworthy account—show the tendency of the natural man to mix truth with error. These civilizations held "the truth in unrighteousness . . . because that, when they knew God, they glorified him not as God, neither were thankful; but became vain in their imaginations, and their foolish heart was darkened" (Rom. 1:18, 21).

Amorite Accomplishments

The Amorites are also noted for their trade in gold, silver, tin, and textiles. They worked with algebra and geometry and made important contributions to the field of **astronomy** (the study of celestial bodies). However, they refused to acknowledge that "the heavens declare the glory of God" (Ps. 19:1). Instead the Amorites tried to interpret human events and destiny by the position

How the Mesopotamians and Egyptians Measured a Year

In Genesis 1:14 we read that God set the sun, moon, and stars in the heavens so that man could measure years. Most of the civilizations of the ancient world did not measure their years by the solar calendar as we do today. It was too difficult for them to judge the different positions of the sun. Instead, they observed the phases of the moon to determine a year. They divided each year into twelve lunar months of 29 1/2 days each. Their months did not actually have half days but alternated between 29 and 30 days. Thus their years consisted of 354 days. One can see that after a few years they were markedly out of step with the solar year of 365 1/4 days. The Babylonians noticed this and sought to correct it by adding an extra month every few years. In a letter written by Hammurabi, one reads that he gave instructions to add an extra month whenever it was noticed that the year was "deficient."

The Egyptians were the first people known to have a solar calendar. Egyptian astronomers noticed that a certain star, Sirius, appeared on the horizon just before sunrise at the time of the annual flooding of the Nile. Counting the days between two such sightings, they arrived at 365 days. Their calendar consisted of twelve months of 30 days each plus 5 extra days called "days of the year." These days were used for feasting and religious festivals.

By the time of the famous astronomer Ptolemy in the second century A.D., even the Egyptian calendar was inaccurate. They failed to realize that they needed to add an extra day every four years. The Egyptians refused to allow Ptolemy to correct it for them—to do so would interfere with the ancient traditions of the gods.

of the planets and stars—a practice that is called **astrology.**

Lacking able leadership after the death of Hammurabi, the Amorite civilization declined in both power and influence. Invaders came into the land and occupied the territory of this once powerful kingdom.

Section Review

1. What did the Greeks call the fertile region between the Tigris and Euphrates rivers?
2. What is the name of the Sumerian wedge-shaped form of writing?
3. Who established the first known empire? What became his capital city?
4. The Amorite civilization centered upon what capital city?
5. What is the difference between astronomy and astrology?

Egypt: Place of God's Preservation for His People

Egypt is a desert land. Were it not for the dry climate, the remains of Egypt—the monuments, the documents, and even the bodies of her rulers—would have crumbled or decayed long ago. Because so much has been preserved from this ancient civilization, we can learn a great deal about her fascinating history and culture.

The land of Egypt served as another type of "preserver." God used Egypt as a special place of preservation for His people. The descendants of Abraham journeyed to Egypt to escape a severe famine in their land. They went with God's promise: "Fear not to go down into Egypt; for I will there make of thee a great nation" (Gen. 46:3). Centuries later Mary and Joseph with the Christ child likewise found safety in Egypt as they fled from the threats of King Herod (Matt. 2:13-21).

The Land of Egypt

Ancient Egypt was not the square-shaped territory that we call Egypt today. It was the narrow strip of land along the banks of the Nile River. It was about seven hundred fifty miles long but in many places less than twelve miles wide. Because the Nile flows northward from the southern plateau, the southern region is called "Upper Egypt" and the northern region, "Lower Egypt." These were really two entirely different lands. Upper Egypt lay close against the Nile, completely cut off from the outside world by desert to the east and west and by rapids (called cataracts) to the south. Lower Egypt, on the other hand, spread out across the Nile Delta in easy contact with other nations by way of the Mediterranean Sea and the Sinai Peninsula.

The Nile River was vital to the existence of the ancient Egyptian civilization. This Egyptian papyrus portrays noblemen hunting and fishing on the river.

One Greek historian called Egypt the ''gift of the river.'' He was exactly right. If there had been no Nile, there would have been no Egypt. Because there was almost no rain there, only the Nile held back the menacing desert wasteland. The river rose and fell every year. As the snow at the river's source in the mountains melted every spring, the river flooded its banks from June through August. This flooding deposited tons of rich silt on Egypt, annually providing fertile soil for the crops.

The Nile was also important as a highway. Boats at the northern end of the river (called the **delta** after the triangular Greek letter delta, Δ) could hoist sails and let the winds from the north push them upriver. To return they needed simply to drop their sails and let the current carry them back. Since nearly all ancient Egyptians lived on the banks of the river, it was easy for those living at one end of the kingdom to communicate with those at the other end. Thus the Nile greatly contributed to a unified Egypt.

The History of Egypt

The people of Egypt descended from Mizraim, the son of Noah's son Ham. In fact, the Hebrews called Egypt ''Mizraim'' (Gen. 50:11). Shortly before 3000 B.C., a man named **Menes** (MEE neez) united the two lands of Upper and Lower Egypt, ruling them from a capital which he called White Walls (later named Memphis).

Old Kingdom

Historians divide ancient Egyptian history into three major phases: the Old, Middle, and New Kingdoms. Each is separated from the others by a time of unrest called an Intermediate Period. The Old Kingdom (ca. 2700-2200 B.C.) has been called ''The Age of the Pharaohs.'' There were **pharaohs** throughout all of ancient Egyptian history, of course, but in the Old Kingdom these rulers were especially powerful. The people considered them to be gods in human form. As ''gods'' they owned all of Egypt and used it for their own purposes. It was during this time that the great pyramids were built, huge tombs attesting to the splendor and might of the pharaohs. The most famous pharaoh of this age was **Khufu** (KOO foo), or Cheops, who built the Great Pyramid at Giza. Its construction required thousands of men working for twenty years.

Middle Kingdom

After a time of rebellion called ''The First Intermediate Period,'' the Middle Kingdom, ''The Age of the People,'' began (ca. 2100-1640 B.C.). Aware of the social unrest that preceded them, the Egyptian pharaohs directed their attention to projects that would benefit the country as a whole. The pharaohs did not have a great concern for the people under their rule; they simply desired a peaceful reign. On the whole, the Middle Kingdom was an age of peace and construction. The Egyptians built irrigation canals and systems of ponds to store the Nile's waters for use in the dry season.

It was during this time of peace that the Israelites moved to Egypt (Gen. 46-50). God used the influence of Joseph (Abraham's great-grandson) to provide a haven for the children of Israel during a time of famine (Gen. 47:1-6). The Israelites stayed in the land of Egypt for four hundred thirty years (Exod. 12:40-41). During that time their numbers grew from a handful to well over a million.

After the Middle Kingdom (in what we call ''The Second Intermediate Period''), an Asian people, the Hyksos (HIK sose), came into the land and eventually became its rulers. It is not known exactly who they were or how they became so powerful. From the Hyksos the Egyptians learned the art of war. The Hyksos brought with them horses, chariots, and bronze weapons.

Periods of Egyptian History

First Intermediate Period

Second Intermediate Period

Foreign Invasions

3000   2000   1000   B.C. A.D.

''The Age of the Pharaohs''   ''The Age of the People''   ''The Age of the Empire''

Limestone stele of Senu; Senu was a high priest during the time of Hatshepsut.

New Kingdom

Egypt eventually expelled these foreign rulers and restored an Egyptian to the throne. This New Kingdom (ca. 1570-1075 B.C.) is also called "The Age of the Empire" because it was in this age that Egypt became a great world power. The pharaohs became "warrior-kings." Using the weapons that the Hyksos had brought, they extended their control to Palestine, Syria, and the lands of the Nile (that is, to the south). In this age Upper Egypt became more important; the Egyptian capital was moved to Thebes in the south.

There are several pharaohs in this age which are of particular interest. One of the early rulers of the New Kingdom was **Hatshepsut** (hat SHEP SOOT), the first great woman ruler of Egypt. She may have been the "daughter of Pharaoh" who discovered Moses in the bulrushes and raised him as her own son (Exod. 2:5-10). Her rule was a peaceful one, and during her reign Egypt carried on extensive trade with nearby nations.

Hatshepsut's reign was followed by that of **Thutmose III** (thoot MO suh), the greatest Egyptian warrior-king. Under Thutmose, the Egyptian armies conquered Palestine and Syria, extending Egyptian rule all the way to the Euphrates River. Modern historians have called Thutmose the "Napoleon of Egypt." Moses, another great leader, lived at this time. But Moses, by faith, "refused to be called the son of Pharaoh's daughter; choosing rather to suffer affliction with the people of God, than to enjoy the pleasures of sin for a season" (Heb. 11:24-25). Thutmose III was probably the pharaoh from whom Moses fled after he killed the Egyptian. Following Thutmose's death Moses returned to Egypt, commissioned by God to lead the Hebrew people out of their bondage. The new pharaoh, probably **Amenhotep II** (AH men HO tep), refused to allow the children of Israel to go. He finally yielded after God sent ten plagues upon the land of Egypt (Exod. 7:8-11:10, 12:29-36). However, Amenhotep changed his mind and pursued the Hebrew people. God overwhelmed pharaoh's chariots and horsemen by returning the waters of the Red Sea upon them (Exod. 14). During the long reign of **Rameses II,** Egyptians once again embarked on building mammoth temples and monuments. Egypt gradually declined from her rank as a Near Eastern power after his death.

The Culture of Egypt

The social structure of ancient Egypt was shaped like a pyramid: at the top was the pharaoh, supremely powerful; below him were the priests and nobles; then came the merchants, the common people, and the foreign slaves, in that order.

Most Egyptians were poor, but anyone from a lower class—even a foreign slave—could rise to a higher class if he gained the pharaoh's favor. This fact is illustrated by Joseph, a Hebrew slave who became the second most powerful man in Egypt.

Stone coffin of Tutankhamen

In 1922 British archaeologists Howard Carter and the earl of Carnarvon found the tomb after many years of digging in the valley. Many experts consider this the greatest archeological discovery of all time: no Egyptian tomb had ever been found in such a marvelous state of preservation. Over a period of eight years, Carter and his assistants removed, catalogued, and restored several thousand objects found in the tomb. (Carnarvon had died in 1923.) Carter and other archaeologists were amazed at the great wealth that they found—especially because Tutankhamen was a relatively unimportant pharaoh. They could only imagine what might have been buried in the tombs of Egypt's great pharaohs.

"King Tut"

About the middle of the fourteenth century B.C., a nine-year old boy named Tutankhamen became the pharaoh of Egypt. After a reign of ten years, he died and was buried in the Valley of the Kings at Thebes. The Egyptians stored great treasures in his tomb, as they did for every pharaoh. They did their best to conceal the burial sites of their pharaohs, but sooner or later most of them were plundered. Shortly after Tutankhamen's death, grave robbers broke into his tomb and stole many of the smaller precious objects that had been placed there. Even so, Tutankhamen's tomb remained nearly intact. Rock chips from another building project nearby soon covered his tomb; it remained forgotten until the twentieth century.

Golden burial mask of Tutankhamen

Unlike women in other ancient cultures, Egyptian women were especially favored in their society. As we have seen, one woman even became a great pharaoh.

The legacy left by the Egyptian civilization is truly great. The Egyptians made important advances in the field of medicine; they increased the knowledge of anatomy and prescribed drugs as remedies for diseases. They also developed a solar calendar, dividing the year into 365 days. They used a form of picture writing called **hieroglyphics** (HY er uh GLIF iks) and developed a type of paper made from reeds of the papyrus plant. (It is from the word *papyrus* that we get our word *paper*.) They drew upon their understanding of geometry and astronomy to build the pyramids, some of the most amazing architectural achievements of the ancient world.

The Aswan High Dam

In 1971 the Egyptians dedicated the Soviet-built Aswan High Dam on the Nile River. They named the lake that the dam created Lake Nasser for the Egyptian president who initiated the project. Many ancient Egyptian monuments were in danger of being covered by water backed up behind the dam. Among those threatened were the temples at Abu Simbel of the Pharaoh Rameses II and his wife. With financial help from around the world, archaeologists were able to move both temples to higher ground. It took several thousand men four and one-half years to move these temples at a cost of forty million dollars. Today they still stand (only a little higher up on the cliff) as they have stood for three thousand years—facing the rising sun. In October, the month Rameses II ascended the throne, the rising sun shines through the temple doorway and strikes the seated statue of Rameses II within.

The damming of the "life line" of Egypt has caused a few problems. For instance, today fertilizer must be used to replace the rich silt that is now trapped behind the dam wall. But modern Egypt enjoys a plentiful supply of water. Egypt does not need to experience, as one Egyptian official put it, "seven years of famine."

The Egyptian religion was polytheistic. The people considered the pharaohs to be gods, but there were many other gods as well: animals, natural forces, and especially the Nile itself. The most important gods were Amen and Ra (who later became one god, Amen-Ra, the sun-god), and Osiris and Isis, the husband and wife who ruled the underworld.

The Egyptians believed that after death they would be judged according to their works. If their works were good enough, they would spend their afterlife in a place of peace—fishing, hunting, and relaxing. The pharaohs' tombs and those of other important men were filled with objects for them to enjoy in the next world. However, the Egyptians believed that these pleasures could not be enjoyed unless the body were preserved. Thus they invented the science of embalming, or preserving dead bodies. Today mummies of the Egyptians lie in museums, preserved by the embalmer's skill and centuries of desert dryness.

The greatness of ancient Egypt is no more. After the New Kingdom, Egypt fell successively to the Assyrians, the Persians, the Greeks, and the Romans. God brought a special judgment upon Egypt: "It shall be the basest of the kingdoms; neither shall it exalt itself any more above the nations: for I will diminish them, that they shall no

The Rosetta Stone and the Unlocking of Hieroglyphics

For centuries men sought to decipher the meaning of the hieroglyphic writing of ancient Egypt. It was not until 1799 that the first glimmer of light was cast on this mystery. In that year a group of French soldiers digging in the sand near the Egyptian village of Rosetta discovered a large black stone containing a proclamation inscribed in three scripts: Greek, demotic (common Egyptian), and hieroglyphics. The Greek text, which scholars readily understood, revealed that the same decree was set forth in all three scripts. By comparing the hieroglyphic text to the Greek text, scholars hoped to finally unlock the secrets of the hieroglyphics. Their task was not easy. They could not tell if the hieroglyphic characters were symbols for entire words or were symbols of an alphabet. Furthermore, the words from the two texts did not match word for word.

The breakthrough finally came when one translator began looking for the proper names within the texts. He discovered that the hieroglyphics for a proper name were contained in a symbol called a cartouche.

The first name he was able to identify was that of Ptolemy (Ptolemaios in the Greek).

This enabled him to determine the next cartouche as Berenice, Ptolemy's wife.

The most famous scholar to study the Rosetta Stone was the French translator Jean Champollion. From his examination of the stone and the cartouches from other Egyptian sources, he devised a preliminary hieroglyphic alphabet that enabled scholars to read other Egyptian inscriptions and documents. With this accomplishment, archaeologists gained a wealth of information about Egyptian history, politics, social customs, and religion.

The Great Pyramid

The Great Pyramid of Khufu (or Cheops) at Giza is a marvelous example of Egyptian architectural skill. It sits virtually astride the thirtieth parallel, or almost exactly one-third of the way from the equator to the North Pole. All four sides of the pyramid face the points of the compass (north, south, east, and west). It rises to a height of 481 feet, and at its base, each side spans a length of nearly two and one-half football fields. It covers approximately thirteen acres, and amazingly, its foundation is almost perfectly flat from side to side; its level varies less than an inch from one corner to another over 1,069 feet away. In its construction the Egyptians used over two million stone blocks, the average weight of each being two and one-half tons. These mammoth blocks were so well placed that between some of them it is impossible to insert the blade of a knife. While the white limestone that graced its exterior has long since been stripped away (to be used in other building projects), the Great Pyramid remains a monument to the genius of the ancient Egyptians.

more rule over the nations. And it shall be no more the confidence of the house of Israel, which bringeth their iniquity to remembrance, when they shall look after them: but they shall know that I am the Lord God'' (Ezek. 29:15-16). God's judgment fell upon Egypt not only because of the false religious beliefs of the Egyptian people but also because of the choice by God's people to rely on Egypt rather than on God for protection and support. God desires His people in every age to put their confidence in Him alone (Ps. 118:8-9). The Bible also speaks, however, of a coming day of blessing for Egypt: ''And the Lord shall smite Egypt: he shall smite and heal it: and they shall return even to the Lord, and he shall be intreated of them, and shall heal them'' (Isa. 19:22).

Section Review

1. To what river was a Greek historian referring when he called Egypt the ''gift of the river''?
2. List the three major periods of ancient Egyptian history.
3. Who is called the ''Napoleon of Egypt''?
4. Who was atop the social structure of ancient Egypt?
5. What important discovery enabled Jean Champollion to read Egyptian hieroglyphics?

Egyptian papyrus

Land of Canaan:
The Promised Land and its Inhabitants

The land of Canaan was the land of promise for God's chosen people, the Israelites. "Every place that the sole of your foot shall tread upon, that have I given unto you. . . . From the wilderness and this Lebanon even unto the great river, the river Euphrates, all the land of the Hittites, and unto the Great Sea [Mediterranean] toward the going down of the sun, shall be your coast" (Josh. 1:3-4). After leaving Egypt, the children of Israel wandered in the wilderness for forty years before they reached the Promised Land. As the Hebrew people entered the land, they encountered numerous peoples. Three of them—the Hittites, the Phoenicians (fih NISH unz), and the Arameans (ARE uh MEE unz; or Syrians)—interacted with the Hebrew people and made notable contributions to the culture of the ancient world.

The Hittites

Before the twentieth century little was known about the Hittites. Many people did not even believe that they had ever existed. The Old Testament was the only source of information concerning this people. The Hittites were the descendants of Heth, the son of Canaan and the grandson of Ham (Gen. 10:15). Biblical references to the Hittites include Abraham's purchase of a burial site from Ephron the Hittite (Gen. 23:1-20; 25:7-10) and King David's murder of Uriah the Hittite to cover up his sin with Bathsheba (II Sam. 11:3-27).

Archaeological discoveries around the turn of this century further affirmed the existence of the Hittite empire. The Hittites began to settle in Asia Minor about 2000 B.C. They were not ruled by priests or gods like the Sumerians and Egyptians. The Hittite king was the commander of the army. His power rested upon the support of the chief warriors. Controlling rich supplies of iron ore, the Hittites excelled in the production of iron. With their military skill and their work in iron, they became feared by other people.

Using iron weapons and horse-drawn chariots, the Hittites extended their empire throughout Asia Minor and into the **Fertile Crescent** (which takes its name from the crescent-shaped fertile region encompassing Mesopotamia and the land of Canaan). They raided the Amorite capital of Babylon and later took control of Syria. This expansion brought them into conflict with the Egyptian Empire, which was also expanding into that area. Constant fighting between the Hittites and the Egyptians weakened them both and led to their mutual decline. This event gave the Phoenicians, the Arameans, and the Hebrews an opportunity to establish independent kingdoms. Once a major power in Asia Minor and the northern Fertile Crescent, the Hittites were absorbed by more advanced cultures and gradually passed into obscurity.

Land of Canaan

Land of Canaan map showing: Solomon's Kingdom, HITTITES, Euphrates R., Mediterranean Sea, PHOENICIANS, Sidon, Tyre, Damascus, ARAMEANS, Jordan R., HEBREWS, Jerusalem, Jericho, Dead Sea, PHILISTINES, SINAI PENINSULA. Scale: MILES 0 50 100 150, KILOMETERS 0 50 100 150

Hittite reliefs from Hattushash

The Phoenicians

O thou that art situate at the entry of the sea, which art a merchant of the people for many isles, . . . thy borders are in the midst of the seas, thy builders have perfected thy beauty. . . . When thy wares went forth out of the seas, thou filledst many people; thou didst enrich the kings of the earth with the multitude of thy riches and of thy merchandise.
—Ezekiel 27:3-4, 33

This is the prophet Ezekiel's description of the city of Tyre. For more than a thousand years, Tyre was the leading city-state of Phoenicia. Comprised of many independent city-states, Phoenicia was located along the eastern coast of the Mediterranean Sea (where Lebanon is today). The Phoenicians were a Canaanite people. The earliest Phoenician city was probably Sidon, founded by Canaan's first-born son, Sidon (Gen. 10:15).

Merchants of the Mediterranean

The Phoenicians became the greatest merchants of their day. With their large merchant fleet, they traded with areas all over the Mediterranean Sea— Egypt, Greece, Sicily, Spain, and North Africa. Spices, fine linen, wheat, cattle, horses, ivory, gold, precious stones, and tin (used to harden copper) were just some of the items handled by these traders.

The Phoenicians also gained great wealth through two valuable natural resources. The first was a type of mollusk (a sea animal similar to a snail) found off the Phoenician coast. The Phoenicians obtained a purple dye from this sea animal. Purple-dyed cloth became one of their chief exports. (The word *Phoenicia* comes from the Greeks, who called these people the "purple people" or the "traders of purple.") The second natural resource was the cedar and fir trees found in the Lebanon mountains. Phoenicia supplied the cedars that King Solomon used to build the temple in Jerusalem. In fact, Solomon used many precious materials from the commercial city of Tyre in building the temple (I Kings 5).

In their travels Phoenician merchants sailed to the farthest reaches of the Mediterranean Sea and to Britain; some historians believe they sailed around Africa and also might have traveled west to the North American continent. The Phoenicians planted colonies all along the Mediterranean coastline. Colonies such as Carthage would later reach greater heights than the Phoenician cities in Palestine.

The Phoenician Alphabet

The Phoenicians are believed to be the originators of the alphabet. By this time the cuneiform writing of the Sumerians and the hieroglyphics of the Egyptians had been in use for centuries. The Phoenicians developed uniform symbols to stand for distinct sounds. By arranging letters representing sounds, they could form an almost infinite number of words. Writing then became simple enough for most people to understand. The Greeks and the Romans later adapted this alphabet for their own use and passed it on to us.

The City of Tyre

Phoenician independence was lost during the ninth and eighth centuries B.C. as the Assyrians invaded the territory along the coast and exacted tribute from the wealthy city-states. However, Tyre, the leading Phoenician city-state, continued to thrive, her trade unhampered by the Assyrians. Long before the Assyrian invasion, Tyre had expanded her city to an island about a half mile off the coast. From her island fortress she was safe from land attack. Massive walls around the island

The broken towers of Tyre: "And I will make thee like the top of a rock: thou shalt be a place to spread nets upon; thou shalt be built no more: for I the Lord have spoken it" (Ezek. 26:14).

city and her strong navy protected her from sea attack as well.

The wealth and prosperity of Tyre was short-lived. The people of Tyre and the other Phoenician cities had perverted the knowledge of the true God by worshiping **Baal,** the pagan god of the Canaan-ites. (In fact, it was Jezebel, the daughter of the King of Sidon, who married King Ahab and intro-duced Baal-worship to Israel.) Because of their great commerce, pride entered their hearts. The prophet Ezekiel addressed them, ''Thine heart is lifted up because of thy riches'' (Ezek. 28:5). Tyre laughed at the calamity of the people of God when Nebuchadnezzar destroyed Jerusalem. For these reasons the prophet Ezekiel declared:

Therefore thus saith the Lord God; Behold, I am against thee, O [Tyre], and will cause many nations to come up against thee, as the sea causeth his waves to come up. And they shall destroy the walls of [Tyre], and break down her towers: I will also scrape her dust from her, and make her like the top of a rock. It shall be a place for the spreading of nets in the midst of the sea: for I have spoken it, saith the Lord God: and it shall become a spoil to the nations.

—Ezekiel 26:3-5

In addition, Ezekiel foretold that Nebuchadnez-zar, king of Babylon, would come and besiege the city (Ezek. 26:7-11). Nebuchadnezzar did come, and he besieged Tyre for thirteen years. He destroyed the mainland portion of the city but failed to destroy the island portion. Alexander the Great, more than two hundred years later, fulfilled the rest of this prophecy. By pushing the ruins of mainland Tyre into the sea (leaving it like bare rock), Alexander's men built a causeway out to the island city. His forces conquered the city, killing thousands and taking many thousands captive. The plunder of Tyre continued in the centuries to follow.

The Arameans

Syria is often called the "crossroads of civilizations." Through the centuries this land has been the link between Asia and Africa, the "melting pot" of the Middle Eastern cultures, and the passageway of the conquering armies. The Arameans (called Syrians in the Old Testament) were descendants of Aram the son of Shem (Gen. 10:22). They settled throughout Syria and northern Mesopotamia, Around 1000 B.C. the Arameans established a number of small independent states. Although of little political importance, this people had a profound effect upon the ancient world in other ways.

As the Phoenicians created a commercial empire by sea, the Arameans established one by land. Damascus, one of the oldest continuously inhabited cities in the world, became a capital of international trade. It was centrally located among the land routes of the Near East. Aramean camel caravans transported goods throughout the ancient world.

To facilitate trade, the language of the Arameans was used as a "go-between" language among the nations of the Fertile Crescent. Later the Aramaic language became the common spoken language of the entire region. This is probably the language which Jesus and His disciples spoke.

The Israelites were the neighbors of the Arameans. David and Solomon conquered many of the Aramean cities, but with the division of the Hebrew nation after Solomon, constant fighting took place between the Syrians and the Hebrews. God used the Arameans to punish His people (II Kings 13:3). Later, because of the wickedness of the people of Damascus, God pronounced the destruction of the Aramean civilization (Amos 1:3-5). In 732 B.C. the Assyrians crushed Damascus and took her people away as captives.

The Hebrews

Abraham of Ur

"For thou art a holy people unto the Lord thy God: the Lord thy God hath chosen thee to be a special people unto himself, above all people that are upon the face of the earth" (Deut. 7:6). God chose **Abraham** of Ur and gave him an unconditional promise to bless him and multiply his descendants into a great nation. Abraham believed and obeyed God, and despite great adversity the nation of Israel was born. These people were God's chosen instruments through whom God manifested His marvelous works, made known His name among the nations, gave the Old Testament (His written Word), and prepared the line through which the promised Messiah (Savior) would come.

Israel's history begins with the birth of Abraham about 2166 B.C. Abraham, a descendant of Shem, grew up in the city of Ur. God called Abraham out of the wicked land of Mesopotamia (Gen. 12:1-3) and directed him to the land of Canaan, the land of promise for Abraham and his descendants. God chose Abraham to be the "father" of a great nation. He fulfilled this promise by providing the aged Abraham with a son, Isaac, through whom this chosen line was to come. This line of blessing

Divisions of Hebrew History	
I. Patriarchal	2166-1876 B.C.
II. Egyptian	1876-1446 B.C.
III. Wilderness	1446-1406 B.C.
IV. Conquest	1406-1389 B.C.
V. Judges	1389-1050 B.C.
VI. United Kingdom	1050-930 B.C.
VII. Divided Kingdom	930-586 B.C.
VIII. Exile	586-538 B.C.
IX. Persian	538-332 B.C.
X. Hellenistic	332-168 B.C.
XI. Maccabean	168-63 B.C.
XII. Roman	63 B.C.—A.D. 70

continued through Isaac's son, **Jacob.** The descendants of these "patriarchs" are called the children of Israel, taking their name from Jacob, whose name God changed to Israel.

Bondage in Egypt

Jacob and his family went down into Egypt to escape a famine in Canaan. God had already provided for His people in Egypt by giving **Joseph** (one of Jacob's sons) a place of leadership. In Egypt Jacob's descendants became a numerous people—the Israelites. Once a place of refuge and prosperity for the Israelites, Egypt became a place of hardship. A pharaoh who did not remember what Joseph had done for Egypt inflicted heavy burdens upon the Hebrew people. God remembered His people, however, and raised up **Moses** to lead them from the

Benjamin West, The Brazen Serpent, Bob Jones University Collection of Sacred Art; Moses erected the brazen serpent to halt a plague of the fiery serpents in the wilderness (Num. 21).

land of bondage to the Promised Land. The children of Israel, in about 1446 B.C., left Egypt and crossed the Red Sea bound for the land of Canaan.

Theocracy

One of the most important events in Hebrew history occurred in the wilderness at Mount Sinai (Exod. 19-20). There God established Israel as a **theocracy**—government directly by God. God established His covenant with the children of Israel, promising to be ever present with them. God governed His people by communicating His will through leaders He ordained, such as Moses and Joshua. God's law gave them instruction, guidelines, and judgments in moral, civil, and ceremonial matters. Unlike human government, which attempts to enforce outward conformity to man's laws, God seeks to rule through the inward obedience of individual hearts. God's law provides a perfect moral standard by which men can distinguish right from wrong.

The Promised Land

Though blessed with the very presence of God, the children of Israel fell into sin. Moses sent twelve spies into the land of Canaan to search out the land (Num. 13:1-16). As the reports came back that the land was filled with giants and walled cities, the people forgot God's promises and rebelled against the Lord. Because of this rebellion, the children of Israel had to wander in the wilderness before entering the Promised Land (Num. 14:20-35).

After forty years the children of Israel finally crossed over the Jordan River into the land "flowing with milk and honey." Under their new leader, **Joshua,** they began their conquest of the land of Canaan. They destroyed Jericho and Ai and defeated the Hittites, the Amorites, the Canaanites, the Perizzites, the Hivites, and the Jebusites. They divided the land among the twelve tribes of Israel (Josh. 14-22).

The Judges

After the death of Joshua "every man did that which was right in his own eyes" (Judges 17:6; 21:25). God had intended that the Hebrew people demonstrate to the ancient world that there is but one living God (**monotheism,** "the belief in one God"), but the children of Israel turned from God to worship the false gods of the Canaanites. Because of their disobedience, God raised up enemies to oppress Israel. This oppression caused the children of Israel to turn back to God and cry out for mercy. God heard their cries and raised up leaders, called judges, through whom He ruled His people and delivered them from their oppressors (Judges 2:16-18).

During the judgeship of Samuel, the Israelites again rejected God's rule, desiring a human king to rule over them instead (I Sam. 8:4-8). Saul became the first king of Israel. He united all the tribes of Israel under his leadership and led Israel in victories over the Philistines and the Amalekites. Nevertheless, he failed to obey the commands of God, and God rejected him as king (I Sam. 15).

David and Solomon

God chose **David,** a man "after God's own heart," as the next king. From his family the promised Messiah would come. King David firmly established the Hebrew kingdom. He conquered Israel's enemies, enlarged Israel's borders, and established peace throughout the land. Jerusalem, the "city of David," became the center of worship and government for the Hebrew kingdom (II Sam. 5:6-10).

The kingdom of Israel reached its peak during the reign of David's son **Solomon.** Visiting dignitaries, such as the Queen of Sheba, marveled at the wealth and wisdom of this Hebrew king (I Kings 10:1-13). Supplied with materials from Phoenicia,

Israelite pottery from the kingdom period of Israel's history (ca. 1000-800 B.C.)

Solomon built the magnificent temple of God that his father David had planned. Much of the wealth of the country was spent by Solomon on other building projects. The burden of building and funding these projects fell upon the Hebrew people.

Division and Judgment

Following the death of Solomon, the Hebrew people came to Rehoboam, the new king, and begged him to lower their taxes. Rehoboam decided to increase the taxes instead (I Kings 12:1-15). Outraged at this decision, the ten northern tribes of Israel rebelled and made Jeroboam their king. The southern tribes of Benjamin and Judah became the kingdom of Judah, remaining loyal to Rehoboam and the house of David (I Kings 12:19-24).

The Hebrew nation, now divided, lost the greatness and peace achieved under the reigns of David and Solomon. Wickedness increased among both the people of Israel and the people of Judah. Peace was replaced by strife and constant warfare. Isaiah and Jeremiah, as well as other prophets, warned God's people of coming judgment, but their warnings went unheeded.

Judgment came upon the disobedient people of God. In 722 B.C. the Assyrians destroyed Samaria (the capital of the northern kingdom of Israel) and carried her people away captive. The Chaldeans (kal DEE unz) under Nebuchadnezzar destroyed Jerusalem in 586 B.C. and carried many of the Jews back to Babylon. This period of exile, known as the **Babylonian Captivity,** lasted seventy years.

Nevertheless, God did not forsake His people. God raised up the Persians to free His people and restore them once again to their land.

Section Review

1. List three civilizations that the Hebrew people encountered as they entered the Promised Land.
2. What two major weapons did the Hittites use as they expanded their empire into Asia Minor?
3. What were the two valuable natural resources that brought wealth to the Phoenicians?
4. What language served as a "go-between," or international language, among the people of the Fertile Crescent?
5. Define a theocracy.

Near Eastern Empires: God's Instruments of Punishment and Preservation

"The most High ruleth in the kingdom of men, and giveth it to whomsoever he will, and setteth up over it the basest of men" (Dan. 4:17). God uses nations to accomplish His purpose in history. We can see in the ancient world how God used the Assyrians and the Chaldeans as His instruments of judgment upon the Hebrews. In a similar manner God used the Persians as His instrument for preserving the Jews. Even so, these kingdoms were not excused from the consequences of their own wickedness. God's judgment eventually fell on them too.

The Assyrian Empire

The Assyrians created the largest empire the world has seen prior to 550 B.C. For centuries they dwelt in northern Mesopotamia along the Tigris River, but by the eighth century B.C. they had built a vast empire that encompassed the Fertile Crescent, Egypt, and part of Asia Minor. Nineveh, the city built by Nimrod shortly after the Flood (Gen. 10:11), became the capital city of the empire.

The Assyrians were indebted to the previous Mesopotamian cultures; their gods, language, art,

architecture, science, and literature were in large part adapted from the Sumerian and Amorite cultures. The Assyrians preserved many contributions of the earlier civilizations and spread these accomplishments throughout the ancient world by their military conquests.

Assyrian military might was unmatched by any other civilization of the day. The Assyrian army was equipped with iron weapons, siege towers, battering rams, and war chariots. Her army of well-trained footsoldiers, spearmen, archers, and cavalry wreaked havoc on the people of the Near East. They terrorized nations with threats of destruction and hoped to gain their submission without the use of force. They earned a reputation for fierceness and cruelty; it was not uncommon for them to butcher, mutilate, and burn at the stake or skin alive their defeated foes. They also practiced mass deportation—removing conquered people from their own land and settling them in a foreign country.

God's Judgment

God used this ungodly, war-loving people as His instrument for venting His wrath against sinful nations and for punishing His disobedient people.

> O Assyrian, the rod of mine anger, and the staff in their hand is mine indignation. I will send him against an hypocritical nation, and against the people of my wrath will I give him a charge, to take the spoil, and to take the prey, and to tread them down like the mire of the streets.
>
> —Isaiah 10:5-6

Under Tiglathpileser (TIG lath puh LEE zer), the Assyrians captured the Aramean capital of Damascus. Ten years later, in 722 B.C., the Assyrian army led by **Sargon II** destroyed Samaria and took captive the ten northern tribes of Israel (II Kings 17). Later, Assyrian armies invaded Egypt and subdued much of her territory.

Mercy and Judgment

The Assyrians did not acknowledge God and were not aware of His workings. They became arro-

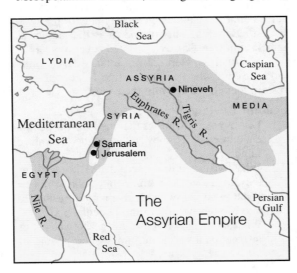

The Assyrian Empire

Reconstruction of the Ishtar Gate of Babylon

me'' (Jon. 1:2). As this heathen city "turned from their evil way" (Jon. 3:10), God turned away His wrath. What a great example of God's mercy, which can save even the vilest of sinners.

The people of Nineveh, however, returned to their wicked ways, and God's mercy turned to wrath (Nah. 1-3). In 612 B.C. Chaldean and Median armies completely destroyed Nineveh and brought the Assyrian Empire to an end.

The Chaldean Empire

Nebuchadnezzar of Babylon

Babylon was one of the oldest and grandest of all the cities of the ancient world. Empires had come and gone, but Babylon had remained. Babylon had been the capital of previous civilizations, but it was not until the sixth century B.C. that she reached the height of her glory.

Shortly before 1000 B.C. a group of Semitic people, the Chaldeans, began to settle around Babylon. Disunited, they were constantly subdued by Assyrian kings. Later, however, the Chaldeans allied themselves with the Medes and helped destroy Nineveh in 612 B.C. During the reign of **Nebuchadnezzar** (NEB uh kud NEZ er), the "New Babylonian" Empire reached its height.

The ancient world was amazed at the sudden rise to power of the Chaldeans. Jeremiah, the prophet of the Lord, explained Nebuchadnezzar's success:

> I [the Lord God] have made the earth, the man and the beast that are upon the ground, by my great power and by my outstretched arm, and have given it unto whom it seemed meet unto me. And now have I given all these lands into the hand of Nebuchadnezzar the king of Babylon, my servant. . . . And all nations shall serve him.
>
> —Jeremiah 27:5-7

God used Nebuchadnezzar, whom He called His "servant," to punish other nations for their disobedience to Him. For example, in 605 B.C. Nebuchadnezzar defeated the Egyptian armies under Pharaoh Necho, who tried to conquer Syria and Palestine. Likewise God allowed Nebuchadnezzar to destroy Jerusalem in 586 B.C. and carry the Jews

gant because of their conquests. Under **Sennacherib** (sih NAK er IB) they tried to take Jerusalem from Hezekiah, king of Judah. As the Assyrians prepared to take the city, the agents of Sennacherib, standing outside the walls of Jerusalem, boasted of the conquests and might of the Assyrian army (II Kings 18:13-35). But God through His prophet Isaiah pronounced: "I will punish the fruit of the stout heart of the king of Assyria, and the glory of his high looks. For he saith, By the strength of my hand I have done it, and by my wisdom; for I am prudent" (Isa. 10:12-13). God sent an angel who slew 185,000 men of Sennacherib's army. Sennacherib went home in defeat only to be murdered by two of his sons.

Although Assyrians were among the most ruthless people of the ancient world, God showed mercy to them. God sent Jonah to Nineveh to preach repentance: "Arise, go to Nineveh, that great city, and cry against it; for their wickedness is come up before

away captive (II Kings 25:8-21). This dispersion of the Jewish people is known as the **Diaspora,** or "scattering." Under Nebuchadnezzar, the Chaldeans became the masters of the Fertile Crescent.

Nebuchadnezzar is remembered not only for his military accomplishments but also for building up Babylon as "the glory of kingdoms, the beauty of the Chaldees' excellency" (Isa. 13:19). The ancient Greek historian Herodotus said of Babylon, "In magnificence there is no other city that approaches it." Inner and outer walls, some of which towered over three hundred feet, surrounded the city. The walls were so thick that chariots, two abreast, could ride on top of them. The city was further protected by a moat surrounding the outside walls.

The Babylonian "hanging gardens" were one of the wonders of the ancient world. The gardens were probably built by Nebuchadnezzar for his Median wife, who missed the trees and flowers of her homeland. Supported by brick arches, these terraced gardens containing tropical plants and trees were the pride of ancient Babylon. The river Euphrates, which ran under the wall and through the midst of the city, watered the gardens and provided a water supply for the city.

Astronomy

The Chaldeans continued the interest in astronomy that had been popular during the Amorite civilization and made further contributions to the field. They charted the positions of planets and stars, named constellations, and predicted eclipses. As did others that preceded and followed them, they accepted the belief that the position of the sun in relationship to the stars and planets influenced human destiny.

From the book of Daniel, we learn that the "wise men"—astrologers, magicians, and sorcerers—had an important place in Chaldean society. They were often called upon to advise the king. Although they claimed the power to interpret dreams and tell the future, these so-called wise men were false prophets. Time and again they proved themselves unable to interpret the king's dreams (Dan. 2:10-11; 5:8). On one occasion Daniel came before King Nebuchadnezzar and said, "The secret which the king hath demanded cannot the wise men, the astrologers, the magicians, the soothsayers, show unto the king; but there is a God in heaven that revealeth secrets, and maketh known . . . what shall be in the latter days" (Dan. 2:27-28).

God's Wrath

The glories of the Chaldean Empire did not last even a century. Nebuchadnezzar had learned of God's power from the Hebrew captive Daniel. But he viewed his accomplishment out of a heart of pride. He said, "Is not this great Babylon, that I have built for the house of the kingdom by the might of my power, and for the honour of my majesty?" (Dan. 4:30). God's judgment fell upon Nebuchadnezzar. He temporarily lost his throne and became like a beast of the field until he recognized the folly of his pride and acknowledged the greatness of God (Dan. 4:31-37).

Under Nebuchadnezzar's successors, Babylon—which had been a "golden cup in the Lord's hand" (Jer. 51:7)—became an object of God's wrath. This mighty empire with its seemingly invincible capital fell in one night. The coruler of the empire, **Belshazzar,** had made a great feast. He used the golden vessels taken from the temple of God in Jerusalem to drink wine and toast the pagan gods of the Chaldeans. Amidst the drunken revelry, fingers appeared and wrote on the palace wall an inscription with the following translation:

> God hath numbered thy kingdom and finished it, . . .
> Thou art weighed in the balances and art found wanting, . . .
> Thy kingdom is divided, and given to the Medes and Persians.
> —Daniel 5:26-28

In the meantime, the Medes and Persians had diverted the flow of the Euphrates River, which ran underneath Babylon's walls. The invading armies, using the riverbed as a passageway, slipped into the city unnoticed. On that night in 539 B.C., Belshazzar was slain and the Chaldean Empire fell.

The Persian Empire

Out of the land of what is today Iran came an empire that spread across the entire Near Eastern

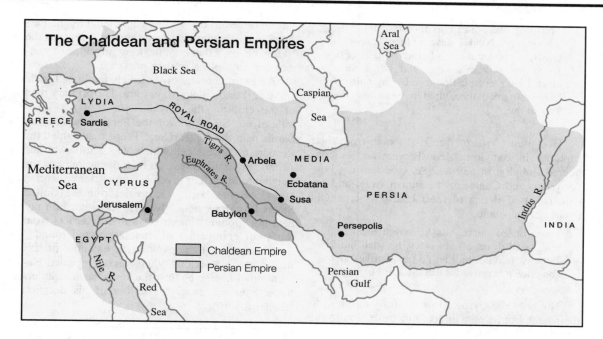

The Chaldean and Persian Empires

- Chaldean Empire
- Persian Empire

world. At its height the Persian Empire stretched from the coastline of Greece to the Indus River Valley in India and from Egypt to Mesopotamia. The rise of this great empire was hastened in the mid-sixth century B.C. by the Persian defeat of the Medes, Lydians, and Chaldeans.

Cyrus the Great

The Persian king **Cyrus** was one of the greatest conquerors who ever lived. Cyrus rose to power among the Persian tribes in the southern region of the Median Empire (see map). After the Assyrian Empire fell in 612 B.C., the Medes had control of the land north and east of Mesopotamia. Cyrus took advantage of a rebellion in the Median army and conquered the Median capital of Ecbatana in 549 B.C. As he extended his conquests into Asia Minor, he came into contact with the Lydians.

The western region of Asia Minor bordering the Aegean Sea was the homeland of the Lydians. Here rich mineral resources, especially gold, were found in abundance. This land was the supposed home of King Midas, who had the legendary touch of gold. The most important contribution made by

the Lydians to the ancient world was the use of coinage as an international medium of exchange. Prior to this time, the barter system (the exchange of one commodity for another) was used. The Persians, Greeks, and Romans later adopted coinage, and its use is still quite popular today.

The Lydian king **Croesus** (KREE sus) confronted Cyrus and the advancing Persian army. Cyrus defeated the Lydian army in 546 B.C. Unlike the Assyrians, who had difficulties ruling their vast empire because of their harsh treatment of conquered peoples, Cyrus was a wise and merciful conqueror. He allowed his defeated enemies some measure of self-rule, tolerated their religious beliefs, and restored captive peoples to their homeland. Instead of killing Croesus, Cyrus took him as a prisoner and allowed him to enjoy the life of the Persian royal court.

Cyrus and the Nation of Israel

The Scriptures refer to Cyrus as the "Lord's anointed." Isaiah, the prophet from Judah, some one hundred and fifty years before Cyrus's birth, prophesied:

Thus saith the Lord to his anointed, to Cyrus, whose right hand I have holden [strengthened], to subdue nations before him. . . . For Jacob my servant's sake, and Israel mine elect, I have even called thee by thy name: I have surnamed thee, though thou hast not known me.
—Isaiah 45:1, 4

God used Cyrus to free His people from their captivity in Babylon. Medo-Persian armies conquered Babylon in 539 B.C. As God had used the Assyrians and Chaldeans to punish Israel and Judah, He used Persia to reestablish His repentant people in their land.

I have raised him [Cyrus] up in righteousness, and I will direct all his ways: he shall build my city, and he shall let go my captives, not for price nor reward, saith the Lord of hosts.
—Isaiah 45:13

Not only did Cyrus allow the Jews to return to their land, but he also directed them to rebuild the temple of God in Jerusalem.

Thus saith Cyrus king of Persia, The Lord God of heaven hath given me all the kingdoms of the earth; and he hath charged me to build him a house at Jerusalem, which is in Judah. Who is there among you of all his people? his God be with him, and let him go up to Jerusalem, which is in Judah, and build the house of the Lord God of Israel, (he is the God,) which is in Jerusalem.
—Ezra 1:2-3

Through the Persians, God protected and provided for His chosen people. It was through Esther and the Persian King Xerxes (ZURK seez), called Ahasuerus (uh HAZ yoo EE rus) in the Bible, that God delivered the Jews from the wicked plot of Haman. Later under Artaxerxes I (AR tuh ZURK seez), Nehemiah was allowed to return to Jerusalem to help rebuild the walls (Neh. 2:1-8).

Persian Government

The Persians developed an effective organization to rule the vast territories that they had conquered. The empire was divided into provinces called **satrapies.** Each province was overseen by a satrap, or governor, who was appointed by the Persian king. The king had secret police, known as the "king's eyes," that kept the king informed of matters that took place in each province.

An excellent network of roads facilitated trade and travel throughout the empire. The primary road of the empire—the Royal Road—ran for 1,677 miles from Susa (one of the Persian capitals) to Sardis near the Aegean Sea. These roads aided the Persian mail service, which was similar to the American pony express. In fact, the account of the Persian mail system given by the ancient historian Herodotus has been used to describe the United States Postal Service: "Neither snow nor rain nor heat nor gloom of night stays these couriers from the swift completion of their appointed round." The book of Esther gives us an example of this mail system in action. When Xerxes repealed Haman's evil decree against the Jews, he sent letters throughout the provinces telling of his decision (Esther 8:3-10).

Description of the Persian Postal System

Nothing mortal travels so fast as these Persian messengers. The entire plan is a Persian invention; and this is the method of it. Along the whole line of road there are men (they say) stationed with horses, in number equal to the number of days which the journey takes, allowing a man and horse to each day; and these men will not be hindered from accomplishing at their best speed the distance which they have to go, either by snow, or rain, or heat, or by the darkness of night.[5]

Persian Culture

Much of Persian culture was adopted from previous civilizations. The Persians borrowed the idea of coinage and gold currency from the Lydians. Their early writing system was the Sumerian cuneiform. Phoenicians and Greeks supplied the Persians with her navy. The Persians also popularized the Egyptian calendar.

Ruins of the ancient city of Persepolis echo the distant glory and grandeur of the Persian Empire. Persepolis (Greek for "city of Persia") was the residence of the kings of Persia from the time of Darius I (521-486 B.C.). The city was destroyed by the armies of Alexander the Great in 330 B.C.

The religion of ancient Persia was founded by and took its name from the religious leader **Zoroaster** (ZOR oh AS ter), who lived during the sixth century B.C. Zoroaster rejected the polytheism prevalent in much of the ancient world and instituted the worship of one god, Ahura Mazda. The sacred writings of Zoroastrianism, called the *Avesta,* consist of myths, regulations, and hymns of praise. Zoroaster taught that good and evil are two opposing forces; the world was their battleground. Every man takes part in this struggle, Zoroaster taught, for he serves either the forces of good or the forces of evil. Like so many of the world's false religions, Zoroastrianism held that at the end of life one would be assured of eternal happiness if his good works outweighed his evil.

The Persian Empire continued some two hundred years after the death of Cyrus. Under Darius the Great, the empire reached its height, expanding all the way to Greece, where the Persian expansion was halted. Although the Greeks stopped the Persian advance, the Persians continued to rule the ancient world until a new world conqueror, Alexander the Great, created an even greater empire toward the close of the fourth century B.C.

Section Review

1. What city became the capital of the Assyrian Empire?
2. What prophet was sent by God to Nineveh to preach repentance?
3. What term describes the scattering of the Jewish people by Nebuchadnezzar?
4. What Hebrew captive foretold the fall of Babylon?
5. What Persian king, called the "Lord's anointed" by the prophet Isaiah, created the largest empire known to his day and earned the title "the Great"?
6. What was the religion of ancient Persia? What was the name of its sacred writings?

A Glimpse Behind and a Glimpse Ahead

The civilizations discussed in this chapter may be viewed almost like the rings that radiate out from a pebble dropped in a pool of water. In this case, the spot where the pebble dropped would be Sumer, site of one of the earliest recorded ancient civilizations. Sumer, in turn, was swallowed by the earliest recorded empire, that of the Akkadians. Successive empires swelled larger and larger, while smaller civilizations, such as the Israelites, existed on their borders or flourished during the lulls in empire building.

The Persian Empire represented in many ways the climax of the civilizations of the ancient Near East. It encompassed the territory held by nearly every other civilization discussed in this chapter and even surpassed them in its expanse. Yet Persia eventually fell to an even greater conqueror—Alexander the Great. He not only exceeded the Persians in empire building but also transformed the cultures of the peoples he conquered. Through Alexander, the Mediterranean world and lands beyond would feel the impact of the culture of the Greeks—the subject of the next chapter.

Chapter Review

Can You Explain?

civilization	empire	pharaoh	monotheism
polytheistic	astronomy	hieroglyphics	Diaspora
cuneiform	astrology	Fertile Crescent	Babylonian Captivity
ziggurats	delta	theocracy	satrapies

Can You Identify?

Sargon I	Amenhotep II	Joshua	Nebuchadnezzar
Hammurabi	Rameses II	David	Belshazzar
Epic of Gilgamesh	Baal	Solomon	Cyrus
Menes	Abraham	722 B.C.	Croesus
Khufu (Cheops)	Jacob (Israel)	586 B.C.	Zoroaster
Hatshepsut	Joseph	Sargon II	*Avesta*
Thutmose III	Moses	Sennacherib	

Can You Locate?

Mesopotamia	Ur	Thebes	Samaria
Tigris River	Babylon	Asia Minor	Fertile Crescent
Euphrates River	Egypt	Tyre	Nineveh
Persian Gulf	Nile River	Damascus	
Sumer	Memphis	Sinai Peninsula	
Akkad	Giza	Jerusalem	

How Much Do You Remember?

1. Identify at least one civilization which began along the banks of the Euphrates and Tigris rivers. What civilization began along the banks of the Nile River?

2. List at least one way in which each of the following civilizations played a role in the history of Israel: Sumerians, Egyptians, Hittites, Phoenicians, Assyrians, Chaldeans, and Persians.

3. Make a list of each of the men listed in the "Can You Identify?" section. Beside each name, identify the civilization to which that person belonged.

4. Arriving at the correct date for an event in ancient history is a difficult task. How did the Hebrews calculate dates? See Isaiah 6:1, 7:1; Ezra 1:1-2; and I Kings 6:1.

5. From Genesis 50:2-3 and 50:26 we find that some of the Hebrews followed one of the Egyptian customs. Which one was it?

6. Outline the civilizations and kings mentioned in the book of Daniel. From the following references, can you name the kings Daniel served? (Dan. 1:1; 5:1-2, 31; 10:1)

What Do You Think?

1. Does the early historical record support or contradict the evolutionary theory that life and civilization progress from simple to complex? Explain your answer.

2. What can be learned about the land of Egypt from the prophecy of its destruction in Isaiah 19:1-10?

3. From Ezekiel 27, list at least five items included in the trade of the Phoenicians.

Notes

1. Samuel N. Kramer, *History Begins at Sumer* (Garden City, N.Y.: Anchor Books, 1959), pp. 8-9.
2. James B. Pritchard, ed., *Ancient Near Eastern Texts Relating to the Old Testament* (Princeton: Princeton Univ. Press, 1969), pp. 164-77.
3. W. J. Martin, trans., "The Law Code of Hammurabi," in *Documents from Old Testament Times*, ed. D. Winton Thomas (Edinburgh: Thomas Nelson and Sons, 1958); reprint ed. (New York: Harper and Row, 1961), pp. 29-35 *passim*.
4. Pritchard, p. 93.
5. Herodotus, *The History of Herodotus*, trans. George Rawlinson, 8. 98.

The Greek Civilization

After the Flood the descendants of Javan (Japheth's son) journeyed westward from Mesopotamia and settled in the land we now call Greece (Isa. 66:19). This land is a mountainous peninsula in the eastern Mediterranean. Between it and Asia Minor lies the island-dotted Aegean Sea. Here was the cradle of Greek civilization. Geography influenced Greek history from its very beginning. Mountains made farming difficult, but abundant natural harbors encouraged the Greeks to become seafarers. Furthermore, the rugged terrain hindered communication among the Greek cities, causing them to remain isolated. As a result the Greeks developed a spirit of independence and local patriotism and became known for their self-sufficient individualism.

The Early Greek World

Aegean Civilizations

Archaeologists have found remains of two remarkable civilizations, the Minoan and Mycenaean, which preceded the Greek civilization in the Aegean region. Although these civilizations did not last long, they left a permanent stamp upon later Greek culture.

Crete

The earliest center of civilization in the Aegean region was located on the island of Crete. By 2000 B.C. the **Minoan civilization** (named after the legendary King Minos) flourished on the island. Through their trade and colonization, the Minoans came into contact with the people of the Fertile Crescent. The Minoans established trade routes with the Egyptians, who desired Cretan olive oil and fine pottery. Many scholars believe that the Philistines, who troubled the Hebrew people in Palestine, were colonists from this Cretan civilization.

The grand palace at Knossos, the capital city, gives us an indication of the wealth and achievement of the Minoans. The palace had hundreds of rooms and covered several acres. Flush toilets, bathtubs, and piped water were some of the "modern" conveniences found there. The beautiful carvings, pottery, and frescoes (paintings done on wet plaster walls) found among the ruins of the palace reflect the Minoan love for beauty.

Mycenae

At Mycenae (my SEE nee) on the mainland of Greece, another center of Aegean culture emerged. The **Mycenaean civilization** was established by invaders from the north. Much of the Mycenaean knowledge of art, building, and commerce came from the Minoan culture. When Knossos was de-

stroyed around 1400 B.C. (possibly by the Mycenaeans), Mycenae became the leading commercial center of the Aegean region.

While the Minoan culture displayed a love for beauty, the Mycenaean culture reflected the military fervor of her people. Her palaces were built on high hills and fortified with massive walls. Rival kings fought constantly. The Mycenaeans expanded their trade through sea raids, piracy, and colonization.

A major commercial rival of Mycenae was the city of Troy. Located on the western coast of Asia Minor, Troy sat on a hill overlooking the Hellespont (HEL us PAHNT), the strait that separates Asia Minor from Europe. (See the map on p. 49.) This strategic site linked the land trade of the Fertile Crescent with the sea trade of the Aegean world.

According to Greek legend the Mycenaeans went to war against the city of Troy. After ten years of bitter struggle, Troy finally fell to the Mycenaeans. They had gained entrance to the city by use of the fabled Trojan horse. The glory of Mycenae was short-lived, however. Around 1200 B.C., invaders

The Lion Gate, entrance into the fortified citadel of Mycenae

The Trojan War

According to ancient Greek legend, the Trojan War began when a Trojan prince named Paris abducted Helen, the wife of a Spartan king. The Greeks set sail for Troy when Paris refused to release her. The war lasted for ten years before the Greeks came up with an ingenious plan to capture Troy. They built a huge wooden horse as a "peace offering"; fully armed Greek soldiers hid within the belly of the horse. Once they were in place, the remaining Greeks closed the trap door and rolled the huge horse up to the city walls. They then withdrew in their ships to a place out of sight of Troy to await darkness, when they would return to the city. Thinking that the Greeks had finally left their land, the Trojans took the horse into the city and celebrated their good fortune. The celebration made the Trojans drunk and careless and enabled the Greek soldiers inside the horse to open the trap door, slip out, kill the drunken guards, and open the city gates to the returning Greek army. In just a few hours, the Greeks were able to burn and sack the city. We remember this event whenever we refer to a "Trojan horse" or when we repeat the familiar saying "Beware of Greeks bearing gifts."

called the **Dorians** came down from the north and conquered the main Mycenaean fortresses. The Dorian invasion marked the decline of the Mycenaean civilization and ushered in a new period of Greek history.

The Greek Dark Ages

The period from 1150 to 750 B.C. is known as the "Dark Ages" of Greek history. During this period there were new intruders in the land. They neglected the great palace fortresses, once the centers of culture in the Aegean world. Instead they adopted a simpler life in local villages and encour-

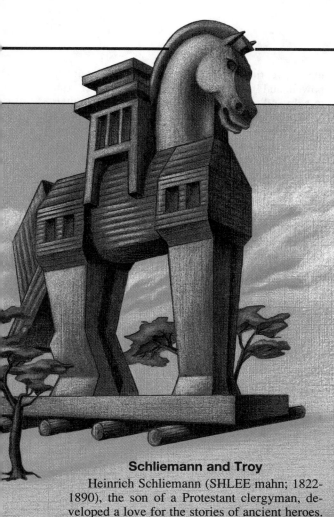

Schliemann and Troy

Heinrich Schliemann (SHLEE mahn; 1822-1890), the son of a Protestant clergyman, developed a love for the stories of ancient heroes.

As a boy, Schliemann had been thrilled as his father told him in a simple and dramatic way about the Trojan War. The stories so fascinated him that Schliemann talked about them regularly. Many of the children his age laughed at him, but young Heinrich determined that one day he would find Troy.

After his commercial ventures had made him a millionaire, Schliemann retired from business and devoted himself to his lifelong ambition—finding Troy. Few scholars in the nineteenth century believed that Troy or even Homer ever existed. Schliemann, however, did not listen to their opinions. He received permission from the Turkish government to carry out excavations.

He first went to the place where Troy was believed by some to be located. Upon reaching the spot, Schliemann was troubled; the landscape was different from that described by Homer. Using the topographical information found in the *Iliad* as a guide, Schliemann found a site about three miles from the sea coast which seemed to harmonize with Homer's description. He hired workmen, and the digging began. After three years' work, Schliemann found not just one city of Troy but nine cities, each built upon the ruins of the previous city. His childhood dream had at last come true.

aged little contact with areas outside the Aegean region. Despite the decline of the Minoan and Mycenaean civilizations, this period did witness the blending of the distinctive elements in the Aegean world into a common Greek culture.

Our knowledge of the Greek Dark Ages rests largely upon the epic poems, the *Iliad* and the *Odyssey*, attributed to the Greek poet **Homer.** Because Homer's poems provide nearly the only glimpse of the early Greek way of life, historians have also called this period the ''Homeric Age.'' With stories of heroic figures, brutal warfare, and adventurous exploits, Homer describes the shaping of Greek culture. Values such as dignity, strength, valor, bravery, generosity, and wisdom as expressed in the lives of Homer's characters are the qualities the Greeks honored most.

Tell me, O Muse, of that ingenious hero [Odysseus] who traveled far and wide after he had sacked the famous town of Troy. Many cities did he visit, and many were the nations with whose manners and customs he was acquainted; moreover, he suffered much by sea while trying to save his own life and bring his men safely home.[1]

Greek Mythology

Greek mythology played a dominant role in shaping Greek culture during the Homeric Age. The Greeks devised stories (myths) to explain their beliefs about life, the world, and God. According to Greek mythology the twelve chief gods and goddesses dwelt on Mount Olympus, the heaven of the gods. **Zeus,** the "king of gods and man," was the ruler of Mount Olympus. His son Apollo was the

Temple of Poseidon on the southern tip of the Peloponnesus; *Inset:* Bronze statue of Poseidon

god of the sun, music, and medicine. **Athena,** patron of the city of Athens, was the goddess of wisdom. Ruling over the sea and earthquakes was the god Poseidon, Zeus's brother.

The Greeks believed in many gods, all of whom were endowed with certain human characteristics (**anthropomorphic,** "having human form or attributes"); yet these gods also possessed extraordinary powers and immortality. The gods had power both to help and to harm man. Zeus, for example, often expressed his anger with men by sending lightning bolts to earth. Because these gods were the invention of sinful men, it is not surprising that they exhibited human sins: they were immoral, impatient, whimsical, unjust, and deceitful. Even so, the Greeks sought the favor of these gods through prayers and sacrifices. How different was the Greek religion from that of the Hebrew people, who worshiped the one true God.

In honor of Zeus, the Greeks held national religious festivals every four years at Olympia, the site of a temple of Zeus. Physical contests, thought to please the gods, became the chief feature of these festivals. The Olympic Games, as they became known, attracted competitors from all over the Aegean world. Each participant represented his home city. The intense competition indicated the high regard the Greeks had for physical prowess. To attain physical perfection was the ultimate goal of every athlete. The games became so popular that the **Olympiad,** the four-year interval between the games, became a Greek means of dating historical events. The Olympic Games were a rare example of cooperation between the Greek city-states.

Section Review

1. Where was the earliest center of civilization located in the Aegean region?
2. What Aegean culture displayed a love for military pursuits?
3. What ancient city did Heinrich Schliemann discover?
4. From what two epic poems do we get a glimpse of Greek life during the period from 1150 to 750 B.C.? To whom are these poems attributed?
5. What athletic contests began as an attempt to please the Greek gods through physical prowess?

Greek City-States

Role of the City-State

Though they shared the same language, customs, and religious beliefs, the Greeks lacked political unity. The Nile River in Egypt had brought the Egyptian people together and had encouraged their political unification. In sharp contrast, the mountains of Greece tended to isolate the Greek city-states, thus hindering national unity.

The Greeks usually built their cities at the foot of a hill. For protection, they would construct a fortress at the top of the hill, to which they could flee when under attack. They called their city a "polis," and the fortified hill, an "acropolis" (from *acro,* meaning "high").

The **polis,** or "city-state," was the basic political unit of Greece. Although relatively small, Greek city-states exercised powers usually associated with national states. The ultimate source of authority, protection, and livelihood for an individual Greek was his city.

The Greek Word *Polis*

The Greek word *polis* had many interesting meanings. It referred not only to a city with its buildings but also included the people and their government. Today we use this Greek word in much the same way.

Polis Greek Usage	*Polis* Our Usage
"City government"	We talk about *politics.*
"City governor"	We talk about a *politician.*
"A citizens' assembly"	We call it the *polity* or *body politic.*
"City"	Some of our cities have the word *polis* at the end of their names.

Some examples of cities that use *polis* in their names are Indianapolis ("city of Indiana"), Minneapolis ("city of water"), and Annapolis ("city of Anne"; named for Queen Anne of England, 1702-14).

The Athenian Pledge

I will not dishonor my sacred weapons, nor will I abandon the one standing beside me where I am positioned in battle. . . . I will not pass on my fatherland inferior, but greater and better. . . . If anyone tries to do away with its laws, I will not allow it, whether I stand by myself or with everyone else.

Government of the City-States

The Greek city-states experienced four basic forms of government. The earliest form was a **monarchy,** "rule *(archy)* by one *(mono),*" which was prominent during the Homeric Age. The king received advice from a council of nobles and a popular assembly. Gradually the council of nobles assumed the king's powers and ruled as the privileged class. This "rule of a few," called an **oligarchy** (AHL ih GAR kee), produced great tension between the wealthy noble class and the lower classes.

The dissatisfaction and unrest of the lower classes often led to **tyranny**. At the head of this government was a tyrant who gained complete control of the government—usually by force. A tyrant was not necessarily a corrupt ruler, as our modern conception of that word implies. He often championed the cause of the common people and brought about reform that allowed more people to participate in government.

A unique political contribution of the Greeks was the development of **democracy,** rule by the people. How different this was from the all-powerful rule of the kings of the Fertile Crescent and the pharaohs of Egypt! Here was a government in which each adult male citizen could share in the responsibility of ruling his city.

Development of the City-States

The period from 750 to 500 B.C. in Greek history saw the development of the Greek city-states. Important in later Greek history, the city-states of Sparta and Athens represented two opposing polit-

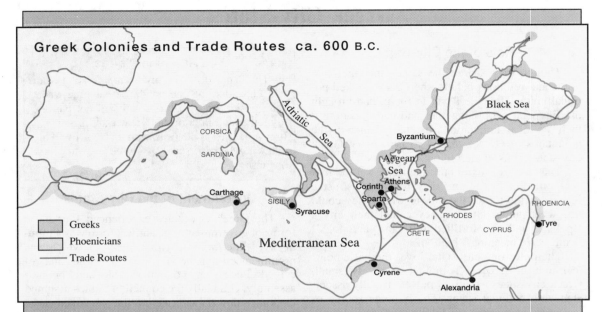

Greek Colonies and Trade Routes ca. 600 B.C.

Black Sea

Adriatic Sea

CORSICA

SARDINIA

Byzantium

Aegean Sea

Carthage

Corinth
Athens
Sparta

SICILY

Syracuse

PHOENICIA

RHODES

CRETE

CYPRUS

Tyre

Greeks

Phoenicians

Trade Routes

Mediterranean Sea

Cyrene

Alexandria

Greek Colonization

Greek settlement was not restricted to the land we call Greece. From about 750 to 550 B.C, Greeks established colonies throughout the Mediterranean world. The most important Greek colony in the western Mediterranean was the city of Syracuse on the island of Sicily. In fact, the Greeks established so many colonies on Sicily and in southern Italy that the area became known as *Magna Graecia* (Great Greece). Some colonies were founded to alleviate overcrowding, some were founded as trading posts, and some were founded as places to send the undesirable members of society.

The colonization procedure was as follows: A mother city—called a metropolis—would choose a leader (often a noble) to direct the expedition. After listening to the reports of merchants, the leader then chose a site for the colony. When final preparations had been made, the colonists, taking with them a small amount of soil as well as fire from the altars of the mother city, boarded the ships and set sail.

Once the colonists arrived at their destination, the leader assigned land and established various laws and religious rites. (Sometimes the people even worshiped their leader after his death in honor of his services to the colony.) Finally, when the colonists were securely settled, they broke their ties with the metropolis. The new city-state was on its own.

ical systems and ways of life. Other Greek city-states were to follow the example and leadership of either Sparta or Athens.

Sparta

Sparta was located in the southern part of Greece on the peninsula called the Peloponnesus (PEL uh puh NEE sus). Conquered by the Dorians,

her inhabitants were made slaves, or **Helots** (HEL uts). The new rulers of Sparta conquered surrounding areas, reducing many of the inhabitants to slave status. Soon the Helots outnumbered the Spartans. In constant fear of an uprising, the Spartans created a thoroughly militaristic state.

The way of life at Sparta centered on the training of warriors. The highest goal of any Spartan was to be the best warrior for the Spartan state. Sparta controlled all aspects of her citizens' lives in order to maintain an army ready for battle. Spartan elders determined whether babies were healthy enough to be reared. An unhealthy baby would be left on a hillside to die. When boys reached the age of seven, the state took them from their homes and placed them in army barracks. Here they underwent rigorous physical training to make them into fit warriors. They were beaten so that they would learn to endure pain. They were encouraged to steal in order to prove their resourcefulness. At the age of twenty, they became a part of the Spartan army but were not full citizens of the Spartan state until they reached the age of thirty. Even then they had to eat and sleep in the army camp instead of at home; they had to be prepared to fight at all times.

Spartan girls went through similar training so that they might learn the same Spartan spirit. Their discipline included running, jumping, and boxing. Their chief goal was to become strong mothers, rearing warriors for the state. Spartan women reportedly sent their sons and husbands off to battle with the words "Return with your shields or on them."

Sparta became the champion of the oligarchical form of government. A board of five Spartan nobles guarded against changes in the Spartan society and any harmful outside influences that would disrupt the *status quo* (existing state of affairs). To ensure the continuing success of her military state, the Spartans often used force or intimidation to help establish oligarchies in neighboring city-states. These city-states organized the **Peloponnesian League,** with Sparta at its head. Its purpose was to thwart the advance of the democratic principles fostered by the Athenians.

Athens

Life in Athens contrasted sharply with the rigid, disciplined life of Sparta. Sparta became associated with militarism, isolation, oligarchy, and glorification of the state. Athens, however, nurtured creativity, commercial endeavors, democracy, and individualism. The Athenians maintained the creative and intellectual heritage of the Minoan and Mycenaean civilizations.

Like other Greek city-states, Athens was ruled by a king during the Homeric Age. Later the noble

---

Greek Language

God chose to use Greek, the language of the ancient world, in writing of the New Testament. To the right is John 3:16 in Greek, with a literal translation.

Greek		English	Greek		English
Α	α	a	Ν	ν	n
Β	β	b	Ξ	ξ	x
Γ	γ	g	Ο	ο	o (short)
Δ	δ	d	Π	π	p
Ε	ε	e (short)	Ρ	ρ	r
Ζ	ζ	z	Σ	σ, ς	s
Η	η	e (long)	Τ	τ	t
Θ	θ	th	Υ	υ	u *or* y
Ι	ι	i	Φ	φ	ph
Κ	κ	k	Χ	χ	ch, kh
Λ	λ	l	Ψ	ψ	ps
Μ	μ	m	Ω	ω	o (long)

Οὕτως γὰρ ἠγάπησεν ὁ Θεὸς τὸν κόσμον, ὥστε
So   for   loved   God   the world,   that

τὸν υἱὸν τὸν μονογενῆ ἔδωκεν, ἵνα
the Son-His the only-begotten He gave, that

πᾶς ὁ πιστεύων εἰς αὐτὸν μὴ ἀπόληται
every one believing into Him not should perish

ἀλλ' ἔχη ζωὴν αἰώνιον.
but should have life everlasting.

Many Greek words have come directly, or almost directly, into English. Using the chart to the left, how many can you recognize?

ἐγώ   κόσμος   μάρτυρος   συναγωγή
εὕρηκα   κρίσις   μυστήριον   φωνή

Greek countryside and harbor; the mountainous terrain of Greece contributed to the political fragmentation of Greek civilization.

sixth century B.C. Charting a moderate course in Athenian affairs, he provided economic and political stability during a time of tension and hostility. Although Solon was of the noble class, he instituted reforms that helped the common man. For example, he forbade the practice of making debtors into slaves. He also created the Council of Four Hundred, which gave representation to all sections of Athens. He later wrote of his years in government:

> On the one hand I gave the common people such privilege as is sufficient, neither detracting from nor adding to their honor. On the other hand I declared that those having power and being admired for their riches should also have nothing shameful done to them. I stood casting a strong shield back and forth between both sides, and I would not allow either an unjust victory.

The moderate policies that Solon instituted satisfied neither political side. After Solon's death tension mounted again between the nobles and the common people. Tyrants supporting the cause of the lower classes arose and seized control of the government. They initiated reforms and reorganized the government to allow greater citizen participation. It was not until the fifth century B.C. under the leadership of Pericles (PARE ih KLEEZ) that Athens established a "rule of the people."

class rose in power and established an oligarchy. Power was vested in a council of nobles, with the chief magistrate, or **archon,** being elected from the nobility. As the nobles gained more and more power, hostility arose between them and the common people.

Under the leadership of the statesman **Solon,** Athens took a step toward democracy. Solon assumed the office of archon at the beginning of the

Section Review

1. What was the basic political unit of Greece?
2. List and define the four basic forms of government found in the Greek city-states.
3. What two Greek city-states represented two opposing ways of life within Greek society?
4. What language did God choose in the writing of the New Testament?
5. What Greek city-state was characterized by creativity, commercial endeavors, democracy, and individualism?

The Fateful Century

The Persian Wars

At the outset of the fifth century B.C., the westward advance of the Persian Empire threatened Greek independence and isolation. The Persians, expanding into Asia Minor, conquered the Lydians as well as the Greek colonies located along the coast bordering the Aegean Sea. The Greek colonies were well treated by the Persians, but the Greeks, who loved freedom, could not tolerate Persian authority. With the support of Athens, the Greek colonies rebelled and overthrew Persian rule.

Under King **Darius I** the Persians not only crushed the revolt but also sought to punish Athens for her part in the rebellion. (This is the same Darius that is mentioned in Ezra 6:1, 6-12. His government order and official assistance aided immensely in the reconstruction of the house of God at Jerusalem.) In 490 B.C. a Persian force landed at the Bay of Marathon, about twenty-five miles north of Athens. Though outnumbered and seemingly doomed for destruction, the Athenian army marched out to meet the mighty Persian army. The Greek historian Herodotus (hih RAHD uh tus) wrote about the Persian Wars and gave this description of the battle:

> So when the battle was set in array . . . instantly the Athenians . . . charged the barbarians [Persians] at a run. Now the distance between the two armies was little short of [one mile]. The Persians, therefore, when they saw the Greeks coming on at speed, made ready to receive them, although it seemed to them the Athenians were bereft of their senses, and bent upon their own destruction; for they saw a mere handful of men coming on at a run without either horsemen or archers. Such was the opinion of the barbarians; but the Athenians in close array fell upon them, and fought in a manner worthy of being recorded.[2]

Surprised by the Greek charge, the Persians were unable to use their cavalry effectively, upon which they heavily relied. Instead, they found themselves engaged in hand-to-hand combat; they were no match for the physical strength and battle skill of the Greek soldiers. The Greeks won a decisive victory.

Battle of Thermopylae

Furious over this setback, Darius organized a full-scale invasion of Greece. He died before this could be carried out, but the struggle was renewed by his son, **Xerxes.** According to legend, Xerxes appointed a slave to sit at his feet and say to him each day, "Master, remember the Athenians!" He amassed a great invasion force of men, ships, and supplies. Crossing the Hellespont upon a bridge made of boats, the Persian army marched toward Greece.

In 480 B.C. the Persians, accompanied by their large fleet of ships, made their way down the Greek coast. The Greeks differed on how best to defend their cities. The Spartans suggested that the Greeks mass their forces across the Corinthian isthmus and defend the Peloponnesus. The Athenians objected to this plan because it would leave Athens exposed to the Persian army. The Greeks finally decided to take their stand at the mountain pass of Thermopylae (thur MOP uh lee), north of most of the city-states. (See the map of the Persian Wars found on the following page.)

At Thermopylae a force of about seven thousand Greeks confronted the advancing Persian army. According to the historian Herodotus, who could never resist improving a story, the Persians numbered about three million. It was more likely that they numbered about two hundred thousand. The Greeks held a good position, however, since only a small number of the Persian army could advance through the narrow pass at one time. The Persians attacked three times but could not take the pass. Then a Greek traitor showed the Persians another way through the mountains. When the Greeks realized that they were almost surrounded, they retreated, but three hundred Spartans remained to hold the pass. These Spartans, all valiant men, fought to the death. According to Herodotus "they defended themselves to the last, such as still had swords using them, and the others resisting with their hands and teeth."[3] A monument at the spot bore these words: "Tell them in Sparta, passerby, that here, obedient to their orders, we lie."

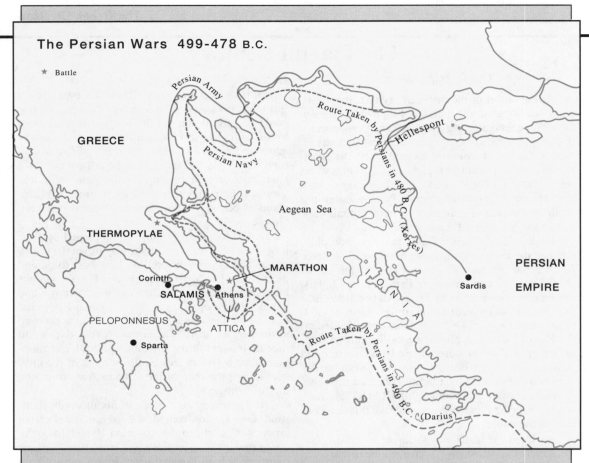

The Persian Wars 499-478 B.C.

★ Battle

Persian Army

Route Taken by Persians in 480 B.C. (Xerxes)

Hellespont

GREECE

Persian Navy

Aegean Sea

THERMOPYLAE

Corinth

SALAMIS   Athens

MARATHON

PERSIAN

EMPIRE

Sardis

IONIA

PELOPONNESUS

ATTICA

Sparta

Route Taken by Persians in 490 B.C. (Darius)

The Hellespont Bridge

To move his army across the Hellespont from Asia Minor to Greece, Xerxes attempted a seemingly impossible feat: to build two bridges over which his army and its supplies could pass. Under the direction of Phoenician and Egyptian engineers, his men anchored a total of 674 ships in two lines across the mile-wide waterway. After tying the ships together with ropes, they laid down a plank roadway across their decks. On the planks they laid brush, which they covered with dirt, pressed down to make a solid surface. The process was nearly completed when a storm destroyed both bridges. The furious Xerxes had the chief engineers beheaded and then had the Hellespont beaten with 300 lashes! Then, under the direction of a Greek engineer, the Persians built two new bridges in the same way. In late May 480 B.C., Xerxes dedicated the bridges by throwing a golden cup, a golden bowl, and a war sword into the water. Then, taking several days, the army marched across one bridge, while the supply wagons used the other. Xerxes, viewing his troops from a nearby mountain, began to weep. When a friend asked him why, he said, "There came upon me a sudden pity, when I thought of the shortness of man's life, and considered that of all this host, so numerous as it is, not one will be alive when a hundred years are gone by." Xerxes and the Persian army were now on the European continent, a step closer to their confrontation with the Greeks.

Battle of Salamis Bay

Once past the Spartan barrier, the Persians swept on to Athens. Xerxes burned it to the ground. The Athenians had left the city, realizing that they would not be able to defend it. They withdrew to an island called Salamis, just off the coast.

Hoping to exploit Xerxes' desire for a quick victory, Themistocles (thuh MIS tuh KLEEZ), the leader of Athens, devised a trap. He sent a trusted slave to Xerxes with the story that the Greeks were frightened and were planning to escape in the morning by sailing northward. The slave also suggested that if Xerxes were to send his ships into the strait between the mainland and Salamis, he would be able to block their escape. The next morning Xerxes ordered his fleet, with many of his soldiers on board, to attack the Greeks. The Persians entered the strait just as Themistocles had hoped. But the rising morning tide made their large ships hard to maneuver. As the Persian sailors struggled to steer their crafts, the Greeks launched their ships from the beaches of Salamis. The small, easily maneuvered Greek crafts created great confusion as they rammed and sank a great many Persian vessels. From a high vantage point overlooking the bay, Xerxes watched as the Greeks carried the day.

The following year the Greeks, led by Sparta, defeated a sizable Persian army, which had remained in northern Greece. Although they had stopped the Persian invasion force, they did little to weaken the vast Persian Empire. The Persians continued to interfere in Greek affairs for two hundred years following the war. Yet the Greeks maintained their hard-fought independence. Freedom bolstered the Greek spirit, furthered the growth of democracy, and encouraged Greek creativity. The way was prepared for the so-called "Golden Age" of Greece—a period of great cultural achievement. Nevertheless, the sinfulness of the Greek people did not change; they retained their pagan ideas.

The Periclean Age

Nowhere in Greece following the Persian Wars was the spirit of patriotism and self-confidence stronger than in Athens. She became the leading city-state of all Greece; because of her heroic efforts

Charles Edwin Long, Vashti Refuses the King's Summons, *Bob Jones University Collection of Sacred Art*

Xerxes

It appears that the disheartened Xerxes returned home from his defeat at Salamis and bemoaned the fact that he had banished his beautiful wife, Vashti. He proposed a beauty contest to find a new wife. Esther, the winner of the contest, proved instrumental in sparing the Jewish people from the wicked plot of Haman (Esther 3). From the book of Esther we can see how God used the Persian defeat by the Greeks to bring safety to His people.

against the Persians, other city-states looked to her for protection. The Athenians encouraged the formation of a defensive alliance among the Greek city-states to protect themselves against any further Persian attacks. This alliance became known as the **Delian League,** and Athens became its leader.

This period of Greek history (460-429 B.C.) is often called "The Age of Pericles." For over thirty years **Pericles** was the influential leader of Athens.

He called Athens the "school of Greece." During Pericles' lifetime Athens attained cultural heights unparalleled in the ancient world. Her climate of freedom inspired excellence in thought, art, science, literature, drama, and architecture. So numerous and notable were the Greek accomplishments during this period that special attention will be devoted to them later in this chapter.

Under Pericles' leadership every adult male citizen of Athens gained the privilege and responsibility of sharing in the Athenian government by being able to vote and hold office. No longer was the government controlled only by those of wealth or of noble birth. Now all adult male citizens could participate in government on an equal basis. The majority of the people of Athens, however—the women, slaves, and foreigners—were still excluded from this privilege.

The Peloponnesian War

The Periclean Age came between two violent upheavals in the fifth century B.C. The first was the Persian Wars, which temporarily united the Greek city-states in a common defense of their liberty. Following the Golden Age came the **Peloponnesian War** (431-404 B.C.), a devastating civil war pitting Greek against Greek. As Athens had grown in influence and wealth, she had transformed the Delian League into an Athenian empire. Sparta became alarmed over the commercial and political power Athens had acquired. The tension between these two rivals and their allies finally flamed into war.

The war has been likened to a struggle between an elephant and a whale. Sparta's strength rested in her land army whereas Athens reigned supreme on the sea with her large fleet. Early in the war a devastating plague wiped out a large portion of the population of Athens, including her leading citizen, Pericles. Though weakened by these losses, Athens continued to fight. Through intermittent fighting, Sparta eventually gained the upper hand by forming an alliance with the Persians. Sparta was finally able to bring Athens to her knees by destroying the Athenian fleet.

Pericles on the Athenian Democracy

Our form of government does not enter into rivalry with the institutions of others. We do not copy our neighbors, but are an example to them. It is true that we are called a democracy, for the administration is in the hands of the many and not of the few. But while the law secures equal justice to all alike in their private disputes, the claim of excellence is also recognized; and when a citizen is in any way distinguished, he is preferred to the public service, not as a matter of privilege, but as the reward of merit. Neither is poverty a bar, but a man may benefit his country whatever be the obscurity of his condition.[4]

Although Sparta emerged victorious, she had nothing but problems after the war. City-states that had looked to Sparta for deliverance from Athenian domination now found themselves under a greater oppressor. Democratic governments were replaced with oligarchies. The Greeks who had experienced freedom found it difficult to submit to Spartan oligarchical rule. Constant uprisings reduced Sparta's control over the Greek city-states, leaving them disunited once again.

Section Review

1. What eastern civilization threatened the Greeks at the outset of the fifth century?
2. At what battle did an unorthodox charge by the Greeks help them to win a decisive victory?
3. Across what body of water did Xerxes make a bridge of boats to move his army?
4. Who was the influential leader of Athens during her so-called Golden Age?
5. What type of war was the Peloponnesian War?

Top: The Parthenon in Athens, temple dedicated to the Greek goddess Athena; **Right:** The Porch of Maidens, one of the fine examples of Greek statuary found on the Acropolis of Athens; **Left Center:** A panoramic view of the Acropolis; **Left Bottom:** Pericles

Alexander's Empire

Rise of Macedonia

North of Greece was Macedonia, inhabited by a people related to the Greeks. King **Philip II** united Macedonia under his rule and extended his kingdom into Greece. Many Greek city-states supported Philip, hoping that he would bring unity to their land. Some resisted him, fearing that their freedom would be lost under Macedonian rule. The weakened and divided Greek city-states were no match for the well-organized army of Philip.

Philip's appreciation for Greek culture led him to treat his many subjects with great tolerance. He hoped to gain Greek support for an invasion of the Persian Empire, the Greeks' constant enemy. But in 336 B.C., before he could fulfill his plans, Philip was assassinated. His son **Alexander** assumed the throne at the age of twenty. As a boy, Alexander had been taught by one of the greatest Greek philosophers, Aristotle, who had instilled in him a love for Greek culture. With his conquering armies he carried this culture to the far reaches of the Near Eastern world.

Conquests of Alexander the Great

With amazing speed Alexander led his army across Asia Minor and confronted the Persian army, led by King **Darius III.** In the heat of one battle, Darius fled, leaving behind his wife, mother, and children to be taken captive by Alexander. Alexander took Syria, destroyed the city of Tyre (see p. 37), and marched unopposed into Egypt. The final blow to the Persian Empire came as Alexander, near the Tigris River, defeated the larger army of Darius. Alexander had accomplished what he had set out to do—to avenge the Persian invasion of Greece and to become the king of Asia.

But his thirst for conquest was not yet satisfied. He marched all the way to India and would have gone beyond, but his weary army refused to go farther. They had been fighting eight years and had

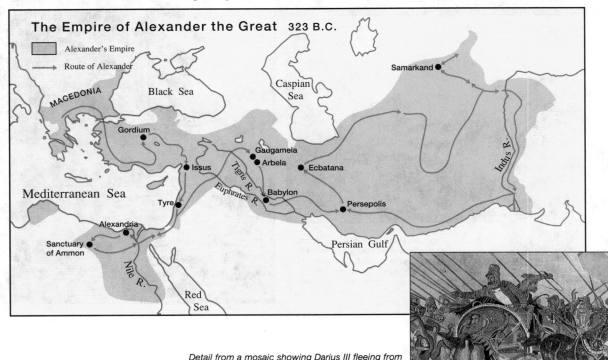

The Empire of Alexander the Great 323 B.C.

Alexander's Empire

Route of Alexander

MACEDONIA • Black Sea • Caspian Sea • Samarkand • Gordium • Gaugamela • Arbela • Issus • Ecbatana • Tigris R. • Euphrates R. • Babylon • Mediterranean Sea • Tyre • Persepolis • Alexandria • Sanctuary of Ammon • Persian Gulf • Nile R. • Indus R. • Red Sea

Detail from a mosaic showing Darius III fleeing from Alexander the Great's forces at the Battle of Issus

marched over eleven thousand miles. Alexander sulked for several days over the unwillingness of his army to continue. Although he had conquered almost all the known world of his day, his achievements had not brought any lasting satisfaction to his heart. How often men have tried to satisfy their soul's desires by seeking the fleeting pleasures of this world. Alexander probably would not have been satisfied even if he had conquered the whole world. God's Word says, "For what is a man profited, if he shall gain the whole world, and lose his own soul? or what shall a man give in exchange for his soul?" (Matt. 16:26).

Division of Alexander's Empire

In 323 B.C., at the height of his power, Alexander died of a fever; he had not yet reached his thirty-third birthday. Over two hundred years before Alexander's death, God's prophet Daniel had foretold that Alexander's empire would be divided into four kingdoms (Dan. 8:21-22; 11:4). Because Alexander left no plans for a successor to his empire, his chief generals fought among themselves to determine who would rule. Four generals emerged victorious and declared themselves kings over portions of the empire; thus Daniel's prophetic vision was fulfilled.

These greedy new kings fought one another as each tried to restore the whole empire under his own rule. From the families of three of Alexander's generals came dynasties that ruled portions of the former empire until the time of the Roman conquests: the Ptolemies (TAHL uh meez) in Egypt, the Seleucids (sih LOO sidz) in Syria and Persia, and the Antigonids (an TIG uh nidz) in Macedonia and Greece.

Alexander will always be remembered as one of the world's greatest military leaders. His empire spread across the ancient world from Greece to India and included most of the capitals of earlier civilizations. He founded cities that became centers of learning and culture. Many of these he named after himself, such as Alexandria in Egypt. Through his conquests he spread the Greek culture and language to the East. Although his empire disintegrated after his death, the Greek culture remained a vital part of the ancient world.

Section Review
1. Over what kingdom did Philip II rule?
2. Who who instilled in Alexander the Great a love for Greek culture?
3. List the three ruling families that ruled portions of Alexander's empire after his death. Identify the region each family ruled.

Greek Culture

The Essence of Greek Culture

The culture of a civilization is a reflection of the values and character of her people. The Greeks cultivated an appreciation for beauty, freedom, justice, truth, and knowledge. They exalted the man who had a creative spirit, versatile talents, a thirst for knowledge, physical ability, and a zest for life. The Greek respect for such qualities as self-control, restraint, balance, and moderation is evident in the Greek motto: "Nothing in excess, and everything in proportion." These were the qualities that characterized Hellenic culture.

The term **Hellenic** is used to describe Greek culture. The Greeks called themselves Hellenes and their land Hellas. The height of Hellenic culture occurred during the Golden Age of Athens. The spirit of freedom, bolstered by the defeat of the Persians, produced the flowering of Hellenic culture in Athens. Most of the Greeks whose achievements history remembers lived in this city.

Ancient Greece has been called the cradle of Western culture. Greek culture left a lasting imprint on the Western world. The Greeks set forth many of the basic concepts of science, mathematics, and philosophy. Greek literature, architecture, and sculpture became models that later civilizations have tried to imitate.

Although the Greek army never conquered the world, Greek culture did. Alexander's conquests spread the Greek language and way of life throughout the ancient world. As a result, Hellenic culture mixed with the cultures of the East. A new culture emerged; it was no longer just Hellenic, meaning "Greek," but **Hellenistic,** "like the Greek."

Hellenistic culture permeated the Near East from the time of Alexander until the coming of the Romans in the first century B.C. Its influence was so great that this period is known as the Hellenistic Age. This culture united the peoples of the Near East by blending their arts, religions, philosophies, and customs. The Hellenistic Age brought the East and West together in learning, in government, and in trade.

The Expression of Greek Culture

Focus on Man

"Wonders are many of earth, and the greatest of these is man." To the Greeks the ability to think and reason made man unique. His "humanity" was thus worthy of special study. The Greeks were among the first to begin the formal study of human thought and culture called the **humanities.** Philosophers and scientists praised the human mind and its reasoning powers. Greek literature dealt with how man lives and acts. The goal of physical activity was to develop the human body toward physical perfection. Greek art focused upon the human form.

The Greeks stressed the dignity and uniqueness of man. They assumed a great truth: man is the highest of created beings. However, they looked upon man's uniqueness apart from God, glorifying the "creature more than the Creator" (Rom. 1:25). As a result they perverted this noble truth into a form of humanism. They did not accept the fact that God created man in His own image; therefore, they praised man for his ability, rather than praising God, who gave man that ability. Similarly, they did not acknowledge their responsibility to their Creator. Instead they believed that "man is the measure [judge] of all things."

Interest in Philosophy

Throughout history men have sought answers to the basic question of life: (1) Where did I come from? (2) Why am I here? (3) Where am I going?

and (4) What is the highest good in life? Early in their history the Greeks developed many myths to help them answer these questions. Following the sixth century B.C., however, many lost confidence in these myths. Men called **philosophers,** "lovers of wisdom," tried to find the answers to these questions through man's reasoning ability. They believed that the highest good was to seek truth and attain knowledge. This, they hoped, would enable men to live properly.

The Greeks believed in the basic goodness of man. They trusted in man's wisdom as a guide for their behavior and as a means for finding happiness. They did not understand that "the wisdom of this world is foolishness with God. . . . The Lord knoweth the thoughts of the wise, that they are vain. Therefore let no man glory in men" (I Cor. 3:19-21). The Greeks relied on man's reasoning ability in their search for wisdom. However, God's Word says that "the fear of the Lord is the beginning of wisdom: and the knowledge of the holy is understanding" (Prov. 9:10).

Thales of Miletus (640?-546 B.C.) is often called the "Father of Philosophy." Among the Greeks, Thales (THAY leez) was one of the first who sought to explain the origin of the universe in natural terms. He concluded that water was the original substance of all things. He and other early philosophers did not deal with the questions of ethics—what is right and wrong. This was left to later philosophers, the most famous of whom are Socrates, Plato, and Aristotle.

Socrates (470?-399 B.C.)—**Socrates** (SAHK ruh TEEZ), a contemporary of Pericles, lived in Athens during her Golden Age. This snub-nosed man with bulging eyes devoted his life to seeking truth and teaching men how to conduct their lives. He took as his motto "Know thyself." According to Socrates, "The unexamined life is not worth living."

Socrates was not a writer but a teacher. We know what he taught by what his students wrote about him. His method of teaching involved the asking of leading questions followed by the analyzing of the students' answers. Socrates believed that truth (absolutes) could be attained through human reason. To Socrates virtue is knowledge, and ignorance produces evil. Thus reason is the best guide to good behavior.

Many in Athens objected to Socrates' questioning of some of the fundamental institutions of the city. They accused him of corrupting the youth and rejecting the gods of Athens. He was tried and condemned to death. Refusing to flee, Socrates calmly drank the cup of hemlock (poison) by which the sentence of death was to be carried out. He died at the age of seventy in the midst of his followers.

Plato (427?-347 B.C.)—The most famous pupil of Socrates was **Plato** (PLAY toh). He established a school of philosophy and science in Athens called the Academy. In the *Republic,* he devised one of the first plans for an ideal society and government. Although Plato lived in democratic Athens, he realized that too much liberty and freedom without restraint often leads to **anarchy** (the breakdown of government and order). He stated that the "excess of liberty, whether in states or individuals, seems only to pass into excess of slavery."

In his works Plato discussed what he considered the nature of true reality. He determined that something would have to be permanent (eternal) if it were to be truly real. Since nothing in this world is permanent, Plato concluded that true reality lies outside the physical world. The things on earth are mere shadows, or imperfect reflections, of their eternal counterparts, or "forms," in the unseen realm of eternity. Through this reasoning process Plato came close to the biblical truth expressed by the Apostle Paul in II Corinthians 4:18—"For the things which are seen are temporal; but the things which are not seen are eternal."

Aristotle (384-322 B.C.)—The last of the three famous Greek philosophers was **Aristotle** (EHR uh STOT ul). Aristotle was not an Athenian like the other two but came to Athens from northern Greece. At the age of eighteen, he began his study at Plato's Academy. Plato called his most famous student "the mind of the school." Like Plato, Aristotle has had a continuing impact on Western thought through his writings. Aristotle, as we discussed earlier, was also the tutor of Alexander the Great and instilled in the young prince an appreciation for Greek culture.

Unlike Plato, Aristotle believed that reality was in the physical world. Therefore, he developed

Jacques Louis David, The Death of Socrates, *Metropolitan Museum of Art, New York*

wide interests in many fields. He wrote treatises on politics, biology, physics, art, drama, mathematics, and ethics. He is best remembered for his works on logic, which are collectively called the *Organon* (''Instrument''). To aid man's reasoning ability, Aristotle developed the **syllogism,** a three-step logical process of thinking. The following is a good example: (1) All Greeks are human; (2) Aristotle is a Greek; (3) Therefore, Aristotle is human.

Epicureans and Stoics—The Epicurean (EP ih kyoo REE un) and Stoic philosophies emerged shortly after the death of Alexander the Great. **Epicurus** believed that great happiness and pleasure could be achieved through the avoidance of pain and fear. **Zeno,** the founder of Stoicism, taught that the affairs of men and the universe were ordered by fixed laws. Man must accept his fate and live a life of duty and self-control. These philosophies had greater impact upon the Roman world than on the Hellenistic world. (See pp. 104-6.) When the Apostle Paul visited Athens in the first century A.D., certain Epicurean and Stoic philosophers mocked him because his preaching concerning the resurrection (Acts 17:18, 32) contradicted their teaching. Paul replied:

> Ye men of Athens, I perceive that in all things ye are too superstitious. For as I passed by, and beheld your devotions, I found an altar with this inscription, TO THE UNKNOWN GOD. Whom therefore ye ignorantly worship, him declare I unto you. God that made the world and all things therein, seeing that he is Lord of heaven and earth, dwelleth not in temples made with hands; neither is worshipped with men's hands, as though he needed any thing, seeing he giveth to all life and breath, and all things; and hath made of one blood all nations of men for to dwell on all the face of the earth, and hath determined the times before appointed, and the bounds of their habitation; that they should seek the Lord, if haply they might feel after him, and find him, though he be not far from every one of us: for in him we live, and move, and have our being; as certain also of your own poets have said, For we are also his offspring.
>
> —Acts 17:22-28

Logic

We remember many things about Aristotle. One of his best-known contributions is the syllogism (a way of reasoning). A syllogism consists of three parts: (1) a major premise (statement); (2) a minor premise; and (3) a conclusion. Here is an example of a syllogism:

Major Premise: All spiders have eight legs.

Minor Premise: A tarantula is a spider.

Conclusion: Therefore, a tarantula has eight legs.

From this simple example we are able to devise a formula for logical reasoning: $(a \rightarrow b, c \rightarrow a, \therefore c \rightarrow b)$. If we do not follow this formula, we could come up with reasoning like this:

Major Premise: All cows have four legs.

Minor Premise: My cat has four legs.

Conclusion: Therefore, my cat is a cow.

Only if the major premise is reversible (true whether you read it forward or backward) can we reason the way we did in the second example. The following is an example of this type of premise: All right angles have ninety degrees; all ninety-degree angles are right angles.

Contributions to Science, Medicine, and Mathematics

The questions raised by the Greek philosophers concerning man and his world encouraged others to seek natural or logical explanations through observation. Even before the Golden Age, **Pythagoras** (pih THAG er us), a philosopher and mathematician of the sixth century B.C., had concluded that the universe could be explained in mathematical terms. His geometric theorem, the Pythagorean Theorem, is still studied by students of geometry.

Hippocrates (460?-377? B.C.), the famed physician of the Golden Age, is known as the ''Father of Medicine.'' After studying in Athens, Hippocrates became a wandering physician who traveled throughout Greece and Macedonia. Contrary to common Greek myths which held that disease was the punishment of the gods, Hippocrates (hih PAHK ruh TEEZ) taught that every illness has a natural cause. He rejected magic and superstition and instead recommended rest and proper diet as the proper treatments. He wrote manuals that preserved his findings for other physicians. On the walls of many doctors' offices today hangs a copy of Hippocrates' oath, which governed his practice of medicine.

The Hippocratic Oath

I swear . . . to fulfill, according to my power and judgment, this oath and this written contract. . . . I will use diets for the help of the sick according to my power and judgment, not for injury or to do an unjust thing. I will not ever give a deadly drug to anyone, even if asked, nor will I lead the way in such counsel; and likewise I will not give a woman a device to cause an abortion. I will keep my life and my art purely and piously. . . . If I fulfill this oath and do not break it, may it be mine to enjoy the fruit of both my life and my art, being honored among all men for all time; but if I transgress and break it, may the opposite of these things come to pass.

Euclid (YOO klid) has often been called the "Father of Geometry." He founded a school of mathematics in Alexandria, Egypt. His textbook *Elements* has been the basis for geometry textbooks up through the twentieth century. The Greek inventor and mathematician Archimedes (AR kuh MEE deez), born in the Greek colony of Syracuse, was known throughout the Hellenistic world for his many discoveries. One of his discoveries was the principle of the lever, the practical value of which is illustrated today by the raising of a car with a jack. Proud of his discovery of the laws of levers, he once boasted, "Give me a spot to stand on and a lever long enough, and I will move the earth." The Greek astronomer and geographer **Eratosthenes** (ur uh TAHS thuh NEEZ) determined the circumference of the globe with amazing accuracy by using the geometry that

Euclid popularized. He also formulated the lines of longitude and latitude that are still used today on maps. The Greeks believed that the earth is round some seventeen centuries before Columbus lived.

Achievement in Literature

History—We get our word *history* from the Greek word meaning "inquiry." The Greeks believed that men could learn lessons from the past to help them live in the present. **Herodotus,** the "Father of History," wrote his history of the Persian Wars in the hope of "preserving from decay the remembrance of what men have done, and of preventing the great and wonderful actions of the Greeks and the Barbarians from losing their due need of glory, and withal to put on record what were their grounds of feud."[5] Although Herodotus tried to present an accurate history, his work contains many myths and exaggerations and an obvious bias toward the Greeks.

Thucydides (thoo SID ih DEEZ), a contemporary of Herodotus, wrote the *History of the Peloponnesian War,* a more accurate and objective record

---

Thucydides on the Writing of History

Of the events of the war I have not ventured to speak from any chance information, nor according to any notion of my own; I have described nothing but what I either saw myself, or learned from others of whom I made the most careful and particular inquiry. The task was a laborious one, because eyewitnesses of the same occurrences gave different accounts of them, as they remembered or were interested in the actions of one side or the other. And very likely the strictly historical character of my narrative may be disappointing to the ear. But if he who desires to have before his eyes a true picture of the events which have happened, and of the like events which may be expected to happen hereafter in the order of human things, shall pronounce what I have written to be useful, then I shall be satisfied. My history is an everlasting possession, not a prize composition which is heard and forgotten.[6]

than Herodotus's work. Although Thucydides was an Athenian and fought briefly for Athens during the war with Sparta, he did not let his personal affections influence his account of the war.

Drama—The Greek achievement in literature was unsurpassed in the ancient world. Homer's epic poems are the monuments of early Greek literature. Later the Greeks excelled in poetic drama. An outgrowth of religious festivals, drama became an important part of Greek life. In Athens, for example, several days were set aside each year for the drama festivals. Shops were closed and schools had a holiday as the entire population of the city attended the outdoor performances. The Greeks held contests to determine the best plays and actors.

Greek drama provided more than just entertainment. The plays educated the Greek people in religious beliefs, moral behavior, and civic pride. Both tragedy and comedy were among the favorite forms of Greek drama. **Sophocles** (SAHF uh KLEEZ), a writer of tragedy, and **Aristophanes** (ARE ih STAHF uh neez), a writer of comedy, were among the most

A Selection from a Comedy of Aristophanes

They're always abusing the women,
  As a terrible plague to men:
They say we're the root of all evil,
  And repeat it again and again;
Of war, and quarrels, and bloodshed,
  All mischief, be what it may:
And pray, then, why do you marry us,
  If we're all the plagues you say?
And why do you take care of us,
  And keep us so safe at home,
And are never easy a moment,
  If ever we chance to roam?
When you ought to be thanking heaven
  That your Plague is out of the way—
You all keep fussing and fretting—
  ''Where *is* my Plague to-day?''
If a Plague peeps out of the window,
  Up go the eyes of the men;
If she hides, then they all keep staring
  Until she looks out again.

Ancient Athenian theater where Greek dramas are still performed

The Winged Victory of Samothrace *(sculpted ca. 190 B.C.) illustrates the sense of movement and emotion that distinguishes Hellenistic Greek art from the calm of classical Greek art.*

famous of the Greek dramatists. Many of the Greek dramas are still enjoyed today; their analysis of human behavior is just as penetrating today as it was in ancient Greece.

Excellence in Art

The Greeks excelled in many forms of art; the most highly prized are their urns, sculpture, and temples. Grecian urns are among the most beautiful ever fashioned. On the exteriors of these graceful forms, the Greeks painted scenes of everyday life, battles, athletic competitions, and activities of their gods.

Greek sculpture falls into three main periods: archaic, classical, and Hellenistic. In the archaic period, Greek sculpture shows a strong Egyptian influence. Figures stand stiff and expressionless, their fists clenched by their sides. From these somewhat crude forms Greek sculpture gradually became more realistic. This change came about during the classical period, a period when Greek sculpture reached its highest achievement. Through their sculpture the Greeks sought to represent the ideal man. In the Hellenistic period Greek sculpture lost its simple beauty. Its calm self-confidence was replaced by a frenzied emotional tone.

The ''Golden Age'' of Greek culture (see pp. 59-60) was also the ''golden'' or ''classical'' age of Greek architecture. The Greek building style became a standard of excellence that later generations copied. Nothing better reflects the beauty of Greek architecture than the buildings of the Athenian Acropolis. During the Persian Wars, Xerxes had destroyed Athens, but under Pericles new and more beautiful buildings were erected. Formerly a fortress for refuge, the Athenian Acropolis became the site of temples to the Greek gods. The most spectacular of these temples is the **Parthenon.** We can get a glimpse of its former beauty and grandeur today, even in its ruined state.

The Athenians dedicated the building to the city's patron goddess, Athena. During the days of Pericles, a forty-foot-high gold and ivory statue of Athena stood inside the temple. The building itself is rectangular in shape and is supported by towering columns in beautiful symmetry. The Greeks gave it the appearance of solidity and symmetry

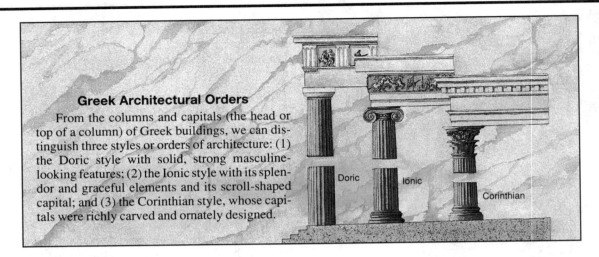

Greek Architectural Orders

From the columns and capitals (the head or top of a column) of Greek buildings, we can distinguish three styles or orders of architecture: (1) the Doric style with solid, strong masculine-looking features; (2) the Ionic style with its splendor and graceful elements and its scroll-shaped capital; and (3) the Corinthian style, whose capitals were richly carved and ornately designed.

Doric   Ionic   Corinthian

through the subtle use of optical illusions. The steps leading to the entrance are slightly curved at the center; this feature gives the eye the illusion of their being flat. (If they were truly flat, they would appear to dip.) The columns are placed closer together at the sides of the building than at the middle. This spacing gives the appearance of regularity. Likewise the floor rises gently at the center, giving the whole the appearance of a swelling, living edifice.

The Parthenon is a symbol of the cultural achievement of the Greek civilization. It is also a symbol of the spiritual blindness of the Greek people. The Apostle Paul visited Athens some five hundred years after her ''Golden Age.'' He preached against the idolatrous practices that the Parthenon and the statue of Athena represented.

God that made the world and all things therein . . . dwelleth not in temples made with hands; . . . we ought not to think that the Godhead is like unto gold, or silver, or stone, graven by art and man's device.

—Acts 17:24, 29

Section Review

1. What was the name given to the new culture that emerged in the Near East that mixed Greek culture with the cultures of the East?
2. What philosopher developed the three-step logical process of thinking called a syllogism?
3. Who is known as the ''Father of Medicine''?
4. Who was the more objective historian: Herodotus or Thucydides?
5. Identify the three styles of Greek architecture.

A Glimpse Behind and a Glimpse Ahead

Greek culture has profoundly influenced Western society. We cannot study art, literature, philosophy, or government without encountering Greek ideas. Unfortunately, the many false beliefs of the Greeks in philosophy and religion have had a lasting influence also. In the next two chapters we will see how the Romans adopted much of Greek culture into their own society. It is this Graeco-Roman culture that formed the foundation of the modern Western world.

Chapter Review

Can You Explain?

anthropomorphic	oligarchy	archon	philosophers
Olympiad	tyranny	Hellenic	anarchy
polis	democracy	Hellenistic	syllogism
monarchy	Helots	humanities	

Can You Identify?

Minoan civilization	Solon	Alexander the Great	Hippocrates
Mycenaean civilization	Darius I	Darius III	Euclid
Dorians	490 B.C.	Thales	Eratosthenes
Homer	Xerxes	Socrates	Herodotus
Iliad	480 B.C.	Plato	Thucydides
Odyssey	Pericles	Aristotle	Sophocles
Zeus	Delian League	Epicurus	Aristophanes
Athena	Peloponnesian War	Zeno	Parthenon
Peloponnesian League	Philip II	Pythagoras	

Can You Locate?

Aegean Sea	Troy	Sparta	Thermopylae
Crete	Hellespont	Peloponnesus	Salamis
Knossos	Mount Olympus	Athens	Macedonia
Mycenae	Olympia	Marathon	

How Much Do You Remember?

1. Draw two columns and list at least three contrasting characteristics of the Spartan and Athenian societies.
2. How did the Persian and Peloponnesian wars affect the unity of the Greeks?
3. How did Hellenic culture differ from Hellenistic culture?

What Do You Think?

1. What are the strengths and weaknesses of monarchy, oligarchy, and democracy?
2. Why was Athens and not Sparta the cultural center during the Golden Age?
3. Read I Corinthians 1:22-31. How does this passage apply to a Christian's study of Greek philosophy?

Notes
1. Homer, *Odyssey*, trans. Samuel Butler, 1. intro.
2. Herodotus, *The History of Herodotus*, trans. George Rawlinson, 6. 112.
3. Herodotus, 7. 225.
4. Thucydides, trans. Benjamin Jowett, 2. 37.
5. Herodotus, 1. intro.
6. Thucydides, 1. 22.

The Roman Republic

Today if you were to travel in Spain, France, Britain, Italy, Greece, Asia Minor, Palestine, Egypt, or North Africa, you could find roads built almost two thousand years ago by the Romans. In fact, some of the modern roads in these lands are built on top of the firm, deep base of the old Roman roads. The Romans constructed a network of roads that connected the far corners of their vast empire with their capital city. It could literally be said of the ancient world that "all roads lead to Rome."

In a figurative sense the road of ancient history also leads us to Rome. Rome was the culmination of ancient civilization. The world had never seen an empire of such power and influence. (The story of the tremendous growth and achievement of the Romans, descendants of Japheth, could be a fulfillment of Genesis 9:27—"God shall enlarge Japheth, and he shall dwell in the tents of Shem; and Canaan shall be his servant.") Though successful in a worldly sense, Rome sank to the depths of spiritual darkness. She readily embraced the pagan gods and false teachings of her many conquered peoples.

The road of God's plan for the ages leads us to Rome as well. God chose to send His Son, Jesus Christ, into the world when the Roman civilization was at its height. God had been at work in the history of the ancient world preparing the world for the coming of the Savior. The Roman world was the cradle of Christianity. From the Roman province of Judea, the truth of the gospel spread to every part of the globe.

As the roads built by the Romans have endured to the present, so has the influence of Rome. In this chapter and the one to follow, we will examine Rome as a city, a republic, an empire, a culture, and a church. In each of these aspects Rome left a lasting imprint on the world. Rome the *city* has remained a prominent metropolitan center to the present day. Rome the *republic* developed many principles of law and government that are practiced by many modern governments. Rome the *empire* contributed to the idea of a one-world government. Rome the *culture* laid the foundation for our Western heritage by conveying the contributions of the ancient world to modern times. And finally, Rome the *church* after the introduction of Christianity, gradually developed into a religious system (Roman Catholicism) that has perverted the truth of Christianity.

Beginning of Roman Civilization

Geographic Features of Italy

The land of Italy, centrally located in the Mediterranean world, was the heart of the Roman Empire. Shaped like a boot, the Italian Peninsula extends into the Mediterranean Sea between the lands of Greece and Spain. At the southern tip of Italy is the island of Sicily, which nearly joins Italy with North Africa.

Geographic obstacles did not hamper the Romans as they did the Greeks. Because of the lack of good soil, the Greeks looked to the sea for their livelihood. However, the soil and climate of Italy were more suitable for farming. The mountains in Greece divided the Greek people and hindered their political unity. The Apennine (AP uh NINE) Mountains, which run down the middle of the Italian Peninsula, are less rugged than the mountains of Greece and did not hamper the growth of trade and travel among the people of Italy. From the Italian Peninsula, the Romans expanded their territory to include all the land surrounding the Mediterranean Sea. It is little wonder that the Romans would later call the Mediterranean *Mare Nostrum,* which means "our sea."

Early Inhabitants of Italy

The earliest inhabitants of the Italian Peninsula had come from across the Alps and had settled in northern Italy. Many of these early settlers—called Latins—moved south and settled in Latium, a plain lying south of the Tiber River near the western coast of Italy. From this region arose a civilization that would one day rule the entire Mediterranean world.

Portions of Italy were also inhabited by the Phoenicians, Greeks, and Etruscans. Both the Phoenicians and the Greeks were known in the ancient world for their sea trade and colonization. Phoenicia established colonies on Sicily and along the coast of North Africa. (The Phoenician colony of Carthage in North Africa later rivaled Rome for mastery of the western Mediterranean world.) The Greeks established independent colonies on the island of Sicily also, as well as along the coast of southern Italy.

Most people have never heard of the **Etruscans.** They came to Italy around the ninth century B.C. and established one of Italy's earliest civilizations. Little is known of their origin, although many historians believe they came from the East, possibly from Asia Minor. The Etruscans settled along Italy's western coast, just north of the Tiber River. They soon became trade competitors with the Greeks living in Italy. The Etruscans learned much about Greek myths, architecture, sculpture, and language. In fact, it was probably the Etruscans who first introduced Greek culture to the Romans. Much of later Roman culture would reflect Greek tradition and customs.

The Founding of Rome

The city of Rome began on the banks of the Tiber River, about fifteen miles from the seacoast. Here trade routes that ran along the western coast of Italy crossed the river. At this point the river was easy to ford. People from Latium began to settle on the hills that overlooked this spot. A colony of Latin people established a village on the Palatine Hill near the Tiber. Soon other Latin villages were founded on the surrounding hills. Sometime during the eighth century B.C., seven of these villages formed a league—the **"League of the Seven Hills."** This was the beginning of the city of Rome.

Like the Greeks, the Romans developed legends to explain their early history. According to Roman tradition, Rome was founded in 753 B.C. by the twin brothers **Romulus** and **Remus.** The legend tells how a relative of Romulus and Remus usurped the throne and ordered the two babes, who were of royal descent, to be drowned. The infants were placed in a basket and thrown into the Tiber River to die. But a wolf saved the boys and cared for them until a shepherd found them and took them in. As young men Romulus and Remus allegedly returned to found a city near the place where the wolf had discovered them. While marking out the boundaries for the city, Romulus, in a burst of jealous anger, killed Remus. (This part of the legend might well have originated from the true story of Cain and Abel.) Romulus founded the city of Rome, named it after himself, and became its first king. Few of the legends concerning the founding of Rome, however, are historically reliable.

Early Roman Society and Government

The basic unit of early Roman society was the family. The family was a small community—self-sufficient and self-ruled. It included not only the father, wife, and children but also all the people who lived in the household, such as slaves. (Even property was considered to be part of the family.) The father (*pater* in Latin) was the sole authority over the family, and his control extended to every aspect of family life. He ruled his family without interference from the state. He was in charge of the family's worship and dispensed discipline and law,

Two Etruscan warriors, bronze statues dating from the fifth century B.C.

mon ancestor are called a **clan.** Likewise, a number of clans united by common beliefs and living in a particular region are called a **tribe.**

Within the Roman society there were two social classes. They differed greatly from each other in the social and political privileges of their members. The wealthy landholders and noble families made up the aristocratic class (a privileged class) called the **patricians.** They held the highest positions in the early Roman society. The majority of the people, however, belonged to a supposedly inferior class called the **plebeians** (plee BEE unz). These were the ''common people''—the farmers, traders, and craftsmen.

The early government of Rome was a monarchy. The king served as the chief priest, the commander of the army, and the administrator of justice. The king's authority was called the **imperium.** A small bundle of rods which enclosed an axe, called the **fasces,** symbolized his power. As far as we know, the kings were elected by the people. The kings could gain advice on official matters from a council of clan leaders known as the Senate. A popular assembly that represented the people at large also existed. It elected and bestowed the imperium on the kings.

holding even the power of life and death over members of his household.

Every Roman took great pride in his family heritage. Parents instilled into their children the values of loyalty, submission to authority, self-control, and duty. Rome's strong families coupled with the patriotism and hardworking spirit of her people provided the foundation for her greatness.

The family also provided the basis for larger social groups. A number of families from a com-

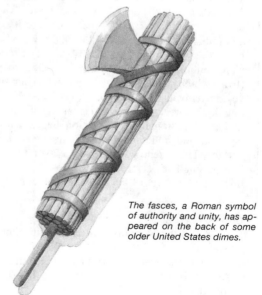

The fasces, a Roman symbol of authority and unity, has appeared on the back of some older United States dimes.

The Appian Way; now paved, the road is used by cars and trucks.

Roman Roads

One of the most important factors in Rome's conquest and control of vast areas of land was her system of roads. Roman engineers constructed over fifty thousand miles of main roads, along with two hundred thousand miles of other roads. The first and most famous road, constructed in 312 B.C., is the Appian Way, which runs over one hundred miles from Rome to Capua. It was along this road that the Apostle Paul traveled on his journey to Rome (Acts 28:14-15). The roads were built in four or five layers, called *strata* (from which we get our word *street*). After surveyors had planned the road's course, laborers dug down three to five feet to create a solid foundation. Occasionally construction began with a layer of sand, called *pavimentum,* to even out the surface. They then began the main layers: first, a bed of small rocks, from ten inches to two feet thick; next, a layer of finer concrete, about a foot thick on the sides and eighteen inches thick in the middle (thus providing an arched pavement for water runoff); lastly, a layer from six inches to two feet thick consisting of large paving stones fitted closely together to provide a smooth ride. This final layer was set into the still moist concrete below. The finished road, anywhere from eight to twenty-four feet wide, was strong enough to bear the weight of the Roman armies as they traveled to the farthest reaches of the empire. The layers made the surface slightly resilient, or flexible, so that it would not crack and break up as our modern roads sometimes do. Drains kept water, which would also harm the roads, out of the way. The Romans built the main roads primarily as highways to speed their armies on their way. However, these roads were later used by the early Christians as they carried the gospel throughout the Roman world.

Section Review

1. What did the Romans call the Mediterranean Sea?
2. In what year was the city of Rome founded?
3. According to legend, what two brothers founded Rome?
4. What were the two main social classes of ancient Rome?
5. What became the symbol of the king's authority in early Roman society?

The Early Roman Republic

Establishment of the Republic

About a century after the founding of Rome, the Etruscans crossed the Tiber River from the north and conquered the Latin villages. During the period of Etruscan rule, Rome grew from a weak league of villages to become the leading Latin city. As the influence of Rome increased, so did the hatred of the Roman nobility for the Etruscan monarch. In 509 B.C. they overthrew the king. In the place of the monarchy, they established a new form of government called a **republic.** Under the Roman Republic the administration of government was divided among three governing branches: the consuls, the Senate, and the assemblies.

Two elected **consuls** (government officials) replaced the king and held the imperium. They supervised the everyday affairs of government, commanded the Roman army, and served as the supreme judges of the land. Power was equally divided between each consul; one could not act without the consent of the other. Each consul served only a one-year term at a time. The shortness of the term prevented a consul from becoming too powerful. During the early years of the republic, members of the patrician class held the office of consul almost exclusively.

The **Senate** became the most important and most powerful body of the republic. Though the Senate served the interest of all the people of Rome, it was in particular an aristocratic body that safeguarded the powers of the patrician class. The Senate was composed of three hundred members who were appointed for life by the consuls. The permanency of the Senate served to increase its powers beyond its early advisory role. It controlled the government's finances, passed laws, and supervised the foreign affairs of the republic.

The republic also had assemblies through which the people could express their views. Wealth, birth, and the place of one's residence determined the membership and voting procedures of these various assemblies. The chief assembly of the early republic was the Assembly of Centuries. This assembly voted on legislation submitted by the consuls, made declarations of war, and elected high-ranking government officials. However, the Senate had veto power over the acts passed by this assembly.

Struggle Within the Republic

The patrician nobles who expelled the Etruscan king took firm control of the government. Patricians held the consulships, dominated the Senate

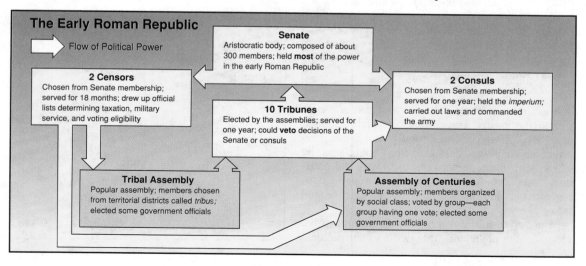

The Early Roman Republic

Flow of Political Power

Senate
Aristocratic body; composed of about 300 members; held **most** of the power in the early Roman Republic

2 Censors
Chosen from Senate membership; served for 18 months; drew up official lists determining taxation, military service, and voting eligibility

2 Consuls
Chosen from Senate membership; served for one year; held the *imperium;* carried out laws and commanded the army

10 Tribunes
Elected by the assemblies; served for one year; could **veto** decisions of the Senate or consuls

Tribal Assembly
Popular assembly; members chosen from territorial districts called *tribus;* elected some government officials

Assembly of Centuries
Popular assembly; members organized by social class; voted by group—each group having one vote; elected some government officials

What is a Republic?

A republic is a form of government in which voting citizens control the power of government through elected officials under law. The word comes from the Latin *res publica,* which literally means ''the people's thing.'' The Romans believed that while kings often advanced themselves and their families, a republic would best protect the interests of the people. There have been many different forms of republics in history. In some only a small portion of the people have held full citizenship and have thus been able to vote. In others the vast majority of the people have had this privilege. You are probably most familiar with the word *republic* in connection with the government of the United States. The framers of the American Constitution feared government by monarchy or oligarchy, for rulers under these types of governments often abused their powers and oppressed the people. Likewise, these men feared pure democracy because it might lead to ''mob rule.'' They studied the Roman Republic and saw the wisdom of a government which blended the elements of monarchy, oligarchy, and democracy into one government under written law. The framers of the Constitution recognized the biblical truth that men are evil by nature and therefore cannot be trusted. For this reason they valued a limited government that would keep any one man or group of men from obtaining absolute power. Many of the principles of government found in the American Constitution came from the model of the Roman Republic.

and social equality. During these two centuries Rome was constantly waging war against her neighbors in Italy. Because the patricians could not handle the burden of war alone, they had to rely more and more on the common people to help in fighting these wars. As the plebeians shared in the dangers of fighting, they wanted to share in the privilege of being represented in the government. By threatening to desert the army, the plebeians gradually gained concessions from the patricians.

One of the first concessions gained by the plebeians was the right to have their own assembly and elected officials. They met as the Council of Plebeians and passed resolutions called **plebiscites.**

Roman Republic to 264 B.C.

Roman territory ca. 326 B.C.
Roman Republic 264 B.C.

ALPS
Po R.
ETRUSCANS
Tiber R.
APENNINES
CORSICA
Adriatic Sea
Rome
LATIUM
SARDINIA
Tyrrhenian Sea
CARTHAGINIANS
SICILY
GREEKS
Mediterranean Sea

and assemblies, made most of the laws, and controlled the courts. In contrast, the plebeians had few social privileges and virtually no voice in government. They were excluded from holding public office, and marriage between plebeians and patricians was forbidden. For failing to repay loans, plebeians could lose their property and even be sold into slavery.

For two centuries following the founding of the republic, the plebeians struggled to gain political

The Roman Forum

These were binding only on the plebeians, however, and not on the patrician class. The Council of Plebeians elected ten men to the office of **tribune.** The tribunes protected the rights and interests of the common people. By crying out **"Veto!"** ("I forbid!"), the tribunes could stop unjust acts of patrician officials.

In the past, patrician judges had taken advantage of the plebeians, who were not familiar with the traditions that made up Rome's unwritten laws. However, continued pressure from the plebeians finally forced the patricians to put the Roman laws into writing. Around 450 B.C. these laws were written down on twelve tablets and hung in the **Roman Forum,** the section of the city that was the center of government. Now all could know the law. Likewise the law was to be applied equally to all. Young boys in the republic memorized the whole code as part of their school work. These tablets of law, called the **Law of Twelve Tables,** became the foundation of Roman civil law.

Gradually the plebeians improved their political and social standing in the republic. They gained the right to hold public offices which had previously been held only by the patricians. A few plebeians even became senators. Debtor slavery was abolished, and the law against intermarriage between plebeians and patricians was repealed. In 287 B.C. the plebeian assembly, now called the **Tribal Assembly,** gained the power to pass laws binding upon all the people of Rome—patricians as well as plebeians.

As the result of these two centuries of struggle, the plebeians officially gained social and political equality with the patricians. The peaceful changes seemed to make the republic more representative of the people. But as the distinctions between patricians and plebeians began to disappear, a new class distinction began to develop—the rich versus the poor. Wealthy plebeians and patricians formed a new alliance that maintained control of the Senate and held the reins of power in the republic.

Section Review

1. In what year was the Roman Republic founded?
2. What was the most powerful body within the governmental structure of the republic?
3. What power did tribunes get to exercise over unjust acts of patrician officials?
4. What was the name of the Roman law that was written down and placed in the Roman Forum?
5. What was the name of the plebeian assembly that gained the power to pass laws binding on all the people of Rome, regardless of their social class?

The Mediterranean—A Roman Sea

The Romans had not originally set out to conquer the world. But through constant warfare from 509 to 133 B.C., Rome grew from a small city along the Tiber River into the largest empire of the ancient world. How did this expansion take place?

Rome—Master of Italy

During the years of internal struggles between the patricians and the plebeians, Rome was also involved in external struggles with her neighbors in Italy. Under Etruscan rule Rome became the leading Latin city. With the expulsion of the Etruscan king in 509 B.C., other Latin cities joined with Rome in a defensive alliance for protection against the Etruscans. Just as the members of the Delian League had revolted against the growing power of Athens, so the Latin cities, fearful of the growing power of Rome, revolted. Rome defeated the Latin cities and secured a strong position in central Italy. She later acquired the land to her north by defeating the Etruscans.

Rome soon began expanding into southern Italy, threatening the Greek colonies located there. The Greek colonies feared Roman conquest and appealed to **Pyrrhus,** a distant relative of Alexander the Great, for help. With the aid of war elephants (the ''tanks'' of ancient warfare), Pyrrhus defeated the Romans twice. In gaining the second victory, however, Pyrrhus's army suffered such great losses that he reportedly exclaimed, ''Another such victory and I shall be ruined.'' Since that time, a ''Pyrrhic victory'' has referred to a victory whose costs outweigh any advantage that may have been gained. Pyrrhus returned to Greece when Rome, joined by another Greek rival, further weakened his force. With Pyrrhus back in Greece, Rome was able to conquer all of southern Italy.

By 265 B.C. Rome controlled all of the Italian Peninsula. Her task now was to rule effectively a land which included Latins, Etruscans, and Greeks. Unlike most conquering people, Rome treated her conquered subjects with mercy and fairness instead of force and oppression. As long as they did not rebel against Roman authority, her subjects lived in relative peace. To many of her conquered subjects in Italy, Rome granted citizenship—the right to vote and hold office. To others Rome allowed a great degree of local independence. Although Rome did not demand tribute (payment of money or grain showing submission) from the conquered states within Italy, she did require them to furnish troops to help her fight her wars. The protection of Roman law and the stability and prosperity that Rome brought to the Italian Peninsula secured the loyalty of her subjects and allies.

Rome—Master of the Western Mediterranean

Rome's conquest of the Italian Peninsula brought her into conflict with Carthage, another power in the western world. This rival of Rome, located in North Africa, possessed good harbors, rich mining resources, and the best navy in the western Mediterranean. While Phoenicia, her mother country, grew weak as a result of Assyrian and Chaldean conquests, Carthage built her own empire in the west. Her empire included the North African coast, southern Spain, the islands of Sardinia and Corsica, and part of the island of Sicily.

Between 264 and 146 B.C., Rome and Carthage fought each other in three wars. Both cities controlled much territory in the western Mediterranean. Both were expanding rapidly. In addition, Rome and Carthage were competing commercially for control of trade in the Mediterranean. This rivalry, which was built upon both jealousy and fear, led to a series of wars known as the **Punic Wars.** (*Punici* was the Roman word for Phoenicians.) The Greek historian Polybius, sympathetic to the Roman Republic, gave this description of the differences between Carthage and Rome.

> The Carthaginians naturally are superior at sea both in efficiency and equipment, because seamanship has long been their national craft, . . . but as regards military service on land the Romans are much more efficient. . . . The troops [the Carthaginians] employ are foreign and mercenary [hired for pay], whereas those of the Romans are native of the soil and citizens. So that in this respect also we must

pronounce the political system of Rome to be superior to that of Carthage, the Carthaginians continuing to depend for the maintenance of their freedom on the courage of mercenary force but the Romans on their own valour and on the aid of their allies. Consequently even if they happen to be worsted at the outset, the Romans redeem defeat by final success, while it is the contrary with the Carthaginians. For the Romans, fighting as they are for their country and their children, never can abate their fury but continue to throw their whole hearts into the struggle until they get the better of their enemies.[1]

The First Punic War (264-241 B.C.)

The First Punic War was fought over control of the island of Sicily. The Romans feared that the Carthaginians would become too strong on the island. A powerful rival force could control the waters between Sicily and Italy and thus hinder Roman trade in the Mediterranean. Sicily could also become a base for a Carthaginian attack on southern Italy. The only way Rome could stop Carthage was to break her naval supremacy.

Using the design of a captured Carthaginian warship, Rome began to build a navy of her own. Although Rome soon possessed the same ships, Roman sailors could not match the experience and skill of the Carthaginians. So Rome developed new tactics for fighting at sea. Up to that time, naval battles were won by ramming and sinking the enemy's vessels. Rome substituted soldiers for experienced sailors. When an enemy ship came near, a plank was dropped (like a drawbridge) so that its spiked tip fastened to the deck of the enemy's ship. Armed Roman soldiers then crossed over and captured the ship. By this method Rome crippled the navy of Carthage.

Despite many setbacks, Rome finally defeated Carthage. Although much of the Roman fleet had been destroyed by fierce storms and though military and diplomatic blunders had prolonged the war, Rome was able to break the spirit of the Carthaginians by overcoming Carthage's naval supremacy. Growing weary from the long war, Carthage sued for peace in 241 B.C. From the peace settlement, Rome gained control of Sicily, and Carthage was forced to pay for Roman losses.

The Second Punic War (218-201 B.C.)

Carthage recovered from her defeat in the First Punic War and extended her control over much of Spain. In 219 B.C. Carthage attacked a Roman ally, a Spanish town on the Mediterranean coast. The city fell after an eight-month siege, and a second war broke out between Carthage and Rome. Rome, who now had the superior navy, planned to isolate Carthage's forces in Spain. By sending one army to Spain and another to Carthage, Rome hoped for a quick end to the war against the divided Carthaginian forces. This strategy might have worked, had it not been for a young Carthaginian commander named **Hannibal.**

Carthaginian coins showing what is believed to be a portrait of Hannibal (top) and a war elephant (bottom)

Historians have likened Hannibal to Alexander the Great. His strong character and leadership won the devotion of his soldiers. This military genius devised tactics that are still being studied by army experts today. (Some of his tactics were used in tank battles during World War II.) Hannibal realized that his only hope of success was to invade the Italian peninsula and capture Rome. By invading Italy, he planned to present himself as liberator of Rome's conquered allies and to give them an opportunity to break with Rome and to gain their freedom. Without the soldiers and resources supplied by her allies, Rome could be conquered—so Hannibal thought.

With cavalry, elephants, and some forty thousand men, Hannibal set out from Spain. He marched his army over the rugged, snow-covered Alps and into northern Italy. The dangerous mountain passes, wintry weather, and attacks from mountain tribes combined to cut his army by about half and left him with only a few supplies and elephants. Nevertheless, he surprised the Romans. They had believed it impossible for any army to cross the Alps—especially during the winter. For the next fifteen years, Hannibal brilliantly led his outnumbered army to many victories in Italy.

Battle of Cannae—In the spring of 216 B.C., the Romans suffered one of the worst defeats in their long history. At Cannae (KAN ee), a small town southeast of Rome, the Roman legions confronted Hannibal's army. Because the Romans outnumbered his army almost two to one, Hannibal had to rely on superior battle tactics. He arranged his forces in the same fashion as the Roman troops—cavalry units on the flanks and infantry at the center. But unlike the Roman line, Hannibal's line bulged forward at the center, inviting the Romans to attack there. The Roman infantry charged the center of Hannibal's line, hoping to break it and divide the Carthaginian forces. While the outside of Hannibal's line held its ground, the center (according to plan) retreated, drawing the advancing Romans into a U-shaped pocket. The Romans soon found themselves hemmed in by the enemy on three sides. Meanwhile, Hannibal's cavalry, which had routed Rome's cavalry, circled around and attacked the rear of the Roman infantry. The surrounded Roman army was almost completely wiped out. It has been estimated that Hannibal lost six thousand men, while the Romans lost nearly sixty thousand. A generation passed before Rome recovered from this terrible defeat.

Following the disaster at the Battle of Cannae, the situation looked very grim for the Romans, who had suffered numerous defeats at the hands of Hannibal. To make matters worse, Rome had to contend with a new Carthaginian ally, Macedonia, and to suppress Syracuse, a powerful Greek city on

A relief sculpture portrays Roman light and heavy infantry from the fourth century B.C. The terms light and heavy refer to the amount and weight of armor worn by each soldier.

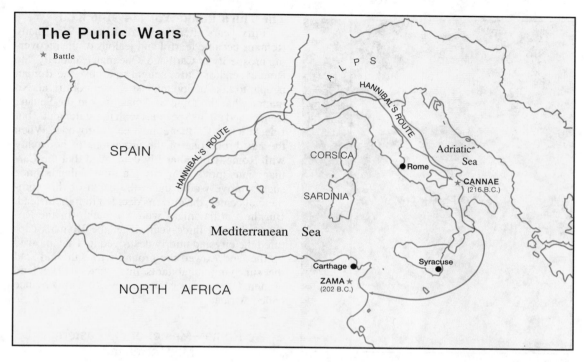

The Punic Wars

★ Battle

A L P S

HANNIBAL'S ROUTE

SPAIN

HANNIBAL'S ROUTE

CORSICA

● Rome

Adriatic Sea

★ CANNAE
(216 B.C.)

SARDINIA

Mediterranean Sea

Carthage ●

Syracuse ●

ZAMA ★
(202 B.C.)

NORTH AFRICA

Sicily that revolted against Rome. Despite these advantages, Hannibal was unable to conquer the city of Rome. He lacked the heavy siege equipment needed to break down her walls. Furthermore, he gained few recruits from the people he freed from Roman rule. Rome's fair and generous treatment of her subjects encouraged them to remain loyal to Rome.

The Siege of Syracuse

When Rome attacked Syracuse during the Second Punic War, the Roman commander Marcellus expected to capture the city with only a five-day siege. However, the Romans found their land-and-sea attack repulsed by a variety of unusual war machines. The land forces were met by stones and other missiles hurled from great distances. The naval attack faced catapults hurling five-hundred-pound stones. Syracuse also used cranes, some of which dropped huge stones on the ships, while others with chains and iron claws picked ships up, spun them around, and smashed them upon the rocks along the shore. Legend tells us that city's defenders also used large mirrors that focused the sun's rays upon Rome's ships and caused them to catch fire. The inventor and director of all this somewhat strange war machinery was Syracuse's most famous mathematician, Archimedes. So effective was his defense that the Romans never tried another assault upon the city. In 212 B.C. Rome finally captured Syracuse, but with a blockade and trickery rather than a direct attack. Part of the reason for the Syracusans' defeat was the fact that they so trusted in their machines that they were unprepared in the final hours to use their more conventional weapons.

Scipio

The Third Punic War (149-146 B.C.)

Fifty years after the Second Punic War, many Romans became fearful and jealous of the recovering prosperity of Carthage. One man especially, the Roman senator **Cato,** sought to arouse the Roman people to take action against Rome's old rival. No matter what the topic of debate was in the Senate, Cato ended all his speeches with the statement "but I declare that Carthage must be destroyed." When the city broke one of the provisions of her treaty with Rome, Rome harshly demanded that the Carthaginians move their city ten miles inland. Since such a move would mean the death of this commercial center, the citizens decided to fight instead. But the Carthaginians were no match for the Romans. After a three-year siege, the Romans captured the city and utterly destroyed it. They plowed up the land, sowed the ground with salt, and sold the surviving inhabitants into slavery. The land around Carthage became a new Roman province called Africa.

Rome—Master of the Eastern Mediterranean

After the Second Punic War, Rome turned her attention to the eastern portion of the Mediterranean. Here the kingdoms carved out of Alexander the Great's empire—Macedonia, Syria, and Egypt—were engaged in a power struggle of their own. Because Macedonia had joined Carthage against Rome during the Second Punic War, Rome sent her legions to deal with Macedonia after Carthage had been defeated. With Macedonia weakened by her wars with Rome, the king of Syria marched into Asia Minor, crossed the Hellespont, and invaded the kingdom of Macedonia. Rome met this challenge by soundly defeating the Syrian armies. Egypt, the weakest of the three, thought it best to make an alliance with Rome. With this completed, Rome became the master of the entire Mediterranean world.

At first, Rome allowed her eastern conquests a certain amount of self-government. But because of constant uprisings and petty rivalries, Rome reorganized her holdings throughout the Mediterranean

Scipio—The turning point in the war came through the daring strategy of a young Roman commander named **Scipio** (SIP ee OH). A member of a powerful family, he became the most famous Roman of his time. After defeating the Carthaginian forces in Spain, he could have moved his army into Italy to take on Hannibal. But instead he crossed over to North Africa and prepared to attack Carthage. Hannibal, who had not lost a battle in Italy, was ordered back home to defend Carthage. By the time he arrived, the Romans had already gained the advantage. Not even the leadership of Hannibal could stop Scipio and the Roman legions. At the Battle of Zama (202 B.C.), the Romans defeated the Carthaginian army. Carthage surrendered and was forced to give up all her territory outside of North Africa, reduce her fleet to only ten vessels, and pay a great sum to Rome for war damages. Rome was now the master of the western Mediterranean world.

into provinces. Governors appointed by the Roman Senate administered these provinces and served as the chief military and civil rulers for each province. The provinces retained local freedom as long as they did not rebel against Roman authority. The main obligation of the provinces was to pay tribute—money or grain—to Rome. In return Rome provided order and protection.

Hair Styles in Ancient Rome

The Romans were down-to-earth and practical people. Their fashions—especially their hair styles—confirmed this fact. During the republic, women wore their hair pulled back in a bun; young girls sometimes wore ringlets. By the time of Octavian, the hair styles had begun to change. Aristocratic women, aided by special slaves, curled (with curling irons) and oiled their hair and then piled it in elaborate fashions on top of their heads. Dark-haired Latin ladies often dyed their hair blonde or red or wore wigs fashioned from the hair of their slave girls. Hair styles changed so often that one Roman poet complained, "I cannot keep track of fashion. Everyday, so it seems, brings a different style!"

Some sculptors, when carving a statue of a lady, made the head with a detachable scalp; by carving different hair pieces, he could keep the statue in the height of style.

Lest you think it was only the women who suffered from vanity, it must be pointed out that men were equally vain. During the republic most men were clean-shaven and wore their hair cropped close. Later when men began to let their hair grow, they too used curling irons to fashion their hair and beards. Like many of their modern counterparts, men who were losing their hair went to great lengths to conceal their baldness. Some grew their hair long on the sides and combed it over the bald spot; others wore wigs. Some even painted the likeness of hair on their heads!

Section Review

1. What man led the defense of Greek colonies against Roman expansion in southern Italy?
2. From the description of the Greek historian Polybius (pp. 80-81), list the differences between Carthage and Rome at the outset of the Punic Wars.
3. Over what island was the First Punic War fought?
4. What famed Carthaginian leader invaded Rome by an unexpected march over the Alps into northern Italy?
5. At what battle during the Second Punic War did the Roman general Scipio decisively defeat the Carthaginians, making Rome the master of the western Mediterranean world?

Rome's Decline into Dictatorship

By the first century B.C., Rome was the greatest power in the Mediterranean world. Nevertheless, during the last two centuries before Christ, the very foundation of the republic was shaken—not by any foreign enemy but by problems that arose within the republic as a result of Roman expansion.

Problems Within the Republic

The economic and military backbone of the early republic was the hard-working citizen-farmer. During the period of Roman expansion, the greatest military burden as well as economic hardships fell upon the small farmers. Many of them lost their land. When these citizen-farmers returned from fighting Rome's wars, they faced numerous obstacles. Some of them lacked the money needed to get their land back in shape; others were unable to pay their back taxes and thus lost their farms to the government. Those who were able to grow crops were unable to compete with the large farms of the wealthy aristocrats or with the cheap grain imported from the new Roman territories. In poverty and in debt, small farmers sold their land (usually for a cheap price) and sought jobs in the cities or as tenant farmers. But jobs were hard to find because of the increased number of slaves that were brought into Italy following Rome's conquests. Landless and unemployed, the citizen-farmers became dissatisfied and restless. Their self-reliant spirit broke down, and they turned to the government for help.

But they received no help from the government. Since its early years, the republic had undergone many changes in order to provide equal rights and privileges for all Roman citizens. The Tribal Assembly, which represented the common people, had greatly increased in power. But no sooner had these gains been achieved than the Punic Wars broke out. The common people failed to assume the responsibilities they had struggled so long to gain. They relied instead on the more experienced and stronger leadership of the Senate to see them through times of crisis. Thus, during the period of the Roman conquests, the Senate was able to increase its power and again dominate the republic.

Frescoes adorned the walls of many Roman homes.

The conditions that devastated the poor provided opportunities for increased prosperity for the already wealthy landholders, whose interests the Senate represented. These wealthy landowners expanded their own estates by buying out the small farmers. They also controlled large tracts of land in the new Roman provinces. Aristocratic senators, once concerned for the best interests of the republic, became greedy and pleasure-loving. The pleas for reform from the masses of unemployed and landless went unheeded by the Senate, whose self-centered interests opposed any change. The Senate was unwilling to address the social and economic problems at home.

The corruption in the government at Rome spread to the Roman provinces. Many of the provincial governors appointed by the Senate used their powers for their own selfish gains. One of the greatest abuses was in the collection of taxes that each province paid to Rome. Roman officials often made agreements with men called **publicans** to collect taxes in a given province. The publicans would agree to pay a fixed amount to Rome. Whatever they collected above this fixed sum they could keep for themselves. In return for a percentage of the extra money received, some senators and governors made deals to see that certain men were appointed publicans. Soon the publicans were the

The Bible's Account of a Publican

There was a man named Zacchaeus, which was the chief among the publicans, and he was rich. And he sought to see Jesus who he was. . . . And when Jesus came to the place, he . . . said unto . . . Zacchaeus, . . . to day I must abide at thy house. And he . . . received him joyfully. And when [the people] saw it, they all murmured, saying, That he was gone to be a guest with a man that is a sinner. And Zacchaeus stood, and said unto the Lord; Behold, Lord, the half of my goods I give to the poor; and if I have taken any thing from any man by false accusation, I restore him fourfold. And Jesus said unto him, This day is salvation come to this house. . . . For the Son of man is come to seek and to save that which was lost.

—Luke 19:2-10

most despised people in the Roman territories; they had become rich, but at the expense of the people. These abuses were still part of Roman society during the time of Jesus Christ in the first century A.D.

The Failure of Reform

The poor found champions for their cause in the brothers **Tiberius** and **Gaius Gracchus** (GRAHK us). The Gracchi (plural form of *Gracchus*) were from one of the noble families of Rome. Their father had been a consul, and their grandfather was Scipio, who had led Rome to victory in the Second Punic War. Elected as a tribune in 133 B.C., Tiberius strove for reforms in the republic and became the spokesman for the common man. In one of his speeches he said,

> The wild beasts that roam over Italy . . . have every one of them a cave or lair to lurk in; but the men who fight and die for Italy enjoy the common air and light, indeed, but nothing else; houseless and homeless they wander about with their wives and children. . . . They fight and die to support others in wealth and luxury, and though they are styled masters of the world, they have not a single clod of earth that is their own.[2]

Tiberius proposed changes in Rome's land policy. For years wealthy aristocrats had monopolized the lands gained through Rome's conquests.

Tiberius wanted these "public lands" to be divided among the poor. He also sought to limit the amount of public land controlled by any one person. Although the Tribal Assembly adopted his reforms, his proposals gained him powerful enemies. Wealthy landholders foresaw their own financial ruin, and senators disliked his reviving the powers of the Tribal Assembly. When Tiberius tried to be reelected as a tribune—an act contrary to Roman tradition at that time—angry senators killed him along with three hundred of his followers and threw their bodies into the Tiber River.

When Gaius became tribune in 123 B.C., he sought to carry on his brother's land reform measures. He also proposed that the government sell grain at low prices to the poor. But the Senate undermined the popular support of Gaius by offering its own programs. (The Senate, however, had no intention of carrying through with these reforms.) During a riot carefully planned by his enemies, Gaius lost his life. Some accounts say he committed suicide to keep from falling into the hands of the senatorial forces. Once again the Senate had prevailed.

Civil War

In the early years of the republic, the Senate, in order to preserve the stability of the government, met the challenges of the plebeians by granting concessions. In response to the new challenge of the Gracchi brothers, the Senate abandoned peaceful measures and resorted to violence to preserve the power and wealth of the aristocrats. The failure of the Senate to deal with reform for the poor further weakened the republic. The disorder of the Roman state finally led to civil war.

The First Civil War

In the first century B.C., three civil wars shook the very foundations of Rome, exposing the corruption in Roman society. The rivalry between the Tribal Assembly and the Senate gave occasion for the outbreak of the first civil war.

Following the deaths of the Gracchi brothers, the common people found a new champion for their cause in **Marius** (155?-86 B.C.). Marius was a well-known military hero who had gained fame for vic-

Expansion of the Roman Republic

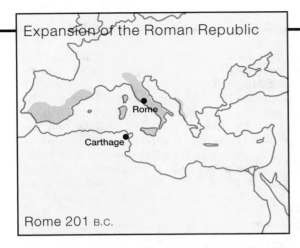

Rome 201 B.C.

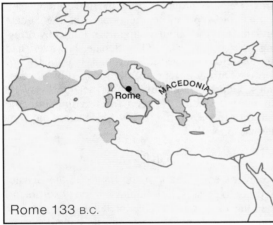

Rome 133 B.C.

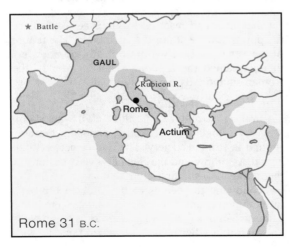

Rome 31 B.C.

tories in North Africa and Europe. He reorganized the dwindling Roman army, allowing the poor and landless to enlist for long terms of service. He promised them a share in the spoils of war—land and money. Up to this time citizens served in the army out of loyalty for their country. Now Marius created a "professional" army, one that served for financial gain rather than for a patriotic cause. Their devotion to the commander of the army was greater than their devotion to Rome. This shift in loyalty would later be the undoing of Rome as generals used their armies to further their own interests rather than those of the people and the state.

In 88 B.C. war broke out in Asia Minor. The Senate appointed **Sulla** (138-78 B.C.), a general who was sympathetic to the senatorial side, to command the Roman army in the east. The Tribal Assembly, however, rejected the Senate's choice and appointed Marius instead. The years that followed saw much bloodshed as the tension between the Tribal Assembly and the Senate, fueled by the rivalry between Marius and Sulla, developed into civil war. In the end Sulla emerged victorious.

Sulla had himself declared dictator. He then set about reorganizing the Roman government. He hoped to restore stability and order by reviving the power and prestige of the Senate. The influence of the Tribal Assembly and the tribunes was now all but gone. With the power of the Senate firmly established, Sulla resigned as dictator. The Senate, however, was unable to maintain control of the government.

The Second Civil War

The first civil war ended with the Senate triumphant over the Tribal Assembly. Yet it was obvious that a powerful man at the head of the army could control the state. Ambitious men sought to gain that control. The people, weary of economic and political crises, were willing to exchange their freedom for temporary relief.

Crassus and **Pompey,** two commanders who served in Sulla's army, competed with one another for fame and power after Sulla's death. Crassus was one of the richest men of Rome. He added military glory to his riches by raising an army and

How the Romans Measured Time

The Romans had two different ways of measuring time. First, they divided the daylight hours into twelve equal parts. (This meant that the "hours" were longer in the summer than in the winter.) Second, the Romans invented a water clock, which kept time in much the same manner as our modern clocks. However, these water clocks were so inaccurate that the Roman philosopher Seneca once observed that it was easier to find two philosophers who agreed than it was to find two water clocks that agreed. It is interesting to note that our use of A.M. (*ante meridiem*) and P.M. (*post meridiem*) comes from the Roman system of counting hours from the middle of the day.

In numbering their years, the Romans started counting from the founding of Rome. After the year number, they wrote A.U.C. *(ad urbe condita),* which means "from the foundation of the city." Their years had 355 days, and even though the calendar was periodically corrected, it was still out of step with the sun. So when Julius Caesar ruled Rome, he asked astronomers to help him set the calendar straight. Upon their recommendations, he decreed that the year 707 A.U.C. (46 B.C.) would have 445 days. This was done so that the Roman year would once again match the solar year. In Roman history that year was known as the "Year of Confusion."

Thus began the Julian calendar, which remained in use for the next sixteen hundred years. Instead of ten months, each year then had twelve months that alternated between thirty and thirty-one days. Even today we still use the same names for the months that the Romans did. The only difference is that the Romans began their year with March and ended with February.

January—Named after Janus, the Roman god of gates and doors.

February—From the Latin word that means "to purify." February was originally the last month of the year. It was during this month that the Romans purified themselves in preparation for the festivals that marked the beginning of the new year.

March—Named after Mars, the Roman god of war.

April—From the Latin word that means "to open." April was originally the second month of the year.

May—Two possible sources of the name: (1) Named after Maia, the Roman goddess of spring, or (2) from the Latin word that referred to older men (majores); the month of May was sacred to these older men.

June—Two possible sources of the name: (1) named after Juno, the Roman goddess of marriage, or (2) from the Latin word that referred to young men (juniores); the month of June was sacred to these young men.

July—Named by Julius Caesar after himself. (It was his birth month.)

August—Named by Caesar Augustus (Octavian) after himself.

September—Means "the seventh month."

October—Means "the eighth month."

November—Means "the ninth month."

December—Means "the tenth month."

Perhaps you have always wondered why February has only twenty-eight days when the rest of the months have thirty or thirty-one days. According to tradition, Julius Caesar named the month of July after himself; because he did not want his month to have fewer days than any other, he took a day from February and added it to July, making a total of thirty-one days. Later, when Octavian named the month of August after himself, he also took a day from February so that his month would be just a long as Julius's month.

defeating a slave revolt that had threatened the Italian Peninsula. But his military glory was surpassed by Pompey, who had many conquests in the east. He had turned Asia Minor, Syria, and Palestine into Roman provinces. He also rid the Mediterranean Sea of pirates.

The wide accomplishments of both Crassus and Pompey, however, failed to win them the popular support that **Julius Caesar** received. This young leader, nephew of the popular Marius, undertook ambitious projects to win the public favor. Caesar (100-44 B.C) was a wise politician who knew how to sway the common people in order to accomplish his aims. Crassus, Pompey, and Caesar each wanted to be sole ruler of Rome. None, though, had sufficient power to assume complete control: Crassus had the money, Pompey had the support of the Senate, and Caesar had the favor of the common people. So in 60 B.C., they formed an alliance called a **triumvirate** (try UM ver it; "rule of three men") to rule Rome together.

Caesar used his position to get himself appointed governor of Gaul (modern France). There he trained a well-disciplined and loyal army. His

The Roman Army

In his conquest of the ancient world, Alexander the Great relied upon the Greek military formation called the "phalanx." This formation packed hundreds of men into a tight wedge with their long spears facing forward. The phalanx was very powerful and almost impossible to defeat on level ground. But it had one weakness that made it almost useless to the Romans: it could not maneuver. It could march forward or backward, but because the men and spears were tightly intertwined, it could not turn easily. Because Rome's enemies used a number of different fighting tactics, Rome needed a formation which could adapt to many different situations. Thus Rome invented the "legion." Each legion (about five thousand men) was divided into several groups. Up front was a line of "skirmishers," carrying short spears. Next came two lines of soldiers, marching in groups called "centuries." Each century, which was headed by a "centurion," stood in a checkerboard formation with the other centuries. These soldiers carried heavier spears. Behind all these soldiers came a line of men carrying heavy thrusting spears with which they could mow down the enemy. As the front lines tired, they could retreat through the gaps in the checkerboard formation and rest behind the last line. There were two advantages to this formation. First, it was much more maneuverable than the phalanx; so it could adjust more easily to variations in the land and the enemy's formations. Second, the men could move in and out more easily, fight more freely, and get rest if they needed it.

military campaigns led him through Gaul and across the channel to Britain. Though away from Rome, he kept his name before the Roman people by sending written accounts of his military accomplishments back to Rome. These published accounts, his *Commentaries on the Gallic Wars,* made him the talk of Rome. Jealous of Caesar's growing strength and popularity, Pompey sought the help of the Senate to weaken his rival. (Crassus had died in a war in Asia.) When the Senate ordered Caesar to return to Rome and disband his army, Caesar crossed the Rubicon (a river in northern Italy) and marched his army toward Rome. By this act Caesar declared war on Pompey and the Senate. Since that day "crossing the Rubicon" means making a fateful decision from which there is no turning back.

Pompey and members of the Senate fled to Greece to give themselves time to raise an army to battle Caesar. When the two armies finally met, Pompey's forces were no match for Caesar's seasoned veterans. Pompey fled to Egypt, where he was later killed. With power firmly in his hands, Caesar had himself proclaimed dictator for life.

Caesar accomplished many reforms during his short rule. He curbed the corruption of the provincial governments, established colonies for the landless army veterans, granted citizenship to many non-Italians living in Rome's new colonies, and initiated many public work programs. He also established the calendar that is the basis for our 365 1/4 days calendar year.

Although popular with the people, Caesar had enemies among the nobles and senators. Some were former followers of Pompey; others feared that Caesar was going to make himself king and do away with the republic. Since the time of the Etruscans, the Romans had regarded kings as evil. Although they permitted a temporary dictatorship, the Romans would not accept a king. On the "Ides" (fifteenth) of March 44 B.C., a group of conspirators assassinated the dictator in the Senate chamber.

The Third Civil War

A third civil war to determine the next ruler broke out after Caesar's death. Caesar's friend and right-hand man, **Mark Antony,** teamed with Oc-

Plutarch's Account of Caesar's Death

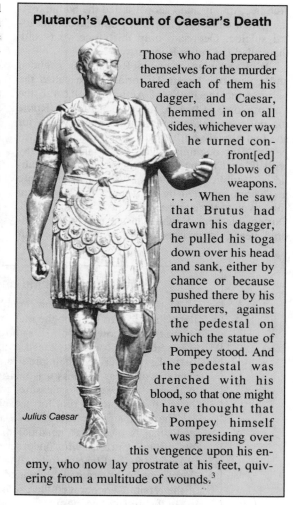

Julius Caesar

Those who had prepared themselves for the murder bared each of them his dagger, and Caesar, hemmed in on all sides, whichever way he turned confront[ed] blows of weapons. . . . When he saw that Brutus had drawn his dagger, he pulled his toga down over his head and sank, either by chance or because pushed there by his murderers, against the pedestal on which the statue of Pompey stood. And the pedestal was drenched with his blood, so that one might have thought that Pompey himself was presiding over this vengence upon his enemy, who now lay prostrate at his feet, quivering from a multitude of wounds.[3]

tavian (Caesar's nephew and only male relative) to capture and punish Caesar's murderers. Octavian and Antony then divided the Roman territory in half—Octavian ruling in the west and Antony (who had fallen under the charm of **Cleopatra,** the queen of Egypt) ruling in the east. Each man, however, was too ambitious to share power with the other. Again civil war was to settle the question of who was to be sole ruler of Rome. In 31 B.C., off the coast of Greece, Octavian's navy won a decisive victory over Antony and Cleopatra at the Battle of

Actium. Antony and Cleopatra fled the battle, realizing their cause was lost. They both later committed suicide. Octavian, only thirty-one years old, then ruled the entire Roman world.

With Octavian, one era of Roman history ended and a new one began. Historians have called the period from the Battle of Actium (31 B.C.) to the Fall of Rome (A.D. 476) the Roman Empire. Rome did not *become* an empire during these years, for she had already built a vast empire under the republic. But beginning with Octavian (some say with Julius Caesar), Rome was no longer a republic—a "public matter"—but was transformed into a government ruled by an **imperator** (an ancient title given to the commander of a victorious army). During this period, which lasted nearly five hundred years, imperators (from which we get our words *empire* and *emperor*) ruled with supreme power. This period of history will be the focus of the next chapter.

Section Review

1. What responsibility did the publicans have in Roman society?
2. What were the names of the two brothers who became spokesmen for reform in the later days of the republic?
3. Who were the two generals who fought in the First Civil War? Identify which one had the backing of the Senate and which one the backing of the Tribal Assembly.
4. Who were the three rulers of the triumvirate?
5. In what battle and year did Octavian defeat Antony in the Third Civil War?

A Glimpse Behind and a Glimpse Ahead

During these years of the republic, Rome grew from a small city along the Tiber to become the master of the Mediterranean world. New prosperity and power resulted from Rome's conquests. But with her rise to prominence, Rome was faced with new challenges. The Roman historian Livy described their predicament: "For true it is that the less men's wealth was, the less was their greed. Of late, riches have brought in avarice, and excessive pleasures the longing to carry wantonness and license to the point of ruin for oneself and of universal destruction."[4]

The foundations of the republic began to crumble. Traditional values, such as discipline, personal morality, and respect for authority, diminished. Citizens who once served their country with a sense of patriotic duty and responsibility now sought their own selfish interests. Corruption in government abounded. The breakdown of the moral fiber of the republic encouraged the use of force to settle Rome's problems.

In the midst of economic and political disorder, the Romans allowed the powers of the state to increase. They surrendered many of their rights and freedoms to obtain political and economic stability. Their industrious, self-reliant spirit was replaced by a reliance upon the state as "the Provider." They looked to the government to solve their problems instead of assuming the responsibilities and privileges that were theirs. They placed their hopes and destiny in the hands of popular leaders instead of realizing the truth found in God's Word: "It is better to trust in the Lord than to put confidence in man" (Ps. 118:8).

The republic was replaced with a dictatorship. Emperors provided temporary stability but at the costly price of liberty.

Chapter Review

Can You Explain?

Mare Nostrum	patrician	republic	veto
pater	plebeian	consul	publican
clan	imperium	plebiscite	triumvirate
tribe	fasces	tribune	imperator

Can You Identify?

Etruscans	Law of Twelve Tables	Cato	Julius Caesar
League of Seven Hills	287 B.C.	Tiberius Gracchus	March 15, 44 B.C.
Romulus	Tribal Assembly	Gaius Gracchus	Mark Antony
Remus	Pyrrhus	Marius	Octavian
509 B.C.	Punic Wars	Sulla	Cleopatra
Senate	Hannibal	Crassus	31 B.C.
Roman Forum	Scipio	Pompey	

Can You Locate?

Italian Peninsula	North Africa	Alps	Britain
Mediterranean Sea	Carthage	Battle of Cannae	Rubicon River
Apennines	Spain	Syracuse	Battle of Actium
Latium	Sicily	Battle of Zama	
Tiber River	Sardinia	Macedonia	
Rome	Corsica	Gaul	

How Much Do You Remember?

1. In what ways is it true to say that "all roads lead to Rome?"
2. Outline the steps by which the plebeians gained a voice in the Roman government.
3. Make an outline of the three Punic Wars. Include dates, causes, major events/battles, and results.
4. For each of the three civil wars that occurred during the first century B.C. of the republic, list the opposing army generals and underline the winner.

What Do You Think?

1. In what way does Daniel 7:7 describe Rome?
2. What do you think were the strengths and weaknesses of the Roman Republic?
3. After reading the conclusion to the chapter, what parallels do you see between the conditions contributing to the fall of the Roman Republic and the present conditions in the American Republic?

Notes
1. Polybius, trans. W. R. Patton, 6. 52.
2. Plutarch, *The Parallel Lives,* trans. Bernadotte Perrin, "Tiberius Gracchus," 9.
3. Plutarch, "Caesar," 66.
4. Livy, trans. B. O. Foster, 1. pref.

CHAPTER 4

"The fullness of time."

יֵשׁוּעַ הַנָּצְרִי מֶלֶךְ הַיְּהוּדִים

ΙΗΣΟΥΣ ΝΑΖΩΡΑΙΟΣ Ο ΒΑΣΙΛΕΥΣ ΤΩΝ ΙΟΥΔΑΙΩΝ

IESUS NAZARÆUS REX ILLE IUDÆORUM

JESUS OF NAZARETH KING OF THE JEWS—By the command of Pontius Pilate, this inscription was placed upon the cross on which the Savior of the world died. It is significant that Pilate had it written in Hebrew, Greek, and Latin; for in this chapter we will see how the Jews, Greeks, and Romans were all part of God's plan to bring world history to its climax in the life, death, and resurrection of His Son, Jesus Christ. We will also see how God used the accomplishments of the Jews (religious), the Greeks (intellectual), and the Romans (political) to pave the way for the growth of His church. This divine preparation culminated during the Roman Empire. This was the time when the world was made ready (Mark 1:15), when the "fulness of the time was come" (Gal. 4:4).

Pax Romana

Octavian's rule brought a period of peace to the Mediterranean world that lasted from 31 B.C. to A.D. 180. During these two centuries the Roman Empire reached its height: its boundaries encircled the Mediterranean Sea and included parts of the old Persian Empire in the east as well as most of western Europe and Britain. In contrast to the period of civil wars that preceded Octavian's reign, the first two centuries of the empire were marked for the most part by internal harmony and unity. Trade prospered, travel and communications improved, and cultural activities flourished. The ancient world experienced a period of peace and prosperity known as the *Pax Romana* ("Roman Peace"). Nevertheless, this was in a sense an artificial peace. Won by war and maintained by force, it did not long endure. But during the *Pax Romana,* the author of peace—Jesus Christ—was born. By His death on the cross, He secured for mankind a true and lasting peace. He said, "Peace I leave with you, my peace I give unto you: not as the world giveth, give I unto you. Let not your heart be troubled, neither let it be afraid" (John 14:27). Of Him the prophet Isaiah foretold, "For unto us a child is born, unto us a son is given: and the government shall be upon his shoulder: and his name shall be called Wonderful, Counsellor, The mighty God, The everlasting Father, The Prince of Peace. Of the increase of his government and peace there shall be no end, upon the throne of David, and upon his kingdom, to order it, and to establish it with judgment and with justice from henceforth even for ever" (Isa. 9:6-7).

Augustus: The "First Citizen" of Rome

With his defeat of Antony and Cleopatra at the Battle of Actium, Octavian brought an end to a century of civil war. He returned to Rome as the triumphant ruler of the Roman world, much as Julius Caesar had two decades earlier. But unlike Julius Caesar, who had made himself dictator for life, Octavian announced in 27 B.C. his desire to restore the republic. He voluntarily chose to share his powers with the Senate. This division of power had existed during the republic. He took the title *princeps* (PRIN keps), or "first citizen." This title was popular among the common people, for it conveyed the idea that he was one of them and not a noble. But in fact, the Roman government was a monarchy disguised as a republic. In his position as the head of the army, Octavian maintained firm control of the government. He was the first Roman ruler to be called an emperor—a title also given to his many successors.

We find in the New Testament (Luke 2:1) two other titles or names of Octavian: "Caesar" and "Augustus." *Caesar* was Octavian's family name—he was the great-nephew and adopted son of Julius Caesar. (The term *caesar* later became a political title used by many Roman emperors.) He is best remembered by the name ***Augustus***. The Senate conferred this title on him when he restored the republic. It was a title of divinity, expressing honor and majesty usually associated only with the Roman gods.

Augustus and the *Pax Romana*

During Augustus's reign (27 B.C.– A.D. 14), the entire Mediterranean world enjoyed economic prosperity. Agriculture remained the livelihood of most of the people. But the unity and stability maintained during the *Pax Romana* also encouraged the growth of trade. Rome established a stable currency of gold and silver coins, which traders could use as a medium of exchange almost anywhere in the empire. Rome freed the Mediterranean Sea of piracy and provided safe travel in Roman territory. Ease of communication also aided trade. Greek and later Latin became almost universal languages. Not only did trade flourish within the empire, but trade also extended to the world outside the empire. The Romans imported such luxury items as silks, spices, and jewels from India and China; they brought in gold and ivory from Africa. During the *Pax Romana* the material wealth of Rome reached its peak.

In addition to prosperity and peace, Augustus's reign brought stability and order to Roman government and society. Attempting to restore honesty and efficiency in government, he placed ability above social class when selecting government officials. Augustus removed unqualified, self-seeking men from office and replaced them with well-qualified officials paid by the state. He created a police and fire service for the city of Rome. In addition, he established a postal service and undertook major building programs.

Augustus also sought to abolish corruption in the provincial governments. He reorganized the provinces of the empire, placing some under the supervision of the Senate and others under his own supervision. To provide fairer methods of taxing the provinces, Augustus ordered a census-taking throughout the empire every fourteen years. From the Scriptures we know that Augustus ordered such a census around the time of the birth of Jesus Christ: "And it came to pass in those days, that there went out a decree from Caesar Augustus, that all the world should be taxed [registered]" (Luke 2:1).

Caesar Augustus

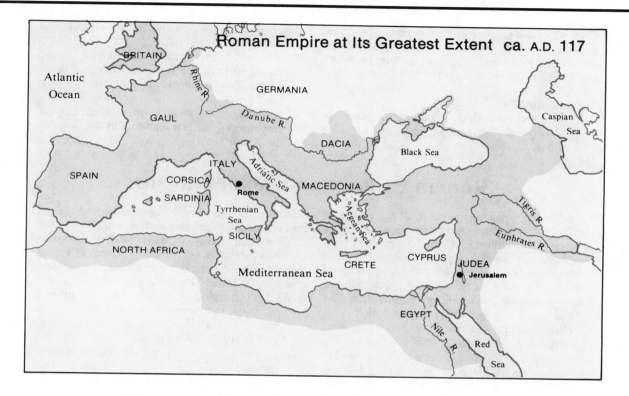

Roman Empire at Its Greatest Extent ca. A.D. 117

Augustus correctly realized that a civilization is only as strong as the moral character of her people. Therefore, he sought social reforms to revive the traditional Roman virtues of duty, discipline, and hard work. He encouraged the passage of laws that promoted family life and rewarded those families that had many children. Other laws punished immorality and placed limits on extravagant living. Despite the laws, Augustus's moral reforms failed. Laws may provide an atmosphere for proper living and may restrain improper behavior, but no law can make sinful men good. True moral reform does not come from outward conformity to good laws but from an inward change in the lives of men produced by faith in Jesus Christ and His saving power (Eph. 2:1-10).

Successors of Augustus

Though Augustus established an effective and well-organized government, he left no plan for choosing a successor. For nearly a half century after his death, men who were in some way related to Julius Caesar occupied the imperial office. Most of these men led wicked lives and squandered the wealth of Rome on their own selfish pleasures. In spite of incompetent leadership, the "Roman peace" continued—it was held intact by the might of the Roman army. Toward the end of the first century, the Roman army began to elevate its favorite generals to the office of emperor. These emperors were men of proven ability. During most of the second century, they provided strong leadership for Rome.

Nevertheless, too much power placed in the hands of ambitious and self-seeking men often leads to corruption. The emperors won popular favor by providing "free" grain and amusements for the people of Rome. The Romans failed to realize however, that these things were not really free. (The necessary funds came out of the public treasury.)

Civil war often erupted as rival generals fought to gain the emperor's crown. For example, from A.D. 235 to 285 Rome had twenty-six different emperors. Of these, twenty-five died violent deaths.

Section Review

1. What was the period of peace in the Mediterranean world lasting from 31 B.C. to A.D. 180 called?
2. List three titles or names by which Octavian was called.
3. What did Octavian institute within the empire in order to provide for fairer taxing of provinces? How often did he order this to take place?
4. How did many of the self-seeking, corrupt emperors of the late empire win the favor of the people?

Roman Culture and Achievement

As Rome expanded from a small city to a large empire, she came into contact with a wide variety of people and cultures. Rome borrowed, copied, modified, and preserved many elements of these cultures. She blended her own values and traditions with those of the Near Eastern and Greek cultures. Rome, a melting pot of ancient culture, was able to hold together an empire of diverse peoples.

Greek culture influenced almost every aspect of Roman life. A Roman poet of the first century B.C. wrote, "Conquered Greece took captive her rude conqueror [Rome] and carried her arts to backward Italy." Rome was actually far from "backward," but the Romans did learn much from the Greeks. The Romans were more practical than the Greeks. While the Greeks built with an eye for beauty, the Romans built with an eye for usefulness. The Greeks made significant contributions in art and philosophy; the Romans, in law and politics.

The Roman Contribution to Law

One of the most valuable and enduring of Rome's achievements was her system of justice. Rome protected the individual rights and property of her citizens. The New Testament writer Luke points out that it was not "the manner of the Romans to deliver any man to die, before that he which is accused have the accusers face to face, and have license [opportunity] to answer for himself concerning the crime laid against him" (Acts 25:16). The Romans believed that all citizens should have equal rights before the law. Cicero, the famous orator of the republic, wrote: "The legal rights at least of those who are citizens of the same common-

wealth ought to be equal. For what is the State except an association or partnership in justice?"

The legal codes of many modern European countries include many principles based on Roman law. Even the American system of justice has benefited from Rome's example. Here are some Roman legal principles. Do you notice any similarity between these and America's laws?

- Justice is a constant, unfailing disposition to give everyone his legal due.
- Liberty is a possession on which no evaluation can be placed.
- Freedom is beloved above all things.
- The burden of proof is upon the party affirming, not on the party denying.
- In inflicting penalties, the age and inexperience of the guilty party must be taken into account.
- No one [is] to be convicted on suspicion alone . . . [for it is] better for the crime of a guilty person to be left unpunished than for an innocent person to be condemned.
- The credibility of witnesses should be carefully weighed.
- In case of equal [conflicting] claims, the party in possession ought to be considered in the stronger position.
- Every individual is subjected to treatment in accordance with his own action and no one is made the inheritor of the guilt of another.[1]

Latin Literature and Language

The Romans modeled their literature after Greek examples. As they studied in Greece or under Greek tutors, many Romans fell under the influence of Greek literature and literary style. They added their own literary ideas and spirit to what they borrowed from the Greeks and thereby created a distinct literature of their own.

Latin literature expresses the life and history of the Roman people. Although Latin literature lacks the originality of Greek literature, the Romans produced some literary masterpieces that are still studied and appreciated today.

The greatest Latin literature was produced during the lifetimes of two of Rome's most famous citizens—Cicero and Augustus. **Cicero** (106-43 B.C.) dominated the first half of this literary age. He was not only one of the leading political figures of the late republic but was also an outstanding scholar, author, lawyer, and statesman. An eloquent and effective speaker, he also won acclaim as the greatest orator of his day. A master of Latin prose, he influenced later Roman writers and students of Latin literature.

The peaceful, stable conditions established during Augustus's reign (27 B.C.–A.D. 14) fostered another outpouring of literary activity. Optimism, patriotism, and appreciation for traditional Roman

---

"The Best of the Bargain"

In his play *Caesar and Cleopatra*, George Bernard Shaw made the following significant observation:

Caesar: [To an Egyptian art collector] Apollodorus, I leave the art of Egypt in your charge. Remember: Rome loves art and will encourage it ungrudgingly.

Apollodorus: I understand, Caesar. Rome will produce no art itself; but it will buy up and take away whatever the other nations produce.

Caesar: What! Rome produce no art! Is peace not an art? Is war not an art? Is government not an art? Is civilization not an art? All these we give you in exchange for a few ornaments. You will have the best of the bargain.[2]

---

values dominated Latin literature. Roman writers of the Augustan Age best expressed these feelings through poetry.

Poetry of the Augustan Age

Virgil—Often called the "Homer of Rome," **Virgil** is considered the greatest Roman poet. He glorified Rome in his epic poem the *Aeneid* (uh NEE id), one of the most widely read Latin literary

---

Cicero on Law

Although Cicero rightly recognized the importance of God's law, "god" to him was Nature and not the one true God. "True law is right reason in agreement with Nature. It is of universal application, unchanging and everlasting; it summons to duty by its commands and averts from wrong-doing by its prohibitions. And it does not lay its commands or prohibitions upon good men in vain, although neither have any effect upon the wicked. It is a sin to try to alter this law, nor is it allowable to attempt to repeal a part of it, and it is impossible to abolish it entirely. We cannot be freed from its obligations by Senate or People, and we need not look outside ourselves for an expounder or interpreter of it. And there will not be different laws at Rome and at Athens or different laws now and in the future, but one eternal and unchangeable law will be valid for all nations and for all times, and there will be one master and one rule, that is, God over us all, for He is the author of this law, its promulgator, and its enforcing judge."[3]

---

works. Virgil modeled the *Aeneid* after Homer's great epic poems the *Iliad* and the *Odyssey*. But while Homer's works stressed the virtues of the Greek ideal man, Virgil's work exalted Rome as the ideal state. The *Aeneid* reflects the common belief of the Augustan Age that Rome was destined to rule the world:

> Others, I doubt not, shall beat out the breathing bronze with softer lines; shall from marble draw forth the features of life; shall plead their causes better; with the rod shall trace the paths of heaven and tell the rising of the stars: remember thou, O Roman, to rule the nations with thy sway—these shall be thine arts—to crown Peace with Law, to spare the humbled, and to tame in war the proud.
> *(Aeneid* 6. 847-853)

Horace—After the death of Virgil, his close friend **Horace** became the ''Poet of the Augustan Age.'' In a poem written in praise of Augustus, he (like Virgil before him) spoke of the triumph of Rome.

> For earth at peace, hath closed Rome's Janus-
>   gate;—
> Curbed license which past ordered limit
>   strays;
>   Uprooted vice, and Rome's old ways
>   Recalled to guide the state;
> The ways whereby Rome's name and fame
>   increased,
> And her great empire's majesty grew strong,
>   Stretching from sunset's couch along
>   Right to the rising East.

Yet Horace did not overlook the seeds of decay in Roman society.

> What benefit are empty walls
> If crime we prune not with a knife severe?
>   Where life is tainted, what avails
> Law without morals?

Horace warned of the danger of luxury and ease: ''As riches grow, care follows, and a thirst for more and more.'' He praised the simple virtues of morality, justice, courage, and moderation. In his satires (works using ridicule or wit to correct or expose human folly or vice), he described the many follies of contemporary Roman society. For example—''This is a fault common to all singers, that among their friends they are never inclined to sing when asked [but] unasked they never desist.''

Ovid—The poetry of **Ovid** is quite different from the poetry of Virgil and Horace. Ovid wrote about mythology and love. His best-known work, *Metamorphoses,* is a collection of over two hundred myths of the ancient world. He skillfully blended these tales to form one continuous story. Ovid became popular among Rome's upper class because of his poetic stories of love and romance. However, his lack of discretion and self-restraint was out of step with the emperor's program for moral reform. Augustus banned Ovid's works from Rome's three public libraries and even exiled him from the city.

History

The historian **Livy,** who also lived during the Augustan Age, wrote a lengthy history of Rome. In some one hundred forty-two volumes, he provides an interesting narrative of the men and events of Roman history from the founding of the city through the end of the republic. Although Livy drew from many unreliable legends, his work offers valuable insight into early Roman customs and history. He saw the traditional virtues and patriotism of the Roman people as the foundation of Rome's greatness.

Livy on the Value of History

What chiefly makes the study of history wholesome and profitable is this, that you behold the lessons of every kind of experience set forth as on a conspicuous monument; from these you may choose for yourself and for your own state what to imitate, from these mark for avoidance what is shameful in the conception and shameful in the result.[4]

Later Roman Writers

The mood of Roman writers changed after the death of Augustus. Latin writers of the first century A.D. were more critical and pessimistic than their predecessors. The poet **Juvenal** wrote bitter satires on the loose morals and social problems of the empire.

> And when could you find more vices
>   abounding?
> When did the gullet of greed open wider?
> When did the dice draw more to the tables?
> They don't bring their wallets along,
> They bring a whole safety deposit box.[5]

Juvenal longed for a return to the days of the republic. He was not alone. The famed historian **Tacitus** favored the old republic over life under the self-centered emperors. His work *Annals* is a valuable but pessimistic history of Rome from the death of Augustus to the reign of Nero. In *Germania,* Tacitus gives us a rare glimpse of the lifestyle of the Germanic peoples, who later conquered the Western Roman Empire. He contrasts the simple

Pompeii

On the afternoon of August 24, A.D. 79, Mount Vesuvius (a volcano about one hundred twenty-five miles south of Rome) violently erupted. Having no advance warning, few of the residents of the nearby city of Pompeii had time to flee. Many died from breathing poisonous gases and fumes. Others were trapped in their houses by the deadly shower of hot cinders and ashes. In three days the entire city was completely buried. This thick layer of volcanic ash hardened, and the city of Pompeii passed from memory.

The site of the city was rediscovered in 1748. Archaeological excavations since that time have uncovered much of Pompeii. The city has been so well preserved that we can almost "relive" that fateful day over nineteen hundred years ago. Through their excavations, archaeologists have gained many insights into everyday life in Pompeii. They have uncovered many houses, complete with what were once beautiful gardens, furniture, utensils, colorful wall paintings, and even "beware-of-the-dog" signs and doghouses. In the city squares are walls covered

the hardened ash. Curious, they filled the air pockets with plaster of Paris. After the plaster dried and the surrounding ash could be removed, the archaeologists realized that the air pockets were forms of the men and women who had been buried by ash during the eruption. When the bodies later decomposed, only air pockets remained in the ash. The plaster casts are a graphic portrayal of the final agonies of the citizens of Pompeii.

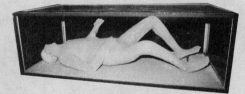

with political posters and advertisements. City streets are lined with shops of all kinds—cloth dyers, cobblers, tanners, potters, surgeons, metal smiths, and many others. There is even a bakery with loaves of bread still in the oven.

In the process of their excavations, the archaeologists also found mysterious air pockets inside

The people of Pompeii enjoyed many conveniences; they also enjoyed many wicked things. They loved immorality. They spent much of their time relaxing at sporting events and worshipping their athletic heroes, even though these "heroes" were wicked men. Many people ate so much at banquets that they went to special rooms where they could vomit and then return to the table to eat some more. Knowing these things about the people of Pompeii, we can recognize the city's destruction for what it probably was: the judgment of God.

virtues and customs of these "barbarians" with the corrupt morals of Rome's upper class.

The importance of Latin did not diminish after the collapse of the Roman Empire. Latin continued as the dominant language of medieval Europe—in learning, government, and religion. From Latin many of the native (or common) languages of Europe arose. Latin was the "parent" of the Romance languages—Italian, French, Spanish, Portuguese, and Rumanian. Although English is not a Romance language, hundreds of English words are of Latin origin.

Greek Contributions During the *Pax Romana*

During the *Pax Romana,* centers of Greek learning, such as Alexandria, Egypt, flourished. **Plutarch** was probably the most famous Greek writer in the Roman Empire. He wrote biographies that compared the lives of important Greek and Roman men. His *Parallel Lives of Illustrious Greeks and Romans* is not only an excellent literary work but also the source of valuable historical information. Advances in medicine continued under the work of the Greek physician **Galen.** Experimenting with animals, Galen studied the lungs, heart, arteries, and blood. His encyclopedia, a collection of the medical ideas of the ancient world, became the accepted medical authority of the Middle Ages. The Alexandrian astronomer and mathematician **Ptolemy** promoted the theory that the earth was the center of the universe. He taught that the sun, moon, and planets revolve around the earth. Although based on false assumptions, his **geocentric** (earth-centered) **theory** of the universe went unchallenged for almost fourteen centuries.

Roman aqueduct

Roman Art and Architecture

As Roman generals returned from their conquests, they brought captured art and artists back to Rome. Greek art became so popular among the Romans that they commissioned artists to make copies of Greek statues. But not all Roman art was imitative. The Romans excelled in portrait busts (head and shoulder statues). These popular statues portrayed Roman heroes, honored statesmen, and valiant soldiers. Unlike Greek sculpture, most Roman statues are realistic. Some even show warts, scars, and wrinkles. The Romans also excelled in relief sculpture (sculpture in which figures project out from a flat background). Realistic reliefs adorned gigantic monuments—triumphal arches and columns—which the Roman Emperors built to commemorate their conquests. The reliefs on these monuments gave a visual story of Rome's military exploits.

Even in ruins, these monuments attest to Roman engineering skill. The Romans used new building techniques as well as techniques borrowed from other cultures. Arches and vaults strengthened with concrete enabled Roman engineers to create large indoor spaces enclosed by massive domes. The Romans built **aqueducts** to supply water to many of their cities. Some aqueducts carried over fifty million gallons daily. They also built bridges and an extensive network of roads. Public baths and large amphitheaters provided relaxation and entertainment for many Romans throughout the empire. Unlike Greek buildings, which are known for their simple beauty, Roman buildings are distinguished for their large size, durability, and practicality.

The Roman Games

In arenas throughout the empire, the Romans flocked to see their favorite events—chariot races, gladiator contests, and wild beast fights. At the Circus Maximus in Rome, over a quarter of a million people gathered regularly to watch the chariot races. At the Roman Colosseum they delighted in the brutal struggles of the **gladiators** and wild beasts. The victors in these life-and-death contests became instant public heroes. In many of these arenas Christians died for their faith as they were slain by the gladiator's sword, thrown to wild beasts, or burned at the stake. These bloody "amusements" were staged by the Roman emperors to win the public favor and keep the unemployed masses of Rome out of mischief.

Without the truth of God, men, no matter how civilized, are bound in spiritual darkness. Roman society had been built on the family, morality, law, and justice; yet the Romans delighted in the bloody spectacles of the arenas. The Apostle Paul explains the apparent contradiction:

> And even as they did not like to retain God in their knowledge, God gave them over to a reprobate mind, to do those things which are not convenient [proper]; being filled with all unrighteousness . . . full of envy, murder, . . . proud, boasters, inventors of evil things, ... who knowing the judgment of God, that they which commit such things are worthy of death, not only do the same, but have pleasure in them that do them.
>
> —Romans 1:28-32

Religious Beliefs of the Romans

Roman religious beliefs gradually changed during her history. In the early days of the republic,

---

Seneca's Account of the Roman Games

I chanced to stop in a midday show [of gladiators], expecting fun, wit, and some relaxation, when men's eyes take respite from the slaughter of their fellow men. It was just the reverse. The preceding combats were merciful by comparison; now all the trifling is put aside and it is pure murder. . . . In the morning men are thrown to the lions and the bears, at noon they are thrown to their spectators. "Kill him! Lash him! Burn him! Why does he meet the sword so timidly? Why doesn't he kill boldly? Why doesn't he die game? Whip him to meet his wounds!" And when the show stops for intermission, "Let's have men killed meanwhile! Let's not have nothing going on!"[6]

The Colosseum

The Roman Colosseum is probably the most famous example of Rome's architectural genius. Shaped much like a football stadium, this mammoth structure originally towered over 160 feet high and covered six acres of land. In many ways the Colosseum was like a modern stadium; however, unlike that of most modern stadiums, admission to the Colosseum was free.

Construction of the building began during the reign of the emperor Vespasian and ended in A.D. 80 during the reign of his son Titus. Father and son were from the Flavian family; therefore, the new stadium was originally called the Flavian Amphitheater. Since the amphitheater had been built on the site of Nero's home, the emperor Hadrian (117-38) erected a large statue (colossus) of Nero outside the building. It is for this reason that the Flavian Amphitheater soon came to be called the Colosseum.

When filled to capacity, the Colosseum could hold nearly fifty thousand people. Spec-

tators poured in through the many numbered gates and took their places in the stadium based upon their social class. In order to increase spectator comfort, workers positioned awnings on top of the stadium wall to give relief from the hot sun. During lunch breaks (these spectacles often lasted all day) the people could buy food and drink at the stadium.

All the activity took place on the large oval floor of the Colosseum. This floor was made of wood and covered with sand. In fact, our word *arena* is the Latin word for sand. Parts of the floor could be quickly raised and lowered to bring up wild animals from their cages below. In addition, the whole arena could be flooded in order to reenact famous naval battles. The "actors" in all these bloody spectacles were usually criminals or war captives. However, professional gladiators also fought in the arena. Here many Christians were martyred for Christ.

the Romans had worshipped gods of nature. Many of the planets in our solar system bear the names of these Roman gods: Mercury, Venus, Mars, Jupiter, Saturn, Neptune, and Pluto. As the Romans came into contact with the Greeks, they associated their gods with the mythical gods of Mount Olympus. But like the Greeks, many Romans grew dissatisfied with the old gods and turned to philosophy to find happiness and meaning in life. The Romans had little concern for the abstract ideas of Greek philosophy; but in two Greek philosophies—Epicureanism and Stoicism—they discovered practical guidelines for living.

Epicureanism

The Epicurean philosophy may be summed up by the following:

There is nothing to fear in God,
There is nothing to be alarmed in death;
Good is easily obtained,
Evil is easily endured.[7]

The founder of this philosophy, Epicurus, taught that true happiness comes only as man frees his mind from fear and his body from pain. Epicurus believed happiness rested in the virtues of simple pleasure and peace of mind. He rejected the ideas of an afterlife and divine judgment. For him, happiness was to be found only in this life.

The poet **Lucretius** was probably the greatest exponent of Epicureanism in the Roman world. In his philosophical poem *On the Nature of Things,* Lucretius preserved the teachings of Epicurus. He hoped to reform the declining moral standards of the republic. However, many Romans interpreted the Epicurean teaching "seek happiness as the only good" as meaning they could do *anything* that would bring them pleasure. What could have restored Rome's traditional values became the excuse for the worst excesses of behavior.

Stoicism

The Stoic philosophy had a stronger and more lasting impact on Roman society than Epicureanism. One of the leading Stoics of the Roman Empire was **Seneca,** the tutor of the emperor Nero and an outstanding writer and thinker. Seneca saw Stoicism as the solution to Rome's moral decline. He wrote:

A brave man fears nothing more than the weakness of being affected with popular glory. His eyes are not dazzled either with gold or steel; he tramples upon all the terror and glories of Fortune; he looks upon himself as a citizen and soldier of the world; and in despite of all accidents and oppositions, he maintains his station. He does not only suffer,

The Maison Carrée, a beautiful Roman temple at Nîmes, France; the temple was built in honor of the grandsons of Caesar Augustus.

but court, the most perilous occasions of virtue, and those adventures which are most terrible to others: for he values himself upon experiment, and is more ambitious of being reputed good than happy.

Stoicism teaches that the highest good is the pursuit of the virtues of courage, dignity, duty, simplicity of life, and service to fellow men. Stoics believed in the brotherhood of man and the moral responsibility of each individual to his society. By proper living, man could bring himself into harmony with the divine law that governs the universe and directs his fate. The Stoics were sincere in their efforts, but they were sincerely mistaken; good behavior does not make a person "good" in the sight of God. It does not change the fact that he is a sinner.

Greek and Roman Deities		
Greek Deity	*Function*	*Roman Deity*
Zeus	King of the gods	Jupiter
Hera	Queen of the gods, wife of Zeus (Jupiter)	Juno
Ares	God of war	Mars
Apollo	God of the sun, the arts, and medicine	Apollo
Aphrodite	Goddess of love and beauty	Venus
Athena	Goddess of wisdom	Minerva
Hermes	Messenger of the gods, god of commerce and travel	Mercury
Poseidon	God of the sea	Neptune
Kronos	God of agriculture	Saturn
Artemis	Goddess of the moon	Diana
Eros	God of love	Cupid

Another eminent Roman devoted to Stoicism was the emperor **Marcus Aurelius**—scholar, philosopher, administrator, and last of the so-called Good Emperors of Rome. (His death in A.D. 180 marks the end of the *Pax Romana*.) Known as the "philosopher-king," Marcus Aurelius expressed the Stoic ideals in his book *Meditations*, a collection of personal reflections.

Influence from the East

With the large number of peoples and land embraced by the Roman Empire came a great variety of religious beliefs and ideas. From the East came the "mystery religions" that won popular acceptance among the Romans. These religions, based upon polytheism and mythology, promised immortality to those who performed secret and mysterious ceremonies. Rome tolerated these foreign religious beliefs as long as the people acknowledged that the Roman emperor was a god too.

Also from the East came the practice of emperor-worship. The Roman emperors held the title *pontifex maximus* ("greatest priest"). In this office, they interpreted the will of the gods in the affairs of state. People expressed their loyalty and patriotism to the state by worshipping the emperors. (Beginning in the Middle Ages, Roman Catholic popes also claimed this title for themselves.) Although Christians were loyal to the state, the government persecuted them because they did not worship the emperors—their first loyalty was to God, for He alone is worthy of worship.

Section Review

1. What culture greatly influenced Roman culture?
2. Who was called the "Homer of Rome"?
3. What city was covered by the volcanic ash of Mount Vesuvius and not rediscovered until the mid-eighteenth century?
4. What was the name of the man and his theory that stated that the earth was the center of the universe?
5. Who was a leading Stoic philosopher of the Roman Empire, who also served as tutor to an emperor? Who was his famous pupil?

The Introduction of Christianity

The World Made Ready

God directed the affairs of men and civilizations in ancient times to make the world ready for the coming of His Son and the spread of the gospel. Roman society at the time of Christ was characterized by safe travel and social and political stability. The widely known Greek language made possible the easy exchange of ideas. While these factors aided the spread of Christianity, other factors encouraged the popular acceptance of Christianity. The moral decay throughout the empire demonstrated the inability of human religions and philosophies to satisfy the longings of man's soul and to provide a worthy standard of moral behavior. Into this climate of despair, God sent His Son, who alone could satisfy that hunger and teach men how to live.

God used the Greeks and the Romans, but the Jews were His special tool. Though sometimes disobedient and rebellious against God, they preserved the knowledge and worship of the one, true God in the midst of a heathen world. They offered the hope of the coming Messiah and through their sacrifices testified to the sinfulness of man and his need of reconciliation to God.

The Babylonians destroyed Jerusalem in 586 B.C. and exiled thousands of Jews from their home land. Separated from the temple in Jerusalem, these "scattered" Jews built new centers of worship called **synagogues**. (Christians later used these synagogues for the preaching of the gospel message.) Like many other peoples, the Jews came under the influence of Hellenistic culture. Many Jews embraced the Greek culture and language. A group of men translated the Hebrew Old Testament into Greek because many Jews could no longer understand the Hebrew language. This translation is called the **Septuagint** (SEP too uh JINT). Through this translation, both Hellenistic Jews and Gentiles were made aware of the hope of the coming Messiah and the moral standard of God's law.

In the Fullness of Time

At the completion of His work of preparation, God sent **Jesus Christ** as a sacrifice to redeem fallen man from his sinful condition and to provide eternal life to those who, by faith, trust in Him. The Bible states that "when the fulness of the time was come, God sent forth His Son, made of a woman, made under the law, to redeem them that were under the law, that we might receive the adoption of sons" (Gal. 4:4-5).

Jesus was born in the small Roman province of Judea during the reign of the emperor Caesar Augustus. The events of His earthly life and ministry are recorded in the four Gospels (Matthew, Mark, Luke, and John). At the age of thirty, Jesus began His public ministry—preaching, teaching, and working miracles—demonstrating to all by word and deed that He was the promised Messiah, the Son of God.

However, most Jews rejected Jesus as their Messiah. The Apostle John tells us that "He came unto his own, and his own received him not" (John 1:11). The Jews looked for a messiah who would free them from Roman rule and reign over them on the throne of King David. They failed, however, to see the Old Testament distinction between the first and second comings (or advents) of the Messiah. At His first coming, Jesus Christ did not come to establish an earthly kingdom but to die on the cross for the sins of mankind. The Old Testament prophet Isaiah foretold this coming:

> He is despised and rejected of men; a man of sorrows, and acquainted with grief. . . . Surely he hath borne our griefs, and carried our sorrows: yet we did esteem him stricken, smitten of God, and afflicted. But he was wounded for our transgressions, he was bruised for our iniquities: the chastisement of our peace was upon him; and with his stripes we are healed.
> —Isaiah 53:3-5

At His Second Coming Christ will come to earth to set up His kingdom.

The Jewish religious leaders, whose blindness and hypocrisy Jesus had denounced, sought to put Him to death. They brought Christ before the Roman governor **Pontius Pilate,** charging that Christ had disrupted the state. They said He claimed to be the Messiah, the King of the Jews, and thus set Himself up in opposition to the Roman emperor **Tiberius** (A.D. 14-37). Although Pilate found no fault in Jesus, he desired to maintain the peace. Giving in to the Jewish demands, he sentenced Jesus to

Mattia Preti, Christ Seats the Child in the Midst of the Disciples, *Bob Jones University Collection of Sacred Art*

death by **crucifixion.** By His death on the cross, Jesus Christ accomplished God's plan of redemption.

The person and work of Jesus Christ are the foundation of the Christian faith. Christ was born of a virgin, lived a sinless life, and died that man might obtain salvation through His blood. But Christians do not worship a dead Savior; they worship a risen Lord. That Jesus Christ arose from the grave is a proven fact of history. Before He ascended into heaven, Christ was seen by over five hundred people (I Cor. 15:6). His life, death, and resurrection are the basis of the gospel; as Paul says, "Christ died for our sins according to the scriptures; and . . . he was buried, and . . . he rose again the third day according to the scriptures" (I Cor. 15:3-4). Men and women since that day have testified to the power of the gospel of Jesus Christ in their lives.

The Spread of the Gospel

"Go ye into all the world, and preach the gospel to every creature" (Mark 16:15). This is a command for Christian disciples of every age. During the first three hundred years of Christian era, the followers of Christ carried the gospel to many parts of the world. Conditions were favorable for the rapid expansion of the Christian faith. It was not until the nineteenth century that the missionary outreach of Christianity again experienced such favorable conditions.

Jerusalem was the center of the early church. Christ told His disciples, "Ye shall be witnesses unto me both in Jerusalem, and in all Judea, and in Samaria, and unto the uttermost part of the earth" (Acts 1:8). Through the disciples' preaching, thousands of Jews at Jerusalem turned from their unbelief and trusted in Jesus Christ as their Savior. But as the number of believers grew, so did the opposition of Jewish religious leaders. They began to persecute the Christians, imprisoning many of the disciples and stoning **Stephen**—the first Christian martyr. But the persecution at Jerusalem served only to spread the Christian faith, scattering Christians and their gospel message throughout Judea and Samaria. The spread of Christianity beyond its Jewish cradle was greatly aided by two events: the conversion of Paul and the Roman destruction of Jerusalem.

The Apostle Paul (A.D. 5?-67?)

Paul, originally named Saul, was born into a Jewish home of Tarsus (in present-day Turkey), inherited Roman citizenship, received one of the best educations a Jew could obtain, and became a Pharisee (a member of the strictest of the Jewish religious sects). His religious zeal made him a persecutor of the Christian church. But one day on his way to Damascus, Saul, the zealous persecutor, became a zealous Christian (Acts 9:1-6).

Perhaps no person has exceeded Paul in the impact of his work for Christ. The Holy Spirit inspired him, as He also inspired certain other men of his day (such as Peter, Luke, and John) to write part of the New Testament Scriptures. Paul wrote a greater number of books than any other biblical writer; most of the New Testament epistles (letters) were written by him. Through his missionary endeavors, Paul introduced the gospel to a large portion of the Roman world. He traveled thousands of miles on Roman roads preaching the gospel and establishing churches in Asia Minor, Macedonia, Greece, and Rome. The success of Paul's labors among the Gentiles demonstrated that the gospel was for all people and not just for the Jews. It was not until the Jewish uprising in A.D. 66-70, however, that the Roman world outside the Judean province was able to distinguish clearly the Christian faith from Judaism.

Italian Mannerist 16th century, Saint Paul, *Bob Jones University Collection of Sacred Art*

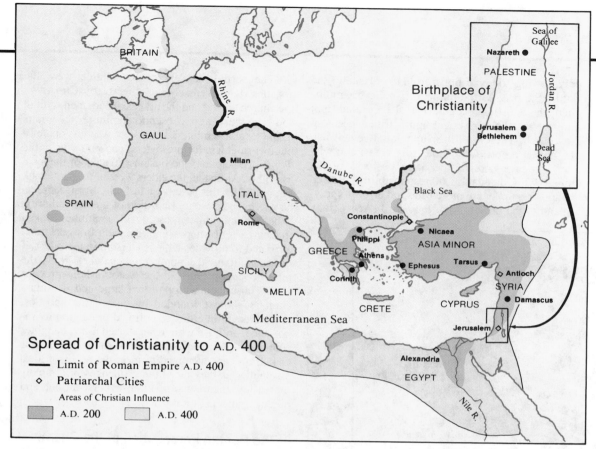

Spread of Christianity to A.D. 400

— Limit of Roman Empire A.D. 400
◇ Patriarchal Cities

Areas of Christian Influence

A.D. 200   A.D. 400

The Destruction of Jerusalem (A.D. 70)

Since the destruction of Jerusalem by Nebuchadnezzar in 586 B.C., Judea had been under the rule of foreign powers—first the Chaldeans, then the Persians, Alexander the Great, the Ptolemies, the Seleucids, and finally the Romans. The Jews tolerated foreign rule as long as they could maintain their religious freedom and administer their own local affairs. But the Jews grew dissatisfied with Roman rule as the Roman governors of Judea gradually became more oppressive and insensitive to the strong religious beliefs of the Jews.

In A.D. 66 Jewish discontent flared into open rebellion. The Jewish historian **Josephus,** who later recorded the conflict between the Jews and the Romans, warned the Jews of the folly of armed resistance against the mighty Romans. But the Jews failed to heed his advice. Roman legions were quickly dispatched to suppress the Jewish insurrection. In A.D. 70 the war came to a climax as the Roman legions under their commander **Titus** breached the walls of Jerusalem, looted the temple, and completely destroyed the city. God had judged the Jews for their rejection of Jesus Christ and their persecution of the early church. The Jews lost their homeland and became wanderers among the nations of the earth—objects of ridicule and persecution. Nevertheless, they retained their distinctiveness as a people. God used the destruction of Jerusalem to separate the early church from its Jewish environment and to scatter Christians throughout the Roman Empire.

The Development of the Organization of the Church

The organization of the early church was very simple. Christians met in private homes or in the Jewish synagogues for fellowship and worship. They gathered to read portions of God's Word, to pray, to sing songs of praise, and to partake of the Lord's Supper. As the number of believers multiplied, the apostles recognized that they could not minister to all the physical and spiritual needs in the church. Therefore, they appointed seven men of "honest report, full of the Holy Ghost and wisdom" to take care of the daily business of the church. This delegation of responsibility allowed the apostles to devote more time and effort to praying and to the preaching of the Word (Acts 6:1-7).

Arch of Titus in Rome

The earliest leaders of the church were the apostles, who were chosen directly by Christ. As the church spread and the apostles died, men of faith and experience were chosen to administer the affairs of the local assemblies. The pastor was just one of a number of elders (or presbyters) chosen to direct the worship, discipline, and business matters of the local assembly. At first all the elders were of the same rank but gradually the pastor, or bishop ("overseer") as he was called, rose to a position of greater authority. When difficult times arose, local assemblies looked to their pastor/bishops to protect them from doctrinal error and to provide stable leadership in the midst of persecution. As the number of churches grew, the influence and prestige of the pastor/bishops grew as well. Those men who pastored large and important churches—those founded by one of the apostles, those located in cities of political or economic importance, or those which had started many daughter churches—had special places of prominence. These church officers attempted to meet the needs of local assemblies as they faced the challenges of a rapidly increasing membership, intense persecution, and heretical attacks upon Christian doctrine.

The Roman Persecution of the Church

Satan has always attacked God by persecuting God's people. Christ told His disciples, "If they have persecuted me, they will also persecute you" (John 15:20). Throughout the history of the Christian church, God's enemies have demonstrated their hatred for God by persecuting Christian people. "All that will live godly in Christ Jesus shall suffer persecution" (II Tim. 3:12).

One of the most severe periods of persecution of the church occurred during the time of the Roman Empire. The ungodly Romans believed that the claims of Christ upon His followers set Christians at odds with the Roman state and society. They charged that Christians were disloyal citizens because they refused to burn incense on the altars of the emperors, acknowledging "Caesar as Lord." The Romans, who worshipped many different gods, opposed the exclusive claims of Christians: "Neither is there salvation in any other: for there is none other name under heaven given among men, whereby we must be saved'' (Acts 4:12).

The Romans considered Christians ''social misfits'' and Christianity a threat to their way of life. Christians did not attend the ''amusements'' of the arenas, celebrate the pagan festivals, or indulge in the many other vices of the day. Because Christians separated themselves from these public activities, the Romans branded them ''haters of humanity.'' They resented the Christians' fervent desire to tell others about Christ and became alarmed over the rapid growth of the Christian church. Christians became the scapegoats for all the evils that plagued the empire, from fires to earthquakes.

The first official Roman persecution of Christianity began under the emperor **Nero** (A.D. 54-68). He accused the Christians of setting fire to Rome, although he himself may have been responsible. What followed was a hideous display of cruelty and death. The Roman historian Tacitus records that Christians were ''torn by dogs, or were nailed to crosses, or were doomed to the flames and burnt, to serve as nightly illumination, when daylight had expired.''

From the time of Nero until A.D. 250, the persecution of Christians was sporadic and confined to small areas. However, beginning in 250, persecution became empire-wide. Thousands of Christians—both the young and the old—met death by sword, crucifixion, wild beasts, fire, and burning oil. But they had the steadfast confidence that it is better to ''fear him which is able to destroy both soul and body in hell'' than to fear ''them which kill the body, but are not able to kill the soul'' (Matt. 10:28).

The last and most violent widespread Roman persecution came under the emperor **Diocletian** (284-305). He turned the full power of imperial Rome against the Christian faith. Diocletian ordered the destroying of Christian churches, the depriving of Christians' political and civil rights, and the burning of all copies of the Scriptures. A later edict ordered all Christians to sacrifice to the pagan gods; those who refused to obey the edict suffered torture and death. Despite these intense efforts, Christianity endured.

Polycarp: "Faithful unto Death"

In his message to the church at Smyrna in Asia Minor, Jesus said, ''Behold, the devil shall cast some of you into prison, that ye may be tried; and ye shall have tribulation ten days; be thou faithful unto death, and I will give thee a crown of life'' (Rev. 2:10). A little more than fifty years later, Christians at Smyrna experienced that tribulation in bloody persecution. Among those ''faithful unto death'' was the leader of the church at Smyrna, Polycarp.

Polycarp had received many spiritual blessings in his life. As a young man, he had heard the Apostle John speak. When he was about forty, Polycarp had received a visit from Ignatius, bishop of Antioch, who was under arrest on his way to Rome, where he died for his faith. After the visit, Ignatius wrote a letter, thanking Polycarp for his hospitality and urging, ''Stand thou firm, as an anvil when it is smitten. It is the part of a great athlete to receive blows and be victorious. But especially must we for God's sake endure all things.''

Around A.D. 160 a wave of persecution swept over the Christians in Smyrna. City authorities seized Polycarp, bishop of the church, and brought him before a howling crowd gathered at the stadium. The Roman official governing Smyrna tried to get Polycarp to publicly disavow his faith. ''Swear the oath [to the emperor],'' he said, ''and I will release thee; revile the Christ.'' Polycarp looked at the official and replied, ''Fourscore and six years have I been His servant, and He hath done me no wrong. How then can I blaspheme my King who saved me?''

When further argument proved fruitless, the official turned Polycarp over to the fury of the crowd. They seized the aged bishop, bound him to a stake in the middle of the stadium, and burned him to death. A faithful witness to his Lord, Polycarp proved worthy of ''a crown of life.''

What effect did the Roman persecutions have upon the Christian church? The Romans believed that persecution would halt the growth of Christianity and force Christians to renounce their faith. Yet the more the Romans persecuted the Christians, the more the Christian faith grew, causing one Christian writer to observe, ''The blood of the martyrs is the seed of the church.''

The church grew not only in numbers but also in purity. In the midst of trials and afflictions, Christians became more devoted to their Lord, more steadfast in their convictions, more abundant in their witness, and more willing to offer their lives, if need be, for the sake of the gospel. Persecution separated the church from the world as well as worldly Christians from the church. In the end the Roman world did not overcome Christianity; Christianity overcame the Roman world.

From Imperial Persecution to Imperial Acceptance

In 313 an event occurred that altered the whole outlook of the church. In the **Edict of Milan,** the Roman emperor **Constantine** (306-337) made Christianity legal, ending almost three hundred years of Roman persecution of Christians. Just a year earlier, before a crucial battle with a rival for the emperor's throne, Constantine claimed to have seen in the sky a vision of a shining cross that bore the inscription, "By this sign, conquer!" Upon defeating his foe, Constantine publicly embraced Christianity, attributing his military success to the Christian God. We do not know what Constantine's true motives were for adopting the Christian faith nor whether he truly became a Christian. But we do know that his outward acceptance of Christianity dramatically changed the history of the church. Rome, previously a persecutor of the church, became the protector and patron of the church. Constantine restored church property that had been confiscated under the Diocletian persecution, made Sunday a legal holiday, contributed funds for new church buildings, and encouraged others to embrace Christianity.

The Catacombs

The early Christians buried their dead rather than cremating them as the pagans did. Because they believed in the resurrection of the body, Christians thought it was wrong to destroy the body deliberately by burning it. They established their own burial grounds, which they called *koimeteria*—a Greek term meaning, "place of rest," or "sleeping place." From this word we get our modern English word *cemetery*. We call the cemeteries that these early Christians established catacombs. (The word *catacomb* derives from the Greek *kata kumbos*, meaning "near the low place." The Italians first used this Greek phrase in reference to a Christian cemetery located near a low place outside the city of Rome.)

The catacombs are underground passageways about a yard wide and six to eight feet tall. In the walls of these passageways the Christians carved openings in which they placed the bodies of their friends and relatives. As more burial space was needed, more of these corridors were dug. Eventually there were many miles of walking space underground. Between the years 150 and 400, over half a million Christians were buried in the catacombs.

As the Roman Empire collapsed and barbarians swept into the Italian Peninsula, the catacombs were abandoned. The church removed some of the remains to safer places, while grave robbers and vandals destroyed the rest. By the year 900 all the tombs were empty.

Today the catacombs are tourist attractions. They contain some of the earliest examples of Christian art. More importantly, the catacombs illustrate the faith of the early Christians. One symbol often found painted or carved on the walls of the catacombs is the fish. The early Christians used the Greek word for fish *(ichthus)* as a confession of their faith in Jesus Christ.

Iesous **Chr**istos, **Theo**u **U**ios, Soter
Jesus Christ, God's Son, Savior

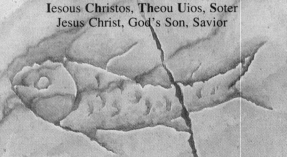

A Governor Seeks Advice

How should Roman officials deal with Christians in their community? This question was raised by Pliny the Younger, a governor of a Roman province in Asia Minor. He wrote the emperor Trajan (98-117) for advice. The following are excerpts from Pliny's letter and Trajan's reply.

Pliny to Trajan:

It is my rule, Sire, to refer to you in matters where I am uncertain. . . . I was never present at any trial of Christians; therefore I do not know what are the customary penalties or investigations, and what limits are observed. I have hesitated a great deal on the question whether there should be any distinction of ages; whether the weak should have the same treatment as the more robust; whether those who recant should be pardoned, or whether a man who has ever been a Christian should gain nothing by ceasing to be such; whether the name itself, even if innocent of crime, should be punished, or only the crimes attaching to that name.

Meanwhile, this is the course that I have adopted in the case of those brought before me as Christians. I ask them if they are Christians. If they admit it I repeat the question a second and a third time, threatening capital punishment; if they persist I sentence them to death. For I do not doubt that, whatever kind of crime it may be to which they have confessed, their pertinacity [stubbornness] and inflexible obstinacy should certainly be punished.

Trajan to Pliny:

You have taken the right line, my dear Pliny, in examining the cases of those denounced to you as Christians, for no hard and fast rule can be laid down, of universal application. They are not to be sought out; if they are informed against, and the charge is proved, they are to be punished, with this reservation—that if anyone denies that he is a Christian, and actually proves it, that is by worshiping our gods, he shall be pardoned as a result of his recantation, however suspect he may have been with respect to the past. Pamphlets published anonymously should carry no weight in any charge whatsoever. They constitute a very bad precedent, and are also out of keeping with this age.[8]

Once threatened by persecution, Christians now found themselves protected by Roman law, favored by the Roman emperor, and granted privileges by the Roman state. But with this official favor also came the increased intervention of the state in church affairs. For example, when a heretic by the name of **Arius** disrupted the unity of the church by challenging the deity of Christ, Constantine intervened and called for a general council of church leaders to settle this doctrinal controversy. In 325, the **Council of Nicaea,** presided over by Constantine, affirmed Christ's deity and the doctrine of the Trinity; it also branded Arianism a heresy. As the emperors became more involved in church matters, the ties between the state and the church increased. Indeed, at the end of the fourth century, Christianity became the official and exclusive religion of the Roman state by edict of the emperor **Theodosius I** (379-395).

As a result of the freedom and privileges granted by the Roman government, the church grew rapidly in membership and material prosperity. Nevertheless, the close alliance between church and state caused a decline in the purity of the church's membership, practices, and organization. Great numbers of people joined the church—some because they embraced the truth, others because it was the popular thing to do. As Christians devoted more attention to the things of this world, their zeal and interest in spiritual matters declined. Church buildings became lavishly decorated. The line of distinction between the church and the world became less discernible.

Although Christianity triumphed over the pagan religions of Rome, some pagan ideas and practices crept into the church. One such practice was **monasticism,** which exercised a strong influence on the church from the fourth century to the end of the Middle Ages. Monasticism is not of Christian origin nor biblically based but from the Eastern pagan religions. Because of the moral and economic decay of the Roman Empire and the growing worldliness of the church, many sought escape

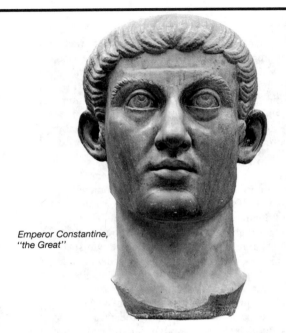

Emperor Constantine, "the Great"

from the turmoil and evil of the world by living apart from society in monasteries. Many men and women sincerely believed that the greatest form of piety and the best means to gain victory over the flesh was to withdraw from all worldly cares and possessions and practice strict discipline and religious exercises.

The organization of the church became more complex as the church grew numerically. By the fourth century, the church had a definite **hierarchical** (HY er AR kih kul) structure—levels of authority among the pastor/bishops and churches in the empire. The organization of the church followed the pattern of the political and geographic divisions of the Roman Empire. The smallest division was the parish, served by a pastor. Next was the diocese (DYE uh sis) or district, a territorial division supervised by a bishop and comprising a number of parishes within and around a city. An archbishop administered a number of dioceses called a province. The largest administrative districts of the church were the patriarchates. The **patriarchs** were the bishops of the most important cities of the empire—Jerusalem, Alexandria, Rome, and Constantinople (the new capital founded by Constantine). These positions had the most prestige and authority within the church. At first the patriarchs were all of equal rank, but over a period of time the patriarch of Rome came to be regarded as the "first among equals."

Because of the close ties between church and state, the worldliness of many Christians, the adoption of pagan ideas, and religious hierarchy, the church gradually departed from the truth of the Christian faith. The seeds of error that took root during the fourth and fifth centuries blossomed during the Middle Ages into the Roman Catholic church—a perversion of biblical Christianity. (In Chapter 7 we will examine the rise and growth of this church and its leader, the pope.)

Section Review
1. What were the centers of worship called for the Jews who were scattered abroad?
2. What two events greatly aided the spread of Christianity beyond its Jewish cradle?
3. What emperor made Christianity a legal religion in the empire? What emperor made Christianity the official religion of the empire?
4. What heresy challenged the deity of Christ? At what council in 325 was the truth of Christ's deity affirmed?
5. What were the pastor/bishops of the most important cities called? List these four cities.

Collapse of the Roman Empire

Reason for Rome's Decline

In the third century a series of political, economic, and social crises shook the foundations of the empire. Signs of internal weakness and decay were already present within the empire. In the fourth and fifth centuries, barbarian invaders entered Roman territory, and Rome was too weak to expel them. What were the reasons for this decline and the eventual collapse of the Roman Empire?

One important reason was Rome's political disorder. By the third century, Rome could no longer boast of a strong and stable government. Inefficiency and waste had accompanied the sharp rise in the size of the government. Rome also suffered from unstable leadership, for the Romans had never adopted a definite plan for choosing a successor to the emperor. Hence, ambitious generals plotted and struggled to gain control of the government. As the army became increasingly involved in political affairs, greedy soldiers were quick to elevate a military leader to emperor in return for rewards. If the army became dissatisfied with an emperor, they could remove him from power and put someone else in his place. In many cases war broke out between different legions as each tried to secure the emperor's throne for its own commander. Political turmoil, assassination, and civil war became commonplace. The army, once the protector of the Roman state, controlled the state in order to satisfy its own greed.

Closely associated with Rome's political problems were her economic troubles. The cost of maintaining an increasingly large army to defend her extensive borders, as well as the expenses of a huge government bureaucracy, drained the Roman treasury. To solve the economic crisis, the government attempted to raise revenue by increasing the tax burden of the people. In addition, emperors reduced the silver content in the Roman coins, adding cheaper metals instead. As the value of coinage declined, prices rose. This inflation was aggravated by Rome's one-sided trade with India and China, which depleted the empire's gold and silver supplies. Because Roman money became almost worthless, the barter system replaced the use of money. Trade slackened, shops closed, and poverty increased. Confidence in the economic future of Rome all but collapsed.

Moral decay was another factor in the decline of Rome. As we saw in the last chapter, Rome's strength during her early history was due in large part to the virtues of her citizens—their discipline, patriotism, self-denial, hard work, and respect for authority. However, the moral decay that began during the days of the republic continued during the *Pax Romana*. Contentment was replaced by greed.

People looked to the government to supply free grain and public amusements. (This also contributed to the large economic burden of the empire.) Family life disintegrated, divorce and immorality abounded, and superstition increased. Once the backbone of Rome, a hard-working patriotic citizen was now hard to find.

Attempts to Reform and Reorganize

By the end of the third century the Roman Empire was at the point of collapse. But two powerful emperors—Diocletian and Constantine—introduced strong reforms that delayed the fall of the empire for almost two centuries. While earlier emperors tried to work within the framework of the old institutions of the republic, Diocletian and Constantine wielded supreme authority over the state in their attempts to restore order and stability to the empire.

In 284 the Roman army proclaimed Diocletian emperor of Rome. Diocletian, an able administrator and organizer, reshaped the political structure of the empire. He realized that the empire was too large for one man to rule effectively. He therefore chose a co-emperor, known as an **augustus,** to rule the western half of the empire while he ruled in the east. Diocletian's plan called for each co-emperor to appoint an assistant, called a **caesar,** to help the augustus and to become his successor. Diocletian divided the empire into four large administrative divisions, called prefectures, which were to be ruled by the two co-emperors, and the two caesars. Through these measures, Diocletian brought temporary stability to the government.

Diocletian also introduced strong measures to combat Rome's economic problems. To curb inflation, he set maximum prices on goods and services. Anyone selling an item above the price limit could be put to death. He tried to revive confidence in Rome's monetary system by introducing new gold and silver coins. He also reformed the tax system, although the people still suffered under an excessive tax burden. In each instance, Diocletian's measures to solve Rome's economic worries involved greater government control and regulations. In the long run, his measures only added to the problems they were intended to solve.

Roman coins: the large sesterce pictures Caesar Augustus. The denarii picture (from left to right) the emperors Claudius, Vespasian, Domitian, and Trajan. The denarius is often mentioned in the New Testament. (See Matt. 22:19.)

When Diocletian retired from office in 305, his system of joint rule fell apart. Civil war broke out among the co-emperors and caesars. After years of struggle, Constantine emerged victorious and became the sole ruler of the empire. Through his political and economic reforms, Constantine continued in the same direction as Diocletian. One of the most significant actions taken by Constantine was the moving of the capital of the empire to the east. He selected the site of the ancient city of Byzantium (bih ZAN tee um) to build his "New Rome," which became known as Constantinople. But this removal of the imperial throne to the east weakened the already struggling western half of the empire.

Diocletian and Constantine prepared the way for the division of the Roman Empire into two separate empires. The empire did not become permanently divided until 395 when the emperor Theodosius I divided it between his two sons. After this division, the Western Roman Empire soon fell. The Eastern Roman Empire—later called the Byzantine Empire—endured for another thousand years, as we shall see in Chapter 5.

Barbarian Invasions of the Empire

During the latter years of the Roman Republic, growing numbers of Germanic peoples had moved down from northern Europe and settled along Rome's borders. These people were divided into independent tribes such as the Angles, Saxons,

Franks, Vandals, and Goths. Roman historians described the Germanic tribes as courageous but restless, given to much drinking and gambling, yet possessing many simple virtues. The Romans called these people "*barbarians*"—a term they used to describe all those outside the empire who did not share in the Greek or Roman cultures.

Rome greatly increased the size of her army in an effort to maintain the security of her borders from barbarian intruders. At first Rome had a hard time finding recruits for this frontier army. To solve the problem, some emperors allowed the most "Romanized" of the Germanic tribes to settle within Roman territory to serve as a buffer between Rome and other barbarian tribes. Other emperors allowed barbarians to enlist in the army. Gradually, this foreign element in Rome's army became Rome's primary means of protecting the empire against the more restless tribes outside her borders.

Out of the Far East in the late fourth century came a new threat to Rome's security—the **Huns.** This fierce nomadic tribe, which had menaced the Chinese empire for centuries, now moved across Asia into Europe, bringing terror and destruction upon all who were in their path. The advance of the dreaded Huns prompted many Germanic tribes to seek refuge in Roman territory.

One such tribe was the **Visigoths,** who crossed the Danube River and settled in the eastern part of the Roman Empire. Because of mistreatment by Roman officials, the Visigoths rebelled. In order to put down the revolt, the emperor led the Roman army against the Visigoths. At the Battle of Adrianople in 378, the Visigoths soundly defeated the Roman army and killed the emperor. This was obviously a disaster for Rome: her legions, thought to be invincible, had fallen in defeat before a barbarian people.

The Fall of Rome

In 410, under the leadership of **Alaric,** the Visigoths moved southwestward into the Italian peninsula and plundered the city of Rome. They eventually settled in what is now Spain. Meanwhile, the Franks moved into northern Gaul, and the Angles and Saxons crossed over into Britain. The Huns, led

Augustine of Hippo

Augustine of Hippo (354-430) was one of the outstanding figures of the early Christian church. As bishop, writer, and preacher he earnestly defended the Christian faith against its many foes.

Augustine was born at Tagaste, in North Africa. His father was a pagan, but his mother was a Christian. Despite his mother's influence, Augustine led a sinful life until his conversion in the year 386. He underwent an intense spiritual struggle. He wanted peace in his soul but loathed giving up his sin. At one point he actually prayed, ''Grant me chastity and continence—but not yet.''

While sitting in a friend's garden, Augustine was in despair over his sin. He prayed, ''But Thou, O Lord, how long ? . . . How long, how long? Tomorrow, and tomorrow? Why not now? Why is there not this hour an end to my uncleanness?'' Then he heard a child nearby chanting in play, ''Take up and read. Take up and read.'' Taking this as a sign from God, Augustine picked up a copy of the Scriptures. His eye fell on Romans 13:13-14—''Not in rioting and drunkenness, not in chambering and wantonness, not in strife and envying. But put ye on the Lord Jesus Christ, and make not provision for the flesh, to fulfil the lusts thereof.'' In the Lord Jesus Christ, Augustine placed his faith and found salvation.

After his conversion, Augustine became a priest (pastor) and eventually bishop of Hippo in North Africa. Augustine opposed the religious falsehoods of his day through his preaching and his writing. For example, about this time a British monk named Pelagius began teaching that man was not sinful and could save himself through his own efforts. Augustine condemned this idea and affirmed the biblical position that man can be saved only by God's mercy and grace.

In 410 barbarian invaders attacked the city of Rome. Pagan Romans blamed this disaster on the Christians. They said that the gods were punishing Rome for abandoning the old ways of

Gasper de Crayer, St. Augustine, Bob Jones University Collection of Sacred Art

worship. Augustine answered this charge in his greatest work, *The City of God*. He said that all human history is the story of two cities representing opposing ways of life. One is the city of earth, the home of sinful, unsaved men. The other is the city of God, namely His church. God's purpose in history is to build His city by saving men from sin. These two cities exist side by side in this life but will be separated by God at the final judgment. The earthly city and its citizens will go to the destruction reserved for sinners. Citizens of the heavenly city will go to eternal glory and bliss with God. With this in mind, Augustine says that we should not look at individual historical events as demonstrating the favor or disfavor of some god. Instead we should see in every event the hand of the true God directing the course of history for His purpose and glory.

by their fierce leader **Attila** (called the ''scourge of God,'' for he was considered to be the instrument of God's wrath upon a sinful people), also invaded Roman territory. However, the Romans with the help of the Germanic peoples were able to stop the advance of the Huns. Just a few years later, the **Vandals**—a Germanic tribe that established a kingdom in North Africa—raided and pillaged Rome

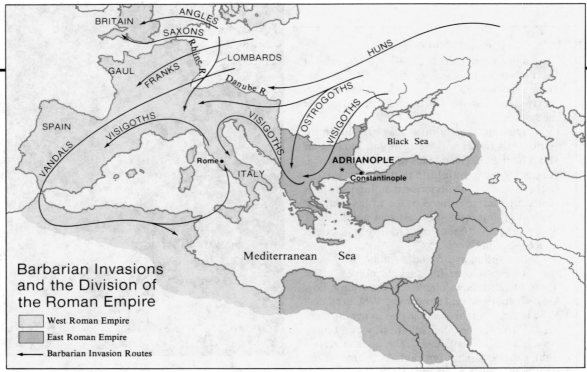

Barbarian Invasions and the Division of the Roman Empire

- West Roman Empire
- East Roman Empire
- ← Barbarian Invasion Routes

again. To later generations, their name came to mean "a destroyer of property."

With the onslaught of the barbarian invasions, the Western Roman Empire collapsed. Many historians give the date 476 for the fall of Rome. In that year, the army ended the long period of Roman rule by placing a non-Roman upon the emperor's throne in the west.

Section Review

1. List three economic problems troubling Rome in the late days of the empire.

2. What emperor sought to solve the political problems of the empire by dividing the empire into four administrative divisions called prefectures?

3. What emperor divided the empire between his two sons, leading to the division of the Roman Empire into two separate empires?

4. What did the Romans call the Germanic peoples who began to settle along the borders of the empire and threatened the security of the empire?

5. In what year did a non-Roman take the imperial throne, signifying the collapse of the Roman Empire?

A Glimpse Behind and a Glimpse Ahead

It must be remembered that the foundation of Rome had eroded internally before collapsing under the pressure of external invasion. The English historian Edward Gibbon, who wrote the monumental *Decline and Fall of the Roman Empire*, stated, "The story of its ruin is simple and obvious; and instead of inquiring *why* the Roman Empire was destroyed, we should rather be surprised that it had subsisted so long."

Some say, however, that Rome never fell. In a sense this is true. Although the political structure of the western empire no longer existed after 476, elements of Roman culture continued into the Middle Ages, preserved by the Roman Catholic church in the west and the Byzantine Empire in the east.

Chapter Review

Can You Explain?

princeps	Epicureanism	Septuagint	patriarchs
geocentric theory	Stoicism	crucifixion	augustus
aqueducts	*pontifex maximus*	monasticism	caesar
gladiator	synagogues	hierarchical	barbarians

Can You Identify?

Pax Romana	Galen	Josephus	Theodosius I
Augustus	Ptolemy	A.D. 70	395
Cicero	Lucretius	Titus	Huns
Virgil	Seneca	Nero	Visigoths
Horace	Marcus Aurelius	313	378
Ovid	Jesus Christ	Diocletian	Alaric
Livy	Pontius Pilate	Edict of Milan	Attila
Juvenal	Tiberius	Constantine	Vandals
Tacitus	Stephen	Arius	476
Plutarch	Paul	Council of Nicaea	

Can You Locate?

Rome	Jerusalem	Asia Minor	Constantinople
Roman Empire	Tarsus	Milan	Danube River
Judea	Damascus	Alexandria	Adrianople

How Much Do You Remember?

1. List four ways Octavian sought to improve Roman government and society.
2. For each of the following names, list the person's occupation and a brief statement of his achievement: Cicero, Virgil, Livy, Plutarch, Galen. (Include any titles of important works they wrote.)
3. List two reasons for the Roman persecution of Christians.
4. List three reasons for Rome's decline.

What Do You Think?

1. Read the following passages from the book of Acts, and tell what you learn about the rights of a Roman citizen: Acts 16:37-38; 19:38-41; 22:25-29; 23:27-29; 25:7-12, 16.

2. How did the Roman games compare to the Greek games?
3. How did God use the Jews, Greeks, and Romans respectively to prepare the world for the coming of His son?
4. Read Micah 5:2 and Luke 2:1-7. How did God use Caesar Augustus to fulfill Micah's prophecy about the birth of Messiah?
5. Arius taught that Christ did not always exist but that He was created by God the Father. How does John 1:1-4 show this teaching to be false?
6. Was the church better off being persecuted by the emperors or being favored by them?
7. By 476 the fall of Rome was complete. When do you think Rome began to decline? Support your answer.

Notes
1. Naphtali Lewis and Meyer Reinhold, eds., *Roman Civilization,* vol. 2 (New York: Columbia Univ. Press, 1955), pp. 535-50 *passim.*
2. George Bernard Shaw, *Seven Plays with Prefaces and Notes* (New York: Dodd, Mead, and Co., 1951), p. 466.
3. Cicero, *De Re Publica,* trans. Clinton Walker Keyes, 3. 22
4. Livy, *History of Rome,* trans. B. O. Foster, 1. pref.
5. Juvenal, *Satires,* trans. L. R. Lind, 1. 93-96.
6. Seneca, *Moral Epistles,* trans. Chester G. Starr, 7.
7. F. F. Bruce, *New Testament History* (Garden City, N.Y.: Doubleday, 1961), p. 42.
8. Pliny, *Letters,* trans. William Melmoth.

UNIT II

Medieval maps of the world, such as the one above, present a view of the world very different from our modern view. In the center stands Jerusalem, the city of God. Around Jerusalem lie Europe (bottom left), Africa (bottom right), and Asia (top half of the map). Medieval Europeans thought of Asia as a mysterious place. Therefore, maps such as this one located Paradise and similar "otherworldly" sites in Asia.

This unit progresses eastward from Rome into the mysterious, alluring Orient as well as southward to the continent of Africa. Beginning with the Byzantine Empire (a blending of Eastern and Western culture), we will move to the Middle East (the realm of Islam), to the faraway lands of India and China, and finally to an examination of early African civilizations. What seemed strange and incomprehensible to the medieval Europeans will become familiar to us.

BYZANTINE EMPIRE		
RUSSIA		
ISLAM		
INDIA	MOHENJO-DARO	ARYAN INVASIONS
CHINA		SHANG DYNASTY (ca. 1500–ca. 1000)
JAPAN		
AFRICA		KUSH Taharqa

2000   1500   100

B.C.

THE EASTERN WORLD

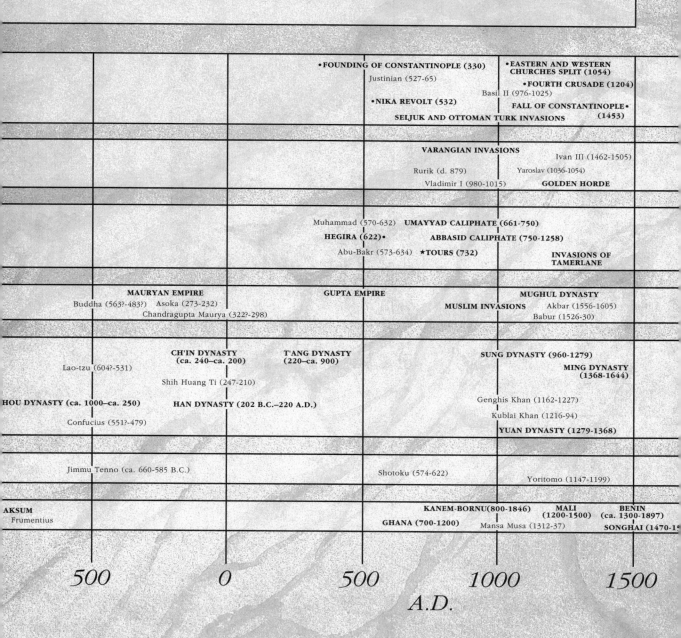

- •FOUNDING OF CONSTANTINOPLE (330)
- •EASTERN AND WESTERN CHURCHES SPLIT (1054)

Justinian (527-65)

- •FOURTH CRUSADE (1204)

Basil II (976-1025)

- •NIKA REVOLT (532)

FALL OF CONSTANTINOPLE• (1453)

SELJUK AND OTTOMAN TURK INVASIONS

VARANGIAN INVASIONS

Ivan III (1462-1505)

Rurik (d. 879)   Yaroslav (1036-1054)

Vladimir I (980-1015)   **GOLDEN HORDE**

Muhammad (570-632)   **UMAYYAD CALIPHATE (661-750)**

HEGIRA (622)•   **ABBASID CALIPHATE (750-1258)**

Abu-Bakr (573-634)   ★TOURS (732)

INVASIONS OF TAMERLANE

MAURYAN EMPIRE   **GUPTA EMPIRE**   **MUGHUL DYNASTY**

Buddha (563?-483?)   Asoka (273-232)   **MUSLIM INVASIONS**   Akbar (1556-1605)

Chandragupta Maurya (322?-298)   Babur (1526-30)

CH'IN DYNASTY (ca. 240-ca. 200)   **T'ANG DYNASTY (220-ca. 900)**   **SUNG DYNASTY (960-1279)**

Lao-tzu (604?-531)   **MING DYNASTY (1368-1644)**

Shih Huang Ti (247-210)

HOU DYNASTY (ca. 1000-ca. 250)   **HAN DYNASTY (202 B.C.-220 A.D.)**   Genghis Khan (1162-1227)

Kublai Khan (1216-94)

Confucius (551?-479)

YUAN DYNASTY (1279-1368)

Jimmu Tenno (ca. 660-585 B.C.)   Shotoku (574-622)

Yoritomo (1147-1199)

AKSUM   **KANEM-BORNU(800-1846)**   **MALI (1200-1500)**   **BENIN (ca. 1300-1897)**

Frumentius   **GHANA (700-1200)**   Mansa Musa (1312-37)   **SONGHAI (1470-1**

| 500 | 0 | 500 | 1000 | 1500 |

A.D.

CHAPTER 5

"Orthodox and infidel."

The Dome of the Rock in Jerusalem, a Muslim mosque standing on the site of the Jewish temple of Solomon

The Byzantine and Islamic Empires

In 476 the Roman Empire collapsed in the West. It endured in the East, however, for another thousand years. This Eastern Roman Empire became known as the **Byzantine** (BIZ un TEEN) **Empire.** The Byzantine civilization was a blending of the cultural heritage of ancient Greece and the cultures of the Near East. Byzantine culture strongly influenced the people of Russia and southeastern Europe. But the Byzantine Empire was not without a rival. During the seventh century the Islamic religion arose in the desert land of Arabia. Its zealous followers, the Muslims, spread their faith through military conquest; they built an empire that stretched from Spain to India. At the same time, they forged a remarkable civilization by combining their own customs and traditions with the arts and learning of the peoples they conquered. This chapter will trace the beginnings, growth, and interaction of these two civilizations.

The Byzantine Civilization

The Rise of "New Rome"

In 330 the emperor Constantine formally dedicated a new capital for the Roman Empire. He called the city **"New Rome,"** but it became more widely known as Constantinople, "Constantine's City." This "second Rome" was ideally located on a peninsula that juts out into the waters of the Bosporus, a narrow strait that separates southeastern Europe from Asia Minor. Constantinople was the meeting place of East and West, the vital link in both land and sea trade routes. Wealth from all over the world passed through her port.

In addition to being a flourishing commercial center, Constantinople also became an important political and religious center. After the days of Constantine, Roman emperors continued to live there. When the emperor Theodosius formally divided the empire into two parts (see p. 116), the city became the permanent capital of the Eastern Roman Empire. It was also recognized as one of the five major patriarchates of the Christian church.

While the Eastern Roman Empire continued to prosper, conditions in the Western Empire steadily declined. During the fourth and fifth centuries bar-

The name of Constantinople, ancient capital of the Byzantine Empire, was changed to Istanbul by the Turkish government in 1930.

barian tribes threatened Rome's borders. The weak Western Empire crumbled under the onslaught, but the richer and stronger Eastern Empire was able to withstand the attacks. Constantinople, the ''queen of the Mediterranean,'' became the foremost city of the empire.

The Byzantine Empire took its name from the ancient Greek city Byzantium, on which Constantinople was built. The inhabitants of this empire still considered themselves Romans, for in many respects their civilization was a continuation of the Roman Empire. In addition to having many of the same customs and traditions, the Eastern Empire retained the political and legal structures of ancient Rome. But Byzantine culture was influenced even more by the Hellenistic culture that still permeated the region; it was more Greek than Roman, more Asiatic than European. While a more civilized way of life declined in the West, it endured and flourished in the East under the Byzantine Empire.

The Reign of Justinian

The first great period of Byzantine history and culture came during the reign of the emperor **Justinian** (juh STIN ee un; 527-65). He rose from humble origins to become one of the most famous Byzantine emperors. However, he owed much of his success to the timely counsel and strong character of his wife, **Theodora.** In 532 a riot broke out in Constantinople, threatening to topple Justinian from power. This riot flamed into a popular uprising, named the **Nika Revolt** after the people's battle cry: *''Nika!''* (''Conquer!''). Justinian was about to flee the capital and admit defeat when Theodora's bold advice encouraged him to stay:

> My opinion then is that the present time, above all others, is inopportune for flight, even though it bring safety. . . . For one who has been an emperor it is unendurable to be a fugitive. May I never be separated from this purple [sign of royalty]. . . . If, now, it is your wish to save yourself, O Emperor, there is no difficulty. For we have much money, and there is the sea, here the boats. However consider whether it will not come about after you have been saved that you would gladly exchange that safety for death. For as for my-

self, I approve a certain ancient saying that royalty is a good burial-shroud.[1]

This was the turning point in Justinian's reign; he remained and crushed the revolt, firmly establishing himself as emperor.

Justinian then turned his attention to his chief objective: restoring the greatness of the Roman Empire. To accomplish this goal, he sought to recover the Roman territory in the West that had fallen into the hands of barbarian tribes. For over two decades his generals led military campaigns throughout the Mediterranean world. His forces defeated the Vandals in North Africa, captured Italy from the Ostrogoths, and penetrated the southern portion of the Visigoth kingdom in Spain. Justinian's conquests extended the boundaries of the Byzantine Empire to their greatest extent; nevertheless, he was unable to recover all the land once held by Rome.

One of the most enduring achievements of the Byzantine Empire was the preservation of Roman law. By the sixth century, the reliable Roman legal system had become a complex and disorganized mass of legal opinions. Its many laws were often confusing and contradictory. Like the New Testament Pharisees, the Romans had created so many regulations that they almost forgot the foundational concepts of truth and justice. For this reason Justinian appointed a commission of ten scholars to compile, reorganize, and condense the vast body of law that had accumulated from the days of ancient Rome. Their work resulted in the **Justinian Code,** a systematic arrangement of laws that clarified Roman legal principles. This code preserved the heritage of the Roman legal system, which was

---

An Excerpt from the Justinian Code

The imperial majesty should be not only made glorious by arms, but also strengthened by laws, that, alike in time of peace and in time of war, the state may be well governed, and that the emperor may not only be victorious in the field of battle, but also may by every legal means repel the iniquities of men who abuse the laws, and may at once religiously uphold justice and triumph over his conquered enemies.

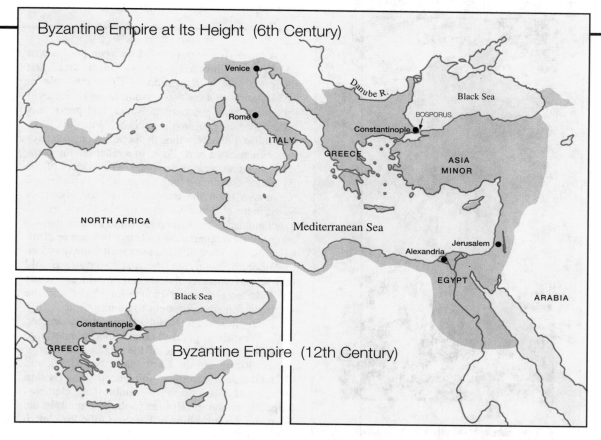

Byzantine Empire at Its Height (6th Century)

Byzantine Empire (12th Century)

to provide a foundation on which most modern European nations would build their political and legal systems.

Justinian's reign marked a golden age of Byzantine culture. Like Constantine, he desired to restore the grandeur of ancient Rome. Sparing no expense, he initiated an extensive building program to construct churches, public buildings, aqueducts, and roads both in the capital city and throughout the empire. He also patronized Byzantine art. From this period comes the finest example of Byzantine architecture, the Church of **Hagia Sophia** (HAH-juh so-FEE-uh), meaning "Holy Wisdom."

Even so, Justinian left his successors with an empire beset by many problems. In his attempts to reclaim the West, he had neglected the defense of the empire's eastern and northern borders. Likewise, his costly military campaigns, coupled with his massive building program, left the empire financially drained. Thus it may be said that Justinian took the Byzantine Empire to the height of glory but left it at the brink of ruin.

Separation of the Eastern and Western Churches

When Constantine founded "New Rome," he established not only a new political capital but also a new religious center. He desired Constantinople to be a Christian city, a "new Jerusalem." Under his influence, Christianity became the favored religion of the Roman Empire. It was quite natural for "Constantine's City" to rise to a place of honor in the structure of the organized church; it became one of the five patriarchal cities, second only to Rome in prestige. The bishop of Rome (later to become the pope) became the most important religious leader in the West; the patriarch of Constantinople held that position in the East.

The Eastern Orthodox Church

The churches in the eastern Mediterranean that refused to recognize Rome's control over them became known as the Eastern Orthodox. The word *orthodox* comes from two Greek words that together mean "straight (*orthos*) opinion (*doxa*)." Although the Orthodox church claims to teach correct doctrine, many of her beliefs are contrary to Scripture.

Unlike the Roman Catholic church, the **Eastern Orthodox church** is made up of various national churches. Today, for example, there is a Russian Orthodox church, a Greek Orthodox church, and a Rumanian Orthodox church, among others. In addition, the Orthodox churches do not recognize one man as their leader as the Roman Catholics recognize the pope. Each patriarch exercises authority over his own national church and is equal in position to every other patriarch.

A bitter rivalry developed between the Eastern and Western churches. Tensions culminated when the pope sent a delegation to Constantinople in 1054 stating that he was assuming authority over the churches in southern Italy that had previously been under the patriarch's authority. When the patriarch refused to accept this, the pope's representatives excommunicated him. Then, in retaliation, the patriarch excommunicated the pope. The leaders of the Byzantine church had long looked with suspicion and resentment upon the interference of the bishop of Rome in the religious affairs of the East. They refused to acknowledge the bishop of Rome's claim that his authority was supreme over all churches (see pp. 180-81). East and West differed over such things as when to celebrate Easter, whether parish priests should marry, and whether the church should use **icons** (EYE kahnz)—painted images of Christ and the saints, which some thought to be idolatrous.

Each church developed a distinctive character. In the West the organized church incorporated into the Christian faith some of the pagan practices of ancient Rome and the Germanic tribes. Greek and Oriental ideas strongly influenced the Eastern church. This adoption of nonbiblical elements helped to create the Roman Catholic church in the West and the Byzantine or Eastern Orthodox church in the East.

The church in the East became one of the most powerful institutions in the Byzantine Empire. Closely linked to the political framework of the empire, it gradually emerged as the state church. The Byzantine emperor was at the same time the head of the state and the protector of the church and its teachings. This relationship was not found in the West after the fall of Rome. People in the West looked to the bishop of Rome, instead of the Western emperor, for leadership.

The Empire Under Siege

The Byzantine Empire experienced both success and failure during the period from the sixth to the fifteenth centuries. She enlarged her empire repeatedly, only to see the gains erased by outside forces. During the fourth and fifth centuries she endured strong barbarian attacks. After Justinian's reign in the sixth century, the empire was besieged on almost every side for several hundred years. From the West came the Lombards, a Germanic tribe that conquered most of Italy. From the North came the Slavs and the Bulgars, who settled in the Balkan Peninsula. Out of the East came the Persians, who sought to restore the glory of the Persian Empire. Although often weak and on the brink of collapse, the Byzantines managed to stave off all these foreign invaders.

In the seventh century the Byzantine Empire had to reckon with a new and energetic force—the Arab Muslims. The Muslims, advancing from the Arabian Peninsula, smashed the Byzantine defenses both on land and at sea. Soon they threatened Constantinople itself. But the "city protected by God" (as it was called) withstood the Arab attacks. Constantinople was aided by its defensible location, its strong fortifications, and a new secret weapon called **"Greek fire."** Though the Byzantines stopped the Muslim expansion into southeastern Europe, they lost Syria, Palestine, Egypt, and North Africa. The Byzantine Empire at one time encompassed the Mediterranean Sea; by the eighth century its territory had been greatly reduced.

Greek Fire

One reason Constantinople was able to withstand enemy sieges was her secret weapon known as "Greek fire." This weapon, which the Byzantines acquired in the seventh century, was an explosive mixture of naphtha oil, sulfur, and saltpeter. Soldiers squirted it from tubes or threw clay pots containing this flammable liquid at the enemy. Greek fire ignited spontaneously and burned even on water. In fact, it could not even be extinguished with water. This weapon proved to be particularly effective against wooden ships and enabled the Byzantines to control the Mediterranean Sea for many centuries.

Between 850 and 1050 the Byzantine Empire gradually recovered her former strength and prosperity. No longer did she remain on the defensive; she pushed back the Muslims and reasserted herself as the dominant power in the Mediterranean. This period of military success reached its height under **Basil II** (976-1025). Known as the "Bulgar Slayer," Basil crushed the Bulgars in the Balkan region and added their kingdoms to the empire. The Byzantines not only reclaimed some of the territory they held during Justinian's day but also revived their commercial and cultural interests. Constantinople abounded with the riches of trade, art, and architecture. Merchants and missionaries carried these achievements to other lands; many of these lands still bear the marks of Byzantine culture.

After two centuries of expansion, new obstacles confronted the empire. The growth of commercial rivals—especially the city of Venice in Italy—challenged Byzantine trade supremacy in the eastern Mediterranean. Competition from Venetian merchants cost the empire sorely needed resources and markets. At the same time, the **Seljuk Turks** emerged as a powerful force in the East. These Turks, originally nomadic tribes from central Asia, had adopted Arab culture and the Islamic religion. The important Byzantine territory of Asia Minor fell to these fierce warriors in 1071, when they annihilated the Byzantine army at the **Battle of Manzikert** (MAN zih kurt). (Since that day, Asia Minor has remained under the control of the Turks.) Fearful that Constantinople would fall, the desperate Byzantine emperor appealed to the Christians in the West for aid. The West responded by sending several military expeditions, known as the **Crusades,** to free the East—especially the Holy Land—from these Muslim invaders.

In 1204 an invading army breached the defenses of Constantinople. The invaders captured and looted the city, slaughtering both young and old. They reveled in drunken orgies before the altars of the Hagia Sophia. Surprisingly, these soldiers were not the infidel Muslims, but supposed Christian warriors from the West on a "holy" crusade. Venetian merchants had enlisted the aid of these greedy crusaders and had transported them to Constantinople so that they might destroy Venice's commercial rival. Neither their cause nor their conduct was holy.

Although Byzantine forces later recaptured Constantinople, the Byzantine Empire never fully recovered from the destruction it suffered. For two

The Fall of Constantinople, May 30, 1453

The Hagia Sophia was crowded. Every able-bodied person was in attendance—even the emperor Constantine XI. The light from many candles illuminated the mosaics of Justinian and his empress. This was a somber occasion. Weary from months of fighting the Ottoman Turks, the people of Constantinople gathered for the last time in their great church and asked God for help on the morrow. When the service was over, every man hurried back to his position on the wall.

At dawn the Turkish bombardment began again. Since April 12, the Turks had been using catapults to hurl rocks weighing up to twelve hundred pounds at the walls of the city. At one particular place they had succeeded in breaching the wall. However, they were unable to enter Constantinople because of the wide moat surrounding the city. As they built bridges over the moat and brought up siege towers to scale the walls, the Byzantines burned them with "Greek fire." The Turks also tried tunneling under the walls, but the Byzantines dug tunnels to meet them and again used "Greek fire" on those underground.

However, the Byzantines knew that the city's downfall was inevitable. The Turks had been able to fill in the moat at the place where the city wall had been broken down. At dawn on May 30, 1453, waves of Turkish soldiers charged the gap in the wall, but the Byzantines repulsed them several times. Sometime during the fighting, Constantine XI joined his soldiers; his presence, however, did not influence the outcome of the battle. The greater number of Turks finally overpowered the city's defenders. By nightfall Constantine XI was dead, and Constantinople was in the hand of the Turks.

centuries the empire continued to exist, but in a state of steady decline. The empire finally came to an end in 1453, when a new wave of Muslim invaders, the **Ottoman Turks,** sacked Constantinople and killed the last Byzantine emperor.

The Contributions of the Byzantine Civilization

When the Turks brought an end to the Byzantine Empire, they destroyed the protective barrier that for hundreds of years had shielded the West against the spread of Islam. This protection had given the West time to recover from the long period of chaos that followed the collapse of Rome. In addition, the Byzantine civilization was important in her own right. She was the means by which the classical heritage of Greece and Rome was preserved and transmitted to the West.

While the size of the Byzantine Empire had gradually diminished from its peak under Justinian, the influence of the Byzantine civilization had expanded. The many achievements of the Byzantine society had attracted the less civilized peoples who came into contact with the empire. They marveled at the material wealth that abounded at Constantinople and tried to copy the effective governmental

Mosaic of Christ from the Church of Hagia Sophia

Novgorod School, Our Lady of Tikhvin, *XVI Century (left), and Anonymous Russian Icon, XVII Century (right), Bob Jones University Collection of Sacred Art*

The Meaning of Icons

A key feature of Eastern Orthodoxy is its use of icons. They occupy prominent places in churches and homes and are held in great reverence by the Orthodox faithful. Religious art in itself is not wrong, but the Orthodox have virtually turned their icons into objects of worship by kissing them and burning incense before them.

Although we frequently speak about looking at a painting, the Orthodox believe that one should not look at icons. Instead, the viewer should direct his mind beyond the icon to the heavenly reality it represents. For example, one viewing a picture of the Apostle Peter should not see a painted figure but should see in his mind's eye the real Peter in heaven.

In an effort to make the painted figures appear otherworldly, the artists, who were usually monks, developed several techniques that remained unchanged for many centuries. For example, there are no shadows in icons because the shadows imply something material and earthly. Second, historical scenes that occurred inside a building are often shown outside with the building in the background. In this way, the painters hoped to elevate the event beyond its historical context and give it universal meaning. Third, the figures in icons are portrayed unrealistically with very thin noses, small mouths, and large eyes. This illustrates the fact that the figures supposedly conquered their five senses (their earthly selves) and lived in holiness according to their spiritual nature.

Even the colors used by the icon painters had special meaning. For example, the monks usually portrayed Christ wearing garments of red, blue, and gold. The red symbolized love, and the blue and gold represented truth and heaven. In pictures of the transfiguration, Christ is usually shown wearing white—a symbol of light and holiness.

Notice the icons pictured here. The one on the left is from the sixteenth century, and the one on the right is from the seventeenth century. Notice that in spite of some obvious differences, both portray the Madonna and child in a similar fashion. (The one on the right has a decorative cover.) Unlike the Western art with its changing styles, icon painting has for centuries remained basically unchanged.

system that the Byzantines had inherited from ancient Rome.

Furthermore, many of the pagan peoples of eastern Europe had embraced Orthodox Christianity along with Byzantine culture. Two Byzantine missionaries, the brothers **Cyril** and **Methodius** (muh THO dee us), had gone to the Slavic peoples of Russia and southeastern Europe. The Slavic

The Church of Hagia Sophia

pieces of glass or stone in wet cement or plaster, artists could form beautiful patterns and pictures.

While the churches housed some of the best examples of Byzantine art, they were in themselves the best examples of Byzantine architecture. Byzantine architects demonstrated a mastery of design and engineering skill. They especially excelled in domed structures. The most famous of Byzantine structures is the beautiful Hagia Sophia, sometimes called the Santa Sophia. In size and rich adornment, no other church in the empire could equal it. It became a model of architectural design that was copied in other cities and lands. Still standing today, its great dome reaches a height of 180 feet and has a diameter of 108 feet. Procopius, a sixth-century historian, describes the splendor of the Hagia Sophia as "a spectacle of marvellous beauty, overwhelming to those who see it, . . . for it soars to a height to match the sky, and as if surging up amongst the other buildings it stands on high and looks down upon the remainder of the city, adorning it. . . . It exults in an indescribable beauty."[2]

tribes did not have a written language; so Cyril and Methodius developed one for them. Their system, a modification of the Greek alphabet, became the foundation of the Slavic written language.

Byzantine art and architecture demonstrate the wealth and splendor of this once-mighty empire. Byzantine art was primarily intended to glorify God; it adorned the interiors of churches. Craftsmen excelled in wall paintings, carved ivory, illuminated manuscripts (manuscripts decorated with ornate letters or designs in bright colors or precious metals), and marble and metal work. A favorite decorative art—the **mosaic**—graced the walls and ceilings of Byzantine churches. By inlaying tiny

Section Review

1. List four titles which were given to the city of Constantinople.
2. What Byzantine emperor sought to restore the greatness of the Roman Empire by extending the boundaries of the Byzantine Empire to their greatest extent?
3. What is the name of the organized church that developed within the Byzantine Empire?
4. What decorative art did Byzantine artists create by using tiny pieces of glass or stone in wet cement or plaster?
5. What is the name of the most famous Byzantine architectual structure?

Early Russia

Beginnings of the Russian State

Looking at a map of the modern world, one cannot help noticing the enormous size of the land of Russia. She occupies a large portion of two continents—Europe and Asia. Within her borders is a population composed of people of many different racial and linguistic backgrounds. The largest group is the **Slavs,** whose ancestors played a major role in establishing the early Russian state.

No one knows for sure where the Slavs first lived. They moved into eastern Europe as the Germanic tribes there migrated farther westward.

Eventually three groups emerged: the West Slavs—the Poles and Czechs—settled in the Danube region; the Yugo-Slavs, or "South Slavs," moved down into the Balkan area; and the East Slavs, the ancestors of the Russians, occupied the territory between the Baltic and Black seas. Running through the land of the East Slavs is a network of rivers along which they built their village communities. The Slavs participated in the prosperous trade that flourished along these river highways.

During the eighth and ninth centuries, bands of Swedish Norsemen, known to the Slavs and Byzantines as **Varangians** (vuh RAN jee UNZ), sailed south from the Baltic Sea using the waterways. Like the Vikings who terrorized western Europe (see pp. 191-92), they plundered Slavic villages along the rivers. Attracted by the possibilities of opening trade routes with the Byzantine and Muslim civilizations, many Varangian warriors settled along the inland waterways. Slavic settlements often hired Varangian warriors to protect their villages from other raiding tribesmen.

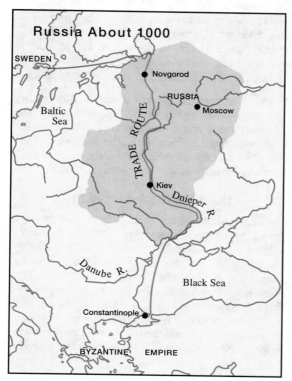

Russia About 1000

In the city of Novgorod (NAWV guh RAWT), according to one traditional account, the Slavs invited Varangian rule: "Our whole land is great and rich, but there is not order in it. Come to rule and reign over us." Whether by invitation or by force, the Varangian warrior **Rurik** gained control of Novgorod about 862. That year is the traditional date for the beginning of Russian history. Rurik established the first ruling dynasty of Russia. His successors captured and ruled other cities in the region, the most important of these being Kiev (KEE ef). Yet despite their military superiority, the Varangians were greatly outnumbered by the Slavs and were soon absorbed by the populace.

Shortly after Rurik's death, Kiev became the center of the early Russian state. This city was located on the shores of the Dnieper (NEE pur) River, the major route for trade with the Byzantine Empire. For three centuries Kiev held the prominent position in a loose confederation of city-states. Established by Varangian princes, this confederation sought to further the region's common commercial interests and protect important trade routes. The area under Kievan influence became known as Russia, perhaps deriving its name from the Slavic designation of the Norsemen, *Rus,* meaning, "rowers" or "seafarers."

Influence of Byzantine Culture

Russian culture bears a strong Byzantine imprint. Because of early commercial contacts, Kiev and Constantinople developed close cultural ties. A significant event in Russian history was the adoption of Byzantine Christianity by the Kievan ruler **Vladimir I** in 988. He ordered the destruction of pagan idols and temples and established Orthodox Christianity as the official state religion. By adopting Orthodox Christianity rather than Roman Christianity, Russia was virtually cut off from the mainstream of Western thought. She came under the influences of the Eastern church and Byzantine culture.

The influence of the Orthodox church upon Russia was great. The Russian language profited from the Slavic alphabet, which the Byzantine missionaries Cyril and Methodius had adapted from the Greek alphabet. This alphabet enabled the Russians to translate Greek works into their Slavic language.

For All the Wrong Reasons

According to legend, the Russian ruler Vladimir decided that he would establish a monotheistic religion among his people to replace their polytheistic, pagan beliefs. Before he decided what that new religion would be, he investigated what the world had to offer. He summoned representatives of Islam, Judaism, Roman Catholicism, and Eastern Orthodoxy and had each of them explain why his particular religion was best. After listening to the claims of each, Vladimir sent out envoys to observe these religions on a firsthand basis. When they returned, he made his decision.

First of all, Vladimir rejected Islam because the Koran forbade the drinking of alcoholic beverages. Second, he rejected Judaism because the Jewish people had been defeated and scattered across the world. Since their God did not seem strong enough to protect them, He could not be counted on to protect the Russian people, thought Vladimir. Third, the king rejected Roman Catholicism because the Catholic churches were dark and damp and the services were dull. Vladimir chose Eastern Orthodoxy.

The reason for his choice was simple. When his envoys returned from Constantinople, they enthusiastically described a service they had attended at the Hagia Sophia. They told him how the whole church seemed to shine as the mosaics reflected the light of the burning candles. They told him of the beautiful music, the clouds of incense, and the gorgeous robes of the patriarch who led the service. Impressed by what he heard, Vladimir adopted Eastern Orthodoxy. The Russian Orthodox church was established, and Vladimir was "converted" to Christianity.

Today many people are just like Vladimir. They choose a religion that makes them comfortable or that appeals to their intellect. However, Christ told His disciples. "If any man will come after me, let him deny himself, and take up his cross daily, and follow me" (Luke 9:23). Since Christ does not promise His followers a life of ease and pleasure, the unconverted world wants nothing to do with biblical Christianity. But those who know Christ as Savior would not exchange the riches of their faith for all the manmade religions the world has to offer.

A Russian Orthodox church in Tallinn, Estonia

It also prompted the growth of native Russian literature. Russian artists made beautiful icons like those adorning Byzantine churches. The Russians even patterned their cathedrals after Byzantine models. One feature of their cathedrals, however, is uniquely Russian—the "onion-shaped" dome.

Height of Kievan Russian

Kiev reached the zenith of its power and prestige during the reign of **Yaroslav** (yuh ruh SLAHV) "the Wise" (1036-54). Yaroslav greatly strengthened the city's position of leadership; Kiev became known as the "Mother of Russian cities." His reign saw the greatest territorial expansion of the early Russian state. He gained international recognition by negotiating marriage alliances between his princely house and the royal families of France, Sweden, Norway, Poland, Hungary, and the Byzantine Empire. He also sponsored the earliest Russian code of laws, which combined Slavic tribal law and Byzantine law.

Yaroslav desired to make Kiev a rival of Constantinople. In size, wealth, and culture, Kiev became one of the leading cities of its day. It was a prosperous center of commerce—a meeting place of the world's merchants. Yaroslav's patronage of art, education, and the church attracted Byzantine painters, architects, teachers, and priests. With the aid of Byzantines, the Russians constructed their own cathedral of Hagia Sophia. Kiev also boasted schools, libraries, monasteries, cathedrals, and fortifications that Yaroslav built.

After the death of Yaroslav, Kiev lost its prominence among the Russian cities. Civil war broke out among Yaroslav's heirs over succession to the throne. Cities that had formerly looked to the Kievan rulers as the Grand Princes of Russia began to assert their independence. New trade routes and commercial centers drew away much of Kiev's wealth and population. The death blow to the early

Russian state came in the thirteenth century, when the **Tartars**—fierce Mongolian warriors from central Asia—swept into Russia (see pp. 164-65). They destroyed Kiev in 1240 and ruled Russia for more than two centuries, up to the late 1400s. After the decline of Mongol power, a new center of Russian society arose in the north—Moscow.

Section Review
1. What ethnic group played a major role in establishing the early Russian state?
2. What city became the center of the early Russian state?
3. What Russian ruler adopted the Eastern Orthodox church as the official religion of the Russian state?
4. What two Byzantine missionaries developed a written language for the Slavic people of Russia?
5. Under whose leadership did the city of Kiev and the early Russian state reach the height of its power and prestige?

The Islamic Civilization

The Land of Arabia

The cradle of Islam was Arabia, a large peninsula that extends south of the Fertile Crescent in the Middle East. This peninsula lies between Asia and Africa, bounded by the Persian Gulf in the East and the Red Sea in the West. In land area, it is about one-third the size of the United States. Much of the land is a barren wilderness of deserts and stony plains. Vegetation is sparse and agriculture is limited because of the extreme heat and lack of adequate rainfall. This uninviting environment kept Arabia in relative isolation until the birth of the Islamic religion in the seventh century.

The land of Arabia is adjacent to the Bible lands. As do the Hebrews, many Arabs trace their beginnings back to Abraham: the Hebrews, through his son Isaac; the Arabs, through his son **Ishmael.** Although he was not the child of God's special promise as was Isaac (Gal. 4:22-23), God blessed Ishmael: "I have blessed him, and will make him fruitful, . . . and I will make him a great nation"

(Gen. 17:20). Ishmael's descendants dwelt in the Arabian Peninsula and became a numerous people, just as God had foretold.

Because they had no organized government, there was little unity among the Arab people before the advent of Islam. Each Arab's loyalty was to his own tribe, and warfare among the tribes was frequent. These tribes did not have a common religion. In addition, there were two distinct lifestyles among the people of Arabia. Many of the Arabs traveled through the harsh desert wilderness in independent bands. These nomads, called **Bedouins** (BED oo inz), roam the desert in search of pastureland and water for their herds of goats, sheep, and camels. Over the centuries the Bedouin way of life has remained relatively unchanged; today they can be seen traveling from oasis to oasis across the desert land.

Not all Arabs were desert nomads, however; some lived a more settled life along the outer rim of the peninsula. They established cities along important trade routes or along the coast, where rainfall was more abundant and the land was more fertile. A few of these cities became important trade centers for camel caravans, which carried goods across the desert to and from other lands. Out of one of these cities arose an Arab religious leader whose teaching united the people of Arabia.

The Founding of Islam

Muhammad

Shortly after the death of the Byzantine emperor Justinian in 565, **Muhammad** (moo HAM id) was born in Arabia. Muhammad (570-632) claimed to be the last and greatest of the prophets of the god **Allah** (AH luh). His teaching became the basis for a new religion known as **Islam** (is LAHM), meaning ''submission'' (that is, to the will of Allah). His followers are known as **Muslims** (or Moslems, ''submitters to Allah'').

Muhammad, whose name means ''highly praised,'' was born to a poor family in the city of Mecca, in western Arabia. Little is known of his

early life except that he became an orphan at the age of six and was reared by his grandfather and uncle. As a young man he entered the employment of a wealthy merchant widow. At the age of twenty-five, he married his employer (fifteen years his senior). For the first time in his life he had financial security. He spent much of his leisure time meditating on religion. The Jewish and Christian influences that he encountered while traveling with caravans impressed him deeply. The Judaeo-Christian belief in one God (monotheism) was quite different from the polytheism so prevalent in Arabia.

The Messenger of Allah

In his fortieth year, Muhammad claimed that he had received a vision in which the angel Gabriel gave him a divine revelation to ''Recite!''

> Recite thou, in the name of thy Lord who created;—
> Created man from Clots of Blood:—
> Recite thou! For thy Lord is the most Beneficent,
> Who hath taught the use of the pen,—
> Hath taught Man that which he knoweth not.

This incident was just the beginning of a series of visions and revelations that allegedly continued throughout his lifetime. Muhammad became convinced that he was the ''messenger of God'' entrusted with a new revelation for man. He began preaching that there was only one god, Allah, and that he, Muhammad, was Allah's prophet.

Muhammad had little success in gaining converts at first. His early followers were family members and close friends. For the most part, the people of Mecca ridiculed him, viewing his teaching as a threat to the city's commercial interests. Mecca was a leading trade center, situated at the crossroads of trade routes in western Arabia. It was also a center of religious worship. At Mecca was located the **Kaaba,** a sacred shrine that housed hundreds of pagan idols. People from all over Arabia made pilgrimages to this shrine. Meccan merchants promoted pagan worship in order to reap financial gain. Large crowds in Mecca meant money in their coffers. The principal attraction was the famous Black Stone, a meteorite built into the wall of the Kaaba. According to later Muslim tradition, the

Worshipers throng the Kaaba, located in the courtyard of the great mosque in Mecca.

Pages from a copy of the Koran, dating from the eleventh century

angel Gabriel sent the stone to Abraham, who, along with his son Ishmael, built the shrine. Fearing that Muhammad's teaching about one god would stop the profitable business surrounding the shrine, the leaders of Mecca persecuted Muhammad and his followers.

The Flight to Medina

In 622 Muhammad made a fateful decision. He and his followers decided to flee Mecca and move to Medina (mih DEE nuh), a city several hundred miles to the north. This move is known as the *Hegira* (hih JIE ruh), or "Flight." (It is celebrated as year 1 of the Muslim calendar.) At Medina, Muhammad's following grew rapidly. The citizens of Medina not only accepted Muhammad as their spiritual leader but made him their political and military leader as well. Once in power, Muhammad the persecuted became Muhammad the persecutor. He had previously presented his cause peaceably through preaching, but now he advanced it by military conquest. With an army of militant Muslim followers, he crushed all opposition. A bitter struggle with the rival city of Mecca ended in 630. Muhammad reentered the city of his birth in triumph. He destroyed the idols of the Kaaba and turned it into the center of Islamic worship. Mecca became the "holy city" of his new religion.

The Teachings of Islam

The Koran

The heart of Islam is the **Koran,** the sacred book of the Muslims. Muslims believe that the archangel Gabriel revealed the words of Allah to Muhammad through numerous dreams and visions. These so-called revelations formed the basis of his teaching. Many of his followers committed his teaching to memory; others wrote it down. After Muhammad's death, they compiled his teaching into a book, the Koran, meaning "recitation." Composed of 114 chapters, or *suras,* the Koran is the primary authority on Muslim belief and practice. Dedicated Muslims memorize the entire Koran, which is about the same length as the New Testament.

Islam is a monotheistic religion. The central doctrine taught by the Koran is the belief in one god, Allah (*al,* "the"; *Ilah,* "god"). Islam recognizes ninety-nine attributes or names of Allah. According to the Koran,

> [Allah] is God beside whom there is no god. He knoweth things visible and invisible: He is the Compassionate, the Merciful.
>
> He is God beside whom there is no god: He is the King, the Holy, the Peaceful, the Faithful, the Guardian, the Mighty, the Strong, the Most High! Far be the Glory of God from that which they unite with Him! (Sura 59:22-23).

Muslims believe that Allah sent more than one hundred thousand prophets to reveal his will to man. But Islam reveres Muhammad as the last and greatest of Allah's prophets and the Koran as Allah's final "revelation," superseding all others.

The moral teaching of the Koran serves as a guide for the conduct of its believers. It encourages Muslims to cultivate humility, duty, kindness, and benevolence. It condemns idolatry, murder, gambling, drinking of wine, and adultery (although the Koran allows a Muslim to have four wives). Muslims are taught to fear Allah, because he will reward good works and punish evil in the life to come. The Koran gives a description of this "day of judgment":

> As for him who shall come before his Lord laden with crime—for him verily is Hell: he shall not die in it and he shall not live.
>
> But he who shall come before him, a believer, with righteous works,—these! the loftiest grades await them:

Gardens of Eden, beneath whose trees the river flow: therein shall they abide for ever. This, the reward of him who hath been pure (Sura 20:76-78).

The Koran reflects many ideas that Muhammad drew from Jewish and Christian sources. It frequently mentions stories and characters of the Old and New Testaments. The Koran honors Noah, Abraham, David, and even Jesus as prophets of Allah. (Muhammad considered Jesus no different from the prophets.) Likewise, the Koran echoes many truths found in the Bible. It emphasizes prayer, moral conduct, a coming day of resurrection and judgment, and the existence of heaven and hell. Islam also stresses the worship of one god and regards the Bible as a holy book.

But while Muhammad used many biblical terms in his teaching, he distorted biblical truth. Satan often uses this tactic to deceive people—he dresses error in the clothes of truth. Muhammad claimed to worship the same God as the Christians. But the god of the Koran is not the God of the Bible, for Muhammad rejected the doctrine of the Trinity and denied that Christ is the Son of God (see I John 4:2-3). In reference to Christians, the Koran says:

O ye people of the book! overstep not bounds in your religion. . . . The Messiah, Jesus, son of Mary, is only an apostle of God. . . . Believe therefore in God and his apostles, and say not, ''Three'': (there is a Trinity)—forbear—it will be better for you. God is only one God! Far be it from His glory that He should have a son! (Sura 4:169).

The Five Pillars

The Koran teaches that heaven is a paradise in which the ''faithful'' will enjoy gardens of delight, rivers of wine, and the company of beautiful women. Islam requires every Muslim to perform certain religious duties in order to reach heaven. These are the **Five Pillars of Islam:**

1. Reciting the simple confession ''There is no God but Allah, and Muhammad is his prophet.'' (This is the central theme of Islam.)
2. Reciting prayers five times a day while facing toward Mecca.
3. Giving alms (money) to the poor.
4. Fasting from sunrise to sunset during the sacred month of Ramadan (RAM uh DAHN).
5. Making a pilgrimage to Mecca. Every able Muslim is commanded to make this pilgrimage at least once in his lifetime.

The Koran teaches Muslims to fear Allah's punishment if these religious practices are not observed.

Islam reflects those characteristics of false prophecy and teaching shown in II Peter 2:1-2:

But there were false prophets also among the people, even as there shall be false teachers among you, who privily shall bring in damnable heresies, even denying the Lord that bought them, and bring upon themselves swift destruction. And many shall follow their pernicious ways; by reason of whom the way of truth shall be evil spoken of.

The Spread of Islam

By the time of his death in 632, Muhammad had united much of Arabia under Islam. But he died without having appointed a successor. This presented a serious problem for Islam and the Arab people. Who should succeed Muhammad as the rightful leader of new religion and the emerging Arab state? The closest friends of Muhammad chose his first four successors from among themselves. These men, who were called *caliphs* (KAY lifs; ''successors''), directed the affairs of Islam, exercising spiritual, political, and military authority. The first caliph was **Abu-Bakr** (AH-boo BAH-kur), father-in-law and early convert of Muhammad. He and the three caliphs who followed him initiated a policy of military conquest that led to the creation of a vast Arab empire founded upon the Islamic religion.

With amazing speed, Arab warriors burst forth from the desert homeland, conquering Palestine, Syria, Egypt, Iraq, and Persia. Many factors contributed to this rapid expansion:

1. A desire for fertile, productive land. Since their land was barren and unable to support a growing population, the Arabs sought an escape from the poverty of the drought-stricken Arabian peninsula through conquest.
2. The weakness of the Byzantine and Persian empires in the seventh century. Years of con-

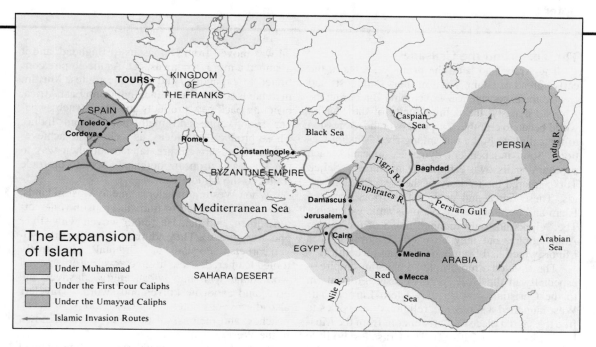

The Expansion of Islam

- Under Muhammad
- Under the First Four Caliphs
- Under the Umayyad Caliphs
- → Islamic Invasion Routes

TOURS★
KINGDOM OF THE FRANKS
SPAIN
Toledo
Cordova
Rome
Constantinople
BYZANTINE EMPIRE
Mediterranean Sea
Black Sea
Caspian Sea
PERSIA
Indus R.
Tigris R.
Baghdad
Euphrates R.
Damascus
Jerusalem
Cairo
EGYPT
SAHARA DESERT
Persian Gulf
Arabian Sea
Medina
ARABIA
Red Sea
Mecca
Nile R.

stant warfare had left those two rivals exhausted and their territories vulnerable to attack.

3. Islam, which united the Arab people around a common cause. The Arabs viewed each conquest as a *jihad* (jih HAHD; "holy war"). With their swords they defended the honor of Islam. Their religious fervor produced a fierce fighting spirit—a fanatical zeal intensified by the promise that a Muslim's death in battle assured him of entrance into paradise.

Umayyad Caliphate (661-750)

In 661 a Muslim general seized the office of caliph (the caliphate). He moved the political capital of the empire from Medina to Damascus and established the rule of the **Umayyads** (oo MY yadz). The Umayyads created a hereditary dynasty, ending the practice of selecting the caliph from among the close friends and relatives of Muhammad.

The Umayyads continued Arab expansion. Muslim forces pushed eastward into India, laid siege to Constantinople, and advanced across North Africa. In 711 they crossed the Mediterranean and invaded Spain. They pressed on into southern France until they were stopped by the Franks at the **Battle of Tours** (see pp. 186-87). The year of this

battle was 732, exactly one hundred years after the death of Muhammad. Although the Muslim advance into Europe was stopped, the Arabs could boast of an empire that stretched from Spain to India.

Abbasid Caliphate (750-ca. 1000)

Discontent over Umayyad rule soon mounted: a growing number of non-Arab Muslims were dissatisfied with being treated as second-class citizens by Arab rulers. In addition, many Arab Muslims did not consider the Umayyads the rightful successors of Muhammad. In 750 Abbas, a descendant of Muhammad's uncle, overthrew the Umayyad caliph and founded the **Abbasid** (AB uh sid) Caliphate. Under the Abbasids, Arab supremacy within the Muslim empire gradually declined. The Abbasids appointed many non-Arabs to high government positions. Also, non-Arabs became increasingly influential in Islamic society.

The Abbasid Caliphate marks the peak of the Muslim empire. The Muslims controlled more territory than the ancient Romans did. Its new capital, Baghdad, became one of the world's leading commercial centers, rivaling the Byzantine capital of Constantinople. Likewise, during the Abbasid rule, Islamic culture flourished.

The Turks and the Crusades

The Arabs had been the primary agents in the early spread of Islam. Their military conquests had created the expansive Muslim empire. But during the Abbasid dynasty, the political unity of the Muslim world began to crumble. Disputes over the succession to the caliphate broke out among rival Muslim factions. Soon independent dynasties appeared, each proclaiming its own caliph. Meanwhile the Seljuk Turks entered the territory of the weakened Abbasids. These fierce and energetic warriors accepted Islam and began a new wave of Islamic expansion. The Seljuks not only reunited much of the former Arab empire, but they also took control of Asia Minor, which had been under Byzantine control.

The revived strength of the Muslim empire—especially in the Holy Land—caused great alarm to the Christian peoples of western Europe. The West launched a series of "religious" Crusades to free the sacred place of Christendom from the Muslim Turks (see pp. 217-22). The Crusades did little to remove the Muslims from Palestine, but they did succeed in weakening the power of the Seljuks. In the thirteenth century the Seljuk's empire came to an end when the Mongols swept into the Muslim world. A short time later, the Ottoman Turks, former subjects of the Seljuks, restored Turkish rule. Once again Muslim forces (now led by the Ottomans) created a large empire. The Ottoman Empire stretched across North Africa, over much of the Middle East, and into southeastern Europe. In 1453 the Ottomans seized Constantinople, causing the collapse of the Byzantine Empire.

The Contributions of Muslim Culture

The Arabs built the Muslim empire through conquest. However, these culturally poor nomads had little to offer the people whom they conquered. Instead, they borrowed, embraced, and added to the rich cultural heritage of the peoples with whom they came into contact—the Persians, the Byzantines, the Egyptians, and the Syrians. By blending the many cultural influences within the empire with the Islamic religion, the Arabs were able to create a unified civilization.

By the middle of the eighth century, the Muslim empire was no longer predominantly Arab. Its capital was moved from Damascus to Baghdad, and it assumed a more Persian aspect. As the empire continued to expand, so did its trade routes. Muslim merchants traveled to China, India, and East Africa, bringing back new products and ideas (such as paper from China and mathematics from India). These products and ideas, as well as the achievements of Muslim culture, later found their way to the West as European merchants opened up trade routes to the Middle East.

When Western travelers came to Muslim lands, they were astounded to find silk, muslin (fine cotton), linen, and damask (cloth woven with silver and gold thread). They admired magnificently woven carpets ("Persian" or "Oriental" rugs), finely tooled leather, delicate filigree jewelry (ornamental work done with fine wire), engraved silver and gold, and exquisite knives and swords. Travelers also discovered dates, oranges, lemons, apricots, peaches, and melons, all of which were unknown in the West at that time.

One of the chief ways the Muslims gained knowledge was to translate manuscripts from other lands into Arabic. They translated the writings of Aristotle, Plato, Galen, Hippocrates, Archimedes, Euclid, Ptolemy, and others. They also translated important works from Persia and India. Many of these manuscripts might have been lost had they not been preserved by the Muslims. They built great libraries to house these manuscripts and their Arabic translations.

Medicine

In the field of medicine, the Muslims profited from the Greek writings of Galen and Hippocrates. Muslim doctors put into practical use what they learned from the classics and developed new medical procedures. Two of the most famous Muslim physicians were **al-Rāzi** (AL RAY-zee) and **ibn Sina** (IB-un SEE-nuh; also know as Avicenna). Both men wrote many medical books in which they recorded their practical experience in identifying and treating various diseases. Al-Rāzi is best remembered for his work with smallpox, and ibn Sina for his work with tuberculosis.

Muslim doctors developed amazing surgical skills. They performed such delicate operations as

A page from an Arabic translation of an ancient Greek medical treatise; such translations helped preserve ancient Greek and Roman learning in Muslim lands while Europe was in her Dark Ages.

removing cancer from the body and cataracts from the eye. The Muslims also built hospitals throughout the empire. Although they did not know about germs, they suspected that dirt led to disease. Therefore they tried to keep their patients and hospitals as clean as possible. Furthermore, Muslims had drugstores that filled prescriptions. Government inspectors supervised the druggists to ensure the purity of the drugs.

Literature

In addition to their religious, scientific, and medical writings, the Muslims produced rich and colorful imagery in both their poetry and their prose. Perhaps the most renowned Muslim poet (also a famed mathematician) was **Omar Khayyam** (OH-mar kie-YAHM). His *Rubaiyat* (roo BY YAHT; a poem with verses of four lines) remains quite popular in the West. Like most Muslim poetry it is very picturesque.

The Moving Finger writes; and, having writ,
Moves on: nor all your Piety nor Wit
Shall lure it back to cancel half a Line.
Nor all your Tears wash out a Word of it.

And that inverted Bowl they call the Sky,
Whereunder crawling coop'd we live and die,
Lift not your hands to It for help—for It
As impotently moves as you or I.

Better known to both young and old is *The Thousand and One Nights* (popularly known as *The Arabian Nights*). Among these fanciful tales gathered from all over the Muslim world are the stories of ''Aladdin and His Wonderful Lamp'' and ''Ali Baba and the Forty Thieves.''

Tales of Arabia

The Thousand and One Nights is about a sultan named Shahriyar who each day weds a new bride and then executes her the next morning. One day he marries Scheherazade, a beautiful and intelligent young maiden. That night for Shahriyar's entertainment, she tells him a story but stops at the climax. Eager to hear the conclusion, the sultan decides to wait another day and then execute her. The next night Scheherazade finishes her story but then begins another, stopping again at an exciting part. Shahriyar once more decides to wait so that he can hear the conclusion. This goes on for a thousand and one consecutive nights. At the end of that time, the sultan is so much in love with Scheherazade that he abandons all thought of executing her, and they live happily ever after.

Mathematics

The Muslims borrowed much of their basic mathematical knowledge from India. The so-called Arabic numerals are of Hindu origin. So are the decimal system and the concept of zero, which the Muslims popularized. The Muslims studied and improved algebra, which came from India, as well as the geometry and trigonometry of the Greeks.

Art and Architecture

Religion plays an important part in Muslim art. Muhammad is said to have forbidden the representation of men and animals in art. He feared that the people might worship the statues or painting of living things. Therefore Muslim artists developed decorative designs that are more abstract than representational. The most common patterns found in Muslim art are abstract designs of stems and leaves and geometric figures. Muslim artists also excelled in **calligraphy**, the art of beautiful writing. They adorned the walls of buildings with verses from the Koran written in beautiful Arabic script. One of the most honored forms of Islamic art was manuscript illumination; Muslim artists used miniature paintings and decorative colors and ornamentation to illustrate or ''illuminate'' their books—especially the Koran.

In architecture, however, Muslim art reached its highest achievement. The Muslim drew from the architectural styles of Persia and Byzantium, but gradually produced their own unique style. The best examples of Muslim architecture are the **mosques** (MAHSKS; places of Muslim worship). Muhammad did not believe Muslims should build elaborate mosques, since these buildings were only places of prayer. He said on one occasion, ''The most unprofitable thing that eateth up the wealth of the believer is building.'' Nevertheless, his followers spent fortunes on their houses of worship.

The typical features of a mosque are its courtyard, minaret, and dome. In the courtyard is a pool for ceremonial washing before prayer. Either as part of the mosque or adjacent to it is a tall **minaret** (or tower). From this tower the **muezzin** (myoo EZ in; ''crier'') calls the faithful to prayer five times a day. One of the characteristic features of Muslim architecture is the dome. It usually covers the main portion of the mosque. Inside, the walls are white and inscribed with quotations from the Koran. Some, however, are highly decorated with tile and mosaic designs. In one wall of each mosque is a niche that indicates the direction of Mecca, toward which a Muslim prays.

Section Review

1. What name is given to the Arab nomads who roam the desert in search for pastureland and water?
2. Who claimed to be the last and greatest of the prophets of Allah?
3. What became the ''holy'' city of the Islamic faith? What was the principal attraction of visitors to this city?
4. What is the name of the ''holy'' book of Islam? What is its central doctrine?
5. List the two caliphates that ruled the Islamic empire from the seventh to the eleventh centuries. Beside each caliphate, write the name of the capital city of its empire.
6. What is the name for the Muslim places of worship, which are the best examples of Muslim architecture?

A Glimpse Behind and a Glimpse Ahead

This chapter has focused on two remarkable yet opposing civilizations. The first—the Byzantine—preserved Roman culture and learning after the Western Roman Empire collapsed. The second—Islam—also preserved much from the classical world. Although the Byzantine Empire gradually declined in size and political influence, her culture spread northward, particularly into Russia. On the other hand, as the Muslims expanded politically, they spread their culture from Spain to India.

As western Europe slowly recovered from the chaos brought about by the barbarian invasions of the fifth century, she renewed her contacts with the East. These ties stimulated the intellectual rebirth called the Renaissance and the spiritual revival known as the Reformation. Before we turn our attention back to western Europe, however, we will take a look at ancient civilizations in the Far East and Africa—civilizations that derived very little from the cultures of the Mediterranean world.

Chapter Review

Can You Explain?

icon	*Rus*	Muslim	mosque
"Greek fire"	Bedouin	*Hegira*	minaret
Crusades	Allah	*jihad*	muezzin
mosaic	Islam	calligraphy	

Can You Identify?

Byzantine Empire	1054	Varangians	Koran
"New Rome"	Basil II	Rurik	Five Pillars of Islam
Justinian	Seljuk Turks	Vladimir I	Abu-Bakr
Theodora	Battle of Manzikert	Yaroslav	Umayyad
Nika Revolt	1453	Tartars	Battle of Tours
Justinian Code	Ottoman Turks	Ishmael	Abbasid
Hagia Sophia	Cyril	Muhammad	al-Rāzi
Eastern Orthodox	Methodius	Kaaba	ibn Sina
church	Slavs	622	Omar Khayyam

Can You Locate?

Byzantium	Venice	Kiev	Damascus
Constantinople	Russia	Arabia	Baghdad
Bosporus	Novgorod	Mecca	
Balkans	Dnieper River	Medina	

How Much Do You Remember?

1. List three achievements of Justinian's reign as Byzantine emperor.
2. The Byzantine Empire was constantly besieged during her history. List six groups of foreign invaders that threatened her borders.
3. List the contributions to Russian history of each of the following: Rurik, Vladimir I, and Yaroslav.
4. List the Five Pillars of Islam.
5. Identify the occupation and contribution to Muslim culture of each of the following men: al Rāzi, ibn Sina, and Omar Khayyam.

What Do You Think?

1. Of what significance is Genesis 16:10-12 to the Arab people?
2. Many in the Orthodox church have held great reverence for icons, often to the point of worship. Is this in keeping with the teaching of the Bible? Explain your answer. (See Exod. 20:3.)
3. Contrast the methods used by Muhammad and his followers to spread their religion with the instructions that Christ gave His disciples in Matthew 28:19-20.
4. Because Muhammad drew many of his ideas from the Bible, esteemed Christ as a prophet, and regarded the Bible as a holy book, is Islam a Christian religion? Explain your answer.

Notes
1. Procopius, *History of the Wars,* trans. H. B. Dewing, 1. 24
2. Ibid., 1. 1

The Civilizations of Asia and Africa

The "unknown lands" of Asia and Africa have fascinated Westerners for centuries. The Orient, with her silks and spices and her unique cultures, has attracted travelers since early days. The resources of Africa have long generated a profitable trade with that continent. In recent times concern for the millions lost in the darkness of Asian and African religions has prompted Western missionaries to carry the gospel to these lands. Despite these contacts, most of Asia remained virtually unaffected by Western influences until the twentieth century, and Africa remained mostly untouched until after the Middle Ages. In this chapter we will examine the early histories of the three major Asian civilizations: India, China, and Japan. We will also consider a less civilized people—the Mongols—who built an empire that stretched from the Pacific Ocean westward to eastern Europe. Finally, we will study the culture and heritage of the enormous continent of Africa.

India

India is a land of great diversity. In its **topography** (the physical features of a land), climate, and population, it is a study in contrasts. This triangular subcontinent extends from southern Asia into the Indian Ocean, forming a giant peninsula. Its terrain varies from subtropical rain forest to barren deserts, from low coastal plains to the highest mountain range in the world, the Himalayas. Between the rugged mountain regions in the north and the coastal plains and tropical plateaus of the south lie fertile valleys watered by two great river systems, the Indus and the Ganges. Like the Mesopotamian and Egyptian cultures, the earliest Indian civilization began along riverbanks. The first inhabitants of India settled in river valleys along the Indus and Ganges rivers.

These people must have felt secure from invaders and foreign influences. They were protected by tall mountain ranges in the north and by seas on the east and west. But despite these natural barriers, India did not remain an isolated land. Throughout her history, merchants, foreign invaders, and wandering tribes crossed the mountains along India's northwestern border (through such mountain passes as the Khyber) and settled in the fertile river valleys. As a result, India became a land of many peoples, customs, and languages. From the diverse elements within Indian society, a unique culture developed.

Early Indian Civilization

India derives its name from the Indus River, along whose fertile banks the earliest Indian civilization flourished (ca. 2300 B.C.). Much of our limited knowledge of this civilization has come from excavations of two of its leading cities: Mohenjo-Daro (moh HEN joh DAH roh) and Harappa (huh RAP uh). These carefully planned cities had wide, straight streets lined with brick houses. Evidence indicates that these cities had elaborate drainage and sewer systems, which were more advanced than those in most modern Indian villages. Although a great distance separates India and the Near East, the early inhabitants of India carried on trade with Egypt and Mesopotamia. We know from archaeological evidence that the Indus civilization ended suddenly—perhaps by flood or by enemy invasion. It was at this time that a warlike people called the **Aryans** migrated into the Indus Valley.

The Aryans were a fair-skinned people who came from central Asia sometime after 1500 B.C. and subdued the non-Aryan people of northwest India. Many historians believe that the Aryans were related to tribes that were invading the Near East, Greece, and Rome about the same time. The Aryans were herdsmen; they kept large numbers of cows and horses. Although they left behind no cities as the Indus civilization did, they did establish a new language in India—**Sanskrit.**

Opposite Page: *A restored section of the Great Wall of China snakes across the Chinese landscape.*

Mohenjo-Daro

When the city of Mohenjo-Daro in the Indus Valley was first built (ca. 2300 B.C.), the founders had carefully planned everything. Wide main streets ran from north to south, and small lanes ran east to west. Houses were built with thick, solid walls to keep the dwellings cool during the long, hot summers. The thick walls also made it possible for buildings to have several stories. The builders used kiln-baked bricks, which were of a higher quality than those dried in the sun. Each house was equipped with a well, and drains took dirty water down the streets and out of the city. In the center of the city were huge public baths, which the men used in religious ceremonies. Also in the center of the town was a large granary.

All this was suddenly and violently destroyed, possibly by Aryan invaders. From unearthed skeletal remains, archaeologists have learned of the swiftness of Mohenjo-Daro's destruction. The remains of two men who were evidently attempting to hide in a well have been found. A group of people, slowed by a small child, died in the streets. Archaeologists have found the skeletons of another group, who thought they could find safety by crouching down behind a wall. One family grabbed all their possessions and tried to escape, but they were caught and brutally murdered. A young couple tried to hide themselves and their child in a corner of the darkest room in the house, but they too did not escape death. The city's destruction was complete. Never rebuilt, it lay forgotten for many centuries; excavations of the site in recent times have revealed the grim ending of Mohenjo-Daro.

Our knowledge of the Aryans and their influence on Indian society comes not from archaeology, but from a collection of religious literature known as the *Vedas* (VAY dus), meaning "knowledge." Preserved in the *Vedas* are early traditions and religious beliefs of the Indians, which were passed down orally from one generation to the next. From Sanskrit literature, we gain insights into the Aryan way of life, which became the basis of Indian culture and tradition. This formative period of Indian history lasted from about 1500 to 500 B.C.

Key Features of Indian Society

India has one of the oldest cultures in the modern world. The basic characteristics of Indian society, described in the *Vedas*, have changed little from ancient to modern days.

Joint-Family

The family has always been one of the most important social units in India. The extended or **joint family** included the children, grandchildren, wives, and close blood relatives of a common ancestor. The oldest male of the group was the dominant authority over the family. When married, sons did not establish their own homes; instead they remained in their father's or grandfather's household. Each family member had his own duties and obligations. The interests of the family came before those of the individual family members. Parents chose the husbands or wives for their children in order to maintain the family's position and honor in society.

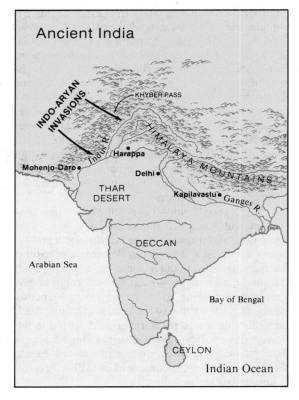

Ancient India

Village Life

Unlike the inhabitants of the Indus civilization, who dwelt in cities, the Aryans settled in small rural villages. Family groups living in a village were governed by a headman or a council of village elders. For the most part, the villages were independent and self-governing. Over the centuries village life has remained a vital part of Indian society. It is said that eight out of ten people in India today live in small villages much as their ancestors did over two thousand years ago.

Caste

Imagine living in a country in which your status in life was determined the moment you were born. India was such a country. Her population was divided into rigid social groups called **castes.** The Indians formulated strict rules governing the life of the members of each caste group: where they lived, what they did (profession), what they wore, what and with whom they could eat, as well as whom they could marry. (Marriage was forbidden outside one's own caste.)

India had between two and three thousand different castes and subcastes. Each one fell into one of four broad "class" groups. The most important group was the priests, called the *Brahmans.* Next in rank were the rulers and warriors, followed by the merchants and traders. The lowest class group was the *Sudras* (SOO dras)—composed of servants and serfs. Outside the caste system and at the bottom of the Indian social ladder were the outcastes, or "untouchables." They performed the most menial tasks in society. Members of the caste structure avoided the "untouchables," for mere contact with them was thought to bring defilement. While anyone could improve his status within his caste, no one could change castes. Thus with the caste system there was little change in the village and family life of India. This fact explains in part why Indian society remained nearly the same for thousands of years.

Religion and the Indian Way of Life

Religion has played a dominant role in shaping Indian culture. From India came two pagan religions that have had a major impact on Asian culture: Hinduism and Buddhism.

Hinduism

Hinduism is ingrained in the Indian way of life. It developed from the early culture and traditions of India: her social structure, literature, arts, and customs. It has not only preserved the traditional elements of India's past but also served as a unifying influence in India's diverse society. Because Hinduism has no formal statement of doctrine, it was able to absorb into its system of belief a wide variety of gods and religious concepts found among the many peoples of India. (Hindus believe all religions to be equally true and equally false.) To this day, the vast majority of the people of India are Hindus.

The basic tenets of Hinduism are found in the religious literature of ancient India, namely the *Vedas* and the *Upanishads* (oo PAN uh SHADZ; philosophical essays elaborating on the teaching of the *Vedas*). Hindus believe that a great god called **Brahman** permeates everything in the universe. The Hindus acknowledge many gods; all deities, however, are considered only manifestations of the eternal, unchanging Brahman. Since Brahman is not a personal being, he is often referred to as the great soul or **world soul.** The ultimate purpose and goal of man, according to the *Vedas*, is to reunite his soul with the world soul. Reunification is accomplished through the process of reincarnation, in which a man's soul passes through many states (or rebirths) before it escapes the physical world and unites with Brahman. This cycle of rebirths is called the **wheel of life.**

The Hindu believes that a person's deeds in this life determine his status in the next. If he has lived a good life (that is, his good works outweigh his bad), then he will move to a higher caste in the next life. The soul of an evil person may be reborn into a lower caste or even into some form of animal life. By observing the religious rituals and ceremonies prescribed by the Hindu priests and by fulfilling the duties and obligations of his caste, a Hindu believes that he (through repeated rebirths) can ultimately gain release from the "wheel of life" and attain union with the world soul.

Buddhism

India was also the birthplace of **Buddhism.** The founder of this new religion was **Siddhartha Gau-**

The many-armed Shiva is one of the major Hindu gods, considered by Hindus to be both the creator and the destroyer. He is shown here as Nataraja ("lord of the dance") and stands on a dwarf, symbolizing his victory over human ignorance.

Central to Buddha's teaching are his **Four Noble Truths:** (1) Suffering is part of all existence. (2) Suffering has a cause—selfish desires. As long as man has a craving for pleasure, possessions, and power, he will have sorrow and misery. (3) Suffering can be overcome by destroying selfish desires. (4) If man follows the Eightfold Path, he will destroy selfish desires and end all suffering. This pattern for living includes correct beliefs, intentions, speech, conduct, livelihood, effort, thoughts, and meditations.

Buddhism is a religion built upon works and moral behavior. Buddhists believe that man does not need the help of the gods or membership in a higher caste in order to obtain freedom from suffering. Once a man has absolutely freed himself from his selfish cravings, he will no longer be reborn but will enter into *Nirvana* (neer VAH nuh), the state of absolute peace and happiness where he loses himself in the world soul.

Both Hindus and Buddhists believe that man can achieve eternal peace if his good works outweigh his bad. The followers of these pagan religions never know, however, if they have done more good works than bad. Moreover they fail to realize that even a large number of good works cannot erase the fact of sin. The only remedy for man's sin is God's saving grace. "For by grace are ye saved through faith; and that not of yourselves: it is the gift of God: Not of works, lest any man should boast" (Eph. 2:8-9).

Lack of Political Unity

While many aspects of Indian society have remained the same for centuries, the political history of India has been one of constant change. Through much of her history India has been little more than a patchwork of small rival kingdoms. Successive waves of foreign invaders have streamed into the Indian subcontinent. The powerful empires established by these invaders have provided brief periods of unity and stability for the Indian peoples.

Mauryan Empire

In 326 B.C. Alexander the Great threatened India. His armies crossed the Indus River and conquered many small kingdoms in India's northwestern region. Alexander intended to advance farther

tama (sid-DAR-tuh GOU-tuh-muh; 563?-483 B.C.), later known as Buddha, the "Enlightened One." At the age of twenty-nine, Gautama became troubled over the misery, poverty, and death that he saw in the world. He became convinced that he should devote all his efforts to find the way of deliverance from suffering. Therefore, he renounced his life of luxury, gave up his princely heritage, left his wife and child, and set out to find peace and true happiness. After six frustrating years, living as a hermit in self-sacrifice and meditation, Gautama was at the point of despair. Sitting down under a tree, he vowed that he would not move until the truth came to him. According to Gautama, he was pondering the questions of life when he realized the truth and attained enlightenment.

into India, but when his army refused to continue, he had to turn back. According to traditional accounts, he met a young man named **Chandragupta Maurya** (CHUN-druh-GOOP-tuh MAH-oor-yuh) while in India. As Alexander's empire began to disintegrate after his death, Chandragupta conquered the disorganized and weak kingdoms in the north and created the first strong empire of India— the Mauryan Empire.

Although it originated in India, Buddhism was unable to displace Hinduism in Indian life and has had a far greater impact on other lands. Shown here is an icon of Buddha from Tibet.

The most famous of the Mauryan rulers was Chandragupta's grandson **Asoka.** He extended the Mauryan Empire to include all but the southern tip of India. Sickened by the results of his own bloody conquests, Asoka renounced war and became a convert to Buddhism. He spent much of his reign promoting the Buddhist religion. Asoka is credited with building thousands of Buddhist shrines called stupas (STOO puz). He also had Buddhist teachings inscribed on stone pillars throughout the empire. Many of these stone pillars still stand, providing valuable information concerning Asoka's reign. One of his most far-reaching acts was the sending of Buddhist missionaries abroad. Buddhism soon spread across much of Southeast Asia, where it became a powerful force in other Asian cultures. It did not gain a wide following in India, however. Hindu priests viewed Buddhist teaching as dangerous to the caste system. Fearing that they might lose their prestige and rank in society, they worked against the acceptance of Buddhist beliefs.

Gupta Empire

The first great period of Indian unity was shortlived. Not long after Asoka's death (232 B.C.), the Mauryan Empire collapsed. The years between the second century B.C. and the third century A.D. witnessed new invasions and the rise of small competing kingdoms. However, during this time of turmoil, India did enjoy a profitable trade with Rome and China. Even so, it was not until the fourth century A.D., with the rise of the **Gupta** (GOOP tuh) **Empire,** that India entered a new, and perhaps her greatest, era of prosperity and achievement.

One historian has stated that "at the time India was perhaps the happiest and most civilized region of the world." The rulers of the Gupta dynasty reunited northern India under a strong and effective government. Trade flourished and the people prospered materially. India's culture spread throughout Southeast Asia. Her universities attracted students from all over the continent, and she made great strides in the fields of textiles and ironwork. The Gupta Age was also one of the finest periods of Indian art, architecture, literature, and science.

Gupta literature became renowned for its adventurous and imaginative fables and fairy tales.

Hindu temples

The foremost Indian poet and dramatist of this period was **Kalidasa** (KAH lih DAH suh), whose plays have earned him the title "the Indian Shakespeare." The popularity of various Indian stories soon spread outside India, where many of them found their way into the literature of other lands. (Western authors such as the brothers Grimm and Rudyard Kipling drew upon Indian stories for ideas for their writing.)

This was also an age of advance in mathematics, science, and medicine. Our so-called Arabic numerals originally came from India. Indian mathematicians were among the first to use negative numbers, the decimal, and the zero. Centuries before Isaac Newton, Indian scientists developed their own theories of gravity. Indian astronomers knew that the earth was round and that it rotated on its axis. If in need of medical attention, the people of the Gupta Empire could go to free hospitals where Indian physicians were able to perform many surgical procedures.

During the sixth century the Gupta Empire collapsed under the repeated attacks of the White Huns (perhaps related to the Huns who plagued the Roman Empire during the fifth century). India again entered a period of political disorder; the country became divided into small warring kingdoms. Waves of foreign invaders again entered the land; but as in the past, Hinduism absorbed these foreign elements into Indian society. However, the history of India took a dramatic turn when northern India fell under the domination of Muslims, who brought with them a religion and culture as strong as Hinduism.

After years of constant raids, Muslim warriors conquered much of northern India, where they established a Muslim kingdom in 1206 near the city of Delhi. Almost immediately a conflict arose between the Muslim and Hindu elements within Indian society. This was a struggle not only between two religions, but between two distinct ways of life. The Hindus believed in many gods, but the Muslims acknowledged only one. The Hindus followed the rigid caste system, while the Muslims believed in the equality of all men before their god, Allah. Although Muslim control of northern India ended at the close of the fourteenth century, the hostilities between Hindus and Muslims in Indian society have continued to the present.

Section Review

1. Along the banks of what river did the earliest Indian civilization begin?
2. List the four broad class groups under the Indian caste system.
3. What is the cycle of rebirths (the process of reincarnation) called?
4. Identify the two empires which brought temporary national unity to India.
5. What famous Indian poet earned the title of "the Indian Shakespeare"?

China

The Land of China

At the heart of eastern Asia is the land of China. In ancient days the Chinese called their land the **Middle Kingdom,** for they believed China to be the center of the earth. Today more people live in China than in any other country in the world—close to one-fourth of the world's population. In land size, modern China is about the same size as the United States; but China's population is four times greater.

China is one of the world's oldest civilizations. The earliest Chinese lived in the fertile valleys of China's two major river systems: The Hwang Ho (or Yellow) and the Yangtze (YANG see). In this respect, ancient China was similar to other early river-valley civilizations—Mesopotamia, Egypt, and India. But while all these were conquered by hostile armies, China during her early history remained relatively free from outside influences.

China was isolated from other centers of civilization until modern times. The vast Pacific Ocean, the tall Himalayan Mountains, and the huge Gobi Desert hemmed in China on all sides. These geographic barriers gave her security from foreign invasion and influences. She did, however, carry on trade with many countries. Because of the relatively small foreign influence upon Chinese society, the Chinese developed and maintained a unique and

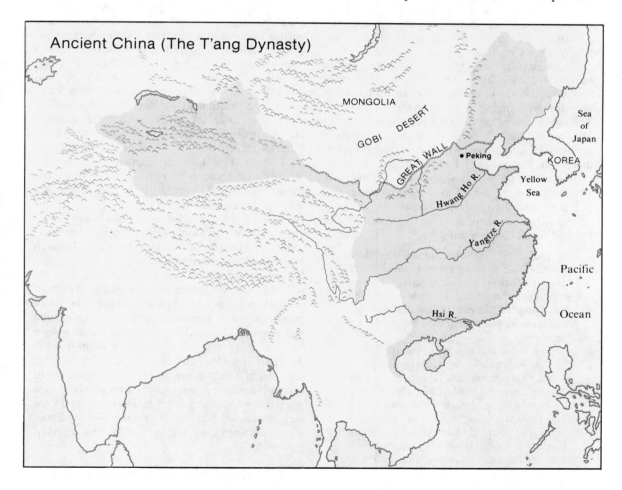

Ancient China (The T'ang Dynasty)

stable culture that has remained virtually unchanged from ancient to modern times.

Important Features of Chinese Society

Strong Family Ties

The family was and still is the center of life in Chinese society. Chinese families were large, embracing many generations: parents and their children, grandparents and grandchildren, aunts and uncles, nephews and nieces, cousins and in-laws. Ancestors were also included in the Chinese concept of the family. Many Chinese could trace their family history back hundreds of years.

A major responsibility of every Chinese was to bring honor to his family. One of the worst offenses that a person could commit was to dishonor his ancestors by bringing reproach on the family name. The cult of **ancestor worship** became the leading religion in China. Every Chinese house contained an ancestral altar before which the Chinese burned incense to the spirits of their dead. By caring for their family graves and worshiping before these altars, the Chinese hoped to receive blessings and guidance from their ancestral spirits.

An American historian gives this description of the traditional Chinese family:

> The family had functions which in the modern West are commonly assumed by the state. It educated its youth, cared for its unemployed, disciplined its erring members, and supported its aged. In turn, the state held the family accountable for the misdeeds of its members. . . .
>
> The individual was of far less importance than the family. The individual member was to make his earnings available to his less fortunate relatives. . . . Marriage was primarily not for the happiness of those who entered into that relationship, but for the purpose of continuing the family line. No sin was greater than that of dying without leaving male issue to revere the memory of one's ancestors.[1]

Language and Learning

The most noticeable feature of Chinese spoken language is their tonal quality. By varying the tone of voice on a particular syllable, the Chinese can convey more than one meaning. For example, *ma* may mean "mother," "hemp" (an Asiatic plant), "horse," or "to scold," depending upon the pitch of the voice. Communication in China is made difficult by variations in the spoken languages from one region to another. It is often impossible for one Chinese to understand what another is saying.

Although the spoken language varies greatly, China does possess a common written language. Traditional Chinese writing is not based on a simple alphabet as our English system is; the Chinese writing consists of some sixty-five thousand **characters** that represent complete ideas, objects, and sounds. For instance, the word for "good" 好 is a combination of the character for girl 女 and boy 子. One has to memorize each character in order to be able to read—a fact that makes reading and writing extremely difficult. Over the centuries the vast majority of the Chinese people have been illiterate. Even the most literate Chinese know only about four thousand characters. It is little wonder that those who master the written language have always been given a place of distinction in Chinese society.

China has been called a "scholar's world." In most other civilizations soldiers, priests, or merchants held prominent positions in society. Through much of Chinese history, however, no social group has exceeded the influence of scholars. For the would-be scholar, education (consisting mainly of memorizing classical Chinese literature) began at an early age and demanded total dedication of time and energy. The goal of the learned man was a career in government service. Scholarship was the determining factor in obtaining a position, whether it be that of a local magistrate or a high government official. Because there were more scholars than government positions, the Chinese developed civil service examinations to choose the best qualified. Those obtaining the highest test scores received positions.

Chinese Thought and Life

Two native philosophies greatly influenced Chinese life: Confucianism (kun FYOO shun iz um) and Taoism (TOU iz um). These systems of

我
們
既
因

信
稱
義、

藉
著
我
們

的
主
耶
穌

基
督、
得
與

上
帝
相
和。

—Romans 5:1

Chinese Characters

When God scattered Noah's descendants throughout the world (Gen. 11:1-9), they carried with them a knowledge of man's earliest history. They knew of creation, the fall, and the Flood. Those who migrated to China preserved some of these truths in their writing system. Since most Chinese characters tell a story, we can break down the more complex characters into simpler ones and discover the meaning of each part.

For example, the Chinese character 禁 means "to forbid." It tells the story of God's command to Adam in Genesis 2:16-17. God planted two special trees in the Garden of Eden: the tree of life and the tree of knowledge of good and evil. God commanded Adam not to eat of the tree of the knowledge of good and evil but gave him permission to eat fruit from any other tree in the garden. It is interesting to note, therefore, that the character "to forbid" is made up of 林, which means "wood" or "tree" (notice that two are indicated) and 示, which is one of the basic Chinese symbols for God. (This character for God also had the idea of "to command" or "to express").

The Scriptural idea of sacrifice (the killing of a spotless animal) is also found in Chinese writing. The word "to sacrifice" 犧 is made up of four major parts: 牛 is "ox" or "cattle," 羊 is "sheep," 秀 is "beautiful" or "unblemished," and 戈 is "spear" (the weapon by which the animal was killed).

Closely associated with the idea of sacrifice is the concept of righteousness. The character 義, which means "righteous" or "righteousness," is made up of 羊, which means "lamb," and 我, which means "me." Notice that when the two characters are combined to create the word righteous(ness), the lamb is placed over the person. In the same manner, Christ, who is the perfect Lamb of God, covers our sins with His blood.

Another interesting study is the character for a boat or ship, 船. It is made up of 舟, which means a "small vessel," 八, which is the number eight, and 口, which means "person," "population," or "mouth." The largest boat built in antiquity (as far as we know) was the ark. It saved Noah and his family—a total of eight persons.

The written Chinese language indicates that at some time in the past the Chinese knew God's truth. Although most Chinese people today do not have access to the Scriptures, the written language preserves not only the truth of man's sin but also the wonderful fact of God's saving grace.

thought became the heart of China's religious beliefs and practices.

Confucianism

K'ung Fu-tzu (KOONG FOO-DZUH; 551?-479 B.C.) is the most honored teacher in Chinese history. The Chinese call him "the Master"; we know him as **Confucius.** Confucius grew up in poverty during a time of social and political unrest in China. Unable to obtain a political office, he devoted his life to teaching. He believed that through proper conduct man could solve the problems of society and live in complete happiness. His disciples recorded and expanded upon his teaching, developing a system of ethics that became a major influence upon Chinese culture.

Fundamental to Confucius's teaching was his belief in five basic human relationships: father and son, elder and younger brothers, husband and wife, friend and friend, and ruler and subjects. Confucius believed that harmony and order in society would result from the maintenance of proper relationships. In addition, he placed great confidence in China's past, trusting it as the basis and guide for human behavior. From the ancients he derived the fundamental principle for all human relationships:

"What you do not want done to yourself, do not do to others."

The major defect in Confucius's teaching was his neglect of the most important relationship of all—man and God. Only as we fulfill our duties and responsibilities to God are we able to properly fulfill those to our fellow men. God's Word teaches,

> Thou shalt love the Lord thy God with all thy heart, and with all thy soul, and with all thy mind. This is the first and great commandment. And the second is like unto it, Thou shalt love thy neighbor as thyself.
> —Matthew 22:37-39

Only by drawing nigh to God is man able to fulfill God's teaching found in Luke 6:31: "As ye would that men should do to you, do ye also to them likewise."

Taoism

Second in importance to the teaching of Confucius was that of **Lao-tzu** (LOU DZUH; 604?-531 B.C.), the legendary founder of **Taoism.** Lao-tzu taught that *tao* (meaning "the way") was the pervading force in nature. He encouraged men to find peace and happiness by living in harmony with nature. According to Taoist teaching, men can achieve this harmony by ceasing to strive after power, wealth, and learning; instead they should adopt a simple, inactive lifestyle. By being passive and submissive, men can accomplish great things. Taoists illustrated this teaching with the example of water: "There is nothing in the world more soft and weak than water, yet for attacking things that are hard and strong there is nothing that surpasses it. . . . The soft overcomes the hard; the weak overcomes the strong."

Confucianism became the guiding philosophy of China's educational, social, and political systems; Taoism became the basis of mystical, magical, and superstitious elements in Chinese society. In many ways the two philosophies are exact opposites. Confucianism promotes an active way of life and teaches that man has social obligations to fulfill. Taoism favors a passive existence and attempts to free man from responsibility. Confucianists strive for improved government and laws and emphasize the importance of education. The Taoists reject external authority and stress noninvolvement in society.

Dynastic History of China

The Chinese have a passion for history. Their interest in antiquity sparked a great tradition of historical writing, much of which traces the history of China's ruling dynasties (or families). From the periods of **dynastic rule,** historians have established the major divisions of Chinese history.

The Chinese were able to maintain a strong sense of national unity, but they experienced numerous periods of political upheaval and disorder. Each dynasty went through the same cycle: it began, matured, prospered, and then declined. The unrest that brought an end to one dynasty prepared the way for the founding of a new one. While each dynasty had its own special qualities and left its mark on Chinese culture, the fundamental character of society remained essentially the same throughout Chinese history.

The Sayings of Confucius

The philosophy of Confucius is contained in a collection of his sayings and activities called the *Analects*. Some of what Confucius said is morally sound advice, demonstrating how human wisdom may in some way discern divine truth.

- When you have erred, be not afraid to correct yourself.
- It does not greatly concern me . . . that men do not know me; my great concern is my not knowing them.
- To go beyond is as wrong as to fall short.
- It is moral cowardice to leave undone what one perceives to be right to do.
- Where there is habitual going after gain, there is much ill-will.
- Learn, as if never overtaking your object, and yet as if apprehensive of losing it.
- The nobler-minded man . . . will be agreeable even when he disagrees; the small-minded man will agree and be disagreeable.
- Impatience over little things introduces confusion into great schemes.
- The cautious seldom err.
- Faults in a superior man are like eclipses of the sun and moon: when he is guilty of a trespass, men all see it; and when he is himself again, all look up to him.
- When you meet with men of worth, think how you may attain to their level; when you see others of an opposite character, look within and examine yourself.
- They who care not for the morrow will the sooner have their sorrows.
- Learning without thought is a snare; thought without learning is a danger.
- With a meal of coarse rice . . . and water to drink, and my bent arm for a pillow—even thus I find happiness. Riches and honors without righteousness are to me as fleeting clouds.

Shang Dynasty

The Shang dynasty, one of the earliest known Chinese dynasties, was established along the Yellow River around 1500 B.C. The rulers of this dynasty united much of northern China. Archaeologists have unearthed fine examples of Shang bronze work and marble carvings. Much of our knowledge of Shang culture comes from early Chinese writing found inscribed on pieces of animal bones and tortoise shells. To obtain answers about the future from their ancestors, the Chinese wrote questions on bones or shells; then they touched them with a hot metal rod, causing them to crack. By "interpreting" the pattern of the cracks, the Chinese believed they could determine the will of their ancestors.

Chou Dynasty

Shortly before 1000 B.C., the people who lived along the Shang's western border overthrew the Shang rulers. The Chou dynasty that they established lasted over eight hundred years—longer than any other dynasty in Chinese history. This period is often called the "Classical," or "formative," age of Chinese history. Much of China's culture, such as family life, ancestor worship, the writing system, and Confucian and Taoist thought, became firmly established during this time.

The Chou government was decentralized. While the Chou rulers retained the ultimate authority, they allowed powerful nobles great freedom in ruling local territories. However, the Chou rulers were un-

A Chinese altar shrine from around the time of the fall of the Han dynasty

able to control the nobles, and fighting broke out among rival states.

Ch'in Dynasty

Order was restored by **Shih Huang Ti** (247-210 B.C.), the founder of the short-lived but memorable Ch'in dynasty—the dynasty that gives China its name. Shih Huang Ti (SHEER HWAHNG TEE), which means "First Emperor," was the first to unite China proper under one strong centralized government. He standardized the Chinese weight, measurement, and coinage systems and brought uniformity to China's writing system. Perhaps the most remarkable achievement of the Ch'in dynasty was the construction of the Great Wall. The wall was twenty-five to thirty feet high and fifteen feet wide. A road ran along its top, providing for rapid movement of troops and swift communication. A consolidation of existing structures, the Great Wall covered over 1,400 miles of often rugged terrain. It was erected as a defensive barrier against the invasions of the barbaric Huns (whose descendants later invaded the Roman Empire). Although Shih Huang Ti brought order and protection to China, he did so through harsh and ruthless measures. Just a few years after his death, the people revolted, bringing an end to the Ch'in dynasty.

Han Dynasty

The next dynasty to rule China was the Han dynasty, established in 202 B.C. This dynasty was so popular that to this day some Chinese call themselves the "sons of Han." The most famous Han ruler was **Wu Ti** (140-87 B.C.). He drove back the Huns and extended China's territory. To meet the growing need for well-trained government officials, the Han rulers introduced a civil service system in which competitive public examinations determined appointments to government posts. The Han established the *Pax Sinica* ("Chinese Peace") throughout China and much of central Asia. During this period trade routes were opened with the West. Over the "Silk Road"—named for China's chief export—traders brought China into direct contact with the Greek and Roman civilizations. The Han period also marked the entrance of Buddhism into China. It soon became one of China's leading religions.

T'ang Dynasty

In A.D. 220 revolts overthrew the last of the Han rulers. For nearly four hundred years China suffered from internal wars and barbarian invasions. Attempts to establish a lasting central government were unsuccessful. At the beginning of the seventh century, however, the T'ang rulers came to power and restored unity and prosperity once again to China. The T'ang dynasty was a golden age in Chinese history. The Chinese enjoyed a stable government, an expanding empire, increased, trade, contact with other civilizations, advances in learning, and magnificent works of arts and literature. The T'ang was one of the finest periods of Chinese poetry. The most popular and prolific poet was **Li Po,** who wrote thousands of poems expressing emotional and sentimental themes.

The glory of the T'ang lasted about three centuries. As self-seeking rulers began squandering much of the country's wealth, the T'ang dynasty lost both prosperity and power. The weakened dynasty collapsed shortly after 900.

Sung Dynasty

Fifty years later a new dynasty—the Sung—restored order. Compared to the other dynasties of China's past, however, the Sung dynasty was politically weak. The Sung rulers were unable to prevent the northern portions of China from falling under barbarian control. Despite these problems, the Sung dynasty carried on active trade, and the Chinese culture flourished. During this period the Chinese excelled in painting, printing, and porcelain.

Chinese Culture and the Western World

Only in recent years has the Western world significantly influenced Chinese society. Over the centuries China had resisted the introduction of foreign elements. This distrust of outsiders is the reason the traditional Chinese way of life remained virtually unaffected by the Western ideas and influences for centuries. The contrast between Eastern and Western cultures caused many Westerners to view China as a land of mystical enchantment.

> Many of [China's] traditional customs are the opposite of those of the Occident [the West] and, accordingly, seem bizarre. In the old China the men wore skirts and long gowns, the women baggy trousers. At banquets what

A Chinese painting on silk, entitled The Tribute Horse, *from the Sung dynasty period*

> we think of as a dessert came first and rice concluded the meal. Men in greeting one another shook their own hands, not the hands of the other (a much more sanitary proceeding than that of the West, be it said). The place of honor was on the left, not on the right. In meeting on the streets gentlemen removed their spectacles and not their hats. White not black was the color of mourning. . . . These, and an almost endless number of other contrasts, seemed to place the Chinese in another world and to baffle any attempt to understand them.[3]

Unlike the Chinese who generally looked with suspicion upon Western ways and ideas, Westerners profited from their contacts with the Chinese. Europe became an open market for many Chinese goods; silk and porcelain were among the most popular. As far as we know, the Chinese were the first to produce silk. They carefully guarded the secret of the silkworm, whose cocoon provided the silk thread needed to make this beautiful fabric. The Chinese also developed the process for making porcelain, a white, translucent form of pottery which is still known as "china." In Europe, Chinese silk became fashionable, and china was one of the most valued possessions.

The West also learned of printing from the Chinese. The Chinese developed a method called block printing in which they carved raised characters on a block of wood. By inking the block and pressing it on paper, the Chinese were able to print multiple copies. However, the printing of new pages involved the slow process of carving another block of wood. To speed up this process, the Chinese invented **movable type**—that is, they carved smaller separate blocks for each Chinese character. The blocks could then be rearranged and reused. However, because there were thousands of characters, movable type was not widely used, nor was it practical.

Like printing, many other products associated with the Western world originated in China. Can you imagine a school classroom without paper or an ink pen? The Chinese were the first to develop paper (as we know it) and one of the first people to use ink. Think what navigation would be like without

The Tomb and Terra-Cotta Army of Shih Huang Ti

Shih Huang Ti, the first emperor of China, died in 210 B.C. His body was entombed in an elaborate mausoleum that had taken workers his entire reign to construct. (Thirty-six years before his death he had drafted nearly a million Chinese laborers for the project.) According to contemporary Chinese historians, it contained a model of his palaces and various government buildings. It also housed a replica of his empire complete with rivers and seas of mercury, which actually flowed by mechanical means.

To protect his grave, the Chinese installed crossbows which would release automatically if an intruder entered the tomb. According to the custom of the day, Shih's son ordered his father's concubines who had not borne him sons to be buried with the emperor. He also ordered those who had worked on the safety devices in the tomb to be buried too. Once the emperor was interred, the Chinese covered the mausoleum with earth and planted trees over it to give the appearance of a hill. Today it is called Mount Li. It stands fifteen stories high in the midst of a plain.

In 1974 a group of Chinese farmers, while digging a well in the Mount Li area, unearthed a subterranean passageway. Inside were huge terra-cotta statues (made of hard, water-proof ceramic clay) of ancient Chinese soldiers. In the years since the discovery, Chinese archaeologists have uncovered about six thousand soldiers—life-size replicas of the men in Shih Huang Ti's army. No two statues are alike. Some are old with wrinkles, and others are young and fair. Some are smiling, and some are serious. In addition to the soldiers, archaeologists have found clay horses and chariots. Because the ceiling of the tomb has collapsed and crushed many of the terra-cotta statues, the task of excavating is a difficult one. When the work of the excavators is completed, the Chinese intend to create a museum on the site.

the Chinese invention of the magnetic compass. Another important Chinese discovery was gunpowder; this substance was first used in the manufacturing of fireworks. While it is true that the West made more productive (and sometimes destructive) use of these inventions, we should remember that they were originally Chinese contributions.

Section Review

1. What did the ancient Chinese call their land? Why?
2. What social group held the most esteemed position in Chinese society?
3. How do historians divide the major periods of Chinese history?
4. What is perhaps the most remarkable building achievement that occurred under the Ch'in dynasty?
5. List seven specific contributions that China made to the Western world.

Japan

Over one hundred miles off the coast of Asia—opposite China, Korea, and Siberia (Russia)—is the island nation of Japan. Japan consists of four main islands and hundreds of lesser ones. If placed alongside the Atlantic coast of the United States, Japan would stretch from Maine to Florida. In land area Japan is about the size of the state of California. Most of this land, however, is mountainous; less than twenty per cent of it is suitable for farming. Through much of her history, Japan was more geographically remote than China; for centuries she remained isolated from the mainstream of the world's civilizations. It was not until the late nineteenth century that Japan made her presence felt in the arena of world affairs.

Japan's Early History

Although Japan is the youngest of the major Asian civilizations, little is known about her early history. Instead of keeping historical records as the Chinese did, the early Japanese passed down myths and legends, many of which played an influential role in shaping Japanese culture. According to Japanese mythology, the god Izanagi and goddess Izanami, while standing on the rainbow bridge of heaven, dipped a jewelled spear into the ocean. Drops falling from the tip of the spear formed the islands of Japan. The god and goddess descended to live on the islands. Their offspring were the Japanese people.

Our first historical glimpse of ancient Japan finds the land divided by a number of warring clans. In early Japanese society, the **clan**—a group of families claiming descent from a common ancestor—was the basic unit of social, religious, and political organization. Each clan had its own land, its own god, and its own chieftain. The chieftain served as both political and religious leader. By the fifth century A.D., one clan had risen in power and prestige over rival clans. Centered on the island of Honshu (the main Japanese island), the **Yamato clan** extended its authority and forged a unified Japanese state.

The leaders of the Yamato clan used Japanese mythology to secure the loyalty of other clan chief-

tains. According to legend the first emperor of Japan, **Jimmu Tenno** (*tenno,* "heavenly prince"), was a direct descendant of the sun goddess. The Yamato clan claimed that its rulers were descendants of Jimmu Tenno; they were, therefore, believed to be divine. From this clan arose the imperial family of Japan. Subsequent Japanese emperors all claim Jimmu Tenno as their divine ancestor. Unlike China, which has many ruling families or dynasties, Japan has had but one imperial family in its entire history. For this reason, the imperial family has served as a symbol of unity and continuity in Japanese society.

Supporting the belief in the divine origin of the emperor was Japan's native religion, **Shintoism** (meaning "the way of the gods"). Shintoism was originally a form of nature worship that attributed deity to anything in nature that was awe-inspiring or extraordinary, such as fire, a waterfall, or a high mountain. However, Shintoism also stressed the supremacy of the sun goddess and the divine descent of the emperor. In many respects it became a religion of feeling, inspiring love for one's home-

Ancient Japan

land, loyalty to one's clan, and reverence for one's emperor. It is little wonder that in modern times the Japanese government made Shintoism into a national cult, which required belief in the ancient myths, encouraged patriotism, and maintained the prestige of the emperor.

Influence of China

Japan remained in relative isolation during her early history. In the fifth to the eighth centuries, however, the Chinese invaded the Japanese islands. This was not a military invasion by soldiers but a cultural invasion of ideas, learning, and art. China was experiencing the golden age of the T'ang dynasty, and the Japanese welcomed the influx of the "superior" Chinese culture.

There were two important vehicles that transmitted Chinese culture to Japan. The first was the Chinese writing system, which the Japanese adopted to complement their spoken language. For the first time, the Japanese were able to keep written records and produce their own literature. From an understanding of Chinese characters, they were also able to read and study Chinese literature and learn of the life and thought of the Chinese people.

Secondly, Chinese culture flowed into Japan through Buddhism. The Japanese learned much about the Chinese way of life from Buddhist monks who came over from China. For example, the Japanese learned to appreciate Chinese art and architecture from the numerous Buddhist temples built in Japan. Buddhism became firmly established in Japan during the seventh century when a member of the imperial family, **Prince Shotoku,** made Buddhism the favored national religion. He had many Buddhist temples, hospitals, and schools constructed. He also sent many young men to China to study Chinese ways: agriculture, science, architecture, law, government, philosophy, and religion. Japan borrowed not only Chinese writing, literature, and religion but also her system of weights and measurements, medical practices, calendar, styles of furniture and dress, and methods of building roads and bridges.

In the mid-seventh century, the leaders of Japan sought to weaken the influence of the local clan chieftains and extend the power of the emperor to all of Japan. They modeled their government after the strong centralized bureaucracy of the T'ang dynasty. This turnabout in the Japanese political and economic structure became known as the "Great Change" or **Taika** (tie EE kuh) **Reform.** Like the Chinese, the Japanese established civil service examinations, granting government posts to men of ability. A new judicial code and tax system came into existence, and at Nara the Japanese established their first permanent capital, which was copied after the main city of China. (Later the capital was moved to Kyoto, where the Japanese emperors maintained their court until 1868).

The Taika reforms changed the nature of Japan's political structure from semi-independent clans to a centralized government headed by the emperor. Or so it was in theory. In actual practice, government authority came to rest in the hands of powerful families who controlled the key posts of government. The **Fujiwara** had married their daughters to the sons of the imperial family. When a male child was born, they forced the ruling emperor to abdicate. The Fujiwara elders then ruled Japan as regents of the infant emperor.

Rise of Samurai

The Fujiwaras enjoyed the wealth and extravagance of the imperial city. However, the luxurious life of the royal court brought corruption and bankruptcy to the government. Disorder followed as the central government was no longer able to provide protection for outlying provinces. Many provincial governors began to rely on strong military clans for protection. Soon power struggles broke out among rival military families. In the twelfth century **Yoritomo,** the leader of the Minamoto clan, became the supreme military leader of Japan when he defeated the only remaining powerful clan. The powerless emperor granted Yoritomo the title of **shogun** ("great general"). Yoritomo created a warrior state, ruled by military rather than civilian officials. Although the line of the imperial family continued, powerful shoguns held the real power over the Japanese government from 1192 to 1868.

With the rise of the office of shogun, the warrior class became the leading class in Japanese society. The Japanese warrior was called **samurai** or *bushi.* Besides mastering the military skills of horsemanship, fencing, archery, and *jujitsu,* the samurai studied history, literature, and the art of writing. He used these skills in providing protection for his master and lord. An unwritten military code known as the **Bushido** (*B*OO*S*H ih DOH; ''the way of the warrior'') governed the conduct of the samurai. It demanded that he live by loyalty, honor, duty, justice, courage, sincerity, and politeness. To avoid

> ### The Way of the Warrior
>
> A Japanese warrior learned *Bushido* almost from birth. One authority on *Bushido* describes the early training this way: ''Does a little [baby] cry for any ache? The mother scolds him in this fashion: 'What will you do when your arm is cut off in battle? What [will you do] when you are called upon to commit *hara-kiri?* ''

the disgrace of capture, atone for deeds of misconduct, or prove questioned loyalty to his master, a warrior could end his life with honor by committing suicide according to the ceremonial practice of *hara-kiri.*

Comparison of the Asian Civilizations

As we have seen in this chapter, each of the major Asian civilizations—India, China, and Japan—had a distinctive culture and history. Nevertheless, there are a few characteristics they share.

Traditionalism

These oriental civilizations have often been referred to as the ''changeless'' lands. So deeply

Kamikaze

In 1274 Mongol ruler Kublai Khan sent a fleet of ships with a large army on board across the Yellow Sea to invade the island nation of Japan. But before his soldiers could land on the islands, a terrible wind called the *kamikaze,* or ''Divine Wind,'' destroyed the fleet. Seven years later he sent an even larger fleet. This time forty-four hundred ships containing one hundred forty-two thousand men set sail for Japan. After a few brief skirmishes at sea, the Mongols looked for a good beach on which to land the army. But before they could do this, another kamikaze blew, once again sinking Kublai Khan's ships. Never again did the Mongol hordes threaten Japan. Like other island nations, she was able to remain relatively free from foreign influence for centuries.

Many years later during World War II, the term *kamikaze* was applied to a special division in the Japanese air force, whose members willingly died for the emperor. These pilots flew suicide missions, crashing their planes loaded with explosives into enemy ships.

A Japanese scroll from the Kamakura period (A.D. 1185-1333)

were their cultures rooted in the beliefs and customs passed down from generation to generation that there remained little room for new ideas and ways. Each possessed its own standard of traditional values—Hinduism and the caste system in India, Confucianism and historical literature in China, and Shintoism and mythology in Japan. Built upon traditionalism, these civilizations frowned upon change; they were content to live in the past. The Asians relied upon human tradition in determining what is true and good. Paul warns of this danger in Colossians 2:8, "Beware lest any man spoil you through philosophy and vain deceit, after the tradition of men, after the rudiments [principles] of the world, and not after Christ."

Stifling of Individuality

Within the Indian, Chinese, and Japanese societies, the group—not the individual—held the prominent place: the caste in India, the extended family in China, and the clan in Japan. The group was responsible for the welfare and actions of its members; likewise each member became accountable to the group. Lacking the initiative and responsibility of individuals, these societies remained static. God desires each individual to be productive: "But let every man prove his own work, and then shall he have rejoicing in himself alone, and not in another. For every man shall bear his own burden" (Gal. 6:4-5). Likewise, God will hold each individual, not a group, accountable for his own actions: "So then every one of us shall give account of himself to God" (Rom. 14:12).

False Religion

The cultures of India, China, and Japan are among the oldest and most enduring in the world today. They are also among the most heathen. This is not to say they are nonreligious, for Hinduism, Buddhism, Confucianism, Taoism, and Shintoism played an important role in shaping the lives of the people in the Orient. But in these lands the vast majority of people live apart from the knowledge of God and His truth. Instead of worshiping the true living God, they follow after polytheism, idols, superstition, vain philosophies, myths, and fables. Their man-centered religions offer no hope beyond

An eighteenth-century Japanese woodcut entitled Teahouse Maid

this life. Only in Christ can man look to the future with confidence and expectation.

Section Review

1. What was the basic social, religious, and political unit in early Japanese society?
2. According to legend, who was the first Japanese emperor? What do the Japanese believe about his ancestry?
3. The culture of what foreign civilization had a profound effect on Japan's early history?
4. What was the name of the reform movement that sought to weaken the influence of local clan leaders while strengthening the authority of the emperor and the central government?
5. What were Japanese warriors called? What was the unwritten military code that governed their conduct?

The Mongol Empire

In this chapter and the preceding one, we have examined the major civilizations of Asia and eastern Europe to the thirteenth century. Despite being separated by great distances and diverse cultural backgrounds, the civilizations of India, China, Byzantium, Russia, and the Muslim empire shared something in common: each land was invaded by fierce warriors coming out of central Asia. Since ancient days, central Asia had been the homeland of many nomadic peoples. Vast grassy plains, known as the **steppes**, stretch from western China to eastern Europe. This pastureland was a highway along which roving tribes moved as they sought food for their flocks and herds.

One of these roving tribes was known as the Huns. They advanced into China and Europe while the Turks, also a nomadic people, moved into Byz-

antine and Islamic territories. By the thirteenth century another group, the Mongols, had united the peoples of central Asia. The Mongols spread across the Asian steppes, creating an empire that stretched from China across central Asia to Russia, southward into Byzantine and Muslim territories, and later into the land of India. In less than a century, the Mongols built the largest land empire in history.

Building the Mongol Empire

The Mongol people arose in the north of China, in the land known today as Mongolia. Their round felt tents dotted the eastern portion of the Asiatic grasslands. They raised sheep, goats, and horses. They had no government but were divided into small tribes. In approximately 1162, Temujin (TEM yoo jin) was born to the family of a tribal

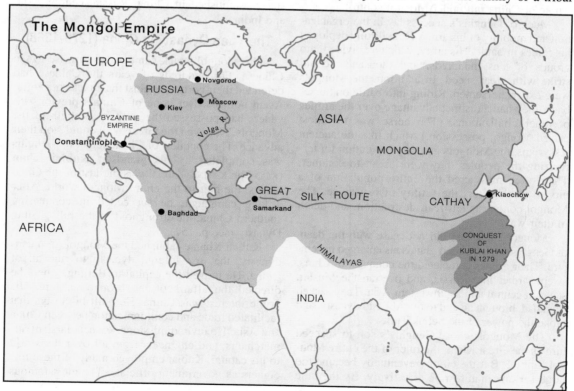

The Mongol Empire

chief. Overcoming many hardships in his youth, Temujin succeeded his father as leader of his tribe at the age of thirteen. He gradually united all the Mongol tribes under his authority and established an empire in the steppes. He became "lord of all the people dwelling in felt tents." In 1206 the Mongols gave him the title **"Genghis Khan"** (JENG-gis KAHN), meaning "universal ruler."

Genghis Khan was one of the greatest conquerors in history. He believed that he had a divine commission to conquer the world. Having organized the Mongols into a well-disciplined fighting force, he conquered northern China. He then turned his army westward. The Mongols overran central Asia, advanced to the banks of the Indus River, pushed into Persia, and crossed into southern Russia. Returning from his western conquests, Genghis renewed his campaign against China. His death in 1227, however, prevented him from seeing the whole of China fall under Mongol control.

Much of Genghis's success lay in the organization and mobility of his army. He skillfully deployed his forces in battle. His army, which he divided into groups of tens, hundreds, and thousands, could strike with great speed. In addition, the Mongols were expert horsemen. Riding into battle on horseback, they had a distinct advantage over the armies of other civilizations. (The horse was the most prized Mongol possession.) Much like the ancient Assyrians, the Mongols gained a reputation for terrorizing the peoples they were about to conquer. They often massacred the entire population of a city to teach others the futility of resistance. The Mongol conquests left fear, destruction, and death in their wake.

Mongol expansion did not cease with the death of Genghis. His sons and grandsons enlarged his empire. Their armies completed the conquest of China, swept farther into Russia, and overran the Muslim states in central and southwestern Asia. They sacked Baghdad, brought an end to the Abbasid dynasty, and broke the power of the Seljuk Turks.

The Mongols chose Genghis's son to succeed him as the Great Khan, the ruler of the entire Mongol Empire. But the empire eventually became too large for one man to rule effectively. By the time

Genghis Khan

of the fifth ruler, the empire had already begun to fragment into many separate Mongol states, each ruled by a descendant of Genghis. In the following pages we will examine separately the Mongol states established in China, Russia, central Asia, and India.

The Yuan Dynasty in China (1279-1368)

The Mongol attack came as no surprise to the Chinese. For hundreds of years the Chinese had defended their borders against the attacks of central Asian nomads. But none of China's previous invaders had possessed the military strength of the Mongols. Not even the Great Wall could stop their advance. The conquest of China begun by Genghis was completed by his grandson **Kublai Khan** (KOO-blie KAHN). Kublai was the last of the Great Khans, the heir to the entire Mongol world. After a long campaign, he succeeded in conquering southern China, the stronghold of the ruling Sung Dynasty (see p. 157).

Kublai Khan established the Mongol (or Yuan) dynasty, the first foreign dynasty to rule all of China. He moved the capital to Beijing, where he directed the affairs of the Mongol empire. His prime interest was China. He built highways that facilitated trade and communication between China and Asia. He invited missionaries, scholars, artists, merchants, and engineers from all over the world to his capital. Kublai employed many of these foreigners as government officials. The most famous

European traveler to Mongol China was Marco Polo (see pp. 307, 308). Polo lived in China seventeen years. Many of those years he spent in the service of Kublai. He later wrote a glowing account of his travels and of the wonders of Kublai's court. His stories gave most Europeans their first glimpse of the land of China.

With the death of Kublai, the world empire founded by Genghis Khan came to an end. The Mongols still ruled most of Asia, but no longer could they boast of a unified empire. The empire had broken into many independent Mongol kingdoms. The descendants of Kublai continued to rule in China. But despite the peace and prosperity that the Yuan dynasty brought to China, the Chinese resented the rule of foreigners. The Mongols had excluded the Chinese from holding positions in the government. Discontent mounted as the successors of Kublai grew weaker and more decadent. Rebellion eventually broke out, and the Chinese drove the Mongol rulers back into Mongolia. A new Chinese dynasty, the Ming ("brilliant") dynasty, restored Chinese rule and reestablished Chinese ways. Reacting to years of Mongol rule, the Chinese adopted an antiforeign spirit that led to the closing of China to outside influences.

The Golden Horde in Russia

While Kublai was occupied with the conquest of China, another grandson of Genghis, **Batu Khan,** led the Mongols into Europe. The Mongols—or Tartars, as the Europeans called them—crushed the Russian defenses and penetrated Hungary and Poland. Western Europe now lay vulnerable to the Mongol attack. But upon hearing of the death of the Great Khan, Batu stopped his advance. He withdrew to the Volga River in Russia, where he consolidated his conquests in central Asia and Russia. His realm, the strongest Mongol state in Western Asia, became known as the "Golden Horde." (The word *horde* comes from the Mongol *ordu,* which means "camp.")

For nearly two hundred fifty years, Russia remained under the yoke of the Golden Horde. The Mongols not only exacted tribute from the Russian cities but also gathered recruits for their army from among the Russian people. During the period of Mongol domination, Russian ties with western Europe and the Byzantine Empire weakened as Asian influences grew stronger.

This period also witnessed the growth of Moscow from an insignificant town to the capital of the Russian nation. Many factors aided Moscow's rise. Moscow stood at the center of Russia's inland waterways. Her location was advantageous for both trade and defense. Furthermore, the leaders of Moscow cooperated with the khans of the Golden Horde. They served as the khan's tax collectors. In return, the khans recognized the prince of Moscow as the Grand Prince of Russia. The Russian church also enhanced the prestige of Moscow. When the head of the Orthodox church moved from Kiev to Moscow, Moscow became the religious center of Russia.

While Moscow grew strong and prosperous, the Golden Horde weakened. By the late fourteenth century, the grand princes began to openly challenge their Mongol overlords. Under **Ivan III,** the Grand Prince from 1462-1505, Moscow refused to pay further tribute to the Mongols. By 1480 Moscow had freed herself from the Mongol yoke and became the political and religious capital of the new state. Ivan extended his control over much of northern Russia. He laid the foundation for an independent Russian state and emerged as its *autocratic* (ruling with unlimited authority) leader. After the collapse of Constantinople in 1453, many people considered Moscow the "Third Rome."

Later Mongol Empires

Tamerlane's Empire

In the late fourteenth century, there arose a central Asian conqueror who attempted to rebuild Genghis's empire. His name was Timur the Lame; he was known to the Europeans as **Tamerlane.** Tamerlane belonged to a Mongol-Turkish tribe and claimed to have descended from Genghis Khan.

Having established his power in central Asia, Tamerlane raised an army and began a new wave of Mongol invasions. His army swept over the Muslim lands in southwestern Asia, capturing Baghdad and Damascus and defeating the Ottoman Turks in

Asia Minor. His march into southern Russia weakened the Golden Horde and indirectly aided the Russian princes in their struggle to gain freedom from Mongol control. Turning to the East, Tamerlane led his army into India, where in 1398 he reduced the city of Delhi to ruins and slaughtered an estimated one hundred thousand people. He died in 1405 while planning an invasion of China.

Tamerlane was an able but cruel conqueror. He left a trail of merciless plundering, destruction, and massacres. His conquests reached from India to Asia Minor. But the size of his empire was much smaller than the earlier Mongol Empire. It collapsed shortly after his death.

The Mughul Empire in India

India was a frequent target of Mongol attacks. From the time of Genghis Khan to Tamerlane, Mongol raiders had terrorized the people of northern India. But unlike most Asian lands, India had not fallen under Mongol rule; not until the sixteenth century did the Mongols gain control of India. **Babur,** "The Tiger," a descendant of the two greatest Asian conquerors, Genghis Khan and Tamerlane, became the leader of the Turkish-Mongol tribes in what today is Afghanistan. With an army of about twelve thousand men, Babur crossed the mountain passes and invaded northern India. Having captured the capital city of Delhi, he established the **Mughul** Dynasty in 1526. ("Mughul" is the name given to the Mongols in India.) Later Mughul rulers extended the empire over all but the southern tip of India.

Under the Mughuls (who were Muslims), Indian civilization flourished. Unlike the cruel destruction inflicted by Tamerlane, the Mughul rulers established law and order, increased Indian unity, and fostered a period of rich achievement in art and architecture. The greatest Mughul ruler was Babur's grandson **Akbar** (1556-1605). Akbar expanded the empire to include all of northern and central India. Not only an excellent military general, Akbar was an able administrator who brought many reforms to the Indian government. He realized that force alone could not win the support of the Indian people. Through his policy of religious toleration, he won the support of the Hindu population.

The Mughul emperor Babur sits in the center of his court in this illustration from his autobiography.

Section Review

1. What name is given to the vast grassy plains that stretch from western China to eastern Europe?
2. Who united the Mongol tribes and established a Mongol empire in the steppes? What title was he given?
3. What Mongol ruler conquered China? What was the name of the Mongol dynasty in China?
4. What city rose to prominence during the period of Mongol domination over Russia?
5. What descendant of Genghis Khan and Tamerlane set up a Mongol dynasty in India? What was the name of this dynasty?

Africa

Although the Mongols spread over Asia and threatened Europe, they left untouched one great "unknown land"—Africa. The second largest continent, Africa covers over one-fifth of the earth's land surface. It is nearly four times the size of the continental United States. Although much of the continent is a large plateau, its mountains, deserts, grassy flatlands, and jungles give Africa a unique beauty.

We have studied some of Africa's history in earlier chapters. The Egyptians established on the banks of the Nile the earliest recorded civilization in Africa. Carthage built a thriving civilization in North Africa in the days of the Roman Republic, and the Romans later made the area part of their empire. After the collapse of Rome, Muslims swept across North Africa and brought the region under Islamic domination.

As important as these events are, they involve only a portion of that great continent. The history of the rest of Africa, known as **sub-Saharan Africa** (so named because it is south of the Sahara Desert), is not so well known but is nonetheless important.

Ancient African Civilization

Centuries before Europeans penetrated into sub-Saharan Africa, several African empires and kingdoms flourished. In ancient times, two important kingdoms arose in northeast Africa, south of the Egyptian civilization. The earliest was the kingdom of Kush, which centered in what is today northern Sudan. (Ruins of its capital, Meroë, still exist near the modern city of Khartoum.) Originally a province of the Egyptian Empire, Kush grew in power until by 700 B.C. it had not only overthrown Egyptian rule but also conquered all of Egypt and established its own dynasty of pharaohs. (The "Tirhakah of Ethiopia" mentioned in II Kings 19:9 is one such Kushite ruler, Taharqa.) The Assyrians drove the Kushites out of Egypt around 660 B.C., but the Kushite kingdom continued for nearly a thousand years longer.

Kush eventually fell to a kingdom to its east known as Aksum (or "Axum"). The ruler of Aksum recorded the shattering defeat he inflicted on the Kushites in A.D. 330:

The pyramids of ancient Kush are smaller than those of Egypt but still stand as visible reminders of the vanished Kushite civilization.

I made war on them. . . . They fled without making a stand, and I pursued them . . . killing some and capturing others. . . . I burnt their towns, both those built of bricks and those built of reeds, and my army carried off their food and copper and iron . . . and destroyed the statues in their temples, their granaries, and cotton trees and cast them into the [Nile].[4]

Aksum was unusual among the early African kingdoms in that it embraced Christianity. Later tradition claimed that the rulers of Aksum were descendants of King Solomon and the Queen of Sheba. Actually the kingdom's conversion to Christianity was the work of a Syrian Christian named **Frumentius** (see the box on p. 169). Aksum's conversion intensified its already extensive trade with the Roman Empire. Later the Muslim invasions in North Africa cut off Aksum from almost all European contact. The civilization nonetheless continued to exist and became the nucleus of the modern state of Ethiopia.

Central and Western Africa

During Europe's Middle Ages several important kingdoms arose in central and western Africa. Our knowledge of these civilizations is somewhat sketchy, because most of their histories were not written down but passed on orally. However, oral tradition, archaeology, and some accounts written

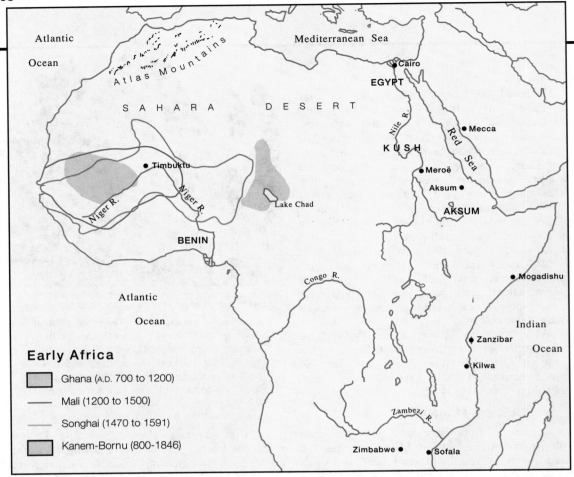

Early Africa

Ghana (A.D. 700 to 1200)

Mali (1200 to 1500)

Songhai (1470 to 1591)

Kanem-Bornu (800-1846)

by non-Africans provide us a general picture of these cultures. In central Africa, for example, the kingdom of Kanem-Bornu thrived on the shores of Lake Chad. Deriving its profit from the camel caravan trade and building a strong military force (including camel-mounted cavalry), this African kingdom lasted a thousand years, from ca. 800 to 1846.

Even more important were the three kingdoms of western Africa—Ghana, Mali, and Songhai, each progressively larger than the previous. All three built prosperous civilizations whose wealth derived from the gold mines within their empires and the camel caravan trade in gold, salt, and other precious items that crossed the Sahara Desert. The Niger (NIE jur) River in particular provided a base for these empires as its waters drew travelers crossing the arid Sahara.

The kingdom of Ghana rose to prominence first, enjoying its heyday from A.D. 700 to 1200. Fanatical Muslims from northern Africa attacked and fatally weakened Ghana in the eleventh century but proved unable to conquer the region. In its place rose the kingdom of Mali, dominating western Africa from 1200 to 1500. The most famous ruler of Mali was **Mansa Musa** (1312-37). Since the Mali rulers had converted to Islam, Mansa Musa made a pilgrimage to Mecca. So splendid was his traveling party that it caught the attention of the non-African world. Mansa Musa took with him sixty thousand men and over ten thousand pounds of gold, and he astonished the Egyptians with his wealth during a stay in Cairo. His capital, Timbuktu, became Africa's most important center of trade. Mansa Musa also encouraged learning in

---

Frumentius, "Apostle to the Abyssinians"

The conversion of Aksum (sometimes known as "Abyssinia") was the result of the ministry of an unlikely missionary named Frumentius. We have little information about his early years. We know that he was a Christian and Roman citizen, probably from Tyre, who was born around A.D. 300. While still a young man, he and his brother were traveling abroad with a relative. Pirates attacked their ship, massacring most of the crew and passengers. The pirates spared the brothers, however, and sold them into slavery in Aksum. Frumentius and his brother, like Joseph in Egypt, rose to high positions in government because of their abilities. As treasurer and secretary to the king of Aksum, Frumentius earned the trust of high officials in government. When the king died, the queen asked Frumentius to help administer the government until the young prince was old enough to rule himself.

While serving the kingdom, Frumentius also promoted his Christian faith. He encouraged Christian merchants from the Roman Empire to hold private services during their visits to Aksum. Under Frumentius's preaching and guidance, the citizens of Aksum also began to convert to Christianity. The young prince whom Frumentius served was probably Ezana, the king who won the great victory over Kush in 330. Ezana seems to have accepted Christianity later in life. Historians note that he did not credit his victory over Kush to pagan gods, as he had done with victories earlier in his reign, but "by the might of the Lord of Heaven Who in heaven and upon earth is mightier than everything which exists." He also praised the "Lord of Heaven, Who . . . to all eternity reigns the Perfect One." Ezana's conversion was perhaps the crowning work of Frumentius, a man since remembered as the "Apostle to the Abyssinians."

his realm, attracting so many scholars to Timbuktu that books began to rival gold as an item for trade.

If rulers such as Mansa Musa enjoyed an exalted status among their people, they also paid a price. A king was supposed to be superior to common men. He often spoke to his court hidden behind a curtain, and no one could watch him eat. Unfortunately, this emphasis on perfection meant that if the king fell seriously ill or became infirm with age, he was expected to commit suicide or be smothered to death.

In the fifteenth century, the Songhai Empire overthrew the Mali Empire. It extended farther than either Ghana or Mali, stretching to the Atlantic in the west and pressing Kanem-Bornu on Lake Chad in the east. Its wealth proved more attractive than its power proved fearsome, however. An invasion by greedy Moroccans in 1591 brought an end to Songhai, and with it, an end to the western African empires.

East African City-States

Along the eastern coast of Africa lay a series of important trading ports, each an independent city-state. These trading ports had existed as early as the days of the Roman Empire, and after the collapse of Rome, they continued to flourish as outlets for gold, iron, ivory, and animal skins to the Arabs and Persians. Prosperous city-states such as Kilwa (in what is today Tanzania) received goods from the tribes and kingdoms in the interior and sold them to Arab sea traders. As a result of this profitable trade, as well as a temperate climate, the seaside city-states grew wealthy and cultured. In the fourteenth century a Muslim visitor wrote, "Kilwa is one of the most beautiful and well-constructed towns in the world." A European visiting in 1500 wrote, "In this land there are rich merchants, and there is much gold and silver and amber and musk and pearls. Those of the land wear clothes of fine cotton and of silk and many fine things, and they are black men."

Although they were independent of each other, the city-states shared a common culture, one that was a mixture of Arab, Persian, and African elements. The architecture, for example, was predominantly Arab. The language of the city-states, **Swahili** (swah HEE lee), was more dominantly native African but contained elements of Arabic, Persian, and Indian. The city-states enjoyed centuries of prosperity, but after 1500 they were crushed between the Europeans attacking the coasts to seize control of trade and the

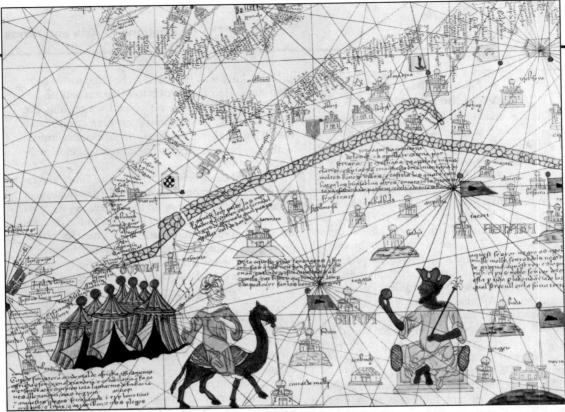

A fourteenth-century map of Africa features Mansa Musa, king of Mali, seated on his throne.

pressure of interior tribes pushing toward the coasts. The Swahili language has survived, however, and the term *Swahili* is used even today to describe the culture of some eastern Africans.

Forest Kingdoms

Providing the goods for the eastern city-states to sell were the "forest kingdoms" of the interior of Africa. Records of these kingdoms are even scarcer than of the central and western empires to the north. The best-known forest kingdoms are those with which Europeans came into contact right after the close of the Middle Ages. Perhaps the most important was the kingdom of Benin, in western Africa (today's southern Nigeria). It arose around 1300 and lasted until the nineteenth century. In addition to being a center for trade, Benin also produced fine statues and relief sculptures in bronze. The metalworking of Benin was in fact one of the highest artistic accomplishments of early African history.

African Culture

Daily life for most Africans centered less on kingdoms and empires than on smaller social organizations. Many Africans knew of little more than life as it existed in their villages. The family, of course, was most basic. Since **polygamy** (marriage of a husband to more than one wife) was common, families were larger and more complex than in Europe at that time. Several families who could trace their descent back to a common ancestor formed a clan. A group of two clans or more, in turn, formed a tribe, or ethnic group. The tribe was perhaps the most important cultural organization. Many African kingdoms were dominated by one ethnic group.

Religious belief in Africa was diverse. As mentioned before, some regions, such as Aksum, embraced Christianity. Unfortunately, as was the case with Roman Catholicism and Eastern Orthodoxy, these African churches declined into superstition and formalism. Islam claimed a large number of converts, but Islamic visitors from the Middle East often complained that much African adherence to their religion was only superficial. Muslim patterns often influenced African kingdoms, however, in structuring their government, organizing their system of education, and establishing their currency.

The majority of the people in sub-Saharan Africa held to traditional tribal religions. In general, these traditional religions taught that there was a high god who created the universe and that below him were a number of lesser gods and the spirits of dead ancestors. Prayers and sacrifices were offered to these gods to ward off illnesses and increase crop yields. In some cases, followers of traditional religions would even offer human sacrifices. During the collapse of the kingdom of Benin, for example, rulers ordered human sacrifices in attempts to please the gods and stave off disaster.

Most Africans relied on farming or herding to sustain themselves and their families. Trade, however, was the mainstay of the African kingdoms. Gold, salt, ivory, and animal skins were perhaps the most valued products. Beginning late in the Middle Ages, African trade began to change. As Europeans began sailing to African ports, the camel caravan trade became less important. More significantly, a new trade opened with Arabs and later with Europeans—the slave trade. Although slavery had existed in Africa for centuries, demand for slaves increased after the Middle Ages. This traffic in human lives unfortunately became the main point of contact for African-European relations after 1500. It eventually led to suffering and exploitation for the African people.

As this survey of early African civilization demonstrates, portrayals of all of Africa as "primitive" are inaccurate. The African kingdoms displayed a level of complexity and organization that compare favorably with contemporary civilizations in Europe and Asia. Like the Asians, though, most Africans (with a few notable exceptions) remained

Three outstanding examples of the metalwork of the African forest kingdom of Benin: a standing figure of a horn-blower (left), a sculpted bronze head (top center), and a leopard (right).

in spiritual darkness apart from the light of the saving truth of God's Word.

Section Review

1. What ancient African civilization conquered the Egyptians for a time? What ancient African civilization converted to Christianity?
2. Name the three western African kingdoms in chronological order. What were the two bases of their wealth?
3. What African kingdom was noteworthy for its fine metalworking in bronze?
4. Name at least three items that were important goods in African trade.

A Glimpse Behind and a Glimpse Ahead

Not since the days of the *Pax Romana* had the contact between the East and West been as great as under the *Pax Mongolica* ("Mongol Peace"). The empire established by Genghis and his successors brought unity to Asia for a time. This made travel safer, improved communications, and encouraged trade. (In 1415, for example, one African kingdom was able to send a giraffe as a gift to the emperor of China. He returned the favor by sending numerous gifts back to Africa in the company of a Chinese fleet.) Many historians believe that it was during this period that such Chinese inventions as gunpowder, the magnetic compass, papermaking, and movable-type printing came to the West. Renewed contact with the East prompted the West to search for new and better ways to reach the lands of silks and spices. Likewise, the Mongol policy of religious toleration encouraged missionaries to travel to the Far East.

Chapter Review

Can You Explain?

topography	Middle Kingdom	movable type	autocratic
joint family	ancestor worship	clan	sub-Saharan Africa
caste system	Chinese characters	shogun	Swahili
world soul	dynastic rule	Bushido	polygamy
wheel of life	*Pax Sinica*	steppes	

Can You Identify?

Aryans	Gupta Empire	Yamato Clan	Golden Horde
Sanskrit	Kalidasa	Jimmu Tenno	Ivan III
Vedas	Muslims (1206)	Shintoism	Tamerlane
Hinduism	Confucianism	Prince Shotoku	Babur
Upanishads	Confucius	Taika Reform	Mughul
Brahman	(K'ung Fu-tzu)	Fujiwara	Akbar
Buddhism	Lao-tzu	Yoritomo	Frumentius
Siddhartha Gautama	Taoism	samurai	Mansa Musa
Four Noble Truths	Shih Huang Ti	Genghis Khan	
Chandragupta Maurya	Wu Ti	Kublai Khan	
Asoka	Li Po	Batu Khan	

Can You Locate?

India	Delhi	Nara	Aksum
Indian Ocean	China	Kyoto	Ghana
Himalayas	Hwang Ho River	Mongolia	Mali
Indus River	Yangtze River	Beijing	Songhai
Ganges River	Gobi Desert	Volga River	Niger River
Khyber Pass	Japan	Moscow	Timbuktu
Mohenjo-Daro	Korea	Afghanistan (modern)	Benin
Harappa	Honshu Island	Kush	

How Much Can You Remember?

1. List three key features that characterized early Indian society.
2. Make a chart of the major Eastern religions (Hinduism, Buddhism, Confucianism, Taoism, and Shintoism). For each religion, list (if possible) its founder, its native territory, and its main teachings.
3. List the Chinese dynasties, and next to each write its main characteristics and/or contributions.
4. Identify the most influential class of people in each of the following civilizations: India, China, and Japan.
5. Identify the key river systems of India and China.
6. List the Mongol rulers. Identify the territory ruled by each one.
7. List three characteristics shared by India, China, and Japan.
8. Why is our knowledge of much of African culture so sketchy? What are three available sources for studying African history?
9. Name the three major religions of Africa.

What Do You Think?

1. How does Hebrews 9:27 refute the Hindu teaching of reincarnation?
2. How does each of the Eastern religions mentioned in this chapter rely upon human effort and works to find happiness in this life and the life to come?
3. The Chinese appointed scholars to government posts. What do you think should be the qualifications of your government officials?
4. What do you think is the most influential class of people in your society today? Explain your answer and relate how it demonstrates the values of your country.

Notes
1. Kenneth Scott Latourette, *A Short History of the Far East* (New York: Macmillan, 1957), p. 158.
2. Lin Yu-t'ang, *The Gay Genius* (New York: Day, 1947), p. 38.
3. Latourette, p. 181.
4. Robert W. July, *A History of the African People*, 2nd ed. (New York: Charles Scribner's Sons, 1974), p. 43.

UNIT III

Writers give various titles to the era in Europe lasting from 500 to 1500. You are probably already familiar with names such as the "Dark Ages," the "Medieval Era," and of course the "Middle Ages." (The term *medieval* itself comes from Latin words meaning "middle age.") The "darkness" of the age lies more in our ignorance of the period than in its real character. The era *is*, however, a "middle" age. The medieval world is the bridge between the ancient world of Greece and Rome, and our modern world. Far from being an unhappy blot on the history of man, the Middle Ages is an important stage in the course of history.

MEDIEVAL CHURCH

Jerome (340?-420)

Patrick (389?-461?)

Boniface (680?-755)

Benedict of Nursia (480?-543?)

Leo I (440-461)

Gregory I (590-604)

HOLY ROMAN EMPIRE

B A R B A R I A N

FRANCE

Clovis (481-511)

Charles Martel (689?-741)

ENGLAND

I N V A S I O N S

★BATTLES

400   500   600   70

THE MEDIEVAL WORLD

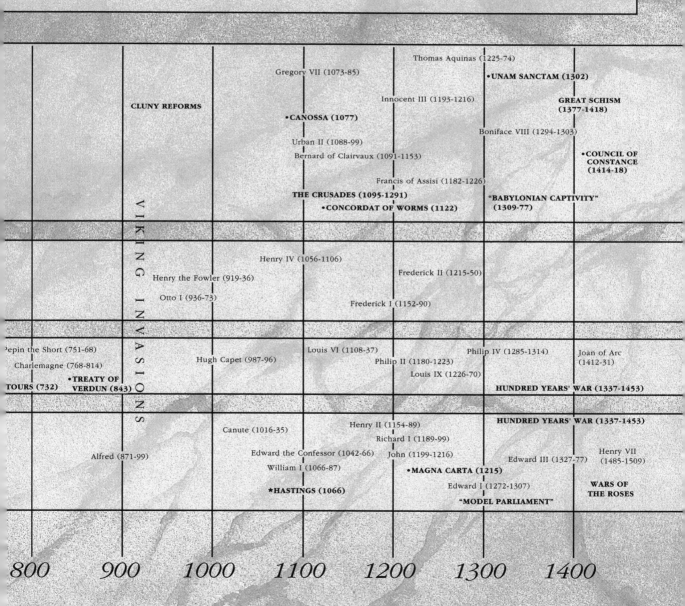

Thomas Aquinas (1225-74)

Gregory VII (1073-85)

•UNAM SANCTAM (1302)

Innocent III (1193-1216)

CLUNY REFORMS

**GREAT SCHISM
(1377-1418)**

•CANOSSA (1077)

Boniface VIII (1294-1303)

Urban II (1088-99)

Bernard of Clairvaux (1091-1153)

•COUNCIL OF
CONSTANCE
(1414-18)

Francis of Assisi (1182-1226)

THE CRUSADES (1095-1291)

"BABYLONIAN CAPTIVITY"
(1309-77)

•CONCORDAT OF WORMS (1122)

Henry IV (1056-1106)

Frederick II (1215-50)

Henry the Fowler (919-36)

Otto I (936-73)

Frederick I (1152-90)

Pepin the Short (751-68)

Louis VI (1108-37)

Philip IV (1285-1314)

Joan of Arc
(1412-31)

Charlemagne (768-814)

Hugh Capet (987-96)

Philip II (1180-1223)

•TREATY OF

Louis IX (1226-70)

TOURS (732)   VERDUN (843)

HUNDRED YEARS' WAR (1337-1453)

HUNDRED YEARS' WAR (1337-1453)

Canute (1016-35)

Henry II (1154-89)

Richard I (1189-99)

Alfred (871-99)

Edward the Confessor (1042-66)

John (1199-1216)

Edward III (1327-77)

Henry VII
(1485-1509)

William I (1066-87)

•MAGNA CARTA (1215)

**WARS OF
THE ROSES**

★HASTINGS (1066)

Edward I (1272-1307)

"MODEL PARLIAMENT"

V I K I N G   I N V A S I O N S

800   900   1000   1100   1200   1300   1400

CHAPTER 7

"Some to pray, some to fight, some to work."

The Making of Medieval Europe

During the Middle Ages, Western society was composed primarily of three classes of people: the clergy, the nobility, and the peasants. Each played an important part in shaping European life and culture. Their roles in society have been described simply: the clergy were called to pray; the nobility, to fight; and the peasants, to work. Accordingly, each group represented an institution of medieval Europe—the church, the feudal system, and the manor.

Growth of the Medieval Church

Outwardly, things looked bleak for western Europe at the outset of the Middle Ages. Rome had fallen; the order and stability she had once provided were gone. Barbarian tribes began to carve out their own kingdoms from the territory once held by the caesars. Monuments of Rome's former grandeur—her aqueducts, amphitheaters, public baths, and roads—were in disrepair. Productivity and trade, as well as thought and learning, were on the decline. The lifestyle of the barbarians was gradually replacing Graeco-Roman culture.

Amidst the confusion and change there remained one stable institution. It represented order and authority and was a means of preserving many elements of classical culture. This institution was the Roman Catholic church. It became the heart of medieval society, influencing almost every aspect of life. As the church grew in numbers and amassed great power, prestige, and wealth, it assumed leadership in political as well as religious matters. The Roman church cared for the poor, sick, and aged and took the leading role in education. (There was little literacy and learning outside the church during the medieval period.)

To fully understand the Roman church, one must examine Christianity and its development in the days of the Roman Empire. The word *church* has two different meanings. Specifically, it refers to a local assembly of believers. There were many such local churches scattered throughout the Roman world. The word also has a universal meaning, namely, the "body of Christ." In this sense, *church* refers to the spiritual body composed of all true believers everywhere who are united by faith in Christ. Scripture presents Jesus as "the head over all things to the church, which is his body, the fullness of him that filleth all in all" (Eph. 1:22-23). Recognizing the unity of their faith, the early Christians described this church as **catholic,** a word meaning simply "universal" or "encompassing all."

In the estimation of most people living in western Europe during the Middle Ages, there was but one church. Unlike the early Christians, Europeans conceived of the church solely as an outward, visible institution, which they called the Catholic church. They viewed the large number of local assemblies merely as part of one large ecclesiastical (religious) organization.

It is difficult to tell precisely when the "universal church" as perceived by Europeans took on the official title of the Roman Catholic church. One thing is certain, however; the *true* universal church and the Roman Catholic church are not synonymous. The former is a spiritual union of all true believers. The latter is an earthly organization; though it has included many believers through the centuries, it is nevertheless the mixed offspring of biblical truth and pagan error. Consequently, the Roman Catholic church in its long history has given increasing importance to the traditions of man at the expense of God's truth. During the Middle Ages, the church was more interested in preserving outward unity among its members than in fostering the inner peace that comes by faith in Jesus Christ. Gradually people began to look to this institutional church for salvation, rather than to the Savior, Jesus Christ.

The Head of the Church

The church and bishop of the city of Rome played key roles in the development of the Roman

Giovanni Serodine, St. Jerome, *Bob Jones University Collection of Sacred Art*

Jerome and the Vulgate

Because most of the people in the Roman Empire spoke Latin, there was a great need for a Latin translation of the Bible. From the earliest days of the church, many people had attempted to meet that need. By the fourth century there had been so many mistakes in translating and copying the Scripture that many Latin manuscripts were no longer reliable. To correct the problem, the bishop of Rome asked a scholar named Jerome (340-420) to revise the Latin text. Jerome agreed to do so and worked for over twenty years, revising existing translations of portions of the Bible and making original translations of other portions. The results of his labor is a translation that came to be called the Latin Vulgate—a name which means "common" or "well known."

Although Jerome's work was also somewhat inaccurate, the Vulgate became the most widely-used Bible of the Middle Ages. Later it became the official Bible of the Roman Catholic church. Through Jerome's work medieval Europe was exposed to the Word of God.

church. As discussed earlier (see p. 114), the church had been organized according to the political and geographical divisions of the Roman Empire. The church of Rome administered one of the five patriarchates, the highest-ranking divisions within the church. (Jerusalem, Antioch, Alexandria, and Constantinople administered the other four.) At first each patriarchate was equal in rank and authority; however, the church of Rome gradually rose to a place of preeminence; its bishop assumed sole authority over the church in the West.

There were many reasons for this rise in power and prestige. The bishop of Rome presided over the largest and wealthiest city in the empire. As the people of the Mediterranean world looked to Rome for political and economic leadership, it was quite natural for them to look to her for spiritual guidance as well. Furthermore, all the other patriarchal bishops were located in the East. With the collapse of the Western Empire in the fifth century, the Roman bishop became one of the few remaining sources of stability in the West. Under Bishop **Leo I** of Rome, the prestige of the office was further enhanced. In 452, when the barbarian Huns threatened the city of Rome, Leo persuaded their leader Attila to spare the city. Leo was hailed as *papa* or **pope** (''Father-Protector''). This title had been applied to other bishops in both the East and the West; by the sixth century, however, it referred almost exclusively to the bishop of Rome.

During the fifth and sixth centuries, the bishops of Rome desired to translate their prestige into authority over all churches. For the most part they were successful. By the end of the sixth century, the bishop of Rome was generally regarded as the pope, the head of the visible church in the West.

To support their claim of primacy (''first in rank''), the bishops of Rome advanced the **Petrine theory.** This theory holds that Christ made Peter the first pope and gave him supreme authority over the church on earth.

> Thou art Peter, and upon this rock I will build my church; and the gates of hell shall not prevail against it. And I will give unto thee the keys of the kingdom of heaven: and whatsoever thou shalt bind on earth shall be bound in heaven: and whatsoever thou shalt loose on earth shall be loosed in heaven.
>
> Matthew 16:18-19

According to this theory, Peter supposedly became the vicar, or substitute, of Christ on earth. As the first bishop of Rome, he transferred his office with all its authority to those who succeeded him.

The Petrine theory rests upon a number of false assumptions. For instance, the Roman church misinterprets Scripture by asserting that in Matthew 16 Christ appointed Peter the first pope. Nowhere

Saints

One of the greatest errors promoted by the Roman church during the Middle Ages was the veneration of ''saints.'' The word *saint* means ''set apart'' or ''holy.'' According to the New Testament, every Christian is a saint through the righteousness of Jesus Christ (e.g., see Rom. 1:7). However, after the time of the apostles, the Roman Catholic church applied the term saint only to Bible characters or to noteworthy Christians (those who supposedly performed miracles or died a martyr's death).

To honor these people, the medieval church held special services and declared certain days to be sacred in their memory. Many of these days—such as St. Patrick's Day and St. Valentine's Day—are still celebrated today. The church taught that dead saints not only help people in time of trouble but also intercede on their behalf before the throne of God. Certain saints became known as ''patron'' saints because they supposedly intercede for a special group of people. The church tells people that they can pray to St. Lucy if they have eye trouble, St. Martha if they need help with cooking, or St. Valentine if they are in love. Likewise, each occupation has a patron saint; for example, St. Sebastian for athletes, St. Hubert for hunters, and St. Matthew for tax collectors. The Roman Catholic church continues to designate saints as patrons for modern times: for example, St. Michael is the patron saint of policemen, St. Joseph of Arimathea is the patron saint of funeral directors, and St. Clare—who died in 1253—is the patron saint of television. Countries, too, have their own special saints: St. George of England, St. Patrick of Ireland, St. Denis of France, and St. Boniface of Germany.

Honored above all saints is Mary, the mother of Christ. To medieval man, Mary was the queen of heaven. Calling her the Mother of God, he prayed to her frequently. He believed that she had never sinned and that she had remained a virgin throughout her life. In fact, Mary became more important in his everyday life than Christ Himself.

in Scripture does Peter ever claim to have such authority. In fact, it is Peter who in I Peter 5:2-3 exhorts God's servants to be of a humble spirit:

> Feed the flock of God which is among you, taking the oversight thereof, not by constraint, but willingly; not for filthy lucre, but of a ready mind; neither as being lords over God's heritage, but being [examples] to the flock.

Another false assumption is that Peter, as the first pope, passed down his authority to succeeding bishops of Rome. There is no historical evidence that Peter ever served as the bishop of the church at Rome.

The Church's Teaching

The Middle Ages is often called an "age of faith." Religion dominated society; nearly every aspect of a person's life was controlled by the Roman church. The power of the Roman bishops grew greater than that of monarchs. And what few bright spots of culture that existed at this time were made possible by the church.

Although there was much church activity, there was little true faith. The church had compromised with the world. Because few people other than the clergy could read and examine the Bible for themselves, the majority of the people placed their trust in the visible church instead of in Christ; they looked to an institution for guidance instead of to the Word of God. Christians began to tolerate spiritual error; without the Bible, they knew no better. Gradually their faith became separated from the truth, and they believed in a distortion of biblical Christianity. This period is perhaps best characterized as an age of spiritual ignorance and darkness.

The Roman church, with the pope as its head, assumed the role of mediator between God and man, between this world and the world to come. It claimed to be the guardian of truth and the final authority in interpreting the Scriptures. The Roman church believed in the inspiration and authority of the Bible as God's Word, but it contended that the traditions of the church had equal authority. As a result, the doctrine and practice of the Roman church was a dangerous mixture of truth and error.

An outgrowth of this mixture of human tradition and Bible doctrine is the **Roman sacramental system.** The Roman church defines a sacrament as a religious act that automatically grants grace (spiritual benefit) by its very performance. The church teaches that the sacraments are necessary for salvation: they were thus made the core of worship and teaching in the Roman church. In addition, the church claims the exclusive right to administer the sacraments and to do so only to those in fellowship with the visible church.

By the end of the twelfth century, the Roman church recognized seven sacraments and taught the following regarding them.

1. *Baptism* initiates one into the church by "washing away original sin."
2. *Confirmation* brings one into full fellowship with the church and confers upon him the Holy Spirit to strengthen his spiritual life.
3. Through *penance* a church member earns forgiveness for sin committed after baptism. Penance includes contrition (sorrow), confession (to a priest), satisfaction (actions done to make amends for sins), and absolution (forgiveness of the guilt of sins by a priest).
4. The *Holy Eucharist* (YOO kur ist), or Holy Communion, is both a sacrament and a sacrifice in which the priest sacrifices Christ anew. During this service, known as the **mass,** the priest supposedly transforms the bread and wine into the actual body and blood of Christ. This "miraculous" change is known as **transubstantiation.**
5. *Matrimony* unites a man and a woman as husband and wife.
6. *Holy Orders* sets an individual apart for the service of the church by ordaining him into the priesthood.
7. *Extreme Unction,* sometimes called the last rites, gives an anointing or blessing to a seriously ill or dying person. Its purpose is to grant absolution from any remaining sin and to offer spiritual comfort.

Through the sacraments, the Roman church wielded great power over the Western world. It maintained that there was no salvation outside the one visible "catholic" church. Because of the Roman sacramental system, salvation became a product of works, not a matter of faith. The church

Francesco Cavazzoni, *Legend of the Finding of the True Cross,*
Bob Jones University Collection of Sacred Art

Medieval Superstitions

Closely associated with the worship of Mary and the veneration of the saints was the importance that the church attached to relics. A relic is an object associated with a saint, such as a piece of clothing or even a part of the saint's body. During the Middle Ages many rulers as well as individual churches made great efforts to secure relics. The reason for such interest was twofold. First, the Roman church taught that mass could not be celebrated unless it were performed upon an altar stone that contained a relic of a saint. Second, the church taught that those who properly viewed and honored the relics would receive time off from their stay in purgatory. This teaching helped to promote pilgrimages to shrines housing the relics of saints.

Many legends and traditions record how these relics supposedly came to be found. One popular story involved the discovery of the true cross when St. Helena, the mother of Emperor Constantine, visited Palestine to visit the holy places. At the emperor's orders, workmen dug up the cave in which Christ's body had been laid. There, so the story goes, they found three crosses and, lying beside them, the wood inscribed with the superscription that Pilate ordered placed over Jesus' cross (Luke 23:38). Not knowing which cross was Christ's, St. Helena had a bishop touch a dead body with each of the crosses in turn. When the touch of the third cross brought the body back to life, she claimed that she had found the true cross. Later, in honor of this "event," the Catholic church established the Feast of the Triumph of the Cross (September 14).

Most of the relics, however, were fakes. Some churches claimed to have Noah's beard, a bit of manna, the bones of Balaam's donkey, and some feathers from the wings of the archangel Michael (to name only a few). In addition, various churches claimed to have relics related to the life of Christ: straw from the manger, some of the wine Jesus made at Cana, drops of sweat from Gethsemane, the crown of thorns, and some of Christ's blood. So many places claimed to have part of the true cross that one sixteenth-century churchman sarcastically remarked that if all the pieces of the "true" cross were gathered together, there would be enough wood to build Noah's ark!

It was such superstition that blinded the minds of the people of the Middle Ages to the truth of God's Word. Against these false teachings the Protestant Reformation directed some of its strongest attacks.

taught that only by participating in the sacraments could one have any hope of heaven, and only through the sacraments could God be properly worshiped. The words of Jesus Christ show the error of this system: "In vain they do worship me, teaching for doctrines the commandments of men" (Matt. 15:9).

Warriors of the Church

In many respects the Roman church was like an army—a religious army that spread across western Europe and held it captive for almost a thousand years. There arose a sharp distinction between the common church members and those who "enlisted" (through Holy Orders) in the special service of the church. The "enlisted" men were called the **clergy;** the "nonenlisted," the **laity.** The medieval world looked upon the clergy as the only servants of the church—its elite "warriors." However, this idea is contrary to God's Word; all Christians are to be active soldiers in the service of God. (See Eph. 6:10-18.)

In any volunteer army, men enlist for many different reasons. So it was in the Roman church. Some wore the uniform but were not in sympathy with the cause; they joined out of ambition, hoping to gain the wealth, luxury, and power that often accompanied prestigious church offices. Others enlisted to find a haven from personal or family problems. Though many had poor motives, some men joined the ranks out of a sincere desire to serve God. Thus the medieval church had both good and bad warriors: the dedicated and the unworthy, the giving and the selfish, those who sought eternal rewards and those who desired material gain, those who furthered the cause of Christ and those who hindered it.

Much like the soldiers in an army, the clergy of the Roman church were organized into different branches of service. The clergy of one branch were called **secular** (from *seculum,* Latin for "world"). These men conducted religious services, administered the sacraments to the laity, and supervised the business and property of the church. Too often, however, the secular clergy mixed the work of the church with worldly pleasure. The Bible admonishes: "No man that warreth entangleth himself with the affairs of this life; that he may please him who hath chosen him to be a soldier" (II Tim. 2:4).

Another of the church's "fighting forces" was the **regular clergy.** This group of clergy renounced the world. Some sacrificed their own personal ambitions in order to maintain an active mission of social service. Others retired to a life of solitude and study. They lived in monastic communities under strict regulations. (The word *regular* comes from the Latin *regula,* meaning "rule.") The most popular system of rules in medieval Europe came from Benedict of Nursia (480?-543?), often called the "Father of Western Monasticism." Characterized by disciple and order, the **Benedictine Rule** strictly regulated the lives of monks. They engaged in such daily activities as manual labor, study, religious services, and prayer. Monks entering this order took vows of poverty, chastity (celibacy), and obedience to the abbot, the leader of the monastery.

The regular clergy, or monks, played an important role in the growth of the medieval church and in the progress of Western society. They were the missionaries of the medieval church. Two of the most renowned medieval missionaries were English monks: **Patrick** (389?-461?), who took the gospel to Ireland, and **Boniface** (680?-755), who was known as the "Apostle of the Germans." Monks also developed new farming techniques and contributed to the preservation of learning by collecting the writings of the ancient world for their libraries.

The "commander in chief" of the medieval "army" was the pope. Perhaps the best representative of the early medieval popes was **Gregory I**

Left: Monks in Cappadocia (modern Turkey) carved monasteries and churches into the rock.
Right: Wall painting from a Cappadocian monastery

Alessandro Magnasco, Monks Before a Fireplace, *Bob Jones University Collection of Sacred Art*

(590-604), called ''the Great.'' He greatly expanded the power and authority of his office. In fact, he is commonly recognized as the first true pope—a title which he, however, disclaimed. Unlike many of his successors, he was a man of deep devotion and fervent piety. Yet, like most of the age in which he lived, Gregory was blinded by superstition and ignorance. He promoted many doctrines that the Roman church later officially embraced: the mass, the equality of tradition and Scripture, the sacrament of penance, and **purgatory** (a place of temporary punishment where souls bound for heaven must go after death to atone for their ''minor'' unconfessed sins or for sins for which they have not done sufficient penance).

Section Review

1. List two reasons for the rise of the bishop of Rome to prominence over other bishops.
2. What term describes a religious act (necessary for salvation) that automatically grants spiritual benefit to the one who does it?
3. List the seven sacraments of the Roman church.
4. Into what two groups were the members of the Roman church divided?
5. Name the two English monks who were known for their missionary activity. (Beside each man's name, write the nationality of the people to whom he ministered.)

A New Western Empire

As the Middle Ages began, western Europe faced widespread invasions, social unrest, and political disorder. The kingdoms established by leaders of Germanic tribes were generally small and lacked strong central governments. By far the most powerful of the Germanic peoples were the **Franks.** They established many independent kingdoms in Gaul (modern-day France). From these Frankish kingdoms arose a new empire that temporarily reunited much of western Europe.

Clovis and the Franks

In 481 **Clovis** became the head of a Frankish tribe in northern Gaul. Through treachery and ex-

ceptional military ability, he conquered other Frankish tribes, uniting them into one kingdom. He soon became known as ''King of the Franks.'' Once Clovis pushed the Visigoths out of southern Gaul, his territory included most of the area of present-day France, which takes its name from the Franks.

Important to the history of both western Europe and the Frankish kingdom was Clovis's ''conversion'' to Christianity. Like the emperor Constantine, Clovis was in danger of being defeated in battle, when he cried out to God for help. He vowed to believe in God and be baptized in His name if granted the victory. Emerging victorious in battle, Clovis remained true to his vow. He even required three thousand of his soldiers to be baptized into the Roman church. The ''conversions'' of Clovis and his men were typical of many medieval conversions made for convenience or by coercion. But Christ reminds us of the fate of such people in Matthew 7:21-23:

> Not every one that saith unto me, Lord, Lord, shall enter into the kingdom of heaven; but he that doeth the will of my Father which is in heaven. Many will say to me in that day, Lord, Lord, have we not prophesied in thy name? and in thy name have cast out devils? and in thy name done many wonderful works? And then will I profess unto them, I never knew you: depart from me, ye that work iniquity.

Clovis gained the support of the Roman church which found him a powerful champion for its cause. Thus began an alliance between the Frankish rulers and the Roman church that lasted for centuries.

The Mayors of the Palace

Clovis died in 511, after having established a strong, unified kingdom. In accordance with Frankish custom, the kingdom was divided among his four sons. Their descendants continued to reign over the Franks well into the eighth century. This royal line of family was known as the **Merovingian House,** taking its name from an early ancestor of Clovis named Merovech. The Merovingian family was plagued by quarrels. The custom of granting a share of the kingdom to each of the king's sons caused brothers to become rivals. Each sought to gain the other's territory, using murder and treachery when necessary. Yet despite the domestic feuds and confusion under the Merovingian kings, Frankish rulers remained in power.

Even so, by the seventh century, they had lost much of their prestige and effectiveness through drunkenness, immoral living, and family strife. They became known as the **''do-nothing kings.''** They reigned, but they did not rule. The real power behind the throne was assumed by the principal palace official, called the *major domo,* the **mayor of the palace.** Originally, the mayor of the palace supervised only the king's household, but he later extended his authority over the financial, military, and administrative functions of government.

Near the end of the seventh century, **Pepin II** became the mayor of one of the stronger Frankish states. He defeated all rival mayors and reunited almost all of the Frankish territories under one rule. The Merovingians still occupied the throne, but they were mere puppets of the mayors. Probably the best remembered of all the mayors of the palace is **Charles Martel,** son of Pepin II. In 732 Charles won his fame by stopping the advance of the Muslims into Europe. He defeated them at the Battle of

The Origin of Names

People have not always had first and last names as we do today. During Bible times, for example, most people had only one name. However, to avoid confusion with another person who had the same name, people often added a second name: for example, Simon the Canaanite (Matt. 10:4) and Alexander the Coppersmith (II Tim. 4:14). During the Middle Ages this practice of adopting a second name continued. Some names were descriptions of a person's appearance or character, such as ''the Pious,'' ''the Fat,'' or ''the Red.'' (The modern English surnames, or last names, Reid, Reed, and Read mean ''Red.'') Some names, such as Cook, Miller, Tailor (Taylor), Carpenter, Smith (from blacksmith, silversmith, coppersmith, etc.), or Clark (from clerk), described a person's occupation. Other names described the place near which a person lived: Stone, Hill, Wood, Ford. Finally, many people took the name of their father as their second name. For example, the son of John became Johnson; the son of Henry became O'Henry; the son of Greg became MacGregor. Later even this naming system became confusing. As a result it became customary for a son to keep his father's last name regardless of his own occupation or where he might live. While most modern surnames still have a particular meaning, for the most part they no longer bear any relationship to one's work, the first name of one's father, or one's place of residence.

Tours in western France. This feat earned him the title *Martel,* or "the Hammer."

Pepin the Short (751-768), like his father Charles Martel, served as mayor of the palace. He possessed all the powers of the king, but he wished to have the title as well. Pepin appealed to the pope, asking him to decide whether he, Pepin, or the "do-nothing" Merovingian king should be the rightful ruler of the Franks. The pope replied that the one who wielded the power should be king. Pepin therefore became king in 751. Three years later the pope traveled to France and sealed the change in ruling families by anointing Pepin "by the grace of God king of the Franks." The **Carolingian House**—named after its most illustrious member, Charlemagne—now officially ruled the Franks.

In return for his support, the pope asked Pepin to protect him against the **Lombards.** They were a Germanic people who through conquest had moved into northern Italy (a region still known today as Lombardy). In the first half of the eighth century, the Lombards had invaded central Italy and had threatened the city of Rome. Coming to the pope's aid, Pepin defeated the Lombards and gave their lands to the pope. Known as the **"Donation of Pepin,"** these lands eventually became the Papal States. The pope, head of the Roman church, became a ruler involved in European politics. His successors continued to rule as kings over this region for the next one thousand years. How different these so-called vicars of Christ were from Jesus Christ, who said, "My kingdom is not of this world" (John 18:36).

The Empire of Charlemagne

Charlemagne's Character

When Pepin the Short died in 768, his sons Carloman and Charles succeeded him as corulers of the Frankish realm. After only a few years, Carloman died, and Charles became the sole ruler of the kingdom of the Franks. Charles was not only the greatest of the Carolingian kings but also one of the outstanding figures of the Middle Ages. His character and accomplishments won him the title **Charlemagne,** (SHAR luh mane) or "Charles the Great."

> ### The Mayor of the Palace
>
> The real power and authority in the kingdom lay in the hands of the chief officer of the court, the so-called Mayor of the Palace, and he was at the head of affairs. There was nothing left [for] the King to do but to be content with his name of King, his flowing hair, and long beard, to sit on his throne and play the ruler, to give ear to the ambassadors that came from all quarters, and to dismiss them, as if on his own responsibility, in words that were, in fact, suggested to him, or even imposed upon him. He had nothing that he could call his own beyond this vain title of King. . . . The Mayor of the Palace took charge of the government and of everything that had to be planned or executed at home or abroad.
>
> —Einhard

According to Einhard, Charlemagne's close friend and biographer, "Charles was large and strong, and of lofty stature, though not disproportionately tall (his height is well known to have been seven times the length of his foot)." Undoubtedly his "lofty stature" did not come from his father, Pepin the Short, but from his mother, who was called *Berte au grand pied,* or "Big-Foot" Bertha. Einhard further described Charlemagne as

> stately and dignified, whether he was standing or sitting; although his neck was thick and somewhat short, and his belly rather prominent; but the symmetry of the rest of his body concealed these defects. His gait was firm, his whole carriage manly, and his voice clear, but not so strong as his size led one to expect. . . . He abominated drunkenness in anybody, much more in himself and those of his household.

Charlemagne possessed many virtues, but he was not without his vices. On one occasion he is reported to have beheaded several thousand prisoners in cold blood. In addition, his personal life was marred by sin. He had little regard for the sanctity of marriage; he married, divorced, and remarried many times.

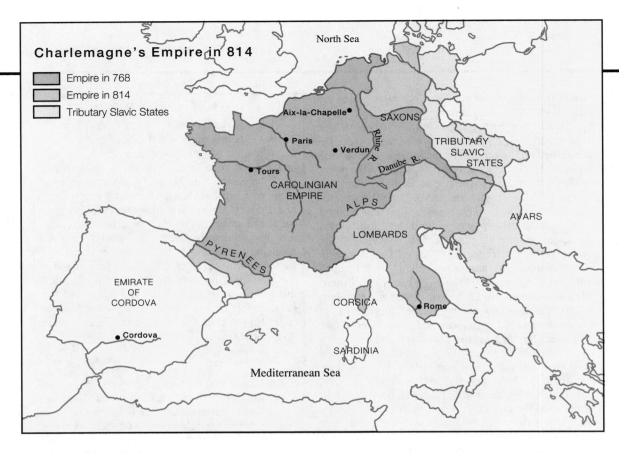

Charlemagne's Empire in 814

- Empire in 768
- Empire in 814
- Tributary Slavic States

North Sea

Aix-la-Chapelle

SAXONS

Paris

Verdun

Rhine R.

TRIBUTARY SLAVIC STATES

Danube R.

Tours

CAROLINGIAN EMPIRE

ALPS

AVARS

LOMBARDS

PYRENEES

EMIRATE OF CORDOVA

CORSICA

Rome

Cordova

SARDINIA

Mediterranean Sea

Charlemagne's Conquests

The Frankish kingdom reached its peak under Charlemagne's rule (768-814). As his father had done, Charlemagne rescued Rome, which had again been invaded by Lombards. He took for himself the title "King of the Lombards." With this foe subdued, he directed his military campaigns against the Saxons, a Germanic tribe in northern Europe. After thirty years of bitter struggle he conquered this people also. Near the Danube River in central Europe, he defeated the Avars, a nomadic people similar to the Huns. And in the south, he drove the Spanish Muslims back across the Pyrenees. By the time of his death, Charlemagne had created an empire that stretched over most of western Europe. He laid the foundation for the modern European nations of France, Germany, and Italy.

Charlemagne divided his empire into hundreds of administrative districts, or counties. He appointed counts to supervise each district. They administered justice, maintained the peace, and raised an army in times of war. To ensure the enforcement of his policies on the local level, Charlemagne created the office of *missi dominici*, or the king's envoys (messengers). He sent pairs of these messengers into the districts to investigate local conditions and to hear complaints leveled against any of the local officials. These *missi dominici* then sent back written reports to Charlemagne.

Because such officials were subject to bribery, Charlemagne chose only men of proven ability and character. Furthermore, he stated that no *missi dominici* could serve in any district in which he held property, nor could two serve together for more than one year.

Charlemagne's Crowning

Since the days of the Roman emperors, no one man in the West had ruled as much territory as Charlemagne. Western Europe looked upon him as another Constantine, ruling and protecting both church and state. While Charlemagne was attend-

Charlemagne

A Revival of Learning

Charlemagne's love of learning prompted him to promote education throughout his empire. His royal court at Aachen (Aix-la-Chapelle; AYKS lah shah PEL) became the leading center of learning in the realm. There he assembled the best scholars of western Europe. The most distinguished of these was **Alcuin** (AL kwin) from York, England. He took charge of the palace school and trained the king's children as well as the children of other noble families. Alcuin also taught the king. Einhard wrote of Charlemagne's "education":

> The King spent much time and labor . . . studying rhetoric, dialectics, and especially astronomy; he learned to reckon [calculate], and used to investigate the motion of the heavenly bodies most curiously, with an intelligent scrutiny. He also tried to write, and used to keep tablets and blanks in bed under his pillow, that at leisure hours he might accustom his hand to form the letters; however, as he did not begin his efforts in due season, but late in life, they met with ill success.

Perhaps it was under Alcuin's influence that Charlemagne developed his deep concern for a better-educated clergy. He encouraged the church to establish schools to upgrade the literacy of the priests and monks. In a letter to church leaders, Charlemagne set forth what has been called the charter of education for the Middle Ages. In it, he said:

> And hence we have begun to fear that, if [the clergy's] skill in writing is so small, so also their power of rightly comprehending the Holy Scriptures may be far less than is befitting; and it is known to all that, if verbal errors are dangerous, errors of interpretation are still more so. We exhort you, therefore, not only not to neglect the study of letters but to apply yourselves thereto with that humble perseverance which is well-pleasing to God, that so you may be able with greater ease and accuracy to search into the mysteries of the Holy Scriptures.

Charlemagne's educational reforms renewed interest in the Bible and the works of classical writers. For several centuries in western Europe

ing a church service in Rome on Christmas Day 800, the pope placed a crown on his head and proclaimed him Roman emperor. The assembly present cried out: "To Charles Augustus, crowned by God, the great and pacific [peaceful] emperor of the Romans, life and victory."

Although the title "emperor" did little to increase the actual power of Charlemagne, it did have an important impact upon later medieval history. His empire fell apart after his death, but Charlemagne's crowning had revived the idea of a restored Roman Empire which would again unite the territories of western Europe. This crowning also raised a serious question: whose authority is supreme—the state's or the church's? Though Charlemagne's authority was unquestioned in his day, popes later insisted that their authority superseded that of the kings, pointing out that a pope had crowned Charlemagne. They claimed the power not only to confirm kings but also to depose them. This struggle for supremacy between the popes and the kings culminated during the late Middle Ages.

there had been little interest in learning; few people could read or write. During that time many ancient manuscripts were lost or damaged; others were full of copyist's mistakes. One of the most important contributions of Charlemagne's reign was the rediscovery and preservation of these ancient works. In addition, God used the Carolingian scholars to preserve copies of the Bible.

Monasteries were the primary centers for studying, copying, and preserving ancient manuscripts; they were the "printing houses" and libraries of the Middle Ages. Monks undertook the painstaking process of making handwritten copies of earlier works. During this period, they developed a new and beautiful style of handwriting known as the **Carolingian minuscule.** This clean and simple writing style became the model for much of our

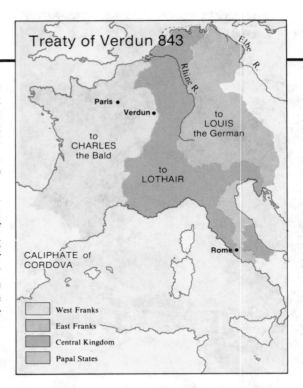

Treaty of Verdun 843

- West Franks
- East Franks
- Central Kingdom
- Papal States

This ivory carving from the ninth century illustrates the brief revival of interest in the arts that took place in Charlemagne's time.

"lowercase" writing today. Many manuscripts were illuminated with colorful illustrations.

Disintegration of Charlemagne's Empire

Although the effects of this renewed interest in learning lasted for centuries, Charlemagne's impressive empire deteriorated rapidly. Within a century after his death, the Carolingian Empire had collapsed, torn by civil war and pillaged by foreign invaders.

Problems From Within

When Charlemagne died in 814, his empire passed to his only surviving son, Louis the Pious. During Louis's reign, a bitter rivalry broke out among his sons over which portion of the empire each would inherit. Even before Louis's death this rivalry led to civil war. The Bible tells us, "A brother offended is harder to be won than a strong city: and their contentions are like the bars of a castle" (Prov. 18:19).

After years of fighting, the brothers met at the city of Verdun, to settle their differences. In the **Treaty of Verdun** (843), they agreed to split the empire into three separate kingdoms: **Charles the Bald** received West Frankland; **Louis the German,**

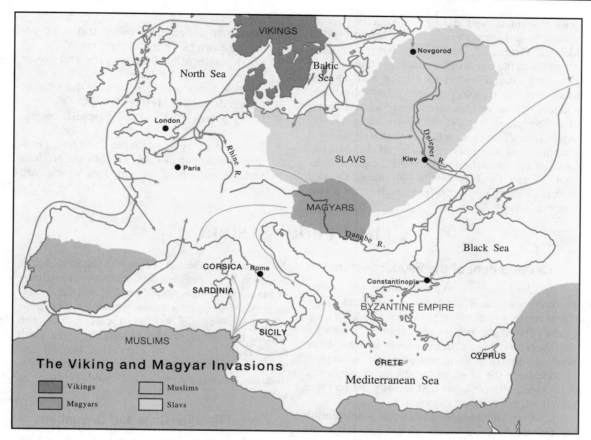

The Viking and Magyar Invasions

Vikings
Magyars
Muslims
Slavs

East Frankland; and the eldest brother, **Lothair,** retained the title of emperor and ruled the land between his brother's kingdoms. (See the map on p. 190.) Notice how closely the modern states of France, Germany, and Italy correspond to these divisions.

When Lothair died, Charles and Louis wasted little time in seizing portions of his kingdom. (Part of this territory is still know today as Lorraine, "Lothair's kingdom.") Political fragmentation characterized the last days of the empire as the Carolingian rulers persisted in their family strife. In addition, the successors to Charlemagne's grandsons were weak and incompetent rulers, as is demonstrated by the disrespectful surnames they were given; Louis the Stammerer, Charles the Fat, Louis the Child, and Charles the Simple.

Problems from Without

During the ninth and tenth centuries, the Carolingian Empire offered little resistance to the foreign invaders that beset it on every side. From North Africa came Muslim raiders who devastated the Mediterranean coast of Europe. They captured Sardinia, Corsica, and Sicily and pillaged southern Italy. From the East came the **Magyars,** a group of Asiatic nomads who later became known as the Hungarians. They swept into the Danube region of southeastern Europe, where they ravaged the eastern borders of the empire.

The most feared invaders were the **Vikings,** or Norsemen. These Germanic tribes swooped down from the north out of the lands known today as Norway, Sweden, and Denmark. Fearless warriors, skilled seamen, and daring adventurers, Viking sailors braved the waters of the Atlantic to sail to Iceland, Greenland, and North America. Some sailed down the rivers of Russia, while others sailed along the coastal waters of Europe and into the Mediterranean region, plundering coastal villages and towns. The Vikings struck terror into the hearts of the people of Europe; their swift raids left villages aflame, homes and crops destroyed, and churches and monasteries ransacked. Few in Europe felt safe from the attacks of the dreaded Norsemen. "From the fury of the Northmen, O Lord deliver us" was a prayer offered in churches across western Europe.

Section Review

1. What man united the Frankish tribes and became known as "King of the Franks"?
2. What palace official became the real power behind the Frankish throne?
3. At what battle and in what year did Charles Martel defeat the Muslims?
4. Under whose rule did the Frankish empire reach its peak?
5. Name the treaty that split the Carolingian Empire into three parts, and identify the brothers and the portion of the kingdom which each received.

The Feudal System

Development of the Feudal System

As Charlemagne's empire disintegrated, powerful nobles replaced the weak Carolingian kings. There arose a new political system in which local rulers offered the people protection in return for their services. This system, known as **feudalism,** was the form of government prevalent in western Europe from the ninth to the thirteenth centuries. It provided relative order and security until a more structured government emerged.

Land was the basis of wealth and power during the Feudal Age. Governing power formerly exercised by a central government gradually passed into the hands of landholding nobles, called **lords.** In theory, the king was the supreme lord, holding all the land in the kingdom by right of conquest or inheritance. But when foreign raiders threatened his territory, the king had to rely on the help of powerful nobles. In return for their services (usually military aid), the king granted them the use of landed estates. The land grants became known as **fiefs,** or in Latin, *feudum,* from which our word *feudal* comes.

A fief could be extremely large or very small. The recipient of such an estate became the king's **vassal** (servant). A vassal did not own the land, or fief, but held it as payment for service rendered to the king. Originally, the king granted his vassal the use of a fief for as long as the vassal lived. When

the vassal died, the fief reverted to the king. Later, however, many fiefs became hereditary, remaining in the hands of the vassal's eldest son upon payment of a fee. Often a vassal parceled out portions of his fief to gain the services of lesser nobles, who became his vassals, and he, in turn, their lord. Each new vassal could likewise partition his fief and become a lord. This process, called **subinfeudation,** could continue until a fief could no longer be subdivided.

Feudal Relationships and Obligations

At the heart of feudalism was the relationship that existed between a lord and his vassal. Solemn ceremonies symbolized the "contract" entered into by these two nobles. **Homage** was the ceremony by which a man became a vassal and thus eligible for a fief. This ceremony usually took place in the lord's court with many witnesses present. The would-be vassal knelt before the lord and placed his hands between his lord's hands; he then professed himself to be the "lord's man." With a ceremonial kiss, the lord recognized him as his vassal. After performing homage, the vassal took an oath of fealty (fidelity), pledging faithfulness and loyalty to his lord. In turn, the lord handed to the vassal a small stick, lance, or clod of earth. By this symbolic act, known as **investiture,** the lord gave to the vassal the right of use of a fief.

In addition to the grant of a fief, the lord was obligated to guarantee his vassal protection and justice. The vassal's primary duty was to provide military service for his lord. He was expected to furnish a specified number of knights (for at least forty days a year) to assist the lord in his battles. Not all of the vassal's responsibilities were military, however. A vassal also agreed to supply financial payments, called **aids,** on special occasions such as when his lord's eldest son became a knight or when the lord's eldest daughter was married. Vassals attended the lord's court to give counsel and to assist in the administration of justice. In addition, the vassal was obligated to pay a ransom if his lord were captured in war. Although a vassal's duties were many and varied, he benefited from this feudal relationship. A fief gave a vassal authority and power; the greater the size of the fief, the greater the vassal's prestige. Often, through subinfeudation, a noble became a vassal of more than one lord. This increased his dignity, but it also increased his obligations. It often led to conflicting loyalties, as when lords warred against one another. In the same way, problems arise when men try to serve two spiritual masters. It is indeed true, as Christ said, that ''no man can serve two masters:

for either he will hate the one, and love the other; or else he will hold to the one, and despise the other'' (Matt. 6:24).

The Life of the Nobility

The Castle

The **castle** was the center of life for the nobility. It was not only the lord's home but also the local jail, the treasury, the armory, the court, and the seat of government. Modern books and films have ro-

Bamberg Castle in England

manticized daily life in the medieval castle. Yet, as impressive as feudal castles may have appeared from a distance, they were often damp, cold, musty, and dark. Tapestries and flowers were used to add warmth and cheer to the otherwise bleak surroundings. Feudal castles had few of the comforts and luxuries that we associate with the elegant, aristocratic palaces of a later day.

Castles were built primarily for defensive purposes. The word *castle* comes from the Latin word *castellum,* meaning ''fort'' or ''fortress.'' At first castles were often just wooden blockhouses set on high mounds surrounded by a stockade and a ditch (moat). It was not until about the tenth century that castles assumed the features that most people think of today: massive stone walls, towering battlements, wide moats, and wooden drawbridges. It was the lord's responsibility to protect the inhabitants of the surrounding countryside. When invaders threatened the land, the local villagers fled into the safe confines of their lord's castle. High atop the castle's battlement, defenders could repel an attack with spears and arrows, or by pouring molten metal or dropping large boulders on the heads of attackers.

Knighthood

Also important to the protection of life and property during the Middle Ages was the **knight.** In the early Middle Ages, anyone brave and strong enough could become one. Later, however, knighthood was restricted to the nobility.

The preparation for knighthood was long and hard. At age seven, a boy's initiation formally began. At that time his parents placed him in the care of a knight (often an uncle) for special training. For the next several years the youth, or **page,** developed both his mind and body. He studied academic subjects such as religion, science, and history; he also spent time learning to fence (to fight with a sword), to ride a horse, and to hunt with falcons and dogs. In his midteens, the page became a **squire,** the personal servant of a knight. His training became more intense and his responsibilities greater. He cared for the knight's armor, weapons, and horse; he dressed his knight each morning and waited on him, his family, and guests as they ate.

When he was about twenty-one, a squire became eligible for knighthood. Occasionally a man was knighted instantly on the battlefield in recognition of unusual bravery. More often, however, a squire received knighthood in a special religious ceremony. The squire spent the night before the ceremony praying before his armor, which lay on the altar of the church. The ceremony climaxed the next morning when the squire, kneeling before an elder knight or priest, was dubbed, or tapped on the shoulders with the flat side of a sword's blade.

Italian armor (left) and a French helmet (right) of the late Middle Ages

The ceremony often ended with a display of the young man's knightly skills.

The Code of Chivalry

The knight promised to live by a strict code of behavior, called the "code of chivalry." The word *chivalry* comes from the French word for *horseman* (i.e., a knight); it is closely related to the English word *cavalry*. A true knight was expected to be brave in battle, skillful with his weapons, honest and generous and loyal to his lord. He never attacked an unarmed knight but gave him the opportunity to put on his armor before engaging him in battle. Likewise, it was improper for an entire company of knights to attack a single knight; they were to fight him one at a time.

The influence of the Roman church gradually pervaded the knightly code. According to the twelfth-century philosopher John of Salisbury, knights were to "defend the Church, assail infidelity, venerate the priesthood, protect the poor from injuries, pacify the province, pour out their blood for their brothers, and if need be lay down their lives."[1] The church tried not only to improve the conduct of the knights but also to place limitations on feudal warfare through decrees known as the **Peace of God** and the **Truce of God.** By the Peace of God the church forbade the pillage of her property and extended protection to all noncombatants in society. The Truce of God sought to limit fighting to specified weekdays by forbidding combat from Wednesday evening to Monday morning. Although often ineffective in enforcing these decrees, the church did help to improve the harsh and brutal conditions of the feudal period.

Tournaments and Jousts

Even in times of peace, the knight maintained his skills. He often went hunting and fishing, but his real love was fighting. When peaceful conditions kept him at home, he sometimes kept fit by staging a mock war, called a **tournament.** The typical tournament included two types of contests: the *joust* and the *melee.* Jousting was a competition between two knights on horseback who charged at each other, carrying lances with which each tried to unseat his opponent. The melee was a team competition. At a signal, the two sides rushed at each other on horseback and fought what amounted to a full-scale battle. Often they fought within a fenced area so that the battle would remain compact and thus more intense and exciting to watch. The weapons were usually blunted, but there were nonetheless many injuries and even some deaths. One historian states that the tournaments "satisfied the craving of both fighters and spectators for 'red-blooded' excitement in a manner that reminds one of the Roman gladiatorial games, the Spanish bullfight, the rougher aspects of American football, and prize fighting."[2]

Section Review

1. What was land granted by kings to nobles in return for their service called?
2. What place was the center of life for the nobility?
3. What two "stages" of preparation did a young man go through to become a knight?
4. Name the strict code that governed knightly behavior.
5. What two types of activities were part of the typical tournaments among knights?

The Manor

Role of the Manor

The **manor** was the home for the vast majority of people living in western Europe during the Middle Ages. It was the center of medieval society, a self-contained farming community controlled by a lord and farmed by peasants. The manorial system arose out of the economic and social conditions of the early medieval period; during that time trade decreased, the size and number of towns diminished, and money was rarely used as a medium of exchange. Most Europeans moved to large estates, where they relied on their own labor to produce their daily needs.

Because of the lack of trade, the manor had to be largely self-sufficient. Each manor usually had its own priest and skilled workers. Craftsmen made such items as furniture, shoes, tools, and woven cloth. The laborers on each manor produced their own food, built their own homes, and made their own clothing. They grew crops and raised cattle, sheep, and pigs; they constructed bridges and roads. About the only items the manor could not provide for itself were salt, iron, and tar, all of which had to be imported.

Manors varied from one locality to another. Factors such as climate and soil influenced the quality of life on the manor; the people on one manor might prosper, while those on another might barely eke out a living. Some manors were large estates composed of many villages and thousands of acres of land. Others were simply small villages with only a few hundred acres. Likewise there was

The manor was the center of medieval society.

a wide range in the population on the manors, from a dozen families to more than one hundred.

Description of the Manor

The center of a typical manor was the village, usually located near a stream or at a crossroad. Here peasants lived in clusters of small cottages, which were one- or two-room huts with thatched roofs and walls of mud and straw. The peasants enjoyed few comforts or possessions; their homes had dirt floors, few if any windows (glass was a luxury), no chimneys, and meager furnishings. Next to each cottage was a small plot on which a peasant family could plant a vegetable garden and build a stable to house any livestock it might own. It was not uncommon for the livestock to be housed inside the cottage.

Two buildings dominated the manor: the lord's residence and the village church. Depending upon the size of the manor, the lord's dwelling might be a castle or a simple wooden building known as the manor house. In either case, it was situated on a high hill or some other defensible site. Usually the village was close by, for when enemies attacked, the villag-

ers sought refuge inside the fortified walls of the lord's house. Not far from the manor house stood the village church and the priest's home. The church steeple towered above the manor, directing the villagers' gaze heavenward. The church was not only the place of worship but also the place for village meetings, court sessions, and social gatherings.

Activities were not confined to the village. Villagers obtained building material and firewood from nearby forests and grazed their livestock in the pastures. They fished in streams and ponds and hunted for game in the manor's woodlands. The lord and villagers divided the cultivated fields on the manor. One-sixth to one-third of the arable land was set apart as the lord's **demesne** (dih MAYN)—the land reserved for the lord; the rest was alloted to the villagers. The village peasants worked together to plow the land, sow the seed, and harvest the crops; no one peasant had enough equipment or oxen to do the job alone. The open fields were divided into long, narrow strips. In each field, a villager held one or more of these strips. Often the lord's demesne was not a separate field, but the most fertile strips in each open field.

During the early Middle Ages, most manors employed a **two-field system** of farming. Villagers planted crops on only half of the cultivated land, leaving the other half to lie fallow for a year to recover its fertility. The following year, they reversed the procedure.

Later, a **three-field system** came into common use, especially in northern Europe. This system established a pattern of rotating planting among three fields. In the spring the peasants planted one field with barley, oats, or beans; in the fall they planted a second field with rye or wheat. In the meantime the third field was left fallow. This rotation of crops increased the productivity of the land, because one crop put back into the soil the nutrients another took out.

People on the Manor

The population on even the smallest manors reflected the medieval class structure: clergy, nobility, and peasantry. Throughout the Middle Ages the highest social status belonged to the clergy and the nobility. Every person on the manor, regardless of his class, had specific duties. The parish priest cared for the religious needs of the villagers, while the local lord provided protection and justice. Both the clergy and the nobility relied upon the support and provision of the peasants.

A small percentage of the people on the manor were **freemen.** These were the more privileged peasants who served as manorial officials, or provided skilled labor, such as blacksmiths, millers, and carpenters. Some freemen owned their own land, while others rented land from the lord of the manor. Freemen did not have the same obligations as the average peasant. For example, freemen were often exempted from laboring in the lord's fields. Furthermore, they had the freedom to leave the manor. Although he had greater privileges, the freeman's living conditions differed little from those of the average peasant.

The majority of those living on a manor were the peasants known as the **serfs** (from the Latin *servus,* which means "slave"). The status of the serf was midway between the ancient slave and the medieval freeman. He had the use of a small por-

Pieter Brueghel (the Elder), The Harvesters, *Metropolitan Museum of Art, New York*

tion of land and had opportunity to provide for himself and his family. Unlike the freeman, the serf was bound to the land on which he was born; he was not free to leave the manor without the lord's permission.

In return for the use of the lord's land and his protection, the serfs owed the lord various services and payments. These services took the form of labor; serfs were bound to work on the lord's demesne. They plowed his fields, sowed and harvested his crops, gathered his hay, and cared for his cattle. The lord might call upon them to build fences, clear woodland, or dig a moat for his castle. Usually the serfs devoted two or three days a week to working for their lord, an obligation known as **week work.**

Serfs also had to pay the lord—usually in produce—for the use of his land and its resources. Serfs gave the lord a portion of their crops, a share of the fish caught in the village stream, cheese in exchange for pasturing their cattle in the lord's fields, and a share of the firewood cut. In addition, the serfs were obligated to use the village mill and bakery owned by the lord. The lord took part of their grain and flour as a fee.

Life on the Manor

The only world most peasants ever knew was the manor on which they were born. It was their home: the place of their work, their worship, and their death—just as it had been for their ancestors before them. In fact, a peasant seldom traveled more than twenty miles from the place where he was born.

Each year there were two major holy days (holidays)—Easter and Christmas. Christmas brought a two-week celebration (alluded to in our carol ''The Twelve Days of Christmas'') and a great banquet at the lord's house. There were also other holidays, such as Mayday (in the spring) and Harvest Day (much like our Thanksgiving).

Despite the holidays, life was hard for the peasant on the manor. He worked from sunrise to sunset. Yet despite all his labors, the average peasant barely managed to subsist. He suffered from both poverty and misery. What little money he could earn usually went either to the lord in rent and fees or to the church in tithes. Famines plagued the land and constant feudal wars ruined crops and killed livestock. Strenuous labor, filthy living conditions, poor diet, and lack of medical care combined to give the average peasant a very short lifespan.

Section Review
1. Where did the vast majority of people in Europe live during the Middle Ages?
2. What two buildings dominated the manor?
3. Name the term that describes the peasant laborers on the manor.
4. Why did the peasants work for their lord and give him part of the crops they raised?

A Glimpse Behind and a Glimpse Ahead

This chapter is the story of everyday life in the early Middle Ages. It was an age dominated by the church, feudalism, and the manor. With the exception of Charlemagne's brief empire, this age experienced little political unity. For the most part, Europe was under the strong authority of the Roman Catholic church. But following the collapse of the Carolingian Empire, several feudal princes began to amass power and to slowly build strong feudal kingdoms in the midst of Europe's political disorder. These princes would one day rival the Roman church in influence and openly challenge the authority of the pope.

Chapter Review

Can You Explain?

catholic	purgatory	investiture	manor
pope	"do-nothing kings"	aids	demesne
Roman sacramental system	feudalism	castle	two-field system
mass	lord	knight	three-field system
transubstantiation	fief	page	freemen
clergy	vassal	squire	serfs
laity	subinfeudation	chivalry	week work
	homage	tournament	

Can You Identify?

Leo I	Franks	Lombards	Louis the German
Petrine theory	Clovis	Donation of Pepin	Lothair
seven sacraments	Merovingian House	Charlemagne	Magyars
secular clergy	mayor of the palace	*missi dominici*	Vikings
regular clergy	Pepin II	800	Peace of God
Benedictine Rule	Charles Martel	Alcuin	Truce of God
Patrick	732	Carolingian minuscule	
Boniface	Pepin the Short	Treaty of Verdun (843)	
Gregory I	Carolingian House	Charles the Bald	

Can You Locate?

Rome	Lombardy	Verdun	Divisions after the Treaty of Verdun
Gaul	Aachen (Aix-la-Chapelle)	Charlemagne's empire	
Tours			

How Much Do You Remember?

1. What were the three institutions of medieval Europe? What social class represented each? What were their roles in society?
2. What did the word *church* mean to the majority of the people living during the Middle Ages?
3. What were the two divisions of the clergy? What were the duties of each?
4. List the names of men who filled the office of mayor of the palace. What role did they play in the history of the Franks?
5. Why was Charlemagne called "the Great"? How did he organize his realm? What were his contributions to the advancement of learning?
6. What three groups invaded Europe in the ninth and tenth centuries? What group caused the most damage? How?
7. What was the difference between a freeman and a serf?

What Do You Think?

1. Does the fact that the church was the dominant influence on medieval life make the Middle Ages an "age of faith"?
2. Why was it difficult for a person to know the gospel during the Middle Ages?
3. According to the Roman church, how is a person saved? Compare your answer with what the Bible teaches in Titus 3:5 and Ephesians 2:8-9.
4. Read Hebrews 10:10-14. How do these verses refute the Roman church's teaching concerning the mass?
5. Feudalism has been described as "chaos roughly organized." Is this description accurate? Explain your answer.

Notes

1. Sidney Painter, *Feudalism and Liberty* (Baltimore: Johns Hopkins Press, 1961), p. 93.
2. Loren C. MacKinney, *The Medieval World* (Reinhart and Co., 1938), p. 230.

"I am the Sun; the emperor, the moon."

Princes and Popes

The collapse of the Carolingian Empire and the declining influence of the church made the ninth century in western Europe a period of widespread political chaos and moral corruption. Reforms beginning in the tenth century, however, strengthened the church and led to greater religious and temporal power for the papacy. Able German rulers revived the imperial tradition by establishing the Holy Roman Empire. In England and France feudal kings gradually increased in influence over the noblemen. These changes brought about a struggle for power in Europe. Popes clashed with kings, and kings challenged nobles as each party sought to make its power supreme. Yet in the midst of the struggle, these rivals joined forces to rescue the Holy Land from the Muslims. Their efforts, called the Crusades, helped bring western Europe out of the "Dark Ages."

Reforms in the Church

By crowning Charlemagne emperor, Pope Leo III established an important precedent. Later popes claimed that this practice demonstrated their superiority over civil rulers. In Charlemagne's day this supremacy existed only in theory. During the political disorder that followed the collapse of Charlemagne's empire, however, the papacy had opportunity to make real its claim of supreme political power. Nevertheless, the church was slow in asserting its leadership. Corrupt popes and worldly clergy caused the Roman church to lose much of its prestige and influence. The reforms of the eleventh through thirteenth centuries restored the church's prestige and brought the papacy to the height of its power.

Need for Reform

During the ninth century and the early part of the tenth, the Roman church had sunk deep in moral corruption. It amassed great wealth as churchmen neglected their religious duties for temporal gain. When the political conditions in Europe became worse, the church needed protection for its large landholdings. The greatest threat to the church's possessions was the Viking raiders. Churchmen secured protection from these and other enemies by entering into feudal relationships. They became vassals; their loyalties were divided between the church and feudal lords. Some kings and nobles were claiming that it was their right not only to appoint church officials but also to invest them with their religious authority—a practice known as **lay investiture.**

Before long it became commonplace for lay lords to appoint men with few spiritual qualifications to church offices in return for their political loyalty and financial favors. Unscrupulous men, enticed by the wealth and power of high church office, bought and sold church positions. The condition of the papacy was little better. Inept and immoral men filled the office, openly committing great wickedness and bringing disgrace upon the church. In addition, striving factions of nobles in Rome squabbled over the appointment of popes.

The scandalous conditions in the church prompted a reform movement. It began in 910 at a monastery in Cluny, France, and spread quickly throughout the Roman church. Members of this movement exposed and sought to remedy abuses within the church. They introduced measures to forbid **simony** (the buying and selling of church offices), to free the church from secular control resulting from lay investiture, and to restore the dignity and authority of the papacy.

One of the most influential of the reforming monastic orders was the **Cistercians** (sih STUR shunz). Monks of this order adopted lives of seclusion and strict discipline. They wore rough garments, abstained from meats, and worked hard in the fields. This order was made popular by its most zealous member, **Bernard of Clairvaux** (1091-

Opposite Page: The Notre Dame Cathedral in Paris

1153). A man of deep piety and sincere devotion, Bernard demonstrated by his life the genuineness of his religious convictions. He was an outspoken critic of worldliness in the church and in society.

Rivalry between Pope and Emperor

A primary goal of church reform was to rescue the papacy from the state of weakness and corruption into which it had fallen. In 1059, the **College of Cardinals** was created so that churchmen, and not the Roman nobles or German kings, could choose the popes. After almost two centuries of worthless popes, men of moral strength and able leadership restored dignity to and increased the power of the papal office. In fact, the papacy soon became the driving force of the reform movement.

Probably the greatest of the reforming popes was **Gregory VII** (1073-85). As a Benedictine monk, Gregory had been a leading advocate of papal reform. He used his influence as pope to curb other abuses in the church and to strengthen his office. Gregory believed that the church was superior to the state; therefore, he wanted to free the church from secular control. This meant doing away with lay investiture.

In 1075 Gregory formally prohibited (on pain of excommunication) any layman from appointing a person to church office or investing a person with spiritual authority. The German emperor **Henry IV** refused to obey, insisting upon his right to appoint the bishops in his realm. He declared that Gregory was not pope but a "false monk." In retaliation, Gregory excommunicated him and freed Henry's subjects from their oaths of loyalty. The struggle between the two might have continued, but growing discontent among the German nobles prompted Henry to seek the pope's forgiveness. In the winter of 1077 at Canossa (a castle in northern Italy), the penitent Henry stood barefoot in the snow for three days, waiting for the pope to speak to him. Gregory had won a great victory for the papacy.

The struggle over lay investiture did not end with Gregory and Henry. It continued until 1122, at which time the pope and the German emperor reached a compromise settlement. At the city of Worms, they signed an agreement—the **Concordat of Worms**—that recognized the right of the church to elect its own bishops and abbots and to invest them with spiritual authority. These elections, however, had to be held in the presence of the emperor or his representatives. In addition, the emperor retained the right to invest church officials with secular authority.

New Religious Orders

In the thirteenth century, new religious orders arose, which continued the reforms begun by the Cluniac and Cistercian movements. Unlike earlier monastic orders whose members sought seclusion from society, the new Franciscan and Dominican orders emphasized service to one's fellow man.

Church-State Relations

Whose power is greater—the church's or the state's? This question has been asked in nearly every age of history. The medieval world viewed both the church and state as God's instruments, each possessing God-given authority and definite responsibilities in society. Even so, the powers asserted by one were often in direct conflict with those claimed by the other. Ever since the emperor Constantine had made Christianity an accepted religion of the Roman Empire, the roles of church and state had become less distinct.

The Bible tells us that God established both institutions. For this reason, the two should not be in conflict. Both are God's ministering agents for the good of society. The church is to be a bulwark of moral righteousness, striving to bring men to Christ through the preaching of the gospel; the state is to be a bulwark of justice and order, providing protection through its God-given authority. The Christian citizen has an obligation to both.

Sin has thwarted man's attempt to achieve an ideal church-state relationship. The church has often failed to provide moral leadership and has become entangled in temporal affairs. Likewise, the state has often overstepped its bounds of authority and has interfered with the church and the home. During the Middle Ages the tension between church and state led to an intense struggle for power. Satan encourages this conflict even today as he attempts to harm God's people and frustrate God's purpose.

Anonymous Lombard, Saint Francis,
Bob Jones University Collection of Sacred Art

They labored to bring about reform by living and preaching among the people—especially those in the growing towns. Members of these orders were called **friars** (''brothers''). Renouncing worldly possessions, they pledged themselves to lives of poverty. Since the friars begged for their daily sustenance, these are sometimes referred to as **mendicant** (''begging'') **orders.**

Francis of Assisi (uh SEE see; 1182-1226), the son of a rich merchant, was the founder of the Franciscan Order. As a young man he exchanged his wealth for beggar's rags and devoted his life to preaching and ministering to the poor and sick. A contemporary of his, a Spanish nobleman named **Dominic** (1170-1221), founded the Dominican order. Dominic devoted his life to battling heresy. He believed that the best way for the church to combat heresy was to educate her members. Consequently the Dominican order earned a reputation in the field of learning; its members taught at Europe's finest universities and supplied the church with some of her greatest scholars. Combining their intellectual training with their zeal for fighting heresy, the Dominicans became the leaders of the Inquisition—a church court established to discover and try heretics.

These mendicant orders pledged their allegiance to the pope. They championed the cause of the papacy in its clashes with powerful bishops and princes. Soon, however, these orders lost most of their zeal. They forsook poverty to gain wealth, abandoned others to serve themselves, and sacrificed spiritual power for temporal authority.

Zenith of the Papacy

The years of reform restored the church's prestige, tightened its hold over its members, and broadened its influence on medieval society. Nowhere was this power more evident than in the papacy. For centuries the popes had contended that their power exceeded that of kings; the truth of that claim was now certain. The battle over lay investiture and the formation of new religious orders had increased papal authority throughout Europe.

Innocent III

Papal power and prestige reached its zenith under Pope **Innocent III** (1198-1216). No pope be-

Francis of Assisi and the Manger Scene

Of all the objects associated with Christmas, none is more familiar than the manger scene. Usually included in this portrayal of Christ's birth are figures of Mary, Joseph, shepherds, three wise men, an ox, and a donkey. The baby Jesus lies on a bed of hay in a wooden manger. From the Scriptures we know that there are several misconceptions in this traditional representation. For instance, the wise men did not come with the shepherds to the manger but arrived some time later (Matt. 2:11). Also, Scripture does not tell us how many wise men there were. Nor do we know what animals were present in the stable when Christ was born. Furthermore, Christ was probably laid in a stone manger, not a wooden one.

The man responsible for unintentionally popularizing these misconceptions was Francis of Assisi. To dramatize for the common people the events surrounding the birth of Christ, Francis tried to physically recreate the scene. He built the manger of wood, for wood was plentiful in his native land. (He had no way of knowing that mangers in Palestine were made of stone.) He had townspeople portray Mary, Joseph, and shepherds, and the wise men. Although the wise men were not actually present at the manger, Francis included them so that he might bring together the events related to the Christ child. Around the manger Francis placed an ox and ass, interpreting Isaiah 1:3 as referring to Christ's birth: "The ox knoweth his owner, and the ass his master's crib." At midnight on Christmas Eve 1223, Francis held an outdoor service using this manger scene. He hoped to show the people how Christ came in poverty and how He was born to a life of suffering and death. Because of his popularity and devout life, Francis's manger scene became the model that others copied.

fore or after him exercised such extensive authority over both church and state. Innocent likened his authority to the sun, and that of kings, to the moon:

> The Creator of the universe set up two great luminaries [sources of light] in the firmament of heaven; the greater light to rule the day, the lesser light to rule the night. In the same way . . . he appointed two great dignities; the greater to bear rule over souls (these being, as it were, days), the lesser to bear rule over bodies (these being, as it were, nights). These dignities are the [papal] authority and the royal power. Furthermore, the moon derives her light from the sun, and is in truth inferior to the sun in both size and quality, in position as well as effect. In the same way the royal power derives its dignity from the [papal] authority.[1]

How was Innocent able to enforce this position when earlier popes had failed? A large measure of his success is due to the strength of the church,

Abbey of Mont-Saint-Michel, located in Normandy on the English Channel

Pietro Martire Neri, Saint Jerome, Bob Jones University Collection of Sacred Art. Even though the office of cardinal did not exist in Jerome's time, he is often portrayed as a cardinal because of his service to Pope Damasus.

which he represented. By the thirteenth century the Roman church had matured into a large, wealthy, and powerful organization. By summoning the wide resources of the church, which were at his disposal, and by exploiting its strong influence on society, Innocent established his authority over all of Europe. He and his successors were especially zealous in humbling unsubmissive kings, even though the Apostle Peter had commanded the believers to "honour the king" (I Pet. 2:17). In addition, they worked to stamp out any individual or group that protested against papal authority.

Papal Weapons

It was difficult for anyone to resist the ecclesiastical weapons that the popes directed against those who offended the church. Chief among the weapons in the church's arsenal were the following:

1. **Excommunication**—the punishment of an individual by depriving him of the sacraments and excluding him from the fellowship of the church. This was an especially powerful weapon in the hands of the pope, for churchmen believed that he controlled the gates to heaven and could through excommunication deprive an individual of any hope of eternal salvation.

2. **Interdict**—the suspension of public church services and of the administration of all sacraments (except baptism and extreme unction) in a given location. Popes often used this weapon against disobedient kings. By placing a king's realm under an interdict, the pope hoped that the suspension of spiritual blessings from the church would bring about a public outcry that would force the erring king to submit.

3. **Inquisition**—a special church court commissioned by the pope to stamp out heresy. Heresy, the holding of beliefs contrary to the teaching of the church, was the greatest of medieval crimes. Inquisitors were given special powers to seek out and judge those accused of heresy. They used torture to make the accused admit to error; those who would not, often faced death.

The Inquisition

It is not without reason that one church historian has called the Inquisition "one of the most terrible engines of intolerance and tyranny which human ingenuity has ever devised."

Started by Pope Gregory IX (1227-41), the Inquisition was an organization of the Roman Catholic church dedicated to uncovering and punishing heresy (teachings contrary to the Roman church). The Inquisitors, usually members of the Dominican order, were often well-educated and respected individuals. Nevertheless, they believed (as did the Roman church) that it was proper to force people to change their views by subjecting them to physical punishment.

The Inquisition operated methodically. A group of Inquisitors would come into a particular town, gather the people together, and then one of them would preach a sermon on the evils of heresy. The preacher urged those who held heretical views to confess them, promising that if they confessed voluntarily, the Inquisition would be lenient with them. After the sermon the Inquisitors took up lodging in the town and waited.

Over the next several days, people came to the Inquisition and confessed their heresies. While doing so they often mentioned the names of others who held similar views. After a set period of time the Inquisition no longer took voluntary confessions but began to call in those who had been accused of heresy by others. The accused person was not required to answer the Inquisition's summons; but if he did not do so, he was presumed guilty and placed under arrest.

The accused then had to stand trial before the panel of Inquisitors. He could not call any witnesses in his defense; he was not told who had accused him of heresy; and his trial was held in secret. The Inquisition did allow him to have a lawyer, but few attorneys ever agreed to help an accused heretic. The lawyers feared, and rightly so, that they too might come under suspicion of heresy. If during the trial the accused person steadfastly maintained his innocence, the Inquisitors used torture to force a confession. For example, they might pull his bones out of joint or burn various parts of his body. Of course, when subjected to such terrible suffering, the poor prisoner often readily confessed to anything.

Once the Inquisitors completed their last trial, they again gathered the whole town together. At this meeting one of the Inquisitors preached another sermon. Then he read the sentences handed down, beginning with the least severe and ending with the most severe. The punishments varied greatly. Some people had to do penance, some lost their property, and some were sentenced to prison. Those who refused to recant, however, were handed over to the secular authorities to be burned at the stake. After the executions, the Inquisitors moved on to the next town and began the process again.

By the end of the fifteenth century the Inquisition began to die out; however, Ferdinand and Isabella revived it in Spain. In addition, the success of the Protestant Reformation (see Chapter 11) prompted Pope Paul III (1534-49) to give the Inquisition a central organization called the Holy Office. Under this new organization, the Spanish Inquisition proved to be particularly barbaric as it tortured and killed suspected Protestants, Jews, and Muslims. By the early nineteenth century the Inquisition finally stopped its bloody activities, but the organization itself continued. Today it is called the Sacred Congregation for the Doctrine of the Faith.

Character and Results of Reform

Sadly, many medieval reformers devoted more effort to rebuilding the church's prestige than to restoring its purity. Many were more interested in obtaining political power than in maintaining spiritual strength. The reforms provided no lasting solution to the church's difficulties, and often they compounded the very problems they were intended to correct. Though churchmen made outward changes, they failed to recognize the need for inward cleansing and forgiveness through Jesus Christ. They failed to see that genuine reform is possible only for regenerate hearts.

Section Review

1. What was the practice called in which kings and nobles appointed church officials and invested them with their religious authority?
2. Which pope and emperor had a showdown at Canossa in 1077? Which man won?
3. List the two new religious orders whose members begged for their daily sustenance. Identify the founder of each.
4. Under which pope did the papacy reach its zenith?
5. List and define the three major weapons used by the papacy during this period.

A European Empire

Since the time of the tower of Babel, men have dreamed of a universal empire that would unite all the peoples of the earth under one government. This concept took form in the tenth century with the founding of the Holy Roman Empire.

Founding of the German Kingdom

After the death of Charlemagne, his grandsons divided the Frankish empire (see pp. 190-91). In East Frankland, the weak descendants of the ruler Louis the German offered little protection against the Magyars—savage horsemen who were terrorizing southeastern Europe. Local tribal leaders called **dukes** assumed the role of protectors. Each duke ruled like a king in his own territory, called a **duchy.** After the death of the last Carolingian king, the dukes elected one of their own to lead them against outside attackers.

The German nobles selected the Saxon duke **Henry the Fowler,** the first of the Saxon line of German kings. According to tradition, Henry was called "the Fowler" because the messengers who brought him the news of his election found him enjoying his favorite pastime—hunting game with hawks. As king, Henry I (919-36) forced the other dukes to acknowledge his royal status, but he permitted them to guide the internal affairs of their own territories. His chief concern was to strengthen his own duchy of Saxony so that he could build a strong base for his royal power. He repelled the raids of the Slavs and Magyars and expanded German territory eastward—a movement that would continue throughout German history.

Holy Roman Emperor Otto I (right) receives from poet and dramatist Hroswitha von Gandersheim copies of her works.

Henry's son, **Otto I** (936-73), often called "the Great," became one of the strongest German kings. Unlike his father, he was not content with the mere title of king but sought to actually assert his royal authority over the other duchies. To aid him in his struggles with rival dukes, he relied on the support of high-ranking church officials, many of whom he had appointed to office. These powerful bishops and abbots served Otto as vassals, giving him their allegiance and supplying soldiers for his army. In addition to his conflict with the nobles, Otto won a great victory over the Magyars. After their defeat, the Magyars no longer menaced German territory. They settled in the lower Danube valley, where they are known today as the Hungarians.

Establishment of the Holy Roman Empire

Tenth-century Italy was divided into many warring factions. Fearing that a rival duke would seize northern Italy and threaten his monarchy, Otto crossed the Alps, took possession of Lombardy, and proclaimed himself king of Italy. Ten years later, in 962, he crossed the Alps again, this time marching his army into Rome. The pope, who had appealed to him for protection against the Roman nobles, crowned Otto emperor. Like Charlemagne, Otto had come to the pope's rescue and in return

had received the emperor's crown. Otto believed that his new role as protector made him superior to the pope, a claim disputed, of course, by the papacy.

The conquests and coronation of Otto revived the memory of the Carolingian and Roman empires. Later German kings considered themselves the successors of Charlemagne and the Roman caesars. Because of its alliance with the Roman church and its symbolic association with the empire of ancient Rome, the German empire became known as the **Holy Roman Empire.** But as the eighteenth-century French author and philosopher Voltaire observed, it was "neither holy, nor Roman, nor an empire." The empire was built on the union of Germany and Italy and on the alliance of the church and state, neither of which could provide a strong foundation.

Conflict Within the Empire

Conflict of Interest

Although the Holy Roman Empire founded by Otto I became the most powerful state in Europe, it experienced many internal conflicts. The first was a conflict of interest. The German rulers often intervened in Italian affairs. Otto's grandson, Otto III, built a palace in Rome and planned to make Rome the capital of the empire. Concerned for Italy's welfare, the German rulers neglected the affairs of their homeland. This lack of attention gave the German nobles an opportunity to increase their power. The divided interests of the Holy Roman emperors ultimately weakened their authority and hindered efforts to create a unified Italy and a unified Germany.

Conflict with Popes

Another conflict that plagued the empire was the struggle between the emperors and the popes. Beginning with Otto I, the emperors actively intervened in papal affairs. They even began choosing the popes. In addition, they continued the long-standing practice of appointing important church officials within their realm (a situation later to be resolved by the Concordat of Worms in 1122; see p. 202). As the Cluniac reforms spread throughout the Roman church, the popes began to challenge the emperor's authority, especially in the matter of lay investiture.

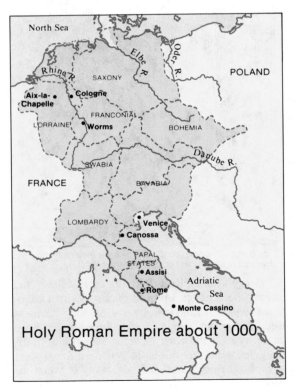

Holy Roman Empire about 1000

The orb (symbol of power and justice) and scepter (symbol of authority) of the Holy Roman emperor

The most famous struggle over investiture was the one between the emperor Henry IV (1056-1106) and Pope Gregory VII. Although Gregory won a great victory over the emperor at Canossa in 1077 (see p. 202), the triumph was only temporary. Henry was humiliated but not defeated. Returning home, he crushed a rebellion of German nobles and then invaded Italy, seized Rome, and installed a new pope. Gregory VII, who fled, died a year later in exile. But the domination of the German emperors over the papacy did not continue. Soon other popes, such as Innocent III, were able to interfere in the political affairs of the empire and weaken the emperor's authority.

Conflict with Nobles

The third and perhaps most damaging conflict within the empire was the one between the German nobles and the Holy Roman emperors. For almost a century, while the emperors had been preoccupied with Italian affairs, the German nobles had enjoyed great independence. The situation began to change, however, when a new royal line, the **Salian House** (1024-1125), succeeded the Saxon kings. The Salian kings (including Henry IV) were unsuccessful in their attempts to establish a strong, centralized monarchy that would weaken the power of the great nobles. After the death of Henry's son, who had

died without an heir, civil war broke out among rival noble families who competed for the crown.

The civil wars further weakened the German monarchy and led to the development of feudalism throughout the empire. The large duchies in Italy and Germany broke up into many small states. Powerful nobles became feudal lords, forcing lesser nobles to become their vassals. During this period, several of the strongest nobles firmly established the practice of electing the German monarch. The power of the nobles was supreme in the land.

The Empire under the Hohenstaufens

In 1152 the German princes hoped to bring an end to the civil wars by choosing as king a member of the **Hohenstaufen** (HO un SHTOU fun) family. **Frederick I** (1152-90), also called Barbarossa ("Red Beard"), sought to restore the glory and stability of what he termed the "holy empire." Like previous German kings, Frederick meddled in Italian affairs. His expeditions brought strong papal opposition. Although most of Frederick's advances into Italy ended in failure, he was successful in forming a marriage alliance between his son and the heiress of the kingdom of Sicily.

The last notable Hohenstaufen ruler was **Frederick II** (1215-50), the grandson of Frederick I. Frederick was heir not only to the German throne but also to the throne of Sicily. The latter kingdom was established by the Normans in the eleventh century and included all of southern Italy. Frederick II grew up in Sicily, where he became acquainted with the Greek and Arab cultures. Later his court would become a leading center of culture. One of the most learned men of his day, he also distinguished himself as a patron of artists and scholars.

As a boy, Frederick II was the ward of Pope Innocent III, the most powerful man in Europe. Innocent recognized the threat of having Hohenstaufen possessions encircling the Papal States. Therefore he secured the German throne for Frederick in return for his promise to give up the throne of Sicily. Shortly after Innocent's death, however, Frederick broke his promise. He devoted almost all his attention to Sicily and Italy, leaving the feudal princes of Germany relatively free from imperial interference. Frederick expanded his Italian holdings and might have united all of Italy under his control had it not been for the resistance of the papacy.

The death of Frederick II in 1250 marked the decline of the Holy Roman Empire. German kings still continued to call themselves Holy Roman emperors, but their contact with Italy was minimal. The attempts of the German emperors to unite Germany and Italy ended in failure. Their lack of success marked the beginning of a long period of disunity for the two countries. Not until the late nineteenth century did Italy and Germany become unified national states.

Section Review

1. What German king founded the Holy Roman Empire? In what year did this take place?
2. What did the French philosopher Voltaire observe about the Holy Roman Empire?
3. What conflict of interest did many of the German emperors have?
4. From what family did the German princes choose a king in hopes of ending the period of civil war? List two emperors who belonged to this family.

Rise of Feudal Monarchies

England

The Anglo-Saxons Settle England

Roman authority over the Celts in Britain came to an end in the early fifth century. After nearly four hundred years of occupation, the Roman legions had to withdraw from the island in order to protect Roman territory on the Continent. Soon afterwards, Germanic tribes from northern Europe, such as the Angles and the Saxons, invaded Britain. They established their own independent kingdoms and transformed "Roman" Britain into England (or "Angle land," meaning the "land of the Angles").

During the ninth century, the Danes (Scandinavian Vikings) began to raid the land. The petty kingdoms of the Angles and Saxons had little success in resisting the Danes—that is, until the time of King **Alfred the Great** (871-99). Alfred, the ruler of the important Saxon kingdom of Wessex, defeated the Danes and pushed them back into northeastern England. He extended his rule over the south of England, laying the foundation for a unified English monarchy.

Alfred's success was not confined to the battlefield. He was an able ruler and a patron of learning. He built a navy to repel future Danish invasions—an undertaking that earned him the title "founder of the English navy." He strengthened the Anglo-Saxon practice of local government. His realm was divided into many local districts called **shires** (counties), governed by officials called *shire-reeves* (from which we get our word **sheriff**). He built churches, founded schools, and invited foreign scholars to his court. During his reign, scholars began to translate important literary works into the common language of the people. In addition, monks began to compile the *Anglo-Saxon Chronicle,* which traces the history of England from Roman times to Alfred's day. The Chronicle was continued after Alfred; monks added current events and revised older passages.

Alfred was a man of strong character. He won the love and respect of his people as well as the admiration of later generations. Unlike many of the men who have been highly praised by historians, Alfred truly deserved the title "the Great." His life demonstrated that the true greatness lies not in wealth or worldly fame, but in a man's character—not necessarily in what a man *does*, but in what he *is*.

Statue of Alfred the Great located in Winchester, England, Alfred's capital

England in the Time of Alfred the Great

SCOTS

North Sea

Irish Sea

York

DANELAW

WALES

London
Canterbury
Winchester
HASTINGS ★

English Channel

Alfred's Territory
★ Battle

On October 14, 1066, the armies of William, duke of Normandy, and Harold, earl of Wessex, met in the famous **Battle of Hastings.** Much more was at stake than the English throne; the outcome of this battle altered the course of English history. Before the day ended, Harold had been killed and the Anglo-Saxons defeated. William, known as "the Conqueror," established a new line of English kings, the Norman dynasty.

William brought to England the centralized feudalism of Normandy and established himself as feudal lord over the entire country, which, in theory, was now his by right of conquest. He divided his holdings among his military followers, feudal vassals called **tenants-in-chief.** To maintain his power over all the feudal nobles, he required that all who became vassals through subinfeudation also swear allegiance to him as their lord. He also extended his authority over the English church; William—not the pope—appointed the bishops of his realm.

To determine the taxable resources that belonged to him as king, William commissioned a great survey. His royal officials traveled throughout the country gathering detailed information about property holders and their belongings. According to the *Anglo-Saxon Chronicle,* "there was not a single hide or rood [1/4 acre] of land, nor even was there an ox or a cow or a pig left that was not set down in his writings." The findings of the survey were collected in a record known as the *Domesday Book.*

Less than a century after Alfred's death, the Danes renewed their attacks. England fell to the Danish ruler **Canute** (kuh NOOT), who made England part of the Danish Empire, which also included Norway. Although Canute ruled England well, his successors were weak. The Anglo-Saxons eventually drove out the Danish rulers and placed **Edward the Confessor** on the throne.

William of Normandy Conquers England

Edward (1042-66) was a descendant of Alfred. He was called "the Confessor" because of his devotion to God. In January of 1066, he died without a direct heir. His cousin William, the French duke of Normandy, claimed the throne, asserting that Edward had promised it to him. The English nobles, however, refused to grant William the crown. Instead they elected **Harold,** the powerful earl of Wessex, king. William refused to be deprived of what he thought was rightfully his. Obtaining the blessing of the pope, he raised a large army, crossed the English Channel, and invaded England.

The *Domesday Book*

Why was William's census called the *Domesday Book?* Some historians have suggested that the name came from *Domus Dei,* the chapel in which the book was kept in Winchester Cathedral. It has also been suggested that because the book represented the official and final record of a person's holdings, it was compared by the common people to the coming Day of Judgment, or "doomsday," when God will open the Book of Life. Nevertheless, most scholars believe that the word *dome* comes from the Anglo-Saxon word *doom,* which means merely the judgment or decision of the king.

The decisive Battle of Hastings as portrayed in the Bayeux Tapestry, an early pictorial record of the Norman conquest of England

Reforms Strengthen Royal Authority

When William's sons William II and Henry I died without heir, the Norman line came to an end. After a period of dispute over rightful succession, the crown passed to the Plantagenet (or Angevin) family, founded by **Henry II** (1154-89), the great-grandson of William the Conqueror. Being a Frenchman, Henry possessed more wealth and territory outside of England than within. Through inheritance and marriage, he had gained landholdings in France that far surpassed those ruled directly by his feudal lord, the French king. This situation provoked jealous rivalry between the French and English thrones.

Henry strengthened royal authority in England by expanding the jurisdiction of the royal courts. Before this time, each lord had his own court for deciding cases concerning his vassals and serfs. Henry established circuit courts with justices who traveled throughout the land hearing cases. During Henry's time, the circuit courts usually heard only cases involving land disputes, but later other cases were handled also.

Before the circuit justices arrived in a shire, a jury composed of men of that district would make a list of **indictments** (accusations) of what crimes had been committed and who the suspected offenders were. (From this practice arose the modern-day grand jury, which decides whether there is suf-ficient evidence to hold an accused person for trial.) When the justice heard a case, he often relied on information supplied by a smaller jury of men acquainted with the facts of the case. Gradually, it became the accepted practice to have "twelve good and truthful men" serve on this jury, the forerunner of our trial juries. Unlike their modern counterparts, however, these men gave evidence upon which the justice could render a verdict, instead of being the ones to hear the evidence and give the verdict.

As a result of Henry's judicial reforms, more cases were tried in the royal courts than in the feudal ones. The decisions of Henry's justices provided uniform laws for all of England and thus superseded the local feudal laws. This **common law** not only helped ensure justice but also helped to draw the English people together into a unified nation.

Henry hoped to strengthen his authority over the church by appointing his friend **Thomas á Becket** archbishop of Canterbury, the highest church office in England. Once in office, however, Becket became a bitter opponent of Henry's interference in church matters. The controversy reached a climax when Henry attempted to bring clerics who committed grave crimes to trial in royal, instead of church, courts. Becket resisted. Outraged by his opposition, Henry reportedly exclaimed, "What a pack of fools and cowards I have nour-

Trial by Ordeal

One way the Anglo-Saxons attempted to determine the innocence or guilt of a person charged with a crime was trial by ordeal. There were four forms of trial by ordeal.

Trial by cold water. The charged person was taken to a pond, which was blessed by a priest. He was bound hand and foot and thrown into the water. If he floated, he was judged guilty, for the "holy water" had rejected him. If he sank, he was judged innocent, for the water had accepted him. He was then rescued—presumably in time to save his life; if not, his innocence supposedly merited entrance into heaven.

Trial by hot water. A person was forced to plunge his arm into boiling water. A priest would then wrap a bandage around his arm. After three days the bandage was removed. If the arm was blistered, the man was judged guilty; but if it had healed, he was judged innocent. Our saying "in hot water" probably comes from this ordeal.

Trial by hot iron. This ordeal was much like trial by hot water, except in this case a person had to carry a red-hot piece of iron a prescribed distance.

Trial by morsel. A person was made to swallow a lump of dough. If he choked, he was judged guilty; if he did not, he was judged innocent.

The people of the Middle Ages falsely believed that God would immediately reveal guilt or innocence through these means. With the rise of the royal courts of Henry II, trial by ordeal gradually came to an end. By the time of King John's reign, it had all but disappeared from England. It then became the practice to determine the guilt or innocence of an accused person by the facts of the case rather than by an ordeal.

ished in my house, that not one of them will avenge me of this turbulent priest!" Four knights, hearing the king's rash words, traveled to Canterbury and murdered the archbishop at his altar. Because of the popular uproar over Becket's death, the king abandoned his plans to control the clergy. Becket became a martyr and his tomb a popular shrine.

Magna Carta Limits Royal Power

After Henry's death his oldest son **Richard I** (1189-99) became king. Richard, known as "the Lion-Hearted," was an able warrior and an admired Crusader. Nevertheless, he contributed little to the English crown. Less than six months of his ten-year reign were spent in England. His participation in the Third Crusade (see p. 220) and the defense of his French holdings from the king of France occupied most of his reign. While he was absent from England, his brother John and the king of France plotted to overthrow him. His reign provides the setting for the adventures of the legendary English hero Robin Hood.

The death of Richard elevated **John** (1199-1216) to the English throne. John was a more able ruler than Richard, but he lacked the strong personal qualities that had won his brother the trust and admiration of the people. John's weak will and cruel, unscrupulous ways brought him nothing but trouble.

John's reign was marked by continual conflict with three formidable opponents: the French king, the pope, and the English nobles—all of whom got the better of him. The French king Philip II took advantage of John's weakness and extended his royal control over many of John's French possessions.

In the meantime, John clashed with Pope Innocent III over who would be the next archbishop of Canterbury. When the archbishop of Canterbury died in 1206 and John failed to appoint a new one, the monks at Canterbury decided that they would choose a new archbishop. (This choice was usually made with the approval of the king and the English bishops.) The monks sent the man of their choice to Rome to be confirmed by the pope. When John heard of this, he was outraged and had the bishops choose another man, who was also sent to Rome. When both men arrived in Rome, Innocent III refused to confirm either. Instead he selected a friend of his, an English cardinal named Stephen Langton, to be archbishop. When John refused to allow Stephen into England (he had been out of the country for several years), trouble broke out.

Innocent placed England under an interdict and excommunicated the king. Having no allies and threatened by a French invasion, John submitted to the pope, even to the point of becoming the pope's vassal and making England a fief of the papacy. Restored to the pope's graces, John was able to

Magna Carta

Certain provisions of the Magna Carta transcended the immediate occasion for which they were framed and became the bases of later political concepts.

No Taxation Without Representation. "No scutage [a feudal tax] or aid shall be imposed in our kingdom save by the common council of our kingdom." (Clause 12)

Trial by Jury and Due Process of Law. "No freeman shall be taken, or imprisoned, or dispossessed, or outlawed, or banished, or in any way injured, nor will we go upon him, nor send upon him, except by the legal judgment of his peers, or by the law of the land. To no one will we sell, to no one will we deny or delay, right or justice." (Clauses 39-40)

avert Philip's invasion of England. However, he was not able to put down a rebellion of the English barons (nobles).

The English barons were dissatisfied with John's reign. They resented his excessive taxes and his disregard for their feudal privileges. In 1215, the infuriated nobles revolted. At Runnymede, a meadow near London, they forced John to set his seal to the **Magna Carta** (Latin for "Great Charter"). Originally intended as a guarantee of feudal rights, the Magna Carta became one of the most important documents in English history. Later Englishmen looked to the Magna Carta as establishing the principle that the king's power is limited: the king is not above the law and can be removed for refusing to obey it.

Parliament Becomes an Important Institution

One of England's most gifted medieval kings was **Edward I** (1272-1307). He attempted to extend English rule over all of Britain—Wales, Scotland, and England. He conquered Wales and made his son Prince of Wales. (Since that time, it has been customary to confer the title "Prince of Wales" on the eldest male heir to the English throne.) Edward's attempts to subdue Scotland, however, met with fierce resistance.

Probably the most important and enduring contribution of Edward's reign was the development

of **Parliament.** It had always been the custom of English kings to seek counsel from a group of advisers. The Anglo-Saxon kings had the **witan,** an assembly of the great men of the kingdom. William the Conqueror established the Great Council—also known as the *curia regis* ("king's council")—a feudal body composed of his chief vassals.

When Edward became king, he enlarged the membership of the Great Council to include representative knights from every shire and representative burgesses (citizens) from every town. The word *parliament* (from a French word meaning "to speak," or "to discuss") came to designate this expanded assembly. The meeting of Parliament during Edward's reign has been called the "Model Parliament," for it had the basic features of later Parliaments.

In the fourteenth century, members of Parliament met in two separate groups: the chief vassals in one, and the knights and burgesses in another. The members of the latter group were called the "Commons," because they represented the community. Their assembly became known as the House of Commons, and that of the chief feudal lords became known as the House of Lords.

Over the centuries, Parliament became more and more powerful. Edward had acknowledged that the king could not propose new taxes without the consent of Parliament. Therefore he, as well as his successors, had to summon Parliament regularly in order to obtain needed revenue. The members of Parliament soon discovered that by withholding their approval of new taxes, they could force the king to hear their grievances. This **"power of the purse,"** as it became called, gradually transformed Parliament from an advisory body into a legislative body. The rise of Parliament served as a check on the king's power and in later centuries helped to convert English government into a limited monarchy.

France

The Capetians and Their Royal House

The kingdom of West Frankland, once the heart of the Carolingian Empire, broke up into many feudal realms soon after the death of Charlemagne. In 987 the great feudal lords chose the count of Paris, **Hugh Capet,** as their king, thus ending the weak rule of the Carolingian monarchs. Hugh founded a new royal line, the Capetian House, whose members built a strong feudal monarchy in France.

Many factors helped the Capetian kings to steadily increase their power over the feudal lords. For instance, for over three hundred years every Capetian king had a son to succeed him. There were therefore no wars of succession to threaten the stability and continuity of royal power. This power gradually increased as the size of the royal domain increased. Capetian rulers enlarged their royal possessions by conquest and through marriage alliances. They also developed an effective system of centralized government, which laid the foundation for the French national state. Furthermore, the Capetians found valuable allies in the church and townspeople. By tapping the wealth of the towns and the church, the Capetians won financial independence from the great feudal lords.

Philip II and Royal Expansion

Although the early Capetians bore the title of king, they actually ruled only a small area around Paris, known as the *Ile-de-France*. Like an island, it was surrounded by feudal lands ruled by the king's vassals. Many of these vassals were powerful lords possessing more land and authority than the French king. (William, duke of Normandy, and Henry Plantagenet are noted examples.)

The early Capetian kings were constantly struggling to maintain control of their feudal holdings. Not until the reign of the fifth Capetian king, Louis VI (1108-37), did the French king become master of his royal domain. For the first time the Capetians had a strong and solid base from which they would extend their royal power over the rest of the kingdom. It was **Philip II "Augustus"** (1180-1223),

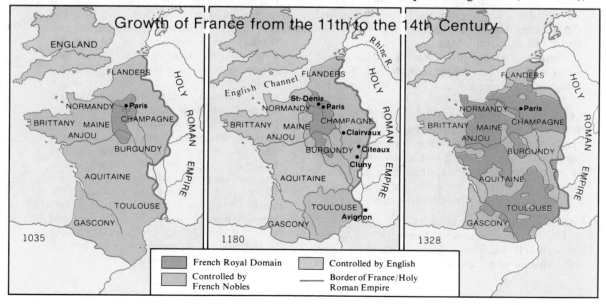

Growth of France from the 11th to the 14th Century

| French Royal Domain | Controlled by English |
| Controlled by French Nobles | Border of France/Holy Roman Empire |

however, who became known as the real founder of France. By enlarging the territory under his rule and by increasing his power over his vassals, he began a period of Capetian greatness.

The chief obstacle to the expansion of royal power in France was the large amount of land held by the English kings. Although the Plantagenets were vassals of the French king, their landholdings in France far exceeded those ruled directly by the French king. Philip II attempted to deprive the English kings Henry II and Richard the Lion-Hearted of their continental holdings but met with little success. He found King John easier to deal with. A controversy broke out between John and one of his French vassals. When John refused to stand trial in Philip's court as the French monarch's vassal, Philip declared John's French lands forfeited. Because John had lost the support of his French vassals and had alienated the English nobles, he was defeated by Philip. John lost Normandy, Anjou, Maine, and Touraine to him. The French king had broken the power of King John in France and, in doing so, had tripled the size of his own royal domain.

Philip also increased the effectiveness of royal government. He replaced local feudal officials with new royal ones called *baillis* (bah YEE), or bailiffs, whom the king appointed and paid. Similar to Henry II's itinerant justices, these bailiffs collected royal taxes, enforced feudal rights, and administered justice, reinforcing the king's authority throughout his realm.

Philip's attempts to increase royal power in France met with one major setback. Shortly after taking a Danish princess as his wife, Philip had his marriage annulled by the French bishops. Pope Innocent III, who seized every opportunity to intervene in the internal affairs of the European states, refused to recognize the annulment. He excommunicated Philip and placed France under an interdict. Forced to back down, Philip took back his Danish wife; but in doing so, he had to put away another wife, whom he had married in the meantime.

Louis IX and Royal Dignity

Philip's grandson, King **Louis IX** (1226-70), has been called the ideal medieval king. He combined sincere piety and just rule to build respect

King Louis IX of France, known as "Saint Louis"

and loyalty for the French throne. His character is demonstrated in the instruction he gave to his son and heir:

Fair son, the first thing I would teach thee is to set thine heart to love God. . . . If God send thee adversity, receive it in patience, and give thanks to our Saviour, and bethink thee that thou hast deserved it, and that He will make it turn to thine advantage. If he send thee prosperity, then thank Him humbly, so that thou become not worse from pride. . . . Maintain the good customs of thy realm, and abolish the bad. Be not covetous against thy people; and do not burden them with taxes and imposts save when thou art in great need. . . . See that thou hast in thy company men, whether religious or lay, who are right worthy, and loyal, and not full of covetousness, and confer with them oft: and fly and eschew the company of the wicked. Hearken willingly to the Word of God and keep it in thine heart. . . . Give often thanks to God for all the good things He has bestowed upon thee, so that thou be accounted worthy to receive more. In order to do justice and right to thy subjects, be upright and firm, turning neither to the right hand nor to the left, but always to what is just.

Concerned about the welfare of his subjects, Louis IX made peace and justice the primary goals of his reign. He sought to protect the rights of all, regardless of their rank in society. Louis further expanded the jurisdiction of the royal courts over the feudal courts. He also established a permanent royal court at Paris, which served as the supreme court of the land. Fearful that his royal agents (the bailiffs) might infringe the feudal rights of his subjects, he appointed special men to search out abuses in the royal government. He was also the first French king to issue ordinances (i.e., legislation) without first consulting his chief vassals. His efforts at judicial reform earned him the title of "the French Justinian."

Louis IX led two crusades against the Muslims in North Africa. Although he was a zealous warrior, both campaigns failed. While on his second crusade, he contracted a disease and died. He is remembered in history as "Saint Louis."

Philip IV and Royal Strength

The climax of Capetian rule came during the reign of **Philip IV** (1285-1314). Known as "the Fair" (because of his handsome features), Philip IV further expanded royal power in France. He strengthened the organization and authority of the central government. As the royal government increased in size, the king needed greater revenue. Philip therefore taxed the French people as no French king before him had done.

The need for revenue led Philip to tax the French clergy also. Pope **Boniface VIII** stepped in and decreed that no king could impose a tax on clergy. Philip countered by refusing to allow gold and silver (especially the tithes of the French church) to be exported from France, thus decreasing the papal revenues. In another controversy, Philip defied Boniface's authority despite the threat of being excommunicated or having an interdict placed on his land (see p. 205). In doing so, he had the support of the French people. Their loyalty was gradually shifting away from the church and the papacy to the state and the French king.

To strengthen popular support for his policies, Philip summoned representatives from the church, nobility, and townspeople to meet at Paris. The meetings of these three estates (or classes) became known as the **Estates-General.** The king sought advice from this representative body, but he did not wait for its consent to enforce legislation or raise taxes. Thus the power of the French monarch grew without restraints such as those the English Parliament imposed on the English kings. This trend partly explains why the French government developed into an absolute monarchy, while the English government became a limited monarchy.

Section Review

1. What man defeated the Danes and laid the foundation for a unified English monarchy?
2. What two men struggled for the English throne in 1066? What was the name of the battle where this issue was settled? Who won?
3. On what document did English nobles force King John to affix his royal seal? In what year did this take place?
4. What is the name of the ruling family in France? List five kings in this section who belonged to this royal family.
5. List the English and the French advisory/representative assemblies that developed during this period and identify each with its respective country.

Rescue of the Holy Land

For centuries tourists have flocked to see the land where Christianity began. Even in medieval times eager pilgrims from Europe journeyed to the Holy Land. They viewed Jerusalem as the center of the earth and revered the sites associated with the life of Christ as sacred and holy places. But these people journeyed to Jerusalem for much the same reasons that the Muslims went to Mecca:

some wanted to demonstrate their piety; others hoped to earn forgiveness of sins. They believed that somehow they could draw nearer to God's presence by visiting the holy places.

> For sure he must be sainted man
> Whose blessed feet have trod the ground
> Where the Redeemer's tomb is found.
> (Scott, *Marmion*, V.21)

Had these pilgrims walked "by faith, not by sight" (II Cor. 5:7), they would have realized that we do not have to travel thousands of miles to draw near to God. God's Word tells us that we can "draw near with a true heart in full assurance of faith" (Heb. 10:22).

The Call

During the eleventh century, the Seljuk Turks advanced into the Near East. Moving into Palestine, they seized the holy places of Christendom and disrupted travel to the sacred sites. They invaded Asia Minor and threatened the security of Constantinople. Seeing his land in peril, the Byzantine emperor appealed to Christians in the West for help against the Turks. Pilgrims returning from the Holy Land also called for the recovery of the holy places, recounting tales of terrible atrocities committed by the infidel Moslem Turks.

In 1095 Pope **Urban II** addressed a council of church leaders and French noblemen at Clermont, France. He called for a holy crusade to free the Holy Land from the Turks: "This royal city [Jerusalem] . . . situated at the center of the earth, is now held captive by the enemies of Christ. . . . She seeks, therefore, and desires to be liberated and ceases not to implore you to come to her aid." He called upon the feudal nobles to stop fighting one another and to join instead in fighting the Turks. He urged them to avenge the wrongs done by this "wicked race," to "enter upon the road to the Holy Sepulcher [the tomb where Christ was buried]," and to "wrest that land from the wicked race, and subject it to yourselves."

The response to Urban's moving appeal was overwhelming; those present enthusiastically answered, "God wills it!" Urban is reported to have replied: "Let these words be your war-cry when you unsheathe the sword. You are soldiers of the cross. Wear on your breasts or shoulders the blood-red sign of the cross. Wear it as a token that His help will never fail you, as the pledge of a vow never to be recalled." During the two centuries that followed, many Europeans were obsessed with the winning of the Holy Land. Wandering preachers spread the idea, causing thousands to answer the call. The people were convinced by the Roman church that their task was "God's work," and that they were fighting a "holy war." They went forth with the symbol of the cross sewn upon their garments. Those marked by a cross were called *Crusaders,* and their military campaigns became known as the **Crusades** (words derived from the Latin *crux,* meaning "cross").

The Crusaders: Their Motives

What prompted the Crusaders to leave their homes and journey such long distances to fight the Turks? Some had a pious desire to serve Christ, to defend the church, and to rescue the Holy Sepulcher. At the same time there were those who desired adventure, seeking an escape from the humdrum life on the manor. Still others hoped to gain fame or fortune. Some knights joined a Crusade because they could enjoy their favorite pastime—fighting—and have in addition the blessing of the Roman church. Some merchants, motivated by a desire for profit, embarked on the Crusades looking for new opportunities for commercial gain.

The Roman church was a powerful force behind the Crusades. The promise of both earthly and heavenly rewards lured many into taking the Crusader's vow. Church leaders guaranteed the protection of the family and property of the Crusader while he was away. Criminals and debtors undertaking the "holy" cause received pardons. In fact, the popes proclaimed that participation in the Crusades was a substitute for penance. Hardened sinners were told they could earn forgiveness of sins by joining one of these campaigns. Furthermore, the Roman church assured the Crusaders that anyone who died while on a Crusade would be granted eternal life. Of course this was a false assurance, given by church leaders who manipulated the credulous people. Notice the similarity of this false

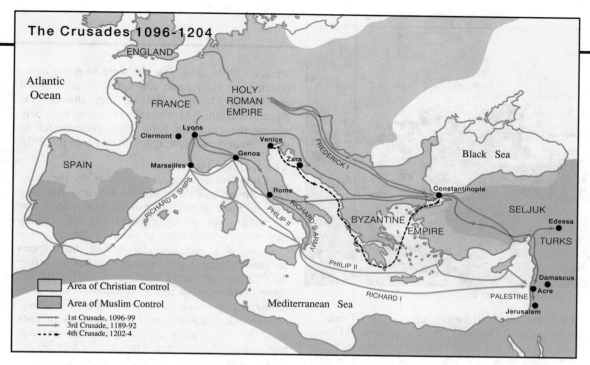

ENGLAND

Atlantic
Ocean

FRANCE

HOLY
ROMAN
EMPIRE

Lyons

Clermont

Venice

FREDERICK I

Black Sea

Genoa

Zara

SPAIN

Marseilles

RICHARD'S SHIPS

Rome

RICHARD'S ARMY

PHILIP II

Constantinople

SELJUK

Edessa

BYZANTINE EMPIRE

TURKS

PHILIP II

Damascus

RICHARD I

PALESTINE

Acre

Mediterranean Sea

Jerusalem

Area of Christian Control

Area of Muslim Control

1st Crusade, 1096-99
3rd Crusade, 1189-92
4th Crusade, 1202-4

teaching of the Roman church to that of the Islamic religion (see p. 139). Both proclaimed their cause to be a holy war. Both promised paradise to their warriors who fell in battle.

The Campaigns

There were eight major Crusades between 1095 and 1291. Some Crusaders traveled alone or in small bands; most, however, joined the large organized expeditions.

The First Crusade

Excitement mounted as the year of departure drew near for the first major expedition (1096-99) to the East. Masses of zealous peasants, eager to reach the Holy City, embarked on the long journey in advance of the main armies. These common people had few supplies and even less fighting experience. Those that survived the perilous journey found themselves no match for the Turks, who completely routed them.

The Crusaders' cause fared much better when the main body of knights reached Palestine. Despite the heat, a shortage of supplies, and dissension among their leaders, the Crusaders broke Muslim

resistance and succeeded in capturing Jerusalem. In taking the city, they slaughtered its inhabitants. According to an exaggerated eyewitness account, the city was filled with corpses and blood. In the temple area alone, "men rode in blood up to their knees and bridle reins. Indeed," the account continues, "it was a just and splendid judgment of God that this place should be filled with the blood of unbelievers, since it had suffered so long from their blasphemies."[2]

Of all the Crusades, the first was the most successful. Besides winning the Holy City, the Crusaders established four small feudal kingdoms along the Mediterranean coastline. It was not long, however, before a new Muslim offensive threatened these "Crusader states." In response the Second Crusade was launched in 1147. Unlike the first, this second campaign ended in miserable failure, with the Western forces suffering defeat at the hands of the Turks.

The Kings' Crusade

In 1187 the Muslims recaptured Jerusalem under their new leader, **Saladin.** News of Saladin's victory stirred the Europeans to organize the Third Crusade (1189-92). Three of the most powerful

A crusader castle near Sidon

kings in Europe led the crusading armies: Frederick Barbarossa of Germany, Philip Augustus of France, and Richard the Lion-Hearted of England. This Crusade began as the largest of all, but troubles plagued the expedition from the start. Frederick accidentally drowned on the way to the Holy Land. Constant strife between Richard and Philip led Philip to return to France with his army shortly after his arrival in the Holy Land. Richard remained and defeated Saladin in many battles, but he did not succeed in taking Jerusalem. Richard and Saladin then agreed to a three-year truce that allowed Western pilgrims free access to the holy places in Jerusalem.

The "Diverted" Crusade

Unlike earlier Crusaders who maintained the pretense of a religious undertaking, the participants of the Fourth Crusade (1201-4) abandoned the ideals of their predecessors and openly pursued political and economic ends. Venetian merchants agreed to transport the Crusaders to the East, but because of miscalculation, the Crusaders were unable to pay the transportation fees. In order to pay their way, they agreed to support a Venetian attack upon the city of Zara, a rival seaport in the Adriatic. The conquest of this city whetted the Crusaders' appetite for plunder and booty and weakened their desire to reach the Holy Land. The Venetians realized this and diverted the Crusaders to Constantinople,

Venice's chief rival. The wayward warriors never reached the Holy Land and never raised a sword against the Muslims. Instead, they attacked the Byzantines, who had originally requested their help against the Turks. In 1204 Constantinople fell to the Crusaders, who pillaged the city (see p. 129).

The Later Crusades

Crusaders continued to journey to the Holy Land throughout the thirteenth century. But they were no more successful than the earlier ones. The expeditions were poorly organized and lacked strong leadership. Meanwhile, attitudes in Europe were changing. With each crusading failure, the religious zeal and fighting spirit so prevalent in Europe before the Crusades gradually subsided. Soon Europe became occupied with new expeditions. These were dominated by strong nations rather than by the Roman church, and motivated by commercial interests more than by religious concerns. The Crusader was replaced by the explorer. The motto "take up the cross" was changed to "seek out and discover." And the recovery of the Holy Land gave way to finding new commercial routes to the Far East.

The Consequences

Although it is impossible to measure with exactness the effects of the Crusades upon western Europe, there is little doubt that they brought about several profound changes. The following are the most evident:

1. The Crusades weakened the feudal structure of Europe. Feudal nobles, seeking to raise money to go on Crusades, allowed the serfs to buy their freedom. Freed serfs left the manors with hopes of finding new opportunities in the growing towns. With the decline of the feudal structure came the emergence of strong nations ruled by kings. Under the pretext of financing the Crusades, several European kings gained the power to tax. Taxation provided badly needed revenues, which monarchs used to extend their powers.

2. The Crusades expanded the commercial activity of Europe. The Crusaders were amazed at the riches they found in the East. They came to know and desire such luxuries as sugar,

The Children's Crusade

In the summer of 1212, children by the thousands gathered in towns throughout France and many of the German states. Filled with religious zeal, they set out for the Holy Land convinced that God wanted to use them to free it from the Muslims. They took as their text Psalm 8:2: "Out of the mouth of babes and sucklings hast thou ordained strength because of thine enemies that thou mightest still the enemy and the avenger." As they went forth, they sang songs of praise to God. Later generations have associated the following song, traditionally known as "the Crusaders Hymn," with the Children's Crusade.

Fairest Lord Jesus,
Ruler of all nature,
O Thou of God and man the Son!
Thee will I cherish,

Thee will I honor,
Thou my soul's glory, joy, and crown!

According to chronicles of the day, a young shepherd boy named Stephen from the town of Cloyes, France, had a vision. He claimed that Christ told him to lead a Crusade of children to the Holy Land. He journeyed to St. Denis just north of Paris, where he encouraged children to join him in a Crusade. Word spread quickly; by August, thousands of children had gathered. He told them that God had promised that the Mediterranean Sea would open for them so they could walk through on dry land just as the children of Israel had walked through the Red Sea. Following Stephen, they marched toward the sea.

When news of Stephen's vision reached Germany, another young boy, Nicholas, felt that he too was called to lead a Crusade. He attracted a large following in the city of Cologne. (Like St. Denis, Cologne was a pilgrim center. It supposedly housed the shrine of the bones of the three wise men!) Of the thousands of children who left with Nicholas, only about a third reached the Mediterranean coast. When the sea did not open, they were sadly disillusioned; too weary to travel home, they remained in Italy.

Meanwhile, Stephen's group reached Marseilles, a Crusader port in southern France. They too discovered that the sea did not open for them. Many returned home, but about five thousand remained, still hoping for a miracle. It was then that two merchants offered the children free passage to the Holy Land. Thinking that this was God's miracle, they accepted. Of the seven ships that set sail, two were wrecked. The other five made their way to the North African coast, where the merchants sold the children into slavery. It was not until eighteen years later that the people of Europe found out what had happened. A priest who had accompanied the children, and who was himself enslaved, escaped and made his way back to Europe and told of the fate of the children.

spices, fruits, silks, cotton, and glass mirrors (which were obtained by Middle Eastern countries primarily through trade with the Orient). The heightened demand for these goods in Europe led enterprising individuals to import them. The increase in trade prompted the rise of a money economy (as opposed to a barter system) and the need for banking services. It also incited Europeans to search for even greater profits by finding new routes to the wealth in the East.

3. The early Crusades strengthened the leadership of the papacy. The popes called for the Crusades, planned them, and collected taxes

Louis IX attacked the city of Damietta, Egypt, in 1249; Louis is pictured on the left with a crown on his head.

the Byzantine and Muslim empires. In addition, the Crusades renewed interest in the knowledge of ancient Greece and Rome—knowledge that had been preserved by the civilizations in the East. And the Europeans' travel experiences and increased understanding of world geography gave impetus to the later period of exploration.

5. The Crusades offered important lessons for the Christian church. The Christian warriors believed that they could accomplish God's work by using the weapons of the flesh. Yet the Bible teaches that the Christian soldier is involved in a spiritual battle. His weapons should not be the weapons of this world. The Apostle Paul admonishes believers in II Corinthians 10:3-4: "For though we walk in the flesh, we do not war after the flesh: (For the weapons of our warfare are not carnal, but mighty through God to the pulling down of strong holds.)"

or tithes for their financing. They were thus able to extend their powers in both secular and sacred matters. As the later Crusades failed, however, people became disillusioned and began to distrust the motives of the papacy. Respect for the crusading ideals and the papacy continued to diminish as popes called for Crusades to battle heretics in Europe and unruly German kings.

4. The Crusades opened new horizons to the people of medieval Europe. Contact with the East changed their narrow-minded attitudes and introduced them to other civilizations, such as

Section Review

1. What pope called for a holy crusade to free the Holy Land from the Turks? In what year did this occur?
2. How many major Crusades were there? Over what years did they span?
3. What is the nickname of the Third Crusade? List the kings (with their country) who went on this Crusade.
4. To where was the Fourth Crusade "diverted"? Who "diverted" the Crusade?

A Glimpse Behind and a Glimpse Ahead

In some ways the Crusades failed dismally. The Holy Land was not permanently won, the Muslims were not driven out, and the breach between the Eastern and Western churches only became worse. Even so, the Crusades were not totally in vain. God in His providence permitted and used the Crusades to accomplish His overall purpose in history. The Crusades combined with other forces already at work in Europe to bring about far-reaching changes in Western life. These changes helped to usher Europe into the modern age while also preparing the people for a great spiritual revival—the Reformation—which you will read about in the next unit.

Chapter Review

Can You Explain?

lay investiture	interdict	sheriff	*curia regis*
simony	Inquisition	tenants-in-chief	"power of the purse"
friars	duke	indictment	*baillis*
mendicant orders	Holy Roman Empire	common law	Estates-General
excommunication	shire	witan	Crusades

Can You Identify?

910	Henry the Fowler	Harold	Hugh Capet
Cistercians	Otto I	Battle of Hastings	*Ile-de-France*
Bernard of Clairvaux	Salian House	(1066)	Philip II
College of Cardinals	Hohenstaufens	*Domesday Book*	Louis IX
Gregory VII	Frederick I	Henry II	Philip IV
Henry IV	Frederick II	Thomas à Becket	Boniface VIII
1077	Anglo-Saxons	Richard I	Urban II
Concordat of Worms	Alfred the Great	John	1095-1291
Francis of Assisi	*Anglo-Saxon Chronicle*	Magna Carta (1215)	Saladin
Dominic	Canute	Edward I	
Innocent III	Edward the Confessor	Parliament	

Can You Locate?

Cluny	Sicily	Runnymede	Constantinople
Canossa	England	Canterbury	Palestine
Worms	Hastings	Scotland	Jerusalem
Lombardy	Normandy	Anjou	Venice

How Much Do You Remember?

1. List three examples from this chapter of the conflicts between the papacy and European monarchs. Identify the names of the popes and rulers as well as the issue that prompted the controversy.
2. Identify the following records/documents in English history: *Anglo-Saxon Chronicle, Domesday Book,* Magna Carta.
3. What did the reigns of Henry II of England and Philip II of France have in common?
4. List at least three motives that prompted Europeans to join the Crusades.
5. List five consequences of the Crusades.

What Do You Think?

1. The conflict between church and state was not just a medieval problem. In what ways is it evident today?
2. Compare the reigns of John of England and Louis IX of France in light of Proverbs 16:12.
3. Of the events discussed in this chapter, which one do you think had the greatest impact upon the church? What event had the greatest impact on each of the following: the Holy Roman Empire, England, France? Explain your answers.
4. What kinds of "holy wars" should Christians be prepared to fight? (See Eph. 6:10-18; II Cor. 10:3-5; I Tim. 1:18-19; 6:12.)

Notes
1. Henry Bettenson, ed., *Documents of the Christian Church* (New York: Oxford Univ. Press, 1947), pp. 157-58.
2. Geoffroide Villehardouin and Jean, sire de Joinville, *Memoirs of the Crusades,* trans. Sir Frank Marzials (London: Dent, 1926), p. 321.

CHAPTER 9

"Town air makes one free."

The Reshaping of Medieval Europe

In the economic, social, and political developments of the Middle Ages we can see the beginnings of modern Western society. During the late medieval period (1200-1500), Europe experienced significant changes. Trade was pursued with renewed vigor, towns grew in size and importance, and a new social class emerged. Contact with other cultures sparked interest in learning and the arts, and national states began to appear. At the same time, the feudal and manorial systems weakened, and the church, once the dominant force in Europe, declined in strength and influence.

Revival of Trade

During the early Middle Ages, trade activity had diminished in Europe. Money was in short supply. Travel was often treacherous, as roads were poor, and robbers and pirates often threatened merchants on the trade routes. Towns, which were once the heart of economic activity, declined in size. The manors became the new economic centers of medieval Europe. Unlike towns and cities, manors did not depend upon trade but were virtually self-sufficient. The few items that could not be made or grown on a particular manor could be obtained by **barter**—exchanging goods for goods. For the most part, trade remained localized and relatively insignificant.

Trade Routes

The reopening of trade routes between western Europe and the East was a major factor in the revival of European commerce. During the early Middle Ages, Byzantine and Muslim merchants had dominated trade in the Mediterranean region. Later, however, enterprising Italian merchants, with their large fleets, began to seize trade rights in the Near East. Soon Italian cities such as Venice, Pisa, and Genoa gained a virtual monopoly on Mediterranean trade.

European commerce expanded as the Italian merchants became the middlemen in trade between Europe and the Orient. Once goods from the Far East reached the Mediterranean, Italian merchants transported them to Europe, where they were distributed to European markets. Traders who brought goods from the Orient reached the Mediterranean by three principal routes:

1. The southern route was almost entirely on water. Ships laden with goods from India and China sailed across the Arabian Sea and northward up the Red Sea. The goods were then hauled overland to the Nile River and transported to the Mediterranean.
2. The central route combined land and sea travel. Ships from the Far East carried goods to the Persian Gulf, where caravans transported the merchandise to Baghdad or Damascus. Other traders then brought them to port cities along the Mediterranean and Black seas.
3. The northern route, known as the "Silk Road," was an overland route across central Asia. It connected Beijing and Constantinople.

Italy controlled Mediterranean trade, but Flanders was the marketplace of northern Europe. The region of Flanders (which included parts of present-day Belgium, France, and Holland) lay at the crossroads of northern European trade routes. The Flemish, who were makers of fine cloth, had easy access to the markets of Europe.

Markets and Fairs

As trade activity increased, so did the need for places where merchants could meet and exchange their goods. On the local level, markets became the primary centers for trade. Once a week traders met along important highways, in church courtyards, or in village squares. The goods sold there benefited both the people on the manor and those in the towns. The market offered incentive for the laboring serfs to produce more, for at the market they could sell their surplus produce. Many saved their money, desiring to buy goods or hoping one day to be able to buy their freedom from the manor. The market also offered craftsmen and merchants an opportunity

Opposite Page: The medieval town of Carcassone

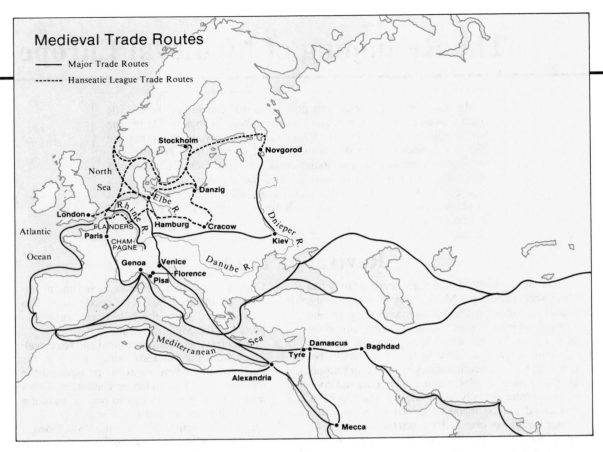

Medieval Trade Routes

—— Major Trade Routes

------ Hanseatic League Trade Routes

to peddle their wares. Thus these places of trade met the demands of the local population. Townspeople obtained surplus food from the manors, and the people of the manor acquired articles made and sold by local craftsmen and merchants.

On a larger scale than the markets were the trade fairs, which attracted merchants from all over Europe as well as many foreign countries. These fairs were sometimes great regional or international events. They were held annually and could last from several days to several weeks. Because they were held in nearly every part of Europe, fairs were often scheduled in sequence so that merchants could attend one after the other.

Fairs provided a meeting place for East-West trade. Italian middlemen and foreign merchants from Constantinople, Damascus, and Alexandria brought spices, silks, precious gems, cotton, linen, rugs, and dyes from the East. Peddlers and town merchants bought these "luxury" items and distributed them locally. In return, foreign merchants purchased local products such as wool, grain, timber, and fish.

The most famous and important of the medieval fairs were held in Champagne, a region in northeastern France. This province became an important trade center for merchants traveling between Flanders and Italy. At almost any time during the year, fairs were being held in the towns of this region, each one lasting about six weeks.

Fairs such as the ones at Champagne were more than just places to exchange goods; they were festive occasions.

> The neighboring lords and their families came to see and to buy and to enjoy the diversions of the fair. The monks from the abbey and the secular clergy mingled with the throng. No doubt many an artisan and many a runaway serf from the neighboring manors was drawn hither by the strange sights and sounds and the gay-colored crowd. Mountebanks, jugglers, and musicians of every de-

scription vied in their efforts to attract the crowd, men with trained monkeys, dogs, or dancing bears, wrestlers, wandering minstrels singing ancient lays, fakers without number were there to entertain and astonish the populace. There were gathered as in modern fairs the thief, the pick-pocket, the cutpurse, the thug, the prostitute, beggars. Often the sergeants were hard pressed to maintain order in this heterogeneous mob.[1]

Money and Banking

The barter system in use during the early Middle Ages could not meet the expanding demands of the trade fairs. Therefore money gained wider use as a means of exchange. This development helped trade and provided a standard of value for the purchase and sale of goods. Feudal lords and commercial towns began minting their own coins. Their values varied greatly, depending upon the amount and purity of the metal contained in them. Certain coins of high quality became widely accepted as mediums of exchange. One, for example, was the **florin,** a gold coin minted by the city of Florence.

Because most merchants did not know the value of coins minted outside their own region, **money-changers** grew in importance at the markets and trade fairs throughout Europe. These men were experienced in judging the approximate value of coins, discovering counterfeit currency, and determining one currency's value in relation to another. Merchants could be assured of the value of a foreign currency that they accepted for their goods. If the merchants wanted that currency exchanged into their own, moneychangers were also ready to perform that service—for a fee, of course.

They did more, however, than just evaluate and exchange money for merchants. They provided many other services that we commonly associate with modern banks. Since they dealt constantly with money, moneychangers went to great lengths to protect their own funds. Realizing this, other merchants began entrusting their surplus cash to the moneychangers for safekeeping. The moneychangers then became moneylenders. Kings, nobles, and even popes borrowed from them to finance their activities. For example, a king might

borrow money to finance a crusade to the Holy Land. He risked great danger, however, by carrying large sums on his journey. It was much safer and more convenient to obtain a letter of credit in Europe. (Letters of credit were much like our modern checks.) Once he reached the Holy Land he could present the letter of credit to another moneychanger and receive cash in return. It is not surprising to learn that our word *bank* comes from the Italian ***banca,*** which means ''bench,'' referring to the table of the moneychangers.

The Medieval Church and Business Practice

There was little economic freedom in Europe throughout much of the medieval period. Most people had little opportunity or incentive to improve

Jan Gossaert, Portrait of a Banker, *National Gallery of Art, Washington, D.C.*

their way of life. Feudal lords held virtual monopolies over the economic life on the manors. In addition, the teaching of the Roman church discouraged economic activity.

In a day when religion dominated society, it was quite natural for the church to shape the economic ideas of Europe. The church viewed with suspicion those individuals involved in trade. Did not the Bible teach "Lay not up for yourselves treasures upon earth . . . for where your treasure is, there will your heart be also" (Matt. 6:19, 21)?

Quentin Metsys, The Moneylender and His Wife, *Museé du Louvre. Paris © Réunion des Musées Nationaux*

Poverty was upheld as a virtue. Since seeking the riches of this world often leads one to greed and the hoarding of wealth, the Roman church sought to place restraints upon business.

Every man had a particular place in society and was expected to work for the common good of society, not just for himself. It was considered selfish and rebellious for one to try to improve his own status in life or to involve himself in trade solely for profit.

Profit resulting from the sale of goods or services was deemed acceptable only if the seller did not take advantage of the buyer. The church advocated a **"just price"** for goods sold—a price that included the cost of materials, a fair return for labor expended, and a reasonable profit. According to the church it was wrong to sell an item for more than it was worth or to buy it for less than its actual value. If any man received a profit greater than his needs, he was expected to give it to charity.

Furthermore, the medieval church prohibited **usury**—the practice of charging interest for the use of lent money. Usury was considered a sin. The church assumed that anyone who borrowed money was in great need. Therefore, for someone to profit from a loan made to a brother in need was definitely wrong. Such a loan should be an act of charity, not a money-making venture. The revival of trade altered this doctrine. Merchants borrowed money not because of poverty but for business investment. Soon it became acceptable to charge interest on loans made for investment purposes. Profit made on such loans was considered a fitting reward for the risk taken, since loss was an equal possibility.

In spite of the church's teaching, the revival of trade and changes in business methods brought new opportunities and incentives to much of Europe's population. Sound economic principles made Europe prosperous: the dignity of labor, the legitimacy of profit, freedom of exchange, and individual responsibility—not group responsibility—for economic matters. More and more people were gaining financial independence.

Section Review

1. What European military campaigns brought about renewed interest in international trade?
2. Who served as middlemen in trade between Europe and the Orient?
3. What were the primary centers of trade on the local level in Europe? What were the centers of trade for large-scale international trade?
4. Where do we get our word for *bank?*
5. What is the term for charging interest for the use of lent money? What institution condemned this practice during the Middle Ages?

Growth of Towns

Towns, like trade, did not entirely disappear in the West during the Middle Ages. Even so, Europe could boast few cities that could compare in size and population to the many bustling cities of the Roman Empire. Renewed trade, however, stimulated the growth of towns. Towns provided needed markets and were important centers of exchange.

By the eleventh century, active forces at work in Europe began to give shape to the forerunners of the modern city. Better farming methods led to increased agricultural production. Townspeople who wished to devote their full energy to a specific trade or craft could depend upon others to produce surplus food. An increased food supply boosted Europe's population. As Europe's population grew, so did her towns. Some towns revived within the decayed walls of old Roman cities, while others sprang up at locations important to trade: crossroads, bridges, fords, river mouths, and harbors. Still others were built near castles, churches, and monasteries.

Townsmen Gain Basic Freedoms

Merchants and craftsmen, who lived in the growing urban centers, did not fit into the medieval class structure. They were not lords, vassals, or

Ponte Vecchio Bridge across the Arno River in Florence, Italy; the bridge is lined with shops of Florentine merchants.

serfs. And their labor contributed little to the agricultural output of the local manor. Nevertheless, nearly every town was subject to some feudal lord.

Townsmen having common interests soon banded together to gain freedom from feudal interference and to secure local self-government. They achieved this independence in a variety of ways. Some towns bought privileges from feudal lords who were willing to grant certain liberties in exchange for large sums of money. Other lords bestowed these privileges freely, for a thriving town meant greater revenues from sales taxes and tolls (a fee paid for some privileges, such as traveling on a road or crossing a bridge). Nevertheless, there were some lords who did not want to relinquish control at any cost. In such cases towns often revolted and fought for their freedom.

The privileges granted a town by a feudal lord were usually written down in a legal document called a **charter.** This document outlined the rights and freedoms of the townspeople. The more favorable the charter, the greater the number of people attracted to settle in the town. While liberties varied from town to town, most townsmen shared certain basic freedoms:

1. *Free Status.* The most important privilege enjoyed by a townsman was that of being a freeman. No matter what his previous status, a man who lived in a town for a year and a day was considered free. A serf, for example, who ran away from his manor and managed to escape capture by living in a town for one year, broke all ties with his manor. An old German proverb says, "Town air makes one free."

2. *Exemption from Manorial Obligations.* Town charters usually exempted townsmen from laboring for the lord of the manor. The townsmen as a group, not as individuals, owed service to the lord. This service was usually rendered in the form of a cash payment.

3. *Town Justice.* Townsmen also won the privilege of administering their own justice. Instead of being tried in a feudal court and judged by feudal customs, a townsman was tried in the court of his town and was judged by town people and town customs.

4. *Commercial Privileges.* The chief commercial freedom granted to townsmen was the right to buy and sell freely in the town market. The merchants were free from feudal interference and were protected from competition by outside merchants.

Merchants and Craftsmen Establish Guilds

Merchants and craftsmen in growing towns banded together to protect their common commercial interests. They formed organizations called **guilds,** whose primary function was to regulate the business activity of a given town. By acting together, town merchants gained greater security, discouraged outside competition, and increased profits. Guilds also provided aid to members in need. They established schools and cared for the poor, widows, and orphans. Powerful guilds helped towns obtain favorable charters and played an important role in town governments.

There were two types of guilds: merchant and craft. The earliest type was the merchant guild. It guarded the trade interests of merchants by giving them a monopoly of a town's trade. The guild restricted outsiders from doing business in town except upon payment of a heavy fee. The guild also fixed prices at which goods could be bought and sold at the town market.

At first each town had only one guild. But as a town's trade grew and became more specialized, each merchant guild divided into many craft guilds. There were guilds for the town's bakers, tanners, shoemakers, butchers, wheelwrights, and other craftsmen. Each craft guild regulated the hours its members worked, the wages earned, and the number of employees hired. Members of a particular craft guaranteed the quality of their products. They punished members who used shoddy materials, dealt dishonestly, or sold goods cheaper than the established price.

Within each craft guild, there were three classes of members; apprentices, journeymen, and masters. A young boy began his training as an **apprentice.** He entered the home of a master craftsman and was expected to work hard in return for his food, lodg-

Guild halls in Ghent, Belgium

ing, and training. It was the master's responsibility to teach the young apprentice not only the skills of the trade but also proper conduct. At the end of his apprenticeship—a period varying from two to seven years—the young man became a **journeyman,** or "day-laborer." He could then seek employment and earn wages as a skilled worker. Usually a journeyman remained at the home of his master and worked at his master's shop.

Every journeyman looked forward to the day when he could become a master himself. This required years of experience, as well as funds to open a shop. To become a **master,** a journeyman had to undergo an oral examination, present an example of his workmanship (called a "master piece"), and take an oath to conduct himself according to the regulations of the guild. Once approved by the other masters of the guild, the new master could open his own shop and take on his own apprentices and journeymen.

Sometimes towns formed associations to promote and protect their mutual commercial interests. The most famous of these was the **Hanseatic League,** composed of more than seventy German cities in northwestern Europe. The *Hanse* (German for "guild") sought to organize and control trade in Sweden, Russia, Flanders, and England. Although the *Hanse* primarily sought commercial privileges, it also became a powerful political force. It negotiated treaties, maintained its own navy, and even waged war against other countries.

A New Social Class Emerges

In early feudal society, a great social and economic gulf had separated the nobility and the peasants. With the growth of towns during the eleventh and twelfth centuries, however, a new social class arose, commonly referred to as the **middle class.** It was composed of merchants, bankers, craftsmen, and skilled laborers. These were the "men of the town" known as *burgesses* in England, *bourgeois* in France, and *burgers* in Germany. (The word *burg* means "a walled town.") The members of this new class had freedom and money. They were energetic, independent, mobile, and growing in number and power. Their world was the town market, and their livelihood was trade. The middle class contributed to the decline of feudalism and helped shape modern society.

Most noblemen considered the middle class a threat to their position in society. Social ranking, formerly determined by birth or landholding, had gradually shifted toward those who possessed the greatest amounts of money and goods. A nobleman's wealth was in his land; a merchant's wealth was his money or goods. While the nobleman usually spent

Lübceck; by the end of the thirteenth century, it was the leading city of the Hanseatic League.

the money he derived from his land, the merchant invested his money, often at great risk, to gain more wealth. Soon many merchants, bankers, and master craftsmen possessed more goods, fine clothes, and comfortable dwellings than the feudal lords.

By challenging the nobility's social position, the middle class also weakened the nobility's political authority. By the twelfth century, most towns had gained some degree of self-government. Although townsmen were able to regulate trade within their own town, they realized that the sectionalism produced by feudalism and the tolls and sales taxes levied by feudal lords hindered widespread trade. As a result, the middle class desired the stable and uniform government a national king could offer rather than the localism of feudal lords. Kings who had previously relied on nobles to supply revenue and soldiers now could draw upon the rich resources of the towns and the middle class, usually in the form of taxes.

Town Life

Medieval towns were small. By the thirteenth century, only a few, such as Paris, Rome, Venice, and Florence, had populations over fifty thousand. The typical town averaged only about five thousand people. Most towns were enclosed by thick walls for protection. As the population of the town grew, conditions became overcrowded. Old walls had to be torn down and new ones built to create more room. Because land space within walled towns was limited, houses were crowded together along narrow

streets. It was not uncommon for houses to be four or five stories high. The upper stories of houses often extended out over the streets. The streets below were dark, crooked, and filthy. The townspeople tossed their garbage into open gutters lining the roads. According to medieval writers, the stench from some towns could be smelled miles away. Poor sanitation caused disease, and epidemics spread rapidly, carried throughout the town by the pigs, rats, and dogs that roamed the streets.

Although town life was not easy or comfortable, it was often exciting. During the day the streets hummed with the noise of merchants and peddlers selling their wares, of craftsmen plying their trade, and of children playing in the streets. The center of activity was the town square. Here

Narrow town street in England

The Black Death

Death swept across Europe in the fourteenth century. A form of plague known as the Black Death (because of the dark blotches it left on its victims) slew fully one-fourth of the population of Europe. Some historians maintain that half of the people of Europe died. So great was the suffering and social upheaval that many people believed that the end of the world was at hand.

The plague spread to Europe from Asia, carried by the rats and fleas in merchant ships. During the Middle Ages, however, men did not know the cause of the disease. This uncertainty made the plague even more fearsome. The Black Death seemed uncaused and unstoppable. People of every social and economic class fell to its onslaught. Men sought above all to save themselves. One witness of the plague wrote, "One citizen avoided another, hardly any neighbor troubled about others, relatives never or hardly ever visited each other. Moreover, such terror was struck into the hearts of men and women by this calamity, that brother abandoned brother, and the uncle his nephew, and the sister her brother, and very often the wife her husband. What is even worse and nearly incredible is that fathers and mothers refused to see and tend their children, as if they had not been theirs."[2]

The widespread destruction brought out the best and worst in mankind. Some devout men viewed the plague as the judgment of God and turned to Him. They devoted themselves to the treatment of the ill and the easing of suffering wherever possible. Others, however, gave free reign to their lusts. Their philosophy became, "Eat, drink, and be merry; for tomorrow we die." Instead of being humbled by the terror, men became bolder in their sin. Even secular historian Barbara Tuchman in her book *A Distant Mirror* notes that this behavior conforms to the picture of the end times given in Scripture by the Apostle John: "And the rest of the men which were not killed by these plagues yet repented not of the works of their hands, . . . neither repented they of their murders, nor of their sorceries, nor of their fornication, nor of their thefts" (Rev. 9:20-21).

visiting merchants displayed dazzling items from foreign lands. Within the square's large open space, the town's militia drilled, boys played soccer, and actors performed. Lining the square were the town hall, various guild halls, and the towering cathedral.

Section Review
1. What factors contributed to the growth of towns in medieval Europe?
2. List four basic freedoms shared by most townspeople.
3. What was the primary function of a guild?
4. What were the three classes of members of craft guilds?
5. What new social class arose with the rise of towns in the eleventh and twelfth centuries? What were the chief occupations of the people of this class?

Medieval Learning and Art

The Middle Ages is often considered an age of ignorance and superstition—a "dark" age of learning. While there was little formal education of the masses throughout much of this period, education never completely died out. Learning continued, primarily under the influence of the Roman church. The monks constituted the vast majority of the educated. The primary centers of education were the monasteries and cathedrals. The church, however, was often more interested in maintaining existing knowledge (no matter how inadequate) than in pursuing new ideas.

A basic part of medieval education was the liberal arts curriculum, which was divided into two groups of studies: the **trivium,** consisting of grammar (Latin), rhetoric (effective speaking), and logic;

and the **quadrivium,** consisting of arithmetic, geometry, astronomy, and music. A medieval bishop-historian described his education:

> [I was taught] by means of grammar to read, by dialectic [logic] to apprehend the arguments in disputes, by rhetoric to recognize the different meters, by geometry to comprehend the measurement of the earth and of lines, by [astronomy] to contemplate the paths of the heavenly bodies, by arithmetic to understand the parts of numbers, by harmony to fit the modulated voice to the sweet accent of the verse.[3]

During the twelfth century, a revival of learning swept across Europe. It was brought about by several factors:

1. Political and economic conditions in Europe were improving, producing a climate more favorable for intellectual and cultural pursuits.
2. Europe's contact with the Byzantine and Arab civilizations exposed Europe to new ideas. These cultures transmitted to Europe not only their own knowledge but also the preserved learning of ancient Greece and Rome. New avenues of study opened as Justinian's code of laws, the works of Aristotle, and Greek and Arab medical writings became available in Europe.
3. As towns grew and the functions of government expanded, there was an increasing need for education. A theological training was no longer sufficient to meet all the needs of law and business. Greater numbers of people—including some from the rising middle class—were seeking entrance into the ranks of the educated.

The Universities

Probably the most important development during this period was the rise of the university. These new centers of learning gradually replaced most of the old monastery and cathedral schools of the Roman church. In the late Middle Ages students were little concerned about the town or school in which they studied. They were more interested in who their teacher was. Students traveled all over Europe to find the best instructor in their subject area. A master teacher attracted many students, who paid him a fee to teach them. As the number of teachers and students grew in a given locality, the scholars—like craftsmen—formed educational guilds for privileges and protection. At first any association of people, such as a guild, was called a *universitas.* But gradually the term came to designate those united for the common purpose of education.

Two of the earliest universities were at Bologna in northern Italy and at Paris. Students organized the university at Bologna and formed a guild to ensure adequate instruction from their teachers and to protect against being overcharged for food and rent by the townspeople. The university at Paris grew out of an old cathedral school. Unlike Bologna, it was supervised by a guild of masters or professors, not students. Each school offered training in specialized areas of study. Bologna became a leading center for the study of law; Paris, for liberal arts and theology. These schools served as models for other universities.

Rules for Teachers Set Down by Students at Bologna

A professor might not be absent without leave, even a single day, and if he desired to leave town he had to make a deposit to ensure his return. If he failed to secure an audience of five for a regular lecture, he was fined as if absent—a poor lecture indeed which could not secure five hearers! He must begin with the bell and quit within one minute after the next bell. He was not allowed to skip a character in his commentary, or postpone a difficulty to the end of the hour, and he was obliged to cover ground systematically, so much in each specific term of the year.[6]

Philosophy and Theology

The schools and universities of twelfth-century Europe provided the home for a new intellectual movement known as **Scholasticism.** It was characterized by a renewed interest in theology and philosophy. In their search for understanding, the "schoolmen" (from which we get the term *scho-*

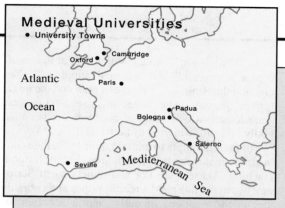

Medieval Universities
- University Towns

Atlantic
Ocean

Mediterranean Sea

University Life

University life has changed significantly over the years. Early universities had no campuses, buildings, laboratories, or athletic facilities. Classes met wherever the teacher could find a place to lecture. All lectures were conducted in Latin. Students sat on the floor, on straw, or on small benches. They took notes on wax tablets or parchment, if they could afford it. Few students had textbooks—books were too scarce and too expensive. Sometimes students pooled their resources to buy a textbook, which they shared.

While the academic setting has changed dramatically over the centuries, some things about university life never change. For example, many students will still write home only when they are in need of money. This letter from a medieval student to his parents could well have been written by his modern counterpart: "This is to inform you that I am studying at Oxford with the greatest diligence, but the matter of money stands greatly in the way of my promotion, as it is now two months since I spent the last of what you sent me. The city is expensive and makes many demands; I have to rent lodgings, buy necessaries, and provide for many other things which I cannot now specify. Wherefore I respectfully beg your paternity by the promptings of divine pity that you may assist me, so that I may be able to complete what I have well begun."[4]

In another letter, a father writes to his son who is away at school. The contents of the letter would not seem out of place in modern society: "It is written, 'he also that is slothful in his work is brother to him that is a great waster.' I have recently discovered that you live dissolutely and slothfully, preferring license to restraint and play to work and strumming a guitar while the others are at their studies, whence it happens that you have read but one volume of law while your more industrious companions have read several. Wherefore I have decided to exhort you herewith to repent utterly of your dissolute and careless ways, that you may no longer be called a waster and that your shame may be turned to good repute."[5]

lasticism) relied upon two sources of knowledge: faith and reason. They tried to harmonize the teachings of the church (faith) and the writings of Greek philosophers (reason). Although the schoolmen or "scholastics" acknowledged the necessity of faith, they attempted to use logic and philosophy to explain and defend the church's teaching. They did not seek to discover new knowledge but sought to support that which already existed. By applying the test of reason to the teaching of the church, they hoped to show the reasonableness of the Christian faith.

Three of the most noted scholastic thinkers were Anselm, Peter Abelard (AB uh LARD), and Thomas Aquinas (uh KWY nus). The earliest of these was **Anselm** (1033-1109), the archbishop of Canterbury whose view of the relationship between reason and faith may be summed up by his following statement:

> I do not try, Lord, to attain Your lofty heights, because my understanding is in no way equal to it. But I do desire to understand Your truth a little, that truth that my heart believes and loves. For I do not seek to understand so that I may believe; but I believe so that I may understand. For I believe this also, that "unless I believe, I shall not understand."[7]

Anselm realized that faith is essential to proper understanding. Nevertheless, he did not reject the use of reason. He is best remembered for his use of logical arguments to support two major doctrines of the Christian faith: the existence of God and the satisfaction concept of the atonement (that Christ's death on the cross satisfied God's holiness and justice and redeemed fallen man).

Unlike Anselm, **Peter Abelard** (1079-1141) advocated the frequent asking of questions as the "first key to wisdom." Abelard, a popular teacher of philosophy and theology at Paris, governed his studies by the following principle: "By doubting we arrive at inquiry (asking critical questions), and through inquiry we perceive the truth." In his most famous work, *Sic et non* ("Yes and No"), Abelard listed 158 questions concerning important articles of faith. With each question he presented pro and con statements of earlier church scholars. He thereby demonstrated that contradictory views existed. Abelard did not attempt to answer the questions that he raised; he did hope that the questions would prompt his students to search for truth through critical reasoning. Nevertheless, many church leaders viewed his emphasis upon reason as dangerous to the teachings of the church.

Scholasticism reached its height under **Thomas Aquinas** (1225?-74), called "the prince of the schoolmen." Aquinas believed that certain truths could be understood by man's reason and that others could be perceived by faith alone. Since both man's reason and man's faith are gifts from God, Aquinas saw no real contradiction between them. In his *Summa Theologica* he attempted to demonstrate in a systematic fashion that the teachings of the church were in harmony with the logic and philosophy of Aristotle.

By reconciling the teachings of the church and the writings of Aristotle, the scholastics hoped to settle the controversy between faith and reason. (The problem, however, was not with faith and reason but was in the scholastics' sources for their faith and reason.) They used Aristotle's system of thought in interpreting their faith. This attempt to apply human reasoning to spiritual truth often led them into error. Many of them placed reason above faith, making spiritual truth dependent upon logical reasoning. Furthermore, their overemphasis on reason took them beyond profitable learning and left them with empty speculations. For example, they asked such foolish questions as "Are angels brighter in the morning or in the evenings?" "At what hour of the day did Adam sin?" and "Will a man at the resurrection recover all his fingernail clippings?" Neglecting the Bible as the source of faith and the guide for reason, they gave "heed to fables and endless genealogies, which minister questions, rather than godly edifying which is in faith" (I Tim. 1:4).

In their attempts to explain their faith, the scholastics revealed many contradictions in the church's teaching. These were not contradictions in Scripture but in the fallible decrees of popes and councils and in the opinions of early church scholars. In later centuries men would take their eyes off the church and look elsewhere for a more reliable source of truth. In this way God used the scholastics to prepare for the coming of the Reformation—a period in which men once again recognized the Bible as the only infallible source of truth.

Medieval Science

In medieval times people devoted little attention to science. Medieval thinkers focused upon the world to come and placed little emphasis upon the present physical world. In their opinion, faith and reason were the only sure guides to knowledge. Science was merely a secondary source of knowledge, which at best could only confirm truths that theology and philosophy had already established.

Magic and superstition clouded medieval science. Astrologers sought to interpret the future from the position of the stars, while alchemists attempted to transform nonvaluable metals into gold. What little scientific knowledge that did exist had been handed down from ancient sources. Churchmen compiled this information into handbooks of knowledge called encyclopedias. Because these compilers did not question the accuracy of their sources or conduct any experiments themselves, they often passed down gross misconceptions and falsehoods.

The body of scientific knowledge increased during the twelfth and thirteenth centuries as Greek and Muslim works began to circulate in Europe. For the most part European "scientists" were content to accept the findings of the past without verification. Nevertheless, there were some who began to critically reexamine inherited scientific ideas. One of the best known of these new scientific thinkers

Symbolism in Medieval Art

In this painting entitled *The Coronation of the Virgin,* the Italian artist Antonia da Imola portrays the Roman Catholic myth of the crowning of the Virgin Mary as the "queen of heaven." A number of Bible characters and medieval "saints" are gathered around Christ and Mary, watching this "event."

Antonio da Imola, Coronation of the Virgin, *Bob Jones University Collection of Sacred Art*

Like many other works of art from the Middle Ages, this painting reflects a mixture of biblical truth and Roman Catholic error.

Most medieval paintings contain a great deal of symbolism. In *The Coronation,* da Imola paints several "saints" with telltale attributes—characteristics that would enable the medieval viewer to easily identify the painted figure. For example, Augustine of Hippo is shown dressed in black, holding a bishop's crosier (a staff similar to a shepherd's crook), and wearing a miter (a tall, pointed hat worn by bishops). The artist portrays Francis of Assisi bearing stigmata (wounds in the hands and feet similar to Christ's). Francis supposedly received these marks because of his great holiness. The martyr Catherine of Alexandria is seen holding a spiked wheel—the instrument of torture associated with her death. Lucy of Syracuse holds her eyes in a dish. According to leg-end, she cut them out because their beauty was a stumbling block to a young man who ardently admired her.

The painting also contains a number of Bible characters. For example, Peter is the older man with a short gray beard. Although da Imola did not do so, many artists portrayed Peter with keys (Matt. 16:18-19), a book (for his epistles), a cross (John 21:18-19), or a fish (Matt. 4:18-19). Da Imola portrays Paul with a brown beard and bald head. He holds a sword, which symbolizes his martyrdom. Mary Magdalene is shown with long hair and ointment in her hand. The medieval world believed that it was she who anointed Jesus' feet and wiped them with her hair (Luke 7:36-38). Lastly, the artist paints the archangel Gabriel with wings, holding a lily in his hand. The lily, found throughout this painting, is a symbol of purity.

was the Englishman **Roger Bacon** (1214?-94). He was keenly aware of the obstacles facing scientific advancement: "There are four principal stumbling blocks to comprehending truth, which hinder well-nigh every scholar: the example of frail and unworthy authority, long-established custom, the sense of the ignorant crowd, and the hiding of one's own ignorance under the show of wisdom."[8]

Although not the first to conceive of the idea, he advocated observation and experimentation as tests for scientific conclusions. Thanks to Bacon and others, science was beginning to free itself from the shackles of mysticism, superstition, and unreliable authority. Nevertheless, it was not until a later day that scholars grasped the full importance of this scientific method.

Roger Bacon and the Future

In a fascinating letter, the thirteenth-century English scientist and philosopher Roger Bacon forecast what he believed would become of the technological achievements of the future. Some of his predictions demonstrate an astonishing foresight.

He predicted, for example, improvements on ships which would "do away with the necessity of rowers, so that great vessels, both in rivers and on the sea, shall be borne about with only a single man to guide them and with greater speed than if they were full of men." The modern reader can easily imagine trains or cars when Bacon describes "carriages [that] can be constructed to move without animals to draw them, and with incredible velocity."

Long before the twentieth century, men dreamed of building flying machines. Bacon was one of these dreamers. His idea, however, was unlike modern airplanes: "Machines for flying can be made in which a man sits and turns an ingenious device by which skillfully contrived wings are made to strike the air in the manner of a flying bird."

Bacon also believed that one day man would learn to make gold. Today nuclear physics has enabled scientists to "manufacture" this precious metal. (The process is very expensive, however, costing more than the value of the gold it produces. Also the manufactured gold is highly radioactive.) Bacon's predictions demonstrate that scientific inquiry is not just experimentation and observation. Scientists need a healthy imagination too.

Language and Literature

The language of the learned during the Middle Ages was Latin. It was firmly established in the universities and governments throughout Europe and was the official language of the Roman Catholic church. It was not the spoken language of the common people, however. The common tongue varied from region to region; French, German, Italian, Spanish, and English were among those spoken. By the twelfth century, writers began to use the common spoken language, or **vernacular**, in literature.

Among the earliest forms of vernacular literature were the heroic epics—long narrative poems that celebrated the adventures of legendary heroes. Many of these epics have become national treasures: the English *Beowulf*, the French *Song of Roland*, the German *Song of Nibelungs*, and the Spanish poem about El Cid. Wandering minstrels called **troubadours** popularized the vernacular in lyric poetry. They traveled from castle to castle singing their songs of love and adventure to noblemen and their ladies. They also popularized stories about knights, chivalry, and love. Probably the best-known of these medieval romances are the tales of King Arthur and the Knights of the Round Table.

The two greatest writers of the late medieval period were Dante and Chaucer. **Dante Alighieri** (DAHN-tay ah-lee-GYAY-ree; 1265-1321) was an

Dante Alighieri, an engraving by Gustave Doré

Italian poet. His *Divine Comedy* ranks as one of the most brilliant works in all literature. In this long poem Dante takes an imaginary journey through hell, purgatory, and paradise. His work reflects the religious beliefs, social order, and political turbulence of the late Middle Ages.

Geoffrey Chaucer (CHAW sur; 1340?-1400) was a prominent English poet. His masterpiece, *The Canterbury Tales*, presents a collection of stories told by pilgrims on their way to visit the tomb

Chaucer's Pilgrims

Chaucer's *Canterbury Tales*, written in the late fourteenth century, gives a wonderful picture of medieval England. The following two selections are from his descriptions of the twenty-nine pilgrims. Because of the changes in the language over the last six hundred years, the English of Chaucer's day is rather difficult for the modern reader to understand.

A KNYGHT ther was, and that a worthy man,
That fro the tyme that he first bigan
To riden out, he love chivalrie,
Trouthe and honour, fredom and curteisie.

A MARCHANT was ther with a forked berd,
In mottelee, and hye on horse he sat;
Upon his heed a Flaundryssh bever hat,
His bootes clasped faire and fetisly.

Portrait of Chaucer from a fifteenth-century manuscript of Canterbury Tales; *reproduced by permission of The Huntington Library, San Marino, California*

of Thomas à Becket at Canterbury (see pp. 212-13). Chaucer used his skill as a storyteller and his insight into human behavior to depict English life and customs. By their masterful use of the vernacular in literature, both Dante and Chaucer aided the development of their native languages.

Art and Architecture

The art of the Middle Ages was primarily religious. Since laymen were illiterate, the church used the visual arts to teach Bible stories. Artists depicted Bible characters and popular "saints" of the church with certain characteristics. These symbols helped the observer identify the painted or sculptured figures. For example, John the Baptist is always shown wearing an animal skin and carrying a staff with a cross on top. The skin illustrates the fact that "John was clothed with camel's hair" (Mark 1:6). The cross symbolizes his message: "Behold the Lamb of God, which taketh away the sin of the world" (John 1:29).

The most prominent form of medieval art was religious architecture. The people of Europe poured much of their wealth and energy into building impressive cathedrals. An eleventh-century French monk described the architectural revival that began about the year 1000:

> There occurred, throughout the world, especially in Italy and Gaul, a rebuilding of church basilicas. Notwithstanding the greater number were already well established and not in the least in need, nevertheless each Christian people strove against the others to erect nobler ones. It was as if the whole earth, having cast off the old . . . were clothing itself everywhere in the white robe of the church.[9]

From 1050 to about 1150 the prevalent architectural style in Europe was **Romanesque** (ROH muh NESK; "Roman-like"). Romanesque builders modified the rectangular Roman basilica (which earlier church architects had copied) and constructed churches in the shape of a Latin cross. Thick walls supported the tremendous weight of stone vaults and ceilings. Other features included rounded arches, heavy columns, and small doors and windows. The interiors of these churches were dark and gloomy.

Beginning about the thirteenth century, architects devised a way to support stone vaults and ceilings by the use of "flying," or external, buttresses. These supports made it possible for cathedrals to have higher ceilings, thinner walls, and larger windows and doors. This new style was

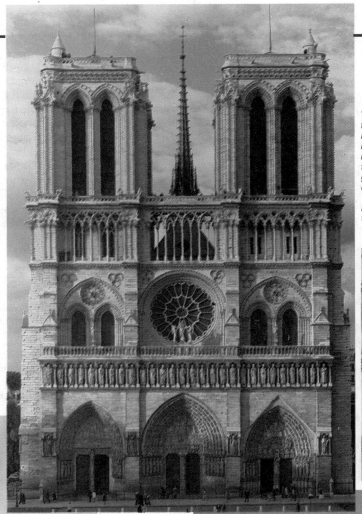

The glories of medieval architecture: the front of the Cathedral of Notre Dame in Paris (top center) and a panoramic side view of the cathedral showing the flying buttresses (bottom right), the lofty pointed arches and stained glass windows of the Rheims Cathedral in France (below right), and the "Leaning Tower of Pisa"—the famous bell tower of the Pisa Cathedral (bottom left)

Medieval Hymns

Although most of the hymns we sing today are of recent origin, there are several medieval hymns that have remained famous to this day. Two of these, probably written by companions of Francis of Assisi, illustrate the religious ideas of the Middle Ages. The first, known as the *Stabat Mater*, is a hymn devoted to the Virgin Mary. Based upon John 19:25, the hymn begins as follows:

At the Cross, her station keeping,
Stood the mournful mother weeping,
Where he hung, the dying Lord.

The second hymn, the *Dies irae* (based upon Zeph. 1:15), portrays the fearful Day of Judgment when both sinners and saints will tremble before the wrath of God. The first few lines of Sir Walter Scott's well-known translation set the tone for this piece:

That day of wrath, that dreadful day,
When heaven and earth shall pass away,
What power shall be the sinner's stay?
How shall he meet that dreadful day?

Although the above hymns are rarely if ever sung in Protestant churches, there are other medieval hymns that are often sung. In 1225 Francis of Assisi wrote his "Canticle of the Sun, and Hymn of Creation"—a poem praising God for His creation. This poem, which has seven stanzas in its English paraphrase, begins as follows:

All creatures of our God and King,
Lift up your voice and with us sing

Alleluia, alleluia!
Thou burning sun with golden beam,
Thou silver moon with softer gleam;
O praise him, O praise him,
Alleluia, alleluia, alleluia!

Another much-loved hymn came from the pen of Bernard of Clairvaux, who wrote a seven-part poem that speaks of Christ's body on the cross. The final part speaks of the head of Christ:

O sacred Head, now wounded,
With grief and shame weighed down,
Now scornfully surrounded
With thorns, Thine only crown;
O sacred Head, what glory,
What bliss till now was Thine!
Yet, though despised and gory,
I joy to call Thee mine.

Finally, there is what many regard to be the finest of all medieval hymns—"Jesus, the Very Thought of Thee." Although tradition has ascribed this poem to Bernard, the authorship is uncertain. It is a hymn that every Christian should be able to sing from the heart:

Jesus, the very thought of Thee;
With sweetness fills the breast.
But sweeter far Thy face to see,
And in Thy presence rest.

Jesus, our only joy be Thou,
As Thou our prize wilt be;
In Thee be all our glory now,
And through eternity.

---

called **Gothic.** In contrast to the dark and heavy elements of the Romanesque, Gothic architecture was light and delicate. The spacious and lofty Gothic cathedrals created an atmosphere of dignity and serenity. Their high towers and pointed arches soared toward heaven, inviting men to turn their thoughts toward God. Another feature of Gothic architecture was stained-glass windows. They added beauty, light, and color to the interior of churches. They also served as a type of "visual Bible." By arranging the glass pieces, artists illustrated biblical stories in vivid colors.

Section Review

1. List three factors that aided a revival of learning during the twelfth century.
2. What were two of the earliest universities begun in Europe? How did they differ?
3. What is the name of the new intellectual movement characterized by a renewed interest in theology and philosophy? What did the philosophers and theologians of this movement try to harmonize?
4. What clouded the work of medieval science?
5. Who were the two greatest writers of the late Middle Ages? Beside each man's name, identify his native country and the title of his important work.

Emergence of National States

Nation-states emerged in the late Middle Ages as people in certain regions became more fully aware of their common traditions, language, and religion. This awareness was the foundation of national feeling. Accompanying the growth of nation-states was the rise of national monarchies. The monarchy served as the symbol of national pride. The independent king ruling a group of people having common interests formed the basis of the early nation-state. Royal power steadily increased in the fourteenth and fifteenth centuries, while feudalism gradually declined. As differences among the various people in Europe became more distinct and as national feeling mounted, boundaries between nation-states began to solidify. By 1500 the major states of Europe were established. The medieval age was passing; the modern age was at hand.

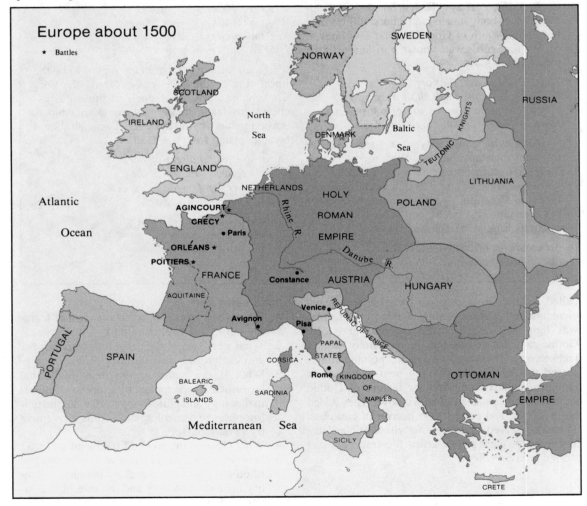

Europe about 1500

★ Battles

War Between England and France

During the fourteenth and fifteenth centuries, England and France were embroiled in a long struggle known as the **Hundred Years' War.** Intermittent battles and broken truces spanned the years from 1337 to 1453. What began as a conflict between feudal lords ended as a rivalry between two emerging nation-states. The war contributed to the decline of feudalism in England and France and stimulated the growth of national feeling in each country.

Causes

For centuries English and French monarchs had confronted one another on the matter of English holdings in France. Although Philip II had drastically reduced the size of the English possessions, the king of England still held on to the duchy of Aquitaine. More fuel was added to this flame of discord when the French monarch attempted to take possession of the rich commercial territory of Flanders. This act threatened England's profitable wool trade. War finally erupted after the last Capetian king of France died without a male heir. The English king, **Edward III,** whose mother was the sister of the three previous French kings, claimed to be the rightful heir to the French throne. But the French nobles were unwilling to give the crown to the long-time rival of the French monarchs. Instead, they chose Philip VI of the house of Valois (vah LWAH) as king.

Conflict

English forces crossed the Channel and won several major victories over the French—at Crécy (kray SEE) in 1346, at Poitiers (pwah TYAY) in 1356, and at Agincourt (AJ in KORT) in 1415. Their success was due largely to new battle tactics and weapons. The English relied on archers armed with **longbows.** Arrows shot by these powerful weapons could penetrate a suit of armor. With the longbow, English archers had greater range and accuracy than their French counterparts, who used the conventional crossbow. Through the strategic deployment of bowmen and knights in battle, the outnumbered English completely routed the French.

Joan of Arc's successful efforts to rally the French were the turning point of the Hundred Years' War

The English nonetheless had little to show from their victories over the French. Decades of constant skirmishes had left them drained of resources. Political unrest at home decreased their zeal for fighting a foreign war. For the French, the war was one of humiliation and destruction. They not only suffered one defeat after another but also saw their countryside pillaged by the English knights.

Even though the English won most of the battles, the French eventually won the war. What turned the tide for the French was a surge of nationalism inspired by a simple peasant girl named **Joan of Arc.** Believing that "heavenly voices" had directed her to drive the English out of France, she roused the weak French king to action, rallied the dispirited French troops, and accompanied the French army into battle. She was captured by the enemy and burned at the stake, but her example stirred the nation. The French succeeded in bringing the war to an end.

Consequences

The English defeat was actually a blessing in disguise. No longer did the English kings concentrate their efforts on holding their French possessions. Instead they began to build a strong nation-

The Battle of Crécy

During the first half of the Hundred Years' War, the outnumbered English forces won a series of impressive victories over the French. Superior English weaponry and discipline made the difference. No battle demonstrates this more clearly than that of Crécy.

In 1346 King Edward III of England invaded France. After landing in Normandy, the English marched along the coast en route to Paris. Edward knew it would be difficult to capture Paris; so he turned his forces northward to join his allies in Flanders. The French pursued them, and the two armies met on August 26 near the village of Crécy, some one hundred miles north of Paris.

The English took up their position on a sloping ridge. Their knights dismounted and prepared to fight alongside the infantry. Armed with deadly longbows, the archers placed themselves slightly forward in wedges. In the center of the English line was a series of irrigation terraces that provided additional protection. The English also lined up a new weapon—the cannon. King Edward directed the battle from his headquarters in a nearby windmill. His troops readied themselves for the enemy attack.

The French forces, however, were in chaos. Three times as large as the English invasion forces, the French army was poorly organized. The French king, Philip VI, was indecisive. Some of his advisors urged an immediate attack. Others advised waiting. According to one account of the battle, Philip ordered the attack but then changed his mind. Unfortunately, by the time he had reconsidered, the army had started moving and could not be easily stopped. Also many of the French knights, hungry for a battle with the English, disregarded the king's order to withdraw.

The large but confused French army moved forward to confront the enemy. The first line of the French forces, mercenary crossbowmen from Genoa, surged up the hill. Before they ever reached the English, a shower of arrows, as one writer put it, "fell like snow" upon them. Trying to escape the "feathered death" of the arrows, the Genoese fell back. Enraged, the French knights behind them slashed at the Genoese with their weapons and rode their horses directly over them toward the English. Some of the angry Genoese began firing their crossbows at the French.

The English longbows continued to pour down death upon the French. The longbow shot with greater accuracy and distance than any other kind of bow and could even pierce armor. Volley after volley from the English archers whistled through the air into the ranks of the French.

The brave French charged on into the slaughter. Waves of knights swept up the slope, only to die in the face of the staunch English defense. At one point the French pressed in on the area commanded by the Prince of Wales, heir to the English throne. The prince sent a message to his father asking for reinforcements. From his windmill, King Edward answered, "Let the boy earn his spurs!" The prince's forces fought on without reinforcements and drove the French back.

The battle continued on into the night. Finally, the weary French army fell back and melted away. King Philip fled the battlefield. The sun came up the next morning on corpses of thousands of French soldiers. The English lost at most only a few hundred. England had scored a decisive victory in her campaign for the French throne.

The Iberian Peninsula 910

☐ Under Moorish rule

FRANCE

KINGDOM OF LEON
NAVARRE
INDEPENDENT MOORISH STATES
COUNTY OF BARCELONA

EMIRATE OF CORDOVA

BALEARIC ISLANDS

Atlantic Ocean

Mediterranean Sea

AFRICA

Spain 1400

☐ Under Moorish rule

FRANCE

NAVARRE

PORTUGAL
CASTILE
AND
LEON
ARAGON

BALEARIC ISLANDS

GRANADA

Taken by Spain in 1492

Atlantic Ocean

Mediterranean Sea

AFRICA

state at home. The war also furthered the cause of nation-making in France. The rivalry over the English presence in France had stirred French nationalism. This bolstered the cause of the French kings as they continued to increase their royal powers.

In England—After a century of fighting on French soil, the English troops returned home only to become involved in civil war. Two rival families, the houses of York and Lancaster, fought for the English throne. The series of conflicts between these noble families is known as the **Wars of the Roses.** (The emblem of the House of York was a white rose; the emblem of the House of Lancaster, a red rose.) The struggle ended after thirty years when Henry Tudor defeated Richard III at the battle of Bosworth Field. Henry was crowned King **Henry VII** (1485-1509). He founded the powerful Tudor dynasty. During the sixteenth century, the Tudors firmly established the power of the English monarchy and built the English nation into a major European power—a position she held for over four hundred years.

In France—Weary of the death and destruction, the Estates-General had during the war allowed the French king to levy a royal land tax called a *taille* (TAH yuh) with which he could maintain a strong army and thereby defeat the English. The eventual success over the English greatly increased the power of the French king. Unlike the English king, who had to depend upon Parliament for funds, the French king could raise money without consent of the Estates-General. There was no check upon his growing power.

Reconquista in Spain and Portugal

Nation-states did not develop as quickly in the Iberian Peninsula (see the map above) as they had in England and France. The peninsula had long been primarily a Muslim land (see p. 139). In the eleventh century a few small non-Muslim states in the north began a concerted effort to drive out the **Moors** (Spanish Muslims). By the late thirteenth century, warriors of the *Reconquista* ("reconquest") had successfully reclaimed all of the peninsula except for the kingdom of Granada.

As the Moors were being driven out, the small northern states expanded into the reclaimed land. Three principal kingdoms emerged: Portugal, Castile, and Aragon. Like most other European states, these kingdoms experienced struggles between a developing monarchy and feudal nobles. There arose in each kingdom the equivalent to an Estates-General or Parliament—the **Cortes,** a council composed of nobles, clergy, and representatives of the cities. The expulsion of the Moors, together with the support from the growing towns and the decline of feudalism, increased the power of each king above that of his feudal nobles and Cortes.

The nation of Spain was created when **Ferdinand,** heir to the throne of Aragon, married **Isabella,** heiress to the throne of Castile. (The kingdom of Portugal remained independent.) Ferdinand and Isabella firmly established their royal power in the new nation. They began the Spanish Inquisition, a systematic persecution of Muslims and Jews. Inquisitors later directed their attacks against Christians who opposed the Roman Catholic church. Ferdinand and Isabella completed the *Reconquista* by driving the Moors out of Granada in 1492. In that same year Christopher Columbus, who sailed under their Spanish sponsorship, landed in the New World.

Disunity in Italy and Germany

In contrast to the rising tide of nationalism and strong monarchies in England, France, Spain, and Portugal, Germany and Italy remained divided into many small regional states. "Germany" and "Italy" were geographic expressions, not unified nations.

The collapse of the Hohenstaufen house in the thirteenth century brought an end to German interference in Italy. Italy was left divided among the kingdom of Naples, the Papal States, and powerful northern cities such as Florence, Venice, Genoa, and Milan. There was little opportunity for national unity while each region struggled to prevent the others from becoming too powerful. Despite its political turmoil and disunity, Italy prospered commercially and later gave birth to the period of cultural achievement known as the Renaissance (see Chapter 10).

Imperial authority declined in Germany with the fall of the Hohenstaufens. Small territorial states emerged. The office of emperor remained, but the real power of government passed into the hands of the great nobles. By the middle of the fourteenth century, a written constitution known as the **Golden Bull** established the **Diet** of the Holy Roman Empire. The Diet was the German equivalent to the English Parliament and the French Estates-General. The most important members of the Diet were the seven electors (three archbishops and four noble princes) who selected the German emperors. The electors generally chose weak men as emperors in order to protect the power of the German nobility. In addition, they passed the imperial crown from one family to another so that no single family would become too powerful. While other lands were striving toward national unity, the German electors sought to avoid it.

Despite the efforts of the German nobles, the **Hapsburg** family built a strong base of power among the southern German states. These states became known collectively as Austria. (Members

of the Hapsburg family ruled from the city of Vienna until after World War I.) After 1438 only members of this family were elected to the German throne. Emperor **Maximilian I** (1493-1519) greatly enlarged the Hapsburg possessions through marriage. His first marriage brought the rich region of the Low Countries (modern Belgium and Holland) under his rule. His second marriage brought him Milan. He also formed a marriage alliance between his son and the daughter of Ferdinand and Isabella of Spain. In this way Spain, the Low Countries, the Holy Roman Empire, and territory in the New World (the Spanish possessions) came under Hapsburg rule.

⋅MAXIMILIANVS⋅

Maximilian I

Section Review

1. What two nations fought during the Hundred Years' War? What were the dates for this war?
2. Which side won most of the battles of this war? What side won the war?
3. What people did the Spanish and Portuguese seek to drive out of the Iberian Peninsula? What was this effort called?
4. What was the German constitution called? What assembly did it establish?
5. Following the collapse of the Hohenstaufen house, what family came to occupy the throne of the Holy Roman Empire and ruled from Vienna until after World War I?

Decline of the Roman Church

Opposition to the authority of the Roman church steadily increased during the fourteenth and fifteenth centuries. The church lost power and prestige not only because of the growing moral corruption of the clergy but also because of the shifting loyalties in European society. With the rise of strong states, national loyalties began to overshadow church loyalty. Many kings no longer tolerated papal interference in their lands. Furthermore, the expansion of knowledge challenged the traditions of the church and a critical spirit of inquiry gradually replaced the passive acceptance of the church's teachings. In addition, the steady growth of wealth in European society turned men's attention from spiritual concerns to earthly gain. In fact, members of the clergy who should have been examples of spirituality were often the ones most desirous of temporal wealth and power.

The growing weakness of the church was most evident in the declining power of the papacy. From its zenith under Pope Innocent III, the papacy had fallen into disgrace. It lost not only its hold on the kings of Europe but also its position of leadership in the church.

Papal Humiliation

The decline of the papacy began under Pope **Boniface VIII** (1294-1303). He sought to control Europe in the highhanded manner of Innocent III. But times had changed; the arrogant demands of Boniface met with resistance.

He suffered a series of humiliating defeats at the hands of the French king **Philip IV.** Trouble began when Philip decided to levy a tax on the French clergy. The pope denounced this, but his words went unheeded. The conflict intensified when Philip arrested a criminal bishop and brought him before a royal court to stand trial. Boniface ordered Philip to release the bishop. When Philip refused, Boniface issued the famous papal **bull** (an official papal document) *Unam Sanctam* (1302). In this strong statement of papal supremacy, Boniface asserted that "it is altogether necessary to salvation for every human being to be subject to the Roman pontiff."

Boniface VIII, statue by Arnolfo di Cambio

Philip, supported by the French people, defied the pope. He accused Boniface of heresy and sought to bring him to trial. Philip's agents, accompanied by a band of soldiers, traveled to the papal residence and took the pope captive. But the people of the town aided Boniface, and he was soon freed. The aged pope, however, did not recover from the shock and humiliation of the ordeal. He died a month later.

Papal Exile

National feeling and royal power triumphed over the demands of the papacy. A short time after the death of Boniface, a Frenchman was elected to the papal office. He, however, never set foot in Rome but moved the papal capital from Rome to Avignon (AH vee NYAWN), a city in modern

France. From 1309 to 1377 the popes—all Frenchmen—resided at Avignon. This period is known as the "**Babylonian Captivity** of the Church," or the Avignon Exile. Although the popes were not actually held captive, they did fall under the influence of the French kings.

During the Avignon years, the papacy declined even further. The rising tide of nationalism caused the English, Germans, and Italians to resent a "French-controlled" papacy. In addition, critics of the church denounced the wealth and corruption that marked the Avignon court. Some of the popes raised new church taxes and sold church offices to maintain their lives of luxury. The Avignon popes were for the most part able administrators of the church bureaucracy, but they had little concern for spiritual matters. Once again calls for reform echoed across Europe.

Papal Schism

The papacy returned to Rome in 1377, but the pope died soon after taking up residence in the city. The French-dominated College of Cardinals, threatened by a Roman mob, elected an Italian as pope. Several months later, the cardinals declared the election invalid and elected a new pope, who moved back to Avignon. The Roman church now had two popes—one in Rome and one in Avignon. Both men claimed to be the rightful pope, and each excommunicated the other. For forty years this **Great Schism** divided the allegiance of the nations of Europe.

In 1409 church leaders met at Pisa to resolve the schism within the church. The council deposed both popes and appointed a new one. But the other two refused to relinquish their office, and the church now had three popes. The matter was finally settled at the **Council of Constance** (1414-18). This large gathering of church leaders succeeded in deposing the other claimants to the papal office and secured the election of Martin V as the sole pope. The council healed the schism and restored the papacy to Rome. But because it was unwilling to initiate any meaningful reforms, it failed to stop the growing criticism of the church's doctrine and

The papal palace at Avignon

Waldo of Lyons

The Waldensians

The increasing corruption of the medieval church was not unnoticed by Christians. Many believers protested strongly against the immorality and worldliness that characterized the institutional church. Many protest movements arose and vanished in the Middle Ages. One which outlasted all others was the Waldensians.

The Waldensians are named for their founder, Waldo of Lyons (died 1217). A prosperous merchant, Waldo was moved by Jesus' words in Matthew 19:21—"If thou wilt be perfect, go and sell that thou hast, and give to the poor, and thou shalt have treasure in heaven: and come and follow me." He sold all that he had and gave the proceeds to the poor. Then Waldo, and others who followed him, began living a life of simplicity and poverty, seeking to do good to all men. As he told a papal representative later, "We have decided to live by the words of the Gospel, essentially that of the Sermon on the Mount, and the commandments, that is, to live in poverty without concern for tomorrow."

In the beginning the Waldensians did not differ from other reform movements such as that of Francis of Assisi. The Waldensians, however, remained laymen instead of becoming priests. They went about preaching and began to translate parts of the Bible into the common language. Their preaching and translating drew the opposition of the church hierarchy, who considered them ignorant laymen, and the pope condemned the movement.

Declaring like Peter and the apostles that they must "obey God rather than men" (Acts 5:29), the Waldensians continued their ministry. They found clever ways to disguise their work from church officials. One Waldensian, for example, went about as a traveling merchant. He would enter a town and display his goods. As he did so, however, he would hint that he had yet more valuable items to share. Curiosity would mount, and the crowd would urge him to show them these hidden treasures. Finally, the merchant revealed his special "wares"—the "pearl of great price" (Matt. 13:46)—and he would preach to them.

Throughout the rest of the Middle Ages, the Waldensians suffered persecution from church authorities, but they managed to survive in the mountains of Switzerland, northern Italy, and southeastern France. After the Reformation, the Waldensians joined forces with the Protestants. Persecution only intensified after the Reformation, though, as Catholic rulers tried to root out the Waldensians entirely from their domains. Some Waldensians fled persecution. One group, for instance, settled in North Carolina in 1893 and built a thriving bakery business. Only in the nineteenth and twentieth centuries were the Waldensians finally able to gain the right to worship freely. As protestors against the corruption of the medieval church even before the Reformation, the Waldensians won the praise of English poet John Milton as "them who kept [God's] truth so pure of old / When all our Fathers worship't sticks and Stones."

practice. As a result, the ''Babylonian Captivity'' and the Great Schism added more fuel to the smoldering discontent that would soon flame into the Protestant Reformation.

Section Review

1. Which pope issued the papal bull *Unam Sanctam?* What did it assert?
2. To what city was the papacy ''exiled''? What is this period called?
3. Name two of the church councils called to settle the Great Schism.

A Glimpse Behind and a Glimpse Ahead

From 1200 to 1500 medieval Europe underwent many changes that helped lay the foundations of modern society. Trade revived, towns grew, and national states came into existence. Though the Renaissance and the Reformation mark the end of the historical period known as the Middle Ages, certain medieval institutions and practices continued to exist for several centuries. For example, Latin remained the language of the educated, and the nobility retained their prominent place in society. Some medieval institutions, such as the jury system, the Roman Catholic church, and the university have continued to the present day. An understanding of the Middle Ages, therefore, helps in the understanding of our own culture.

Chapter Review

Can You Explain?

barter	journeyman	vernacular	Cortes
banca	master	troubadours	Golden Bull
''just price''	middle class	Romanesque	Diet
usury	*trivium*	Gothic	bull
charter	*quadrivium*	nation-state	''Babylonian
guilds	*universitas*	*taille*	Captivity''
apprentice	Scholasticism	*Reconquista*	Great Schism

Can You Identify?

florin	Dante Alighieri	Henry VII	Boniface VIII
moneychangers	Geoffrey Chaucer	Moors	Philip IV
Hanseatic League	Hundred Years' War	Ferdinand	*Unam Sanctam*
Anselm	Edward III	Isabella	1309-77
Peter Abelard	longbow	1492	Council of Constance
Thomas Aquinas	Joan of Arc	Hapsburgs	
Roger Bacon	Wars of the Roses	Maximilian I	

Can You Locate?

medieval trade routes	Crécy	Portugal	Avignon
Flanders	Poitiers	Castile	Pisa
Champagne	Agincourt	Aragon	Constance
Paris	Iberian Peninsula	Austria	
Bologna	Granada	Low Countries	

How Much Do You Remember?

1. Name three factors that encouraged the revival of trade in medieval Europe.
2. In what ways did the church influence business practice?
3. Identify the important contributions and written works of the Scholastics thinkers Anselm, Peter Abelard, and Thomas Aquinas.
4. List characteristics distinguishing the difference between Romanesque and Gothic architecture.
5. What were the causes of the Hundred Years' War? What effect did this war have upon England? upon France?
6. Give the key events and people in the following outline of the decline of the medieval church from 1302 to 1418.
   I. Papal humiliation
   II. Papal exile
   III. Papal schism

What Do You Think?

1. Compare modern labor unions with medieval guilds.
2. Was medieval science truly "scientific"? Explain your answer.
3. Why was the period of the exile of the papacy in Avignon called the "Babylonian Captivity of the Church"?

Notes

1. James W. Thompson, *An Economic and Social History of the Middle Ages* (New York: The Century Co.), p. 602.
2. Boccaccio, *Decameron*, trans. Richard Aldington (New York: Garden City Pub. Co., Inc., 1930), p. 4.
3. Gregory of Tours, *History of the Franks*, trans. Ernest Brehant (New York: Octagon Books, 1973), p. 248.
4. C. H. Haskins, *Studies in Medieval Culture* (Oxford: Oxford Univ. Press), p. 10.
5. Ibid., p. 15.
6. James W. Thompson and Edgar Nathan Johnson, *An Introduction to Medieval Europe* (New York: Norton, 1937), p. 730.
7. Anselm, *Proslogion*, trans. M. J. Charlesworth, 1.
8. Thompson and Johnson, p. 716.
9. E. G. Holt, ed., *Literary Sources of Art History* (Princeton Univ. Press, 1947), p. 3.

Following Pages: Eyre Crowe, Wittenberg, October 31, 1517, *Bob Jones University Collection of Sacred Art*

THE AWAKENING WORLD

"The Awakening World" may seem a strange title for Unit IV. Had the world been asleep before? The word *awakening* here signifies a new expansion of man—geographically, mentally, and, most important, spiritually. The Renaissance recaptured the artistic excellence of the ancients and taught men again to use their God-given talent and reason. The explorers revealed the immensity of the world and brought exciting, unknown lands to the attention of Europe. In the midst of these achievements of mind and body, God sent an "expansion" of the soul, the spiritual revival known as the Reformation. Greater than all the beautiful works of the Renaissance artists, more dramatic than all the discoveries of the explorers, more influential than all the kings and wars of the era was a simple sentence penned by the Apostle Paul and proclaimed by a former German monk named Martin Luther: "The just shall live by faith."

Detail from Eyre Crow, Wittenberg, October 31, 1517, Bob Jones University Collection of Sacred Art

	RENAISSANCE	Giotto (1266?-1337)	Petrarch (1304-74)
	REFORMATION		Wycliffe (1320?-84)
	AGE OF EXPLORATION		* Indicates Date of Important Discovery

1250   1300   135

THE AWAKENING WORLD

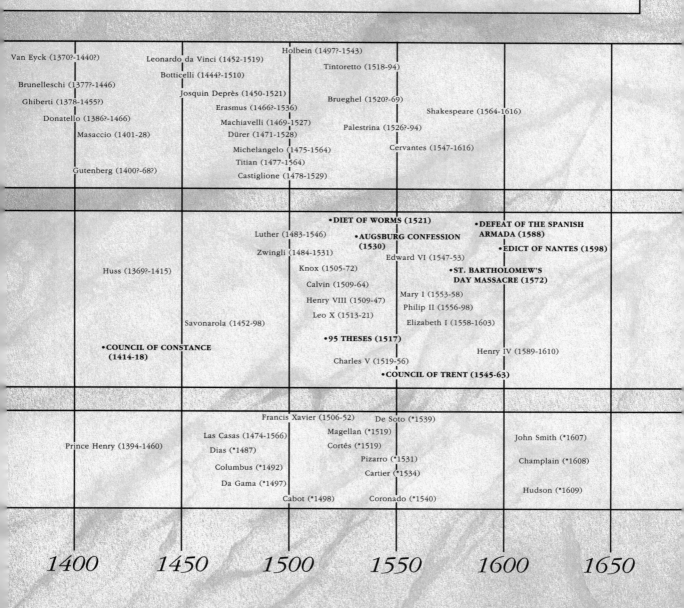

Van Eyck (1370?-1440?)

Leonardo da Vinci (1452-1519)

Holbein (1497?-1543)

Tintoretto (1518-94)

Brunelleschi (1377?-1446)

Botticelli (1444?-1510)

Ghiberti (1378-1455?)

Josquin Deprès (1450-1521)

Brueghel (1520?-69)

Erasmus (1466?-1536)

Shakespeare (1564-1616)

Donatello (1386?-1466)

Machiavelli (1469-1527)

Palestrina (1526?-94)

Dürer (1471-1528)

Masaccio (1401-28)

Michelangelo (1475-1564)

Cervantes (1547-1616)

Titian (1477-1564)

Gutenberg (1400?-68?)

Castiglione (1478-1529)

•DIET OF WORMS (1521)

•DEFEAT OF THE SPANISH
ARMADA (1588)

Luther (1483-1546)

•AUGSBURG CONFESSION
(1530)

Zwingli (1484-1531)

•EDICT OF NANTES (1598)

Edward VI (1547-53)

Huss (1369?-1415)

Knox (1505-72)

•ST. BARTHOLOMEW'S
DAY MASSACRE (1572)

Calvin (1509-64)

Henry VIII (1509-47)

Mary I (1553-58)

Leo X (1513-21)

Philip II (1556-98)

Savonarola (1452-98)

Elizabeth I (1558-1603)

•COUNCIL OF CONSTANCE
(1414-18)

•95 THESES (1517)

Henry IV (1589-1610)

Charles V (1519-56)

•COUNCIL OF TRENT (1545-63)

Francis Xavier (1506-52)

De Soto (*1539)

Las Casas (1474-1566)

Magellan (*1519)

John Smith (*1607)

Prince Henry (1394-1460)

Dias (*1487)

Cortés (*1519)

Champlain (*1608)

Pizarro (*1531)

Columbus (*1492)

Cartier (*1534)

Da Gama (*1497)

Hudson (*1609)

Cabot (*1498)

Coronado (*1540)

1400   1450   1500   1550   1600   1650

CHAPTER 10

"What is man, that thou art mindful of him?"

A new age was dawning in Europe in the fourteenth century. The Western world was on the threshold of a widespread revival of learning and a brilliant flowering of the arts. This period of change in Europe from the fourteenth century through the sixteenth century is known as the **Renaissance** (REN uh sahns), a French word meaning "rebirth." (The Latin form of this word is found in the Vulgate in John 3:3, where Jesus said to Nicodemus, "Except a man be *born again*, he cannot see the kingdom of God.") The spirit of this age is evident in the confident outburst of a young German: "What a century! What genius! It is sheer joy to be alive. . . . Learning flourishes, men are spiritually quickened. O Barbarism, take a rope and prepare for extinction!"[1] This chapter focuses on the intellectual and artistic developments that constituted this transformation in Western civilization.

Characteristics of the Renaissance

Contrast with the Middle Ages

The Renaissance man considered the time in which he lived a sharp break with the ignorance and superstition of the Middle Ages. To him the medieval period was merely a backward, unimportant interval between the achievement of classical culture and the glory of his own "modern" age. He failed to realize that the Renaissance was the culmination of gradual changes that had begun during the Middle Ages.

The Renaissance attitude toward life differed sharply from the medieval outlook. The Renaissance man's hearty zest for living was a far cry from the sober, otherworldly concerns of earlier generations, who were consumed with the welfare of their souls and with the work of the church. People during the Middle Ages fixed their thoughts on the future joys of heaven. The dusty past and the troubled present were of little interest or importance. The Renaissance man, on the other hand, gloried in the past and lived with enthusiasm in the present. The future could take care of itself, or so he thought.

Focus on Man

The Renaissance emphasized human individuality, ability, and dignity. In medieval times the group—not the individual—had been all-important (for example, the church, a guild, or a particular social class). During the Renaissance, however, the reverse was true. People of this age praised the wonders of human achievement. They conceived of the ideal man as one with diverse interests and talents.

This renewed focus on man's capacities has been called **humanism**. Unlike modern secular humanism, Renaissance humanism did not abandon belief in God. But like every movement that puts undue emphasis upon human ability, it led to the false assumption that man is basically good. "There is nothing to be seen more wonderful than man," wrote an Italian humanist. Shakespeare's immortal character Hamlet exclaims, "What a piece of work is man! How noble is reason! How infinite is faculty, in form and moving! How expressive and admirable in action! How like an angel in apprehension!"

Created in God's image and given dominion over creation, man does possess a unique position in God's universe. But God's image in man was badly marred by the fall in the Garden of Eden. Because of Adam's disobedience man is basically sinful. He is in need of a Savior.

The godly man acknowledges that God is the source of all wisdom and the giver of all talents and abilities (James 1:17). The psalmist David said to God, "I will praise thee; for I am fearfully and wonderfully made" (Ps. 139:14). He humbly recognized man's true character and the source of man's understanding.

Opposite Page: Florence, Italy—birthplace of the Renaissance

When I consider the heavens, the work of thy fingers, the moon and the stars, which thou hast ordained; what is man, that thou art mindful of him? and the son of man, that thou visitest him? For thou hast made him a little lower than the angels, and hast crowned him with glory and honor. Thou madest him to have dominion over the works of thy hands; thou hast put all things under his feet. . . . O Lord our Lord, how excellent is thy name in all the earth!

—Psalm 8:3-6, 9

Because many people in Renaissance society misunderstood man's true nature, much of their culture was devoid of eternal values, biblical ethics, and godly living.

Humanism

Humanism is an overemphasis on human worth and ability, leading man to glorify himself instead of God. There have been many historical expressions of humanism. The Greek humanists, for example, emphasized the uniqueness of man above the animals; they taught that man's reason was the standard of truth. Like the Greeks, most of the Renaissance humanists praised human accomplishment and talent. Although most of them were church members and acknowledged the existence of God, many Renaissance humanists were primarily interested in classical learning.

While its historical forms may vary, humanism inevitably leads people away from God and spiritual concerns. It promotes the false idea that man is good and that he is superior to God. Secular humanism of the twentieth century altogether rejects belief in God and worships man as God. The pride of humanism, however, will not go unpunished.

The lofty looks of man shall be humbled, and the haughtiness of men shall be bowed down, and the Lord alone shall be exalted in that day. For the day of the Lord of hosts shall be upon every one that is proud and lofty, and upon every one that is lifted up; and he shall be brought low.

—Isaiah 2:11-12

Revival of Learning

The expansion of trade and the growth of town and national governments during the later Middle Ages increased the need for well-educated laymen with professional skills. Merchants, bankers, lawyers, clerks, and diplomats—to name only a few—needed a well-rounded education to meet the demands of an increasingly complex society. Renewed business activity also indirectly sparked interest in classical literature. Lawyers needing to draw up business contracts and other legal documents turned to Roman law to see how the ancients had handled such matters. In the process of their research, they discovered the writings of Cicero and other Latin authors. Interest in classical literature prompted men to collect and study this literature.

Soon a new course of study—the **humanities**—became popular in the West. The humanities, also known as the liberal arts, included the study of history, science, and grammar, as well as classical literature and philosophy. Those who studied the liberal arts were known as **humanists.** Unlike the scholastics of the Middle Ages, most Renaissance humanists did not study to prepare for service in the church. Instead they prepared themselves for life in the secular world.

The goal of Renaissance education was to develop well-rounded individuals. Humanists, who considered ignorance the source of evil, looked to education as the remedy for sin. They criticized medieval man for being ignorant and narrow-minded, and they praised men of their own day for their zest for life, wide interests, and quest for knowledge. They scorned the medieval practice of passively accepting ideas without questioning their accuracy. Renaissance man was more critical. He examined established ideas to discern whether they were trustworthy.

Renaissance humanists greatly admired the classical age of ancient Greece and Rome. They praised the amazing versatility that the ancients had possessed. Cicero received special honor, for he was not only a renowned scholar, lawyer, and statesman but also an eloquent orator and master of literary expression. By following the example of the ancients, the humanists believed they could re-

IMAGO · ERASMI · ROTERODA
MI · AB · ALBERTO · DVRERO · AD
VIVAM · EFFIGIEM · DELINIATA ·

ΤΗΝ · ΚΡΕΙΤΤΩ · ΤΑ · ΣΥΓΓΡΑΜ
ΜΑΤΑ · ΔΙΞ ΕΙ

· M D X X V I ·

Albrecht Dürer, Erasmus of Rotterdam, *National Gallery of Art, Washington, D.C.*

shape their own age according to classical values. They stimulated a "rebirth" of interest in literature, art, and philosophy of the classical age.

This fascination with classical culture led to an intense search for ancient manuscripts. Men went to great lengths and spent vast fortunes to obtain classical works. They found many Latin manuscripts in the libraries of monasteries where they had lain neglected and forgotten for centuries. Although Greek works were rare in the West, many had been preserved in the East by the Byzantine and Muslim civilizations. As the humanists recovered these precious works, they examined them to determine their accuracy and authenticity. Essential to such an investigation, of course, was a thorough knowledge of the classical languages. This need gave rise to the renewed study of Greek and classical Latin during the Renaissance period.

Section Review

1. What is the name of the period during the fourteenth through the sixteenth centuries in European history in which learning and the arts revived and flowered?
2. Define humanism.
3. What new course of study became popular in Europe during the Renaissance? What disciplines were included in this course of study?
4. What was the goal of Renaissance education?
5. What period of history did the Renaissance humanists admire?

Course of the Renaissance

The Renaissance began in Italy. This land had been the center of the ancient Roman Empire; even in the fourteenth century, the Italians thought of themselves as Romans. In their long history Italians had also come into close contact with the Byzantine and Islamic civilizations. Several cities in northern Italy had maintained trade and cultural ties with the East during the Middle Ages. When commerce began to revive throughout Europe during the eleventh and twelfth centuries, the Italian cities rose to prominence. Their control of the Mediterranean trade routes to the East brought them great riches. To display their newly

acquired wealth, these cities commissioned talented artists to design buildings, decorate churches, and carve statues for public squares. Affluent bankers and merchants became the sponsors or **patrons** of these artists. Artists no longer depended solely on the church for support.

Perhaps the most famous of the Renaissance patrons, apart from the church itself, were the members of the **Medici** (MED uh CHEE) **family.** The Medici were prominent Italians who had become extremely wealthy through commerce and banking. Their riches gained them political control of the

Medici Chapel, Florence

city of Florence. They also used their vast financial resources to promote learning and the arts. They sponsored searches for manuscripts, established a public library (one of the first in Europe), and commissioned great works of painting, sculpture, and architecture. The most notable and most generous patron of the Medici family was **Lorenzo de Medici,** called *Il Magnifico* ("The Magnificent"). During his rule the city of Florence became the most influential city of the Renaissance movement.

Until about 1500 the Renaissance was primarily an Italian movement. By the sixteenth century, however, enthusiasm for art and learning had spread throughout Europe. It was carried abroad by students who had studied in Italy and by merchants who traded with Italian cities. The Renaissance took hold in England, France, Germany, and the Netherlands. At first the people of these lands copied the Italians, but before long they developed their own ideas and styles.

Thought and Literature

Italian Humanist Writers

The city of Florence, home of the powerful Medici, was the birthplace of the Renaissance. This bustling city was the center of Italian commerce. Members of her wealthy class, who sponsored art and learning, made Florence the center of culture in Italy. Most of the writers, painters, sculptors, and architects of the early Renaissance lived in this city.

At the beginning of the fourteenth century, Florentine writers gave expression to the growing secular attitudes. They looked to the literature of ancient Greece and Rome for inspiration. Their study of the classics stirred a rebirth of learning in Europe.

Petrarch—The pioneer of the Renaissance humanism and one of the most important figures in Italian literature was **Francesco Petrarch** (1304-74), the son of a Florentine merchant. As a youth he followed his father's wishes and entered law school. But his real love was the classical writings of Greece and Rome. His father did not approve of his spending more time reading these ancient works than studying law. One day he found his son's copies of the classics and threw them into the fire. But, moved by Petrarch's grief, he managed to snatch two works from the flames.

After his father's death, Petrarch gave up his study of law and devoted his life to classics. He searched monastic and church libraries to find ancient manuscripts, which he collected and studied. He composed his own Latin poems, modeling them after

Terra-cotta bust of Lorenzo de Medici by Andrea Verrocchio

classical poetry. These he considered his best works. Later generations, however, remember him best for his vernacular writings. In sonnets (fourteen-line poems) and letters to his friends, he expressed human interest and emotions. Petrarch wrote about nature, his pride in his homeland, and his love for Laura (the woman he idealized). His love poetry had an immense influence on later writers. Of Laura he wrote the following:

> He for celestial charms may look in vain
> Who has not seen my fair one's radiant eyes,
> And felt their glances pleasingly beguile.
> How can Love heal his wounds, then would again,
> He only knows who knows how sweet her sighs,
> How sweet her [conversation], and how sweet her smile.

In letters addressed to his heroes of the past—Cicero, Virgil, and Livy—Petrarch places his own day on an equal plane with the days of ancient Rome. Because Petrarch led the way in reviving interest and study in classical literature, he is known as the "Father of Humanism."

Castiglione—Another Italian, **Baldassare Castiglione** (CAHS tee LYOH nay; 1478-1529), wrote one of the most famous books on etiquette (social behavior) published during the Renaissance. The topic of good manners was popular at that time. As more people acquired wealth and moved into a higher social class, they were eager to behave in an acceptable manner. In his book *The Courtier,* Castiglione describes the ideal Renaissance gentleman. He presents the courtier or gentleman as a man of character, well educated, courageous, and courteous. Such a man should demonstrate the nobility of his character whether on the battlefield or in the fashionable places of society. *The Courtier* became an immediate best seller and was translated into many different languages. It set the standard for courtly behavior all over Europe.

Machiavelli—One of the most influential Renaissance writers was the Florentine public official and political thinker **Niccolo Machiavelli** (MAH kyah VEL ee; 1469-1527). From 1489 to 1512 he worked as a diplomat for the Florentine Republic.

During these years he was able to observe firsthand the political developments in Europe.

He was deeply disturbed by the unrest and division in his native land. Italy at this time was divided into a number of competing, warring states. Many of these relied on mercenary soldiers led by men called *condottière* (KAHN duh TYEHR ee) to fight their battles. Even the papacy was involved in these petty conflicts. The popes acted like secular

---

Rules for Proper Conduct

Besides The Courtier, *other books of etiquette circulated in Europe during the Renaissance. The* Book of Manners, *written by Giovanni della Casa (1503-56), is typical of such publications. These excerpts typify the author's advice.*

A man should never boast of his birth, his honors or his wealth, and still less of his brains.

It is not a polite habit . . . to carry your toothpick either in your mouth, like a bird making its nest, or behind your ear.

You should also take care, as far as you can, not to spit at mealtimes, but if you must spit, then do so in a decent manner.

Refrain as far as possible from making noises which grate upon the ear, such as grinding or sucking your teeth.

Anyone whose legs are too thin, or exceptionally fat, or perhaps crooked, should not wear vivid or parti-colored hose, in order not to attract attention to his defects.

A man must . . . not be content to do things well, but must also aim to do them gracefully.[2]

---

rulers as they sought to expand the boundaries of the Papal States. The kings of France and Spain added to the political and economic turmoil by fighting a series of wars over this troubled land.

Machiavelli wrote several important and influential works on government. The most important and controversial of these is an essay called *The Prince.* In this work Machiavelli reflects upon the political conditions of his day. He tells his readers that the successful ruler must do what is expedient

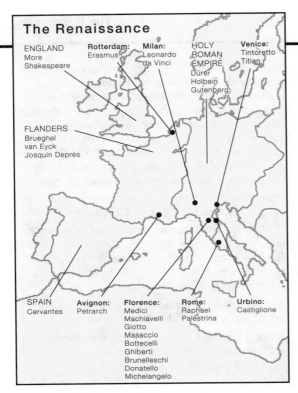

The Renaissance

ENGLAND
More
Shakespeare

Rotterdam:
Erasmus

Milan:
Leonardo
da Vinci

HOLY ROMAN EMPIRE
Dürer
Holbein
Gutenberg

Venice:
Tintoretto
Titian

FLANDERS
Brueghel
van Eyck
Josquin Deprès

SPAIN
Cervantes

Avignon:
Petrarch

Florence:
Medici
Machiavelli
Giotto
Masaccio
Bottecelli
Ghiberti
Brunelleschi
Donatello
Michelangelo

Rome:
Raphael
Palestrina

Urbino:
Castiglione

and not be governed by principles of right and wrong. Such a man uses force when necessary, for "it is much safer to be feared than loved." Although Machiavelli probably wrote *The Prince* as merely an objective description of Italian politics, later rulers took his "advice" and embraced this wicked system as the ideal political philosophy.

Perhaps a better source of Machiavelli's own political views is his *Discourses on the First Ten Books of Livy.* In this work he examines the politics of ancient Rome and derives lessons for rulers of his day. Favoring a republican form of government, he writes that "when there is combined under the same constitution a prince, a nobility, and the power of the people, then these three powers will watch and keep each other reciprocally in check."

Whatever Machiavelli's motives were, his works, particularly *The Prince,* promoted the concept of the secular state—one freed from moral restraints and religious principles. In succeeding centuries the idea that "might makes right" became popular with many of Europe's rulers. They justified the use of any method necessary (including deceit and brute

force) to maintain their political power. The ideals of morally responsible governments and rulers seemed to fade from view as Europe entered what is called the "Age of Absolutism." (See Chapter 13.)

Northern Humanist Writers

Despite the strong Italian influence over the Renaissance in northern Europe, the emphasis of northern humanists differed from that of their Italian counterparts. The northern humanists generally had a greater interest in religious matters than the Italian humanists. Their religious concern led to a greater emphasis upon church reform in the north. Accordingly, northern humanists gave more attention to Christian rather than classical sources. They placed the study of the Hebrew Old Testament and the Greek New Testament above the writings of Cicero, Virgil, and other ancients.

Erasmus—Perhaps the most honored and influential scholar of the Renaissance was **Erasmus** of Rotterdam (1466?-1536). As a young man he entered a monastery, but he spent little time there. Instead he traveled throughout Europe obtaining an education in Latin and Greek. He distinguished himself as the foremost scholar of Europe and was widely acclaimed as the prince of humanists.

Erasmus did much to prepare the way for the Protestant Reformation, even though he himself refused to break with the Roman Catholic church. In his most famous work, *Praise of Folly,* he uses satire to point out the evils and follies of Renaissance society. He became a leading advocate of

" FOLLY " AS PROFESSOR.

A selection of Hans Holbein's illustrations for Erasmus's Praise of Folly

Gutenberg

A resourceful German named **Johannes Gutenberg** helped to change significantly the course of history. He is generally recognized as the man to put movable-type printing into use in Europe. The Chinese had developed movable-type printing in the eleventh century, but there is no evidence that their accomplishments were known in Europe. Gutenberg's greatest achievement was his edition of the Bible, printed in 1456.

The advent of movable-type printing is a landmark in the history of the Western world. The cost of books dropped dramatically because they no longer needed to be copied by hand and because they could be produced in large quantities. In addition, printing eliminated many of the errors which characterized older hand-written books. It paved the way for the rapid spread of ideas and stimulated the growth of education. In the past students had to memorize everything they heard in the classroom because the teacher was usually the only one who had a book. With printing, students could afford to purchase their own books. It is no coincidence that between 1450 and 1517 a total of twenty-five new universities and colleges were established in Spain, France, Germany, and England.

In the seventeenth century Sir Francis Bacon, an English philosopher and author, wrote that there were three inventions that "changed the appearance and state of the whole world." They were the compass, gunpowder, and movable-type printing. These inventions may not seem significant to us, but they shaped Europe almost to the same extent that television and computers are shaping the present age.

church reform and was an outspoken critic of monasticism, the ignorance and worldliness of the clergy, and the church's empty ritualism. His interest and skill in biblical studies led him to publish his first edition of the Greek New Testament in 1516. In the preface Erasmus tells his readers his position on translating Scripture:

> I strongly dissent from those who are unwilling to have the Scriptures translated into the vernacular and read by the ignorant, as if Christ taught so complicated a doctrine that it can hardly be understood even by a handful of theologians. . . . It is perhaps reasonable to conceal the mysteries of kings, but Christ seeks to divulge his mysteries as much as possible. I should like to have even the most humble women read the [Gospels] and the Epistles of St. Paul. . . . Would that the plowboy recited something from them at his plowshare, that the weaver sang from them at his shuttle, and that the traveler whiled away the tedium of his journey with their tales.[3]

The great reformer Martin Luther used Erasmus's Greek New Testament in making his German trans-

PILGRIM FOLLY.

lation of the New Testament. Many others, including the translators of the King James Version, have used Erasmus's text as the basis for translating the New Testament into the common languages of the people.

More—A close friend of Erasmus was the English humanist Sir **Thomas More** (1478-1535). More was a man of deep piety who spent regular hours in prayer. He exercised his responsibility as a father to "train up a child in the way he should go" (Prov. 22:6). He held daily devotions in his home, requiring even the household servants to attend. Before each meal he had one of his children read a portion of Scripture.

More devoted much of his life to the service of his country. His interest in social and political matters prompted him to write a book setting forth his views on the ideal government. This work, entitled *Utopia* (meaning "nowhere"), is the story of an imaginary state built upon Christian principles and Plato's philosophy. More was dismayed by the greed of the nobility and the plight of the poor in English society. He believed that if men would govern themselves by a sense of community and brotherly love, they could achieve political, social, and economic equality. According to More, the three deadliest sins of the English community were sloth (laziness), greed, and pride. In Utopia, all men would be compelled to work. Thus everyone would have economic security, and all sloth and greed would be eliminated. All pride was to be centered in the state.

More was not the first nor the last person to conceive of an ideal state. Throughout history men have set forth a variety of views. Nevertheless, to have a perfect state, society must be composed of perfect men and women. Since "all have sinned, and come short of the glory of God" (Rom. 3:23), it is impossible for man to achieve this goal.

More entered the service of King Henry VIII of England because, as he said, "If better men did not go into politics, worse ones would." Although he served Henry well, he was beheaded for treason when he refused to take an oath recognizing Henry as head of the church in England. At the scaffold he said, "I die the king's loyal servant, but God's first." Despite the corruption in the Renaissance pa-

pacy, More still believed in the pope's supremacy in the church.

Cervantes—The foremost Spanish writer of the late Renaissance is **Miguel de Cervantes** (sur VAN teez; 1547-1616). His novel *Don Quixote* (DAHN kee-HO-tay) is one of the most enduring works in all of literature. It is a satire on chivalry and on the chivalric literature that was popular in Cervantes's day. The main character, Don Quixote, imagining himself to be a knight, puts on a suit of armor, mounts an old horse, and gallops around the Spanish countryside seeking to right the world's wrongs. In doing so he makes a fool of himself. Accompanying Don Quixote on his many adventures is his faithful squire Sancho Panza, whom Cervantes presents as the more practical, down-to-earth person. Through this work Cervantes pokes fun at outmoded medieval ideas. At the same time he presents a vivid picture of life in sixteenth-century Spain.

Shakespeare—Renaissance literature reached its peak in the works of **William Shakespeare**

William Shakespeare

(1564-1616), who is generally considered the greatest playwright of all time and the finest poet in the English language. Shakespeare, the son of a prosperous trader, was born and reared in Stratford-upon-Avon, a small town northwest of London. As a young man he went to London, where he became a successful actor and playwright. His fame spread during his early career after he published two long narrative poems. Shakespeare gained financial success as a leader and a stockholder in a prominent London theatrical group called the Lord Chamberlain's Men, later known as the King's Men. He purchased stock in two playhouses, the most famous of which was the Globe Theatre, where most of his plays were performed.

Shakespeare's lifework includes 154 sonnets and thirty-eight plays. His dramatic works are classified into histories, comedies, and tragedies. The tragedies *Hamlet, Othello, King Lear,* and *Macbeth* are generally recognized as his greatest works. Fourteen of his plays are set in Italy. This delighted English audiences, for in true Renaissance spirit they looked to Italy as the birthplace of learning. Several of Shakespeare's plays reflect the surge of national pride in England. In his history play *Richard II,* he penned these words:

> This royal throne of kings, this sceptred isle,
> This earth of majesty, this seat of Mars,
> This other Eden, demi-paradise,
> This fortress built by Nature for herself
> Against the infection and the hand of war,
> This happy breed of men, this little world,
> This precious stone set in the silver sea,
> Which serves it in the office of a wall,
> Or as a moat defensive to a house,
> Against the envy of less happier lands;
> This blessed plot, this earth, this realm, this
>   England.

Shakespeare has left an indelible print upon Western culture. His writings had an enormous impact upon later authors. Few libraries in the world could contain all of the books that have been written about his life and work. Shakespeare's poems and plays have been the object of careful study by every generation since his death. His literary genius enriched the English language and influenced its development. Many of the phrases and expressions that he coined are part of everyday speech in modern society. His plays, which have been translated into many languages, have worldwide appeal. A master of character portrayal, Shakespeare probed the depths and complexity of human existence as few writers ever have.

Section Review

1. Apart from the church, what family became the most famous patron (sponsor) of Renaissance learning and art? Who was the most noted patron of this family?
2. Who is called the "Father of Humanism" because he led the way in reviving interest and study in classical literature?
3. What contribution did Johannes Gutenberg make to European history?
4. What work of Erasmus did later reformers and Bible translators use?
5. What Englishman is generally considered the greatest playwright of all time?

The Visual Arts

The visual arts clearly express the spirit and attitudes of the Renaissance. As in any age, some men honored the Lord in their work and some dishonored Him. Many artists during this period used their God-given talents to bring glory to their Creator. Others, however, used their abilities to make a name for themselves, arrogantly trying to outdo one another. These were quick to boast of their ability. They measured themselves by the praise of men and had little concern for God's standard:

> For we dare not make ourselves of the number, or compare ourselves with some that commend themselves; but they measuring themselves by themselves, and comparing themselves among themselves, are not wise. But we will not boast of things without our measure, but according to the measure of the rule which God hath distributed to us. . . . Not boasting of things without our measure, that is, of other men's labours. . . . But he that glorieth, let him glory in the Lord. For not he that commendeth himself is approved, but whom the Lord commendeth.
> —II Corinthians 10:12-13, 15, 17-18.

SICMORIENSVIRVS DE ERSIC OTVLIT VORVS
IC • XC

A medieval painting of the crucifixion from the altarpiece of St. Mark's Basilica in Venice

Renaissance artists drew their inspiration and ideas from the classical world. They broke with the artistic traditions of the Middle Ages in the following ways:

1. Renaissance art emphasized the present physical world. Medieval art had emphasized the spiritual realm and the life to come.

2. Secular patrons often supported the Renaissance artists. During the Middle Ages the church of Rome had almost exclusively patronized the artists.

3. Most Renaissance artists were extremely proud of their work and wanted their names known and their works praised. Medieval artists, on the other hand, had worked primarily for the glory of God and the church and usually did not gain any personal recognition.

4. Renaissance artists gave a realistic, three-dimensional aspect to their works. Medieval art was flat and two-dimensional.

5. Most Renaissance portrait painters frequently painted kings, merchants, and other important secular individuals. Medieval painters usually portrayed church leaders, biblical characters, or saints of the church.

6. Painting and sculpture were the most popular media during the Renaissance. The glory of medieval art was its architecture.

Early Italian Painters

Giotto—**Giotto di Bondone** (JAWT-toh DEE bone-DOH-nay; 1266?-1337) is the most famous painter of the early Italian Renaissance. He is often called the "Father of Renaissance Painting." He opened a new era of art in the Western world. Before his time, figures in paintings were stiff and flat; medieval artists painted expressionless people and set them against a plain gold background. This practice created an impression of calm serenity— a heavenly atmosphere. Giotto, however, sought to make painting more natural. His figures were more realistic and exhibited human feelings. He also tried to add a three-dimensional look to his paintings by making greater use of backgrounds.

Giotto, Madonna and Child, *National Gallery of Art, Washington, D.C.*

Sandro Botticelli, The Adoration of the Magi, *National Gallery of Art, Washington, D.C.*

Giotto is most famous for his **frescoes** (paintings on wet plaster) on the walls of the town church at Padua. Although he tried to make his painting as realistic as possible, he never fully mastered the technique of **perspective**—portraying a three-dimensional appearance on a flat surface.

Masaccio—Florentine artists of the fifteenth century achieved greater realism in their paintings by creating works that gave a sense of life, action, depth, and feeling. Early in the century **Masaccio** (meh SAH chee OH; 1401-28) added new techniques to painting. By means of shading (contrasting light and dark), he created a three-dimensional effect in his painting. This technique enabled him to portray human figures with a realism that had been missing in the works of previous painters.

Botticelli—In the late fifteenth century, **Sandro Botticelli** (BOT ih CHEL ee; 1444?-1510) added an-

other dimension to Renaissance art: movement. He depicted forms with bold line and gave clarity and a sense of activity to his characters. With their flowing hair and wispy garments, his painted figures seemed to move and sway. Botticelli's early paintings reflected the humanistic spirit prevalent in the Medici court. He painted pagan themes of classical mythology. But when the Medici family was expelled from Florence, Botticelli fell under the influence of the preaching of the monk Savonarola. (See box on p. 268.) He became one of Savonarola's converts, and his painting, as a result, took on a more religious and moral outlook.

High Renaissance Painters

The artistic achievement of the Italian Renaissance culminated in the early sixteenth century. During this period, known as the High Renais-

Savonarola: Preacher of Righteousness

A generation before the Reformation, a Dominican friar named **Girolamo Savonarola** (1452-98) sought to bring moral reform to the city of Florence and to the Roman church. He opposed the corrupt rule of the Medici family and severely criticized Pope Alexander VI, a man notorious for his bribery, fornication, robbery, blasphemy, and murder. Savonarola warned the Florentines of a coming day of judgment and called upon them to repent of their wicked ways. At the height of his popularity, crowds of ten to twelve thousand people flocked to hear his sermons. He soon became the leading religious figure in the city.

As a result of his preaching, the secular culture that dominated the city began to change. For example, people built great bonfires into which they threw playing cards, gambling dice, immoral books and pictures, and objects of luxury. Not everyone, however, enthusiastically accepted the reforms that Savonarola had begun. Alexander VI, perhaps the most wicked of all the popes, sought to silence him. He prohibited him from preaching, but Savonarola continued to boldly denounce the sins of Rome. Alexander then tried to buy his silence by offering to make him a cardinal, but Savonarola refused. He finally excommunicated him, but Savonarola ignored his action.

The people of Florence, intimidated by the pope's action and weary of Savonarola's strict preaching, abandoned the friar. He was arrested, tortured, tried, and condemned to die by hanging. The crowds that had once gathered to hear him preach gathered to watch him die. Savonarola was hanged, his body was burned, and his ashes were cast into the Arno River. (His ashes were scattered so that nobody could preserve them as relics.)

In the eyes of his contemporaries, Savonarola was a failure. The city had cast aside his reforms and had consented to his execution. God, however, does not measure success or failure on the basis of popular approval. He rewards those of His servants who are faithful—even unto death.

sance, the center of culture shifted from Florence to Rome. The papacy became the major patron of Italian artists. High Renaissance artists mastered the painting techniques that the Italian artists of the fifteenth century had pioneered. The most famous High Renaissance painters are Leonardo da Vinci, Raphael, and Michelangelo.

Leonardo da Vinci—**Leonardo da Vinci** (DUH VIN-chee; 1452-1519) is probably the best example of the so-called Renaissance man. He displayed interests in a wide range of fields. He was an accomplished sculptor, architect, painter, musician, and poet. He also studied anatomy, botany, geology, astronomy, engineering, and mathematics.

As a young man Leonardo received training in painting and sculpture at Florence. Distinguishing himself as a painter, he was admitted into the Florentine painter's guild. But he believed that the restrictions of the guild stifled his creative talents.

A self-portrait by Leonardo da Vinci

Leonardo da Vinci, Mona Lisa

He was eager to explore new ideas; the city of Florence, he thought, was too dependent upon the classical age. Therefore in 1482 he sought a position in Milan under the sponsorship of the duke of Milan. In a letter he wrote to his prospective patron, Leonardo proudly listed his qualifications:

> And in short, according to the variety of cases, I can contrive various and endless means of offence and defense [that is, weaponry]. . . . In time of peace I believe I can give perfect satisfaction and to the equal of any other in architecture and the composition of buildings, public and private; and in guiding water from one place to another. . . . I can carry out sculpture in marble, bronze, or clay, and also I can do in painting whatever may be done, as well as any other, be he whom he may.[4]

While in Milan Leonardo painted his famous mural *The Last Supper* on a wall in a monastery. The painting illustrates his mastery of perspective and exemplifies the Renaissance love for balance. He vividly depicts the intense feelings of the dis-

ciples when Christ announced that one of them would betray Him. Although in a deteriorated state, this mural remains one of the most famous religious paintings of all time. Perhaps Leonardo's most famous work is his painting the *Mona Lisa.*

Raphael—Raffaello Sanzio (1483-1520), better known as **Raphael** (RAF ay el), completed an enormous number of paintings and frescoes in his short lifetime. His interest in painting undoubtedly began at home, for his father was a painter. As a young man Raphael studied the works of the masters in order to perfect his own technique. He soon became one of the most beloved painters of his time.

Raphael is famous for his paintings of sweet-faced Madonnas in which he idealized motherhood. He sought to express the peace and quiet joy of life rather than its anguish and strain. He is also known for the magnificent frescoes that he painted to decorate the papal residence in Rome. *The School of Athens* is an excellent example of his work; it displays balance, harmony, and perspective. In this painting he creates a spacious setting in which are gathered the great philosophers and scientists of the classical world.

Michelangelo—**Michelangelo Buonarroti** (MY-kul-AN-juh-lo BWAWN-uh-RAW-tee; 1475-1564) is one of the most famous artists in all of history. His contemporaries praised his artistic masterpieces. As a young boy he exhibited unusual skill in sculpting. It is said that he learned how to handle a chisel and hammer before he could read and write. When he told his father that he wanted to study painting and sculpture, his father was furious. His father believed manual labor was beneath the dignity of the family. But when Michelangelo displayed little interest or ability in school, his father apprenticed him to a leading Florentine artist. While an apprentice, the talented youth caught the eye of Lorenzo de Medici, who took Michelangelo into his household as his adopted son.

In 1508 Pope Julius II asked Michelangelo to paint the ceiling of the **Sistine Chapel** in the Vatican (the papal residence in Rome). Protesting that he was a sculptor and not a painter, Michelangelo began the mammoth project reluctantly. After four years of working along on scaffolds nearly seventy

Leonardo da Vinci and His Notebooks

Though remembered primarily for his great artistic abilities, Leonardo da Vinci was extremely interested in science and technology. He studied nature and conceived of numerous inventions, recording all his thoughts and observations in notebooks. Today we have about 5,700 pages of his notes, all of which are written in "mirror script." Since Leonardo was left-handed he found it easier to write from right to left. His notes may be read properly—that is, from left to right—only when viewed in a mirror.

Leonardo originally began his notebooks to help him in his painting. He studied plant life and the human body in order to make his paintings more realistic. Some of his plant drawings are so accurate that they could be used in any modern botany textbook. He often used cross-section and cutaway views to better understand the objects of his study.

While much of Leonardo's work was designed to improve his artistic abilities, he was also interested in knowledge for its own sake. An intelligent and imaginative man, he invented many things. With the help of modern technology—as well as some alterations—many of them have proved workable. He devised, among other things, a chain drive (used on bicycles), ball bearings, a jack, an odometer, a device for measuring humidity, and a life belt for those who were shipwrecked. His work foreshadowed prefabricated houses, submarines, and automobiles. In the area of military science, Leonardo invented a tank which was powered from the inside by hand cranks, and a triple-tier machine gun. While one set of guns was being fired, another was cooling, and the third was being reloaded.

Of all Leonardo's inventions, those that proved to be the least workable were his flying machines. Although flying fascinated Leonardo almost more than any other subject, he never fully grasped its principles. He did, however, diagram two objects that are used today in modified form. One of them is a helical screw (from the Greek word *helix*—"spiral"). This object is the forerunner of the propeller as well as the helicopter. The second object is Leonardo's version of the parachute.

Michelangelo, The Last Judgment, *from the Sistine Chapel*

Sea. Numerous canals dissect the city; these serve as streets along which gondolas, or flat-bottomed boats, transport people about the city. Her merchant fleet was once the strongest sea power in the Mediterranean region. Her merchants controlled the important trade routes to the East. The economic prosperity she enjoyed encouraged cultural activity. Wealthy merchants built grand palaces and commissioned artists to adorn the city with great works of art. The beautiful, wealthy, and proud city of Venice became known as the "Queen of the Adriatic."

Venice, however, was wicked and materialistic. Her citizens eagerly sought after luxury, pleasure, and prestige. Each year the city staged elaborate pageants; beneath all the glitter and pomp was a city sunk deep in moral decay.

Even the art of Venice mirrored her materialism. It attested to the Venetian love for money, precious gems, rich clothing, decoration, and festive occasions. Artists painted wealthy merchants, proud city officials, and beautiful women. These paintings, filled with radiant color and light, reflect the city's secular and sensuous spirit.

Titian—Tiziano Vecelli (1477-1576), known as **Titian** (TISH un), was the leading figure of the Venetian school of painting. He ranks with Michelangelo as one of the foremost painters of the

feet above the floor, he finished painting the 5,800-square-foot ceiling. The original plan had called for only twelve figures; however, when Michelangelo finished the project, he had painted over three hundred figures, most of which were ten to eighteen feet tall. This magnificent fresco depicts the story of creation, man's fall, the Flood, and the redemption of man as prophesied by the Old Testament prophets. Nearly a quarter of a century later he painted the front wall of the chapel with his conception of the Last Judgment. This painting is filled with violent, frenzied action portraying a dynamic Christ calling the saved to heaven and condemning the lost to hell.

Venetian Painters

During the late Renaissance the city of Venice became a leading center of culture. It is located on a cluster of islands at the northern end of the Adriatic

Titian, Doge Andrea Gritti, *National Gallery of Art, Washington, D.C.*

Il Tintoretto, The Visit of the Queen of Sheba to Solomon, *Bob Jones University Collection of Sacred Art*

Renaissance. A prolific painter known for his rich use of color, Titian is especially remembered for his portraits. His work contains a freshness, warmth, and vitality missing in the serene Renaissance portraits of southern Italy. He captured on canvas the personality of his subject, not just the physical appearance. His fame spread throughout Europe. He painted pictures for the Holy Roman emperor and the kings of Spain and France, becoming one of the few Renaissance painters to grow wealthy through his work.

Tintoretto—**Tintoretto** (1518-1594) was the last of the great sixteenth-century Venetian painters. He was born Jacopo Robusti but is known by his nickname Tintoretto (Italian for ''little dyer'') because his father was a dyer by profession. In his painting he sought to combine the bright colors of Titian and the masterful drawing of Michelangelo. His work exhibits a dramatic excitement full of tension and action.

Northern European Artists

Dürer—The German painter **Albrecht Dürer** (DOOR ur; 1471-1528) is sometimes called the ''Leonardo of the North.'' Like Leonardo, he was accomplished in many different fields: writing, de-

Albrecht Dürer, Knight, Death, and Devil, *National Gallery of Art, Washington, D.C.*

Jan van Eyck, The Marriage of Giovanni (?) Arnolfini and Giovanna Cenami (?), *Reproduced by courtesy of the Trustees, The National Gallery, London. Van Eyck's masterful painting of an Italian financier and his wife displays the enormous advance in realism that the artist achieved through his use of oil paints. In addition, the subject matter—devoid of any religious elements—illustrates the secular interests that grew during the Renaissance. Note the realistic details, such as the mirror in the background showing the backs of the artist's subjects.*

signing, engraving, and painting. He had a high regard for Italian art and was the first northern artist to travel to Italy for the express purpose of studying art. His painting illustrates his love for both classical and religious themes. He also had a keen interest in nature, an interest reflected by his amazingly accurate watercolors of floral scenes. Although Dürer is a celebrated painter, he is best remembered for his woodcarvings and engravings, which were used to illustrate printed books. He is the first artist to sign even his most insignificant drawings. His "signature" consisted of a capital *A* straddling a capital *D*.

Holbein—Another celebrated German painter is **Hans Holbein** (HOHL bine) the Younger (1479?-1543). He is considered the finest portrait painter of the Northern Renaissance. He traveled throughout Europe working in many countries—especially England. Holbein became the official court painter

of Henry VIII, the king of England. He not only painted the portrait of Henry, his wives, and his son, but he also designed Henry's clothes, jewelry, and tableware. This German master also painted the portraits of leading figures of the Northern Renaissance, such as Erasmus and Sir Thomas More.

Van Eyck—One of the founders and an outstanding representative of the Flemish school of painters was **Jan van Eyck** (van IKE; 1370?-1440?). In his early career he illustrated manuscripts; this art form required careful attention to minute details. Van Eyck's concern for detail carried over to his large paintings. He was one of the first to use oil paints, a medium that allowed him to achieve greater realism in his painting.

Brueghel—During the fifteenth century, Flemish painters created a distinctive style of art known for its realism, landscapes, and scenes of contemporary life. In the sixteenth century **Pieter Brue-ghel** (BROY gul; 1525?-69) helped develop and perfect this style. He is best remembered for his **genre painting,** a type of painting that depicts scenes of everyday life. These works show the peasants in their daily activities: farming in the fields, hunting in the woods, and dancing in the village square. When he painted biblical events, he depicted them as though they took place in Flanders.

Renaissance Architects and Sculptors

Both architects and sculptors were influenced by the spirit of humanism. They greatly admired the art of the classical world. Renaissance architecture and sculpture, like painting, also reflected the new secular concerns of the Renaissance Age. In the medieval period the primary function of architecture had been to glorify God through the building of magnificent cathedrals. During the Renaissance, however, architects also designed and built spacious palaces and comfortable villas for powerful princes and wealthy merchants. Similarly, sculpture which had been used during the Middle Ages to decorate

churches now graced town squares and homes of the wealthy.

Ghiberti—About the year 1401 the leading men of Florence held a contest to select an artist to design a set of bronze doors for one of the entrances to the baptistery of Florence. Among the many artists who entered the competition were **Lorenzo Ghiberti** (gee BEHR tee; 1378-1455) and **Filippo Brunelleschi** (BROO nuh LES kee; 1377?-1446). According to the contest rules, each participant had to present a sculptured relief depicting the story of the sacrifice of Isaac. Ghiberti's work was judged the best. He gloated over his victory:

To me was conceded the palm of victory by all the experts and by all those who had competed with me. To me the honor was conceded universally and with no exception. To all it seemed that I had at that time surpassed the others without exception, as was recognized by a great council and an investigation of learned men . . . highly skilled from the painter and sculptors of gold, silver, and marble. There were thirty-four judges from the city

The Florence Cathedral, showing Brunelleschi's dome (left) and Giotto's bell tower (right)

and the other surrounding countries. The testimonial of the victory was given in my favor by all. . . . It was granted to me and determined that I should make the bronze door for this church.[5]

Ghiberti, however, would have done well to heed God's admonition in I Samuel 2:3 "Talk no more so exceeding proudly; let not arrogancy come out of your mouth: for the Lord is a God of knowledge, and by him actions are weighed."

For the next two decades Ghiberti worked on the doors. The finished doors contained twenty-eight panels depicting New Testament stories. The city later commissioned him to do a second set of doors. This time he chose to depict stories from the Old Testament. According to Michelangelo, Ghiberti designed the ten panels on these doors "so fine that they might fittingly stand at the Gates of Paradise." Ghiberti himself said that "of all my work it is the most remarkable I have done and it was finished with skill, correct proportion, and understanding."

Brunelleschi—Disgusted with losing the competition to design the doors of the baptistery in Florence, Brunelleschi turned from sculpture to architecture. He traveled to Rome where he studied Roman monuments. He later returned to Florence and defeated Ghiberti in a competition to design and construct a dome for the cathedral of Florence. Not since the days of ancient Rome had such a magnificent and lofty dome been constructed in the West. His dome was the crowning glory of the Florence cathedral. Most of the domes designed during the Renaissance conformed to his model.

Donatello—Donatello (1386?-1466) was the leading sculptor of the early Renaissance. He was born in Florence and as a young boy served as an assistant to Ghiberti. He later accompanied Brunelleschi to Rome, where both studied classical statues. Although strongly influenced by these classical works, he gave to his sculpture a new realism and expression. He mastered the art of sculpting freestanding statues. One of his most revolutionary works was his statue of David, which he depicted as a young Florentine shepherd boy. Donatello also cast the first full-scale equestrian statue (man on horseback) since Roman times. His realistic, free-

Michelangelo's Pietá

standing statues later inspired the most outstanding sculptor of the Renaissance—Michelangelo.

Michelangelo—Michelangelo was a man of many talents. He was a noted painter, sculptor, architect, engineer, and poet. While in his early twenties, he completed one of his most famous masterpieces, the *Pietà* (PYAY tah; an Italian term meaning "pity" or "compassion"). It depicts the virgin Mary mourning over the crucified Christ. When the work was unveiled, one viewer exclaimed, "This cannot be the work of some unknown artist. It must be the work of our master in Milan." Hearing this, Michelangelo returned later that night and carved into the ribbon across Mary's chest, "Michelangelo Buonarroti, Florentine, made this."

In sculpting the *Pietà,* Michelangelo went beyond usual artistic methods of portraying subjects realistically because he wanted to express what he considered to be the ideal. The sculpture contains a number of contradictions. For example, Michelangelo portrays Christ after the Crucifixion without any disfigurement; in fact, the figure of Christ is a model of physical perfection. Though dead, He looks full of life. Perhaps Michelangelo had in mind the teaching of Scripture in Revelation 1:18—''I am he that liveth, and was dead; and, behold, I am alive for evermore.'' Another interesting feature is that Mary is presented as a young girl—one too young to be the mother of Christ. Michelangelo created this distortion of historical fact in order to emphasize the purity of Mary. Furthermore, though the figure of Christ is life-size, Mary is larger than life. It is estimated that if she were to stand, she would be eight to nine feet tall. When questioned about these discrepancies, Michelangelo said, ''The hands execute but the eye judges.'' To the admiring eye these distortions are not readily apparent.

Another famous work by Michelangelo is his marble statue of David. Like many of the Renaissance artists, Michelangelo glorified the human body. His David, standing eighteen feet high, is the embodiment of Michelangelo's vision of a perfect specimen of young manhood.

Music

The most prominent type of musical composition during the early Middle Ages was known as **plainsong**, or Gregorian chant. Sung to Latin words, these simple, single-lined melodies became the official music of the Roman Catholic church and were a vital part of medieval church services. For the most part, medieval music was mystical and spiritual in nature; its purpose was not to appeal to the senses and emotions of its listeners but to their spirits. Medieval music attempted to remove the listener from the cares of the world.

Renaissance music was more secular. Like the visual arts, it did not remain under the exclusive patronage of the church. With the advent of the printing press, copies of music became more readily available. Both the number of musicians and the popular interest in music increased. Music moved into the palaces of the nobles and the homes of the middle class. Even ordinary people could purchase printed song books. ''How-to-do-it'' books instructed would-be musicians how to play a musical instrument. By far the most popular instrument of

the day was the lute. This instrument, which resembles a pear-shaped guitar, was most widely used to accompany singers. More music was composed and performed during the Renaissance than in any previous period in history.

Josquin Deprès

One of the leading figures in music during the early Renaissance was the Flemish composer **Josquin Deprès** (duh PREH; 1450?-1521). His life and music mark the transition between medieval and modern times. His contemporaries hailed him as one of the foremost composers of the day. Martin Luther said of him ''He is the master of notes; they do as he bids; as for the other composers, they have to do as the notes will.''

With a simple and charming style, Deprès composed both sacred and secular works. He is best remembered for his masses (music sung during the mass service), hymns, and more than one hundred **motets**—unaccompanied Latin songs that combined different melodies and words with a plainsong melody. Less serious were his **chansons**, lighthearted songs that set secular lyric poems to music.

In the latter part of his life, Deprès served as the court composer for his good friend King Louis XII

JOSQVINVS PRATENSIS.

Josquin Deprès

of France. On one occasion when Louis forgot to fulfill a promise that he made to Josquin, the composer devised an unusual way to remind the king. At the next church service the choir sang a newly composed motet about those who break their promises.

Palestrina

The most famous composer of church music during the Renaissance was the Italian composer Giovanni Pierluigi (1526?-94). He is better known as **Palestrina,** taking his name from the town of his birth. As a boy he sang in his town's church choir; later he served as the organist and choirmaster of the Palestrina Cathedral.

During his lifetime, Palestrina composed more than nine hundred musical pieces. He also revised many of the old Gregorian chants. By the sixteenth century, church music had become so complicated that it was difficult to understand what the choir was singing. Commissioned by the papacy, Palestrina simplified much of the church's official music. He was the master of **polyphonic** music (consisting of many melodies), which he composed for choirs to sing without accompaniment. In his own day he was hailed as the "Prince of Music."

Giovanni Battista Beinaschi, Saint Cecilia and Angel Musicians, *Bob Jones University Collection of Sacred Art*

Section Review

1. During the High Renaissance, what city became the cultural center of Italy?
2. List the three most famous painters of the High Renaissance period; beside each, give the title of one of his masterpieces.
3. What beautiful, wealthy city, called the "Queen of the Adriatic," became the center of culture during the late Renaissance? Identify two leading painters from this city.
4. Identify a Northern Renaissance artist for each of the following characteristics: portrait painter, genre painting, woodcarvings and engravings, and detailed realism through oil painting.
5. Who was the most famous composer of church music during the Renaissance? What type of music did he master?

Consequences of the Renaissance

The Renaissance and the Reformation that followed it are in many respects exact opposites. The Renaissance was a secular age; men placed confidence in human ability and gloried in human achievement. Artists and scholars, who looked to classical Greece and Rome for inspiration and authority, helped stir a great revival in learning and the arts. The Reformation was a religious age; men placed confidence in God and gloried in God's salvation. Men of God, who looked to the Bible as the sole authority, helped stir a great spiritual revival.

Despite these differences, it would be wrong to assume that there was no connection between the Renaissance and the Reformation. Every period of history is preparatory to the age that follows. In God's providence, the age of the Renaissance prepared western Europe for the coming age of the Reformation (which we will discuss in the next chapter).

Positive Consequences

The Renaissance, in a sense, made the Reformation possible. *First,* the Renaissance provoked a spirit of inquiry. Men no longer meekly accepted the authority of the Roman church. Instead they critically evaluated her teaching for themselves. This critical spirit encouraged men to turn their attention back to the simplicity of first-century Christianity.

Second, it revived interest in the literature and languages of antiquity. In their search for classical sources, Renaissance humanists recovered many Christian sources—manuscripts of the Old and New Testaments. The discovery of these manuscripts led to a renewed interest in the biblical languages (Greek and Hebrew) and in the study of the Bible itself.

Third, the Renaissance developed movable-type printing, which made possible the inexpensive production of written material. The printed page helped spread the ideas of the reformers throughout Europe. *Fourth,* it made education more widely available. Now even common people were now able to read what was being printed. *Fifth,* the Renaissance stressed the importance of the individual, thus restoring the proper emphasis on individual responsibility—the obligation each man has to God and to his fellow man.

Negative Consequences

The Renaissance's secular emphasis helped weaken moral restraints and thereby made the need for reform more readily apparent. The church, which should have been the example of moral righteousness, was steeped in worldliness and wickedness. Renaissance clergy and popes reveled openly in luxury and immorality. It has been said that "the moral corruption of Rome and Italy in the latter half of the fifteenth century and the early part of the sixteenth is the best justification of the Protestant Reformation." Similarly, the humanists, who sought to imitate the best of the classical world, often embraced its evils.

The revival of classical literature and art carried in it the danger of a revival of heathenism in religion and morality. The worship of classical forms led to the worship of classical ideas. Some humanists and artists combined culture with Christian faith and devoted their genius to the cause of truth and virtue, but the majority silently or openly sacrificed to the gods of Greece and Rome rather than to the God of the Bible. The dazzling glory of classical antiquity obscured the humble beauty of Christianity.[6]

A Glimpse Behind and a Glimpse Ahead

Throughout history people have sought to reach a proper balance between life on earth and life in the world to come. The medieval world "tipped the scale" toward the world to come; they were often careless about the past, believing that it had little bearing on their lives. They merely existed in the present and fixed their eyes on the future, anticipating the glories that awaited.

The people of the Renaissance reacted to the otherworldly focus of the Middle Ages by placing too much emphasis on this world. They gloried in the past, finding there the inspiration and example for the present. Their enthusiasm for life led them to exalt the present, often to the neglect of the future.

It was the Reformation that sought to restore the proper balance between this life and the life to come. The reformers found their guide for life in the Word of God, which puts past, present, and future in proper perspective:

For the grace of God that bringeth salvation hath appeared to all men, teaching us that, denying ungodliness and worldly lusts, we should live soberly, righteously, and godly, in this present world; looking for that blessed hope, and the glorious appearing of the great God and our Saviour Jesus Christ.

—Titus 2:11-13

Chapter Review

Can You Explain?

Renaissance
humanism
humanities

humanists
patrons
frescoes

perspective
genre painting
plainsong

motets
chansons
polyphonic

Can You Identify?

Medici family
Lorenzo de Medici
Johannes Gutenberg
Francesco Petrarch
Baldassare Castiglione
Niccolo Machiavelli
condottière
Erasmus

Thomas More
Miguel de Cervantes
William Shakespeare
Giotto di Bondone
Masaccio
Sandro Botticelli
Girolamo Savonarola
Leonardo da Vinci

Raphael
Michelangelo
  Buonarroti
Sistine Chapel
Titian
Tintoretto
Jan van Eyck
Albrecht Dürer

Hans Holbein
Pieter Brueghel
Lorenzo Ghiberti
Filippo Brunelleschi
Donatello
Josquin Deprès
Palestrina

Can You Locate?

Florence
Rotterdam
Stratford-upon-Avon

Padua
Rome

Milan
Venice

Adriatic Sea
Flanders

How Much Do You Remember?

1. How did the Renaissance man's attitude toward life differ from medieval man's?
2. List three reasons that Italy was the early home of the Renaissance.
3. Identify the title of one important work authored by each of the following: Petrarch, Castiglione, Machiavelli, Erasmus, More, Cervantes, and Shakespeare.
4. In what ways did the northern European humanists differ from the humanists in Italy?
5. List four ways Renaissance art differed from medieval art.

What Do You Think?

1. Many of the Renaissance artists boasted of their talent and ability. What should be the Christian's attitude toward his talents and abilities? What does the Bible say about this in II Corinthians 10:12-18?
2. The Renaissance men believed it was important to have a broad education in the humanities. Today many educators emphasize the importance of specialized study. What are the strengths of each position?
3. "The printing press was the most important invention of the Renaissance period." Do you agree or disagree with this statement? Why?

Notes

1. Lewis W. Spitz, *The Renaissance and Reformation Movements* (Chicago: Rand McNally, 1971), p. 5.
2. Selections from *The Renaissance: Maker of Modern Man* (National Geographic Society, 1970), p. 93, and John R. Hale, et al., *Renaissance* (New York: Time-Life Books, 1965), p. 57.
3. *The Renaissance: Maker of Modern Man*, p. 300.
4. E. G. Holt, *Literary Sources of Art History* (Princeton: Princeton Univ. Press, 1947), p. 170.
5. Ibid., pp. 87-88.
6. Spitz, p. 17.

CHAPTER 11

"Scripture alone, faith alone, grace alone."

The Reformation

On November 10, 1483, in the mining town of Eisleben located in the heart of Germany, a son was born to Hans and Margaretta Luther. Before this boy had reached the age of ten, European explorers had sailed to the southern tip of Africa and had landed in the New World. The age of exploration and discovery had begun. Meanwhile, the Renaissance was flourishing in Italy and was beginning to spread to northern Europe. Throughout Europe a spirit of nationalism was stirring. Men busied themselves in much religious activity; even so, there was little true godliness.

This was the age in which the young Martin Luther grew up. This son of a German peasant became one of the leading figures of the sixteenth century. Through God's leading he initiated the Protestant Reformation and was its outspoken leader during the early years. This religious movement began during the early sixteenth century as a protest against the corruption in the Roman Catholic church. Luther and other Protestant reformers exposed the false doctrines of Roman Catholicism that had clouded God's truth for centuries. The reformers reasserted biblical truth and the authority of the Word of God. Through their efforts and the moving of God in the hearts of men, Europe experienced a great spiritual awakening. The hold of the Roman Catholic church on the populace was broken, and many Protestant churches came into existence.

Forerunners of the Reformation

The spiritual revival that swept across Europe during the sixteenth century was the culmination of centuries of activity. For many generations men had attempted to curb the abuses in the church. Most reforming efforts, however, were directed only against its most visible evils. Only a few men recognized the need for doctrinal purity and deeper moral reform. Attempting to stir inward reform, they attacked the church's corrupt teaching as well as its corrupt practices. These brave men held to the Bible as the sole authority for the Christian faith. Asserting that Christ was the only head of the church, they rejected the authority of the pope. God used these stalwarts of the Faith to prepare the way for the later reformers of the Reformation Era.

John Wycliffe

One of the strongest voices of protest against the wickedness in the Roman church came from the Englishman **John Wycliffe** (WIK lif; 1320?-84). Wycliffe was a fearless preacher, a distinguished scholar, and a patriotic leader. Long associated with the University of Oxford, he earned

John Wycliffe

Opposite Page: Edward Matthew Ward, Martin Luther Discovering Justification by Faith, *Bob Jones University Collection of Sacred Art*

fame as a teacher, lecturer, and theologian. Nevertheless, it is for his work as a religious reformer that he is best remembered. Because many of his convictions and teachings were later embraced by the sixteenth-century reformers, he has been called the "Morning Star of the Reformation."

From his study of the Bible, Wycliffe became convinced that the church as it came to be dominated by Roman Catholicism had strayed from its original purity both in doctrine and practice. Through sermons, lectures, and writings, he opposed the temporal power and wealth of the Roman church. He sought to purge the church of its corrupt clergy. Wycliffe denounced monastic orders, criticized the practice of confessing sins to a priest, and denied the doctrine of transubstantiation (the belief that during the Holy Eucharist the bread and wine are transformed into the actual body and blood of Christ). He, as well as other Englishmen of his day, resented the claims of the papacy upon the church in England. But Wycliffe went a step further than his countrymen in proclaiming the papacy to be an institution "full of poison." He preached Christ as the only head of the church. The pope, he said, "is not the head, life or root except perchance of evildoers in the church." He called the pope "the antichrist" and "the leader of the army of the devil."

Wycliffe upheld the Bible as the supreme authority for all believers, clergy as well as laity. He believed that every Christian should study the Bible and that God's Word is the only source of spiritual truth and the only accurate presentation of the way of salvation. Wycliffe contended that a knowledge of Scripture would expose the error in the practice and teaching of the Roman Catholic church and would start true reform. For this reason, he initiated the translation of the Bible from Latin into English so that more people could discover the truths found in Scripture. This first complete English translation of the Bible—known as the Wycliffe Bible—was finished in 1382. Wycliffe also trained men, mostly laymen, to preach the gospel. By groups of twos, these servants of the Lord, barefoot and clad in coarse garments, went out with staffs in hand (a symbol of their pastoral office) to live and preach among the people.

Wycliffe's reforming efforts met with stiff opposition. Church leaders sought to suppress his teaching, which they condemned as heretical. In 1384 Wycliffe died from a stroke, but his death did not end the persecution. For more than a century after his death, the church attempted to completely eradicate his teaching and followers in England. Many of his followers, known as **Lollards,** were imprisoned, tortured, and burned at the stake.

John Huss

The flame of truth could not be extinguished. Wycliffe's views soon spread to the Continent (mainland Europe), where they influenced the Bohemian reformer **John Huss** (1369?-1415). From the city of Prague, Huss challenged the Bohemian people to oppose the worldliness in the church. Huss, who taught and defended many of Wycliffe's beliefs, was accused by church leaders of spreading heresy. Though excommunicated, he remained steadfast in his beliefs and continued to be a popular preacher.

In 1414 church leaders met in the city of Constance to settle the pressing disputes over the papal schism (see p. 248) and church reform. Sigismund, the Holy Roman emperor, wishing to settle the question of heresy in Bohemia, summoned Huss to the **Council of Constance,** giving him a promise of imperial protection. Huss traveled to Constance expecting to have opportunity to defend his teaching from the Word of God. But soon after his arrival, church leaders had him imprisoned and placed on trial for teaching heresy. Not shown from God's Word that he was in error, Huss refused to renounce his beliefs. In spite of the emperor's promise of protection, the council condemned him to die at the stake.

The day of execution came, and Huss was led to the stake. Moments before the fire was kindled, he was asked to **recant** (renounce his beliefs) and thereby save his life. He responded, "I shall die with joy today in the faith of the gospel which I have preached." Although the flames ended his earthly life, his influence remained strong, and the work for reform continued. His Bohemian brethren, stirred by his death, vigorously adhered to his

Chaucer and Wycliffe

In The Canterbury Tales *Geoffrey Chaucer, a contemporary of John Wycliffe, ridicules the clergy of his day. His description of a monk and a friar displays the popular contempt for the selfish desires and worldly interests of many members of the clergy. In contrast to these examples of religious hypocrisy, Chaucer presents the tale of a town parson who is materially poor but rich in true godliness. Chaucer may have used the life of Wycliffe or one of his followers as the model for this passage.*

A good man was there of religion,
And a poor PARSON OF A TOWN,
But rich he was of holy thought and work.
He was also a learned man, a clerk,
That Christ's gospel truly would preach;
His parisshens devoutly would he teach.

This noble ensample to his sheep he gave,
That first he wrought, and afterward he taught.
Out of the gospel he the words caught,
And this figure he added eke thereto,
That if gold rust, what shall iron do?
For if a priest be foul, on whom we trust,
No wonder is a lewed [ordinary] man to rust.

To drawen folk to heaven by fairness,
By good ensample, this was his business.
But if were any person obstinate,
What so he were, of high or low estate,
Him would he snybben sharply for the nonys.
A better priest I trowe that nowhere none is.
He waited after no pomp and reverence,
He maked him a spiced conscience,
But Christ's lore and his apostles twelve
He taught, but first he followed it himself.

teaching despite increased persecution by the Roman church.

The same council that condemned Huss to death also reexamined the writings of Wycliffe. The Roman church formally condemned Wycliffe as a heretic on 260 different counts and ordered his writings to be burned. His enemies at the council also ordered his body to be dug up and burned—an act that supposedly signified his condemnation to hell. More than a decade passed, however, before this order was carried out. In 1428, forty-four years after his death, Wycliffe's bones were dug up and burned. His ashes were thrown into a nearby stream.

The Roman church seemingly triumphed over Wycliffe and Huss. Both men had called attention to

Left: The house in Constance in which John Huss lived prior to his arrest; **Right:** Statue of John Huss that stands in Prague; **Right (inset):** Lichen-covered rock that marks the place where Huss was burned at the stake

the deplorable condition of the church; neither, however, had been able to initiate any widespread or lasting reform. In the providence of God, the time was not yet ripe. The task of breaking the iron grip of the Roman church was left for a later generation. Nevertheless, these "reformers before the Reformation" faithfully stood for truth and boldly opposed the errors of Roman Catholicism. In doing so, they prepared the way for the Protestant Reformation.

Section Review

1. What Englishman's protest against the Roman church prior to the Reformation period earned him the title "Morning Star of the Reformation"?

2. What did this "pre-reformer" uphold as the supreme authority for all believers? What great work did he do in order to expose the corruption of the Roman church to the English people?

3. What English author presented contrasting views of the clergy of his day—the hypocrisy of wealthy, worldly monks with the godliness of a poor town parson? What was the title of his work?

4. What city is associated with the life and ministry of John Huss?

5. What council condemned Huss to be burned at the stake? What other man did this council condemn as a heretic?

Beginning of the Reformation

The name **Martin Luther** is inseparably linked to the Reformation period. His courageous stand against the Roman Catholic church sparked the religious upheaval known as the Protestant Reformation.

Luther's Early Life

Strict discipline characterized Martin Luther's early training both at home and at school. At the age of eighteen he entered the University of Erfurt, where he became acquainted with both scholastic and classical studies. It was also at the university that he saw a complete Bible for the first time. He rejoiced to discover that it revealed much more about God than he had ever previously imagined.

After graduation Luther planned to obey the wishes of his father and prepare for a legal career. But these plans, as well as the course of his life, changed suddenly during the summer of 1505. While returning to Erfurt after a visit with his parents, Luther was caught outside in a violent thunderstorm. When a lightning bolt struck nearby, Luther, thinking himself near death, cried out in terror, "Saint Anne, help me! I will become a monk." To the shock of his parents and friends, Luther remained true to his vow. Soon after returning to Erfurt, he entered an Augustinian monastery.

Luther spent his days in the monastery zealously performing good works, which he hoped would earn him his salvation. In 1507 he was ordained a priest. A few years later he was made professor of Bible at the newly formed university at Wittenberg and became a pastor of the town church. Though a respected monk, pastor, and teacher, he was filled with doubt and despair over his own salvation. How could he, a sinner, stand before a just and holy God? His good works offered no relief from his burden of guilt and sin. Through his study of Scripture, however, Luther soon discovered that no amount of good works could justify a sinner before God; justification was by faith alone. Luther later described his spiritual awakening:

> Night and day I pondered until I saw the connection between the justice of God and the statement that "the just shall live by faith" [Rom. 1:17]. Then I grasped that the justice of God is that righteousness by which through grace and sheer mercy God justifies us through faith. Thereupon I felt myself to be reborn and to have gone through open doors into paradise. The whole of Scripture took on a new meaning, and whereas before the "justice of God" had filled me with hate, now it became to me inexpressibly sweet in greater love. This passage of Paul became to me a gate to heaven.[1]

This doctrine transformed Luther's life, and to the day of his death, it was the heart of his preaching. **"Justification by faith alone"** became the rallying cry of the Reformation movement.

Controversy over the Sale of Indulgences

In 1514 Pope **Leo X** (1513-21) launched a campaign to complete the rebuilding of St. Peter's Basilica in Rome. Because of the lavish spending of the Renaissance popes, the papal treasury was

Raphael, Pope Leo X and Two Cardinals, *Scala*

drained of funds. In order to raise the needed money, Leo sent out agents to sell certificates of **indulgences,** which supposedly granted pardon from the punishment of sins. In 1517 one of these agents, a Dominican friar named **Johann Tetzel,** began selling indulgences near Luther's parish at Wittenberg. People flocked to see Tetzel, believing they could purchase forgiveness for sins. He told them that by buying an indulgence a person could free a relative from suffering in purgatory. He is said to have preached, "As soon as a coin in the coffer rings, right then a soul from purgatory springs." Martin Luther, who had experienced salvation as God's free gift, resented the exploitation of his people. From his pulpit he railed against the abuses accompanying the sale of indulgences.

Leo X's issuance of indulgences was nothing new for the Roman church. For centuries, popes had granted certificates of pardon. It was the position of the Roman church that although Christ died to save men from hell, they still had to do penance or suffer in purgatory as punishment for their individual sins. The popes maintained that they had the power to suspend these punishments for specific individuals. This practice rested in the theory that the saints did more good works than necessary to get themselves into heaven. Their "excess works," along with the merits of Christ's perfect life, were supposedly collected in a type of bank, the **treasury of merits.** The pope served as "treasurer" and could dispense these extra good works. At first, popes granted indulgences only to those people who performed some special work, such as giving money to charity or fighting on a crusade. However, by the time of the Renaissance, popes were selling indulgences to raise money for their own projects.

Though Tetzel's methods were scandalous, his cash boxes overflowed with money for Leo's building program. Nevertheless, there were a few sincere church members who questioned the practice of selling indulgences. They wondered why the pope, if he were truly the keeper of the treasury of merits, did not give these merits out freely to all, or why, if he could pardon one soul from purgatory, he did not pardon everyone. Luther raised these

same questions. He had been dismayed to find that members of his congregation who had purchased indulgences were unwilling to change their wicked ways. Concern for the spiritual well-being of his parishioners prompted Luther's protests. His opposition to the sale of indulgences shook all of Christendom.

Luther's Break with Rome

The Ninety-five Theses

On October 31, 1517, Martin Luther, dressed in his professor's gown, stood outside the castle church in Wittenberg, Germany. On the church's wooden door, which served as a kind of public bulletin board for the university and town, he posted a lengthy document. It contained a list of ninety-five theses, or statements, concerning the sale of indulgences, which Luther proposed as topics for a scholarly debate. Little did he realize he would stir up a great controversy. Almost overnight the **Ninety-five Theses** became a symbol of defiance against the corruption and hypocrisy of Rome. By questioning indulgences, Luther inadvertently—but providentially—challenged the whole system of Roman Catholicism.

St. Peter's Cathedral in Rome

Luther's Trip to Rome

In the fall of 1510, while still a monk, Luther traveled to Rome on business for the Augustinian order. He had eagerly anticipated the trip; in Rome there would be many opportunities to visit sacred shrines and venerate relics of the saints. Luther considered Rome a holy city—a place where he could draw closer to God.

What he found, however, deeply disturbed him. Renaissance Rome was a city given over to wickedness. Even church leaders indulged in sins of every kind. Prostitution and other forms of sexual immorality flourished. Greed and ambition controlled the actions of both clergy and laity. During his visit Luther encountered stories of how Pope Alexander VI (1492-1503) had used treachery and murder to accomplish his purposes.

As a reformer Luther used his experiences in Rome and other cities to illustrate the corruption of the Roman Catholic church. On one occasion in 1537 Luther told a group of friends, "I wouldn't have missed being in Rome for a great deal of money. I wouldn't have believed it if I hadn't seen it for myself. For so great and shameless is the godlessness and wickedness there that neither God nor man, neither sin nor disgrace are taken seriously. All godly persons who've been there testify of this, and this is the witness of all the ungodly who have returned from Italy worse than they had been before."[2]

The hammer blows that nailed Luther's protest to the church door rang throughout Germany. Within weeks, printed copies of his Ninety-five Theses circulated widely in Germany and received a sympathetic welcome among the people. Many of them were disgusted with Tetzel's evil ways; others looked for an occasion to stop the flow of German money into the papal coffers at Rome. Indulgence sales dropped off sharply, a fact that angered Tetzel and upset church officials. They denounced Luther as a heretic and urged the people to take action against him. At first Pope Leo X refused to get involved in what he considered a minor quarrel among monks. But when funds stopped coming in for St. Peter's Church, he was prompted to action.

The Leipzig Debate

Opponents of Luther, thinking him to be nothing more than an ignorant and misguided monk, sought to engage him in debates in order to show him the error of his ways. But Luther, armed by years of diligent study of the Scriptures and guided by the Spirit of God, was more than their match. The climax of this confrontation occurred in the debate at Leipzig (LIPE sig) during the summer of 1519. Here Luther met the formidable scholar **John Eck,** a champion of Roman Catholicism. The three-week debate centered on the question of authority in the church. Luther asserted that the pope had human rather than divine authority and that he could err just as any other man. The great reformer insisted that Scripture is the only reliable authority. Eck charged that Luther was holding views similar to those of John Huss, whom the Council of Constance had condemned as a heretic a century earlier. In response Luther maintained that not all of Huss's teachings were heretical—a position that led him to the conclusion that even church councils might err.

The Leipzig debate only widened the breach between Luther and Rome. Luther had entered the debate believing himself to be a good Roman Catholic; in his mind all he had done was to call attention to a few corrupt practices that other sincere Catholics had found equally offensive. But because he renounced the authority of popes and councils, he was driven to the Scriptures for guidance. He soon became even more firmly convinced that the Bible alone is the sole authority for the Christian faith.

In the months that followed, Luther wrote a series of pamphlets intended to rouse the German people to action. He wanted them to take a stand against the corrupt Roman system. Because the papacy failed to take the initiative, he called upon civil rulers to reform the church. He attacked the sacramental system of the church, stating that it distorted the true meaning of salvation. He maintained that every believer was a priest and that each had the freedom to approach God personally through faith (Eph. 2:18; I Pet. 2:9).

Left: Portrait of Martin Luther; Center: The Ninety-five Theses;
Right: Luther nailing his Ninety-Five Theses to the door of the
church at Wittenberg

The Road to Worms

The pope was unable to take serious action against Luther. One reason for this was that Luther was the subject of one of the most respected and powerful territorial princes in all of Germany, Frederick the Wise, Elector of Saxony. Frederick opposed the idea of having any of his subjects stand trial outside of Germany—especially if that trial were to take place in Italy.

In June of 1520, the pope finally heeded the counsel of his advisers. He issued a papal bull that condemned Luther for advancing heretical doctrines and gave him sixty days to recant. If he did not do so, he would be excommunicated. At a public gathering near the city gate of Wittenberg, Lu-ther responded to the pope's ultimatum; he ceremoniously tossed the papal bull into a bonfire. By this act he sealed his separation from Rome. As expected, a few weeks later he was formally excommunicated from the Roman church.

The newly crowned German emperor, **Charles V,** sensing Luther's strong public support, refused to condemn him without a hearing. In the spring of 1521 he summoned Luther to the city of Worms to appear before the German diet. The emperor gave Luther the promise of imperial protection to and from Worms, but Luther's friends reminded him of what had happened to John Huss in a similar situation. Despite their warnings, Luther proceeded to Worms to defend the truth before the imperial Diet.

On the afternoon of April 17, 1521, Luther stood before the emperor, princes, and bishops of the Holy Roman Empire at the **Diet of Worms.** He was given no chance to defend his teaching. Instead he was simply asked whether a number of books lying on a table in front of him were his writings and whether he would recant the heresy contained in them. To the first question Luther answered yes; to the second, he asked for time to consider his answer. On the next day the questions were again put to him, and he was asked to give a clear and simple reply. With firmness of conviction, he gave his memorable declaration:

> Unless I am convicted of error by the testimony of Scripture or (since I put no trust in the unsupported authority of pope or of councils, since it is plain that they have often erred and often contradicted themselves) by clear reason I stand convicted by the Scriptures to which I have appealed, and my conscience is taken captive by God's word, I cannot and will not recant anything, for it is neither safe nor right to act against the conscience. Here I stand. I can do no other. God help me! Amen.

Martin Luther before Charles V at the Diet of Worms

Luther left the city. The emperor soon afterwards issued an edict declaring Luther an outlaw of the empire. He banned Luther's writings, forbade anyone to give him aid, and demanded that he be seized and turned over to the authorities. If captured, Luther was to suffer the fate of a condemned heretic—death. God, however, was not through with this man. Luther lived for twenty-five years under the imperial edict and died a natural death in 1546. During these years the truth of God's Word, which he so boldly defended, took root in the hearts and lives of men and women all over Europe.

Progress of the Reformation in Germany

Continuation of Luther's Work

Despite the Edict of Worms, the doctrines of the Reformation continued to spread rapidly. They were proclaimed from pulpits, heralded from street corners, and circulated in printed pamphlets. Perhaps the greatest help to the reforming cause in Germany was Luther's translation of the New Testament (and later the whole Bible) into German. This work, based upon Erasmus's Greek New Testament, created widespread enthusiasm for the Bible among all classes of German people. The power and beauty of its expression helped to create a standard German language for all Germany.

Luther's work did not stop with his translation of the Bible. In order to make the principles of the Scripture so clear that even a child could understand them, he wrote his *Shorter Catechism.* In question-

Charles V

Philipp Melanchthon, an engraving by Albrecht Dürer

and-answer form, this catechism gives instruction in the fundamental doctrines of Scripture. Luther also used music as a means of teaching the gospel. He urged the people to sing doctrinal hymns at home, work, and church. His own hymn "A Mighty Fortress is Our God," called the "victory hymn of the Reformation," is one of the best-known and most-loved hymns of the Christian church.

As the followers of Luther's teaching increased in number, it soon became necessary to frame an official statement of Lutheran beliefs. In 1530 **Philipp Melanchthon,** Luther's close friend and co-worker, drew up the **Augsburg Confession,** which clearly sets forth the chief doctrines for which Luther and his followers contended. This document became the doctrinal standard for the Lutheran church and remains that church's most highly respected statement of faith.

Preoccupation of Charles V

One reason for the rapid spread of Lutheran doctrine was Charles V's preoccupation with the political affairs of Europe. Charles, the crowned ruler of the Holy Roman Empire, was also the ruler by inheritance of the Hapsburg possessions of Spain, Sicily, Naples, the Netherlands, and Austria, plus territory in the New World. His vast holdings gave him great power, but many problems as well. He was constantly defending the borders of his far-flung possessions, putting down revolts, and repelling invasions.

Between the years 1522 and 1546, Charles fought several wars with his chief rival, **Francis I,** the king of France. The French king was particularly concerned that his country was encircled by Charles's possessions. Meanwhile, Charles was faced with another threat: the Ottoman Turks, led by **Suleiman,** invaded the eastern portion of his empire. By the early 1540s Charles had halted the Turkish advance and had signed a truce with the French king. He could now turn his attention to the religious situation in the German states. But over twenty years had elapsed since the Diet of Worms. Lutheranism was firmly established.

In 1546, the year of Luther's death, Charles began his attack on the German Protestants. For nearly nine years his imperial and pro-Catholic forces waged war against the anti-imperial and Protestant forces of German princes. In 1555 a compromise settlement was finally reached in the **Peace of Augsburg.** It allowed each prince the right to choose whether his territory would be Lutheran or Roman Catholic. The people within a

The Term *Protestant*

The term *Protestant* dates back to the early days of the Reformation. In April of 1529 representatives of the German states gathered in the city of Speyer to discuss the religious situation in Germany. At that meeting the Roman Catholic majority attempted to halt the progress of the Reformation, hoping to eventually suppress it altogether. They passed an edict which, among other things, required the Lutheran princes to guarantee the religious liberty of Roman Catholics living under their rule. At the same time, however, Roman Catholic princes could deny religious liberty to Lutherans living in their territories. The Lutheran princes opposed the entire edict, stating that they would "protest and testify publicly before God" that they would agree with "nothing contrary to His Word." It is from their courageous protest that the word *Protestant* comes. Today the term refers to anyone who holds to the biblical teachings of the Reformation in opposition to Roman Catholicism.

given territory had to either accept the choice of their prince or move elsewhere. The peace only postponed the religious and political problems in Germany; in 1618 war would break out once again.

Section Review
1. What pope launched a fund-raising drive to rebuild St. Peter's Basilica? What did his agents sell in order to raise the needed money?
2. What did Luther post on the door of the castle church in Wittenburg? Give the day, month, and year in which this event took place.
3. At the Leipzig debate, Eck charged that Luther was holding views similar to what earlier reformer? What conclusion did Luther reach as a result of this debate?
4. To what city was Luther summoned to appear before the princes, bishops, and emperor of the Holy Roman Empire? Who was the emperor who presided over the assembly?
5. What settlement ended the civil war that broke out among the Catholic and Protestant princes of Germany? What compromise was reached by this settlement?

Spread of the Reformation

The Protestant Reformation was not confined to the land of Germany. Neither was Luther its only leader. God raised up reformers in many lands who protested the abuses of Roman Catholicism and sought to restore biblical Christianity. Though the reformers often differed on matters of biblical interpretation, they were in agreement with the key doctrines of the Reformation movement: "Scripture alone, faith alone, grace alone!"

The Reformation in Switzerland

Switzerland was one of the first places outside Germany to feel the influence of the Protestant Reformation. The Swiss Confederation began in 1291 when three cantons (or states) banded together for their mutual defense. By the time of the Reformation, the number of cantons had grown to thirteen. Switzerland enjoyed a remarkable degree of independence, even though in theory it was still part of the Holy Roman Empire.

Zwingli in Zurich

An early leader of the Swiss Reformation was **Ulrich Zwingli** (ZWING lee). He was born in 1484 in a small village in the northern, German-speaking region of Switzerland. He studied at several leading universities, where he developed a keen interest in the classics. His training acquainted him with Erasmus, under whose influence he began to study the Bible. As a young man, Zwingli was ordained a Roman Catholic priest. Early in his ministry, however, he realized that there was corruption in the Roman church. He soon became an outspoken critic

Ulrich Zwingli

of its abusive practices. In 1519 Zwingli became the priest of the largest church in Zurich, one of the leading towns in the Swiss Confederation.

While in Zurich, Zwingli was exposed to Luther's writings for the first time. Through Luther, he came to understand that salvation comes only by the grace of God through faith. With the support of the Zurich city council, Zwingli began to make significant changes in his church. These changes aroused Roman Catholic opposition, but Zwingli ably defended his position at several public debates. For one such occasion, he drew up his *Sixty-seven Conclusions.* These articles, similar in style to Luther's Ninety-five Theses, set forth Zwingli's belief in the Bible as the sole rule of faith. He rejected Roman Catholic teaching concerning the mass, celibacy of priests, purgatory, and the primacy of the pope. He declared that Christ is the only way to salvation—that He alone is the eternal high priest, the only mediator between God and man.

Although Zwingli had received a great amount of enlightenment through reading Luther's writings, he disagreed with Luther's view of the Lord's Supper. In an effort to create a united Protestant front and to settle their doctrinal differences, Zwingli and Luther met at Marburg, Germany, in October of 1529. Both men were in general agreement on the doctrines of the Trinity, the person of Jesus Christ, the work of the Holy Spirit, justification by faith, original sin, and baptism. However, at this meeting Zwingli maintained that the Lord's Supper is only a symbolic remembrance of Christ's death. Luther, on the other hand, believed that in the Lord's Supper, Christ is literally present *in, with,* and *under* the elements of bread and wine. (Non-Lutherans call this view *consubstantiation.*) Neither reformer would change his mind, and so after three days of discussion the conference ended without resolving the issue.

Zwingli did not live long after this meeting. Civil war broke out in Switzerland between the cantons that embraced Protestantism and those that remained Roman Catholic. In 1531 Zurich went to war against some neighboring Catholic districts. Zwingli accompanied the troops as a chaplain and was killed at the Battle of Kappel as he sought to aid a wounded soldier. Others carried on Zwingli's reforms in Zu-

rich. Some of his followers joined the ranks of the Lutherans, while others merged with the followers of another famous reformer, John Calvin.

The Anabaptists

Although Zwingli and his followers dominated the religious and political life of Zurich, there were those who were not satisfied with his reforms. Some of them met together in 1525 and organized their own congregation, calling themselves the Swiss Brethren. Among other things, these men opposed the practice of infant baptism. All those who joined their ranks and who had been baptized as infants were rebaptized. For this reason their enemies called them **Anabaptists** (from a Greek word which means "baptize again"). The Swiss Brethren did not call themselves "Rebaptizers" because they did not believe infant baptism to be valid in the first place. When the city council tried to force the Zurich Anabaptists to conform to the religious practices of the city, the men refused to change their beliefs. Persecution followed. Some of them were imprisoned, others fled the city, and several were martyred.

Other groups that opposed infant baptism sprang up in Europe. These various religious bodies were grouped together under the common title "Anabaptist," even though on other issues they were often in sharp disagreement. Some Anabaptists had revolutionary ideas and twisted Scripture to support their false doctrines. Others wanted nothing more than to be left in peace to worship God freely and to study His Word. Because of the wrongdoing of a few, however, all Anabaptists had a bad reputation. The Apostle Paul reminds us in the New Testament that if we are not careful to guard our actions, we can bring reproach upon the "name of God" (I Tim. 6:1) and upon the "word of God" (Titus 2:5).

In spite of their wide differences, most Anabaptist groups held certain beliefs in common. For instance, most believed that only true believers should be members in the local church. In most areas of Europe at this time all the inhabitants of a particular community were considered church members regardless of their spiritual condition. Second, most Anabaptists believed in the separation of church and state—that is, they rejected state interference in their affairs. In addition, many of them believed it was wrong for Christians to hold political office. Third, many Anabaptists believed that a Christian should not take up arms against anyone, even in time of war. This belief is called **pacifism.**

Unfortunately, many of the early Anabaptists also questioned the doctrine of justification by faith alone. They feared that this teaching might encourage men to think that justification apart from good works allowed them to sin as much as they wanted and still have forgiveness from God. These Anabaptists did not understand, as most of the other reformers did, that the Bible teaches that justification—although by faith without works (Gal. 3:11; Eph. 2:8-9)—always *results* in good works in the life of the justified believer (Eph. 2:10).

Most of the Anabaptist groups died out. However, the Mennonites, founded by Menno Simons, and the Amish, founded in the seventeenth century by Jacob Amman, have continued to the present day.

Calvin at Geneva

The most famous and influential Protestant reformer after Martin Luther was **John Calvin.** He was born in 1509 in northwestern France. As a young man, he studied both law and theology at the universities of Orléans, Bourges, and Paris. The Reformation was in full swing during his student days: Luther's ideas were undoubtedly being discussed at the French universities. From his later writings, it is evident that Calvin diligently searched the Scriptures during these years to determine the validity of Reformation doctrine. Sometime around 1533 Calvin was converted and became a Protestant.

His **Institutes**—About a year after Calvin's conversion, the king of France intensified his persecution of French Protestants. Calvin fled his native land and sought refuge in the Swiss city of Basel, where he finished one of the most significant and influential books on theology ever written. *The Institutes of the Christian Religion,* published in 1536 when Calvin was just twenty-six, sets forth Christian doctrine in a systematic outline.

At the heart of Calvin's system of theology is his strong belief in the sovereignty of God. Calvin believed that God "predestines" all things accord-

John Calvin

ing to His own will. As the sovereign Creator of the universe, God foreordains or predestines who will be saved (the "elect"). Everything God does is for His glory, although finite man does not understand God's ways.

His Years at Geneva—In 1536, while returning from a visit to France, Calvin stopped for the night at the beautiful city of Geneva in the French-speaking part of Switzerland. He intended to spend only one night there, but God had other plans. The Protestants of Geneva asked Calvin to stay and become their pastor and teacher. Though hesitant at first, he finally agreed, taking up the work of the Reformation that others had already begun in the city.

Calvin applied his teaching concerning God's sovereignty to everyday life in Geneva. He sought to build a Christian community based upon the Word of God. Taking the Bible, especially the Old Testament, as his law book, Calvin made sure that the city statutes conformed to scriptural teaching. He stressed the independence of church and state, but he believed that both were subject to the rule of God. He asserted that the duty of the state was to promote piety, punish evildoers, and assist the church by providing an atmosphere that would encourage godliness in the lives of church members. The Geneva city council adopted his teaching and issued orders forbidding dancing, drunkenness, and gambling and requiring everyone to attend church services. Opposition mounted to Calvin's strict discipline, however, and in 1538 the city council banished him. Later, problems in Geneva prompted the city to beg Calvin to return and become their spiritual leader once again. In 1541 Calvin returned; he remained there until his death in 1564.

Under Calvin's leadership, the city of Geneva became a leading center of the Protestant Reformation. Calvin's influence, however, reached far beyond Geneva. During his lifetime, many Protestants who had fled Catholic persecution in other countries came to Geneva for protection. Others came to study Calvin's theology. As they returned to their native lands, they passed Calvin's ideas on to others. Many Protestant churches adopted Calvin's system of theology, calling themselves the Reformed churches. This name is still widely used today.

The Reformation in England

Cries for reform had echoed in England since the days of John Wycliffe. His persecuted followers, the Lollards, opposed papal tyranny and preached the authority of the Word of God. During the sixteenth century, efforts for reform intensified in England as Luther's writings were widely circulated and read. The English Reformation, which did not have a dominant leader like Luther or Calvin, was influenced by two important factors.

The first factor was *the publication of English translations of the Bible*. One cannot overemphasize the importance that the Word of God had in bringing about spiritual revival in Europe. The Bible itself instructs us that "faith cometh by hearing, and hearing by the word of God" (Rom. 10:17). During the late fifteenth and early sixteenth centuries, the Bible was translated and printed in the native languages of almost every European country. In England a number of versions of the Bible were published and distributed. These were translated from the ancient tongues into the common language of the English people. A readable, understandable Bible helped increase knowledge of God's Word and helped show the English people (as it did people in other lands) the false teaching of the Roman Catholic church.

The second factor was *the involvement of the English rulers*. The English Reformation began as

a political movement under the direction of the English crown. During the sixteenth century, members of the **Tudor family** occupied the throne. There were five Tudor rulers in all: Henry VII, the founder of this royal line; his son Henry VIII; and Henry VIII's three children—Edward VI, Mary I, and Elizabeth I. Under the Tudors, England broke with the papacy—the authority of the pope over the church in England was no longer recognized. For the most part, the English people supported the crown. They were filled with national pride and resented the claims of a foreign pope on their land. At first the majority of Englishmen remained in the Roman Catholic church. But a growing number became increasingly dissatisfied with Rome and embraced Protestantism. Political motives gradually gave way to spiritual concerns as the truth of God's Word found acceptance in the hearts of a growing number of English people.

The Break with Rome Under Henry VIII

King **Henry VIII** (1509-47) was on the throne of England when the Protestant Reformation began in Germany. He branded Martin Luther a heretic

Hans Holbein the Younger, Portrait of Henry VIII, Thyssen-Bornemisza Collection, Castagnola, Switzerland

and wrote a book attacking Luther's teaching. The pope promptly proclaimed Henry "Defender of the Faith." Nevertheless, Henry later broke with Rome, though not for the same reasons that motivated Luther. Henry wanted to divorce his wife Catherine of Aragon, the daughter of Ferdinand and Isabella of Spain. Catherine had been married to Henry's older brother, who had died soon after the wedding. Contrary to church teaching, the pope permitted Henry to marry Catherine. Because she had borne him no sons to continue the Tudor line, Henry felt that he had sinned and that God was punishing him (see Lev. 20:21).

The pope, not wishing to offend Catherine's nephew, the powerful emperor Charles V, refused to grant Henry the divorce. Therefore, Henry decided to take matters into his own hands. He appointed a new archbishop of Canterbury, **Thomas Cranmer,** who declared Henry's marriage to Catherine invalid and legalized his new marriage to Anne Boleyn. In 1534, Henry had Parliament pass the Act of Supremacy, which made the king the "supreme head" of the church in England. This act completed the break between England and the papacy. It also placed the English church under the direct control of the state. Even so, during Henry's day, the English church remained true to Roman teaching and practice.

Protestant Gains Under Edward VI

When Henry VIII died in 1547, his son **Edward VI** succeeded him to the throne. Edward, a frail boy, was only nine years old when he became king. He was strongly influenced by his advisers, who were sympathetic to the Protestant Reformation. As a result, sweeping changes were made in the English church. Parliamentary acts legalized the marriage of clergymen, abolished many Catholic ceremonies, and required church services to be in English rather than in Latin. In addition, the clergy were required to use the *Book of Common Prayer* in their churches. This prayer book was drawn up by Thomas Cranmer, who had become a leading voice of Protestantism in England. It contains Bible readings and prayers for special occasions and prescribes orders of worship for various church services.

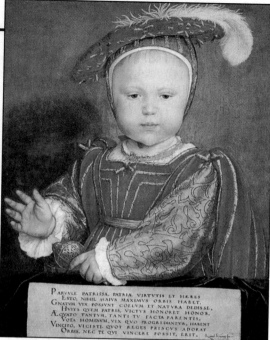

Hans Holbein the Younger, Edward VI as a Child, *National Gallery of Art, Washington, D.C.*

The statement of faith known as the *Forty-two Articles* reveals the extent of Protestant gains during Edward's reign. Formulated by Cranmer and issued by Edward, it became the official creed of the English church. The document sets forth the major Protestant doctrines of justification by faith alone and the sole authority of the Bible. It renounces transubstantiation and recognizes only two sacraments—baptism and the Lord's Supper.

Catholic Reaction Under Mary I

The sickly Edward died of tuberculosis at the age of sixteen (1553). His half sister Mary succeeded him to the throne. **Mary I,** the daughter of Henry VIII by Catherine of Aragon, was a devout Roman Catholic. She sought to restore Roman Catholicism to England by compelling Parliament to repeal the religious laws passed during Edward's reign. She removed several thousand clergymen from office who had Protestant sympathies or who had married.

As political and religious opposition mounted against Mary's pro-Catholic policies, she revived laws against heresy and began to persecute the Protestants. Hundreds of Englishmen fled to Germany and Switzerland. Those who remained in England were imprisoned; some became martyrs at the stake. The most famous victims of Mary's persecution were two bishops, Hugh Latimer and Nicholas Ridley. They were condemned to be burned at the stake. As the fire was lit, Latimer said to Ridley, "We shall this day light such a candle, by God's grace, in England, as I trust shall never be put out." Mary next turned her fury to Thomas Cranmer, the man who had declared her mother's marriage invalid. Charged with heresy and facing death, Cranmer weakened. He signed statements renouncing his Protestant beliefs and acknowledging the authority of the pope over the church in England. Nevertheless, he was sentenced to die at the stake. On the day of his execution he publicly condemned his previous weakness and boldly reaffirmed his Protestant convictions. As the flames came up about him, he thrust the hand that had signed the recantations into the fire so that "this unworthy hand" was consumed first.

Persecution continued until Mary's death in 1558. During her five-year reign, nearly three hundred leaders were martyred. But instead of wiping out Protestantism in England, her actions only increased anti-Roman sentiment and earned her the name "Bloody Mary."

Break with Rome Confirmed Under Elizabeth

When Mary I died, her half sister **Elizabeth I** (1558-1603) became queen. Her forty-five year reign marks one of the greatest periods in English history. Elizabeth never married, but she was so devoted to her country that it has been said she was married to the throne of England. A strong and determined woman, she ruled England effectively during a crucial period of its history. During her long reign she was a symbol of stability and strength. The English people affectionately called her "Good Queen Bess."

The Church of England—Though reared a Protestant, Elizabeth favored a moderate solution to England's religious problems. She restored Protestantism to England; yet she did not totally alienate the English Roman Catholics. Like her father,

History of the English Bible

The history of the English Bible begins with John Wycliffe, who believed that everyone should have the opportunity to read God's Word. In 1382 he and his followers produced the first complete English translation of the Scripture—a translation made from the Latin Vulgate. (Wycliffe knew no Hebrew or Greek.) Although the common people wanted to know what the Bible had to say, the clergy strongly opposed Wycliffe's work. The archbishop of Canterbury called Wycliffe "the very herald and child of anti-Christ, who crowned his wickedness by translating the Scripture into the mother tongue." Nevertheless, the religious and political authorities could not destroy God's Word. Wycliffe's translation survived, and some of its wording even found its way into the King James Version. For example, the phrase "strait is the gate, and narrow is the way" (Matt. 7:14) and the words "beam" and "mote" (Matt. 7:3) come from Wycliffe's translation.

William Tyndale (1492-1536), an able Hebrew and Greek scholar, produced the first English Bible translated directly from the ancient biblical languages. Forced to flee his native England, Tyndale went to Germany, where his New Testament was published in 1525. The authorities in England, however, made every effort to

she had Parliament pass an Act of Supremacy (1559) which rejected papal authority. This act affirmed the queen's position over the church of Eng-

seize or purchase these New Testaments as they were smuggled into the country. On one occasion, a London merchant who was Tyndale's friend sold numerous copies at a high price to the bishop of London. Although the bishop had the copies destroyed, Tyndale used the money he received from the sale to finance a better printing of the New Testament! He also managed to publish part of the Old Testament, but before he could translate and publish all of it, he was captured in Belgium. Condemned as a heretic, he was strangled and then burned at the stake.

Tyndale died, but his work was not in vain. Others used what he had done to produce new translations. A year before Tyndale died, Miles Coverdale (1488-1569) published a translation of the entire Bible. Since he did not know Greek or Hebrew, he relied heavily upon Luther's German translation, the Latin Vulgate, and Tyndale's work. Two years later one of Tyndale's friends, John Rogers, produced the so-called Matthew's Bible. (He published it under the pseudonym of Thomas Matthew.) This was not really a new translation, because Rogers simply combined parts of Coverdale's work with sections of the Old Testament that Tyndale had translated but never published. In 1539 Coverdale himself revised the Matthew's Bible. When it was published, it measured 16 1/2 by 11 inches and received the name Great Bible because of its size. This was the first version of the English Bible specifically authorized to be read publicly in the churches. For almost thirty years it was the only version that could be used legally in England.

Bible translation work did not cease, however. During the reign of Mary I, some of the most important Protestant leaders fled to Geneva to escape death. While there, these men produced a Bible in 1560 that contained, in their words, "most profitable annotations upon all the hard places." Known as the Geneva Bible, this was the first English version to have numbered verses. This version also used italics to indicate words that were not actually found in the Greek and Hebrew manuscripts. Within a short time, the Geneva Bible became very popular, especially among the Puritans.

In an effort to weaken the popularity of this unauthorized version, the Church of England commissioned a new translation. It came out in 1568 and became known as the Bishops' Bible. In spite of its official status, it never gained wide acceptance.

The culmination of all this early translation work occurred at the beginning of the seventeenth century. King James I authorized a group of about fifty scholars to produce a new revision of the Bible. Following the king's orders, these men used the Bishops' Bible as their guide and consulted other English translations and certain Hebrew, Greek, and Latin manuscripts—especially the Greek New Testament that had been edited by Erasmus.

To make their work more efficient and to guard against errors, the translators divided themselves into six committees. Each committee was assigned a particular task. For example, one group translated Genesis through II Kings. Once a particular committee completed a portion of its work, it would send it to the others for evaluation and revision.

In 1611 the scholars delivered their work to the king's printer for publication. The King James Version was a masterpiece, but at first many people resented it. For example, the Pilgrims rejected it. They had grown to love the familiar phraseology of the older English versions and did not want to change. But with the passage of time, this beautiful translation won the hearts of the English-speaking world.

land; however, it changed her title from "Supreme *Head*" to "Supreme *Governor*," the latter being less offensive to the Roman Catholics. Under Elizabeth, Cranmer's *Forty-two Articles* were revised to become the *Thirty-nine Articles*—another Protestant statement of faith.

The attempt by Elizabeth to settle England's religious problems through compromise is known as the **Elizabethan Settlement.** It laid the foundation for the Church of England, also known as the **Anglican church.** This institution became the established state church of England and has as its creed the *Thirty-nine Articles.* While the Anglican church embraced Protestant doctrines, it did not alter its church government, nor did it abolish certain established rituals that were not expressly forbidden in Scripture. The Anglican church retained such things as clerical vestments (robes) and candles on the communion table.

War with Spain—England's shift toward Protestantism did not go unopposed by the Roman Catholics outside of England. England's most formidable Catholic opponent was King Philip of Spain. **Philip II** (1556-98) was the son of the Hapsburg emperor Charles V. When Charles abdicated in 1556, Philip became the ruler of the Hapsburg territories in Spain, the Netherlands, and the New World. One of the strongest defenders of the Roman Catholic church, he worked hard to stamp out Protestantism. He stopped the spread of the Reformation in his realm by turning the Spanish Inquisition against the Protestants. As leader of the strongest Catholic country in the world, Philip sought to bring Protestant England back into the fold of the Roman Catholic church.

Shortly before becoming king, Philip had married Mary I, the Roman Catholic queen of England. A child born of that union would no doubt have been reared a Roman Catholic and would have been by right the next ruler of England and Spain. But in God's providence Mary died childless, and her Protestant sister Elizabeth became queen. Philip sought to marry Elizabeth. But while he was wooing her, Elizabeth was secretly working against Spain. She encouraged her sea captains (men such as Francis Drake) to plunder Spanish ships returning with treasure from the New World. She also aided the Dutch in their revolt against the Spanish ruler.

Because Elizabeth opposed Philip's political and religious involvement in various parts of Europe, he began plotting her overthrow. He conspired to have Elizabeth killed and have her cousin Mary Stuart— the former queen of Scotland—crowned queen of

Queen Elizabeth I

England. The plot was discovered, however, and Elizabeth had Mary put in prison and later executed.

Exasperated and angry, Philip decided to invade England. He amassed a great fleet of 130 ships which was to sail to the Netherlands, pick up a large Spanish army, and transport the invasion force to England. In 1588 this fleet, called by some the "Invincible Armada," set sail from Spain with the pope's blessing. Philip is said to have spent hours on his knees praying for the success of his plans. But God did not hear his pleas. The large, unwieldly Spanish galleons were no match for the smaller, more maneuverable English ships, some of which were commanded by the daring Sir **Francis Drake.** The battered Spanish fleet turned north only to be overtaken by fierce storms that wrecked many Spanish vessels along the coast of Scotland and Ireland. The "Invincible Armada" limped back to Spain with only about half the number of ships with which it had set out.

The defeat of the **Spanish Armada** had a significant impact upon world history. First, it preserved England from both Spanish and Roman Catholic domination. Second, it accelerated the decline of Spain, which during the period of exploration had been one of the richest and strongest European countries. The battle weakened Spanish sea power and as a result weakened Spain's position in the New World. Finally, it established England as a sea power at the very time English colonial expansion was under way. The way was opened for English Protestants, instead of Spanish Catholics, to settle in America.

English Protestants acknowledged God's help in their victory. They had no doubt that the "Protestant wind" that had wrecked the Spanish fleet came from God, for "the Lord hath his way in the whirlwind and in the storm, and the clouds are the dust of his feet" (Nah. 1:3). They could agree with II Chronicles 16:9—a verse that applies to both individuals and nations: "The eyes of the Lord run to and fro throughout the whole earth, to shew himself strong in the behalf of them whose heart is perfect toward him."

The Spanish Armada

The Puritans—Though Protestantism had triumphed in England, not all Protestants were in agreement with the Church of England. Many believed that the Anglican church retained too many of the "trappings of popery." They wished to "purify" the church of those practices that reminded them of Roman Catholicism. Thus originated their nickname—the **Puritans.** Other Englishmen saw no hope of bringing about change in the English church. Those who removed themselves from the church were therefore known as **Separatists.** Eng-

lishmen with Catholic leanings were not satisfied with the Church of England either. They hoped to bring the Church of England back in line with Roman Catholicism.

Neither the Protestants nor the Catholics were satisfied with Elizabeth's solution to England's religious problems. As a result, England experienced much political and religious agitation during the seventeenth century.

The Reformation in Scotland

The leader of the Protestant Reformation in Scotland was **John Knox** (1505-72). In 1547 he was taken prisoner by the French; he served for nineteen months as a galley slave on a French ship. When released he went to England, where he became a noted preacher during the reign of Edward VI. When Mary I came to the throne, he fled to Geneva, where he was greatly influenced by John Calvin.

He returned to Scotland in 1559. Through fiery preaching, he attacked the evils of Roman Catholicism. It was said of him, "Others lop off branches, but this man strikes at the root." Under his leadership Scotland threw off Roman Catholicism and became a Protestant nation. The Scottish parliament rejected papal authority, abolished the mass, and adopted for the Scottish church a Calvinistic statement of faith drawn up by Knox. They established the Presbyterian church in Scotland.

The Reformation in Scotland flourished even though Scotland had a Catholic queen, **Mary Stuart** (1542-87). Mary was less than a week old when her father, King James V, died and she was proclaimed queen of Scotland. She grew up in France, however, the homeland of her mother, while her mother acted as her regent in Scotland. In 1561 the young queen returned to Scotland only to find that her Catholic and French upbringing alienated the nationalistic Scottish Protestants.

Her downfall came when she was implicated in plotting her husband's death. To make matters worse, she married her husband's suspected murderer. Forced to abdicate, she fled to England, leaving behind her infant son James VI, the next king of Scotland. When Elizabeth I died in 1603, James VI was invited to assume the English throne; he was crowned King James I of England.

*Left: Edinburgh, Scotland; **Below Right:** John Knox monument in Edinburgh*

The Reformation in the Netherlands

The Netherlands (including at that time the modern-day countries of the Netherlands and Belgium) was one of the many territories ruled by Charles V. When Charles abdicated, this territory came under the control of his son Philip II. Because Philip was both Spanish and Catholic, many of his subjects disliked him. Not long after he became king, Protestant unrest in the Netherlands prompted him to send troops to put down the trouble. His troops severely persecuted the Protestants there, causing them to break out in armed revolt in 1568. The Protestants fought bravely under their leader William of Orange, also called **William the Silent,** and for a time even many of the Roman Catholics living in the southern part of the Netherlands turned against Spanish rule.

The war dragged on for years, but the Netherlands, aided by the English, managed to hold off the Spanish troops. In 1581 the Protestant areas of the Netherlands declared their independence from Spain. The Roman Catholic area (modern Belgium) remained under Spanish control. William was murdered a few years later, but the Dutch Protestants, nevertheless, won a truce with Spain in the early seventeenth century.

The Reformation in France

The writings of Luther flowed into France, arousing widespread interest in the Reformation. The works of John Calvin also had a strong influence there. By the middle of the sixteenth century, there were over two thousand Protestant congregations in France, and perhaps as many as one-half of the nobility had become Protestants. Despite these gains, France remained a thoroughly Catholic country. The government, fearful of the growing political and religious power of Protestantism, fiercely persecuted the **Huguenots** (HYOO guh NAHTS; French Protestants).

One of the most shocking incidents occurred in 1572. Catherine de Medici, the mother of the French king and the real power behind the throne, instigated a massacre of the Huguenots in Paris. Very early on the morning of August 27 (St. Bartholomew's Day), bands of Roman Catholics began roving the city, breaking into homes and murdering their unsuspecting and helpless occupants. These grisly deeds occurred throughout France. By the time the massacre had ended, an estimated twenty thousand Huguenots had been murdered. Although many people condemned the **St. Bartholomew's Day Massacre,** Philip II of Spain praised it, stating that it was "of such value and prudence and of such service, glory, and honor to God and universal benefit to all Christendom that to hear of it was for me the best and most cheerful news which at present could come to me." Even the pope ordered a special celebration in Rome.

The massacre, needless to say, increased the tension between the French Roman Catholics and the Protestants whose differences had already led to civil war. Civil war broke out once again, this time over the question of who would rule France. The Valois family, which had ruled France since the fourteenth century, was dying out. Two other families were seeking the throne. One of these, the Guise family, was Roman Catholic and traced its line back to Charlemagne. Another family, the **Bourbon,** was Huguenot and traced its ancestry back to Louis IX (St. Louis).

Henry of Navarre, the head of the Bourbon family and the leader of the Huguenots, emerged victorious in the struggle for the throne. He declared himself to be Henry IV (1589-1610), the king of France. However, there was one serious problem. The majority of Frenchmen were Roman Catholic and did not want a Protestant king. To please the people and secure the throne he had so eagerly sought, Henry IV became a Roman Catholic. He supposedly remarked, "Paris is well worth a mass."

Although Henry IV deserted his Huguenot followers, he did grant them a certain amount of religious toleration in the famous **Edict of Nantes** (1598). But, as we shall see in Chapter 13, this period of toleration did not last.

Section Review

1. What city and country are associated with the ministry of the reformer Ulrich Zwingli?
2. List three beliefs that many of the early Anabaptist groups held in common.
3. What influential work on theology did John Calvin write? What city associated with his ministry became a leading center of the Protestant Reformation?
4. Following England's break with the Roman Catholic church, what became the state church of England?
5. Who was the fiery Scottish preacher who advanced the cause of the Reformation in Scotland? What Protestant church became the state church in Scotland?

Challenge to the Reformation: The Counter-Reformation

In the early stages of the Reformation it seemed as if the Roman Catholic church might be destroyed. Northern Europe as well as many areas of eastern Europe had rejected the Roman church. A strong Protestant movement was progressing in France. There were even small Protestant groups in such Catholic strongholds as Spain and Italy. In an effort to prevent further losses to the Protestants, the Roman Catholic church promoted reforms of its own. In the late Middle Ages, as criticism against corruption in the church mounted, Catholics attempted to correct the problem. However, it was not until the sixteenth century, when large numbers left the Roman church, that its leaders became seriously concerned about the need for reform.

The Catholic Reformation is often called the **Counter-Reformation.** (The prefix *counter-* means "to oppose.") The Protestant leaders had directed their efforts primarily against false doctrine. The Catholic reformers, on the other hand, attempted to clean up the church by correcting some of the outward moral problems. They failed to see that the root of their problems was doctrinal error.

The Jesuits

The Society of Jesus, or the **Jesuits,** was instrumental in promoting the Counter-Reformation. This new religious order was founded by the Spanish soldier **Ignatius Loyola** (loy OH luh; 1491?-1556). While recovering from a battle injury, Loyola underwent a religious experience in which he determined to devote his life to the Roman church. In 1540 the Jesuit order officially came into existence. Unlike those in other religious orders, the Jesuits took a special vow of absolute obedience to the pope.

From its beginnings the purpose of the Jesuit order was to suppress heresy and to promote Roman Catholic education. The Jesuits realized the importance of careful training. Those who wanted to become members of the organization had to undergo a two-year period of probation. During that time the prospective member studied the *Spiritual Exercises* written by Loyola and learned to be completely submissive to those in authority. "We ought always to be ready to believe that what seems to us white is black if the hierarchical Church so defines it," Loyola once said. If the two-year probation period ended successfully, an individual became a member of the Jesuits. He usually continued his studies, sometimes spending a total of fifteen years in preparation for his work.

The Jesuits used every means available to promote their own order and to turn men back to the Roman church. They believed it is perfectly proper to do wrong in order to accomplish something good. For example, some Jesuits taught that it is acceptable to murder someone—even a ruler—if that death furthers Roman Catholic purposes. They infiltrated schools and government circles, attacking Protestantism and spreading the Counter-Reformation wherever they went. They were also zealous missionaries. Of the many Jesuit missionaries, the best known is Francis Xavier (1506-52), who traveled to India, China, and Japan.

The Inquisition

To stop the spread of Protestantism, Pope Paul III (1534-49) reorganized the **Inquisition.** It brought terror and death to Protestants in strong Roman Catholic areas such as Spain.

The Inquisition operated on the assumption that anyone accused of heresy was guilty until proved innocent. After the arrest (which usually occurred at night), the accused would stand before an inquisitor. Without knowing what charges had been brought against him or who had brought them, the accused person would be asked to confess his wrong. If mild methods of persuasion failed to produce a confession, the Inquisition used barbaric torture. Those who still refused to cooperate with the Inquisition were burned at the stake. The family of the accused often suffered as well, through arrest or loss of property.

The Index

When Gutenberg introduced movable-type printing in Europe, the price of books and pamphlets dropped sharply. Previously only the rich could afford books, but by the sixteenth century many people could purchase printed material. Printed copies of the Bible and books written by the reformers circulated throughout Europe. Realizing the impact that the printed page was having upon the spread of the Reformation, the Roman church tried to regulate what its members read. In 1559 the Roman Catholic church established the *Index of Prohibited Books,* which condemned, among other things, forty-eight allegedly ''heretical'' editions or versions of the Bible. Only those books that received an ecclesiastical license had official church approval. Even today, books officially sanctioned by the Roman church contain inside the front cover the Latin words *imprimatur* (''let it be printed'') and *nihil obstat* (''nothing hinders'').

The Council of Trent

Twenty-five years after the beginning of the Protestant Reformation, Pope Paul III called a church council to discuss doctrinal questions and to propose needed reform. Charles V, the Holy Roman emperor, had demanded such a council because the religious division in Germany was increasing. He wanted to end the division and to restore unity to his land. Fearful of what a general church council might do, Pope Paul III structured it in such a way that the pope's representatives, as well as the other Italian delegates, controlled the proceedings. The outcome was predetermined. In 1545 the council held its first meeting in Trent, a city of northern Italy. Church leaders did not meet on a continuous basis but gathered for an extended period of time on three separate occasions. In 1563 the Council of Trent held its last session.

The **Council of Trent** is significant for two major reasons. The council explicitly condemned many of the biblical principles upon which Protestantism is based. Most importantly it rejected the doctrines of justification by faith alone and the sole authority of the Scripture. This sealed the break between Protestant and Roman Catholic churches. Also the council set forth a complete doctrinal position of the Roman church. It made its position binding upon all Roman Catholics. The Roman Catholic church did not tolerate any deviation from the decrees of the council.

Giambettino Cignaroli, Ecstasy of John of the Cross, *Bob Jones University Collection of Sacred Art. The Catholic church used the arts—such as painting and music—to attract her former members back to the church. John of the Cross was a Spanish mystic and leader of the Spanish Counter-Reformation.*

Section Review

1. What was the name for the Catholic Reformation that sought to stop the spread of the Protestant movement?
2. What new religious order was formed to suppress heresy and promote Roman Catholic education? Who was the founder of this order?
3. What church court of the Roman Catholic church focused its attention on finding out and punishing those accused of holding Protestant beliefs?
4. What did the Roman Catholic church issue to regulate what its members could read?
5. At what council did the Roman Catholic church set forth its doctrinal position? Who was the pope who called this council?

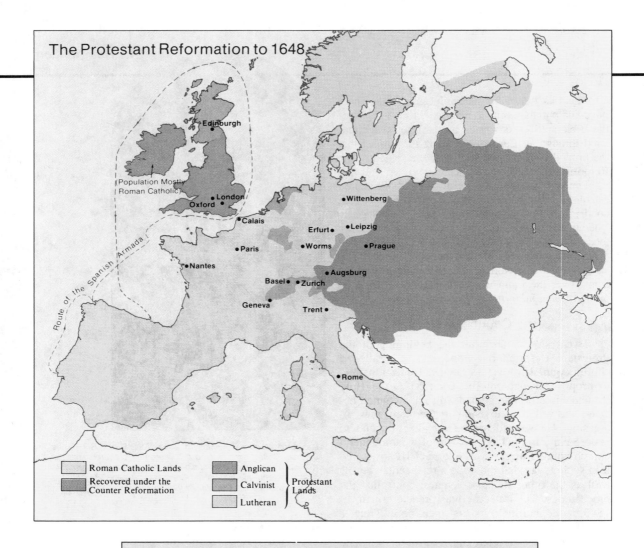

The Protestant Reformation to 1648

- Edinburgh
- (Population Mostly Roman Catholic)
- London
- Oxford
- Calais
- Wittenberg
- Erfurt
- Leipzig
- Paris
- Worms
- Prague
- Nantes
- Augsburg
- Basel
- Zurich
- Geneva
- Trent
- Rome

Route of the Spanish Armada

Roman Catholic Lands
Recovered under the Counter Reformation
Anglican
Calvinist — Protestant Lands
Lutheran

A Glimpse Behind and a Glimpse Ahead

The Reformation broke the hold of the Roman Catholic church on religious life in western Europe. This religious upheaval, however, produced changes in all areas of European society. It reasserted the dignity of everyday labor and encouraged the spread of lay education and the founding of schools. The Reformation's emphasis upon individual responsibility furthered the growth of capitalism and republican forms of government. The inquisitive spirit it helped foster led to the birth of modern science. Thus many of the freedoms and privileges that we enjoy today come directly or indirectly from the Protestant Reformation.

Chapter Review

Can You Explain?

recant	indulgences	pacifism	Counter-Reformation
justification by faith alone	treasury of merits	Elizabethan Settlement	

Can You Identify?

John Wycliffe	Augsburg Confession	Edward VI	St. Bartholomew's
Lollards	Francis I	Mary I	Day Massacre
John Huss	Suleiman	Elizabeth I	Bourbon
Council of Constance	Peace of Augsburg	Anglican church	Henry of Navarre
Martin Luther	(1555)	Philip II of Spain	Edict of Nantes (1598)
Leo X	Ulrich Zwingli	Francis Drake	Jesuits
Johann Tetzel	Anabaptists	Spanish Armada (1588)	Ignatius Loyola
October 31, 1517	John Calvin	Puritans	Inquisition
Ninety-five Theses	*The Institutes of the*	Separatists	*Index of Prohibited*
John Eck	*Christian Religion*	John Knox	*Books*
Charles V	Tudor family	Mary Stuart	Council of Trent
Diet of Worms	Henry VIII	William the Silent	
Philipp Melanchthon	Thomas Cranmer	Huguenots	

Can You Locate?

Oxford	Wittenberg	Switzerland	Netherlands
Bohemia	Leipzig	Zurich	Navarre
Prague	Worms	Basel	Scotland
Constance	Augsburg	Geneva	Trent
Erfurt			

How Much Do You Remember?

1. List three beliefs that Wycliffe and/or Huss held that caused the Roman Catholic church to condemn them as heretics.
2. In contrast to the position of the Roman Catholic church, what did Luther teach concerning salvation, the priesthood, the Bible, and the authority of the pope and church councils?
3. For each of the following reformers, identify the country in which he ministered and any important works he authored: Wycliffe, Huss, Luther, Zwingli, Calvin, Knox.
4. Identify the response of each of the following monarchs of England toward the Protestant Reformation: Henry VIII, Edward VI, Mary I, Elizabeth I.
5. List four ways the Roman Catholic church sought to advance the Counter-Reformation in opposition to the Protestant Reformation.

What Do You Think?

1. We know that history is under God's control. Can you list some evidences of how God made the world ready for the Protestant Reformation?
2. How do you account, humanly speaking, for the fact that Huss died a martyr's death, while Luther lived a full life and died a natural death?
3. What part did the Word of God have in bringing about the Reformation?
4. Analyze the response of European rulers to the Protestant Reformation. List various motives that you think they had in supporting or opposing the Reformation.

Notes

1. Roland H. Bainton, *Here I Stand: A Life of Martin Luther* (New York: Mentor Books, 1950), pp. 49-50.
2. Martin Luther, *Table Talk,* ed. and trans. Theodore G. Tappert, *Luther's Works* (Philadelphia: Fortress Press, 1967), 54:237.

Exploration and Discovery

> They that go down to the sea in ships, that do business in great waters; these see the works of the Lord, and his wonders in the deep.
> —Psalm 107:23-24

The two hundred years from 1450 to 1650 marked the great age of European exploration and discovery. Men crossed uncharted waters, braved violent storms, and suffered starvation and disease as they sailed to distant parts of the globe. What prompted these explorers to face untold perils? Most desired wealth; some sought adventure and fame; others sought to spread the gospel to heathen lands. But whether motivated by greed, pride, or compassion, these explorers helped open up the continents of North and South America, the coast of Africa, and part of Asia to European trade and colonization.

Preparation for Discovery

Several developments in Europe gave rise to this Age of Exploration. The Crusades awakened interest in lands beyond Europe's borders. Travelers such as **Marco Polo** (see the box on p. 308) stirred the popular imagination with tales of strange customs and unbelievable riches in the Far East. The Renaissance provided western Europe with the means, namely navigational equipment and finances, to reach the Orient. In the endeavor to reach the East, Europeans discovered the New World.

Motives for Exploration

Search for New Trade Routes

Spurred by the Crusades and the stories of Marco Polo and others, Europeans reopened trade routes with the East. They imported numerous luxury items from China, India, and the Spice Islands (located north of Australia). Merchants traded for diamonds, rubies, and other gems; for silk; and for expensive porcelain (china). Spices, such as cloves and cinnamon, were in great demand. Europeans used them to flavor and preserve food and as ingredients in drugs and perfumes.

All these items came across Asia to Europe by way of the Middle East. But there were many problems for traders along this long route. Much of the terrain was rugged and difficult to cross. In addition, local rulers charged trading caravans for the privilege of passing through their territory; taxes and tolls drove up the prices of the products. Furthermore, the Italians held a monopoly on oriental trade. Merchants from Genoa controlled the northern routes that came overland from Asia, and those from Venice controlled the southern routes that ran along the coast of India, up the Persian Gulf, and across the desert to Palestine. (See map on p. 226.) Not only were Italians draining gold from the rest of Europe, but they were also keeping traders from other European countries from getting a share of the profits.

In the 1400s these problems became more acute when the Ottoman Turks became a major power in the Middle East. These fierce people attacked caravans and destroyed trading posts. The Europeans, who still craved Eastern luxuries, needed to find a new route to the Orient. Some wondered if it might be possible to get to the East entirely by sea, avoiding the Turks, the Italian traders, and all the tolls and taxes. The quest began in earnest in the late fifteenth century. Adventurers sailed south and east around Africa; others sailed west across the Atlantic; and some even tried to find a Northwest Passage through Arctic ice.

Quest for Gold

For many years there had been stories circulating in Europe that there was gold—lots of gold—somewhere in Africa. Europeans, however, knew very little about this huge continent. The northern coast, naturally, was well known to travelers. But few, if any, Europeans had traveled south into the heart of the continent. Occasionally African traders arrived in Mediterranean ports, bringing gold from the interior, but no European knew exactly where this gold came from. Not surprisingly, many wanted to find it. Explorers were willing to take great risks to obtain wealth, but they often suffered great losses instead. They should have heeded Proverbs 15:16 which says, "Better is little with the fear of the Lord than great treasure and trouble therewith."

Desire for Adventure and Glory

While some explorers craved great riches, others sought the thrill of adventure and the praise of men. Undoubtedly the Renaissance, which encouraged a spirit of curiosity and emphasized individual achievement, played a part in these desires. Men risked their lives, sailing through unknown waters and traveling to distant lands. Through their daring adventures, they hoped to achieve worldly fame. While several explorers did become famous for their exploits, many more died in the quest for glory. The Bible teaches that glory or fame is not something one should look for. The writer of Proverbs reminds us that "for men to search their own glory is not glory" (25:27). How much better it is for men to seek the praise of God rather than the praise of men.

Religious Concerns

Though overlooked or neglected by some historians, religious concern also motivated many explorers. The crusading spirit was alive in Europe, for the Muslim threat was still very real. Even as late as the fifteenth century, the Moors still controlled the southern portion of the Iberian Peninsula. After the fall of Constantinople to the Ottoman Turks in 1453, Europeans feared a full-scale Muslim invasion of eastern Europe. European rulers searched for ways to stop further Muslim victories.

There were rumors of a king in Africa named **Prester John,** supposedly a wealthy and powerful Christian who wanted to help the Europeans fight the Muslims. During the fifteenth century, explorers sailed along the west coast of Africa searching for Prester John's kingdom. They hoped to enlist his help; by attacking from both the north and south, their combined forces could defeat the Muslims. Prester John was not to be found.

Not all of Europe's religious zeal was directed against the Muslims. Some explorers went out

Marco Polo and the Awakening of Curiosity

Marco Polo was only seventeen when he set off on a journey that would revolutionize the world. He was accompanying his father, Nicoló, and his uncle Matteo, both Venetian traders, on their second voyage to the little-known kingdom of Cathay (China). The year was 1271.

For four years the three men traveled eastward, finally reaching the city of Cambulac (Beijing), the capital of Cathay. Young Marco Polo quickly became a favorite of the ruler, Kublai Khan. He learned the languages of the court and at the age of twenty-three became the Khan's adviser. The Polos lived in Cathay for seventeen years, traveling and seeing sights that few Europeans had ever dreamed of. In 1292 they began the long journey home. When they arrived in Venice, their old friends did not recognize them; most at first refused to believe their stories, but the travelers convinced them by producing a wealth of gems that they had received in Cathay.

Three years after his return to Italy, Marco was captured while fighting in a local war and jailed in Genoa. To pass the time, he recounted his adventures to a fellow prisoner, who recorded them in what was soon to become a very popular book: *The Book of Sir Marco Polo Concerning the Kingdoms and Marvels of the East.* The work was far more accurate than the few other books about Cathay that were available in Europe at that time. Its readers were astonished by the tales of a strange black rock (coal) that the Mongols burned. They thrilled to the description of fantastic riches in gold, spices, and many other luxuries. They wondered about the islands of "Cipango" (Japan) that Polo described. More important, they learned of the great sea (the Pacific) that lay beyond Asia.

Nearly two centuries after Polo, a man from Genoa read this book and wondered if the ocean to the west—the Atlantic—might be the same one that Polo saw. This man's name was Christopher Columbus.

seeking to spread the gospel to heathen people, who needed to hear of salvation in Jesus Christ alone. Unfortunately, most of the early explorers were Roman Catholics. Instead of leading people to Christ, they won converts to the Roman Catholic church.

Competition Among European Nations

Exploration was also sparked by the commercial rivalry among the nations of Europe. As Italian merchants brought precious gems, spices, and silks from the East, Europeans were filled with great excitement, but also with great envy. Non-Italian merchants wanted to profit from the oriental trade, and kings wanted to increase their country's wealth and power. As the explorers traveled to unknown regions, they claimed their discoveries for the country they sailed for. The European countries were eager to start trade with the people of newly discovered lands. Nations established trade settlements and encouraged colonization in order to protect their commercial interests.

Tools for Exploration

Navigational Aids

Three things were of great importance to explorers: accurate maps to guide them to their destination, a compass to tell them in what direction they were actually going, and some kind of "locator" instrument to tell them their position. On a trackless and featureless ocean, they needed accurate and trustworthy instruments.

Maps—Maps of the known world became much more accurate in the fifteenth century. Italian mapmakers drew up sailing charts based upon the reports of traders and fishermen. These maps were fairly reliable guides for sailing in the Mediterranean Sea or along the European coast, but they were of little help to the explorers. These men sailed in uncharted waters. As they returned from their voyages, they updated their maps to include their discoveries. With the invention of printing, these maps were widely distributed, opening the door for further exploration.

"A new description of America, or the New World"

Instruments—The **compass** greatly aided sailors in navigation and mapmaking. Invented by the Chinese, the early compass was a magnetized needle floating in a bowl of water on a piece of reed or cork. In the late 1300s, Europeans mounted the compass on a stiff card marked with the cardinal points (north, south, east, and west). This small improvement made a great difference to sailors, who could now use the instrument easily on a moving ship. The compass became an invaluable tool; it helped sailors determine direction and follow a definite course.

Sailors also relied on more complicated instruments to determine their position on an unmarked ocean. The three most common instruments—the astrolabe, the quadrant, and the cross-staff—measured the angle between a star (usually the North Star) and the horizon. From this information the sailor could determine his **latitude**, or distance from the equator. With any one of these instruments, the captain of a ship, even though out of sight of land, could compute his position with some degree of accuracy. They did have two major drawbacks, however. They were useless in cloudy weather, and they were not very accurate when used on the rolling deck of a ship.

Seagoing Vessels

It was not until about 1400 that ships were built to sail long distances over wide and sometimes stormy seas. Early ships in the Mediterranean Sea

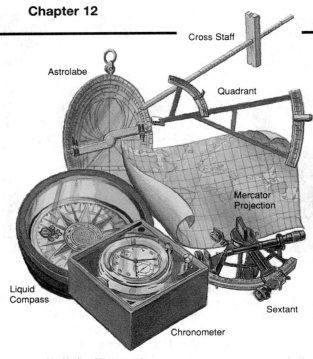

Cross Staff

Astrolabe

Quadrant

Mercator
Projection

Liquid
Compass

Sextant

Chronometer

Navigational instruments

The Arabs used triangular sails, which made their boats easily maneuverable, even when the wind changed directions. This kind of sail, however, could power only a small craft. Such vessels would not be large enough to carry the needed supplies and then return with enough spices to make a trip profitable. On the other hand, the northern sailors, such as the Vikings, used square sails, which could power a larger ship and required a smaller crew. But these ships were not very maneuverable.

The solution came in the middle of the fifteenth century with the building of the versatile **caravel.** This light, fast vessel was popular with the early explorers. It had several masts on which were mounted large square sails to provide power and smaller triangular sails to provide maneuverability. The caravel's high sides and its broad and deep construction made it suitable for ocean travel.

Section Review

1. List five motives that prompted European explorers to ''seek out and discover.''
2. What man's account of his travels awakened European curiosity in the Orient? In what Asian land did he spend seventeen years?
3. What three things were of great importance to the early explorers?
4. What light, fast vessel was popular with the early explorers of the late fifteenth century?

had made great use of oars. An oared ship would need such a large crew to travel the ocean that it could not possibly carry enough supplies to feed all the men. Ocean-going vessels, therefore, needed to use sails. But of the two types of sails in use, neither would be right for a long ocean voyage.

Process of Discovery

The early explorers were pioneers. They set sail across vast, unexplored oceans with uncertain prospects of ever returning home. While some never returned, others brought back the exciting news of their discoveries. They told of new routes to the Orient, of great riches to be gained, of new lands to be explored, and of heathen people who needed to be evangelized. Europe eagerly responded to the challenge. The explorers were followed by merchants, soldiers, settlers, and missionaries. Through trade along the African coast and in Asia, and through colonization in the New World, Europe rapidly extended its influence around the world.

Portugal and Spain

Portugal and Spain were the leading nations of the Age of Exploration. Several factors accounted for their early success. Shipping had long been a principal industry in these lands; Portugal and Spain were bounded by the waters of the Atlantic Ocean and the Mediterranean Sea. Because the Italians had gained a monopoly on trade in the Mediterranean, sailors from the Iberian Peninsula turned southward to the coast of Africa and westward across the Atlantic in search of new trade routes to the East. Furthermore, the experienced Portuguese and Spanish sailors were greatly aided by the navigational and mapmaking skills they had learned from the Moors. A strong motivating force behind their drive for discovery was the crusading spirit, which was still very much alive in the peninsula. (The last Muslim stronghold in the Iberian Peninsula was not conquered until 1492.) The Portuguese and Spanish sailors set sail to spread Roman Catholicism and to battle the Muslims.

Portugal Rounds Africa

Prince Henry the Navigator—**Prince Henry** (1394-1460), called "The Navigator," was largely responsible for Portugal's early success in exploration. Although he never went on an expedition, he has been called "the greatest figure in the history of exploration." As a youth, he was fascinated with the great land of Africa to the south. How big was it? Where was the source of the gold that came out of its interior? Where was Prester John's kingdom? These questions led Prince Henry to start a school of navigation on the coast of Portugal. It was not a *school* in our sense of the word; it was more like a *bank* of knowledge about navigation. He attracted to his palace geographers, astronomers, mapmakers, and sea captains. Under his sponsorship, these men improved navigational instruments, drew up more accurate maps, and de-

veloped the caravel. Henry sent sailors out to explore the coast of Africa and to bring back all the information they could find. On each voyage, Henry's sailors went farther south along Africa's coast. They had not yet reached the equator when he died in 1460, but his accomplishments laid the foundation for the achievements of two other men who would finish the job that he had begun.

Bartholomeu Dias—In 1487, nearly thirty years after Prince Henry's death, the king of Portugal sent **Bartholomeu Dias** down the coast of Africa to find a sea route to India. As he neared the southern tip of the continent, a fierce storm blew his ships out of sight of land for thirteen days. When he finally sighted land again, he noticed that the sun rose on the ship's right instead of its left; he was therefore heading north. He rightly concluded that he had rounded the tip of Africa during the storm and that indeed there might be an all-water route to the Orient. When his men refused to go any farther, he turned around and headed back to Portugal. As he rounded the tip of Africa again, he sighted a huge rocky cape, which he named "The Cape of Storms." The king later changed its name to "The Cape of Good Hope" because he hoped that Dias had finally found a direct water route to India.

The Cape of Good Hope

Vasco da Gama—Ten years after Dias's discovery, the king of Portugal selected **Vasco da Gama** to lead an expedition around the Cape of Good Hope to India. In 1497, with a fleet of four ships, da Gama set sail from Lisbon, Portugal. He did not follow the African coast all the way to the Cape of Good Hope as Dias had done. Instead, he made a great westward sweep to gain more favorable winds and currents. At one point he was actually closer to South America than to Africa. He stayed out of sight of land for fourteen weeks before reaching the tip of Africa. (In following centuries, wind-driven vessels followed this route pioneered by da Gama.)

Nearly a year after leaving Portugal, da Gama arrived in India. He was the first European to reach the great subcontinent by sailing around Africa. He told those who met him, ''We have come to seek Christians and spices.'' But he found Muslim merchants living there who controlled trade in the region and opposed his efforts to trade with the Indians. Despite many obstacles, he was able to trade for spices—enough to pay for the voyage sixty times over!

The Portuguese swiftly took advantage of da Gama's discovery of the ocean route to India. They soon not only controlled this water route but also broke the Muslim trade monopoly in the Indian Ocean. The Muslim fleet was no match for the heavy artillery on the Portuguese ships. It was not long before ships laden with spices were a familiar sight in Portuguese ports.

Spain Sails Westward

Christopher Columbus—When Dias returned from his voyage around the Cape of Good Hope, an Italian named **Christopher Columbus** heard his report: India could be reached by sailing around the tip of Africa. But Columbus, who had studied the writings of the ancient geographer Ptolemy and the traveler Marco Polo, believed that he could reach Japan and China by sailing west—that Japan was perhaps as close as three hundred miles from Portugal. For many years he tried without success to persuade the king of Portugal to finance his voyage westward. But the king's advisers declared the undertaking to be impossible. In Spain Columbus was finally able to secure support for his voyage from King Ferdinand and Queen Isabella. In August of 1492 he set sail from Spain with three ships: the *Niña,* the *Pinta,* and the *Santa Maria.*

Columbus was a man of religious devotion who believed that he was commissioned by God to spread the gospel in distant lands. He was confident

Christopher Columbus at the court of Ferdinand and Isabella of Spain

that his voyage would be a success. His men, however, did not share his optimism. After weeks of being out of sight of land, they demanded that the ships turn back. Columbus was able to persuade them to continue for two or three more days. Two days later, on the morning of October 12, he sighted land and named it San Salvador ("Holy Savior"). He thought that he was near the East Indies; actually he was in the Bahamas. He sailed south to Cuba, which he thought was Marco Polo's Cathay, and to Hispaniola, which he identified as Cipango (Japan).

In three later voyages he explored further in the Caribbean and landed on the South American continent in what is now Venezuela. He never found the great riches for which he looked, and as long as he lived, he believed that he had reached Asia. Although he was mistaken as to where his voyages had taken him, his discovery was nonetheless of great importance. He opened up a "New World" that attracted European exploration and colonization for centuries following.

Columbus was not the first to discover the New World, however. The Vikings made the voyage from Europe in the tenth and eleventh centuries. A few historians even think that the ancient Phoenicians landed in South America before the time of Christ. But in God's plan, the lands of the New World remained virtually unknown to Europe until the sixteenth century—a time when Europe was also rediscovering the truth of God's Word. During the seventeenth century the New World, especially North America, became a haven for Christians who fled from political and religious persecution in Europe.

Line of Demarcation—As a result of Columbus's discoveries, Spain began to compete with Portugal for trade rights and new territory. To avoid disputes with Portugal, Spain asked Pope Alexander VI to divide the world between them. In 1493 he issued a bull, that drew a **Line of Demarcation** running north and south down the middle of the Atlantic Ocean. (See map on p. 314.) Portugal, he said, could claim lands to the east of the line, while Spain could claim those to the west. After negotiations between Spain and Portugal, it was agreed the following year to move the line farther to the west. This agreement between Spain and Portugal had several important results.

The Naming of America

When Columbus landed on an island in the Caribbean in 1492, he mistakenly assumed that he had succeeded in reaching Asia. Upon his return, most Europeans believed his reports, but when later expeditions failed to bring back any riches, doubts began to arise. An Italian merchant named Amerigo Vespucci sailed west to settle the uncertainty. What he found was not a water route to the Orient but a new continent. He was the first European to reach and explore the landmass that now bears his name—South America.

Hearing of Amerigo Vespucci's discovery, a German mapmaker named Martin Waldseemöller began to sell maps of the new continent. Proposing that the land be named after its discoverer, he referred to it as "America." The name was accepted, and before long people applied it to the large landmass to the north of the Spanish possessions as well. They called it "North America."

1. It encouraged Portugal to colonize in Africa and the East Indies, which were east of the line.
2. It gave Spain the right to nearly all of the New World with one exception—the line cut across Brazil, giving that land to the Portuguese, who later explored and settled there. That is why even today the people of Brazil speak Portuguese, while the rest of South America speaks Spanish.
3. It cut Spain off from going east around Africa to get to India and China. Spain had to find a westward route. It was not long before she found a sailor who would do it.

Ferdinand Magellan—In September of 1519 **Ferdinand Magellan** set out with a fleet of five ships to do what Columbus had failed to accomplish. By this time he knew that Columbus had found not the Orient, but an intervening landmass. He thought that he could sail around its southern end and then get to the Spice Islands through Spanish territory. He sailed from Spain to the coast of South America, where he spent the winter. There he saw natives who were so large that he named them Patagonians ("Big Feet"). He then sailed around the southern tip of South America through what we now call the Strait of Magellan. There one of his five ships deserted, and he lost a second in a severe storm. When he finally reached the ocean

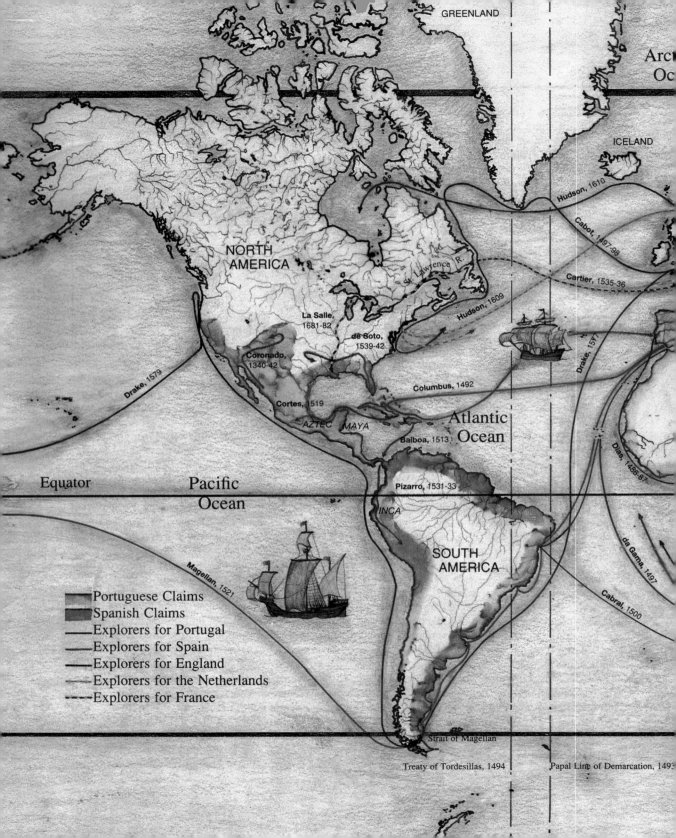

GREENLAND

ICELAND

Arctic Oc

NORTH
AMERICA

St. Lawrence R.

Hudson, 1610

Cabot, 1497-98

Cartier, 1535-36

Hudson, 1609

La Salle,
1681-82

de Soto,
1539-42

Coronado,
1340-42

Drake, 1577

Drake, 1579

Columbus, 1492

Cortes, 1519

AZTEC   MAYA

Atlantic
Ocean

Balboa, 1513

Dias, 1486-87

Equator

Pacific
Ocean

Pizarro, 1531-33

INCA

SOUTH
AMERICA

da Gama, 1497

Magellan, 1521

Cabral, 1500

Portuguese Claims
Spanish Claims
Explorers for Portugal
Explorers for Spain
Explorers for England
Explorers for the Netherlands
Explorers for France

Strait of Magellan

Treaty of Tordesillas, 1494

Papal Line of Demarcation, 1493

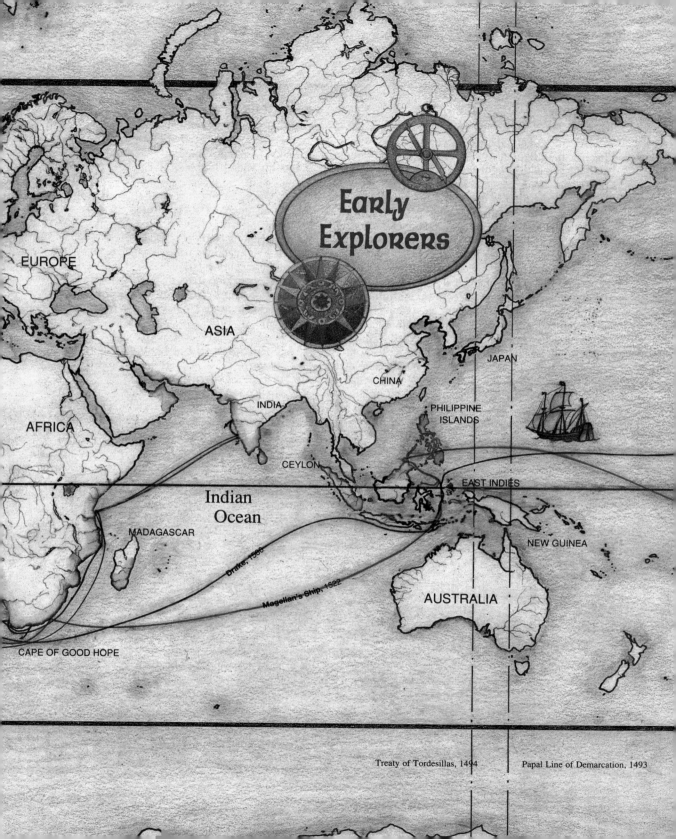

Early Explorers

EUROPE

ASIA

JAPAN

CHINA

INDIA

PHILIPPINE
ISLANDS

AFRICA

CEYLON

EAST INDIES

Indian
Ocean

MADAGASCAR

NEW GUINEA

Drake, 1580

Magellan's Ship, 1522

AUSTRALIA

CAPE OF GOOD HOPE

Treaty of Tordesillas, 1494   Papal Line of Demarcation, 1493

to the west, he appreciated its calmness so much that he named it *Pacific* (''peaceful'').

As the three ships sailed westward across the Pacific, they ran out of supplies, and many sailors starved to death. Finally they reached the Philippines, but there Magellan was killed by natives when he tried to help a local ruler in a tribal war. Magellan's crew continued without him, reaching the Spice Islands, where they took on a large cargo of spices. With only one ship left, they sailed around Africa and back to Spain. The ship returned with only eighteen of the more than two hundred men who had started the trip. This three-year-long, tragic voyage, the first **circumnavigation** of the earth, has been called ''the greatest single human achievement on sea.'' It demonstrated that one great body of water covered the earth and confirmed the fact that the world was round—something the Bible had already affirmed: ''It is he that sitteth upon the circle of the earth'' (Isa. 40:22). Magellan's voyage also made it clear to Europeans that the discoveries of Columbus were not as near to Asia as Columbus had hoped.

Section Review

1. What two European nations led the way during the Age of Exploration?
2. What member of the Portuguese ruling family greatly aided the Age of Exploration? What nickname did he earn?
3. Da Gama's discovery led to the Portuguese establishment of an all-water route to what land?
4. For whom is North and South America named? What German mapmaker popularized the name for these continents?
5. Who settled the trade disputes between Spain and Portugal by dividing the world between the two countries? What was the dividing line called?

Europe and the New World

Amerindian Civilizations

When Columbus landed in the Bahamas, he thought he had reached the East Indies. He thus called the natives whom he found there ''Indians.''

George Catlin, Bull Dance, Mandan Okipa Ceremony, *National Collection of Fine Arts, Washington, D.C.*

George Catlin, Buffalo Chase in Winter, *National Collection of Fine Arts, Washington, D.C.*

These peoples had lived in North and South America for several thousand years before the Europeans arrived. They had probably crossed the Bering Strait between Asia and Alaska and had then moved slowly southward.

Of the Indian groups in North America, some were farmers and lived in villages; others, because they were hunters, followed the herds. They worshiped nature: the sun, the moon, the wind, and the mountains. Most tribes believed in a "Great Spirit" as well as a number of lesser spirits, which they believed watched over them. The North American Indians did not normally form large nations but lived in small groups or tribes. All the tribes in a particular region, however, were very similar. There are five main regions in which these Indians lived: the Northeast, the Southeast, the Plains, the Southwest, and the West Coast.

1. The Northeastern Indians, unlike other tribes, formed a five-tribe confederation led by the Iroquois (IHR uh KWOY). They are known for their use of wampum, or shell money, and for their birch-bark canoes.

2. The Southeastern Indians were most famous as "mound builders"; they built burial and ceremonial mounds, many of which still exist.

3. Farther west, the Plains Indians roamed the grasslands, hunted buffalo, lived in tepees, and fought often with other tribes. They did not use horses, however, until the Spaniards brought them to the New World.

4. The Indians of the Southwest are often called "cliff dwellers." They built villages, called pueblos, out of adobe, or sun-dried brick. Many of these villages were built into the sides of cliffs in order to provide protection from would-be attackers. The cliff dwellers were the most peaceable of the North American Indians.

5. The last major group of Indians, those of the West Coast, are remembered for their totem poles, which they carved out of tree trunks to depict their local gods.

The Indians of Central and South America were more highly civilized than those in North America. They built large cities, traded with their neighbors, and created art and literature of extremely high quality. Nevertheless, they remained very pagan and superstitious peoples. Three cultures in particular—the Maya, Aztec, and Inca—are of special importance.

Maya—The Mayan civilization, which flourished from the fourth century through the tenth century, was noted for its artistic and intellectual achievements. Like that of the ancient Greeks, the Mayan civilization was not a unified nation but consisted of many city-states located in the Yucatán

(YOO kuh TAN) Peninsula in southeastern Mexico. They built great pyramids, temples, altars, paved highways, and other structures. The Maya developed hieroglyphics and studied astronomy with as much dedication as the ancient Egyptians. They computed the length of a year almost exactly (to 365 1/4 days), built astronomical observatories, and developed a system of mathematics that even included the concept of zero as a place holder. The Maya worshipped many false gods, the most common of which was a feathered serpent. During the ninth and tenth centuries, the Mayan civilization declined; her centers of culture were abandoned. The Indians themselves lived in the area until the coming of the Spaniards. When the Spanish arrived, they found only traces of the Mayan civilization.

Aztec—The Aztecs established their civilization after the Mayan civilization had declined. About 1345 they founded the city of Tenochtitlán (tay NAWCH tee TLAHN) on an island in the middle of a lake in central Mexico. This walled city, connected by several four-mile-long bridges to the mainland, had a huge pyramid temple as well as about twenty other beautiful temples. Describing the network of canals throughout the city, one of the first Europeans to see the city called Tenochtitlán "the Venice of the New World."

The Aztecs were fighters. Every able-bodied Aztec man had to serve in the army. With a vicious and well-trained force, they conquered more than five million people and collected tribute from them all. They were better fighters than governors, however, and never developed a real empire. The army often took prisoners of war to sacrifice to their gods. Sometimes the priests even ate the flesh of their human sacrifices.

Inca—The Inca empire, which was at its height from about 1380 to 1570, flourished along the western coast of South America where Peru is today. Inca families lived in tightly organized communes in which several families shared possessions. Most Inca were farmers, raising maize (corn), potatoes, and cotton. All of the communes were closely controlled by the ruler—"the Inca"—whom the people worshiped as a god.

Unlike the Maya and the Aztecs, the Inca ruled a genuine empire. They not only conquered neigh-boring peoples but also took over their lands and ruled them absolutely. Among the peoples they conquered, they abolished human sacrifices and cannibalism. They planned their cities carefully and connected them with well-constructed roads. Of the road between Cuzco, the Inca capital, and Quito, one Spanish conqueror said, "The roads constructed by the Romans in Spain . . . are not to be compared to it." The roads even crossed deep canyons on a type of suspension bridge, which was strong enough to hold up under heavy use. Along these roads the Inca set up a courier system that could deliver messages over one hundred fifty miles per day.

Spanish Exploration

The early Spanish explorers who came to the New World found that the Indian tribes could be easily conquered. Spain, which claimed rights to this land, sent **conquistadors** ("conquerors") to search for riches, to evangelize the Indians, and to establish Spanish authority. By using their firearms and horses, which the terrified Indians had never seen, small bands of Spanish soldiers were able to subdue entire Indian tribes and empires.

But the conquistadors were often cruel to the Indians they had come to "convert." Many of these men used the same ruthless methods to gain both riches and "converts." They saw no conflict in their quest for both, even though God's Word instructs us that "no man can serve two masters: for either he will hate the one, and love the other; or else he will hold to the one, and despise the other. Ye cannot serve God and mammon [riches]" (Matt. 6:24). Often their desire for wealth and fame overshadowed their religious zeal, making their evangelistic efforts a mockery of the gospel.

Balboa—The first notable conquistador was **Vasco Núñez de Balboa.** He came to the New World in search of adventure but soon found himself working on a farm on the island of Hispaniola. Dissatisfied and heavily in debt, he stowed away aboard a ship bound for the mainland, where a new colony was to be established. He joined the colony as a soldier, but by plotting against those in charge, he was able to win control of it. Under his leadership the colony moved to a site on the coast of Panama.

Balboa knew that complaints had been lodged against him before the king of Spain. The only way

The ruined city of Machu Picchu (meaning "old peak") in the Andes Mountains of modern Peru is one of the best preserved treasures of Inca culture. Located nearly eight thousand feet above sea level, Machu Picchu was apparently unknown to the Spanish and was discovered by an American explorer in 1911. The city may have served as both a fortress and a center of Inca religion. It may have also provided a haven for some Incas after the Spanish invasion.

to gain royal favor, he concluded, would be to find gold or make some striking discovery. He heard rumors of a great ocean to the west and of a people wealthy with gold. In 1513, with a force of some two hundred men, he began cutting his way westward across what is today Panama, making his way through the heavy jungle of the isthmus (a narrow strip of land connecting two larger landmasses). After three weeks he and his men neared the western coast. Balboa, wanting to be the first European to see the new ocean, ordered his men to wait while he walked to the crest of a small mountain. There he saw a great body of water, which he named the "South Sea"; Magellan renamed it "Pacific" seven years later.

Balboa sent word of his discovery back to Spain, hoping to receive a royal commendation. But in the meantime he was arrested on trumped-up charges made by a jealous rival and was beheaded.

Cortés—In 1519 **Hernando Cortés,** called "the greatest of the conquistadors," landed on the shore of Mexico. After sinking his ships so that none of his soldiers would desert, he moved his army inland toward the Aztec capital. When the Aztec king **Montezuma** heard of their approach,

Hernando Cortés

he thought that Cortés might be the returning god Quetzalcoatl (ket SAHL koh AHT ul), or at least his representative. (Their chief god, Quetzalcoatl, was supposed to return to them someday from across the sea.) Instead of fighting Cortés, Montezuma welcomed him with gifts of gold and jewels, which only intensified the Spaniard's greed. Cortés himself had said, "We Spaniards suffer from a disease that only gold can cure."

After a time of uneasy peace, war broke out. The Spanish guns took their toll as the Spaniards massacred hundreds of Aztecs. Montezuma was stoned to death by his own people as a traitor. In 1521, after a four-month siege, Cortés finally defeated the Aztecs and destroyed the city. On its ruins he began to build what is now Mexico City. This city later became one of the capitals of New Spain. One of the several **viceroys,** or "assistant kings," which the Spanish king appointed to oversee affairs in the New World, lived here.

Cortés and his men were not satisfied with their successes. Some soldiers headed north, still lusting for gold. Others fought over their newly acquired treasures. Cortés finally returned to Spain in 1539 and died eight years later, a discouraged and frustrated man. He had found great riches, but he was not satisfied. The writer of Ecclesiastes reminds us, "He that loveth silver shall not be satisfied with silver; nor he that loveth abundance with increase: this is also vanity" (5:10). Cortés spent his life acquiring treasure on earth, but he had laid up no treasure in heaven (Matt. 6:19-21).

Pizarro—**Francisco Pizarro** (pih ZAHR oh) was probably the cruelest of all the conquistadors. He came to the New World for one reason: to find gold. He accompanied Balboa in his march across the Isthmus of Panama. After Balboa's execution, he decided to find the people to the south—the Inca—who were rumored to be very wealthy. In 1531 he and his men set out for Peru. After landing by ship on the coast, they marched through jungles for six months, plundering villages as they went. Raiding the Inca empire, they captured **Atahualpa** (AH tah WAHL pah), the Inca ruler, and held him for ransom. Atahualpa promised to fill a room with gold and silver to buy his release. After receiving a ransom of over thirteen thousand pounds of gold

Pizarro appears before Emperor Charles V after his conquest of the Incas.

Las Casas—Not all Spaniards who came to the New World were after gold. In 1502 **Bartolomé de las Casas** (1474-1566), a Roman Catholic friar, arrived in the Americas as a missionary to the Indians. Deeply distressed over the cruelty of his countrymen, he wrote several works decrying the abuse of the Indians in the New World. He described, for example, the death of one Indian chief who was being burned at the stake. A priest told him to become a Christian so he could go to heaven. The man refused, saying that he did not want to go to any place where there were Christians. Unfortunately, the Indians, like many people today, were

and nearly twice as much silver (enough to make all his men rich), Pizarro broke his promise and executed the Inca. With only a handful of men, he had conquered the great Inca empire.

Two years later Pizarro founded the city of Lima, which is today the capital of Peru. Soon afterwards other Spaniards, as greedy as Pizarro and jealous of his gold, attacked and killed him in his home. Pizarro had found more gold in the New World than anyone else, but greed—his own greed and that of others—prevented anyone from enjoying it. Like Pizarro, most other conquistadors died violently, fighting to keep the gold which they thought would help them to enjoy life. The Bible tells us

> Labour not to be rich: cease from thine own wisdom. Wilt thou set thine eyes upon that which is not? for riches certainly make themselves wings; they fly away as an eagle toward heaven. . . . He that hasteth to be rich hath an evil eye, and considereth not that poverty shall come upon him.
> —Proverbs 23:4-5; 28:22

The Requirement

Before the conquistadors made war on the Indians, they were required to read to the Indians a document issued by the king of Spain. The statement, known as the *requerimento,* informed the Indians that the eternal God gave the pope in Rome the authority over all men. The pope in turn had given Spain authority over the New World. It invited the Indians to embrace the Roman Catholic religion and to become loyal subjects under Spanish rule. If they refused, the document warned that "with the help of God, we [the Spanish] shall powerfully enter into your country and shall make war against you in all ways and manners that we can, and shall subject you to the yoke and obedience of the Church and of Their Highnesses. We shall take you and your wives and your children, and shall make slaves of them, and as such shall sell and dispose of them as Their Highnesses may command. And we shall take your goods, and shall do you all the mischief and damage that we can, as to vassals who do not obey and refuse to receive their Lord and resist and contradict him."

The *requerimento* gave legal justification to those Spaniards who massacred unsubmissive Indians. It mattered little to them that none of the Indians were able to understand the document because it was read in Spanish. Nor did it seem to bother the conquistadors to sometimes read the document when no Indians were present to hear it.

turned away from the gospel by the lives of people who claimed to be Christians but were not.

Las Casas devoted his life to improving the plight of the Indians in the New World. In 1542 he helped pass the "New Laws," which protected the Indians from being made slaves. Previously, the Spanish had forced the natives to work on plantations where they were overworked and mistreated. These laws forbade this practice. Las Casas also opposed the common Roman Catholic practice of winning converts by force or enslavement. No man, he said, could be converted by force; real conversion comes only to those who are persuaded gently. Though he was correct, he saw conversion only as "joining the church" and relying on good works, rather than repenting from sin and turning to Jesus Christ, who alone can give salvation.

Further Spanish Explorations—Spanish exploration was not confined entirely to Latin America. Rumors of "a land of gold" to the north enticed other explorers to the regions of what is now the United States. In 1539 **Hernando de Soto,** who served with Pizarro in Peru, landed near Tampa Bay, Florida, in search of "golden" cities. In his exploration of the southeastern United States, he discovered the great Mississippi River. Though he did not find gold, his expedition led the way for further exploration of the North American continent.

Another explorer of the lands to the north was **Francisco Vásquez de Coronado** (KOR uh NAH doh). He set out from Mexico in 1540 to find the "Seven Cities of Cibola," which were reportedly rich in gold. He led his expedition into what is now New Mexico and Arizona and then on through what is now Kansas and Texas. Some of his men went westward and discovered the Grand Canyon.

Neither de Soto nor Coronado realized the value of the lands they explored. Since there was no gold, they said it was a waste of time to explore further. Because of these two expeditions, the Spaniards decided to concentrate their efforts on the land they already held, leaving most of North America open for other European nations to explore.

French, Dutch, and English Exploration

When the pope gave Spain and Portugal rights to all newly discovered lands in 1493, the other nations of Europe objected. King Francis I of

The Legend of El Dorado

Many early explorers came to the New World with one thing in mind: gold. The story that excited them more than any other was the legend of El Dorado. According to American Indian folklore, El Dorado ("the gilded one") was the name of both a wealthy ruler and his fabulous city. This land supposedly possessed untold amounts of gold dust—so much, in fact, that each morning the ruler sprinkled his body with gold dust and each evening washed it off in a lake. It was said that his people threw golden statues and jewelry into the lake as offerings to their gods and that gold was so plentiful that gold dust clung to the roots of plants when they were pulled up.

Explorers hunted all over northern South America in search of this magnificent ruler and his country. Many men lost their lives in this land of rugged mountains and fierce Indian tribes. No one ever found El Dorado, of course, for it did not exist except in legend. Years later American poet Edgar Allan Poe wrote a somber poem about the search for El Dorado. In his poem an explorer, wearied by years of vain searching, "met a pilgrim shadow" and asked "Where can it be— / This land of Eldorado?" The shadow grimly answered:

> *"Over the mountains*
> *Of the moon,*
> *Down the valley of the shadow,*
> *Ride, boldly ride,"*
> *The shade replied—*
> *"If you seek for Eldorado!"*

Those who searched for El Dorado were much like the rich fool of Christ's parable in Luke 12:16-21. They devoted their lives to gain, and in the end lost all they had in death. The Bible asks, "For what is a man profited, if he shall gain the whole world, and lose his own soul?" (Matt. 16:26).

France commented sarcastically, "I should like to see Adam's will, wherein he divided the earth between Spain and Portugal." After Magellan's voyage, most Europeans realized that the land to the west was indeed not Asia, but a new world; and the French, Dutch, and English sought to claim some of it for themselves.

French Explorers—The first great French explorer in the New World was **Jacques Cartier** (kar TYAY), who made three voyages to what is now eastern Canada. In 1534 he sailed to Newfoundland and Labrador, which was so desolate that he remarked, "I am rather inclined to believe that this is the land God gave to Cain." He did not find what he was searching for—a northern passage to the Pacific Ocean.

On his second voyage (1535) he sailed up the Saint Lawrence River to an Iroquois Indian village. The view from a nearby mountain was so impressive that Cartier named the site "Mount Royal." Today one of the largest cities in Canada, Montreal, stands there. Like many explorers of his day, Cartier was certain that there existed a water route—the so-called Northwest Passage—which would take him to the Pacific Ocean and from there to the Orient.

Some seventy years after Cartier, **Samuel de Champlain** (sham PLANE), called the "Father of New France," explored and colonized the area around the Saint Lawrence River. In 1608 he founded the city of Quebec. He worked closely with the local Indians, who led him to two of the Great Lakes (Ontario and Huron) and to what we now call Lake Champlain. Like Cartier, he was looking for a route west to China.

Another noted French explorer was the Jesuit missionary **Jacques Marquette** (mar KET). In 1673 he and a friend, **Louis Joliet** (JOH lee ET), explored the Mississippi River. They paddled canoes downstream to a point in southern Arkansas before turning back. In 1682 Sieur de La Salle (luh SAL) traveled to the mouth of the Mississippi River and claimed the entire Mississippi Valley for France. He called it "Louisiana" in honor of King Louis XIV of France.

Dutch Explorers—The most famous explorer for the Netherlands was the Englishman **Henry Hudson,** whom the Dutch hired to find a shorter route to the East. He explored the northeastern coast of America in his ship the *Half Moon.* In 1609 he entered the Hudson River, thinking it might be the Northwest Passage. He continued upriver to where Albany, New York, now stands. His exploration gave the Dutch a claim to the region. In 1621 the Dutch founded the city of New Amsterdam, which is today New York City.

English Explorers—The English began exploring the New World soon after Columbus's first voyage. They hired an Italian sailor named **John Cabot** to lead the first English expedition to North America. After a six-week voyage across the Atlantic, Cabot dropped anchor off the coast of Canada. The first European after the Vikings to set foot on the North American mainland, he returned to England and was rewarded by King Henry VII. In 1498 Cabot made a second voyage to the New World, this time accompanied by his son Sebastian. They explored the northern coast of North America. Though they did not find gold or spices, they found rich fisheries off the Newfoundland coast. The two expeditions to the New World were the basis for England's claim on America. The Cabots paved the way for the founding of English colonies on the North American continent a century later.

Like the Spanish, the English also looked for gold. But they went about obtaining it much differently. For the most part, the English did not engage in the extreme cruelty to the natives that was typical of the Spaniards. The English brought their families and sought to develop the land, not exploit it. Their first permanent settlement was **Jamestown,** founded in 1607 near the mouth of Chesapeake Bay. Under the leadership of Captain **John Smith** they built a village and began to explore the land. In 1608 much of the village burned down, and the few settlers had almost given up when a new governor, Lord de la Warr, arrived. The influx of new settlers and fresh supplies gave new life to the struggling colony.

This first of many English settlements in the New World was the beginning of what would later become the United States of America. Most of the freedoms that Americans have enjoyed—freedom of religion, freedom of speech, and many others—came from the influence of Protestant settlers who came to North America during the seventeenth century.

Europe and the Orient

The West Reaches the East

Europe's exploration efforts were not limited to the New World; her main interests were on the other side of the world in the Orient. Spain was largely excluded from this area by treaty with Portugal (although she did colonize the Philippines).

THE PORTRAICTUER OF CAPTAYNE IOHN SMITH / ADMIRALL OF NEW ENGLAND

These are the Lines that shew thy Face; but those
That shew thy Grace and Glory, brighter bee.
Thy Faire-Discoueries and Fowle-Overthrowes
Of Salvages, much Cwilliz'd by thee
Best shew thy Spirit and to it Glory Wyn;
So, thou art Brasse without, but Golde within.

Captain John Smith

Portugal, the Netherlands, and England, however, traded and colonized extensively in the East.

The Portuguese—Soon after da Gama returned from his historic voyage, the Portuguese, under the leadership of **Pedro Cabral,** established a trading post in India. From this small beginning they were able to establish numerous trading posts throughout the Indian Ocean. Their fully armed ships gave them an insurmountable advantage over Muslim and native traders in the region.

In 1506 **Affonso de Albuquerque** (AL buh KUR kee) was named the viceroy of Portuguese holdings in the East. He discouraged cruelty to the natives and led his men in setting up trading posts and plantations along the trade routes to support and protect Portuguese traders. Under his leadership the Portuguese began to build a vast commercial empire. They captured and controlled the entrances to the Persian Gulf and the Red Sea. Shortly after Albuquerque's death they pushed farther eastward. By 1520 they had taken Ceylon (present-day Sri Lanka) and the town of Banten on the island of Java. The latter controlled one of the two water entrances to the Far East. Since the Portuguese already controlled the other entrance at the straits of Malacca, they were in an excellent position to dominate all of the sea trade between Europe and Asia. In 1542 they began trading with Japan; in 1557 they founded the colony of Macao on the Chinese mainland.

The Portuguese "eastern empire," however, had some fatal weaknesses. It was spread out too widely for the little country of Portugal to administer and defend effectively. Furthermore, since many sailors died at sea, Portugal's manpower was drained to a critical point. (About one voyage in seven ended in disaster.) Finally, the cruelty of the traders—despite Albuquerque's reforms—caused the Asians to hate them. With the lack of cooperation essential for successful trading, Portuguese commercial interests were hampered. When other European nations began to compete for the business in the East, the Asians granted it to them.

The Dutch—The Dutch were not a wealthy people in the sixteenth century, but they were experienced sailors. When prices soared under the Portuguese monopoly, the Dutch decided to go directly to the source for their Asian goods. In 1596 they settled on Java and Sumatra and expelled the Portuguese from the key city of Banten. They later captured the main Spice Islands and founded the city of Batavia, which became a key port and trading post in the East Indies. They soon became the only nation with which Japan would trade. They also began trading with Formosa (modern Taiwan) and seized the island of Ceylon. By the middle of the seventeenth century, Dutch control extended from Persia to Japan.

In order to provide fresh water, vegetables, and meat for ships making the long voyage around Africa to the Indies, the Dutch in 1652 established a settlement at the Cape of Good Hope at what is now Cape Town, South Africa. The mild climate of the cape attracted many settlers; before long it became a sizable colony.

The English—When England defeated the Spanish Armada in 1588, she realized that she had enough sea power to carry on a busy trade with the East. In 1591, almost a century after da Gama, English merchant-seamen made a trading voyage to India. Although they started late, the English far surpassed the Portuguese in long-range influence in the Orient. They followed the Dutch into the East Indies, trading alongside them for several years. Soon, however, they turned their main attention to India. England seized control of the Persian Gulf and opened trade on both the east and west coasts of India. This was the beginning of England's influence in India—an influence that she continued to expand well into the nineteenth century.

The East Responds to the West

China and Japan resented Western intervention in their affairs. The same satisfied attitude that had kept them from exploring other lands also kept them from welcoming traders to their own land. They had been secure in their traditions, and they did not take kindly to European sailors who attempted to claim their properties for unknown

Portrait of a family, painted during the Ming dynasty

kings and their souls for Roman popes. The Portuguese, who were the first to come to the East, were especially tactless and cruel, and by 1550 there had already been several bloody battles between Chinese and Portuguese soldiers. The people of China resisted the European way of life as well as Christianity. They wanted to be left alone. The Chinese did allow, however, the Portuguese to colo-

Life at Sea

Life at sea was full of hardships during the Age of Exploration. In return for their hard labor, sailors were paid very little and were fed the worst sorts of food imaginable. Since many ships remained at sea for long periods of time, the sailors often had to live for months on a dreary diet of biscuits (hardtack), salt beef, salt fish, and beer. The salted meat was tough, usually stank, and often had maggots in it. The biscuits were usually of poor quality. Some sailors jokingly refused to eat those biscuits that were not infested with maggots, stating that they did not want to eat something that even the maggots had refused. All ships carried barrels of water, but within a short time the water became stagnant and undrinkable. It became discolored, gave off a terrible odor, and was full of tiny organisms. Unfortunately, the only thing onboard that did not spoil was the liquor.

One disease that plagued sailors and brought death to many was a vitamin-C deficiency called scurvy. It caused the gums to become swollen and bloody (loosening the teeth in the process) and caused the limbs to become swollen and discolored. Although no one knew about vitamin C at the time, various sea captains stumbled upon a cure for scurvy, finding that fresh fruit and vegetables stopped it. Since fresh produce could not be carried on long sea voyages, the British navy made it compulsory in 1798 for their ships to carry lime juice. Because of this practice, British sailors acquired the nickname ''limeys.''

nize the port city of Macao, but for this privilege the Portuguese had to pay $30,000 per year in tribute. Except for isolated instances, there was no direct trade between China and the European countries for many years.

Japan at first was more friendly to the Europeans than China was. The Japanese welcomed **Francis Xavier,** the famous Jesuit missionary. Later, however, the government, influenced by Buddhism, expelled the foreign missionaries who had followed Xavier to Japan. Those who stayed were severely persecuted. More trouble broke out in 1639 when the Japanese emperor learned that Portuguese trading ships were smuggling in Catholic missionaries disguised as merchants. Furious, he commanded that any Portuguese who came to Japan be killed on sight. Some traders who did not think the emperor was serious learned otherwise and paid with their lives. The Japanese did allow a few Dutch ships to trade in their ports, but for the most part Japan, like China, was a "closed" country to European travelers.

Section Review

1. List the five major groups of Indian tribes in North America before the coming of the Europeans.
2. What were the three major native Indian cultures of Central and South America?
3. After crossing the Isthmus of Panama, what body of water did Balboa see? What did he call it? Who gave it its present name?
4. By each of the following explorers, list the country for which they sailed and claimed territory in the New World: Jacques Cartier, Samuel de Champlain, Henry Hudson, and John Cabot.
5. List the Oriental possessions gained by each of the following countries during the Age of Exploration: Portugal, Netherlands, and England.

Parallel to Discovery: The Commercial Revolution

During the fifteenth and sixteenth centuries, Europe underwent many political, social, religious, and aesthetic changes. There were also many economic changes. The ownership of land no longer was considered the basis of wealth. Money became the medium of exchange in trade. As new sources of gold and spices were discovered in distant lands and used as a medium of exchange, wealth was redefined. Soon after the earliest explorers had returned home, commercial ventures were organized to establish trade ties with newly found peoples across the seas. Before long, great wealth was coming into Europe from around the world. Europe's business thinking and practice changed. These changes are known as the **Commercial Revolution.**

Mercantilism: Nations Acquiring Wealth

The dominant economic system of the Age of Exploration is known as **mercantilism.** Mercantilists believed that the newly found wealth should benefit the mother country. As a result, European nations kept tight control over their country's economy. A nation's strength and greatness were believed to rest upon its wealth, that is, the amount of gold and silver it possessed. For this reason, the goal of mercantilistic nations was to obtain as much precious metal as possible. To achieve this goal, nations sought to acquire colonies, to become self-sufficient, and to maintain a favorable balance of trade.

Under mercantilism, colonies existed for the good of the mother country. They supplied the mother country with raw materials and provided markets where goods from the mother country could be sold. The colonies were not allowed to produce anything that the mother country produced, for that would be competition. Nor were the colonies allowed to trade with anyone but the mother country. Mexico, for example, had to buy everything it needed from Spain, and whatever it produced had to be sold to Spain. Likewise, it was not allowed to trade directly with other Spanish colonies; for Mexican products to reach Peru, for example, they had to be shipped across the ocean to Spain and then back again to Peru. Thus the

Spanish gold doubloons and pieces of eight salvaged from a 1715 wreck; the pieces of eight are cut from an eight-ounce piece of molten silver and stamped with the shield of Philip V of Spain and with the cross.

mother countries became wealthier and wealthier, and the colonies usually suffered.

By establishing colonies, European nations hoped to become self-sufficient. They did not want to purchase goods from other European countries, for that would drain their own supply of gold and silver. Instead they desired to export more than they imported and thus bring more gold and silver into their national treasury. This was considered to be a "favorable balance of trade."

But mercantilism had its weaknesses. Under this system the government regulated a nation's economic activity, creating national monopolies that deterred competition. More often than not, the interests of the government superseded the interests and welfare of the people—especially those in the colonies.

Mercantilists did not view trade as a "two-way street" benefiting both buyer and seller. They thought of it only in terms of the seller, who obtained gold and silver for his product. This one-sided foreign trade, in which goods went out of a country and gold and silver came in, was often a detriment to a country's agriculture and industry. Under this system the goods and crops a nation produced were deemed important only if they could be traded abroad for gold and silver.

Once gold and silver were obtained by a mercantilistic country, the wealth was seldom used to benefit the people. These precious metals were hoarded. But as Solomon (who possessed great amounts of gold and silver) says in Ecclesiastes 5:13: "There is a sore evil which I have seen under the sun, namely, riches kept for the owners thereof to their hurt." God does not want us to hoard the resources and riches which He has provided for our use. He wants us to invest and use what we have for His glory and not just for our own selfish gain.

Capitalism: Individuals Advancing Wealth

The opportunity for acquiring great wealth was open not only to national states but also to private individuals. During this period another economic system, **capitalism,** developed side by side with mercantilism. Unlike mercantilism, the goal of capitalism was not simply to acquire wealth, but to advance wealth. Enterprising individuals used what money they had to make more money. They invested their wealth, often at great risk, in hopes of making a profit.

Many of the early capitalists were bankers. They made money by buying and selling bills of exchange, by safeguarding money for others, and by exchanging money. They often invested their own resources in business ventures such as financing trade voyages. But sea travel at this time was perilous: it was not uncommon for the stormy seas to send ships to the bottom of the ocean or for pirates to seize a ship's cargo. Such disasters could bring financial ruin to an individual. For this reason, men organized **companies** in which they pooled their resources; they shared the gains as well as the losses.

From this practice arose the **joint-stock company.** People invested money in such companies; in return they were issued stock certificates showing the amount of money they invested. The invested money became part of the company's **capital,** or supply of money. The company then used this capital to finance a business venture. If a profit was made, it was given to the stockholders, or contributors (also called investors), in the form of **dividends.** They shared in both the profits and the losses.

There were many joint-stock companies during the Age of Exploration. Three are especially important. The English East India Company, founded in 1600 with only a small amount of capital, began trading mostly in India. It was astonishingly successful. Profits for the years 1609-13, for example, averaged almost 300 per cent each year (that is, investors received back every year dividends three times their original investment). The Dutch East India Company, founded in 1602, traded in the East Indies (such as Java and Sumatra). It too made great profits, paying dividends of 18 per cent each year for many years. The French Company of New France traded in Canada, mainly for furs. All these companies did more than just trade, however. They set up bases, or settlements, to make their work more permanent.

Another method of getting people to help finance an enterprise was to post in a public place a **prospectus**—details of a proposed business venture. People wrote their names below the prospectus, stating that they would help share the cost of the enterprise. If it were a success, they would share in the profits; if it were a failure, they agreed to sustain the loss. It is from this practice that we get the word **underwriter,** which today we use to describe an insurance company. One of the earliest insurance companies was Lloyds of London. It was founded in 1688 by a group of men who underwrote voyages to the New World.

Section Review

1. What are the changes in Europe's business thinking and practice during the fifteenth and sixteenth centuries called?
2. What was the dominant economic policy of most European nations during the Age of Exploration?
3. What was the purpose of colonies under this economic policy?
4. The use of wealth to make more wealth defines what economic policy?

A Glimpse Behind and a Glimpse Ahead

It was not accidental that the Age of Exploration occurred at the same time as the Reformation. While explorers were discovering new lands across the seas, men were rediscovering the truth of God's Word. In God's timing these discoveries enabled Europeans to carry the gospel to distant parts of the globe. Furthermore, the discovery of the New World—in particular, North America—provided a haven for those who were persecuted for the name of Christ on the European continent.

Chapter Review

Can You Explain?

compass	circumnavigation	mercantilism	capital
latitude	conquistadors	capitalism	dividends
caravel	viceroy	company	prospectus
Line of Demarcation	Commercial Revolution	joint-stock company	underwriter

Can You Identify?

Marco Polo	Maya	Atahualpa	Louis Joliet
Prester John	Aztec	Bartolomé de las Casas	Henry Hudson
Prince Henry	Inca	Hernando de Soto	John Cabot
Bartholomeu Dias	Vasco Núñez de	Francisco Vásquez de	Jamestown (1607)
Vasco da Gama	Balboa	Coronado	John Smith
Christopher Columbus	Hernando Cortés	Jacques Cartier	Pedro Cabral
(1492)	Montezuma	Samuel de Champlain	Affonso de Albuquerque
Ferdinand Magellan	Francisco Pizarro	Jacques Marquette	Francis Xavier

Can You Locate?

Spice Islands	Cuba	Tenochtitlán	Quebec
Cathay (China)	Brazil	Peru	New Amsterdam
Cape of Good Hope	Strait of Magellan	Isthmus of Panama	Jamestown
Lisbon	Pacific Ocean	Lima	Ceylon
Indian Ocean	Bering Strait	Mississippi River	Java
Bahamas	Yucatan Peninsula	Montreal	Formosa
Hispaniola	Mexico	Saint Lawrence River	

How Much Do You Remember?

1. What new navigational instruments aided the explorers in their travels?
2. List four reasons that Portugal and Spain led other European nations in the Age of Exploration.
3. List the important contribution that each of the following explorers made to the Age of Exploration: Bartholomeu Dias, Vasco da Gama, Christopher Columbus, and Ferdinand Magellan.
4. How did the Indians of Central and South America differ from those of North America?
5. What was the Chinese and Japanese attitude toward the European traders?

What Do You Think?

1. In what ways do you think the Renaissance influenced the Age of Discovery?
2. How does I Timothy 6:9-10 relate to the motives of many of the explorers? How does Proverbs 16:16 relate to their goals?
3. What discovery of the Age of Exploration do you think had the greatest impact on history?
4. What effect did the defeat of the Spanish Armada in 1588 have on the history of North America?
5. Mercantilism and capitalism are economic policies—how do they differ?

Following Pages: Prise de la Bastille le 14 juillet 1789. Arrestation du Gouverneur, Monsieur de Launay. © *Réunion des Musées Nationaux*

UNIT V

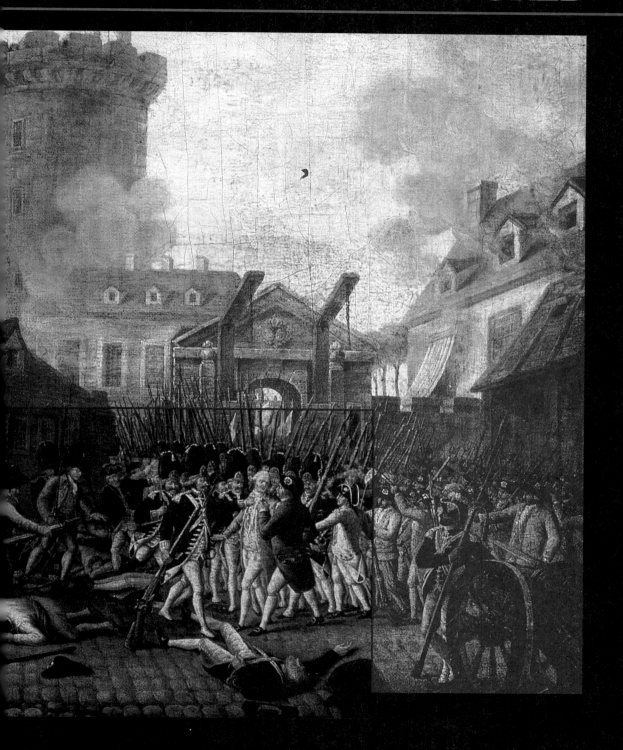

Europeans living from 1600 to 1800 believed that they were living in an "enlightened" age. During this period, political and economic conditions hastened the decline of feudalism and eroded the power of the nobility. Consequently, strong absolutist monarchs were able to grasp political power. At the same time, this period—known as the Age of Reason—saw outstanding scientific and artistic accomplishments. Men expanded on the concepts of individual dignity and responsibility to which the Renaissance and Reformation had given expression. Philosophers popularized the concept that "all men are created equal." In harmony with this "enlightened" attitude, people began to challenge the absolutist ways of kings in search of individual freedom. This spirit of liberty and equality gave rise to the American and French revolutions.

AGE OF REASON

Monteverdi (1567-1643)   Rubens (1577-1640)   Bernini (1598-1680)
Harvey (1578-1657)   Rembrandt (1606-69)
El Greco (1541-1614)   Galileo (1564-1642)
Kepler (1571-1630)   Descartes (1596-1650)
Francis Bacon (1561-1626)

ENGLAND

Cromwell (1599-1658)
James I (1603-25)
KING JAMES VERSION (1611)

WARS

FRANCE

★BATTLES

Henry IV (1589-1610)   Louis XIII (1610-43)
Richelieu (1585-1642)   Mazarin (1602-61)

AUSTRIA

PRUSSIA

RUSSIA

Ivan IV (1533-84)

1550   1600

THE ENLIGHTENED WORLD

Locke (1632-1704)　Swift　　　　　　Pope (1688-1724)　Rousseau (1712-78)　　　　Mozart (1756-91)
　　　　　　　　　　(1667-1745)　　　　　　　　Voltaire (1694-1778)　　　Gibbon (1737-94)
Molière (1622-73)　　　　　　　Watteau　　　　　　　　　　　　　　　　Lavoisier (1743-94)
　　Newton (1642-1727)　　　　(1684-1721)　　　　　Haydn　　　　　Priestley (1733-1804)
　　　　　　　　　　　　　　J. S. Bach (1685-1750)　(1732-1809)
Boyle (1627-91)　　　　　　　　　　　Handel (1685-1759)　Diderot (1713-84)　　Jenner (1749-1823)

Charles II (1660-85)　•BILL OF RIGHTS (1689)

Charles I (1625-49)　　　•HABEAS CORPUS　　　George I (1714-27)　　　　　　George III (1760-1820)
　　　　　　　　　　　　ACT (1679)　　　John Wesley (1703-91)
CIVIL WAR (1642-49)　　　•GLORIOUS REVOLUTION (1688)　　　　　　　　　　AMERICAN
　　　　　　　　　　　　　　　　　　　　　　　　　　　　　　　　　　REVOLUTION (1775-83)

THIRTY YEARS' WAR　　　　　THE WAR OF THE
(1618-48)　　　　　　　　SPANISH SUCCESSION (1701-13)　　SEVEN YEARS' WAR　WARS WITH FRANCE
　　　　　　　　　　　　　　　　　　　　　　　　　　(1756-63)　　　(1792-1814)
　　　　　　　　　　　　　　　　　　THE WAR OF THE
　　　　　　　　　　　　　　　　　AUSTRIAN SUCCESSION (1740-48)

Louis XIV
(1643-1715)　　　　　　　　　　　　　　　　　　　　　　Louis XVI　　★AUSTERLITZ (1805)
　　　　　　　　　•EDICT OF NANTES　　Louis XV (1715-74)　　(1774-92)　　Napoleon (1799-1815)
　　　　　　　　　REVOKED (1685)
　　　　　　　　　　　　　　　　　　　　　　　　　　　　　　　★REVOLUTION BEGINS
　　　　　　　　　　　　　　　　　　　　　Robespierre (1758-94)　(1789)　　★WATERLOO (1815)

　　　　　　　　　　　　　　　•PRAGMATIC SANCTION　　Joseph II (1765-90)
　　　　　　　　　　　　　　　　　　Maria Theresa (1740-80)

Frederick William, the Great Elector　　Frederick William I
(1640-88)　　　　　　　　　　　(1713-40)
　　　　　　　　Frederick I (1688-1713)　　　　　Frederick II (1740-86)

　　　　　　　　GREAT NORTHERN WAR (1700-21)
　　　　　　　Peter I (1682-1725)　　　　　　　　Catherine II (1762-92)　　Alexander I (1801-25)

1650　　　1700　　　1750　　　1800

CHAPTER 13

"I am the state."

> Let every soul be subject unto the higher powers. For there is no power but of God: the powers that be are ordained of God. Whosoever therefore resisteth the power, resisteth the ordinance of God: and they that resist shall receive to themselves damnation. For rulers are not a terror to good works, but to the evil. Wilt thou then not be afraid of the power? do that which is good, and thou shalt have praise of the same: for he is the minister of God to thee for good. But if thou do that which is evil, be afraid; for he beareth not the sword in vain: for he is the minister of God, a revenger to execute wrath upon him that doeth evil.
>
> —Romans 13:1-4

Most Europeans living in the seventeenth and eighteenth centuries accepted the fact that God had established governments. In their day, the governments of Europe were controlled by monarchs. Though these monarchs boldly proclaimed that they ruled by "divine right," they did not always rule their people justly. They emphasized their *right* to power but often failed to properly exercise the *responsibility* of power. God had given them authority to be used for the good of their people; often, however, they used their authority to satisfy their own pleasures and to increase their personal power. They claimed to have absolute authority over their people—an attitude evident in the boastful statement "I am the state," attributed to Louis XIV of France. Monarchs also sought to increase their power and prestige by seizing additional territory—a practice that usually led to war. In order to prevent stronger rulers from taking their land, kings formed diplomatic alliances to maintain a balance of power in Europe. In this way they hoped to ensure that no one nation would become strong enough to dominate the entire continent of Europe.

Power of Kings: Absolute or Restrained

During the Middle Ages royal power in Europe was limited. Popes fought with kings over the question of whose authority was greater. Feudal nobles competed with kings for power within a territory. But with the papacy's decline in power and the passing of feudalism, opposition to royal power decreased.

During the seventeenth and eighteenth centuries, European rulers worked to make their political power **absolute** (unlimited and unrestrained). They sought to increase their royal authority by (1) increasing their control over their nation's finances, religion, and nobility; (2) increasing the size of the standing army and/or developing a strong navy; (3) increasing the size of the government bureaucracy and making it an instrument of their royal will; and (4) increasing the size of their territory—through war if necessary. They justified the extension of

their power on religious grounds. They asserted that God had established their authority; therefore, they ruled by **"divine right."** This right, they said, gave them absolute authority: they were not bound by any manmade laws but were responsible only to God for their actions.

Absolutist rule was accepted by most Europeans, who believed that a strong ruler was the best way to ensure security, order, and prosperity. Nevertheless, some feared an unrestrained increase in royal power. Their cause was often championed by representative assemblies, which had developed alongside the national states. But with the exception of the English Parliament, these assemblies had little success in restraining royal power. Most absolutist kings were able to crush any opposition to their authority.

Opposite Page: Louis XIV in his robes of state

Absolutism Triumphs in France

France was the leading absolutist nation in Europe during the seventeenth century. Much of the power wielded by French kings was secured through the efforts of two chief advisers to the French throne: cardinals Richelieu and Mazarin. For several decades, Richelieu and then Mazarin guided both French policy and French kings. They sought to increase their personal power by strengthening royal power in France and French power in Europe. Their efforts encouraged the growth of absolutism in France. The beneficiary of a stronger French crown and realm was King Louis XIV. For more than seventy years he ruled France with unparalleled pomp and power; he was the leading absolutist ruler of Europe.

Growth of Absolutism: Richelieu and Mazarin

The man who helped lay the foundation for absolutism in France was the **Bourbon** king **Henry IV.** After his victory in the French civil wars (see p. 301), Henry worked to strengthen royal power. He reduced the privileges of the nobility and increased government control of the economy. However, he was assassinated by a Catholic extremist in 1610,

Philippe de Champaigne, Louis XIII, *Bob Jones University Collection of Sacred Art*

and his nine-year-old son **Louis XIII** (1610-43) came to the throne. During the years of Louis's youth, his mother, Marie de Medici, ineffectively ruled France. But in 1624 the Duc de Richelieu (RISH uh LOO)—better known as **Cardinal Richelieu**—became Louis XIII's chief minister.

Richelieu's Aims—Richelieu set about to strengthen the power of the king by destroying the

Huguenots, whom he viewed as a danger to the state. He also wanted to weaken the great nobles and to prevent them from regaining their lost power. Richelieu sought to accomplish the first of his policies by putting extraordinary burdens on the Huguenots. For example, he forced them to house French soldiers, while he allowed Roman Catholics to be exempt from such obligations. Richelieu ordered Huguenot children to be taken from their

Philippe de Champaigne, Triple Portrait of the Head of Richelieu, *Reproduced by courtesy of the Trustees, The National Gallery, London*

homes and to be reared by Roman Catholics. He also sent spies to Huguenot churches to listen for any criticism of the government. Critics were either arrested or heavily fined.

The Huguenot reaction to these harsh measures varied. Some Huguenots left France, while others remained and suffered under the government's persecution. Others participated in violent, though unsuccessful, uprisings against Richelieu's policies. Finally, there were Huguenots who were weak or insincere about their religious beliefs and as a result abandoned their convictions rather than suffer persecution.

Richelieu partially accomplished his second objective—weakening the nobility—by removing them from positions of authority in local govern-

ment. He replaced them with **intendents,** officials directly responsible to the king. In addition, Richelieu destroyed many of the castles of the nobility. Those who defied him were imprisoned, and some were executed.

The Thirty Years' War—To increase the prestige and power of France, Richelieu brought France into the **Thirty Years' War** (1618-48). This war was the last great religious war fought in Europe. It began in Bohemia, the proud land of John Huss. Protestant Bohemian nobles revolted against the newly crowned Catholic emperor, who had revoked their religious freedoms. The emperor sent his troops into the country and ruthlessly crushed all Protestant resistance. Before long the war had spread to other parts of the Holy Roman Empire; Protestantism seemed to be on the verge of collapse.

The Protestant cause was rescued by **Gustavus Adolphus** (gus-TAY-vus uh-DAHL-fuss; 1611-32), king of Sweden. With a small band of troops, Gustavus landed in northern Germany, recruited some additional soldiers, and marched against the emperor's pro-Catholic, pro-imperial forces. Gustavus won several important victories but then was killed in battle. It was soon after his death that France entered the war—on the side of the Protestants.

Although France was a Roman Catholic country, Richelieu feared what would happen if the Holy Roman emperor solidified his power by subduing all his Protestant opponents. France would then be surrounded by two strong Hapsburg powers—Spain and the Holy Roman Empire. For this reason, Richelieu joined the Protestant cause in 1635, making the war more a political than a religious conflict.

After several more years of fighting, the war ended in 1648 with a Protestant-French victory. The peace treaties, collectively known as the Peace of Westphalia, contained several important provisions. First, the treaties recognized the independence of the Protestant provinces of the Netherlands and the Swiss confederacy. (Switzerland had been virtually independent of the Holy Roman Empire since 1291). Second, Germany became more politically fragmented; the Peace of Westphalia recognized over three hundred independent German states. It also reaffirmed the principle that each prince determines the religion of his territory.

Third, France emerged as the strongest nation on the continent of Europe.

Richelieu's Successor—Richelieu died in 1642; King Louis XIII died only five months later. The crown of France passed to Louis's five-year-old son, **Louis XIV** (1643-1715). During Louis XIV's youth, the government was controlled by a new chief minister, **Jules Mazarin.** Mazarin maintained the absolutist policies of his predecessor Richelieu. Shortly after the wily Cardinal Mazarin and the young king came to power, France began to experience unrest. Those who opposed the growing power of the crown participated in a series of riots, civil wars, and antigovernment plots. These upheavals, known as the **Frondes,** were unsuccessful in destroying French absolutism and ended in 1653. They were the last serious attempt to limit the power of the king until the outbreak of the French Revolution in 1789. (See Chapter 15.)

Epitome of Absolutism: Louis XIV

When Mazarin died in 1661, Louis XIV appointed no one to replace him. Instead, Louis became his own chief minister. He told his advisers, "You will assist me with your counsels when I ask for them." Louis believed in "one king, one law, and one faith." These three were wrapped up in the person of the king and his power over the state. Although he probably never said, "*L'état, c'est moi*" ("I am the state"), these words reflect Louis's view of himself. From 1661 until his death in 1715, Louis dominated European affairs to such an extent that historians sometimes call these years "the Age of Louis XIV."

Financial and Military Policies—One of the first things Louis did after the death of Mazarin was to set French finances in order. The French government was close to bankruptcy because it was spending money faster than it took it in. To remedy this

Europe in 1648

Brandenburg—Prussia
Spanish Hapsburgs
Austrian Hapsburgs
Sweden
Boundary Line of the Holy Roman Empire.
Provincial Borders

Louis XIV's Palace of Versailles as it appeared in 1668

dangerous situation, Louis appointed **Jean-Baptiste Colbert** (kohl BEHR; 1619-83) as his minister of finance. Colbert brought temporary fiscal order to France by tighter government control of the French economy. He encouraged commercial activity and economic self-sufficiency. A proponent of mercantilism, Colbert favored limiting imports and increasing exports. He also encouraged the building of a navy to protect French trade abroad.

Louis also set about to reorganize the French army so that the soldiers would owe their loyalty to him rather than to the colonel of their regiment, as had been so in the past. To weaken the influence of the nobility over the troops, Louis placed lieutenant colonels over each regiment. (The word *lieutenant* comes from two French words: *lieu,* ''place,'' and *tenir,* ''to hold.'' A lieutenant colonel is one who holds the place of a colonel.) Through these lieutenants, who were responsible to the king and not to the colonels, Louis gained control of the army. He required his troops to wear identical uniforms rather than allowing them to wear the colors of their colonels. His well-trained, well-paid, and loyal troops became the finest soldiers in seventeenth-century Europe.

Revocation of the Edict of Nantes—In his efforts to create religious uniformity in France, Louis XIV revoked the Edict of Nantes in 1685. Since 1598 it had guaranteed religious toleration of French Protestants. As a result of its revocation, Huguenots lost their freedom to worship. Louis also forbade all Protestant education, tore down Huguenot churches, and forced some Huguenots to serve as galley slaves on French ships.

Persecution came to the Huguenots because the French king viewed their business skill, growing political power, and Christian testimony as a threat to his power. Under similar circumstances, Christians have suffered persecution throughout history. The Apostle Peter admonished persecuted Christians:

> Think it not strange concerning the fiery trial which is to try you, as though some strange thing happened unto you: but rejoice, inasmuch as ye are partakers of Christ's sufferings. . . . Yet if any man suffer as a Christian, let him not be ashamed; but let him glorify God on this behalf. For the time is come that judgment must begin at the house of God: and if it first begin at us, what shall the end be of them that obey not the gospel of God? And if the righteous scarcely be saved, where shall the ungodly and the sinner appear?
> I Peter 4:12-13, 16-18

In spite of Louis's sincere belief that such persecution was for the good of France, his revocation had the opposite effect. More than 250,000 Huguenots—many of them merchants, small businessmen, and craftsmen—left France. Since they made up the spiritual, moral, and economic backbone of the country, their departure was a devastating blow to the French nation. The lands the Huguenots settled in benefited from their spiritual fervor and productive skills. Some of these lands were the rivals of France; thus, Louis's actions indirectly strengthened his enemies. "Evil shall slay the wicked: and they that hate the righteous shall be desolate" (Ps. 34:21). God's judgment came upon France; in less than a hundred years, this nation suffered a violent and bloody revolution.

Life at Versailles—Louis XIV took the sun as the symbol of his reign. As the "Sun King," he considered himself the center of European life, with

Royal chapel in the Palace of Versailles

everyone else "revolving" around him. Louis was a proud man who loved to glorify himself and his own accomplishments. He loved luxury and the attention of the people of his court.

To show his power and splendor, Louis had a great palace built about twelve miles southwest of Paris. When completed, the palace of **Versailles** (vehr SYE) was an awesome sight. Around the palace were elaborate formal gardens. The building itself was nearly a half mile long and contained hundreds of grandly decorated rooms. Dazzling works of art adorned the palace's interior. To maintain the building's symmetrical appearance, Louis refused to allow chimneys to be seen from the front of the palace even though their shortness meant smoky rooms. Elegance and grandeur were important, not utility.

Louis used his palace to impress his subjects. He also used it to keep the nobility subservient to him. He required them to live at Versailles for at least part of each year. While they were there, Louis kept the nobility so busy that they did not have time to plot against him. There were plays, balls, and frivolous activities that kept their minds distracted from the affairs of state.

From the time Louis rose in the morning until he went to bed at night, the nobility flocked around him. They vied with one another for the privilege of performing some small task, such as handing him his shirt in the morning or bringing him a cup of hot chocolate at night. Everything in Louis's life became a pompous ritual designed to make the king the absolute center of attention.

In spite of all its grandeur, Versailles was the center for all that was base and immoral. Adultery on the part of the king was expected. Homosexuality was practiced openly by members of the court. Gambling was commonplace. Every sort of vice could be found in the king's palace. Louis enjoyed seeming prosperity; God, however, warns that "it is an abomination to kings to commit wickedness: for the throne is established by righteousness" (Prov. 16:12).

Foreign Policy—In order to expand French territory and to increase his influence in Europe, Louis XIV engaged in a number of wars. He tried to extend French borders to what he said were their natural boundaries: the Rhine, the Alps, and the Pyrenees. Although he did gain some territory, these wars brought much harm to France. Their cost, in addition

Louis's Vanity

A nobleman who lived in the royal palace described Louis's vanity.

[It was] without limit or restraint; it colored everything and convinced him that no one even approached him in military talents, in plans and enterprises, in government. Hence those pictures and inscriptions in the gallery at Versailles which disgust every foreigner; those opera prologues that he himself tried to sing; that flood of prose and verse in his praise for which his appetite was insatiable; those dedications of statues copied from pagan sculpture, and the insipid and sickening compliments that were continually offered to him in person and which he swallowed with unfailing relish; hence his distaste for all merit, intelligence, education, and most of all, for all independence of character and sentiment in others; his mistakes of judgment in matters of importance; his familiarity and favor reserved entirely for those to whom he felt himself superior in acquirements and ability; and, above everything else, a jealousy of his authority which determined and took precedence of every other sort of justice, reason, and consideration whatever."[2]

to Louis's extensive building programs, brought France close to bankruptcy. On his deathbed, Louis said to his heir: "Try to remain at peace with your neighbors. I have loved war too much. Do not copy me in that, or in my overspending."

Louis died in 1715. He reigned longer than any European king before him or since him. He had outlived both his son and grandson, who were heirs to the throne. His great-grandson **Louis XV** (1715-74), who was five years old when Louis XIV died, succeeded him to the throne. During the early years of the young king's reign, capable regents kept France out of war and rebuilt her economy. But Louis XV, following the example of Louis XIV, later involved France in disastrous and humiliating wars, which once again drained the royal treasury. This bankruptcy was a major factor in the eventual overthrow of the absolute monarchy in France.

Section Review

1. What right did rulers of this period claim that gave them absolute power and placed them above manmade laws?
2. What two chief advisers to the French kings Louis XIII and Louis XIV helped strengthen the power of France and the French monarch?
3. What was the last great religious war fought in Europe? On what side did France enter the war? Why?
4. What French king's reign became the model of absolutism throughout Europe? What was the name of his new palace?
5. What did the French king revoke in 1685? What people were persecuted as a result?

Absolutism Spreads in Europe

French absolutism influenced other European monarchs, who gradually embraced not only absolutism, but the French language, French fashions, and French morals. Three territories in particular came under the rule of absolutist monarchs: Brandenburg-Prussia, Austria, and Russia. Following the example of Louis XIV, known as "the Grand Monarch," the rulers of these territories were determined to increase their personal and national power. As we shall see in later chapters, popular discontent with absolutism finally led to open revolution.

Absolutism in Brandenburg-Prussia

After the Thirty Years' War, Germany remained a fragmented land made up of hundreds of small, weak states. One of these, Brandenburg-Prussia, gradually obtained enough power and territory to become the strongest of the German states. Brandenburg-Prussia (later called simply Prussia) was an unlikely candidate to become a major European power. Her soil was poor, her economic resources were few, and her territories were scattered. She had no natural frontiers such as mountains or rivers to provide protection. Yet she did have energetic and capable rulers (called electors) who used whatever means necessary to increase their power and the size of their territory. These rulers built up a large standing army and established an efficient bureaucracy. They also gained the cooperation of the Prussian nobility, called

Junkers (YOONG kurz), who worked closely with the electors in governing the country and serving as officers in the Prussian army.

The Great Elector—The first important Prussian ruler was **Frederick William** (1640-88), called "the Great Elector" because he was the most powerful of the German princes who elected the emperor. He was responsible for forging Prussia's scattered territories into a unified state. His chief source of power was the standing Prussian army, which numbered about thirty thousand men. Taxes had to be raised in order to support such a large army; in fact, Prussians paid twice as much in taxes as did French citizens. The army became a chief instrument by which Prussian rulers obtained and demonstrated their absolute power. During the next two centuries, militarism played a major role in creating and shaping a German national state.

Frederick I—Under Frederick William's successor, **Frederick I** (1688-1713), the army continued to grow. Frederick I however was more interested in the arts than in warfare. He sought to imitate Louis XIV in as many ways as possible. He had a new palace built for himself and beautified Berlin, the capital of Prussia, with many new public buildings.

Although Frederick I did little to increase the actual power of Prussia, he did increase Prussia's prestige among the other German states. After the War of the Spanish Succession (see pp. 353-54), Frederick acquired for his successors the title of "King in Prussia." (The title "King *of* Prussia" would have been unacceptable to the Holy Roman emperor, who officially ruled all the German states.) This royal title helped to enhance the Prussian rulers' prestige among the nations of Europe.

Frederick William I—Building upon the foundation of his predecessors, **Frederick William I** (1713-40) firmly established Prussian absolutism. He was a violent-tempered man who believed in discipline and routine. He not only reduced court luxury and created a strong centralized bureaucracy but also demanded absolute obedience from all citizens. "Salvation belongs to the Lord," he said. "Everything else is my business."

Frederick William I spent most of his time building up Prussia's military forces. During his reign the army grew to 83,000 men. It was a highly trained and battle-ready force, but Frederick William was not eager for war. He had spent so much money and energy on the military that he could not bear to see his men killed in battle. At the end of his life Frederick William had one of the five largest armies in Europe, despite the fact that Prussia did not rank in the top ten in population. "Prussia," said one of his contemporaries, "is not a state with an army but an army with a state."

Frederick II—Although Frederick William I loved military life, his son **Frederick II** (1740-86) seemed to have no interest in the army. As a young man, Frederick II loved to compose music, play the flute, write French poetry, and follow French fashions. His father opposed such pursuits, and the two quarreled constantly. Though Frederick II never abandoned his interest in culture, he did become one of Prussia's greatest military heroes. He became known as Frederick "the Great," the greatest soldier of his day. During his reign he tripled the size of

Frederick II

the Prussian state. Frederick also strengthened Prussia's economy by establishing a silk industry and stabilizing grain prices. He enacted a wide variety of political and social reforms. For example, he abol-

This home of the Hohenzollern kings was rebuilt in the nineteenth century; Frederick William I and Frederick the Great lie buried here.
Top Left: *Heraldry of the province of Brandenburg*

ished the torture of prisoners and granted religious freedom to Roman Catholics and Jews. Yet despite these and other reforms, Frederick remained firmly dedicated to the principle of absolutism.

By Frederick II's day, Prussia was a strong rival to the Hapsburg rulers of Austria. The **Hohenzollern** (HO uhn ZAHL urn) rulers had built Prussia into a first-class European power. Both Prussia and Austria competed for control of the many German states. Eventually Prussia's military might won out, and the Hohenzollern rulers united the German states into one unified country during the nineteenth century.

Absolutism in Austria

By the beginning of the eighteenth century the **Hapsburg** rulers of Austria not only controlled a large amount of territory but also held the title of Holy Roman Emperor. Although this title gave them no additional power, it did give them an added measure of prestige.

Despite these advantages, Hapsburg rulers were unable to create a strong absolutist state. There were many obstacles to hinder them. First, the Roman Catholic church and the nobility held great power and opposed any limitation upon their traditional rights. Second, Austria was surrounded by greedy neighbors (particularly France and later Prussia) who desired to seize Hapsburg territories that bordered on their own. Since the Austrian rulers needed the support of the nobles to defend the country, the rulers dared not upset them by increasing their own royal power. Third, the Hapsburgs ruled so many different nationalities that it was almost impossible to create a strong, unified government. The Hungarians especially resented Austrian control and did not willingly cooperate with their Hapsburg rulers.

During the eighteenth century, the emperor **Joseph II** (1765-90) made a strong effort to create an absolutist state in Austria. He began his reign as coruler with his mother, Maria Theresa (1765-80).

Schönbrunn Palace, Vienna

During the years of joint rule, Maria Theresa made gradual and careful changes. After her death, Joseph II embarked on a bolder course of action, directing his efforts against the power of the nobility and the Roman Catholic church. He forced both groups to pay higher taxes, while reducing the tax burden on the peasants. At the same time, he made the government more centralized by weakening local authority.

Many of Joseph's actions were directed specifically against the Roman Catholic church. For example, he dissolved hundreds of monasteries, allowing to remain only those that performed what he termed a useful service, such as teaching or ministering to the sick. He altered the church's organization and in 1781 granted religious freedom to non-Catholics. Since many of Joseph's changes were both sudden and drastic, few of them continued after his death. In fact, the nobility and the Roman Catholic church regained many of their old privileges and reasserted their authority. Absolutism was never as strong in Austria as it was in many other European nations.

Absolutism in Russia

Soon after Russia gained her independence from the Mongols (see Chapter 6), **Ivan IV** (1533-84), called Ivan ''the Terrible,'' became the ruler. He expanded Russian territory and built the beautiful St. Basil's Cathedral in Moscow. A cruel tyrant, Ivan had many of the Russian nobility murdered, and in a fit of rage he murdered even his own son. He heavily taxed the people of Russia, treating them like slaves of the state. To glorify himself and his position, Ivan took the title of **czar,** a term that comes from the word *caesar*.

After Ivan's death Russia underwent a period of upheaval. Rival groups fought for control of the government, while bands of peasants roamed across Russia, killing and plundering. This turmoil finally ended in 1613, when the **Romanov** dynasty came to the throne. (This dynasty ruled Russia until it was overthrown by the Revolution of 1917.) **Peter I** (1682-1725), one of the early Romanovs, did much to turn Russia into an absolutist state.

Peter the Great—When Peter became czar, Russia was out of step with the rest of Europe. She was isolated and backward, her economy was weak, and her government was disorganized. Peter determined that if Russia were to become a great power, she would have to adopt Western ways. Therefore, in 1697 he decided to travel in western Europe and learn all that he could. He visited Holland, France, and England, and when he returned to Russia (to put down a revolution), he brought back over seven hundred western Europeans with him. Many of them were shipbuilders, mathematicians, and engineers.

With this outside help, Peter began a Westernization and modernization program in Russia. The

Peter the Great

and his successors controlled the Synod, making sure that the Orthodox church remained in line with the policies of the czar.

Catherine II—After the death of Peter, absolutism continued to develop in Russia under Empress **Catherine II** (1762-96), who also came to be called ''the Great.'' Catherine II was a hardworking and very capable ruler, but she was openly immoral and was driven by uncontrolled ambition. She had her husband, the czar, arrested and murdered. Like Peter I, she sought to increase the authority of the monarchy. She allowed the nobles to retain their privileged positions as long as they served the state. In 1766 Catherine gave the nobles the right to exile rebellious peasants to Siberia. The harsh treatment of these peasants produced several violent uprisings during her reign, but the government savagely put down each one. Discontent continued to mount, but it was not until the twentieth

Russians, with the help of these Western experts, worked to improve the Russian economy; they encouraged production of consumer goods such as paper products and textiles. They also began building a navy and a new capital, which they called St. Petersburg.

Peter himself tried to force Western ways upon his people. He outlawed long beards and oriental costumes such as long robes on men. In 1699 he introduced the Western calendar, which brought an end to the Russian tradition of celebrating New Year's Day on the first of September (a date the Russians believed marked the first day of creation). Many Russians resented these changes.

In addition to his Westernization program, Peter had another major goal: to expand Russian territory and acquire warm-water ports. In the **Great Northern War** (1700-1721) the Russians defeated Sweden and won additional territory along the Baltic Sea. Because of this victory, the Russians gave Peter the title of ''the Great.''

Peter strengthened his absolute powers in Russia by seizing greater control of the Russian Orthodox church. When the head of the church (the patriarch) died, Peter did not allow anyone to fill the vacancy. Instead he created the Holy Synod, which governed the church like a board of directors. Peter

Catherine the Great

century that the Russian people finally overthrew the tyranny of the czars. But as we shall see in Chapter 20, the Russian people simply exchanged one form of repression for another.

Catherine seemed to be an "enlightened" reformer. She encouraged education and corresponded with some of the notable scholars of her day. Though she supported certain social reforms, she was an absolutist monarch at heart. Among other things, she formally instituted government censorship for the first time in Russian history. She weakened the Russian Orthodox church by transferring church property to the government. She also completed the Westernization of Russia that Peter the Great had begun.

In foreign affairs, Catherine continued Russia's expansion program, particularly at the expense of the Poles and the Turks. One of her major territorial goals was to secure additional seaports. During her reign the Russians took from the Turks some territory on the north shore of the Black Sea. The desire of later Russian czars to control the Black Sea completely and to compete in Mediterranean trade became an important issue in international diplomacy.

Section Review

1. What three countries followed the example of France and came under absolutist rule?
2. By what name were the nobility who aided the Prussian rulers known?
3. What Austrian ruler sought to create an absolutist state by attacking the church and nobility?
4. How did Peter the Great propose to get Russia in step with the rest of Europe?
5. Give the name of the ruling family in each of the following countries: Prussia, Austria, and Russia.

Absolutism Defeated in England

Unlike the other countries we have discussed so far, England did not become an absolutist state. English kings had to contend with a Parliament that over the centuries had gradually increased its power and that refused to surrender its hard-won rights. Of special significance was its right to grant or deny a king's request for additional taxes.

During the sixteenth century the Tudors worked with Parliament to gain their desired goals. They relied upon skillful politicians to advise them, and they remained sensitive to public opinion. As a result they were able to control parliamentary legislation. During the last years of Queen Elizabeth's reign, however, tension began to grow between Elizabeth and Parliament. The issue that provoked these tensions was whether the crown or Parliament should have the ultimate responsibility for directing government policy.

Since Elizabeth was the last surviving member of the Tudor dynasty, she made sure to name a successor. Her choice was King James VI of Scotland, the son of Mary Stuart. Although Elizabeth had ordered Mary to be beheaded for treason (see p. 298), her selection of the Stuart family to take the throne of England was not surprising. James was Elizabeth's cousin and her closest living relative. Parliament, therefore, invited James to become the king of England after Elizabeth's death. When James (1603-25) became the king of England, he took the title **James I** because England had never before had a king by that name.

James I—While James was riding toward London to receive the English crown, a group of **Puritans** met him. They presented the king with a petition expressing their desire to see the Church of England purified from "popish" ceremonies. Knowing James had been reared a Presbyterian in Scotland, they hoped he would be sympathetic to their requests. James was not a Presbyterian at heart, however. He ignored all of their requests except for one. He appointed a group of fifty scholars to make a new English translation of the Bible. When completed in 1611, it was called the Authorized Version, although today it is commonly referred to as the King James Version.

James made it very clear from the beginning of his reign that he expected everyone to conform to the Anglican church. On one occasion he told the Puritans that if they did not cooperate, he would "harry them out of the land." True to his threat, James harassed all those who refused to compromise their religious convictions. A small group of Separatists escaped James's persecution. Known as the Pilgrims, they sailed to the New World in search of a land where they could practice their religious beliefs without government opposition.

Not all of James's problems were religious ones. His private life was scandalous. He spent govern-

Solomon's Advice to Kings

At the beginning of King Solomon's reign, God came to him and said, "Ask what I shall give thee." If Solomon had been like most kings in history, he probably would have asked for great riches or absolute power. Instead, he realized the great responsibility he had as ruler and asked for wisdom: "Give therefore thy servant an understanding heart to judge thy people, that I may discern between good and bad: for who is able to judge this thy so great a people?" (I Kings 3:9). God answered his prayer and gave him great wisdom so that there was no king like him before or after him (I Kings 3:12-13). In the book of Proverbs, Solomon gives wise advice to rulers:

- A king that sitteth in the throne of judgment scattereth away all evil with his eyes (20:8).

- A wise king scattereth the wicked, and bringeth the wheel over them (20:26).

- Take away the wicked from before the king, and his throne shall be established in righteousness (25:5).

- The prince that wanteth [lacks] understanding is also a great oppressor: but he that hateth covetousness shall prolong his days (28:16).

- The king by judgment establisheth the land: but he that receiveth gifts overthroweth it (29:4).

- The king that faithfully judgeth the poor, his throne shall be established for ever (29:14).

- Many seek the ruler's favor; but every man's judgment cometh from the Lord (29:26).

Most European rulers of the seventeenth and eighteenth centuries did not follow Solomon's advice. They sought power and wealth rather than wisdom. As a result, their subjects and nations suffered. They "did not choose the fear of the Lord: they would [accept] none of [God's] counsel: they despised all [His] reproof. Therefore shall they eat of the fruit of their own way, and be filled with their own devices" (Prov. 1:29-31).

Since James had financial problems (due in part to the debts that he inherited from Elizabeth), he was forced to call Parliament into session and ask for additional funds. But each time Parliament met, it debated James's foreign and domestic policies. This so infuriated him that he dismissed the House of Commons time after time. "That which concerns the mystery of the King's power is not lawful to be disputed," James said. The only thing that his hasty actions accomplished, however, was to unite his opponents against him.

Charles I—James's son, **Charles I** (1625-49), inherited his father's religious and political views. Charles's policies intensified the tension between the king and Parliament. During his reign the persecution of the Puritans became more severe, causing thousands of them to leave the country and sail for America.

Charles I

ment money extravagantly and relied on personal favorites rather than veteran politicians to give him political advice. James believed he was king by "divine right"—a fact which Parliament did not dispute. But Parliament did question the extent of his authority and was angered over the highhanded manner in which he governed the kingdom.

Like his father, Charles wanted to be an absolute ruler but did not have the army or the bureaucracy to enforce his will. When he convened Parliament, many of its members proved to be quite uncooperative. They demanded that the king recognize their rights to free speech and freedom from arrest. Charles responded to their request by dismissing them. Later he reconvened Parliament, but when they repeated their demands, he dismissed them once again.

In need of funds, Charles was forced to recall Parliament a third time. Angry with the king, members of Parliament drew up a document called the **Petition of Right** (1628). Among other things, it stated that the king did not have the right to make people pay taxes without parliamentary consent and that Parliament would not tolerate arbitrary imprisonment of any subjects. They instructed Charles that if he refused to sign the document, they would not grant him any additional funds. Charles signed the petition, but when Parliament made further demands, he dismissed them once again. From 1629-40 he tried to govern England without calling Parliament into session. He used every means possible to raise money apart from Parliament. He sold knighthoods, forced various individuals to lend him funds, and established high taxes on shipping. In the process, however, he further alienated merchants and landowners.

In spite of everything Charles tried to do, he had to recall Parliament when Scotland rebelled against him. His agents had tried to force the Scottish church to use the Anglican prayer book. The Scots had responded by raising an army to defend their religious liberties. In a very weak position, Charles was ready to make concessions to Parliament. He was forced by financial necessity to sign various acts that greatly strengthened Parliament's power. These acts guaranteed (1) that Parliament would meet every three years even without royal permission; (2) that Parliament could not be dissolved without its own consent; and (3) that no taxes were legal except those passed by Parliament. In addition, Parliament abolished those royal courts that had become tools of Charles's absolutist policy.

Civil War—In the following months the Puritans in Parliament also began to attack the organization of the Anglican church. They demanded an end to episcopal church government and severely criticized the Anglican prayer book. At the same time, Parliament extended its political power by placing the military under its control. Realizing that his power was slipping away, Charles decided to act.

In January of 1642 he foolishly marched into the House of Commons with four hundred armed men. He demanded that five of his strongest critics be put under arrest. These men, however, could not be found. They had escaped from the chamber only minutes before. Charles's rash behavior in this regard served only to antagonize Parliament further.

Each side began gathering an army, and before the year was over, civil war had broken out. Parliament's cause was supported by the Puritans, the lesser gentry, and the merchants. Their opponents called them **Roundheads** because few of them had long hair. Those who supported the king included most members of the nobility. The Roundheads called them **Cavaliers**—a term that referred to the Spanish soldiers, the *cavaliero,* who had killed many Protestants in Europe.

At first the king's forces were victorious. But when Parliament reorganized its army and removed incompetent leaders, the New Model Army, as it was called, gained the upper hand. Under the able leadership of **Oliver Cromwell** (1599-1658), the Roundheads defeated Charles at the Battle of Naseby (1645). This defeat proved to be the deathblow to the Royalist cause. Eleven months later Charles surrendered.

The victory of Parliament's forces did not bring an immediate end to England's problems. The leaders of Parliament and the commanders of the army disagreed over how the new government should be run. Not all who had opposed the king wanted to destroy the monarchy; many simply wanted to limit the king's power. The parliamentary army, however, envisioned a republic where every man would have equal opportunities and privileges. They saw nothing wrong with boldly experimenting with England's longstanding political traditions to attain that end.

When the conservatives (those who wanted only to curb Charles's power) in Parliament realized that the Civil War had gone further than they had intended, they tried to dissolve the army. The

Robert Walker (attributed), Oliver Cromwell, *Bob Jones University Collection of Sacred Art*

error. At first he and the "Rump" jointly governed England, but problems soon arose. Cromwell found, just as Charles I had before him, that it was very difficult to rule with an independent-minded Parliament. So Cromwell dissolved Parliament and ruled without it until his death in 1658.

Taking the title Lord Protector, Cromwell established what is called the **Protectorate.** He ruled in accordance with a written constitution, the *Instrument of Government.* Although his rule was sometimes arbitrary, he was a man of deep religious conviction who sincerely tried to do what he thought was best for the people. Nevertheless, the Protectorate came to an end soon after his death. His son Richard succeeded him as Lord Protector, but he did not have the same forceful personality or leadership ability that his father had. In addition, most Englishmen were dissatisfied with the country's political condition. They wanted the Stuart monarchs to return to the throne.

The Restoration—Sensing the sentiment of the people, Richard allowed the Parliament that Charles I had called in 1640 to reconvene. The members in turn asked Charles's son to take the throne. He accepted their offer, and in 1660 England had a new king—**Charles II** (1660-85).

The reestablishment of the Stuart monarchy is called the **Restoration.** In reality the old monarchy was not restored, because Parliament retained much of the power it had won earlier. In 1679, for example, Parliament again passed the **Habeas Corpus Act** (it had been first passed under Charles I), which made it illegal for the government to arbitrarily hold someone in jail. By obtaining a writ of habeas corpus, a prisoner could force the government to officially charge him with a crime or else release him. This act meant that English monarchs could no longer imprison a person simply for being critical of their policies. Juries could issue verdicts without fear of being imprisoned for rendering unpopular decisions, and the press could openly criticize royal policy.

Although his power was limited, Charles II did his best to remain financially independent of Parliament. He received grants of money from Louis XIV and in return promised to support the objectives of French foreign policy. He also told Louis that he

army, however, refused to disband. It occupied London and expelled several conservatives from the House of Commons. In 1648 the conservatives who remained in Parliament made an alliance with Charles, who had just escaped from captivity and was willing to make several concessions to regain his throne. But Cromwell's army easily put down all resistance. They recaptured Charles and expelled some 140 conservative members from the House of Commons, leaving a governing body of less than one hundred men. (At the beginning of the Civil War the House of Commons had over five hundred members.) The remaining members, together known as the Rump Parliament, set up a special court that tried and condemned the king for treason. On January 30, 1649, Charles I was beheaded.

Oliver Cromwell—The next eleven years (1649-60) were a time of experimentation in new forms of government in England. Cromwell, the leader of the army, had no program for governing the country. Consequently, he ruled by trial and

Studies in Adversity: The Lives of John Milton and John Bunyan

John Milton (1608-74) and John Bunyan (1628-88) are towering figures of seventeenth-century English literature. Each overcame great adversity to write works of literature that have endured for hundreds of years.

Milton is one of the greatest of all English poets. Keenly aware of the political and religious issues of his day, he spent much of his early career writing tracts and pamphlets. He supported the Puritan cause and argued against the corrupt clergy of the Church of England. During Cromwell's Protectorate, he served as Latin secretary to the Council of State. In this position he had opportunity to use his literary skills to defend the Puritan government.

Milton's official duties, however, were soon overshadowed by personal tragedies. In 1651 his infant son died. A year later his wife died, leaving him responsible for the care of three young children. Throughout this period his eyesight steadily weakened; by 1652 he was completely blind. Milton nevertheless continued in his government post and in the writing of poetry. He remarried in 1656, but this wife died also. He lost his position in government in 1660 when the English monarchy was restored under Charles II.

A man of immense scholarship and energy, Milton now devoted himself wholly to his writing. His greatest work, the epic *Paradise Lost,* was published in 1667. This powerful poem recounts the creation, the rebellion of Satan, and the fall of man in the Garden of Eden. The mature Milton, whose life had been one of painful struggles, was not bitter against his Maker. His trust in God is evident in his statement of purpose in the opening lines of *Paradise Lost:* to ''assert Eternal Providence, / And justify the ways of God to man.''

John Bunyan was a preacher. Unlike Milton, he was a man of humble origin and little formal education. During the English Civil War he had served briefly as a soldier in Cromwell's army, taking part in skirmishes with Royalist forces.

After leaving the military, he married and settled down as a tinker (one who repairs metal utensils) in the small village of Bedford. Soon thereafter Bunyan was converted to Christ. He joined a little Baptist church and began studying the Scriptures. Eventually he became pastor of the tiny congregation.

In 1660 he was arrested by government officials. Because he refused to stop preaching, Bunyan was put behind bars. His wife and four children were forced to take care of themselves. (One daughter was blind, and another child died at birth shortly after Bunyan was jailed.) His imprisonment lasted nearly twelve years. During that time he began to write. By the time he was freed from jail in 1672, his masterpiece *The Pilgrim's Progress* was almost complete. Largely autobiographical, this simple but exciting narrative relates the journey of a man named Christian from the City of Destruction to the Celestial City. Translated into more languages than any other book except the Bible, it has encouraged and guided readers for centuries.

would publicly declare himself a Roman Catholic. But despite his promises, Charles did very little that really helped France, and he did not profess Roman Catholicism until he was on his deathbed.

Since Charles II had no legitimate children, he was succeeded by his brother **James II** (1685-88). James was an ardent Roman Catholic and a firm believer in absolutism. In spite of his tactless actions, Parliament decided to tolerate him since he was old and his only heirs were two Protestant daughters. But the political picture changed dramatically in 1688, when James's second wife, a Roman Catholic, gave birth to a son. Members of Parliament feared that England would be brought back into the fold of Rome and that absolutism would be reestablished.

The Glorious Revolution—In June of 1688, leaders of Parliament invited William of Orange (the leader of Protestant Netherlands and husband of James II's daughter Mary) to come to England and take the throne. William accepted and landed in England with a small Dutch army. Many English rallied to support him; when James tried to send his troops against William, he found that even his officers had deserted to the other side. Having no other recourse, James fled to France with his wife and son.

The House of Commons now declared that "King James II, having endeavored to subvert the constitution of the kingdom by breaking the original contract between king and people, and by the advice of Jesuits and other wicked persons having violated the fundamental laws, and having withdrawn himself out of the kingdom, has abdicated the government, and that the throne is vacant." The House also added that "it hath been found by experience to be inconsistent with the safety and welfare of this Protestant kingdom to be governed by a popish prince."

England had undergone a "bloodless" revolution: James II had been dethroned. Parliament invited **William and Mary** to become joint rulers of England. Their reign marked the only time in English history that the country had corulers.

Before members of Parliament officially granted the throne to William and Mary, they drew up a set of conditions that had to be met. Those conditions were embodied in a document called the **Bill of Rights** (1689), which limited royal power, established certain civil liberties, and forbade future kings or queens from being Roman Catholics. William and Mary accepted Parliament's conditions and were crowned William III (1689-1702) and Mary II (1689-94).

In 1701 Parliament passed the **Act of Settlement,** which had far-reaching consequences for the English crown. By this act, Parliament established its right to grant the throne to whomever it wished. The concept of kings ruling by "divine right" had passed away. England had become a nation ruled by constitutional law—that is, law established by tradition and acts of Parliament.

Sir Godfrey Kneller, Mary II, *Bob Jones University Collection of Sacred Art*

The Bill of Rights

In 1689 William III and Mary II signed their names to ''An Act for Declaring the Rights and Liberties of the Subject and for Settling the Succession of the Crown''—a document better known as the Bill of Rights. The English struggle for rights and liberties can be traced all the way back to 1215 when King John signed the Magna Carta at Runnymede. The Bill of Rights of 1689 is a landmark of English constitutional history. It marked the first time that the demands on the monarch were made on behalf of a representative assembly. Among the ''ancient rights and liberties'' declared in the Bill of Rights are the following:

- That the pretended power of suspending of laws . . . without consent of Parliament is illegal.

- That levying money for or to the use of the crown by pretence of prerogative without consent of Parliament for longer time or in other manner than the same is or shall be granted, is illegal.

- That it is the right of the subjects to petition the king, and all commitments and prosecutions for such petitioning, are illegal.

- That the raising or keeping a standing army within the kingdom in time of peace unless it be with consent of Parliament, is against law.

- That the subjects which are Protestants may have arms for their defence suitable to their conditions and as allowed by law.

- That election of members of Parliament ought to be free.

- That the freedom of speech and debates or proceeding in Parliament ought not to be impeached or questioned in any court or place out of Parliament.

- That excessive bail ought not to be required, nor excessive fines imposed, nor cruel and unusual punishments inflicted.

- And that for redress of all grievances and for the amending, strengthening and preserving of the laws Parliament ought to be held frequently.

Cabinet Government—After the reign of Mary's sister, Queen Anne (1702-14), the throne passed to a German, George of Hanover (a descendant of James I). Because the new king, who took the title of George I (1714-27), could not speak English, he had to rely on others to carry out many of the responsibilities of government. During his reign and the reign of his successor, George II (1727-60), the cabinet system of government developed in England.

Cabinet government first began during the reign of Charles II, who often called his closest advisers to his office—called a ''cabinet''—to discuss matters of state. George I, who had little interest in political matters, did not attend cabinet meetings. He left the affairs of government in the hands of his chief minister, Robert Walpole, who is regarded as the first prime minister of England. Executive powers gradually shifted from the king to the chief ministers of the king's cabinet. Later the prime minister and the cabinet, who were originally responsible only to the king, became accountable to Parliament.

Section Review

1. What body in England competed with the monarchy for authority? What special privilege did that body hold over the monarchy?
2. What family succeeded the Tudors to the throne of England? What member of this family succeeded Queen Elizabeth to the throne?
3. What English king was beheaded during the English Civil War? Who was the leader of the Roundheads, the parliamentary forces?
4. Who came to the English throne as a result of a ''bloodless'' revolution?
5. What English document placed limits on royal power, guaranteed fundamental liberties of the English people, and prohibited future English monarchs from being Roman Catholic?

The Whigs and the Tories

As the English Parliament grew in power and influence, factions developed within its ranks. These competing groups were the forerunners of Britain's first political parties—the Whigs and the Tories.

After the Restoration in 1660, Parliament was sharply divided over the policies of Charles II. Some members disliked the favoritism he showed toward the Roman Catholics and France. Many were opposed to the idea of having the throne pass to the Roman Catholic James, duke of York. The leader of this opposition, the earl of Shaftesbury, realized that if he could influence a majority of votes in Parliament he could control the government and the king. His group became known as the Country party.

Another group consisted of those who considered the person of the king and his rightful heir sacred. Led by the king himself, this group became known as the Court party. It came into open conflict with the Country party as the years passed and Charles did not produce a legitimate son. Those opposing the succession of James introduced a bill into Parliament excluding him from the throne.

The fight over the bill was intense, but the Court party succeeded in stopping it. In the heated debates each side had begun to call the other names. Those against James were called "Whigs"—a name applied to Scottish robbers who killed their victims before plundering them. Those supporting James were called "Tories"—a name applied to Irish rebels. Soon the opposing parties adopted these nicknames as their official titles.

The Whigs led the Glorious Revolution of 1688, but some Tories also supported it. Once the matter of Protestant succession to the throne had been settled by act of Parliament, the two parties shifted their attention to other issues.

The divisions between them were never as sharp again. The Tory party continued to favor the king and the Anglican church and opposed great change in the status quo. The Whigs were now willing to support the king, but they also favored a policy of religious toleration and were eager to see certain changes made in government policy. Although the Whig party died out, the Tory party has continued to the present.

Balance of Power

To increase their power on the Continent, some European monarchs used their armies to seize the territories of weaker nations. Each ruler watched his neighbors closely, making sure they did not become too strong. Nations formed alliances in an effort to preserve the **balance of power,** thereby hoping to ensure that no one nation would dominate the other countries of Europe. When they felt is was necessary, they went to war in order to maintain this balance. Because war often demonstrated new strengths and weaknesses in nations, there were many shifts in diplomatic alliances. Countries that had previously been enemies often became friends, and nations that were once allied squared off against each other. Despite the many changes in alliances during the eighteenth century, Prussia remained the constant foe of Austria, and England was always aligned against France. The workings of this system of alliances are demonstrated by the three major wars of this period.

War of the Spanish Succession

In 1700 the Hapsburg king of Spain died, leaving no direct heir to the Spanish throne. In his will he granted the throne to his young grandnephew Philip, who was also the grandson of Louis XIV of France. Louis, seeing an opportunity to make political and territorial gains, claimed the Spanish throne for Philip. Other nations in Europe—especially England and the Netherlands—feared what the union of France and Spain might bring. They formed the **Grand Alliance** to block Louis's actions.

The armies of the Grand Alliance won many victories on the European continent. At Blenheim in 1704, they almost wiped out the French force. In 1705 England captured Gibraltar, a post on the southern tip of Spain. The English also fought the French in North America in what was called Queen Anne's War. The war ended in 1713 with the signing of a series of agreements called the **Treaty of Utrecht,** which included the following provisions:

1. Philip was allowed to retain the throne of Spain as long as the crowns of France and Spain were not united.
2. Spain had to surrender her possessions in the Netherlands and in the Mediterranean area to Austria.
3. Britain won various Canadian territories from France: Newfoundland, Nova Scotia, and the Hudson Bay territory. In addition, Britain kept the strategic Mediterranean port of Gibraltar. (During the war England and Scotland were united into a single kingdom called Great Britain. From that time on it is proper to speak of Britain rather than England.)

Maria Theresa

War of the Austrian Succession (1740-48)

"Because a Monarch robbed a neighbor he had promised to defend, red men scalped each other by the Great Lakes of America, while black men fought on the [Indian] coast of Coromandel." These words by the British historian Thomas Macaulay describe the War of the Austrian Succession—a conflict that spread to three continents.

In 1713 the emperor of Austria, Charles VI, drew up a document called the **Pragmatic Sanction.** It was designed to prevent Austria's neighbors from taking advantage of his daughter, Maria Theresa, once she came to the Austrian throne. The rulers who signed the document agreed to respect the territorial boundaries of Austria, allowing Maria Theresa to rule in peace.

One ruler who had no intention of abiding by the agreement that his father had signed was Frederick II of Prussia. He desired the rich mining area of Silesia, which belonged to Austria, and decided to seize it by force. In August of 1740, after Maria Theresa had been empress for only two months, Frederick invaded the province. By the following year Prussia had firmly established its hold on Silesia and had signed a peace treaty with Austria.

The situation in Europe became more complicated when France entered the war against Austria, hoping to gain territory at Austria's expense. Spain also entered the war; she wanted to retrieve the Italian lands she had lost to Austria in 1713. Britain, fearful of French power and Prussia's threat to George II's Hanoverian domains, entered the war on the side of Austria.

The war was not confined to the European continent, however. It spread to North America, where the British defeated the French, and to India, where the French defeated the British. Weary of war, the nations of Europe finally decided to end the conflict. The **Treaty of Aix-la-Chapelle** was signed in 1748. This treaty did not settle the differences among the nations; it merely ended the fighting temporarily. Except for Silesia, which Frederick was allowed to keep, the treaty restored the *status quo ante bellum* (how things were before the war).

Seven Years' War (1756-63)

In 1754 fighting (called the French and Indian War) broke out between France and Britain in the New World. At the same time, Frederick II decided to take some more of Austria's territory. He assumed that France would not interfere, for France and Austria had been bitter enemies for centuries. Neither did he fear British reprisals, for he had just signed a defensive alliance with Britain in January of 1756. But Frederick miscalculated. France unexpectedly reversed her foreign policy. Fearing the growing threat of Prussia's might, France put aside her old antagonism for the Austrian Hapsburgs and joined with Austria to stop Prussian expansion. This radical change in alliances is called the **Diplomatic Revolution**. It set the stage for the **Seven Years' War**.

Soon after the fighting broke out, the British statesman **William Pitt** the Elder devised a system for winning the war. His strategy called for supplying Prussia with financial aid and using that nation to keep French troops preoccupied in Europe. In the meantime, Britain would attempt to destroy French sea power, making it easier to defeat the French in North America and India.

Britain had tremendous success with her part of the plan. In North America she had over forty thousand regular and colonial troops. By the end of the war, they had seized many French forts and had captured the key French city of Quebec. In India, British forces under the leadership of Robert Clive defeated the French and the Indian princes who had allied with them.

On the continent of Europe, however, Prussia ran into difficulties. Open hostilities began when Frederick II invaded the neighboring kingdom of Saxony. He soon found himself surrounded by enemies. Russia, Sweden, most of the German states, and Spain had joined France and Austria in opposing Prussia. At first Frederick's superior army and his brilliant leadership kept his enemies at bay. But his opponents outnumbered him, and although he

The British won the Seven Years' War in North America (where it was known as the French and Indian War) with the capture of the French fortress of Quebec in 1759. Shown in this eighteenth-century engraving is the climactic Battle of the Plains of Abraham outside the city.

The Duke of Marlborough and the "Toothpick Wars"

Historian John Keegan described the wars between the rulers of Europe in the 1600s and 1700s as "two hundred years of toothpick campaigning for advantage in each cavity and crevice of each other's borderlands." Unlike modern "total wars" of huge armies and massive destruction, these "toothpick wars" were more like chess matches. Rulers considered their armies too valuable to risk lightly in fighting. Armies marched and countermarched trying to gain some advantage in position over their opponents. A successful "campaign" might consist of a series of marches which threatened an enemy's supply line and forced him to retreat—without offering battle. Avoiding battle was surprisingly easy because fortifications were so much more advanced than artillery that an army in its defense works was almost invulnerable. This situation made it easy not to lose a war but rather difficult to win one. Only a remarkable commander could achieve great victories under such circumstances. One soldier who succeeded in winning resounding triumphs was Englishman John Churchill, duke of Marlborough (1650-1722).

Marlborough was the supreme commander of the diverse forces of the Grand Coalition during the War of the Spanish Succession. He had to be both soldier and politician because he not only commanded British, Dutch, and German forces but also had to please the respective rulers of the nations of the Grand Alliance. The Netherlands, for example, would not let her troops stray far from Dutch territory, no matter how hard her allies might be pressed by the French.

Marlborough needed outright victories to win the war; he had to destroy the French ability to fight. Yet the French were perfectly content to stay behind their fortified lines and make Marlborough attack them. Faced with all his difficulties, he had to devise a way to draw the French out while uniting his diverse forces. No campaign of Marlborough's illustrates his skill better than that which climaxed with the Battle of Blenheim.

The ruler of Bavaria surprised the Grand Alliance by joining forces with the French. This meant that the French were suddenly only a few

days' march from Vienna, the Holy Roman Emperor's capital. In addition, the Alliance's forces were divided between the Netherlands and southern Germany. Brilliantly, Marlborough turned this grave situation to his advantage. He made it his opportunity to bring the French to battle—and defeat.

Marlborough arranged for his German allies to gather in southern Germany. Meanwhile he prepared to move his British-Dutch force of forty thousand men from the Netherlands. It marched over two hundred miles right in front of the French army to unite with the other Alliance forces. The commander painstakingly organized deposits of food and supplies along the march ahead of his troops. All the while he confused the French by making it appear that he intended to attack France directly. He even had a bridge built across the Rhine River at one point to reinforce this idea.

At last, his united forces faced a surprised and outmaneuvered French-Bavarian army near the town of Blenheim on the River Danube. In a sharp attack, Marlborough's forces pinned the two wings of their enemy's army and broke through its center. Those French and Bavarians who could do so, retreated. Fourteen thousand, however, had to surrender to the Alliance forces, and twenty thousand were killed or wounded. It was the most shattering defeat ever inflicted on the armies of Louis XIV. As commander and diplomat, Marlborough delivered the nation of England from peril. Two hundred years later, one of his descendants, Winston Churchill, would perform the same service for that nation during the dark days of World War II.

won battles, he despaired of ever winning the war. In addition, when George III became the new British monarch in 1760, he cut off all subsidies to Prussia. By the end of that year, the Russian army had burned Berlin, and all seemed lost. Frederick and Prussia, nevertheless, survived the conflict because Russia dropped out of the war. In 1762 a new czar who greatly admired Frederick II came to the throne. He withdrew his troops from Prussian territory and signed an agreement with Frederick. Unable to continue without Russian support, Frederick's other opponents withdrew from the conflict one by one. The Treaty of Hubertusberg (1763) brought the war to a close on the continent of Europe; it allowed Frederick to maintain his hold on Silesia.

In that same year, France, Britain, and Spain signed the **Treaty of Paris.** This settlement had a number of important consequences:

1. France lost all territory on the mainland of North America. Britain acquired all of Canada, as well as French territory east of the Mississippi.

2. France lost most of her commercial holdings in India. The Battle of Plassey (see p. 483) paved the way for the British East India Company to eventually take over all of India.

3. Spain lost Florida to Great Britain but received New Orleans and Louisiana from France in return.

As a result of the Seven Years' War, England became not only the leading European power but also a major world power.

The Partition of Poland

The balance of power was not always maintained by war; sometimes diplomatic negotiations proved to be more effective. One such case in the eighteenth century involved the nation of Poland. Poland was a large, independent nation that lacked natural boundaries by which her people could easily defend their territory. In addition, the Polish government was weak and inefficient. Her greedy neighbors—Prussia, Russia, and Austria—all plot-

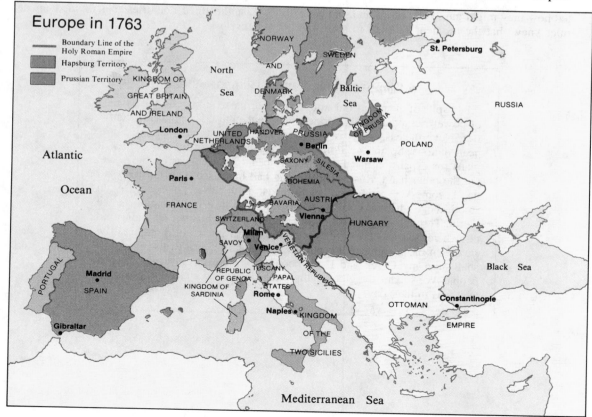

Europe in 1763

Partition of Poland

1772
1793
1795

Baltic Sea

St. Petersburg

RUSSIA

Dvina R.

Danzig
(to Prussia 1793)

EAST PRUSSIA

PRUSSIA
Berlin

TO PRUSSIA

Warsaw
TO AUSTRIA

TO RUSSIA

Oder R.

Vistula R.

Dnieper R.

AUSTRIA

Vienna

Dniester R.

OTTOMAN EMPIRE

territory he wanted, the others would step in to stop him. So through secret negotiation, Prussia, Russia, and Austria agreed to partition Poland among themselves. On three separate occasions during the years 1772 to 1795, these nations seized Polish territory until finally Poland disappeared from the map of Europe. It was not until after World War I that Poland again became an independent nation.

Section Review

1. What did European monarchs seek to preserve in order to make sure that their neighbors did not become too strong and thus able to threaten their borders?
2. What treaty ended the War of the Spanish Succession? What territory did Britain receive as a result of this war?
3. What country and monarch was the Pragmatic Sanction designed to protect?
4. What is the dramatic change in alliances among the major European powers prior to the Seven Years' War called?
5. List the three countries that divided up defenseless Poland.

ted how they might gain parts of Poland, but each ruler knew that the moment he tried to seize the

A Glimpse Behind and a Glimpse Ahead

In spite of the greed and ambition of European monarchs, the balance of power remained intact during the seventeenth and eighteenth centuries. Nevertheless, there was a realignment of power among the European nations. Spain and Portugal greatly declined in influence. French plans for expansion had failed, and Hapsburg power was on the wane. On the other hand, Russia and Prussia had increased their territory and had become key nations on the European political scene. Great Britain stood above all others as the most powerful and richest nation in the world. Through her acquisition of territory in North America, India, and elsewhere, she was laying the foundation for a great world empire. The statement of an eighteenth-century Englishman reflects British pride: ''I shall burn my Greek and Latin books. They are the histories of little people. We subdue the globe in three campaigns and a globe as big again as it was in their day.''

Chapter Review

Can You Explain?

absolute power	lieutenant	Roundheads	balance of power
divine right	Junkers	Cavaliers	*status quo ante bellum*
intendents	czar	cabinet government	Diplomatic Revolution
Frondes			

Can You Identify?

Bourbon	Frederick I	Puritans	War of the Spanish
Henry IV	Frederick William I	1611	Succession
Louis XIII	Frederick II (''the	Charles I	Grand Alliance
Cardinal Richelieu	Great'')	Petition of Right	Treaty of Utrecht (1713)
Thirty Years' War	Hohenzollern	Oliver Cromwell	War of the Austrian
(1618-48)	Hapsburg	Protectorate	Succession
Gustavus Adolphus	Joseph II	Restoration (1660)	Pragmatic Sanction
Louis XIV	Ivan IV	Habeas Corpus Act	Treaty of Aix-la-Chapelle
Cardinal Mazarin	Romanov	James II	Seven Years' War
Jean-Baptiste Colbert	Peter I (''the Great'')	Glorious Revolution	William Pitt
1685	Great Northern War	(1688)	Treaty of Paris (1763)
Versailles	Catherine II (''the	William and Mary	
Louis XV	Great'')	Bill of Rights (1689)	
Frederick William	James I	Act of Settlement	

Can You Locate?

Rhine River	Austria	Gibraltar	Aix-la-Chapelle
Brandenburg	St. Petersburg	Utrecht	Saxony
Prussia	Baltic Sea	Silesia	Poland
Berlin	Black Sea	Hanover	

How Much Do You Remember?

1. What two groups did Richelieu attack in order to increase royal power in France? What methods did he use to accomplish his attacks on these groups?

2. List one major accomplishment for each of the following Prussian rulers that strengthened the Prussian state: Frederick William, Frederick I, Frederick William I, and Frederick II.

3. List one domestic and one foreign goal or policy for both Peter I and Catherine II of Russia.

4. Explain how each of the following documents/laws passed by the British Parliament restrained British monarchs from increasing their royal power: the Petition of Right, the Habeas Corpus Act, the Bill of Rights, and the Act of Settlement.

5. Explain how the policy of balance of power is demonstrated in each of the following wars: War of the Spanish Succession, War of the Austrian Succession, and the Seven Years' War.

What Do You Think?

1. In what ways was the Thirty Years' War a religious war? In what ways was it a political war?

2. Do you think that Louis XIV helped create a stronger, more unified country by revoking the Edict of Nantes?

3. Like Huguenots and Puritans, Christians in every age have faced some degree of government persecution. What should be a Christian's response to government persecution? (Note the response of Daniel's three friends in Daniel 3:16-17.)

Notes
1. James Harvey Robinson and Charles A. Beard, *Readings in Modern European History* (Boston: Ginn and Co., 1908), 1:6-7.
2. Ibid., p. 10.

"Let not the wise man glory."

> Thus saith the Lord, Let not the wise man glory in his wisdom, neither let the mighty man glory in his might, let not the rich man glory in his riches: But let him that glorieth glory in this, that he understandeth and knoweth me, that I am the Lord which exercise lovingkindness, judgment, and righteousness, in the earth: for in these things I delight, saith the Lord.
>
> —Jeremiah 9:23-24

When God created man in His image, He gave him (among other things) the gift of reason. Because of sin, however, man's understanding is darkened, and he is filled with spiritual blindness (Eph. 4:18). It is only by the entrance of God's Word into the heart that a person receives light and understanding (Ps. 119:130). Unfortunately, during the seventeenth and eighteenth centuries, known as the **Age of Reason,** many individuals refused to acknowledge the authority of Scripture and instead exalted their reason to a place of supreme authority. On the other hand, there were those who did not reject the importance of reason but at the same time accepted the authority of Scripture. Such individuals used their reason to reject the false traditions of the past and did not use it to attack biblical truth. In this chapter we will examine the effects of these two attitudes upon science, philosophy, religion, and the arts.

Scientific Discoveries

During the Middle Ages, people relied on two principal authorities for their understanding of the universe: ancient philosophers and church tradition. Few questioned the validity of what the ancient philosophers or the Roman Catholic church had to teach. No one sought to uncover new knowledge about God's world. Instead they simply sought to lend support to established ideas.

The intellectual atmosphere in Europe had changed by the sixteenth century. The Renaissance had rekindled a desire for learning, and the Reformation had reasserted the Bible as the trustworthy authority for man's understanding. Thoughtful individuals began to find errors and inadequacies in church tradition and the writings of pagan philosophers. They discovered that these accepted "authorities" were unreliable. Realizing that they could no longer trust what the Roman church had to say about the Bible, they wanted to search out the truths of God's Word for themselves. Similarly, as they could no longer depend on what ancient philosophers had to say about God's universe, they wanted to seek out the laws of nature for themselves. Many of these men saw in science a means

of glorifying God: they could examine the handiwork of His creation and find practical knowledge to help their fellow man. It was this renewed search for understanding of the physical world that led to the birth of modern science.

The Scientific Method

Scientists use the **scientific method** when seeking answers to their questions about the physical world. This method is a pattern of thinking that includes the following steps:

1. Recognizing the inadequacy of existing knowledge to explain a given question.
2. Gathering observations in an attempt to find possible answers.
3. Seeking to find a pattern in the observations upon which to base conclusions or theories.
4. Choosing the most appropriate conclusion to explain the observations.
5. Verifying the derived conclusion by further observation and experimentation.

Through this method of inquiry, scientists are able to gain a better understanding of the orderly function of God's universe. But although science is a useful tool in obtaining knowledge, it has its limitations. It can explain *how* something happens, but it cannot explain *why* it occurs that way. Nor can it make moral judgments. Science is limited to what men observe about the physical world; it cannot, for example, deal with the origin of the universe. In addition, scientific inquiry is limited by man's nature. Men are finite and fallible: scientists are limited in their observations and may reach wrong conclusions. Because scientific knowledge is constantly expanding, scientific "facts" are often proved incorrect. This happened frequently during the late Reformation period when scientists dispelled many ancient and medieval superstitions.

The Scientific Tools

New tools helped seventeenth-century scientists in their investigation of the physical world. Astronomers developed telescopes, which allowed them to study the movement of stars and planets. With microscopes scientists could see bacteria and other organisms not visible to the naked eye. The thermometer and barometer presented new opportunities for a closer study of weather. These and other inventions gave scientists access to a wealth of new and more accurate data.

With the expansion of scientific knowledge, scientists needed a more precise way to express their theories about their observations. Mathematics soon became the language of science. Calculus, analytical geometry, logarithms, and the slide rule enhanced scientific investigation and made possible further scientific discoveries.

Isaac Newton's telescope

The Scientific Revolution

From the Renaissance to the eighteenth century, scientific inquiry and achievement advanced so rapidly that historians often speak of a **scientific revolution.** This "revolution" greatly increased man's knowledge of the physical universe. Old myths and legends were discarded as men discovered the principles that God established to govern His creation.

Astronomy

Astronomy, the study of celestial bodies, is a very ancient science. Even the Magi (Matt. 2:1-12) seem to have been astronomers. Until the sixteenth century, astronomers usually relied on the theories of the ancient Greek geographer Ptolemy. He taught that the entire universe revolves around the earth—a theory known as the geocentric or "earth-centered" theory. The changes that came with the scientific revolution transformed astronomy, radically altering it as a science.

Copernicus—The Polish astronomer **Nicolaus Copernicus** (kuh PUR nih kus; 1473-1543) questioned Ptolemy's theory of the universe. Copernicus, who did not have a telescope to study the heavens, used instruments such as the astrolabe to measure the position of stars and planets in the skies. He found that the movements of heavenly bodies would be difficult to explain if the earth were the center of the universe. The Polish scholar, therefore, concluded that the sun is the center and that the earth and other planets orbit around it. This view is called the **heliocentric** (sun-centered) **theory.** The Roman Catholic church, which had officially embraced the old geocentric approach, opposed the publication of Copernicus's findings. Men who accepted the heliocentric theory risked being branded as heretics by the church.

Kepler—The noted German astronomer **Johannes Kepler** (1571-1630), a Lutheran, did not fear the threats of the Roman church. Although he agreed with Copernicus that the earth revolves around the sun, he disagreed with him on the nature of the orbit. Copernicus had taught that the orbits of the planets are circular. Kepler, however, found that the orbits are elliptical (oval-shaped). A devout

Comets

Until well into the sixteenth century, most people had a superstitious fear of comets. In fact, from ancient times people viewed them as evil omens. Even as late as 1556 Thomas Digges wrote, "Comets signify corruption of the stars. They are signs of earthquakes, of wars, of changing of kingdoms, great dearth of corn, yea, a common death of man and beast."

Since disastrous events sometimes coincided with the appearance of a comet, such superstitions persisted. The Roman emperor Vespasian believed that a comet seen in A.D. 79 was an evil sign, but he supposedly remarked, "This hairy star does not concern me; it menaces the king of the Parthians [Rome's enemy], for he is hairy and I am bald."[1] Yet it was Vespasian who died in A.D. 79, and in that same year an eruption from Mount Vesuvius buried the cities of Pompeii and Herculaneum. Thus the course of events reinforced some people's fear.

In 1066 another comet appeared in the sky, greatly alarming the English Saxons. They had just experienced the death of their king, Edward the Confessor, and wondered what else the year had in store for them. In October the Saxons

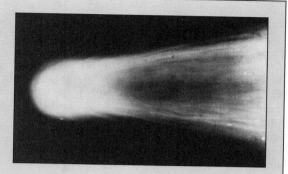

were defeated at the Battle of Hastings and King Harold was killed. William of Normandy went on to become the new ruler of England.

The comet that had appeared in 1066 was the same one that the Englishman Edmund Halley viewed in 1682. Halley's observation and study indicated that the comet he had seen moved around the sun in an elliptical orbit. He further calculated that it appeared on a regular basis approximately every seventy-five years. When the comet appeared again in 1758 as Halley had predicted, astronomers appropriately named it Halley's Comet. It reappeared in 1835, in 1910, and in 1986; its next appearance should be in 2061.

Christian, Kepler prayed that God would keep his investigations free from personal bias: "I ask God to make my spirit strong so that I direct my glance at the pure truth, from whichever side it should be presented, and do not let myself be misled, as so often happens today, by the admiration or contempt of persons or sides."[2]

Galileo—The best-known astronomer in history is probably the Italian **Galileo Galilei** (GAL-uh-LAY-oh GAL-uh-LAY-ee; 1564-1642). Galileo made important contributions to other scientific fields as well—notably physics. As a young man he observed a lamp swinging in the Pisa cathedral. As he watched, he wondered if there was a regular rhythm to the swing. After repeated experiments with pendulums, he found that though he increased the size of the arc, the pendulum still swung in

rhythm. Galileo, therefore, suggested the use of the pendulum to measure time. The results of his work

View of the Pisa cathedral and baptistry from the famous Leaning Tower

can be seen today in timepieces such as the grandfather clock.

Galileo improved upon a Dutch invention, the telescope, and used it in his own work. He confirmed the heliocentric theory and agreed with Kepler that the planets move in elliptical orbits. When Galileo published his findings, however, he also came into conflict with the powerful Roman Catholic church, which tried him for heresy. He was told that unless he retracted his contention that the earth moved, he would be excommunicated. Kneeling before the Inquisitors, he publicly retracted, but according to legend, as he rose from his knees he muttered, ''But it does move!''

Newton—The same year that Galileo died, **Isaac Newton** (1642-1727) was born in England. Like Galileo, he was an astronomer who also contributed to several other fields, such as physics and mathematics. For example, he demonstrated with a prism that ''white light'' is actually composed of many different colors. With his invention of the reflecting telescope and his development of calculus, Newton was able to make more accurate observations and to apply mathematics to the study of the universe.

We remember Newton best for his discovery of the laws of gravity. According to a story related by the French philosopher Voltaire, Newton once observed an apple falling from a tree. Intrigued by this event, he began to wonder why objects fall. From his observation and experimentation, he formulated his famous theory of gravitation. He explained not only why objects fall to the ground but also how planets are held in their orbits by the pull of gravity. Newton expressed these ideas in his greatest work, *Principia,* published in 1687. His contributions won him the esteem of his day; the English poet Alexander Pope praised his achievements: ''Nature and nature's Laws lay hid in Night: / God said, 'Let Newton be!' and all was light.''

Medicine

While astronomy led the way for scientific development in the Age of Reason, there were many important discoveries in other fields. The study of medicine, which involved the practical application

Isaac Newton

of these discoveries, was greatly affected by the scientific revolution.

Vesalius—In 1543 **Andreas Vesalius** (vuh SAY lee us; 1514-64) of Flanders published his great treatise on human anatomy, *On the Fabric of the Human Body.* He gained his information for this monumental work from the dissection of cadavers (corpses). By examining the actual structure of the human body, Vesalius disproved many ridiculous ancient theories, such as the idea that the heart contained a bone. With a clearer understanding of how the human body functions, doctors were better able to treat illness and disease. For his contribution to science, Vesalius has been called ''the Father of Anatomy.''

Paracelsus—The Swiss-born P.A.T. Bombast Van Hohenheim (1493-1541) made the first clinical study of disease and established the use of chemicals in the treatment of illness. He became better known by his self-given name, **Paracelsus** (PEHR uh SEL sus), which means ''better than Celsus,'' a famous Roman physician. Paracelsus suggested that since the human body is chemical in nature, chemicals should be used to treat disease. Although not all his prescriptions were safe or effective, he advanced the science of medicine.

Harvey—The Englishman **William Harvey** (1578-1657), called ''the Father of Experimental Biology,'' helped prepare the way for modern medicine. He carefully studied the heart and circulation of the blood. Ancient theory held that both the heart and the liver prepared different kinds of blood, which were sent to the different parts of the body to be consumed. Harvey discovered that the heart alone acts as pump, pushing blood through the arteries and the veins. In this way blood is not ''consumed'' but constantly circulated.

Jenner—Another Englishman, **Edward Jenner** (1749-1823), developed the smallpox vaccination. His work in his field is a model of the scientific method. First, he observed that milkmaids who contracted the disease cowpox did not contract smallpox, a dreaded disease that kills or horribly disfigures its victims. Jenner speculated that if a person were inoculated with the fluid from a cow-

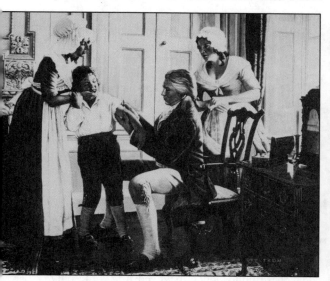

Edward Jenner practicing his method of vaccinating against smallpox

pox sore he would then be immune to smallpox. He tested his theory by inoculating a boy with cowpox, from which the child contracted only a mild case. Later he inoculated the same boy with smallpox. The child did not contract this disease. Jenner called this method of inoculation against

disease **''vaccination''** after the Latin word *vaccinia,* meaning ''cowpox.'' Today, because of Jenner's work, smallpox has been nearly wiped out.

Chemistry

The modern concepts of chemistry developed out of the medieval ''science'' of alchemy. This practice owed more to magic than to science; alchemists mixed chemical ''elixirs'' and ''potions'' in an attempt to achieve some fantastic results—such as changing lead into gold. Needless to say, their attempts failed miserably. With the coming of the scientific revolution, scientists no longer practiced alchemy. Instead they analyzed chemicals to determine their properties.

Boyle—The Irishman **Robert Boyle** (1627-91) was the first to publish the law of inverse gas pressure. Boyle found that increasing pressure upon a gas reduces its volume, while lessening the pressure causes the volume to expand. Scientists call

Robert Boyle

this principle "Boyle's law." In addition to his study of chemistry, Boyle, who was a sincere Christian, diligently studied the Bible. He lectured in defense of Christianity and sought to refute, as he put it, "notorious infidels." He even left money in his will so that these lectures could be continued after his death.

Priestley—English chemist **Joseph Priestley** (1733-1804) discovered several important chemical substances: ammonia, oxygen, nitrous oxide (better known as "laughing gas"), hydrochloric acid, and carbon dioxide, among others. Modern carbonated beverages owe their existence to his work with carbon dioxide. Priestley, who was influenced by his friend Benjamin Franklin, also performed experiments with electricity.

Lavoisier—"The Father of Modern Chemistry" was the Frenchman **Antoine Laurent Lavoisier** (luh VWAH ZEE AY; 1743-94). He used logical rather than fanciful terminology for chemicals. For example, he named one substance hydrogen ("water former") because it forms water vapor when mixed with air. Lavoisier also formulated the law of conservation of matter, which states that matter cannot be created or destroyed; it only changes in form.

Contributions in Other Scientific Fields

Many other scientists contributed to the scientific revolution. **Anton van Leeuwenhoek** (LAY wun hook; 1632-1723) of the Netherlands greatly improved the microscope by making lenses that could magnify up to 160 times. With these lenses

Lavoisier in his laboratory

he discovered the existence of microbes and bacteria. **Gerhardus Mercator** (mur KAY tur; 1512-94) from Flanders devised a way to map the earth on a flat surface. Today the Mercator projection, as it is called, is still a standard pattern for mapmaking.

Section Review

1. What were the two principal authorities for truth during the Middle Ages?
2. List three new instruments that aided scientific investigation of the physical world.
3. What Polish astronomer challenged the earth-centered theory of the universe? What is his view called?
4. What contribution did Edward Jenner make to the field of medicine?
5. Who is "the Father of Modern Chemistry"?

Intellectual Attitudes

Scientific discoveries prompted philosophers to apply the scientific method to their study of man and to their search for truth. In doing so, they placed such a strong emphasis on the power of human reason that this period of history is known as the Age of Reason. It culminated in an eighteenth-century intellectual movement called the **Enlightenment**.

Philosophers of the Enlightenment looked to human reason as the solution for all of life's problems. They praised reason for making possible the achievements of science and providing new ap-

proaches to learning. Reason, they believed, was the gateway to human progress. No longer was reason considered just a method of gaining knowledge; these philosophers believed it was the only sure source of knowledge and truth—an attitude known as **rationalism**.

Forerunners of the Enlightenment

Approaches to Learning

New approaches to learning aided the expansion of knowledge during the seventeenth century.

Irrational Fashions

If one were to judge the Age of Reason by the hair styles of the period, the age would be considered anything but reasonable. Early in the seventeenth century, Louis XIII, who was bald, introduced the wearing of wigs. When Louis XIV began to go bald, he too began wearing wigs. He had a number of large, elaborate ones for each occasion.

While some men wore wigs over their own short hair, many others shaved their heads, and, like the king, had wigs for all occasions. In the eighteenth century, powdered wigs became fashionable. Not only did the men powder their wigs, but they also powdered their faces. They hoped such powdering would disguise their age, making them look younger.

If men's hair fashions appear to be a little ridiculous, they cannot be compared with the absurd women's styles. Women's hair was dressed over pads of wire frames so that it could be supported to great heights. (Some hair styles, it is said, were five feet high!) The hair was kept in place with a kind of clay paste. It was then powdered and decorated with fruit, flowers, jewels, or sometimes with models of such things as stage sets and ships. Because it took hours to fashion these follies, women did not take down their hair for months. As a result, lice, spiders, and even mice would take up their abode in the hair. Ladies who wanted more than one of these hair styles shaved their heads and wore wigs.

Other fashions, in addition to hair styles, illustrate the vanity of the age. Men outfitted themselves in silks, satins, and laces and strutted around very much like the peacocks they kept in their gardens. Women sometimes wore small black patches in the shapes of moons, stars, and comets on their faces. Both men and women carried looking glasses so that they could admire themselves from time to time.

Two methods of reasoning—the inductive and the deductive—assisted scientists in their investigation of the physical world and aided philosophers in their quest to understand that world.

Inductive Reasoning—One of the leading advocates of the inductive method of reasoning was the English philosopher Sir **Francis Bacon** (1561-1626). In his important work *Novum Organum,* he criticized the manner in which many ancient and medieval philosophers arrived at their conclusions about the natural world. Their hasty generalizations, he asserted, created great obstacles for later generations. Believing that men must get rid of all false ideas before they can arrive at truth, Bacon questioned all existing knowledge. He advocated the use of careful observation and experimentation before arriving at general conclusions. Scientists, he asserted, should form tentative conclusions and then gather more information in order to verify their results. Reasoning like this—from specific cases to a general conclusion—is called the **inductive method.**

Bacon believed that man, using this rational approach, could discover and understand truth.

Likewise, he could dispel superstition and error. Many of Bacon's contemporaries, however, objected to his insistence that all knowledge should be questioned. They considered his method an assault on religion. Bacon answered this charge: "If the matter be truly considered, natural philosophy is, after the word of God, at once the surest medicine against superstition and the most approved nourishment for faith; and therefore she is rightly given to religion as her most faithful handmaid, since the one displays the will of God, the other is his power." Unfortunately, less than a century later, men exalted reason as the highest authority, placing it above faith in God and His Word.

Deductive Reasoning—Another method of gaining knowledge was advanced by the French philosopher and mathematician **René Descartes** (day KART; 1596-1650). He feared that man could be deceived by his senses and that observation and experimentation were therefore unreliable. While Bacon let observation and experience guide his rea-

son, Descartes relied on reason aided by the methods of mathematics. Like Bacon, however, Descartes believed that every false idea and prejudice had to be discarded before one could arrive at truth. This led him to doubt everything. The first step in his system of thought was to find some truth or idea that could not be doubted. No one, he believed, could doubt that man is a thinking being, capable of understanding truth. Thus he began his quest for truth with the premise, "I doubt, therefore I think; I think, therefore I am." On this premise he built his system of thought. He taught that by starting with such a simple premise, through careful logic, men could arrive at another, more complex truth. This system is called the **deductive method** of reasoning.

Explanations of Reality

Inductive and deductive reasoning were vital elements of the scientific method, helping scientists to understand the natural world. But could these same reasoning processes be applied to the study

of man and society? Through reason, could man comprehend the spiritual realm? And what was the relationship between the physical and spiritual worlds? Philosophers of the seventeenth century sought answers to these questions.

Descartes—From a man-centered perspective, René Descartes constructed a system of philosophy known as **dualism** (*dual* meaning "two"). According to Descartes there are two types of reality: mind (the spiritual world) and matter (the physical world). While Descartes admitted that there are certain spiritual truths (such as the existence of God) that reason cannot discover, he taught that man can discover truths about the physical world only by using his reason. In fact, Descartes emphasized reason so strongly that he stated, "We should never allow ourselves to be persuaded of anything except by the evidence of our reason."

Spinoza—Another philosopher who emphasized the importance of reason was **Baruch Spinoza** (spih NOH zah; 1632-77). Like Descartes, Spinoza used mathematical deduction to develop his ideas. But unlike Descartes, Spinoza did not regard mind and matter as distinct. He taught that everything in the universe, whether it be spiritual or physical, is all part of one great substance called "God." This view is called **pantheism**.

The Bible, of course, teaches that God is everywhere (see Ps. 139:7-10; Jer. 23:24), but it also teaches that God is separate from His creation (Col. 1:17; 3:1-2). Spinoza did not recognize God as a personal being but thought of Him as an abstract system of truths. In short, Spinoza had no use for the biblical concept of God as a heavenly Father.

Locke—Another influential philosophy of the seventeenth century was empiricism. **Empiricism**—the idea that all knowledge comes through experience—was the philosophy of the Englishman **John Locke** (1632-1704). Locke rejected the idea that God has implanted certain truths within each person from birth. Instead, he maintained that the mind of a baby is like a "blank tablet" on which the experiences of life are written. Thus Locke argued that given the right experiences and education, a child would grow into the right kind of person. He rejected the doctrine of original sin, choosing to believe that man is basically good. Divine revela-

tion is vital, said Locke, but it can never contradict man's reason:

> Nothing that is contrary to, and inconsistent with, the clear and self-evident dictates of reason, has a right to be urged or assented to as a matter of faith, wherein reason hath nothing to do. Whatsoever is divine revelation, ought to overrule all our opinion, prejudices, and interests and hath a right to be received with full assent. Such a submission as this, of our reason to faith, takes not away the landmarks of knowledge; this shakes not the foundation of reason, but leaves us that use of our faculties for which they were given us.

Spokesmen of the Enlightenment

The scientific discoveries and philosophic ideas of the seventeenth century gave rise to a spirit of optimism in the eighteenth century. Doubts gave way to a false self-confidence as men looked to their own reason as the hope for the future. The most prominent spokesmen of the "enlightened" attitude were the eighteenth-century French writers and social critics known as the *philosophes* (FEE luh ZAWFS). These men were more than mere thinkers; they were social reformers. They openly challenged established values and institutions in hope of molding society to conform to their ideas. They contended that certain religious beliefs restricted man's freedom to think and express himself. They championed a secular society, religious toleration, freedom of speech, and the natural rights of all men. The *philosophes* mistakenly believed that man could solve society's problems and that progress and perfectibility were attainable for society and for man.

Locke

Political reform was one of the chief concerns of the eighteenth-century *philosophes*. Many of the French writers were influenced by the political ideas of the seventeenth-century English philosopher John Locke. Locke advanced the idea that men possess certain natural and unalienable rights—rights that cannot be transferred or surrendered. In his *Two Treatises of Government*, he stated that the basis of government is the consent of the governed. People

Opposite Page: Nicholas Lancret, Picnic After the Hunt, *National Gallery of Art, Washington, D.C.*

enter into a social contract with government; if government violates the people's trust, the people have a right to change their government.

Montesquieu

Locke's ideas, which were advanced as a justification of the Glorious Revolution in England, inspired the *philosophes*. Among the men influenced by his rational defense of natural rights and his promotion of the idea that men could change their government was the French baron de **Montesquieu** (MAHN tes KYOO; 1689-1755). He believed that England was the symbol of political freedom. The liberty of the English, he concluded, resulted from the separation of the three powers of government: the executive, the legislative, and judicial. In his famous work *The Spirit of Laws,* he stated the following:

> The political liberty of the subject is a tranquility of mind due to the assurance each person has of his safety. In order to have this liberty, it is [required] that the government be so constituted that no man need be afraid of another. . . . There would be an end of everything, were the same man, or the same body, whether of the nobles or of the people, to exercise those three powers,—that of enacting laws, that of executing the public resolutions, and that of trying the suits of individuals.[3]

Montesquieu's political theory on the separation of powers had a great impact on the framers of the Constitution of the United States.

Voltaire

The leading figure of the Enlightenment was Francois-Marie Arouet, better known as **Voltaire** (vawl TEHR; 1694-1778). He used his clever wit to criticize other people. As a young man Voltaire was thrown into prison for insulting a French noble. Later he was banished from France. He went to England, where he became an admirer of the ideas of Isaac Newton and John Locke. The atmosphere of intellectual freedom that he found in English society made a strong impression on him.

Voltaire became an outspoken critic of the abuses in society, especially religious and political intolerance. He hated organized religion—partic-

Voltaire

ularly the Roman Catholic church. He did not reject religion altogether but advocated a religion ruled by reason. He was a popular champion of the freedom of the press. His cutting wit made him a favorite in many aristocratic and scholarly circles. But because of his scathing attacks on the arbitrary rule of kings and nobles, he was forced to flee country after country.

Diderot and the *Encyclopédie*

The chief instrument for spreading the ideas of the *philosophes* was the French *Encyclopédie*. Like its modern counterparts, the *Encyclopédie* included articles on almost every conceivable subject. This multivolume work was edited by **Denis Diderot** (DEE duh ROH; 1713-84). He wrote several hundred articles himself, but over two hundred other writers also contributed to the work. The articles expressed the Enlightenment philosophy, often in its most radical form. The French government and church officially opposed the publication because it undermined their authority.

Rousseau

Another *philosophe* who contributed to the *Encyclopédie* was Jean Jacques Rousseau (roo SOH; 1712-78). Even though he was a friend to the other *philosophes,* he was out of step with most of them. He favored emotion and sentiment above reason. He had many ideas about the proper treatment and education of children, yet he left his own children to be raised in an orphanage. Rousseau has often been called "the Father of Romanticism." His slogan "back to nature" set the pattern of thought for the first half of the nineteenth century which was called the Romantic Age (see Chapter 16).

Rousseau was also an influential political writer. He believed that man is born free and that he should be able to do whatever he wants to do. He also believed in the basic goodness of man. Personal liberty and order in society, he contended, would come as man freely obeys the laws of society. In his work *The Social Contract,* he maintained that government should be built upon and should carry out the "general will" of the people. By "general will" Rousseau meant majority rule. Unlike most political thinkers of his day, he favored a democracy rather than a representative government or an absolute monarchy. His political ideas influenced the leaders of the nineteenth-century political movements that advocated popular participation in government.

The Religion of the Enlightenment

Many scientists and philosophers of the Enlightenment put their faith in reason instead of God's revelation, the Bible. Though they did not deny the existence of God, they refused to accept orthodox Christianity, for it did not conform to their new ideas. They rejected the supernatural, ridiculing both the miracles and prophetic elements in Scripture. They also denied the fact that man is born in sin, believing instead that man is basically good. Reason was their standard of truth: it was their guide to understanding the universe and the proper way to worship God. This new religion was called **Deism.**

Deists viewed the universe as a machine. God was its "First Cause," or "Grand Architect." He designed the universe as a self-sustaining mecha-

---

Man's Wisdom Versus God's Wisdom

Where is the wise? where is the scribe? where is the disputer of this world? hath not God made foolish the wisdom of this world? For after that in the wisdom of God the world by wisdom knew not God, it pleased God by the foolishness of preaching to save them that believe. . . . For ye see your calling, brethren, how that not many wise men after the flesh, not many mighty, not many noble, are called: but God hath chosen the foolish things of the world to confound the wise; and God hath chosen the weak things of the world to confound the things which are mighty; and base things of the world, and things which are despised, hath God chosen, yea, and things which are not, to bring to nought things that are: that no flesh should glory in his presence. But of him are ye in Christ Jesus, who of God is made unto us wisdom, and righteousness, and sanctification, and redemption: that, according as it is written, He that glorieth, let him glory in the Lord.

—I Corinthians 1:20-21, 26-31

---

nism and established the natural laws by which it operates. Deists asserted that once God had finished creation, He no longer intervened in human affairs. To the Deist, God was merely an impersonal being, much like a clockmaker who, having made a clock and wound its spring, sat back and let it run.

Deists had little use for a personal God or His salvation. They asserted that the truths of religion could be discovered naturally. They believed that a virtuous life guided by human reason would be rewarded in the life to come. Voltaire stated,

> The great name of Deist, which is not sufficiently revered, is the only name one ought to take. The only gospel one ought to read is the great book of Nature, written by the hand of God and sealed with his seal. The only religion that ought to be professed is the religion of worshipping God and being a good man. It is as impossible that this pure and eternal religion should produce evil as it is that the Christian fanaticism should produce it.[4]

Despite these boastful claims, Deism was built upon mere human wisdom. The Bible warns against such error:

Your faith should not stand in the wisdom of men, but in the power of God. . . . [For] the natural man receiveth not the things of the Spirit of God: for they are foolishness unto him: neither can he know them, because they are spiritually discerned. . . . For who hath known the mind of the Lord, that he may instruct him? But we have the mind of Christ.
—I Corinthians 2:5, 14, 16

Section Review

1. What English philosopher was one of the leading advocates of the inductive method of reasoning? Give the name of his important book.

2. Define pantheism. Who was the leading advocate of the pantheistic philosophy?
3. What were the most prominent spokesmen of the "enlightened" attitude called? What country were they from?
4. What aspect of English government did the French philosopher Montesquieu credit as aiding political liberty? What famous work did he write?
5. What aspects of biblical Christianity did some Enlightenment philosophers and scientists reject? What became the new religion of the Age of Reason?

Spiritual Awakening

Not everyone living in the Age of Reason trusted in human wisdom as the only way to find truth. Many realized that although science could improve man's standard of living, it could not improve man; neither could man through his own wisdom understand the things of God. True enlightenment came as men discovered the truth of God's Word and believed it. "The statutes of the Lord are right, rejoicing the heart: the commandment of the Lord is pure, enlightening the eyes" (Ps. 19:8).

This enlightenment produced several spiritual revivals that changed the lives of men and women and altered the moral climate of several countries. As a result, religious groups in parts of Europe and America taught that a purely intellectual knowledge of Christ or simply belonging to a church did not bring salvation, but that true repentance of sin and faith in Christ alone made one a child of God. These groups emphasized that Christians should not only live holy lives in conformity to God's Word, but that they should also earnestly seek to bring others to salvation as well.

Revivals in Germany: The Pietists

In the seventeenth century a movement known as **Pietism** arose in Germany. (The word *pietism* originated in 1689 as a term of ridicule for those who gathered together for Bible study.) By the middle of the century the Lutheran church had fallen into spiritual decay. The clergy, often poorly trained and sometimes unconverted, neglected the

spiritual needs of their people. Their dull, lifeless sermons produced no change in the apathetic attitudes of many church members.

In the midst of this spiritual decline, a Lutheran minister in Frankfurt named **Philipp Spener** (SHPAY nur; 1635-1705) became concerned for his congregation. Realizing that those who had experienced personal conversion needed close Christian fellowship, Spener organized special meetings in his home for Bible study and prayer. In addition, he published his famous work entitled *Pia Desideria* ("Pious Wishes"), in which he outlined the failures of the church and issued a call for spiritual renewal. Though many church officials attacked his ideas, concerned Christians throughout Germany followed the example of Spener and organized themselves into groups known as *collegia pietatis* ("assemblies of piety").

As the movement continued to grow, **August Francke** (FRAHNG keh; 1663-1727), a professor at the University of Halle, became a leader in the training of Pietistic pastors and missionaries. Through his efforts student lay preachers carried the gospel throughout Germany, and mission works were established in America and India. In addition to his teaching responsibilities, Francke helped establish and supervise an orphanage, elementary and secondary schools, and an organization for printing Bibles. In all, he established twenty-one different types of educational institutions that emphasized godliness and Christian wisdom. Though persecuted by various civil and religious authorities, he turned Halle into the most influential center of German Pietism.

A man who studied under Francke at Halle was Count **Nikolaus von Zinzendorf** (TSIN tsen DORF; 1700-1760). He left the Lutheran church and became the leader of the Moravians. This group,

Count Nikolaus von Zinzendorf

which began in Bohemia and Moravia during the time of John Huss, had virtually died out by the eighteenth century. In 1722, however, a small group of Bohemians settled on Zinzendorf's estate and established a religious community which they called Herrnhut (''Lord's Lodge''). From this humble beginning the movement grew as zealous Moravian missionaries traveled around the world, not only preaching the gospel but also seeking to unite all Christians. It was through the Moravians that John Wesley came to a personal assurance of salvation.

Pietism was not simply a reaction against the rationalism of the day; it was also a movement built upon the work of the sixteenth-century reformers and a renewed interest in the Word of God. Unfortunately, the Pietists exalted experience above doctrine—an attitude that led to the eventual downfall of the movement.

Revivals in England: The Methodists

By the eighteenth century spiritual fervor had died out in England. Throughout the country, Anglican clergy sought personal comfort and ease, and many seemed interested primarily in secular pursuits. Smaller denominations were just as complacent as the Anglicans, and few pastors preached salvation by grace through faith. Moral corruption, which permeated every aspect of English society, seemed to worsen with every passing year. Nevertheless, during the eighteenth century a mighty spiritual awakening shook England as God blessed the preaching of faithful men.

John Wesley

Probably the best known of these preachers is **John Wesley** (1703-91). During his lifetime he traveled about 250,000 miles on horseback and preached about 42,000 sermons. Ordained as an Anglican minister in 1728, Wesley returned to Oxford University as a student. There he joined a club

John Wesley

that his brother Charles had helped to establish. Although most were unconverted at the time, the members of this "Holy Club" tried to live righteous lives. They met often for mutual encouragement. Many students mocked their orderly lifestyle and often referred to them in a derisive manner as "Methodists"—a term that Wesley's converts later gladly accepted.

His Conversion—In 1735 Wesley sailed for the American colony of Georgia to be a missionary to the Indians and to serve as pastor in the town of Savannah. During the voyage and then later in Savannah, however, Wesley came into contact with the Moravians, who impressed him with his own spiritual need. Though he had tried to live a good life, he realized that something was still lacking. Wesley records in his journal that soon after he arrived in Georgia, the head of a Moravian settlement there spoke to him:

> "Do you know Jesus Christ?" I paused, and said, "I know He is the Saviour of the world." "True," replied he; "but do you know He has saved *you*?" I answered, "I hope He has died to save me." He only added, "Do you know *yourself*?" I said, "I do." But I fear they were vain words.

Because of conflicts with some of the colonists, his ministry in America soon failed. As he returned to England, he wrote in his journal, "I went to convert the Indians; but O! who shall convert me?" Back in England he made contact with some Moravians in London, and on May 24, 1738, "went very unwillingly" to one of their meetings on Aldersgate Street

> where one was reading Luther's preface to the Epistle to the Romans. About a quarter before nine, while he was describing the change which God works in the heart through faith in Christ, I felt my heart strangely warmed. I felt I did trust in Christ, Christ alone, for salvation; and an assurance was given me that He had taken away my sins, even mine, and saved me from the law of sin and death.

His Ministry—After his conversion, Wesley began to travel throughout the British Isles, preaching as often as four times a day. Since most Anglican churches soon closed their doors to him, he began to preach to large crowds in the open air and saw many conversions. Opposition to his preaching increased, however, and on numerous occasions he faced stone-throwing mobs, hostile clergymen, and unsympathetic civil officials. Yet his ministry never faltered. Each day he rose at 4:00 A.M. and usually preached his first sermon of the day at 5:00 A.M. At the age of seventy, he spoke on one occasion to thirty thousand people, and all heard him clearly. At eighty, he still traveled four to five thousand miles a year in order to meet his preaching responsibilities.

Although Wesley did not intend to leave the Anglican church, he is the founder of the Methodist church. He originally planned for the Methodist societies, which his converts had organized, to remain within the church as the *collegia pietatis* in Germany had remained within the Lutheran church. The Anglican hierarchy, however, refused to ordain Wesley's lay preachers, and in the end the Methodist societies were forced out of the Anglican church. At the time of Wesley's death, the Methodists had 630 lay preachers and about 175,000 members.

Wesley's work and the work of others like him had a tremendous impact on Britain. Spiritual revival broke the apathetic attitudes among professing Christians and led to an interest in domestic reform and foreign missions. The revival also improved the moral condition of England and helped to restrain the type of social upheaval that soon engulfed France. (See Chapter 15.) The spiritual awakening stimulated an interest in Christian education, led to the establishment of the first Sunday schools, and encouraged the production of good Christian literature and music.

George Whitefield

One of John Wesley's contemporaries was a dynamic evangelist named **George Whitefield** (WHIT feeld; 1714-70). The son of a tavern keeper, Whitefield was converted in 1735 and ordained an Anglican minister the following year. Like Wesley, who once wrote, "I look upon all the world as my parish," Whitefield traveled constantly, preaching the gospel wherever he went. He not only preached throughout Britain but also crossed the Atlantic seven times to carry out preaching tours in the

Susanna Wesley (1669-1742)

Susanna Ann Wesley was born in London on January 20, 1669. Although her father was a Nonconformist minister, Susanna later joined the Anglican church. Samuel Wesley, whom she married in 1689, was also reared in the home of a Nonconformist minister. Later, however, he too joined the established church, becoming an Anglican minister.

For almost forty years Samuel and Susanna served the rural parish of Epworth in Lincolnshire. Samuel devoted his time to scholarly pursuits, while Susanna managed the household and reared the children. (She had nineteen children, nine of whom died in childhood.) She carefully budgeted the family's meager income, but in spite of her efforts the Wesleys were always poor and often in debt. To add to the financial burdens, their house burned down twice and had to be rebuilt each time.

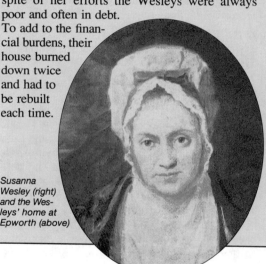

Susanna Wesley (right) and the Wesleys' home at Epworth (above)

Since poverty prevented her sons from attending school until they were about twelve years old (there were no schools for girls), Susanna taught all her children at home. As soon as a child could talk, she taught him to pray and to memorize Scripture. Realizing that her busy schedule made it difficult to spend sufficient time with each child individually, Susanna set aside a special time in the evenings for each one of them. In later years, after he had left home, John Wesley wrote to his mother, telling her that he would give anything to be able to spend Thursday evenings (his special time) with her again.

Although Susanna Wesley never achieved earthly wealth or fame, she reared two sons who through God's grace brought revival to eighteenth-century England. She said of her life, "I am content to fill a little space if God be glorified." The space she filled as a dedicated Christian mother was certainly glorifying to God, and she, along with many other Christian mothers, will reap a rich reward in heaven.

American colonies. His efforts helped further the Great Awakening in America.

Revivals in America: The Great Awakening

During the first half of the seventeenth century many Puritans fled England and settled in North America. For several years the spiritual zeal of these colonists remained strong, but by the end of the seventeenth century their descendants were no longer fervent for the Lord. During the eighteenth

century George Whitefield summed up the condition of the American churches this way: "I am verily persuaded, the generality of preachers talk of an unknown, unfelt Christ. And the reason why congregations have been so dead, is because dead men preach to them."

During the years 1740-42, as the Methodist revival progressed in the British Isles, America experienced the climax of a tremendous revival known as the **Great Awakening.** Through the preaching of Whitefield and other traveling evangelists, thousands of people heard the message of

Isaac Watts and Charles Wesley

From the Reformation until the eighteenth century, English Protestants did not use hymns in their church services. Instead they sang rhymed settings of the Psalms, believing that church music should be drawn directly from Scripture. Many of these psalm settings, however, were poorly written and hard to sing. Determined to improve the music in his own congregation, a minister by the name of Isaac Watts (1674-1748) began to write hymns. Although at first many Protestants of all denominations rejected this "innovation," Watts persevered in his efforts. He is known today as "the Father of English Hymnody."

Watts believed that hymns should be doctrinally sound and easily understood. Sometimes he paraphrased a psalm; for example, "O God, Our Help in Ages Past" is based on Psalm 90, and "From All That Dwell Below the Skies" is based on Psalm 117. On other occasions he composed hymns that were based upon a particular scriptural theme, such as "When I Survey the Wondrous Cross." In everything he wrote, Watts tried to direct the worshipers' attention to Christ.

Churchgoers in the early eighteenth century did not have hymnals. Therefore the pastor or someone else had to read the lines of the psalm or hymn aloud. After each line was read, the congregation would sing it, and then the reader would proceed to the next line. For this reason Watts made sure that each line of his hymns made sense when read by itself.

Joy to the world! the Lord is come;
Let earth receive her King;
Let every heart prepare him room,
And heaven and nature sing.

While Watts laid the foundation for English hymnology, it was Charles Wesley (1707-88) who popularized hymn singing in England. Like his brother John, Charles traveled as an evangelist, but his health forced him to retire early. Charles, therefore, settled down to a pastoral ministry and continued to write hymns. By the time of his death he had written over six thousand.

Charles Wesley is considered to be the greatest English hymn writer of all time. With his hymns he sang the Methodist revival into the hearts of the people and helped strengthen them in Christian doctrine. While Watts's hymns are formal and reserved (reflecting the age in which he lived), Wesley's are filled with emotion. For example, Watts wrote,

Come, sound his praise abroad
And hymns of glory sing;
Jehovah is the sovereign God,
The universal King.

Wesley, on the other hand, penned the following words on the first anniversary of his conversion.

O for a thousand tongues to sing
My dear Redeemer's praise,
The glories of my God and King,
The triumphs of His grace!

Wesley wrote hymns to fit every occasion. He wrote Christmas hymns ("Hark! the Herald Angels Sing"), Easter hymns ("Christ the Lord Is Ris'n Today"), and communion hymns. He also wrote hymns of praise, comfort, and contemplation. In all of his compositions, however, Wesley primarily emphasized the theme of love. For example, "Jesus, Lover of My Soul" and "Love Divine, All Loves Excelling" proclaim the love of Christ. Many of Wesley's hymns also contain such words as *grace, light,* and *joy.*

---

salvation. The real key to the long-term spiritual success of the Great Awakening, however, lay with local pastors who faithfully ministered to the needs of their own congregations.

One such pastor, whose name is inseparably linked with the Great Awakening, is **Jonathan Edwards** (1703-58). A brilliant man who graduated from Yale at the age of seventeen, Edwards used his considerable talents to further the cause of Christ. In 1729 he succeeded his grandfather as the pastor of the Congregational church in Northampton, Massachusetts. Through his sermons and books, he advocated the need for personal conversion. Throughout his life he remained a diligent student, often studying thirteen hours a day and writing works of great theological and philosophical depth.

Probably the most famous sermon Edwards ever preached was "Sinners in the Hands of an Angry God," delivered in 1741 at Enfield, Connecticut. Basing his sermon upon the phrase "their foot shall slide in due time" (Deut. 32:35), Edwards warned his unrepentant hearers that it was only God's mercy that kept them from instantly plunging into hell:

> O sinner! consider the fearful danger you are in. . . . Are there not many here who have lived long in the world, and are not to this day born again? . . . Therefore, let every one that is out of Christ now awake and fly from the wrath to come.

As Edwards preached, the Spirit of God brought such conviction upon the congregation that people began to cry out, "What shall I do to be saved?" Many people began to weep. In fact, the noise became so loud that Edwards had to stop preaching several times and urge the people to be quiet in order that he might continue with his sermon. Edwards did complete the sermon, and many in Enfield came to salvation.

This incident is only one example of the spiritual awakening that swept through the American colonies. Although many political and social benefits derived from the Great Awakening, the most significant results were spiritual. A large percentage of the colonists were converted. For example, in New England alone, which had a population of 300,000, between 25,000 and 50,000 people were converted, and 150 new churches were established. Christians became more and more concerned about mission work and made renewed efforts to reach the American Indians with the gospel. In addition, several groups established schools for the training of Christian ministers. The Presbyterians, for example, established the College of New Jersey, which later came to be known as Princeton University. In spite of several denominational splits, the revival also helped to draw Christians of various denominations together in a bond of fellowship and cooperation. This Great Awakening was only the first of several major revivals that were to come to America in succeeding generations.

Section Review

1. List three major Pietist leaders in Germany.
2. Who was the founder of the Methodists?
3. What man is known as "the Father of English Hymnody"? What man is considered the greatest English hymn writer of all time?
4. What was the name of the spiritual revival in America that climaxed in the 1740s?
5. What man from Massachusetts was the most famous preacher during this American revival? What famous sermon did he deliver?

Artistic Reflection

Between the Renaissance and the Enlightenment, Europe underwent great social, political, religious, and intellectual changes. These changes produced tension and restlessness among the people of Europe. But with the coming of the Enlightenment, doubt and uncertainty gave way to an emphasis on order and restraint. The values, attitudes, and concerns of these historical periods are reflected in their architecture, painting, music, and literature.

The Baroque Age in Art

The doubts and contradictions of the sixteenth century and the new ideas and discoveries of the seventeenth century found expression in two styles of art: mannerism and baroque. These styles illustrate different aspects or moods of the troubled and changing times.

Mannerism was the artistic style that was prevalent throughout much of the sixteenth century. It reflected the political and religious tension of the Reformation era. Unlike Renaissance artists, mannerist artists did not strive for realism and balance. Instead their works are filled with distortions and exaggerations: colors are often unnatural or clashing, and the human form is often distorted. An outstanding painter in this style was **El Greco** (1541-1614), a Greek who settled in Spain. His painted figures have elongated bodies and limbs. He often created a mystical atmosphere with dramatic and sharply contrasting colors.

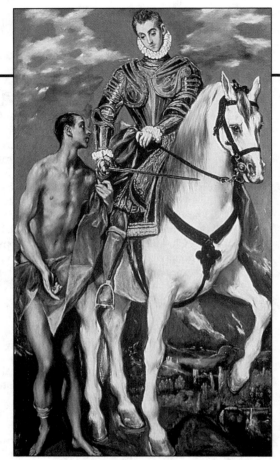

El Greco, St. Martin and the Beggar, *National Gallery of Art, Washington, D.C.*

The art of the seventeenth century captured the mood of the time and is as varied as the personalities of the artists who created it. This new style is called **baroque,** a term probably originating from a Portuguese word meaning ''an irregularly shaped pearl.'' The term, originally used in a negative sense, refers to the period in art history that stretches from 1600 to about 1750. (Nineteenth-century art critics regarded the art of the seventeenth century as theatrical, deformed, and too ornamental.) The baroque style is grand, dynamic, heroic, active, swirling, sensual, and emotional. It engages the complete attention of the viewer. It includes everything from the rippling façades (fronts) of buildings to beautiful fountains; from lifelike sculpture to somber, storm-tossed landscapes; from gigantic canvases that seem to reach out and include the viewer, to arrogant portraits; and from dazzling church domes to lofty, painted ceilings that appear to reveal views of paradise.

Bernini

The baroque style originated primarily as an architectural style and soon spread to painting, sculpture, and music. One of the most famous architects of the seventeenth century was the Italian **Giovanni Bernini** (behr NEE nee; 1598-1680). He designed beautiful fountains for Roman plazas and the expansive colonnades outside St.

Top: Bernini's Cathedra Petri *("Chair of Peter") in St. Peter's Basilica in the Vatican; **Bottom:** The* Cathedra Petri *as seen through the* Baldacchino, *an enormous bronze canopy also made by Bernini; the* Baldacchino *contains nearly one hundred tons of bronze.*

Peter Paul Rubens, The Meeting of Abraham and Melchizedek, *National Gallery of Art, Washington, D.C.*

Peter's Basilica. He was also an accomplished sculptor and painter. His sculpture captured subjects in motion: their hair flowing, their muscles rippling, and their robes billowing.

Rubens

While Bernini popularized the baroque style in architecture and sculpture, a Flemish artist, **Peter Paul Rubens** (1577-1640), popularized the baroque style in painting. As a young man he traveled to Italy and studied the works of the master painters of the High Renaissance. Later he traveled throughout Europe as a diplomat. His ability as a painter, however, did not go unnoticed. He received so many requests for his works that he was forced to employ other artists to help him meet the demand. These assistants worked under his direction to complete parts of his paintings; he put on the finishing touches. His canvases are dramatic and often contain rich landscapes and robust figures.

Rembrandt

No discussion of baroque painting is complete without mention of **Rembrandt van Rijn** (REM-brant VAN RINE; 1606-69), perhaps the greatest Dutch painter of all time. His paintings are usually filled with gold tones and warm browns. By contrasting light and dark (a technique known as chiaroscuro), he created subtle moods on canvas. His

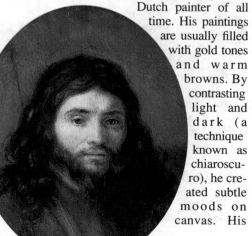

Rembrandt van Rijn, Head of Christ, *Bob Jones University Collection of Sacred Art*

portraits reveal a psychological insight into man's inner nature; many of his subjects he portrays deep in contemplation.

The themes of many of Rembrandt's paintings were inspired by biblical stories. Rembrandt grew up in a Protestant country and was undoubtedly introduced to the Bible by his mother, whom he often painted with her Bible. Early in his career, he looked to the Bible only as a source for ideas. In his later religious works, however, he attempted to give a visual interpretation of Scripture. He sought to convey a message rather than simply to please the eye of some patron.

The Rococo Style

The grand baroque style of Rubens gave way to a delicate style known as **rococo.** This term comes from a French word that literally means ''a pebble.'' (It refers to the small, shell-like ornaments that characterize rococo decoration.) Rococo is essentially a French style and was used most often in interior decoration. (It later spread to several German states and to Austria.) The rococo exchanges the power and grandeur of the baroque for refined elegance; it is delicate and feminine. Where the baroque style shouts at the beholder, the rococo style whispers.

The leading rococo painter was the Frenchman **Antoine Watteau** (wah TOH; 1684-1721), whose works reflect the frivolous, decadent, and artificial court life of the eighteenth century.

The Neoclassical Period in Art

In contrast to the emotionalism of baroque art, much of the art of the eighteenth century was orderly, formal, calm, and balanced. It expressed the conviction of the Enlightenment that the universe is a rational and orderly system. Since the universe runs according to fixed laws, reasoned eighteenth-century man, art should also conform to certain restrictions. Artists of this period, like Renaissance artists, imitated the classical ideals of ancient Greece and Rome. Thus developed the new artistic style of the **neoclassical** (or ''new classic'') period. Interest in classical art was further heightened by the discovery of the ancient cities of Pompeii and Herculaneum (see p. 101).

The Baroque Age in Music

Like baroque art, baroque music expresses the vigor of the seventeenth and early eighteenth centuries. Many of the adjectives that describe baroque art (see p. 378) also apply to baroque music. Ba-

Monticello, the home of President Thomas Jefferson in Virginia, is one of the finest examples of neoclassical architecture in North America. Jefferson, a great admirer of classical architecture, designed the home himself.

roque music broke with past tradition, initiating a radical departure from the music of the fifteenth and sixteenth centuries.

1. Baroque composers gradually turned from **polyphony** (music in which several melody lines of equal importance are intertwined) to **homophony** (music with one basic melody line and several supporting harmony parts—much like a hymn).
2. Although some of the greatest composers still wrote primarily for the church, the trend was toward secular music commissioned by royalty and the aristocracy.
3. New types of musical compositions were developed during the baroque era, such as the opera, the ballet, and the oratorio.
4. Instrumental music became more important during this period, giving rise to the development of the orchestra. Also during this age, craftsmen perfected the techniques of organ building and violin making.
5. Before the baroque era, vocalists often sang *a cappella* (without accompaniment). During the baroque period, instrumentalists usually accompanied vocal numbers.
6. Since many of the earliest baroque composers were Italian, Italian musical markings (which are still used today) became the standard markings for music throughout Europe. For example, *adagio* tells the performer to play slowly, while *forte* tells him to play loudly.

Monteverdi

One of the leading composers of Italian baroque music was **Claudio Monteverdi** (MAHN tuh VEHR dee; 1567-1643). He is especially famous for his operas. In 1607 he wrote his first opera, *Orfeo*. In this work, as in his other operas, he skillfully combined text, music, scenery, and dances into a unified masterpiece. It was partially through his influence that opera became a popular form of entertainment. Opera houses were built in many Italian cities, and for a small charge almost anyone could enjoy this new musical form.

Handel

One of the most famous ''English'' opera composers was a German immigrant to England named **George Frederick Handel** (1685-1759). He spent his early years as a composer of Italian-style operas. Later he turned to composing **oratorios—** musical compositions for solo singers, chorus, and orchestra that tell a sacred story without the dramatic action employed in operas. In all, Handel wrote about twenty oratorios, of which the best-known and best-loved is the *Messiah*.

The *Messiah* was written in 1741 for a charity concert in Dublin, Ireland. Handel, who was fifty-six years old at the time, finished the oratorio's more than fifty numbers in twenty-four days. He wove majestic passages of Scripture together with beautifully composed choruses and arias (melodic sections sung by solo voices). The central theme of the oratorio is Jesus Christ, the Messiah, the fulfillment of God's plan of redemption. Among the best-loved numbers from the *Messiah* are the aria ''I Know That My Redeemer Liveth'' and the ''Hallelujah'' chorus. During one performance, attended by George II, the king was so moved by the ''Hallelujah'' chorus that he rose to his feet, beginning a tradition that is still followed today. The popularity of the *Messiah* has endured to the present, and it remains one of the most frequently performed of all oratorios.

J. S. Bach

Born the same year as Handel was another great baroque composer, **Johann Sebastian Bach** (1685-1750). Bach came from a very musical family who lived in a strongly Lutheran section of Germany. In fact, Martin Luther as a young man lived in the same area some two hundred years before; his music and theology had a strong influence on the Bach family. Most of Bach's musical career was spent in performing, conducting, and composing music for the Lutheran church. Bach's own personal faith and knowledge of the Scriptures shine forth in his religious music.

Bach was a prolific composer. While serving as music director in the city of Leipzig, for example, he was expected to produce a new cantata for the worship service each Sunday. (Bach's cantatas were twenty- to thirty-minute compositions based on a scriptural text and performed by choirs, soloists, and instrumentalists.) In all, he wrote over two

While playing the organ (which he called his pulpit) and while composing, he sought to create music that would spiritually strengthen and uplift the listener. He knew the Scriptures well, and at his death his library contained over eighty books on theological or devotional subjects.

On the manuscripts containing his sacred compositions, Bach often wrote two sets of initials. On the first page of a manuscript he usually wrote the letters *J.J.* which stood for *Jesu Juva* (''Jesus help''), and on the last page he usually wrote *S.D.G—Soli Deo Gloria* (''to the glory of God alone'').

Although he composed most of his music for use in church, Bach believed that all his musical efforts should be for God's glory. On one occasion he put together a small book to teach music to his oldest son. On the title page he wrote the initials *I.N.J.—In Nomine Jesu* (''in the name of Jesus''). Bach believed that all activities—even those that seem to be secular—should be done in the name of Jesus Christ.

To the Glory of God

Johann Sebastian Bach was a man of strong Christian faith who dedicated his talents to God.

hundred cantatas and several oratorios, as well as organ, chamber, and orchestral music.

Bach did not travel widely, and his work was not as well known or as appreciated as that of some other composers of the age. It is said that a local butcher used copies of his music to wrap meat. Later generations, however, have recognized the greatness of Bach's musical style. One of his most famous compositions is the *Passion According to St. Matthew,* an oratorio that he wrote for Good Friday, April 15, 1729. In this work Bach used Matthew's Gospel to tell the story of Christ's crucifixion. In twenty-eight poems and fifteen chorales centered on this scriptural text, he created a massive, dramatic masterpiece that lasts about two and a half hours.

The Classical Age in Music

The classical age in music covers the period from 1750 to the early 1800s. Classical music turned away from the elaborate style of J. S. Bach to an elegant style that showed precision, clarity of composition, and emotional restraint. The main types of compositions—sonatas, concertos, string quartets, and symphonies—reflected the order and balance of the Enlightenment. This music became a popular pastime among the aristocracy and rich middle class. In addition, a new instrument, the piano, became a favorite.

Haydn

The man who played a major role in setting the style for classical music was the Austrian composer **Franz Joseph Haydn** (HYE dun; 1732-1809). During his lifetime he wrote a large amount of music, including 104 symphonies, 83 string quartets, over 50 piano sonatas, several operas, and 2 oratorios. He set the style for symphonic composition, using large orchestration and dividing the work into four movements. Although he was not the first to compose a symphony, he has been called ''the Father of the Symphony.'' His musical works influenced other composers, including two of his most famous pupils—Mozart and Beethoven.

Mozart

Wolfgang Mozart (1756-91) was a musical genius. He learned to play the harpsichord at the age of four and composed pieces at the age of five. When six years old, the young Mozart traveled with his father on a European tour. For three years he played before princes and monarchs of Europe, winning their hearts. It was said that he could listen to a piece of music once and later reproduce it from memory. On one occasion a member of his father's string quartet was absent. With no difficulty, the young Mozart filled in as second violin. The visitors present were astonished at his ability, to which he replied, "Surely you don't have to study and practice to play second violin, do you?"

Mozart was a versatile composer and excelled in many different types of musical compositions. Of his

Wolfgang Amadeus Mozart

twenty-two operas, many are still performed today—especially popular are *The Marriage of Figaro, Don Giovanni,* and *The Magic Flute.* He also composed forty symphonies, instrumental music, and chamber music. His works for piano helped to popularize that new instrument. Despite the early fame he won as a child prodigy, Mozart died in poverty at the age of thirty-five and was buried in an unmarked grave.

The other great composer of this period was Ludwig van Beethoven (1770-1827). His early works reflect the classical style. But he became caught up in the momentous events of the early nineteenth century, and his later compositions reflect the trend toward what would be called romanticism. (See Chapter 16.)

Literature in the Age of Reason

As was true for art and music, the literature of the Age of Reason was characterized by an imitation of the classical works of ancient Greece and Rome. Writers established definite rules, based on classical models, which they tried to follow in order to express themselves reasonably and clearly. This was the age of neoclassical literature.

One of the most famous French writers of the seventeenth century was the playwright **Molière** (maw LYEHR; 1622-73). He is best remembered for his comedies, in which he pokes fun at the hypocrisy and vices in society.

The Age of Reason was an age of satire. The foremost poetic satirist was the Englishman **Alexander Pope** (1688-1744). In his biting and witty satires, he exposes the follies of his day.

> Of all the causes which conspire to blind
> Man's erring judgment, and misguide the mind,
> What the weak head with strongest bias rules,
> Is pride, the never-failing vice of fools.

Pope was one of the most quoted poets of his age. Even today many of his phrases are familiar, such as "To err is human, to forgive divine" and "A little learning is a dangerous thing." Though a brilliant writer, Pope was steeped in the humanistic philosophy of the Enlightenment. He wrote, "Know then thyself, presume not God to scan; / The proper study of mankind is man."

Another popular English satirist was **Jonathan Swift** (1667-1745). As Pope was a master of verse, Swift was a master of prose. His greatest work, *Gulliver's Travels,* recounts the exciting but strange adventures of a man named Gulliver. Although it has become a favorite children's story, Swift intended the book as a satire on human behavior. How could man, who has the capacity of reason, be so complacent and inhumane? Swift mistakenly thought that society's problems resulted from man's failure to use his capacity of reason.

Prose writing gained in popularity during this period. The works of two writers in particular helped lead to the development of the modern novel. *Robinson Crusoe,* written by **Daniel Defoe,** and *Pamela,* by Samuel Richardson, are considered forerunners of this literary form.

Another English writer, **Edward Gibbon** (1737-94), wrote perhaps the most famous historical book of the eighteenth century—the six-volume *Decline and Fall of the Roman Empire.* He traces the history of Rome from the reign of Augustus to its eventual overthrow by barbarian tribes. As a lover of classical culture and a critic of religion, Gibbon blamed not only the barbarian tribes but also the Christians for Rome's decline. He claimed that Christianity reawakened the fighting spirit of the Romans and caused religious controversy, which brought about internal disorder within the empire.

Section Review

1. What artistic age spanning from 1600 to 1750 is characterized by its grand, heroic, sensual, and emotional style?
2. Who was one of the most famous architects of the seventeenth century? What did he design?
3. List three characteristics of the rococo style.
4. Who is the most famous composer of oratorios of this period? What is his best-known and best-loved oratorio?
5. Who wrote *Robinson Crusoe?* Of what literary form was this book a forerunner?

A Glimpse Behind and a Glimpse Ahead

The seventeenth and eighteenth centuries were a period of outstanding accomplishments in science and the arts. This period was also an "enlightened" age. But there were two types of enlightenment—one reflecting human wisdom and producing an age of reason, the other reflecting God's wisdom and producing an age of revival. The book of James gives a fitting summary to these two types of enlightenment by contrasting true and false wisdom.

Who is a wise man and endued with knowledge among you? let him shew out of a good conversation his works with meekness of wisdom. But if ye have bitter envying and strife in your hearts, glory not, and lie not against the truth. This wisdom descendeth not from above, but is earthly, sensual, devilish. For where envying and strife is, there is confusion and every evil work. But the wisdom that is from above is first pure, then peaceable, gentle, and easy to be intreated, full of mercy and good fruits, without partiality, and without hypocrisy. And the fruit of righteousness is sown in peace of them that make peace.

—James 3:13-18

Chapter Review

Can You Explain?

Age of Reason	deductive method	Pietism	polyphony
scientific method	dualism	Great Awakening	homophony
heliocentric theory	pantheism	mannerism	oratorio
Enlightenment	empiricism	baroque	
rationalism	*philosophe*	rococo	
inductive method	Deism	neoclassical	

Can You Identify?

Nicolaus Copernicus	Anton van	August Francke	Claudio Monteverdi
Johannes Kepler	Leeuwenhoek	Nicholas von	George Frederick
Galileo Galilei	Gerhardus Mercator	Zinzendorf	Handel
Isaac Newton	Francis Bacon	John Wesley	J. S. Bach
Andreas Vesalius	René Descartes	George Whitefield	Franz Joseph Haydn
Paracelsus	Baruch Spinoza	Jonathan Edwards	Wolfgang Mozart
William Harvey	John Locke	El Greco	Molière
Edward Jenner	Montesquieu	Giovanni Bernini	Alexander Pope
Robert Boyle	Voltaire	Peter Paul Rubens	Jonathan Swift
Joseph Priestley	Denis Diderot	Rembrandt van Rijn	Daniel Defoe
Antoine Lavoisier	Philipp Spener	Antoine Watteau	Edward Gibbon

How Much Do You Remember?

1. List five steps that make up the scientific method.
2. List the two methods of reasoning that assisted scientists in their investigation of the physical world. Give a brief explanation of each.
3. List four evidences of the influence of the Wesley/Whitefield revivals on England and the American colonies.
4. List characteristics distinguishing the following artistic styles: mannerism, baroque, rococo, and neoclassical.
5. The Age of Reason in literature was known for its plays, satires, prose, and historical writings. Name an important author for each of these literary mediums.

What Do You Think?

1. Is science a completely trustworthy source for gaining knowledge? Explain your answer.
2. What did the *philosophes* criticize about eighteenth-century society? How did they propose to improve society? Were their methods successful?
3. Many political ideas of the Enlightenment influenced American government. List examples.
4. How would you account for the fact that during the Age of Reason, England and America experienced great spiritual revivals and other countries did not?

Notes
1. Patrick Moore, *Comets* (New York: Scribner, 1976), p. 15.
2. Max Caspar, *Kepler* (London: Abelard-Schuman, 1959), p. 373.
3. James Harvey Robinson and Charles A. Beard, *Readings in Modern European History* (Boston: Ginn and Co., 1908), 1:191.
4. John Herman Randall, Jr., *The Making of the Modern Mind,* rev. ed. (Boston: Houghton Mifflin, 1940), p. 292.

"Yearning to breathe free"

People have always yearned for freedom, for Adam's sin brought bondage to the whole human race. At the time of the Reformation, the Protestant reformers reasserted the truth that true liberty is found only in Jesus Christ. ''Stand fast therefore in the liberty wherewith Christ hath made us free'' (Gal. 5:1). These reformers realized that people did not have to be bound by the traditions established by Roman Catholicism. Jesus Christ, by His death on the cross, has secured spiritual liberty for mankind—that is, freedom from the penalty and power of sin.

During the Enlightenment, men asserted that God had provided political liberty as well. Thomas Jefferson stated, ''The God who gave us life gave us liberty at the same time.'' Enlightenment philosophers claimed that man was endowed with certain ''natural rights,'' the most cherished being the rights to life, liberty, and personal property. But in the eighteenth century, few people enjoyed these rights; ecclesiastical and political absolutism was the order of the day. The desire for personal and political liberty, however, prompted a series of revolutions.

This chapter tells of two eighteenth-century revolutions: the American and the French. Unlike modern revolutions, the so-called American Revolution was a conservative movement tempered by the Protestant background of the colonists. Americans attempted to preserve time-honored traditions of religious and political liberty. The event is therefore more accurately described as the War for Independence. The French Revolution, on the other hand, became radical. The French sought to overthrow the power of a corrupt monarchy, aristocracy, and church. Like many modern revolutions, the French Revolution did not establish liberty but led to social upheaval and dictatorship.

American Struggle to Preserve Liberty

Colonial Liberties

Unlike the French and Spanish settlements in the New World, English settlements were formed by individuals and groups of individuals seeking freedom. These people sought an escape from oppression, poverty, and absolutist governments. Some, of course, looked for adventure; others for wealth. Most of the early settlers, however, came to the New World seeking a haven from the religious persecution in Europe. At great personal risk, they left their homelands for a wilderness where they hoped to begin a new life—a life grounded in religious and political liberty.

In 1620 a group of English Separatists called **Pilgrims** set sail for America. They sought a land where they would be free to worship God without government opposition. Though they had been granted permission to settle in the Virginia Colony, navigational errors and storms forced them north to Massachusetts. Here they settled and founded the Plymouth Colony. From the outset, the Pilgrim leaders realized the need for discipline to maintain order among themselves. They knew that unrestrained liberty leads to anarchy. While still on board the *Mayflower,* they drafted a temporary agreement called the **Mayflower Compact,** establishing civil authority for the Plymouth Colony.

Having undertaken, for the glory of God, and advancement of the Christian faith, and honor of our king and country, a voyage to plant the first colony in the northern parts of Virginia, [we] do by these presents [witnesses] solemnly

---

Opposite Page: *Napoleon crosses the Alps in this famous painting by Jacques Louis David. Although he eventually became a dictator and later an emperor, Napoleon helped spread revolutionary ideas across Europe.*

A replica of the Mayflower, *the ship that brought the Pilgrims to North America*

and mutually in the presence of God, and of one another, covenant and combine ourselves together into a civil body politic, for our better ordering and preservation and furtherance of the ends aforesaid; and by virtue hereof to enact, constitute, and frame such just and equal laws, ordinances, acts, constitutions, and offices, from time to time, as shall be thought most meet and convenient for the general good of the colony, unto which we promised all due submission and obedience.

Ten years after the Pilgrims landed at Plymouth, a steady migration of Puritans crossed the Atlantic. They, too, longed for a land where they could freely practice their religion. In 1630, under the leadership of Governor John Winthrop, more than one thousand Puritan men and women settled in New England—most in Boston. Like the Pilgrims, these Puritans believed that they had been sent on a divine mission. They sought to establish an ideal state based on biblical principles. The purpose of government, they believed, was to promote piety and restrain evildoers. The state was to assist (not interfere with) the church in molding godly character in the community. But their ideal society eventually failed as later Puritan generations professed, but did not possess, the religious convictions of their parents and grandparents. Nevertheless, Puritan morality and theology had a great impact on the culture of the American colonies.

In addition to the Pilgrims and Puritans, other Englishmen settled along the North American coastline. They were joined by Irish, Scottish, German, Dutch, and French settlers. As the number of colonies grew, so did their differences. Divisions soon appeared—the natural result of the wide variety of geographic and climatic conditions within the colonies. Each section—from the New England Colonies to the Middle Colonies and down to the Southern Colonies—developed its own lifestyle and trade pattern;

each had a unique appeal for immigrants of different religious and vocational backgrounds.

Despite their diversity, the American colonists shared a common European background and a Protestant heritage. In spite of their different types of organization, their forms of government were remarkably similar. This similarity, no doubt, resulted from a common respect for English law and a love for local self-government.

For almost 150 years after the founding of the first colony, the American colonies prospered under English protection, support, and encouragement. During this time, England permitted the colonies great religious and political liberty. England's permissive attitude was due in part to (1) the colonies' relative unimportance in the growing British Empire, (2) their failure to show a profit in their overseas trade, and (3) the focus of English attention on more important matters in other parts of the world. Thus, under the benevolent but generally neglectful eye of their homeland, the American colonists remained loyal Englishmen and were permitted the luxury of governing themselves in nearly all colonial matters.

British Restrictions

Until 1763 an English colonist living in America under the authority of the British Crown and Parliament enjoyed great freedom and prosperity. But after a series of wars on the European continent (see Chapter 13), the direction of Britain's policy toward her colonies changed. Britain was faced with the development of a worldwide empire that was neither planned nor organized. Furthermore, she was nearly bankrupt because of the French and Indian War, or the Seven Years' War (1756-63). She therefore looked to her colonies to "pay their own way" by making financial contributions to the mother country in exchange for the benefits Britain provided.

Between 1763 and 1774, Parliament passed a series of new laws placing restrictions on colonial trade. The colonists raised their voices in protest; yet they remained loyal to both king and country. They recognized that Britain was their bulwark of defense against both French and Spanish designs on the West and against unfriendly Indians on their

The United States 1775-1800

☐	Original Thirteen States
☐	Territories and Added States
☐	British (after 1783)
☐	Spanish (after 1783)
☐	Disputed Territory
★	Battles

frontiers. Furthermore, they did not object to the amount of taxes they had to pay, for they paid very little in comparison to their English relatives. So what was the cause of their protest? After nearly 150 years of noninterference, the American colonists resented the new parliamentary measures as an invasion of their internal affairs. They believed that Parliament had overstepped its authority and had violated the colonial charters. These charters specified that all powers of taxation rested with the colonial assemblies and not with the Houses of Parliament. Thus the issue was not the amount of the taxes, but who should levy and collect the taxes. "No taxation without representation" became a popular rallying cry in the colonies.

In December 1773 colonial opposition to parliamentary acts mounted to action. Under the cover of night, a group of colonists dressed as Indians dumped a shipload of tea into Boston Harbor to protest a new tax on tea. In response to the Boston Tea Party, Parliament closed the port of this vital colonial city to all shipping. Other laws reduced colonial liberties in Massachusetts. Martial law was imposed, and the colonists were forced to house and support financially the British troops sent to enforce the unwanted edicts of **George III** and Parliament. These acts the colonials viewed as ''intolerable.''

Another act detested by the colonists was the Quebec Act. Parliament extended the territory of Quebec, a former French colony, into the American interior. This act gave favored status to Roman Catholicism and reinstated French law in this territory. The colonists perceived this act as a dangerous threat to their religious and political freedoms, as well as a violation of their colonial charters.

The colonists fully expected to see these new laws repealed, for previously Parliament had backed down after firm colonial resistance. But now the

Concord Bridge, where the first shots of the American War for Independence were fired

louder the colonial protest grew, the more British troops arrived to enforce the decrees of the king and Parliament. Some colonists viewed armed resistance as an option to defend their homes from the interference of British troops sent to oppress them. They began to stockpile munitions in the event that such resistance proved necessary. When the British learned of one of these stockpiles, they sent troops to destroy it. Along the way, these troops encountered colonial militiamen, and two skirmishes ensued near Boston at Lexington and Concord in April of 1775. Thus began a war that neither side had planned nor desired.

American Independence

Attitude Toward War

When it became necessary to resist the British, the colonists did so reluctantly, reservedly, but purposefully. They did not want a rebellion or a war. Nevertheless, they believed that their English rights had been violated, and they would not bow to parliamentary pressure, despite the threat of military force. But not all colonials favored armed resistance against Britain. Though they disliked British interference in colonial matters, they remained loyal subjects.

The Christian people of the colonies were likewise divided in their views of resistance. On the one hand, many believed that they should be loyal to their elected representatives in the colonial legislatures. Therefore, when their representatives called for opposition to the edicts of Parliament and king, these Christians were able to support the colonial cause in good conscience. Other Christians, however, believed that their first loyalty lay with the British government in London. When war broke out, many of them sided with Britain.

Before fighting broke out, few colonists had thoughts of separating from Britain. But as fighting continued, the mood among the colonists gradually changed. Their cause became a struggle to preserve their freedom and to secure independence from Britain. This spirit was clearly stated on July 4, 1776, in the **Declaration of Independence.** This document, written primarily by Thomas Jefferson and adopted by the Continental Congress, firmly declared,

Reenactment of the fighting between the colonists and the British

That these United Colonies are, and of Right ought to be, Free and Independent States; that they are Absolved from all Allegiance to the British Crown, and that all political connection between them and the State of Great Britain, is and ought to be totally dissolved; and that as Free and Independent States, they have full power to levy War, conclude Peace, contract Alliances, establish Commerce, and to do all other Acts and things which Independent States may of right do.

Course of the War

The fighting, which broke out more than a year before the signing of the Declaration of Independence, dragged on for seven years. During the early years of the conflict, it seemed as though Britain would crush American resistance. The small and poorly equipped American army suffered great hardships and often had to retreat from the more numerous British forces. The American cause, however, was strengthened by the determined leadership of General **George Washington.** Also, the American soldiers were fighting for their homes and freedoms. This strong personal motivation could not be matched by the British troops, many of whom were hired German soldiers.

The turning point in the war came in October of 1777, when the American forces won a major victory over the British at Saratoga, New York. After hearing of this victory, France openly declared her support for the American cause and provided the colonies with badly needed aid. (Later

Emanuel Leutze, Washington Crossing the Delaware, *Metropolitan Museum of Art, New York*

Spain and the Netherlands also entered the war against Britain.) At Yorktown, Virginia, in 1781, the combined French and American forces forced the British army commanded by Lord Cornwallis to surrender. When news of the surrender reached London, the British government, which was involved in a struggle with the French, Dutch, and Spanish around the world, was willing to bring the war to an end.

After two years of negotiations, the **Treaty of Paris** (1783) was signed. The British made many concessions to the Americans—many more than could have been anticipated. Most important, though, they officially acknowledged the independence of the American colonies. The Americans had won their war for independence. Theirs was the first significant revolution of the modern era; it was the only one on such a large scale that was successful. Its success was due in large part to its conservative nature, not to its ''rebellious'' nature. Its protest was not against government, but against too much government and a government that had violated its own rules. The colonists did not fight an offensive war; they simply wanted to defend their homeland and preserve the freedoms they had enjoyed for over 150 years.

Constitutional Republic

After the war, the American colonists had their independence, but they lacked a strong national government. At first they organized themselves as independent states in a weak confederation. But under the Articles of Confederation, the states had so much power that the central government was ineffective. In 1787 delegates from the various states met for the purpose of amending the Articles. Instead they adopted a new constitution.

After carefully examining the strengths and weaknesses of governments throughout history, the delegates to the Constitutional Convention chose a republican form of government modeled after the Roman Republic. They divided the powers of government among three branches: executive, legislative, and judicial. To make sure that no one branch became too powerful, they gave each branch specific functions and specific checks on the other branches.

To remedy the problems they experienced under the Articles, the convention established the principle of **federalism,** delegating specified powers to the national government and reserving all other powers for the state governments. They gave the central government sufficient power to function on behalf of the mutual interests of the states. At the same time, they left to the states the freedom to act in matters affecting their individual interests.

The framers of the Constitution stressed such concepts as **popular sovereignty** (government based upon the consent of the governed) and the "natural rights" of all men. In this regard they reflected the influence of the political ideas of the Enlightenment. But while Enlightenment philosophy taught that man was essentially good, the constitutional fathers had a healthy fear of human nature and the power of government. Their Protestant-Puritan heritage taught them that man cannot be trusted.

Although the new Constitution placed checks and balances on the federal government, it contained no specific guarantees that government would not threaten the personal and religious liberties for which the Americans had fought so valiantly. Many states refused to ratify the new Constitution unless such provisions were made. Therefore the constitutional leaders promised that among the first acts of the new Congress would be the introduction of several amendments to the Constitution. The first ten amendments, called the **Bill of Rights,** clearly defined these liberties and placed restraints on governmental interference. The most cherished personal liberties were listed in the first amendment:

Congress shall make no law respecting an establishment of religion, or prohibiting the free exercise thereof; or abridging the freedom of speech or of the press; or the right of the people peaceably to assemble and to petition the government for redress of grievances.

The Constitution, formally adopted in 1789, established a new nation—the United States of America. Under this constitution, American citizens enjoyed greater freedom and prosperity than any other people on earth. From the days of their early settlement, through their difficult years of war, in the framing of their government, and in the developing of their new nation, the American people looked to God for guidance, deliverance, and strength. As a result, later generations of Americans can sing,

> My country, 'tis of thee,
> Sweet land of liberty,
> Of thee I sing:
> Land where my fathers died,
> Land of the pilgrim's pride,
> From every mountain side
> Let freedom ring!
>
> Our fathers' God, to Thee,
> Author of liberty,
> To Thee we sing:
> Long may our land be bright
> With freedom's holy light;
> Protect us by Thy might,
> Great God, our King!

Section Review

1. List three reasons that England permitted her American colonies great religious and political liberty.
2. Following the Seven Years' War, what did England expect from her colonies in exchange for the benefits England provided?
3. What was at the root of the colonial protest against the actions of Parliament?
4. What battle fought in October of 1777 was the turning point in the War for Independence? What European country openly supported the American cause as a result of this victory?
5. Define the principle of federalism as it relates to the American government.

Independence Hall, Philadelphia

French Destruction of the Old Regime

Throughout the eighteenth century, France was the cultural center of Europe. European monarchs imitated the French absolutist government; they fashioned their royal courts after Versailles. French fashion, art, and learning were the envy of Europe. France had one of the largest populations and most active trade economies in all of Europe. But underneath the surface of this seeming prosperity were roots of unrest and turmoil. French *philosophes* had espoused the ideas of personal rights and liberties. But under the authority of an absolute monarch and the dominion of the Roman Catholic church, few Frenchmen enjoyed such freedom. "When the righteous are in authority," the writer of Proverbs says, "the people rejoice: but when the wicked beareth rule, the people mourn" (Prov. 29:2).

The Enlightenment had raised expectations of reform in French government and society. The American War for Independence gave hope to Frenchmen who desired the same freedoms for themselves. Yet the French political and social order remained the same. In addition, extravagant government spending and heavy taxation brought the country to the brink of economic collapse. Such were the conditions in France on the eve of the French Revolution.

Reasons for Discontent

Of the many factors that caused the French Revolution, none by itself was sufficient motivation for revolt. But when heaped together, they stirred widespread discontent with the **Old Regime** (the name given to the political and social order in France before the French Revolution). Revolution was only a short step away.

Social Inequality

As late as 1789, French society was still organized according to the old feudal class divisions of estates. The inequality of social privileges and taxation, which were determined by one's social class, caused deep-seated resentment among the underprivileged.

The First Estate—The **First Estate** consisted of the clergy of the Roman Catholic church. (Since the revocation of the Edict of Nantes in 1685, the Roman Catholic church had been the only recognized church in France.) The church had great wealth: she controlled vast land estates and was exempt from taxation. Part of this wealth was used to provide education and to care for the sick and needy; yet there were many of the upper clergy (such as the bishops) who considered the church's wealth their own. This wealthy group of clergy made up part of the aristocratic group that often advised the king in state matters. On the other hand, the lower clergy (the parish priests) were poor and in some cases destitute.

The Second Estate—The nobility made up the **Second Estate.** They too were a privileged class. They were exempt from many of the taxes levied by the French king. They held some of the highest positions in government and society.

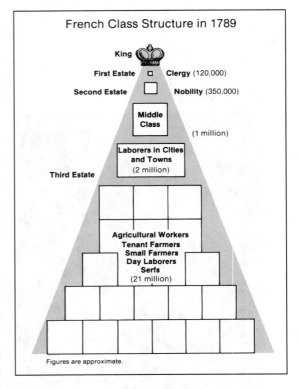

French Class Structure in 1789

King

First Estate — Clergy (120,000)

Second Estate — Nobility (350,000)

Middle Class (1 million)

Laborers in Cities and Towns (2 million)

Third Estate

Agricultural Workers
Tenant Farmers
Small Farmers
Day Laborers
Serfs
(21 million)

Figures are approximate.

The nobility owned vast estates, amounting to an estimated forty per cent of France. Most of the nobles, however, were not interested in improving their land but were interested only in exploiting it. Many nobles lived extravagantly at Versailles and paid agents to extract as much as they could from the impoverished tenants who lived on their estates. Because nobles could lose their titles for participating in trade, they sought to increase their income by assuming the best and most financially rewarding posts in the army, church, and legal professions. Many of the nobles who took such posts did not do any of the work that their positions demanded; they let others do the work while they drew the income.

The Third Estate—The **Third Estate** was by far the largest estate, comprising approximately ninety-eight per cent of the French population. Of the three estates, this class had the greatest social and economic diversity among its members. It was subdivided into three groups. At the top were the lawyers, doctors, bankers, and wealthy businessmen. Below them came the workers in the cities and towns. At the bottom of the social structure were the peasants, who comprised about eighty per cent of the population. While some of the peasants owned their land, the majority were extremely poor, working as tenants on the large estates of the wealthy elite. Although their wages were low and they generally had few material possessions, the peasants bore the heaviest tax burden. In addition, the peasants suffered under lingering feudal obligations. They were required to do the following:

1. pay an annual fee to the noble who owned or had owned the land on which they lived and worked.
2. pay a fee to the former owner when the land changed hands.
3. pay an annual fee for the use of mills, ovens, and winepresses, even if they did not use them.
4. perform the *corvée*—a system of forced labor. During the Middle Ages, the peasants had performed the *corvée* for their feudal lord. In eighteenth-century France, the peasants worked for the government, building and maintaining roads and canals.
5. respect the nobles' hunting privileges. From ancient times, the nobles had been allowed unlimited freedom to hunt; property rights did not restrict them. Peasants, however, were forbidden to kill rabbits, crows, or foxes, even if these animals ruined their crops.

Political Inefficiency

Neither King Louis XV (1715-74) nor King **Louis XVI** (1774-92) had the character or the inclination to rule France in the absolute fashion of Louis XIV. They were indifferent to the affairs of

Louis XVI

government. They had little sense of responsibility, interested more in the frivolous pleasures of life at Versailles. When they did turn their attention to matters of state, they often followed the capricious advice of their mistresses or fell prey to the intriguing schemes of the nobles in their court. Local rulers still imposed old feudal obligations, increasing their power while further restricting the freedom of the French people. The central government, which should have been a unifying force, was thus incompetent and inefficient.

The different social groups, hoping to take advantage of this confused situation, were eager to assume political power. The nobles felt that Louis XIV had unlawfully deprived their ancestors of their positions of authority. The middle class, well versed in the thought of the Enlightenment, wanted political power equal to their economic wealth. The lower classes felt that they were unfairly burdened with numerous and outdated feudal obligations.

Economic Irresponsibility

Unbalanced Tax System—The French system of taxation was grossly unbalanced. The privileged classes were exempt from most taxation. Those who had the least—the peasants—bore the greatest part of the tax burden. The peasants resented not only the unequal assessment of tax obligations but also the wasteful manner in which the taxes were collected and used.

The most common and important taxes levied by the French government were the *taille,* the *capitation,* and the *vingtième.* The *taille,* originally levied for military purposes, was a tax on real and personal property. The *capitation,* or poll tax, was a tax on each person; and the *vingtième* was an income tax. Some of the nobles, clergy, and wealthy middle class either purchased or were granted exemptions from many of these taxes. Others, because of their privileged status, evaded their tax responsibilities altogether. Their failure to share the tax burden not only increased the financial strain upon the peasants but also lessened the income the government received and thus contributed to the national debt.

Verge of Bankruptcy—In spite of heavy taxation, the French government continued to sink deeper into debt. The successors of King Louis XIV continued to wage war and spend extravagantly. Louis XV plunged France into the Seven Years' War, which cost France most of her colonies and overseas trade. Louis XVI, who had no sympathy for the American colonists' cause, nevertheless aided the Americans in hopes of weakening Britain. In addition, both monarchs continued to spend money from the public treasury for their personal luxuries at Versailles.

In order to lessen the national debt, the French government levied more taxes, debased the French currency, and borrowed more money from private banks. But these steps only contributed to the financial problems. To make matters worse, no one knew exactly how much money France actually needed to pay her bills, for France did not have a budget. Finally, in 1787, the private banks refused to extend any more credit to the French government. It was this financial crisis that sparked the outbreak of the revolution.

Rumors of new taxation sparked a workers' riot on April 6, 1789.

Outbreak of the Revolution

Calling of the Estates-General

From the beginning of Louis XVI's reign, able finance ministers had tried to solve France's economic problems. They told Louis that there was no money in the treasury and urged him to tax those who were paying no taxes. Louis, however, was a weak king who did not wish to offend anyone. Therefore, when the economic proposals of his finance ministers proved to be highly unpopular with the nobility, Louis dismissed his ministers. The nobles accused Louis of mismanagement and said that only the Estates-General could change the tax laws. This representative body, however, had not met since 1614. Desperate to find a solution to France's economic problems, Louis sent out a decree instructing the people to choose deputies (representatives) for a meeting at Versailles in May 1789. He told the people to give to their deputies lists of grievances (called *cahiers*) that they wished him to consider. Little did he realize what trouble he was inviting.

In towns and villages across France, the people met to choose deputies to represent them at Versailles. Excitement ran high at the meetings of the Third Estate. Led by the educated middle class, the people drew up their *cahiers*. These lists of grievances were very similar from province to province; most called for a written constitution, equal taxation, equal justice, and the destruction of the remnants of feudalism. The First and Second Estates chose deputies too. For the most part their *cahiers* contained ideas different from those of the Third Estate. They did, however, call for a constitution that would stop the king from infringing upon their rights and privileges.

By Order of the King

Our beloved and faithful, we need the cooperation of our loyal subjects in surmounting all our financial difficulties and in establishing, according to our wishes, a constant and invariable order in all branches of the government which affect the welfare of our subjects and the prosperity of our kingdom. Such worthy motives have induced us to convoke the assembly of the states of all the provinces of our dominion to advise us in whatever is presented to them, and to inform us of the wishes and grievances of our people, so that . . . an efficacious remedy for the ills of the State may be obtained.[1]

—Royal Letter of Convocation
January 24, 1789

Convening of the Estates-General

The deputies made their way to Versailles in late April of 1789. They arrived armed with their *cahiers,* fully expecting the king to listen carefully to their complaints and to right the wrongs so readily apparent in French society. The deputies of the Third Estate, however, were soon disillusioned. At the formal reception given by the king, they were kept waiting for hours. Unlike the richly attired nobles and clergy, they had to dress in black, keep their hats off, and enter the hall through a side door. When they were finally presented to the king, Louis stood in silence as they filed by.

The opening meeting on May 5 was also a disappointment. Louis, instead of assuring the deputies that he would be interested in their ideas for reform, was noncommittal. His only instructions were that they should meet as estates and vote as estates—each estate receiving one vote.

The deputies of the Third Estate objected. They wanted each delegate's vote to be counted separately, regardless of his estate. They would thus have the majority vote, for the deputies of the Third Estate outnumbered those of the First Estate 578 to 291; the Second Estate had only 270 deputies. They realized that if each estate received only one vote, their reforms had little chance of passing. The First and Second Estates were not interested in the grievances of the Third Estate; thus the Third Estate could be outvoted two to one.

Forming of the National Assembly

The disagreement over voting continued until June 17, when the delegates of the Third Estate proclaimed themselves the National Assembly. Since they were sent by the people, they claimed to speak for the people. They asserted the principle of popular sovereignty and denounced the unfair social order of France. They invited the members of the other two estates to join them, and a few did.

On June 20, when the members of the Third Estate arrived at their assembly room, they found the doors locked. Undaunted, the deputies gathered in the nearby indoor royal tennis court. There they swore the famous **"Tennis Court Oath,"** declaring that they would not disband until a written constitution was established.

Three days later, at a joint meeting of the Estates-General, Louis again stated his opposition to a meeting of the three estates as a group unless it were for the purpose of raising taxes. While he made some reforming concessions, he insisted that the "old distinction" between the estates be maintained. He then dismissed the deputies and left. Most of the members of the First and Second Estates left with him, but the deputies of the Third Estate remained. By now they were in a defiant mood. When the king's messenger returned to tell them to go home, one of their leaders said, "Go and tell those who sent you that we are here by the

The Tennis Court Oath

The National Assembly, considering that it has been summoned to establish the constitution of the kingdom, to effect the regeneration of public order, and to maintain the true principles of monarchy; that nothing can prevent it from continuing its deliberations in whatever place it may be forced to establish itself; and, finally that wheresoever its members are assembled, there is the National Assembly;

Decree that all members of this assembly shall immediately take a solemn oath not to separate, and to reassemble wherever circumstances require, until the constitution of the kingdom is established and consolidated upon firm foundations.[2]

Tennis Court Oath, June 20, 1789

will of the people, and that we will go only if we are driven at the point of the bayonet!'' When this message was conveyed to the king, he responded, ''Well, let them stay.''

On June 27, Louis ordered the First and Second Estates to join the National Assembly, which now called itself the National Constituent Assembly. The Assembly immediately set about to draw up a constitution. For a while it looked as if the king had surrendered to the Third Estate. But this was not so. Upon the advice of some in his court, he ordered troops to Versailles and Paris, supposedly for protection. What Louis actually had in mind when he called up the troops was to close down the Assembly. This double-mindedness was typical of Louis. He did not hesitate to change his mind to keep the peace or avoid offending someone. The book of James warns about the folly of such inde-

cisiveness: ''A double minded man is unstable in all his ways.''

Storming of the Bastille

On July 12, Paris was the scene of rioting and looting by angry mobs. Angered by high prices for bread and by rumors that Louis's troops intended to murder them, the Parisians began searching for weapons so that they could defend themselves. The disturbance lasted well into the next day, when the mob heard that there were arms at the Hôtel des Invalides (a hospital for soldiers) and the Bastille (a royal prison for political prisoners). On the morning of July 14, 1789, part of the mob stormed the Invalides; others laid siege and captured the Bastille. When the gates to the Bastille were opened, the mob stormed in and murdered the governor of the prison and his men.

The storming of the Bastille was the action of a frenzied mob. Yet it came to symbolize the downfall of the Old Regime. When Louis heard of the incident, he said, "This is a revolt." His aide replied, "No, Sire. This is a revolution!"

The storming of the Bastille, July 14, 1789

Phases of the Revolution

Destruction of the Old Regime

The storming of the Bastille intensified uprisings throughout the French countryside. Peasants unleashed their frustration by plundering the homes of the nobility and destroying the feudal records that obligated them to service. In hopes of stemming fear and halting the increasing violence, the National Constituent Assembly passed legislation that made sweeping changes in French society, bringing the Old Regime to an end. From 1789-91 the Assembly passed more than two thousand laws. One of the first steps it took was to abolish feudalism. Many of the nobles in the Assembly, frightened by the peasant uprisings, renounced their feudal rights and privileges.

Most prominent among the Assembly's early actions was the adoption of the **Declaration of the Rights of Man** on August 27, 1789. This declaration derived its ideas partly from the English Bill of Rights; partly from the ideas of Montesquieu, Locke, and Rousseau; and partly from the American Declaration of Independence. In the Declaration of the Rights of Man, the Assembly listed what is considered to be the natural rights of all people and the rights that they possess as citizens.

> Men are born and remain free and equal in rights. Social distinctions can be based only upon public utility.

> The aim of every political association is the preservation of the natural and imprescriptible rights of man [rights that cannot be taken away]. These rights are liberty, property, security, and resistance to oppression.

> Liberty consists in the power to do anything that does not injure others.

> Law is the expression of the general will. All citizens have the right to take part personally or by their representatives in its formation. It must be the same for all, whether it protects or punishes.

> Every individual [is] presumed innocent until he has been proved guilty.

> No one should be disturbed because of his opinions, even in religion.

Louis, however, refused to give his consent to the recent legislation passed by the Assembly. His refusal, added to continued food shortages in Paris, brought mobs out into the streets once more. When a crowd of women could not get bread at a bakery, they decided to march to Versailles to protest their plight. Their number swelled to several thousand. On the way they were joined by many French soldiers. Upon reaching Versailles, they burst into the meeting of the Assembly and demanded bread. Getting little satisfaction there, a group of the marchers the next day broke into the royal palace and murdered two of the king's guards. They insisted that the royal family accompany them back to Paris. The king gave in, and he and his family traveled back to Paris. A few days later the delegates of the Assembly moved to Paris as well.

In response to this latest uprising, Louis gave his approval to the decrees of the Assembly. But the problem that had ignited the Revolution—

France's bankruptcy—had not been solved. In fact, it had become worse. The people refused to pay the king's tax collectors, and the Assembly had not devised any new system of tax collection. Finally the Assembly came up with a solution. Since the Roman Catholic church was extremely wealthy and owned vast quantities of land, the Assembly confiscated its land. It then issued paper money, called *assignats,* which was backed by the value of that land. They used these *assignats* to pay off the debts of the government.

Besides taking church lands, the Assembly passed the **Civil Constitution of the Clergy** (July 1790). This bill placed the church under state control, provided for the election of all the clergy by the people, and required the clergy to take an oath of loyalty to the state. When the pope condemned the constitution, many clergy refused to take the oath. As a result, there arose two groups of Roman Catholic clergy in France: juring clergy (those who took the oath) and nonjuring clergy (those who did not take the oath). In many areas of France the people would not recognize the juring clergy. Thus, while the Assembly had destroyed the power of the Roman Catholic church in France, it had antagonized many of the French Roman Catholics, creating yet another problem.

Overthrow of the Monarchy

Although 1790 was a rather peaceful year by revolutionary standards, 1791 proved to be another turbulent year. The king, seeing his powers being taken away and fearing for his life, tried to escape from France. Once out of the country, he hoped to enlist the aid of foreign monarchs and restore his power in France. He and his family disguised themselves and slipped out of the palace on the night of June 20, 1791. Their carriage was almost to the border when they were recognized by a postmaster. They were captured and escorted back to Paris by an armed guard.

In September the National Constituent Assembly completed the constitution over which it had labored for two years. This document completely restructured the French government. The king's power, formerly absolute, was now limited by a constitution. The constitution also guaranteed equal taxes, ended special privileges, created a fairer system of justice, and established a new governing body called the Legislative Assembly. Louis was compelled to agree to this constitution, and he issued a proclamation calling upon all Frenchmen to support it.

Problems of the Legislative Assembly—In October of 1791, the Legislative Assembly convened

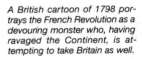

A British cartoon of 1798 portrays the French Revolution as a devouring monster who, having ravaged the Continent, is attempting to take Britain as well.

Course of the French Revolution

DATE	GOVERNMENT	CONTROLLED BY
May and June 1789	King and Estates General Absolute Monarchy	Louis XVI
1789-1791	National Assembly and King Limited Monarchy	Upper Middle Class
1791-1792	Legislative Assembly and King Limited Monarchy	Upper Middle Class
1792-1795	National Convention Republic	Parisian Mobs Robespierre
1795-1799	Directory Oligarchy	Upper Middle Class
1799-1804	Consulate Dictatorship	Napoleon
1804-1815	Empire Dictatorship	Napoleon

for the first time. Its newly elected members had no experience in governing France. In addition, the body was divided into several factions. One group of legislators wanted to maintain the limited monarchy as established by the constitution. Because they were satisfied with the accomplishments of the revolution and sought no further changes, they were known as the conservatives. Another group wished to completely rid France of the monarchy and to establish a republic in its place. These radicals advocated sweeping changes in the government. The third group, the moderates, sided with the conservatives on some issues and with the radicals on others.

Few Frenchmen supported the new government. The king and some of the nobility and clergy hoped to turn back the clock and restore the Old Regime. Other Frenchmen, however, believed that the revolution had not gone far enough. They wanted even more reforms. Some wanted to do away with the monarchy altogether. Those who advocated the most radical changes were the **Jacobins,** members of the Jacobin clubs. (These clubs took their name from an empty Jacobin convent that the Paris club used as its place of meeting.) Although the Jacobins gathered followers from all over France, it was the group in Paris that proved to be the most influential. Its most prominent leaders were Jean-Paul Marat (mah RAH), **Georges-Jacques Danton,** and **Maximilien de Robespierre** (ROHBZ pee EHR).

To achieve their radical goals, the Jacobins often stirred up mobs in the cities, especially in Paris. Jacobin rabble-rousers appealed to Paris workers known as the *sans-culottes*—literally, "without breeches." (Unlike the men of the upper and middle classes, the men of these lower classes did not wear fashionable knee breeches but wore full-length trousers instead.) They believed that the new constitution favored only the middle class. They wanted for themselves a greater share of the wealth of France and more of a voice in the French government.

War with Austria and Prussia—In April of 1792, the Legislative Assembly, backed by the king, declared war on Austria. (From this time until the final defeat of Napoleon in 1815, there was almost constant war in Europe.) Each political faction within France had a different reason for wanting war. The king, for example, hoped that Austria would defeat the Assembly's forces and come to his rescue. The Assembly hoped that a quick defeat of Austria

Right, Left, and Center

Three terms used today to describe various political philosophies originated, surprisingly enough, from the seating arrangement in the French National Assembly. When this legislative body first convened, a group called the Girondins sat on the speaker's right. The conservatives of their day, the Girondins were satisfied with the Constitution of 1791 and wished to see it preserved. The Jacobins, on the other hand, wanted the king removed and a republic introduced. Those who espoused this liberal philosophy sat on the speaker's left. The moderates, who wanted some changes but not radical ones, were seated between the Girondins and the Jacobins. From this arrangement we derive the terms right for conservatives, left for liberals, and center for moderates.

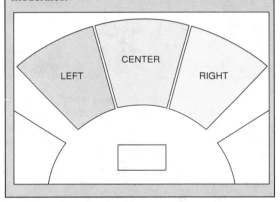

would gain the French people's support for the Assembly government. The Jacobins, however, did not want war, for they feared that a French victory would destroy their hopes of seizing power. Therefore, Marat and Danton deliberately sabotaged the war effort by delaying requests for army supplies.

Things did not go well for France early in the war. Prussia soon joined with Austria. The Austrian and Prussian armies, under the leadership of the Duke of Brunswick, invaded France. In July of 1792, the duke issued the famous **Brunswick Manifesto,** calling upon the French people to rally behind their king and to protect him from the leaders of the Revolution. He threatened to punish those who harmed the king and promised that he would restore Louis XVI to authority when Paris was captured.

Execution of the King—The Brunswick Manifesto, along with early military defeats, made the people of Paris distrustful of Louis. On August 10, 1792, a mob under the leadership of Danton invaded the palace, and murdered the king's Swiss guards. (Louis temporarily found refuge with the Assembly.) The mob demanded that the Legislative Assembly call for another convention to write a new constitution for France. Facing tremendous pressure from the radicals, the Assembly called for elections to a new body that was to be called the National Convention.

In August and September, while new deputies were being chosen, Danton became the virtual dictator of France. During this time many supporters of the monarchy met violent deaths by the radical mobs. In September widespread massacres took place. The mobs emptied the prisons of nobles and nonjuring clergy who were suspected of working against the Revolution. They mercilessly slaughtered them without benefit of trial.

On September 22, the newly elected National Convention abolished the monarchy and proclaimed 1792 to be Year One of the French Republic. The new government, faced with internal disorder and foreign invasion, took action against Louis XVI. Tried and found guilty of treason, the king was sentenced to death. On January 21, 1793, Louis XVI, who had once been called "Good King Louis," was taken by coach to a square in the middle of Paris. There, clad in a brown jacket, white waistcoat, and black breeches, he was led to the guillotine. He was allowed a few last words: "I die innocent," he said; "I pardon my enemies." As drums rolled, the blade did its work, and the head of the former king was held up for the crowd to see. The people threw their hats into the air and shouted, *"Vive la nation!"* ("Long live the nation!")

The Reign of Terror

The French Revolution now took a more destructive and bloody turn. The rebellion and violence in French society were not without their consequences—national suffering was sure to follow. The prophet Isaiah describes a similar situation.

None calleth for justice, nor any pleadeth for truth: they trust in vanity, and speak lies; they

conceive mischief, and bring forth iniquity. . . . Their feet run to evil, and they make haste to shed innocent blood: their thoughts are thoughts of iniquity; wasting and destruction are in their paths. The way of peace they know not; and there is no judgment in their goings: they have made them crooked paths: whosoever goeth therein shall not know peace. . . . For truth is fallen in the street, and equity cannot enter.
—Isaiah 59:4, 7-8, 14

The Committee of Public Safety—Faced with unrest at home and a critical situation on the battlefront, the National Convention appointed twelve men to take over the everyday affairs of government and, in particular, the war. With Robespierre as their leader, these men made up the **Committee of Public Safety.** They set about to create a new order in France. But "while they promise[d] . . . liberty, they themselves [were] the servants of corruption: for of whom a man is overcome, of the same is he brought in bondage" (II Pet. 2:19).

This Committee gave the Revolutionary Tribunal orders to suppress opposition to the Revolution. Anyone suspected of being an "enemy of the people" was arrested. Most suspects, whether guilty or not, were hastily tried and executed—some were drowned, others shot, and many more were guillotined. It has been estimated that between twenty and forty thousand died at the hands of the Tribunal. Surprisingly, the largest percentage of those executed were peasants or *sans-culottes*. The slogan of the Revolution, "Liberty, Equality, and Fraternity" (brotherhood), had become virtually meaningless.

The Committee responded to the looming threat of foreign invaders by mobilizing the entire nation in a unified effort to defeat its enemies. In August of 1793, the Committee issued a decree of ***levée en masse.*** It stated that "the young men shall go to battle; the married men shall forge arms and transport provisions; the women shall make tents and clothes, and shall serve in the hospitals; the children shall turn old linen into lint; the old men shall [go] to the public places to stimulate the courage of the warriors and preach the unity of the Republic and the hatred of kings." This was one of the first instances of a nation calling upon all its citizens to take an active part in the war effort.

The citizen army won a series of victories over the forces of the European **coalition** (a temporary alliance of nations), which was bent on keeping the Revolution from spreading throughout Europe. News of the victories lessened the tension back in Paris. Men such as Danton no longer felt that the Reign of Terror was necessary. Danton appealed to Robespierre to stop the bloodshed. But Robespierre had him arrested as a traitor and then guillotined. Members of the Convention became alarmed when Robespierre stood in the assembly and declared that there were still many traitors in their own ranks. "These must be weeded out," he said, "in order to save the Republic." Fearful of their own lives and weary of the Reign of Terror, the Convention had Robespierre and his followers arrested and sent to the guillotine. Like so many other revolutions, the French Revolution illustrates the saying that "a revolution devours

---

The Guillotine

During a debate in the National Assembly about the equality of all Frenchmen, a man named Dr. Joseph Guillotin rose to express his views on capital punishment. Under the Old Regime, he said, nobles received special treatment. When the situation called for their execution, they were decapitated by ax or sword, while the common man suffered execution by burning at the stake or hanging. If all Frenchmen were equal, Guillotin pointed out, all those condemned should be given a humane means of execution. The Assembly agreed and appointed Dr. Antoine Louis to develop an instrument of execution. After much research and experimentation on sheep and cadavers, he developed the guillotine, which was named for Guillotin. (This was not a new instrument. It had been used in Scotland, Germany, and Italy; Louis developed a new, streamlined model.) In March 1792 the National Assembly adopted the guillotine as the official instrument of execution in France. In later years of the Revolution, thousands of "equal" Frenchmen mounted the scaffolds to be "shaved by the national barber."

Revolutionizing a Nation

The leaders of the French Revolution attempted many political and economic changes. They destroyed the old provincial system of government and divided France into "departments." These departments, which were efficiently governed, helped diminish provincial loyalties that might hamper the new government. The old royal system of weights and measures was replaced with the newer, simpler metric system. These reforms outlived the Revolution itself.

Some of the social changes made during this period were not so long-lived. For instance, the new government's most visible reform was the new revolutionary calendar. The old months were replaced with twelve new thirty-day months (with five extra holidays at the end of the year to keep the calendar accurate). The old system of numbering years from the birth of Christ was replaced by numbering from the beginning of the Republic. Hence, September 22, in the year of our Lord 1792, became the first day of the month of *Vendémiaire* ("Vintage") in the year of the Republic 1. Those in power abolished the divinely established seven-day week (Gen. 2:2-3; Exod. 20:8-11) and instituted a ten-day week (called a *decade*) in which the tenth day was a day of rest. This calendar system never spread beyond France and lasted less than fifteen years there.

The more radical of the revolutionary leaders also attempted to change the state religion. Robespierre hoped to replace all forms of religion in France with a "cult of reason" in which men would worship wisdom. He even held a "Festival of Reason" in the Notre Dame Cathedral to establish his new "faith." The cult of reason, like the revolutionary calendar, proved a dismal failure.

its own." Proverbs 11:5 states, "The wicked shall fall by his own wickedness."

The End of the National Convention—In 1795 a new constitution was enacted, bringing an end to the Convention and establishing the **Directory.** This new government provided for a two-chamber legislature: the Council of Five Hundred and the Council of Ancients. The executive branch was a group of five men called the Directors. These men were to be nominated by the Council of Five Hundred and elected by the Council of Ancients.

The Directory inherited many problems. Constant warfare had brought France once more to the edge of bankruptcy. Internal unrest was threatening to cause another revolution. As had previously been the case, various groups worked to overthrow the new government in order to gain their selfish ends. Though Prussia had made peace with France in 1795, France still faced the threat of Austrian and British forces. The Directory placed the hopes of the defense of France in the hands of a young general named Napoleon Bonaparte.

Section Review

1. Define the "Old Regime."
2. Who bore the greatest tax burden under the French system of taxation? List and define the three types of taxes that they had to pay.
3. What is the name for the list of grievances which the delegates took to the convening of the Estates-General? List four of the most common grievances listed by the delegates of the Third Estate.
4. What action of the Parisian mob is considered the beginning of the French Revolution? Give the month, day, and year of this event.
5. List the three most prominent members of the Jacobin clubs.

The Napoleonic Era

Few individuals have so influenced and dominated the continent of Europe as did **Napoleon Bonaparte** (1769-1821). So strongly did he make his presence felt in Europe that the period from 1796 to 1815 is often called "the Napoleonic Era."

Napoleon was born on the island of Corsica. He attended a military academy in France, and during his early career in the army, he spent many hours studying military strategy. He served in the revolutionary army and later distinguished himself when he suppressed a Paris riot in 1795, helping to pave the way for the establishment of the Directory. As a result, the Directors of the new government chose him to lead the French forces against the Austrians. Instead of directly attacking Austria, Napoleon launched a campaign in northern Italy, which was under Austrian domination. Fighting by what his opponents called ''new rules''—marching at night, fighting on Sundays, and fighting in the rain—he won victory after victory. He extracted a heavy toll from his defeated foes, allowing his poorly equipped soldiers to take booty. In 1797 Austria made peace with France, and Napoleon returned to Paris as a hero.

Members of the Directory were jealous and fearful of Napoleon's popularity. To get him out of Paris, they directed him to invade England. Rejecting this idea, he decided instead to attack Egypt in order to cut off Britain's trade with the Near East. In 1798 he invaded Egypt with an army of some thirty-five thousand men. After some early victories by Napoleon, the British fleet under the command of **Lord Nelson** destroyed the French fleet anchored at Alexandria. The British then blockaded Napoleon and his troops in Egypt, cutting them off from needed supplies. In this desperate situation, Napoleon received word that a new European coalition composed of Britain, Russia, the Ottoman Turks, and Austria had been formed to renew the war against France. Leaving his army in Egypt, Napoleon made his way back to France.

Overthrow of the Directory

Napoleon landed in southern France, where crowds welcomed him as a new Caesar returning in triumph. (They did not know of his defeats nor of the fate of his army in Egypt.) Declaring that he had come to save France, he triumphantly made his way to Paris. Once there, he and his supporters staged a successful *coup d'état* (KOO day TAH)— a sudden and illegal seizure of power by force. By the end of 1799 a new government, called the Consulate, was formed under yet another constitution. When Napoleon submitted the constitution to the people for confirmation in a vote called a plebiscite, they overwhelmingly approved. This constitution established a three-man Consulate modeled after

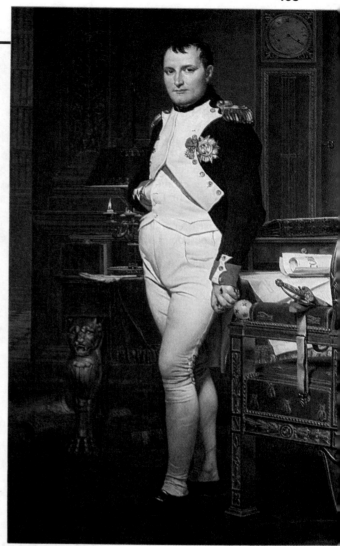

Jacques Louis David, Napoleon in His Study, *National Gallery of Art, Washington, D.C.*

the Roman government. The real power, however, was concentrated in the First Consul, Napoleon.

Promising peace and the restoration of internal order, Napoleon first worked to establish peace with France's external foes. After long negotiations, France signed peace treaties with Austria (1800) and Britain (1802). Meanwhile, Napoleon initiated many domestic reforms. He began public works programs (constructing roads, bridges, and canals); founded the Bank of France, which standardized the monetary system; and set up a more equitable tax system, which helped to stabilize the national debt. He also established a system of public education supervised by an agency called the University of France. Perhaps his most famous accomplishment was the codification of French laws, later to be named the **Code Napoleon.** Napoleon appointed a commission to arrange in an orderly system the various laws that came out of the Revolution. This code established the civil, criminal, and commercial laws of France, many of which exist today.

Since most Frenchmen remained loyal Roman Catholics, Napoleon realized that he could increase his popularity and influence by restoring certain privileges to the Roman Catholic church. Therefore, in 1801 he made an agreement with the pope that returned certain lands to the church, allowed seminaries to operate, and permitted church services to be held openly. In addition, the agreement specified that the state would nominate the bishops and pay the salaries of all the clergy. Although the agreement looked good on paper, Napoleon undermined it with other laws that were hostile to the church.

Creation of Napoleon's Empire

Napoleon's Crowning

After seizing the French government in 1799, Napoleon worked to increase his personal power. In 1802 he held a plebiscite in which the people overwhelmingly agreed to make him First Consul for life. Then in 1804 the Senate proclaimed Napoleon the emperor of France. In a spectacular ceremony on December 2, 1804, in Notre Dame Cathedral, Napoleon took the imperial crown from the hands of the pope and placed it on his own head. Napoleon's assumption of imperial power officially brought the Republic to an end. France, which had begun the revolution with the weak rule of an absolute king, now had an emperor who ruled with strong dictatorial power.

Napoleon's Conquests

Napoleon's unbridled ambition would not be satisfied until he became master of all Europe. His chief obstacle, however, was Great Britain. Napoleon began planning an invasion of Britain, but his

Napoleon as emperor

plans were thwarted by a decisive naval battle in 1805. The British fleet, under the leadership of Admiral Lord Nelson, encountered the French fleet off the Cape of Trafalgar on the southern coast of Spain. Nelson was killed in the ensuing battle, but his fleet ensured Britain's control of the seas by soundly defeating the French.

Abandoning his English invasion, Napoleon launched an all-out campaign against British allies on the Continent. Austria, Russia, and Sweden had joined with Great Britain in 1805 to form the Third Coalition against France. But Napoleon's army crushed the combined armies of Austria and Russia at Austerlitz. In 1806 Napoleon dissolved the Holy Roman Empire and set up the Confederation of the Rhine, composed of western German states under Napoleon's protection. When Prussia entered the war against France, its armies were likewise defeated.

By 1808 Napoleon had truly become the master of the mainland of Europe, and his personal power was at its height. Nevertheless, Great Britain still controlled the seas. Thus Napoleon could not directly attack the British Isles. Instead, he devised a plan of attack that became known as the **Continen-**

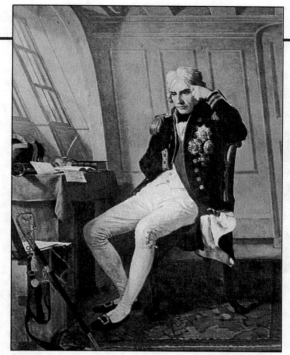

British admiral Horatio Nelson aboard his flagship Victory

tal System. Using his superior land forces, he attempted to close Europe's ports to British ships. He hoped that such a blockade of British trade would cause the British economy to collapse.

Napoleon's Downfall

As Napoleon's armies swept through Europe, many Europeans welcomed the French troops as "liberators" come to free them from the oppression of their absolute rulers. They soon found, however, that they were merely under a new form of oppression. In many European countries, Napoleon replaced the national rulers with one of his relatives. He demanded that these subject lands furnish him with soldiers and supplies. He also looted many lands of their national art treasures, which he took back to France. Overall, he showed little concern about their national feelings or interests.

Nationalistic pride soon began to stir across Europe, and people began to seek freedom from French domination. Furthermore, they resisted the Continental System, for although it was aimed at destroying the British economy, they were suffering under the loss of British trade. Conflict broke out in the Iberian Peninsula when Portugal violated the blockade against British trade and Spain revolted against the rule of Napoleon's brother. French troops were sent to crush the uprisings, but they met with fierce resistance from small bands of Spanish troops, who attacked the French garrisons and then retreated into the hills. These attacks were called *guerrillas* (Spanish for "little wars"). In addition, British troops soon landed in Portugal and began a campaign that eventually drove the French out of the peninsula.

Disaster in Russia

The Portuguese were not the only ones who refused to cooperate with the Continental System. In 1810 Russia broke with the system too. When Czar Alexander I refused to suppress British trade, Napoleon declared war on Russia. He amassed a huge army, called the "Grand Army," totalling about six hundred thousand men (including many non-French soldiers), and in 1812 invaded Russia.

Napoleon planned to engage the Russians in one decisive battle near their western border. But when the Russians realized that their forces were outnumbered, they slowly retreated, drawing the Grand Army deeper and deeper into Russia. As the Russian army retreated, they left nothing behind, burning everything that might be of value to the enemy. (This strategy is called the **scorched-earth policy.**)

Napoleon continued to press on, hoping that if he could capture Moscow, the czar would come to terms. He won several battles along the way, but he could not destroy the Russian army, which kept retreating. Finally, in September of 1812, his army reached Moscow. When Napoleon entered the city, he found it abandoned. That night fire swept through the city, destroying most of it. Napoleon remained in Moscow more than a month, thinking that the czar might still surrender. Winter was approaching, however, and Napoleon knew that his troops were clad only in summer uniforms and did not have enough supplies to spend the winter in Moscow. Frustrated, he finally gave orders to retreat.

As the Grand Army made its way back across the Russian plains, the bitter cold and snow of the Russian winter set in. The Russians, like packs of wolves, picked off the stragglers one by one. At the

Austerlitz—Napoleon's Greatest Triumph

Napoleon Bonaparte was the greatest military commander of his day. He consistently defeated opponent after opponent for almost twenty years. Napoleon's method was to move with speed and flexibility, keeping his forces spread out for easy movement, yet close enough to join quickly for battle. Napoleon believed that by concentrating on a single weak point in the enemy's position, he could defeat his opponent. Above all, he planned his campaigns in a daring manner that confused and frustrated his opponents. No battle illustrates Napoleon's military genius more clearly than the Battle of Austerlitz.

In 1805 the French faced the combined armies of Austria and Russia, called the Allies. Napoleon responded by suddenly invading Austria with seventy thousand French troops. He surrounded and captured thirty thousand stunned Austrian troops at Ulm and then turned northward to face the Russians and remaining Austrians. He decided to try to bait a trap for them. First Napoleon selected a site for the battle, near the town of Austerlitz. Then he made his army look smaller by sending twenty thousand men one day's march behind him. He ordered his main forces to fall back slowly, luring the Allies forward to the chosen battlefield. Finally he tempted the Allies to attack the right end of his line by crowding his troops at the foot of a plateau and exposing his line of retreat to the enemy.

In the Allied camp, Czar Alexander I arrived and took command of the forces. Seeing the apparently weak French position, he assumed that Napoleon had blundered and ordered an attack. On December 2, the Russian and Austrian forces rolled forward. They planned to swing around the southern end of the French line, cut off Napoleon's retreat, and then crush the French emperor's force—which was exactly what Bonaparte expected them to do.

Napoleon was ready. He had already called back the twenty thousand men he had hidden. As the Allies moved forward, the French retreated from the heights. Meanwhile, an early morning fog covered the movements of the other French forces as they prepared a surprise blow. When the Allies were halfway down the slope chasing the ''retreating'' French, Napoleon sent his other forces forward in a sharp counterattack. Surprised and confused, the Allies began to give way. The center of the Allied line broke, and the French swept south, ''rolling up'' the enemy's line and driving them back. Thousands of panicking Russian troops had to flee across frozen lakes whose icy surface cracked and broke under their weight. By the end of the day, thousands of prisoners had fallen into French hands, and the Allied armies fell back in disorganized retreat.

Napoleon's Empire

- French Empire
- Ruled by Napoleon
- Allied with Napoleon
- Independent States (European)
- ★ Battle Sites

Berezina River they burned the bridges, further delaying the French retreat until new bridges could be built. Some tried to swim across the river but were frozen to death. Here Napoleon abandoned his army and sped on to Paris to maintain control of the government before the people heard the dreadful news. In the end, fewer than one hundred thousand of his soldiers returned safely from Russia.

Defeat and Exile

The following year Napoleon once more persuaded the French people to raise an army to defend his empire against a new coalition of European powers. In a long campaign in 1813, Napoleon's forces were finally defeated at Leipzig, Germany, in what was later called the Battle of Nations. After a series of negotiations, the European Coalition forced Napoleon to abdicate. They allowed him to go to the small island of Elba just off the western coast of Italy. They granted him the title "Emperor of the Isle of Elba," and he agreed to spend the rest of his life on the island.

Meanwhile the European powers met in Vienna to try to restore order to Europe. But in February of 1815, while the Congress of Vienna was meeting, word reached them that Napoleon had escaped from Elba and was making his way to Paris. He entered Paris in triumph and once again raised an army to go against the armies of Britain and Prussia. On June 8, 1815, the armies clashed on the plains of Waterloo in what is today Belgium. The allied forces, under the leadership of the British **Duke of Wellington,** won a decisive victory. Napoleon was banished to St. Helena, a little island in the middle of the South Atlantic. There he lived out his days under guard. He died on May 5, 1821, and was buried on the island. In 1840 his body was moved to Paris. Napoleon had said in 1804, ''Death is nothing; but to live defeated and inglorious is to die daily.'' How he must have ''died'' during those six years on St. Helena!

Section Review

1. What is the period from 1796 to 1815 often called in European history?

2. What event officially brought an end to the French Republic? In what year did this occur?

3. What battle illustrates the military genius of Napoleon and is often called his greatest triumph?

4. What country did Napoleon invade in 1812? What policy did this country practice to impede the French invasion?

5. In what battle was Napoleon defeated for the final time? Who led the allied forces? To where was Napoleon banished?

A Glimpse Behind and a Glimpse Ahead

Historians today often associate the French Revolution with the American Revolution. They hail the spirit of liberty that both revolutions stirred. Although at the outset the two revolutions had much in common, their paths diverged. Both were influenced by Enlightenment ideas. But the Protestant-Puritan heritage of the Americans helped protect America from the wanton destruction that took place in France. In addition, the leadership of the American cause recognized the *responsibility* that accompanies liberty.

The radicals who seized control of the French Revolution, on the other hand, simply emphasized liberty itself. This attitude fostered an atmosphere of unrestraint. Unlike the Americans, they sought to overthrow a tradition of tyranny; in doing so, their efforts led to a ''reign of terror'' and eventually to a dictatorship. Thus we must be cautious in comparing the two revolutions, for their outcomes were entirely different.

We must also remember that true liberty does not come through revolution but through regeneration. God's Word establishes the principle: ''Ye shall know the truth, and the truth shall make you free'' (John 8:32). That Truth is the Lord Jesus Christ, who said, ''I am the way, the truth, and the life: no man cometh unto the Father, but by me'' (John 14:6).

Chapter Review

Can You Explain?

federalism
popular sovereignty
Old Regime

corvée
cahiers
assignats

sans-culottes
coalition
coup d'état

Continental System
guerrillas
scorched-earth policy

Can You Identify?

Pilgrims
Mayflower Compact
George III
July 4, 1776
George Washington
Treaty of Paris (1783)
Bill of Rights
First Estate
Second Estate

Third Estate
Louis XVI
Tennis Court Oath
July 14, 1789
Declaration of the
    Rights of Man
Civil Constitution of
    the Clergy
Jacobins

Georges-Jacques
    Danton
Maximilien de
    Robespierre
Brunswick Manifesto
September 22, 1792
Reign of Terror
Committee of Public
    Safety

levée en masse
Directory
Napoleon Bonaparte
Lord Nelson
Code Napoleon
Duke of Wellington

Can You Locate?

Plymouth Colony
Boston
Saratoga
Yorktown

Corsica
Alexandria
Trafalgar

Austerlitz
Berezina River
Leipzig

Elba
Waterloo
St. Helena

How Much Do You Remember?

1. List three reasons that colonists settled in North America.
2. List the three estates in French society and identify what groups of people belonged to each estate.
3. List three major causes of the French Revolution.
4. Identify each of the following terms: *levée en masse, sans-culottes, coup d'état,* and *guerrillas.*
5. Beginning with the absolute monarchy under Louis XVI and going through the dictatorship of Napoleon, identify the various stages of the French Revolution and the person/people in control of each phase.

What Do You Think?

1. How were the American and French Revolutions similar? How did they differ?
2. What is the source of liberty? What is the only way people can have true liberty?
3. Does a Christian have the right to rebel against his government, especially if his cause is just and his government is unjust and oppressive? Consult such passages as Romans 13:1-7, Daniel 3 (concerning Daniel's friends and Nebuchadnezzar), and I Samuel 15:23.

Notes
1. John H. Stewart, *A Documentary Survey of the French Revolution* (New York: Macmillan, 1951), p. 29.
2. Ibid., p. 88

UNIT VI

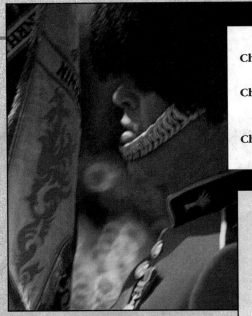

The European World

Chapter 16: Reaction and Revolution
"When France sneezes, all Europe catches cold."

Chapter 17: Industrial Revolution and
European Society
"The best of times, . . . the worst of times."

Chapter 18: Expansion and Evangelism
"Unto the uttermost part of the earth"

Except for Australia, Europe is the smallest continent in the world. But in cultural, economic, and political influence, Europe ranked second to none in the nineteenth century. Nearly every important nineteenth-century movement in art, politics, or any other field originated in Europe. The Industrial Revolution made Europe the unquestioned economic and military leader of the era. Europe flexed its new-found muscles too. Colonialism in Asia and Africa expanded as producers sought new sources for raw materials and markets for their goods. Europe's Christian heritage, derived from the work of the reformers and men such as Wesley, also spread throughout the world as missionaries carried the gospel to "the uttermost part of the earth." The nineteenth century was indeed the "European century."

NINE-TEENTH CENTURY

REVOLUTIONS OF 183

ROMANTICISM

GREEK REVOLT
(1821-29)

David (1748-1825)

SOUTH AMERICAN
INDEPENDENCE

• CONGRESS OF VIENNA
(1814-1815)

Constable (1776-1837)

INDUSTRIAL
REVOLUTION

• LOUISIANA PURCHASE (1803)

REFORM BI
OF 18

Beethoven (1770-1827)

Turner
(1775-1851)

Carey (1761-1834)

Wordsworth
(1770-1850)

• MONROE
DOCTRINE
(1823)

WARS

1800   1810   1820   18

THE EUROPEAN WORLD

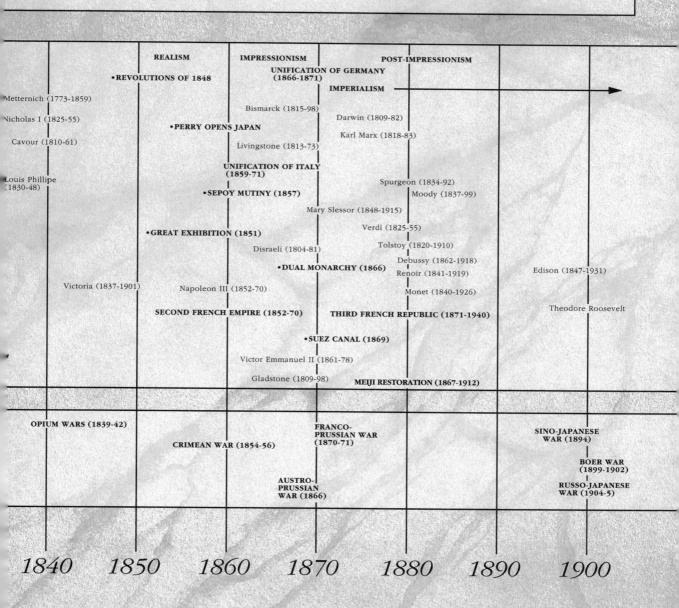

REALISM   IMPRESSIONISM   POST-IMPRESSIONISM

UNIFICATION OF GERMANY
(1866-1871)

•REVOLUTIONS OF 1848

IMPERIALISM

Metternich (1773-1859)

Bismarck (1815-98)

Nicholas I (1825-55)

Darwin (1809-82)

•PERRY OPENS JAPAN

Cavour (1810-61)

Karl Marx (1818-83)

Livingstone (1813-73)

UNIFICATION OF ITALY
(1859-71)

Louis Phillipe
(1830-48)

•SEPOY MUTINY (1857)

Spurgeon (1834-92)

Moody (1837-99)

Mary Slessor (1848-1915)

•GREAT EXHIBITION (1851)

Verdi (1825-55)

Disraeli (1804-81)

Tolstoy (1820-1910)

Debussy (1862-1918)

•DUAL MONARCHY (1866)

Renoir (1841-1919)

Edison (1847-1931)

Victoria (1837-1901)

Napoleon III (1852-70)

Monet (1840-1926)

SECOND FRENCH EMPIRE (1852-70)

THIRD FRENCH REPUBLIC (1871-1940)

Theodore Roosevelt

•SUEZ CANAL (1869)

Victor Emmanuel II (1861-78)

Gladstone (1809-98)

MEIJI RESTORATION (1867-1912)

OPIUM WARS (1839-42)

FRANCO-
PRUSSIAN WAR
(1870-71)

SINO-JAPANESE
WAR (1894)

CRIMEAN WAR (1854-56)

BOER WAR
(1899-1902)

RUSSO-JAPANESE
WAR (1904-5)

AUSTRO-
PRUSSIAN
WAR (1866)

1840   1850   1860   1870   1880   1890   1900

CHAPTER 16

"When France sneezes, all Europe catches cold."

Reaction and Revolution

The spirit of rebellion did not cease with the defeat of Napoleon. From 1815 to 1848 violent uprisings continued to break out on the streets of Paris and spread like a virus all over Europe, causing one European statesman to remark, "When France sneezes, all Europe catches cold." The "cold" he referred to was the spirit of revolution that was being stirred by liberalism and nationalism—forces calling for further change in the social and political structure of Europe.

Conservative elements, however, were opposed to these forces of change. The reactionary rulers of Europe sought to suppress reform and restore the social and political order present in Europe before 1789. But their task was not an easy one. They tried to stamp out revolts with their armies; for the most part, they were successful in the early part of the nineteenth century. But they could not stamp out revolutionary ideas. Such ideas found expression in virtually every aspect of European culture—especially in the literature, art, and music of the romantic movement. As a result, the second half of the nineteenth century saw the forces of liberalism and nationalism triumphing over the forces of conservatism.

Search for Stability

Napoleon had created a new Europe. His conquests had shattered existing national boundaries and had overthrown ruling families. His military campaigns had unleashed nationalism and liberalism all across Europe. But with his downfall in 1814, Europe was ready for peace; there had been almost constant fighting for twenty-five years. The victorious nations of the Grand Alliance—Britain, Austria, Prussia, and Russia—were now faced with restoring order and stability in Europe. They decided to convene a congress of European leaders in order to draw up a settlement.

Congress of Vienna: Restoration of the Old Order

In September of 1814 leading statesmen of Europe gathered in Vienna, Austria. Many of the rulers of Europe were present, and hundreds of diplomats and their wives from nearly every European country crowded into the city. The **Congress of Vienna** was a glittering social occasion. When the delegates were not involved in the difficult negotiations, they and their wives spent much time at lavish parties, festive balls, and musical performances.

The delegates did not meet in large formal sessions. Most of the negotiations were conducted in small, informal, and often secret gatherings. These gatherings were dominated by the spokesmen for the great powers: the foreign minister of Britain, **Lord Castlereagh** (KASS ul RAY); Czar **Alexander I** of Russia; and the Austrian minister of foreign affairs, **Prince Klemens von Metternich.**

Metternich (1773-1859) was the leading figure at the congress. He was a **reactionary** who wished to reverse the trends begun by the French Revolution and restore Europe to its pre-Revolution conditions. So strong was his influence over the congress and over later European politics that the period from 1815 to 1848 is called the "Age of Metternich."

Another important figure at Vienna was **Charles Maurice de Talleyrand** (1754-1838). Talleyrand, the representative of defeated France, was a shrewd and opportunistic politician. He had been a delegate to the Estates-General in 1789, a prominent figure in the National Assembly, and later foreign minister under the Directory and Napoleon. He attended the congress as the new foreign minister of the French king Louis XVIII, the restored Bourbon monarch. Talleyrand took advantage of the disagreement among the great powers at the congress to secure a favorable settlement for France.

Opposite Page: France's tricolor flag, adopted during the French Revolution, became a symbol of revolutionary ideas not only in France but also all across Europe.

Delegates to the Congress of Vienna; Talleyrand is seated on the right with his arm resting on the table. Metternich, in white breeches, is standing on the left.

Redrawing the Map of Europe

Many Europeans hoped that the Vienna peace settlement would support some of the rights and freedoms championed by the French Revolution. But the leading diplomats at Vienna were more concerned about restoring order to Europe. They sought to reestablish political stability, maintain the balance of power among the leading European nations, and respond to the revolutionary ideas spread by France.

Safeguards Against France—In dealing with defeated France, the congress was fairly lenient. Members feared that harsh punishment would only infuriate the French and thus hinder any chances of working out a lasting peace in Europe. The congress did, however, strip France of her conquests, reducing her territory to its 1792 borders. In addition, she had to pay **indemnities**—compensation to other nations for war damages.

While the members of the congress agreed to this moderate settlement, they still feared the French. In order to prevent any further acts of French aggression, they sought to encircle France with a buffer of strong powers. They united the Austrian Netherlands (Belgium) with the Dutch Netherlands in order to form a protective barrier to the north. To the east, they gave Prussia territory along the Rhine River and retained the Confederation of German States established by Napoleon. On France's southern border, they enlarged the Kingdom of Sardinia. (See map on p. 419.)

Restoration of Legitimate Rulers—During his conquests, Napoleon had deposed many European rulers, placing his relatives on their thrones. Following the principle of **legitimacy,** the congress removed these rulers and, where possible, restored those whom Napoleon had unseated. In France, for example, the monarchy was reestablished, and Louis XVIII was invited to assume the throne of his brother Louis XVI. (Louis XVI's young son, considered ''Louis XVII'' even though he did not rule, died in prison during the French Revolution.)

Grants of Compensation—The victors of the Napoleonic Wars and those nations that lost territory in the encirclement of France were compensated with additional territory. In return for giving up her holdings in the Netherlands, Austria received territory in northern Italy. Sweden allowed Russia to keep Finland and received Norway in return. (Norway was taken from Denmark, which had sided with Napoleon.) Although Great Britain did not receive any territory on the Continent, she retained control of some French and Dutch colonies seized during recent wars.

Balance of Power—Another chief concern of the Congress of Vienna was to maintain the balance of power in Europe. The delegates wanted to prevent any nation from becoming so strong that it could threaten the security of Europe as France had done. This concern was increased by jealous rivalries among the major European powers. Metternich, for example, was especially fearful of the growing power of Prussia, which threatened Austria's domination over the German Confederation. In addition, the ambition of Czar Alexander I, who claimed all of Poland for Russia, caused further alarm. Talleyrand urged Castlereagh and Metternich to take action, and France, Austria, and Britain signed a treaty pledging to use force if necessary to prevent Prussia or Russia from gaining more power. As a result, both Russia and Prussia backed down from many of their demands.

Final Settlement at Vienna

The congress was close to reaching a final peace settlement in March of 1815, when news reached Vienna that Napoleon had left the island of Elba and was on his way to Paris. The leaders of the Grand Alliance decided to bring together their armies and once more rid Europe of Napoleon. In June the allied forces, commanded by the duke of Wellington, defeated Napoleon's army at Waterloo (in present-day Belgium). In the same month, the delegates of the congress put the finishing touches on the peace settlement.

Although the Congress of Vienna had settled the matters of encirclement, legitimacy, compensation, and balance of power, its delegates made few concessions to the causes of nationalism and liberalism. They redrew the map of Europe with little regard for the interests of various national

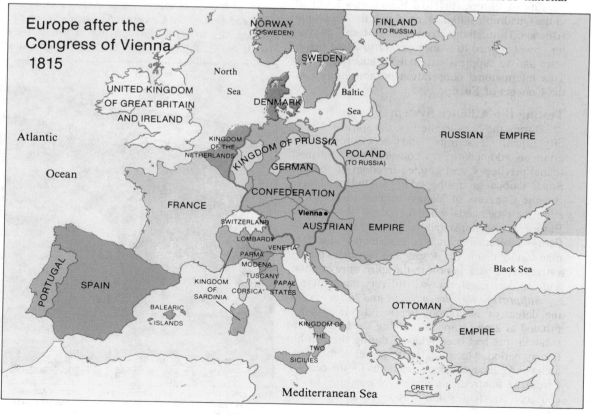

Europe after the Congress of Vienna 1815

groups. Though the major powers consented to co-operate to prevent a major war, a very explosive situation had been established in Europe. Soon the forces of nationalism and democratic liberalism ignited widespread revolt in Europe.

Concert of Europe: Protection of the Old Order

Establishing the Alliance System

In their concern to preserve peace in Europe, the delegates at the Vienna Congress established the **Quadruple Alliance.** In November of 1815 the four nations of the Grand Alliance—Austria, Prussia, Russia, and Great Britain—signed an agreement designed to maintain the Vienna settlements. They agreed to convene new congresses when necessary to resolve problems affecting the peace and stability of Europe. In 1818 France was admitted to the Quadruple Alliance, making it the Quintuple Alliance. Through this **"congress system"** the major powers hoped to work together to avoid major wars and to suppress nationalism and liberalism. This international cooperation became known as the **Concert of Europe.**

Testing the Alliance System

During the Napoleonic Era, the spirit of "Liberty, Equality, Fraternity" had swept Europe. Governments adopted written constitutions, abolished feudal privileges, and granted freedom of speech. Small national groups hoped to gain independence. But the Congress of Vienna refused to acknowledge their demands when it redrew the map of Europe. It also reinstated the powers of **conservatism**—absolute monarchy, the aristocracy, and Roman Catholicism. Yet despite the fact that conservatives were back in power, the spirit of revolution and democratic reform was still very much alive.

Suppressed Revolts in Spain and Italy—After the defeat of Napoleon, Ferdinand VII was reinstated as king of Spain. Ignoring the liberal constitution that had been adopted during the revolutionary period, which limited the power of the monarchy and guaranteed basic freedoms for the people, Ferdinand reintroduced repressive measures to the country. The Inquisition was revived, and those

who spoke out for reform were punished. In 1820 an uprising broke out. The Spanish people demanded that the king restore the constitution. Ferdinand, having lost the support of the Spanish army, gave in to their demands. The Spanish revolt also sparked a similar uprising in Italy. In the Kingdom of the Two Sicilies, the people forced the king to grant a constitution.

Word of the revolts spread alarm among the rulers of Europe. Metternich feared that one revolution would lead to another and that soon all Europe would be caught up in the revolutionary fervor. He called for a meeting of the Concert of Europe. At a congress in 1820, the Quintuple Alliance decided to send Austrian troops into Italy to suppress the revolution and restore the king's authority. Two years later it sent French troops into Spain to crush the revolt. In both instances, the forces of the Quintuple Alliance were successful.

Weakness of the Congress System—When the alliance met to settle the uprising in Spain, they also discussed the problem of the Spanish colonies

The Arch of Triumph in Paris, begun during the reign of Napoleon Bonaparte as a monument to French military victories, was completed in 1836 during the reign of King Louis Philippe.

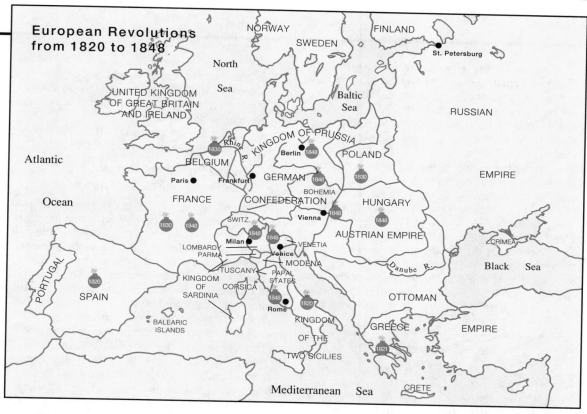

European Revolutions from 1820 to 1848

in the New World. Several of the colonies in Latin America had revolted during the Napoleonic Era. By the early 1820s they had won their independence. Such success, in the eyes of Europe's leaders, set a bad example for Europe. One ardent supporter of monarchical government wrote, "If the New World ever becomes entirely Republican, the monarchies of the Old World will perish!" The congress decided to send troops to help restore the colonies to the Spanish monarchy.

Not every member of the Quintuple Alliance agreed with the plans for intervention in Latin America. Since the Congress of Vienna, Britain had become disenchanted with the congress system and more sympathetic to liberal reforms. She had not cooperated with the congress in suppressing the Spanish revolt. Now she strenuously objected to plans to restore the colonies to the Spanish monarchy. Their independence had broken the Spanish trade monopoly in Latin America. As a result, Britain enjoyed a flourishing trade with this region. She

threatened to use her navy to stop any European intervention in the New World.

In addition to British objections, President James Monroe in a speech to the United States Congress warned the European nations that any attempt to establish or reestablish colonies in the Western Hemisphere would be considered an "unfriendly" act of aggression. Although the United States did not have the power to enforce the **Monroe Doctrine** (1823), the British navy was able to block any attempt on the part of European alliance.

Weaknesses now appeared in the congress system. The Concert of Europe was successful only when it did not infringe upon the special interests of one of the major powers. In that day, as well as today, national interests superseded international cooperation. The defection of Britain signaled the decline of the congress system. Although Austria, Prussia, Russia, and France continued to suppress uprisings in Europe, their efforts were considerably less effective.

Success of the Greek Revolt—In 1821 the Greeks rebelled against the Ottoman Empire. During the early years of their struggle, European rulers basically ignored the revolt. It did not immediately affect their national interests. But news of Turkish massacres of the Greek people began to stir the sympathies of Europeans. The Greek struggle captured the imagination of European artists and writers, and it became the subject of many of their works. When the brutal methods of Turkish oppression seemed to doom the cause for Greek freedom, Britain, Russia, and France came to the Greeks' aid. They defeated the Turkish forces and in 1829 secured the Treaty of Adrianople, which recognized Greek independence. The Greek revolt was another example of the weakness of the congress system. In this incident, the major powers of Europe supported the cause of revolution which they opposed at home.

Metternich's Advice to European Rulers

Let the great monarchs strengthen their union, and prove to the world that while it exists, it is beneficent, and insures the political peace of Europe; that it is powerful only for the maintenance of tranquility at a time when so many attacks are directed against it; that the principles which they profess are paternal and protective, menacing only the disturbers of public tranquility. . . . To every great State determined to survive the storm [of revolution] there still remain many chances of salvation, and a strong union between the States on the principles we have announced will overcome the storm itself.[1]

Section Review

1. List the four major powers of the Grand Alliance that defeated Napoleon.
2. In what city did representatives of the victorious nations gather to decide how to restore the order and stability of Europe? Who was the leading figure at this congress?
3. What principle guided the congress as they sought to restore those rulers whom Napoleon had ousted?

4. The cooperation among the member nations of Europe to avoid wars and to suppress nationalism and liberalism was known as what?
5. Name the two countries in which the alliance system suppressed uprisings in the 1820s. What country did members of the alliance system assist in its revolt during the 1820s?

New Phases of Revolution: Rebellion Against the Old Order

Two leading forces stirring discontent with the old order during the first half of the nineteenth century were liberalism and nationalism. **Liberalism** stressed individual rights such as life, liberty, and property, and personal freedoms such as those of religion, speech, and the press. Liberals advocated democratic reforms such as written constitutions that guaranteed rights and freedoms and limited the power of autocratic rulers. They promoted parliamentary government and an increased public participation in government.

The middle class were the primary supporters of these liberal goals. They wanted a voice in government equal to their economic clout in society. Joining with the middle class to advance the liberal cause against the forces of conservatism were the masses of urban factory workers and peasants. They, however, often differed with the upper middle class concerning the goals and extent of reform. Instead of the gradual, moderate changes advanced by the middle class, the lower classes desired more immediate, radical changes. They hoped to gain a voice in government in order to improve their social and economic standing in society.

Closely associated with the cause of personal liberty was the cause of national liberty. A strong spirit of **nationalism** stirred the ambitions of small and large groups alike to seek their independence or to defend their ethnic interests. The cause of nationalism also promoted a strong drive for unification in both the Italian and German states.

Despite the resistance of conservative leaders to political change in Europe, discontent with the old order continued to grow, leading to new revolts. In the early 1830s and again in 1848, a series of revolutions broke out on the Continent. In both instances the revolutionary fires sparked first in France and soon spread throughout Europe. Although the congress system was no longer effective in dealing with these outbreaks, individual rulers following Metternich's example actively sought to suppress liberalism and nationalism within their borders.

Revolts of the 1830s

When **Louis XVIII** (1814-24) ascended the throne of France following the defeat of Napoleon, he accepted many of the reforms that had come out of the French Revolution. He granted a constitution that guaranteed freedom of the press and religion, insured equality before the law for all Frenchmen, and set up a legislature similar to the British Parliament. But toward the end of his reign, he began to suppress these liberal trends. He muzzled the press, introduced a secret police, and raised property qualifications that determined voter eligibility. By the time of his death in 1824, France once again was beginning to simmer with discontent.

But it was the reactionary policies of the new king, **Charles X** (1824-30), that brought things to a boiling point. Charles was a firm believer in the "divine right" of kings. He sought to restore not only absolute rule but also the privileges of the church and nobility. In July 1830, the people of Paris rose in rebellion in what is called the **July Revolution.** They raised barricades in the streets and resisted the government soldiers. After three days of fighting, Charles X fled to England. The duke of Orléans, **Louis Philippe** (1830-48), was made king under a more liberal constitution. Popular with the Frenchmen, Louis was hailed as the "citizen king." Many of the participants in the revolution, however, soon became disillusioned because Louis Philippe catered to the interests of the upper middle class.

News of the July Revolution soon ignited a series of revolts throughout Europe. One of the nations whose smoldering discontent burst into the flame of revolution was Belgium. This tiny state had been given to the Dutch Netherlands by the Congress of Vienna. But the Belgians were dissatisfied; there were many cultural differences that separated them from the Dutch people. Whereas the Belgians were Roman Catholics, the Dutch were predominantly Protestants. The Belgians were farmers and textile workers; the Dutch were bankers and traders. The Belgians spoke Flemish. Dutch was the official language of the schools, government, and courts.

When news of the July Revolution reached the city of Brussels, rioting broke out. Belgian nationalists declared their independence and drew up a liberal constitution. The leading European nations, facing unrest at home, were not able to come to the aid of the Dutch government. Leaders of these coun-

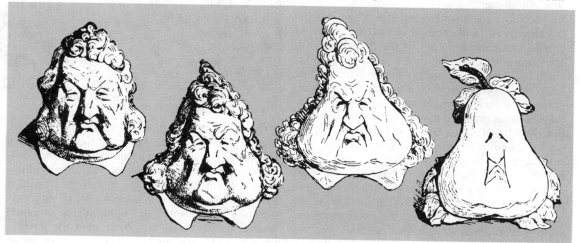

Louis Philippe's pear-shaped face gave occasion for this political cartoon drawn by Charles Philipon in 1831. (The French word for pear is also slang for simpleton.)

tries, however, did meet at a congress in London. There they signed the **Treaty of London,** which recognized the independence of Belgium. This treaty also declared Belgium to be a perpetually neutral state. Thus the balance of power would be maintained, and Belgium would be protected from any act of foreign aggression. (The leaders still feared that France might take over the small state.)

Stirrings of nationalism and liberalism caused revolts to break out in many central European states. But in this region, the rulers of Austria, Prussia, and Russia zealously suppressed any disruption of the *status quo.* Austrian and Prussian troops put down small uprisings in the Italian and German states. In Poland, nationalist leaders tried, without success, to throw off the yoke of Russian control. Czar Nicholas I sent in the Russian army and brutally crushed the Polish rebellion.

Revolts of 1848

The revolts of the 1830s were suppressed, but resentment remained among the lower classes. They were bitter against the rich middle class, who excluded them from the moderate gains the upper middle class had received during earlier revolts. In addition, poor harvests and rising unemployment increased the discontent among the peasants and city workers. In 1848 barricades went up across Europe as revolution once more rocked the European continent.

As before, the revolutionary fires began in Paris. In February of 1848 unemployed workers and disgruntled students gathered in the French capital. They protested Louis Philippe's policies which favored the interests of wealthy businessmen. When Louis refused to listen to their demands for reform, rioting broke out. Barricades blocked the streets of Paris as mobs prepared to meet government troops. But when the National Guard joined the side of the workers, Louis Philippe fled to England.

The revolutionary leaders proclaimed the establishment of the Second French Republic. They set up a temporary government to restore order in Paris and to draw up a new constitution for France. At the urging of radical leaders, the government established "national workshops," a social program meant to provide food, shelter, medical care, and jobs for the growing number of unemployed workers. But instead of providing useful jobs, the workshops became a public-relief program. This was one of the earliest modern examples of government-financed socialistic programs.

The new French constitution established universal manhood suffrage (all men could vote). When elections were held for a new legislature, the voters sent a fairly conservative assembly to Paris. The message was clear—the rural areas of France did not agree with the more radical ideas of the city workers and students. They objected to being taxed to support the unemployed in Paris when they were facing famine themselves. Thus the newly elected conservative majority abolished the workshops. In reaction, unemployed workers sought to overthrow the government. For three days in June, Paris was the sight of a bloody battle. During these **"June Days,"** thousands of Frenchmen lost their lives as the army restored order to the city.

French soldiers attempt to subdue a Parisian mob during the "June Days" uprising of 1848.

In December elections were held for the position of president of the Second Republic. Perhaps because of recent violent uprisings, the French people voted for a man whose name symbolized authority. Louis Napoleon, the nephew of Napoleon Bonaparte, won by an overwhelming majority. Seeming to champion the rights of the common people, he increased his power over the government. In 1852 he staged a *coup d'état,* proclaiming himself Emperor **Napoleon III** of the Second French Empire. (Napoleon Bonaparte's son, who died in 1832, was considered Napoleon II.) Once again French attempts to achieve democratic reforms through revolution led to widespread violence and to the establishment of a dictatorship.

Napoleon III

Metternich's prediction about France again proved true: the infection of revolution spread, causing further revolt. Despite Metternich's precautions, revolutions broke out in all parts of the Austrian Empire in 1848. There were strong nationalistic uprisings in Hungary and Bohemia, while Venice and Milan declared their independence from Hapsburg control. When demonstrations by university students and workers broke out in Vienna, Metternich was forced to resign.

Emperor Ferdinand I, a feeble-minded ruler, readily gave in to the revolutionary demands. He granted a liberal constitution, abolished serfdom, and promised self-rule for the Hungarians. But as the summer wore on, differences among the revolutionaries gave reactionary forces an opportunity to put down the revolution. Ferdinand was forced

to abdicate his throne in favor of his nephew, **Francis Joseph I** (1848-1916). The young emperor renounced the concessions of his predecessor and, with the backing of the army, crushed the nationalist revolts throughout the empire.

The Napoleonic Wars had exposed the Russian people to the revolutionary battle cry ''Liberty, Equality, Fraternity.'' Peasants in Russia still suffered under the burden of serfdom that bound them to the land. Likewise, the many national groups within Russia's borders still yearned for their independence. But democratic and nationalistic reforms made little progress in Russia.

Czar **Nicholas I** sought to head off uprisings by instituting a policy of ''Autocracy, Orthodoxy, and Nationalism.'' This domestic program called for increasing the czar's control over the state, recognizing only the Russian Orthodox church, and uniting the diverse national groups within Nicholas's territory around the culture and traditions of Russia—a policy called **Russification.** Nicholas, as well as later Russian czars, suppressed domestic problems instead of trying to find a workable and just solution. Although Russia did not experience revolution in the 1830s and 1848, she experienced devastating social upheaval in the early twentieth century.

The Napoleonic Era also had awakened liberalism and nationalism among the Italian and German states. They sought freedom from repressive rulers, worked for democratic constitutions, and longed for national unification. But in these states, as in most of Europe, the bright prospects of concessions won soon dimmed. Conservative monarchs regained the support of the army and crushed the uprisings—but only temporarily. The force of nationalism would triumph later in the century. (See pp. 429-33.)

Failure of the Revolts

The period following the Napoleonic Wars was very turbulent. Discontent, uprisings, and bloodshed became commonplace. For the most part, those who took part in the revolts of the 1830s and 1848 shared the common desire of advancing the causes of liberalism and nationalism. But the revolts that swept across Europe shared something else—most ended in failure.

Ferdinand   Metternich   Louis Philippe, Frederick William   Ludwig

ROYALTY IN DISTRESS.   DIE FÜRSTEN IN DER KLEMME.

"Royalty in Distress," a nineteenth-century political cartoon

Forces of discontent led to violent protests and uprisings, often winning concessions from weakened and frightened rulers. But these gains soon were threatened as the revolutionaries quarrelled among themselves. Conflicting goals and backgrounds divided the forces that had previously joined in opposition to the government. Taking advantage of the disagreement and disunity among revolutionary factions, government forces were able to rally and suppress the revolts.

Underlying this period of turmoil was the failure of governments and their citizens to fulfill their God-ordained civic responsibilities. Government should promote righteousness in a land. Righteousness includes not only right moral conduct but also justice, equity, and liberty. "Mercy and truth preserve the king," says the Scripture, "and his throne is upholden by mercy" (Prov. 20:28). Many European rulers oppressed their subjects instead of showing mercy. The book of Proverbs describes such rulers: "The prince that wanteth [lacks] understanding is also a great oppressor" (28:16).

Likewise, many Europeans acted contrary to God's plan by rebelling against governmental authority. The Apostle Paul instructs citizens to honor civil authority, for in so doing they honor God:

Let every soul be subject unto the higher powers. For there is no power but of God: the powers that be are ordained of God. Whosoever therefore resisteth the power, resisteth the ordinance of God: and they that resist shall receive to themselves damnation.

—Romans 13:1-2

Rebellion and revolution, though seemingly for a good cause or directed against an oppressive government, have at their roots a rebellious spirit against God. Such rebellion, whether directed against divine authority or human authority, God condemns: "Rebellion is as the sin of witchcraft, and stubbornness is as iniquity and idolatry" (I Sam. 15:23).

Section Review

1. In what country did the revolution fires of the 1830s and 1848 first spark?
2. What country gained its independence from the Netherlands through the revolts of the 1830s?
3. Following the violence of the "June Days," whom did the people of France elect as president of the Second French Republic?
4. Name the young Austrian ruler who renounced the concessions of his predecessor and crushed nationalistic revolts throughout his empire.
5. What policy did Czar Nicholas I institute in Russia to strengthen his control over the state?

Triumph of Nationalism

By 1850 the spirit of conservatism and international cooperation established by the Congress of Vienna had waned, and the spirit of liberalism and nationalism had intensified. During the second half of the century, the mood of European politics gradually changed. The years of revolution had dispelled the zeal of romantic idealism; in its place there arose a hardened realism. Like Machiavelli's *Prince,* European politicians and diplomats adopted a politics of necessity, known as **realpolitik** (''the politics of reality''), in which they used whatever means necessary—including force—to advance their national goals. Although Europe as a whole escaped widespread war during the nineteenth century, the spirit of nationalism precipitated several smaller wars among the major powers.

Crimean War

The first major international conflict after the defeat of Napoleon was the **Crimean War** (1854-56). This war pitted Britain, France, and the Kingdom of Sardinia against Russia with her policy of expansion

Sidelights of the Crimean War

Despite its relative insignificance upon the course of European events, the Crimean War endures as one of the most famous conflicts in history. One reason for this is that one of the last major cavalry charges in warfare took place during that struggle. It has been immortalized by the poet Alfred, Lord Tennyson in ''The Charge of the Light Brigade.''

The war is also remembered for the fashions established at the time. The British general, Lord Raglan, wore an overcoat in which the sleeves went directly to the neck without shoulder seams. Today we call such sleeves ''raglan sleeves.'' The leader of the Light Brigade, Lord Cardigan, popularized a sweater that buttoned down the front and could be easily slipped on under a uniform jacket. Sweaters of this type are now known as cardigans. Even the ordinary soldiers in the British ranks introduced a new item. Cold and shivering on the plains of Balaclava, they kept themselves warm by pulling woolen socks over their heads. They cut holes in them for their eyes and mouths. The soldiers called them ''Balaclava helmets.'' We call them ski masks.

The Crimean War was the first war to be extensively reported in the press. Daily reports were sent to Paris and London over the newly invented telegraph. It was also the first to be photographed and the first in which base hospitals were used.

Florence Nightingale

Florence Nightingale (1820-1910) established the modern nursing profession through her efforts to help the sick and wounded British soldiers during the Crimean War. Newspaper reports detailing the appalling conditions in the Crimea shocked the British public; many people demanded that something be done to alleviate the suffering. The British government responded by recruiting thirty-eight nurses, many of whom had little or no training, to accompany the well-trained Florence Nightingale to the Crimea.

When this small band of nurses arrived, they found that the ''hospital'' was a filthy and damp former army barracks. The wounded soldiers, wrapped in their bloody, vermin-covered blankets, died by the hundreds from their wounds and from disease. Florence began her work. At first she had few supplies, but through donations from Britain she was able to purchase many necessities. Florence believed in efficient organization and hard work, and before long her efforts began to save lives.

Strain and overwork, however, ruined her health, and after returning from the Crimea, a national heroine, she rarely ventured out into public again. During the American Civil War, however, Florence advised the United States on how to set up military hospitals. Having received many honors in her lifetime, Florence Nightingale in 1907 became the first woman to receive the British Order of Merit.

in the Near East. For centuries the Ottoman Empire had controlled this region. But by the nineteenth century, the Turks were no longer a mighty power. Weak and corrupt government, as well as strong nationalistic feeling among those Europeans under Turkish control, signaled doom for the Ottoman Empire. Referring to that empire, Czar Nicholas remarked, "We have on our hands a sick man, a very sick man, who can die suddenly." Nicholas tried to hasten that death by provoking a war with the Turks. He also hoped to expand Russia's borders to the Mediterranean.

In 1853 Nicholas demanded that the Orthodox church in the Ottoman Empire be placed under Russian "protection." When the Turks refused, fighting broke out. Russian victories within the first months of fighting created concern elsewhere in Europe. Britain feared that a Russian victory would upset the balance of power and threaten her control of the Mediterranean region. The French entered the war primarily because Napoleon III wanted to do something glorious to enhance his prestige. Count Cavour, the prime minister of the Italian kingdom of Sardinia, sided with Britain and France in hopes of gaining their support for the cause of Italian unification.

For two years the war continued on the Crimean Peninsula. Both sides were hampered by poor organization, supply difficulties, disease, and inept leadership. The war ended soon after the Russian fortress of Sevastopol surrendered. At Paris in 1856, the nations that had taken part in the war met to discuss the peace settlement. Besides losing territory, Russia agreed to abandon her claim as "protector" of the Orthodox church within the Ottoman Empire. She also agreed not to build any forts along the Black Sea or to station any warships in those waters. In addition, the major nations promised to keep the Ottoman Empire from being destroyed, in order to preserve the balance of power.

Nationalism in Italy and Germany

The Crimean War illustrated the failure of the congress system. Selfish national interests divided the congress members, leading to war instead of peace. But while nationalism decreased international cooperation, it increased the drive for unification in both Italy and Germany.

Italian Unification

By the mid-nineteenth century, Italy was still what Metternich contemptuously called a "geographic expression." The Italian Peninsula re-

mained politically divided; small kingdoms competed with one another, and foreign powers controlled large sections of the country. Nevertheless, the spirit of nationalism was on the rise, fueled by a nationalistic movement called *Risorgimento* ("resurgence"). In 1832 **Giuseppe Mazzini** (maht TSEE nee; 1805-72) started a patriotic society called Young Italy, determining to fight, if necessary, for Italian unification. But as late as 1851 an Italian historian wrote, "The patriotism of the Italians is like that of the ancient Greeks, and is love of a single town, not of a country; it is the feeling of a tribe, not of a nation. Only by foreign conquest have they ever been united. Leave them to themselves and they split into fragments."[2]

The man primarily responsible for unifying Italy was Count **Camillo di Cavour** (1810-61), the prime minister of the Kingdom of Sardinia. Cavour was a wily diplomat who used whatever means were necessary to promote Italian unification. When the Crimean War broke out in 1854, Cavour

Count Camillo di Cavour

joined with Britain and France in sending troops to fight Russia. He had no quarrel with the Russians but hoped that the peace negotiations following the war would give him the opportunity to enlist support for his cause of unification. Cavour knew he would need an ally in order to wrest the provinces of Lombardy and Venetia from Austrian control. He found his ally in Napoleon III of France, a man seeking to win both military glory and territory.

Napoleon III secretly agreed to help Sardinia gain the Austrian-controlled provinces of Lombardy and Venetia. In return, Cavour promised to cede him the provinces of Nice and Savoy. In 1859 Cavour provoked the Austrians into declaring war on Sardinia. As the Franco-Sardinian armies successfully drove the Austrian troops out of Lombardy,

revolts broke out across northern Italy. Rulers of small Italian states were overthrown as Italians joined Cavour's efforts for unification. Fearful of a strong, unified Italy, Napoleon III made a separate peace with Austria. Despite this infuriating setback, Cavour had made considerable progress in unifying most of northern Italy to the Kingdom of Sardinia.

Meanwhile in southern Italy a follower of Mazzini, **Giuseppe Garibaldi** (GAR uh BAWL dee; 1807-82), rose to prominence. Strongly patriotic and bent on unifying Italy, Garibaldi gathered a band of loyal followers called ''Red Shirts'' and invaded the island of Sicily in 1860. Having conquered the island, they landed on the Italian mainland and took Naples. Garibaldi next planned to march on Rome and take possession of the Papal States. At that point Cavour quickly intervened, fearing that an attack on Rome would draw the French into the conflict on the pope's side. (Since the days of Charlemagne, French troops had guarded the papal city.) Rushing southward with Sardinian troops, Cavour persuaded

Giuseppe Garibaldi

Garibaldi to hand over his conquests to **Victor Emmanuel II,** the king of Sardinia. On March 17, 1861, just a few months before Cavour's death, an Italian parliament officially proclaimed the establishment of the Kingdom of Italy with Victor Emmanuel II as the first king. With the exception of Venetia and Rome, Italian unification had been accomplished. By 1870 these last two territories were added to the Italian kingdom, and in 1871 the city of Rome became the capital of the nation of Italy.

Monument to Victor Emmanuel II in Rome

German Unification

Despite the failure of the revolts of 1848, the cause of German unification continued to advance. But it was in the economic realm, not the political, that great strides were initially made. Under the leadership of Prussia, the German states established a trade union called the **Zollverein.** The favorable results of this economic cooperation lent support to the movement for political unification.

The architect of political unification in Germany was Count **Otto von Bismarck** (1815-98), a loyal Prussian who was both crafty and opportunistic. Bismarck was not a romantic idealist but was devoted to the practice of realpolitik. He believed that the most practical way to achieve his goals was through the hard-nosed policy of "blood and iron," not through idealistic speeches. In 1862 King William I made Bismarck the chancellor of Prussia. Bismarck immediately began seeking opportunities to promote German unification under Prussian domination.

Count Otto von Bismarck

War with Denmark and Austria—Bismarck's first opportunity came in 1864, when he deliberately involved Prussia in a dispute with the king of Denmark over the small territories of Schleswig and Holstein. The king of Denmark wanted to incorporate these territories into his kingdom, but Bismarck protested, claiming them as German territories. Posing as the protector of the German people, he persuaded Austria to join Prussia in a war against Denmark. The brief war ended in a Danish defeat. Following the Danish surrender, Austria and Prussia divided the spoils: Austria took control of Holstein, while Prussia administered Schleswig.

Next Bismarck sought for a way to discredit Austria and to strengthen Prussia's influence in German affairs. He sought to isolate Austria from other European nations and then use the superior might of the Prussian army to assert Prussian domination. Through skillful diplomacy, Bismarck persuaded both Russia and France to remain neutral in the event of war between Prussia and Austria. He then enlisted the aid of the Italians in a war against Austria, promising Venetia in return for their support. Though Bismarck was now prepared for war, he did not want to appear the aggressor. So he stirred up trouble in Holstein, angering the Austrians to such a degree that they declared war first.

The **Austro-Prussian War,** also known as the Seven Weeks' War, broke out in 1866. In short order, the Prussians gained the victory and forced the Austrians to agree to the Prussian peace proposal. Prussia acquired Holstein as well as additional German territory. Furthermore, Austria agreed to end the German Confederation established by the Congress of Vienna. In its place, a Prussian-dominated North German Confederation was established.

The Franco-Prussian War—With Austria now out of the way, Bismarck began working to bring the southern German states under Prussian control. To accomplish this goal, he sought an opportunity to provoke a war with France. Such a war, he believed, would stir up such nationalistic feeling among the German states that it would be relatively easy to persuade them to join with Prussia. In France, an increasingly ill Napoleon III allowed himself to be pushed into war by a prowar party. They wanted to diminish Prussian power before it became too strong for France to handle.

The immediate cause for the **Franco-Prussian War** (1870-71) was the throne of Spain. A liberal revolution had overthrown the corrupt Spanish

monarchy in 1868, and the new provisional government invited Leopold, a Hohenzollern prince, to become king. The French opposed such a plan, for the Hohenzollern family also ruled Prussia. If Leopold became king of Spain, France would be encircled by the Hohenzollerns. Amidst all the furor and cries for war on the part of the French, Leopold withdrew his candidacy.

Yet the French were not satisfied. The French ambassador went to see the Prussian king, William I, who was vacationing at Ems in the Rhineland. He demanded that William promise in writing that no Hohenzollern would ever sit on the Spanish throne. William refused and sent Bismarck a dispatch (report) of his discussions, granting him permission to publish it in the newspapers. Bismarck did publish the dispatch, but not before he slightly changed the wording to make it appear as if William and the ambassador had insulted each other. This **"Ems dispatch"** so angered the French that they declared war on the equally infuriated Prussians.

As Bismarck had hoped, the southern German states joined with Prussia in the war effort. The

Unification of Germany 1866-1871

- Prussia before 1866
- Annexed to Prussia, 1866
- Confederated with Prussia, 1867
- States added to complete the German Empire, 1871
- ─── Boundary of the German Empire, 1871

North Sea

Baltic Sea

DENMARK

SCHLESWIG
HOLSTEIN

NETHERLANDS

Rhine R.

KINGDOM OF PRUSSIA

• Berlin

Oder R.

Elbe R.

RUSSIAN EMPIRE

BELGIUM

SEDAN ★

• Ems

Versailles • Paris

SADOWA ★

LORRAINE
─ (Annexed in 1871)
ALSACE

Danube R.

SWITZERLAND

AUSTRIAN EMPIRE

The Prussian Army: The Industrial Revolution Comes to War

The unification of Germany was accomplished not only by the diplomacy of Bismarck but also by the overwhelming success of the Prussian army under Field Marshal Helmuth von Moltke (1800-1891). Moltke's army achieved a series of astonishing triumphs by applying the new technology of the Industrial Revolution to the art of war. Moltke, a tightlipped Prussian known as the Great Silent One, was not a bold, dashing leader like Alexander the Great or Napoleon. His greatest skill was in efficient organization. A thorough and superior planner, Moltke won quick and decisive victories.

Moltke and his staff took advantage of Prussia's growing industrial power. For example, he used the nation's many railway lines to move and organize his troops. In both the Austro-Prussian and Franco-Prussian wars, Prussia's speed in mo-

bilization gave her an advantage over her opponent. The railroad had become a weapon of war.

The Prussians made improvements in weaponry too. Other countries used muzzle-loading rifles, which required a soldier to stand up and go through several steps to load it. The Prussian army adopted a breechloading rifle, which could be loaded simply by inserting a cartridge into a chamber near the trigger. A soldier could load while kneeling or even lying down, and he could fire much more quickly. In the Austro-Prussian War, the Prussian guns could fire six shots for every one shot for the Austrian weapons. The Prussians also used steel breechloading cannons instead of the bronze muzzle loaders used by most other nations. By World War I, Germany had the finest artillery in Europe.

Moltke made full use of the telegraph, an obvious improvement over carrying messages by horse. The Prussians also realized the importance of the growth in population that accompanied the Industrial Revolution. Unlike other countries, Prussia required nearly every male in the country to undergo military training. In time of war, Prussia was able to raise a larger army than any of her opponents—even though the enemy might have a larger population.

The success of Moltke's army persuaded the rest of Europe to follow his example. In a few years, the armies of Europe were more evenly matched, and decisive victories like those of Prussia became harder to achieve. The end result of these "improvements" was the long, drawn-out, and bloody conflict known as World War I. Unintentionally, Moltke's success also destroyed the myth of war being a glorious, noble, and exciting adventure. As one historian wrote, "Moltke killed war by making it so serious, so dull and so deadly."

Germans invaded Alsace and Lorraine (French provinces) and in less than two months had trapped Napoleon III at the fortress of Sedan. Here Napoleon III and his army of 83,000 men were forced to surrender. Upon hearing of the surrender, mobs in Paris declared an end to the Second French Empire and established a republic, vowing to continue the war. But the Germans advanced to the outskirts of Paris, and the French cause was hopeless. On January 28, 1871, Paris surrendered after a 132-day

A mosaic from the Kaiser Wilhelm Church in Berlin shows the three Hohenzollern emperors of the unified Germany: Kaiser William I (second from the left), Kaiser Frederick III (with the dark beard, standing directly behind William I), and Kaiser William II (with the mustache, standing next to his wife). The cracks in the mosaic are the result of bombing during World War II.

siege. Ten days earlier in the Versailles Palace outside Paris, King William I had been proclaimed emperor of the German Reich (Empire), fulfilling Bismarck's plans for unification.

Reforms in Austria and Russia

The Dual Monarchy

The Austrian Hapsburgs ruled over a varied and increasingly restless group of nationalities. Of these nationalities, the Hungarians created the most problems for the Austrian government. In 1848, under the leadership of Louis Kossuth (KAH SOOTH), they had staged an unsuccessful revolt. Later, after the Prussian victory over Austria in the Austro-Prussian War (1866), the Hungarians again demanded self-government. But this time the Austrians were in no position to reject their demands. They made the Hungarians equal partners within the empire. Both countries remained under the Hapsburg monarchy and cooperated in matters of finance, foreign affairs, and defense. However, they each had their own constitution, official language, flag, and parliament. The Austrian Empire now became the Austro-Hungarian Empire, or **Dual Monarchy,** ruled by Francis Joseph I.

Russia Under Alexander II

When Nicholas I died in 1855, his son **Alexander II** (1855-81) became the Russian czar. He recognized that his father's policy of ''Autocracy, Orthodoxy, and Nationalism'' had caused widespread discontent. It had also weakened Russia's position as a major European power, resulting in Russia's defeat during the Crimean War. Consequently, Alexander implemented several social reforms. The most important one came in 1861, when he abolished serfdom, giving the serfs personal freedom and grants of land. Revolutionaries pressed him for further reforms, but he did not give in to all their

Alexander II

demands. In 1881 he was assassinated. When his son Alexander III (1881-94) became czar, he returned to the harsh policies of Nicholas I.

Section Review

1. What three European nations fought on the side of the Turks against Russia in the Crimean War?
2. Name the prime minister of Sardinia primarily responsible for the unification of Italy.
3. Who was the Prussian politician primarily responsible for the unification of Germany? Against what three European countries did he take Prussia to war in order to achieve his goal?
4. As a result of Austria's military defeat, what nationality within the Austrian Empire was able to achieve self-government?
5. What was Czar Alexander II's most important social reform?

Protest of Romanticism

The powerful feelings unleashed by the political revolutions of the late eighteenth and early nineteenth centuries gave birth to **romanticism.** This cultural movement gave literary and artistic expression to the concepts of "Liberty, Equality, Fraternity." Romanticism was also a movement of reaction—reaction against the restraint of the Age of Reason, the violence of the French Revolution, the repression following the Napoleonic Wars, and the often harsh working conditions caused by the rapid growth of the Industrial Revolution.

In contrast to the Age of Reason, the Romantic Age turned from rationalism to idealism, from the intellectual to the emotional. Romantics emphasized originality above imitation, nationalism above internationalism, and self-fulfillment above the common good. Their attitude shifted from optimism to uncertainty; from contentment to desire.

But in reacting against rationalism and restraint, the romantics went too far in the opposite direction. They became rebels against all forms of rules and laws, and therefore rebels against God. They made their feelings their authority—if it *felt* good, it must *be* good. Although emotions are part of the natural make-up of man, people are not to be ruled by their emotions; they are not to give them free rein. This was one error of the romantics. They exchanged the mind-centered humanism of the Enlightenment for a heart-centered humanism. The Bible, however, warns that "the heart is deceitful above all things, and desperately wicked: who can know it?" (Jer. 17:9).

Romanticism in Literature

The works of romantic writers exhibited a variety of themes. The most popular were longing for distant lands or the distant past, fascination with the supernatural and the mysterious, glorification of the "noble savage," emphasis on nature, love of freedom, and pride in one's nation. Most of these themes were not new; writers had expressed them in previous centuries. But for the most part, voices of protest against the *status quo* had been few. During what we call the Romantic Age, however, scores of well-known writers from many countries contributed to this movement of protest. We will examine only a representative sample of them as we look at the themes of romanticism.

Longing for Distant Lands and the Distant Past

Sir **Walter Scott** (1771-1832) is one of the most famous romantic novelists. As a boy he loved to visit the ruins of castles and monasteries that dotted the countryside of his native Scotland. Some romantics were enthralled with the beauty of nature, but Scott could not look on a scene without wondering about the people who had lived there or the events that had taken place there in the past. His novels reflect this fascination. Many of his stories are set in Scotland and England during the Middle Ages. One of his most popular novels is *Ivanhoe,* which he set during the reign of the English king Richard the Lion-Hearted.

Home of Sir Walter Scott in Scotland

A leading French romantic who was influenced by Scott was **Victor Hugo** (1802-85). He wrote one of the most widely read romantic novels, *The Hunchback of Notre Dame.* This story takes place in medieval Paris and centers on the Cathedral of Notre Dame. It tells a tale of mystery, suspense, and love.

The poetry of the Englishman **Samuel Taylor Coleridge** (1772-1834) reflects the romantics' interest in faraway places. The exotic stanzas of his poem "Kubla Khan" describe the palace of the thirteenth-century Mongol ruler of China. Another of his poems, "The Rime of the Ancient Mariner," relates the fantastic voyage of an old seaman.

Fascination with the Supernatural and Mysterious

Early in the nineteenth century two brothers, **Jacob** and **William Grimm,** compiled a two-volume collection of German fairy tales. These tales, drawn primarily from German folklore, include such favorites as "Hansel and Gretel," "Cinderella," and "Little Red Riding Hood." All of them contain elements of the mysterious and supernatural. The supernatural is also reflected in the plays of the German author **Johann Wolfgang Goethe** (GUR tuh; 1749-1832). His play *Faust* is based on an old folktale about a man who sold his soul to the Devil in return for twenty-four years of youth.

The poems and short stories of the American writer **Edgar Allan Poe** (1809-49) illustrate the mysterious. To enhance the effect of his writing, he emphasized one major emotion in each work. For example, his poem "The Raven" conveys a feeling of melancholy, while his short story "The Fall of the House of Usher" is filled with terror. Today Poe is considered the father of modern mystery and detective fiction.

Glorification of the Noble Savage

The romantic concept of the noble savage began during the Enlightenment. Many of the *philosophes,* especially Jean Jacques Rousseau, assumed that civilization had corrupted man. Rousseau believed that man is at his best when living in a primitive environment apart from civilization. He held up the American Indian as the best example of the primitive yet uncorrupted noble savage. The romantics readily accepted these ideas and made them a part of their philosophy.

The novels of the American writer **James Fenimore Cooper** (1789-1851) reflect the concept of the noble savage. In a series of five novels known as the Leatherstocking Tales, Cooper recounts the exploits of an American frontiersman (Natty Bumppo) and his Indian companion. These characters live far from civilization and experience a life of freedom close to nature. Of all the novels in this series, the best known is *The Last of the Mohicans.*

Emphasis on Nature

Closely associated with the concept of the noble savage was the romantic emphasis upon nature. Like the *philosophes,* the romantics denied original sin, believing that man was innately good. To them, society and education had corrupted man. They taught that the good in man could be restored by contemplating nature. One romantic writer who promoted this philosophy was **William Wordsworth** (1770-1850). He expresses his deep love for nature through poetry, which he describes as "the spontaneous overflow of powerful feelings."

Love of Freedom

Another characteristic of the romantics was their rebellion against the constraints of society. Many sought to live a life free from all restraints. The English romantic poet **George Gordon, Lord Byron** (1788-1824) was such a man. He indulged in loose living and soon became enslaved to his own passions. Yet his "free" lifestyle was not free from sin or its consequences. "For when ye were the servants of sin, ye were free from righteousness. What fruit had ye then in those things whereof ye are now ashamed? for the end of those things is death" (Rom. 6:20-21). As a result, his life was filled with personal tragedy and sorrow.

Byron not only wrote about freedom but also actively supported the cause of freedom during his short lifetime. He tried to help the Italians in their fight for unification. He later went to Greece to aid the Greeks in their struggle for independence from the Turks. He died there of a fever in 1824. One of his poems written in 1820 reveals his feelings about freedom:

> When a man hath no freedom to fight for at
>   home,
>   Let him combat for that of his neighbours;
> Let him think of the glories of Greece and of
>   Rome,
>   And get knock'd on the head for his labours.
> To do good to mankind is the chivalrous plan,
>   And is always as nobly requited;
> Then battle for freedom wherever you can,
>   And, if not shot or hang'd you'll get
>   knighted.

"The Tables Turned"

Up! up! my Friend, and quit your books;
Or surely you'll grow double:
Up! up! my Friend, and clear your looks;
Why all this toil and trouble?
        . . . .
Books! 'tis a dull and endless strife:
Come, hear the woodland linnet,
How sweet his music! on my life,
There's more of wisdom in it.

And hark! how blithe the throstle sings!
He, too, is no mean preacher:
Come forth into the light of things,
Let Nature be your teacher.
        . . . .
One impulse from a vernal wood
May teach you more of man,
Of moral evil and of good,
Than all the sages can.
        . . . .
Enough of Science and of Art;
Close up those barren leaves;
Come forth, and bring with you a heart
That watches and receives.

—William Wordsworth (1798)

The Castle of Chillon on Lake Geneva, immortalized by Lord Byron in his poem "The Prisoner of Chillon"

Like Byron, the English poet **Percy Bysshe Shelley** (1792-1822) sought to throw off all restraints. Opposing what he called "religious, political, and domestic oppression," Shelley advocated "the sacred cause of freedom." The "oppression" that he so strongly condemned included the Christian faith, the rule of government, and traditional customs and ideas. Several of his poems, particularly *Queen Mab,* reflect his destructive attitudes.

Pride of Nationalism

The theme of nationalism runs throughout romantic literature. It is particularly evident in the writing of the greatest Russian poet, **Alexander Pushkin** (1799-1837). His influence upon Russian literature is similar to that of Shakespeare's upon English literature and Dante's upon Italian literature. He is considered to be the founder of modern Russian literature.

Many of Pushkin's works are based upon Russian folklore and history. In them he expresses the romantic longing for freedom. A rebel by nature, Pushkin supported the Decembrist Revolt in 1825. Frequently sent into exile, he was later pardoned by Czar Nicholas I.

Though Russian poetry is difficult to translate into English, these verses from "Message to Siberia" convey the sorrows of the exiles' cries:

Deep in the Siberian mine,
Keep your patience proud;
The bitter toil shall not be lost,
The rebel thought unbowed.

. . . .

The heavy-hanging chains will fall,
The walls will crumble at a word;
And Freedom greet you in the light,
And brothers give you back the sword.[3]

Romanticism in Music

Romantic composers revolted against the accepted rules of regularity, balance, and restraint that defined classical music. While the musical styles of such classical composers as Haydn and Mozart sound very much alike to the untrained ear, the individualistic styles of romantic composers are more readily distinguished. As do romantic literature and art, romantic music seeks to stir the emotions of its listeners. Romantic composers composed for the public enjoyment. During this age, popular interest in music increased as new musical instruments such as the accordion, harmonium (reed organ), and piano became more accessible to the general public. Music lovers attended solo recitals by such popular performers as the pianist Liszt and the singer Jenny Lind, as well as the performances of national and city orchestras. For example, the London Philharmonic Orchestra was formed in 1813, and the New York Philharmonic in 1842.

Nationalism was a major influence on romantic music. Almost every country could boast of a national composer: Poland had Chopin, Hungary had Liszt, Bohemia had Smetana, Russia had Tchaikovsky, and Italy had Verdi. These composers often used national folk songs and popular dance tunes in their compositions. Many romantic composers are still well known, and their music is still greatly enjoyed.

The man who bridged the gap between classical and romantic music was **Ludwig van Beethoven** (1770-1827). Although born in Bonn, Germany,

Ludwig van Beethoven

Beethoven spent most of his life in Vienna. His early music reflected the classical influence of his teacher, Franz Joseph Haydn. Later, however, his music became more dramatic and explosive, blending classical and romantic elements. It was Beethoven who increased the size of the orchestra and added two new instruments: the trombone and the piccolo. He also helped establish the piano as a popular instrument. In his late twenties he began to lose his hearing, and by his fiftieth birthday he was completely deaf. In spite of this handicap, he continued to compose for the rest of his life. His works include thirty piano sonatas and nine symphonies.

Composers of Piano Music

The Polish composer **Frederick Chopin** (sho PAN; 1810-49) has been called the "poet of the piano." In 1830 he left his beloved homeland on a concert tour of Europe. He never returned, for in the same year the Russians suppressed the Polish revolt for independence. Chopin refused to return and be subject to such repressive rule. Yet in spite of his self-imposed exile, his love for Poland did not diminish. His musical compositions express his deep affection for his homeland. He drew many of his melodies from Polish folk dances. Today he is

still considered the national composer of Poland, and his works a symbol of Polish nationalism.

Much of the piano music of **Franz Liszt** (1811-86) was inspired by his native land, Hungary. The best known of his compositions are his Hungarian Rhapsodies. While he was recognized as a composer, Liszt was also hailed as the most accomplished pianist of his time. He transcribed many orchestral works for the piano, and his dazzling virtuosity drew large crowds to his concerts.

Franz Liszt

Composers of Orchestral Music

The orchestral works of the Russian composer **Peter Ilich Tchaikovsky** (chy KAWF skee; 1840-93) include symphonies, ballets, and overtures. Of his ballets, the *Nutcracker* is particularly beautiful. His *1812 Overture,* written to mark the anniversary of Napoleon's defeat in Russia, is vibrant with Russian melodies. Its glorious finale features thundering cannons and pealing bells.

Like Tchaikovsky, the German composer **Johannes Brahms** (1833-97) produced brilliant orchestral works. Besides composing chamber music and symphonies, Brahms also wrote over three hundred songs. Though his compositions are unquestionably romantic, he often drew upon musical forms that were popular during the baroque and classical periods.

Richard Wagner

Johannes Brahms

Composers of Opera

During the nineteenth century, Italians longed for a unified nation free from foreign control. The operas of **Giuseppe Verdi** (1813-1901) stirred this dream. Verdi incorporated into his operas the theme of good triumphing over evil. Often when the villain in the opera was defeated, the audience would cheer, seeing in this action the destruction of Austria, which controlled much of northern Italy. Even Verdi's name became associated with the resurgence of Italian nationalism, because it suggested ''*Victor Emmanuel Re* (king) *d'Italia.*'' (Victor Emmanuel was the man whom the Italians hoped would become the ruler of a unified Italy.)

The operas of **Richard Wagner** (1813-83) also had a nationalistic flavor, though not a revolutionary one. Wagner based much of his work on ancient Germanic myths, seeking to unite the Germans around a common culture. He expanded the function of the orchestra and wrote vocal parts that demanded singers with very powerful voices. One characteristic of Wagner's musical dramas is his use of short melodies, called motifs. Each motif, which recurs often throughout the course of the opera, represents a particular character, action, or idea.

Romanticism in Art

Like their literary counterparts, romantic artists appealed to the senses and feelings of the beholder. Their use of bright colors was intended to elicit an emotional response. Their subjects were often scenes of local landscapes or faraway places. They chose themes from national legends and folklore as well as from the medieval past. Their works demonstrate an appreciation for nature and a deep sensitivity to the feelings of the common man.

Eugène Delacroix, French, 1798-1863, The Combat of the Giaour and Hassan, *oil on canvas, 1826, 59.6 x 73.4 cm, Gift of Mrs. Bertha Palmer Thorne, Mrs. Rose Movius Palmer, and Mr. and Mrs. Arthur M. Wood, 1962.966* © *1993 The Art Institute of Chicago, All Rights Reserved.*

Most French painters of this period continued in the neoclassical style. The most famous neoclassical painter was **Jacques Louis David** (dah VEED; 1748-1825), whose works demonstrate the neoclassical interest in themes from classical Greece and Rome. (For examples of David's work, see pp. 65, 386, and 405.) The painter **Eugène Delacroix** (duh lah KRWAH; 1798-1863), called "the Great Romantic," broke with the neoclassicism of David. Delacroix's paintings are filled with bold colors and portray exciting or violent scenes. One of his most popular works is "Liberty Leading the People." In it he depicts liberty as a Roman goddess carrying the red, white, and blue flag of the Revolution. She is leading the mobs of Paris over the dead bodies of their fallen comrades.

In contrast to the wild, exciting canvases of Delacroix, the painting of the Englishman **John Constable** (1776-1837) illustrates another aspect of romanticism—love for nature. Constable is most famous for his landscape paintings. He made frequent use of green, breaking with the ideas of artists who believed that landscapes should be painted in browns. Throughout most of his career, however, Constable was overshadowed by another English artist, **J.M.W. Turner** (1775-1851). His water-color and oil paintings of landscapes and sea-scapes were greatly admired and eagerly bought. He frequently painted with yellows and oranges, causing one Italian to remark, "The English sell us mustard to eat, and their painters paint with it."

Top: John Constable, Wivenhoe Park, Essex, *National Gallery of Art, Washington, D.C.;* **Bottom:** J.M.W. Turner, Junction of the Thames and the Medway, *National Gallery of Art, Washington, D.C.*

As he matured, Turner's technique changed—his later work foreshadowed the impressionistic style. (See pp. 467-68.)

One of Turner's best-known works is the "Fighting *Téméraire*." The *Téméraire* was one of the sailing ships that fought in the Battle of Trafalgar. With a melancholy mood, he paints the vessel thirty-three years after the battle, as it is being towed away by a steamship to be junked. The painting combines many romantic elements: the sailing ship symbolizes the past; the tugboat, the arrival of the Industrial Revolution; and the sea, nature.

Section Review

1. What is the name of the cultural movement that gave literary and artistic expression to the concepts of "Liberty, Equality, Fraternity"?

2. List six prominent themes prevalent in the works of Romantic writers.

3. What man bridged the gap between classical and romantic music?

4. Romantic musicians often expressed their affection for their homeland through their musical compositions. Identify the national backgrounds of each of the following: Frederick Chopin, Franz Liszt, Peter Tchaikovsky, Giuseppi Verdi, Richard Wagner.

5. What aspect of romanticism did the paintings of Constable and Turner illustrate?

A Glimpse Behind and a Glimpse Ahead

"The beginning of strife," says the writer of Proverbs, "is as when one letteth out water: therefore leave off contention, before it be meddled with" (Prov. 17:14). The violent uprisings that swept across Europe during the nineteenth century illustrate how "the beginning of strife" is like the opening of a floodgate. Revolutionaries hoped that their revolts would bring about change. But like a flood, their revolts often did more harm than good, destroying everything in their path. Discontent led to rebellion, rebellion to strife, and strife to destruction. Though some needed reforms were accomplished, there was often much wrong done to obtain them. Men sought to right injustice on their own instead of looking to the Lord, who is Truth and Justice.

Come and see the works of God: he is terrible [awesome] in his doing toward the children of men. He turned the sea into dry land: they went through the flood on foot: there did we rejoice in him. He ruleth by his power for ever; his eyes behold the nations: let not the rebellious exalt themselves.

—Psalm 66:5-7

Chapter Review

Can You Explain?

reactionary
indemnities
legitimacy

Concert of Europe
conservatism
liberalism

nationalism
Russification
Risorgimento

realpolitik
Dual Monarchy
romanticism

Can You Identify?

Congress of Vienna
Lord Castlereagh
Alexander I
Prince Klemens von
  Metternich
Charles Maurice de
  Talleyrand
Quadruple Alliance
congress system
Monroe Doctrine
Louis XVIII
Charles X
July Revolution
Louis Philippe
Treaty of London

June Days
Napoleon III
Francis Joseph I
Nicholas I
Crimean War (1854-56)
Giuseppe Mazzini
Camillo di Cavour
Giuseppe Garibaldi
Victor Emmanuel II
Zollverein
Otto von Bismarck
Austro-Prussian War
  (1866)
Franco-Prussian War
  (1870-71)

Ems dispatch
Alexander II
Walter Scott
Victor Hugo
Samuel Taylor
  Coleridge
Jacob and William
  Grimm
Johann Wolfgang
  Goethe
Edgar Allan Poe
James Fenimore Cooper
William Wordsworth
George Gordon, Lord
  Byron

Percy Bysshe Shelley
Alexander Pushkin
Ludwig van Beethoven
Frederick Chopin
Franz Liszt
Peter Ilich Tchaikovsky
Johannes Brahms
Giuseppe Verdi
Richard Wagner
Jacques Louis David
Eugène Delacroix
John Constable
J.M.W. Turner

Can You Locate?

Vienna
Austrian Netherlands
Dutch Netherlands
Sweden

Finland
German Confederation
Brussels
Kingdom of the Two
  Sicilies

Sardinia
Crimea
Sevastopol
Schleswig

Holstein
Alsace
Lorraine

How Much Do You Remember?

1. List four concerns that guided Europe's leaders at the Congress of Vienna as they sought to restore the stability of Europe.
2. List the nations involved in the Quintuple Alliance. What was the purpose of this alliance system?
3. List three goals of liberalism.
4. List the significant events that led to the unification of Italy and of Germany.
5. Contrast the Romantic Age with the Age of Reason.

What Do You Think?

1. What were the strengths and weaknesses of the Vienna peace settlement of 1815?
2. What parallels do you see between the congress system and the United Nations?
3. Should national interests come before international cooperation? Explain your answer.
4. What characteristics did Cavour and Bismarck have in common?
5. What are the dangers of letting feelings be the guiding authority in your life?

Notes
1. James Harvey Robinson and Charles A. Beard, *Readings in Modern European History* (Boston: Ginn and Co., 1908), 1:387.
2. Denis Mack Smith, *Italy: A Modern History* (Ann Arbor: Univ. of Michigan Press, 1959), p. 5.
3. Ruth M. Weeks, Rollo L. Lyman, and Howard C. Hill, eds., *World Literature* (New York: Scribner, 1938), pp. 844-45.

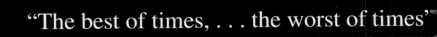

Industrial Revolution and European Society

It was the best of times, it was the worst of times, it was the age of wisdom, it was the age of foolishness, it was the epoch of belief, it was the epoch of incredulity, it was the season of Light, it was the season of Darkness, it was the spring of hope, it was the winter of despair, we had everything before us, we had nothing before us, we were all going direct to Heaven, we were all going direct the other way.

These lines from the opening of Charles Dickens's *Tale of Two Cities* aptly describe European society in the second half of the nineteenth century. In the eyes of many Europeans, this period was the "best of times." Nationalism and democratic liberalism were bringing about great changes. In addition, the Industrial Revolution was dramatically transforming European society. Industrialism joined with science and technology to increase productivity and to raise the material standard of living for the majority of Europeans. The advances in industrial development gave rise to a belief in progress that affected both intellectual and religious attitudes. Many believed that both man and his society were getting better and better. Yet for many Europeans, this period was the "worst of times." Crowded slums and unhealthy working conditions caused many urban workers to despair. To them it was all too apparent that the evils of society had not been remedied.

The situation became worse as many intellectual and religious leaders began to question the authority of God's Word. This gradual shift away from God and His Word gave rise to a secular humanism that abandoned belief in God for faith in human potential.

This chapter traces the development of the Industrial Revolution and examines its impact on European society. We will devote special attention to Great Britain, where the Industrial Revolution began. We will also look at the response of European society to the dramatic changes caused by industrial development and at the changing outlooks and values that transformed European society.

The Industrial Revolution

Shortly before the French Revolution, Great Britain began to experience some sweeping changes of her own. Unlike the French Revolution, which was sudden and violent, the **Industrial Revolution** occurred gradually over several decades. Power machines began to replace hand tools, and the modern factory system came into existence. These technological developments were revolutionary, not because of the speed with which they occurred, but because of their tremendous impact on society.

Beginnings of Industrialism

During the eighteenth century, conditions in British society were favorable for industrial development. Three important factors combined to make possible the "Industrial Age":

1. *An adequate food supply.* The Industrial Revolution was preceded by a revolution in agriculture. New machines and better methods of farming led to an increased food supply that

Opposite Page: Houses of Parliament, London

was able to meet the demands of the growing urban population.

2. *A large and mobile labor force.* As a result of the increased efficiency and productivity in agriculture, fewer people were needed to produce the food. The unemployed farm workers moved to the centers of industrial development and formed the labor force of industry.

3. *Expansion of trade.* Throughout the eighteenth century foreign trade became an increasingly vital part of the British economy. This trade expanded as the number of British colonial possessions increased. The newly acquired colonies not only created a demand for British goods but also provided an open market for British industry.

In addition to these factors, Britain's social and political climate provided a favorable setting for industrial development. Because of Britain's geographic isolation from the Continent, she escaped the destruction of the Napoleonic Wars. While other nations experienced revolution in the nineteenth century, British society remained relatively stable and peaceful. Reforms came gradually through parliamentary measures rather than by violent uprisings. Furthermore, the British government encouraged industrial development by issuing patents for new inventions and removing many regulations that had previously hindered economic growth. Likewise, taxes were not excessive, and interest rates were low. These conditions encouraged businessmen to invest in new business ventures.

Agricultural Revolution

Jethro Tull and **Charles Townshend** are important figures in the history of agriculture. In the eighteenth century Tull invented a seed "drill," or planter, that did away with the wasteful scattering of seed. Later Townshend developed a new system of crop rotation. Instead of leaving a field fallow for a year, he planted clover and turnips in the field. These crops returned needed minerals that other crops removed from the soil. In addition, the yield of turnips and clover could be used to feed farm animals. Townshend also used fertilizer in connection with his system and found that the crop yield per acre was much higher as a result.

Through the use of selective breeding, **Robert Bakewell** produced larger and healthier farm animals. Since more feed was available (as a result of Townshend's system of growing turnips and clover), farmers no longer had to slaughter most of their animals in the winter. They now had the means to feed them until spring. Because of the work of Bakewell and others, today we have such well-known breeds as Hereford cattle and Berkshire hogs.

Another factor that influenced agricultural production was the **enclosure movement**. In the past, small farmers had benefited from using certain open fields as common pasture. In the eighteenth century, however, Parliament made it much easier for wealthy landowners to incorporate these common grazing lands into their own estates and form large farms. The small farmers, unable to survive on what little land they owned, often had to sell out. These farmers and their families had no choice but to move to the cities to look for work there. In

The Industrial Revolution in Great Britain

Major Industrial Areas—1850

Railroads

North Sea

SCOTLAND

Glasgow

Irish Sea

IRELAND

Dublin

Newcastle

ENGLAND

Liverpool

Manchester

Sheffield

Birmingham

Humber R.

Trent R.

WALES

Ouse

Severn R.

Thames R.

London

English Channel

Workers make cloth from wool, mid-eighteenth century.

spite of all the hardships and upheaval, the enclosure movement made agriculture more efficient and profitable. Likewise, it helped to provide workers to fill positions in Britain's growing industries.

The Textile Industry

The Industrial Revolution made its breakthrough in the cotton industry. In the eighteenth century cotton manufacturing was new to Britain and faced a strong challenge from the established wool industry. The manufacturers of woolen goods enjoyed government support and even had persuaded Parliament to pass laws that were designed to hinder domestic cotton production. But with the invention of new machines, cotton production accelerated and was soon able to overshadow the wool industry.

Improvements in the textile industry began in 1733, when **John Kay** invented a "flying shuttle." This invention made it possible for a weaver to work faster and to weave cloth of greater width. One weaver, however, now needed four spinners to keep him supplied with thread. In 1769 **James Hargreaves** solved this problem with the invention of the spinning jenny. (The word *jenny* may be derived from *gin,* a local dialect term for *engine.*) This machine could spin up to eight threads at a time. But the thread it spun was coarser and weaker than the thread the old spinning wheel spun. It did not take long, however, for someone to find a so-

lution to that problem too. That same year, **Richard Arkwright** invented a spinning frame that not only produced thread superior to the spinning jenny but was also powered by water. Because his spinning frames were too large for home use, he built special factories for them. For this contribution to the textile industry, Arkwright is often called the "Father of the Industrial Revolution."

Other improvements began to come to the cotton industry in quick succession. For example, in 1779 **Samuel Crompton** invented an even larger spinning machine, called the "spinning mule." This machine, operated by one person, could spin a thousand threads at a time. Six years later both spinning and weaving machines were converted to steam power. The only remaining bottleneck in the production process was the harvesting of cotton. This involved a slow process by which cotton seeds had to be separated by hand from the cotton fiber. It was not long before the demand for cotton exceeded the supply. But in 1793 the American inventor **Eli Whitney** devised a simple cotton gin. With this machine, one man could do the work of fifty "pickers." Now spinning, weaving, and the preparation of raw cotton could keep pace with one another. As a result, the manufacture of cotton goods went on at a furious pace.

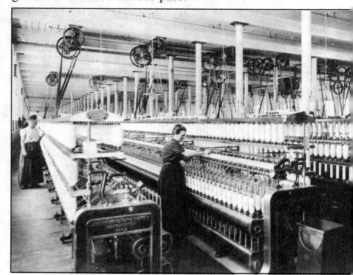

Early twentieth-century cotton mill

Righteousness Exalteth a Nation

In 1851 Great Britain staged the first world's fair, sponsored by Prince Albert. The exhibition hall, designed like a huge greenhouse, was itself a tribute to British achievement. Erected in just four months, the great iron and glass structure covered nineteen acres and was high enough to enclose the tall elms in Hyde Park, where it stood. The British magazine *Punch* dubbed it the "Crystal Palace."

On opening day, May 1, 1851, twenty-six thousand invited guests crowded into the building. (Over six million visitors came to the exhibit before it finally closed.) The short opening program included the singing of the national anthem and a prayer by the archbishop of Canterbury. A huge choir accompanied by a pipe organ and a two-hundred-piece orchestra closed the ceremony by performing the "Hallelujah" chorus from Handel's *Messiah*.

The fair housed exhibits from all over the world, but Britain's industrial machinery drew the most attention. British visitors, however, could not help admiring the exquisite workmanship displayed at other exhibits: Belgian lace, French furniture, and German porcelain. Industrial mass production could not match the beauty of handcrafted items. One observer remarked that "what England as a nation lacks is taste!" Notwithstanding her "lack of taste," however, it was obvious that Great Britain was the leading industrial nation in the mid-nineteenth century.

As the opening ceremony for the exhibition indicated, Victorian England was a place where God was honored and thanked for the great blessings that the nation enjoyed. The queen set a fine example: she forbade the sale of alcohol at the exhibit's refreshment stands and prohibited the exhibition to be open on Sundays. Most people in Victorian society believed the Bible to be the inspired Word of God. They advocated self-improvement, thrift, and hard work. They supported missions as well as evangelistic efforts in their own country. They emphasized family life and viewed divorce as a social disgrace. Of course, Victorian England had her faults too; but in spite of them, the country was an example of the truth that "righteousness exalteth a nation: but sin is a reproach to any people" (Prov. 14:34).

The Factory System

In the earliest stages of the Industrial Revolution, there were no factories in the modern sense of the word. Workers lived in rural areas. They labored at home, using their own hand tools. For the most part, they were able to set their own work schedules and determine how much they wanted to produce. But the size and expense of the new industrial machinery made it impossible for this **domestic system** to continue.

The **factory system** brought the workers, raw materials, and machinery under one roof. Factories were usually located near transportation routes, sources of water power, or natural resources.

As the factory system replaced the domestic system, four significant changes took place for the worker. First, the worker often moved into an urban environment in order to be near the factory. Second, he no longer owned his own tools but used those provided by the factory owner. Third, he no longer controlled the number of hours he worked per day nor the pace at which he worked. Fourth, he now more often performed his work while separated from his family. Although these changes were a necessary part of industrialism, they created problems both for workers and for society.

Development of Industrialism

During the last half of the nineteenth century, industrialism spread throughout much of western Europe. Britain remained the leader, but Germany became a fierce competitor. Other European countries built factories and railroads; yet Russia, eastern Europe, and southern Europe remained economically backward and poverty-stricken. The United States, Japan, and to some extent Canada showed signs of industrial growth. In South America, Africa, and most of Asia, however, modernization and industrialization were a long way off. In these latter areas traditional economic patterns continued relatively unchanged by the new economic developments in Europe.

Iron and Steel Production

One of Britain's most abundant natural resources was iron ore. During the early stages of the Industrial Revolution, however, the production of cast-iron objects remained very costly. Before the Industrial Revolution, charcoal (a wood by-product) had been used in the smelting of the ore. Charcoal, however, was becoming increasingly scarce. Ironmakers therefore began to use coke (a coal by-product) in the smelting process. Britain had large coal deposits, and coke became a cheap fuel. In 1784 **Henry Cort** invented a process by which iron ore was "puddled" (stirred) in the furnace to rid it of impurities. In addition, he developed a method of rolling and hammering the iron to produce a versatile product called wrought iron.

Not until 1856 was an inexpensive and efficient steel-making process devised. The man responsible was Sir **Henry Bessemer.** He found that shooting a jet of air into molten iron would help to rid it of more of its impurities. Then, by adding carbon and other metals, he developed steel. With this process, steel production increased tremendously. For example, Britain, Germany, France, and Belgium produced 125,000 tons of steel in 1860; in 1913 they produced over 32,000,000 tons. For this reason, the first stage of the Industrial Revolution has been

MAJOR INVENTIONS 1700-1850

Date	Inventor	Invention	Industry
1705	Thomas Newcomen	steam engine	mining
1733	John Kay	flying shuttle	textile
1769	Richard Arkwright	spinning frame	textile
1769	James Watt	*successful steam engine	all industry
1770	James Hargreaves	spinning jenny	textile
1779	Samuel Crompton	spinning mule	textile
1785	Edmund Cartwright	power loom	textile
1793	Eli Whitney	cotton gin	textile
1800	John McAdam	crushed stone roads	transportation
1801	Richard Trevithick	steam locomotive	transportation
1807	Robert Fulton	*successful steamboat	transportation
1825	George Stephenson	*successful locomotive	transportation
1831	Michael Faraday	electric dynamo	all industry
1834	Cyrus McCormick	reaper	agriculture
1844	Samuel Morse	telegraph	communications
1844	Charles Goodyear	vulcanization of rubber	transportation

☐ English   ☐ Scottish   ☐ American   *Commercially successful

called the "age of iron"; the later stage, the "age of steel."

New Sources of Power

Many of the early factories were located near rivers, streams, or lakes so that they could use water power to run their machinery. Discoveries of new sources of power made possible the modern factory system. In 1769 a Scotsman by the name of James Watt designed the first practical and efficient steam engine. He improved the design of an earlier steam engine, making one that would provide enough power to run heavy machinery. Steam power made it possible for factories to be strategically located near markets or sources of raw materials instead of near a source of water power.

By the late nineteenth century, new energy sources began to replace the steam engine. Through the invention of the electric dynamo (a machine that turned mechanical energy into electrical energy), many factories converted to electrical power. By 1914, one-half of all the power used in British and German industries was supplied by electricity. Another energy source was oil. The beginning of oil production followed the drilling of the world's first commercial oil well near Titusville, Pennsylvania, in 1859. Although much of the oil was used in the production of kerosene for use in lamps, the development of the internal combustion engine in 1885 provided new uses for the product.

Transportation

Improvements in transportation aided the progress of the Industrial Revolution. Between 1754 and 1788, British roads were greatly improved under a system of turnpike trusts. In a turnpike trust, a group of men financed the building of a road and then charged a toll to those traveling on it. By 1788 Britain had eighteen thousand miles of roads, many of which were built using a method devised by **John McAdam.** Constructed with crushed rocks tightly packed down, macadamized roads provided a smooth and durable surface. Travel by stagecoach was faster than ever before.

The development of canals made it easy to transport heavy or bulky industrial goods. Canals made the routes shorter, and the cost of transportation decreased. England built her first canal in 1757, and by 1850 five thousand miles of canals crisscrossed the nation, joining major rivers.

In addition to building roads and canals, Britain took the lead in constructing railroads. The early "rail" lines were rather short, usually running from coal mines or stone quarries to a nearby port. The first "trains" moved to their destination with the help of gravity and horse power. In 1804, however, **Richard Trevithick** built a steam-powered locomotive, and ten years later the locomotive of **George Stephenson** pulled a train of cars for the first time.

As industry grew in the nineteenth century, the need for transportation grew as well. To meet this need, railroad building increased dramatically. For example, in 1860 there were about 30,000 miles of railroad in the entire world, but by 1890 there were 213,000 miles of railroad just in the United States, Britain, and Germany.

About the same time that Trevithick put a steam engine on wheels, the American **Robert Fulton** put a steam engine in a ship. Although not the first person to do that, he was the first to operate a steamboat as a commercial success. By the middle of the century, iron steamships were crossing the Atlantic Ocean in less than ten days. (It is interesting to note, however, that at first these ships still

carried sails, since few people trusted the new steam engines.)

The steamships and railroads met transportation needs in the nineteenth century. But two developments at the beginning of the next century pointed the way to the future. In 1903 two brothers, **Orville** and **Wilbur Wright,** carried out the first successful airplane flight at Kitty Hawk, North Carolina. In 1908 **Henry Ford** began production of his famous Model T automobile.

Mass Production

In addition to the scores of inventions that improved industrial output, new production techniques helped manufacturers to produce more goods at cheaper prices. Between 1870 and 1914, industrial production in Europe and North America more than tripled. Several new manufacturing methods made this tremendous growth possible.

1. **Automation**—In the early stages of industrialization, new machines helped workers perform their functions more quickly and efficiently. As the years progressed, other machines were invented to run the first machines. One result of this increased automation was that workers in many factories spent their time making sure the machines functioned properly rather than making the products themselves.

Assembly line in Henry Ford's automobile plant

2. **Interchangeable parts**—The expanding role of machines in industrial production gave rise to interchangeable parts. While handcrafted items varied, machine-produced items were all the same. Previously, if some part of a product were damaged, the whole product had to be replaced, or a new part custom-made. But with interchangeable parts, a product needing repair could be fixed easily and cheaply by replacing the broken piece with an identical piece.

3. **Division of labor**—In the past, skilled craftsmen worked on their products from start to finish. During the last part of the nineteenth

century, this procedure changed. Instead of one man making an entire product, a number of workers divided the manufacturing process into several simple procedures.

4. **Assembly line**—Another method devised to speed up production was the assembly line. Workers stationed along a conveyer belt would assemble a specific part of a product. The item would then move down the line, where other workers assembled different parts. One of the first industries to use this new procedure was Henry Ford's automobile plant. By 1913 Ford workers were able to assemble a car in ninety-three minutes.

Science and Industry

As science made new discoveries, factory owners eagerly sought to apply the new knowledge to their particular area of manufacturing. In the field of chemistry, for example, scientists discovered how to make synthetic products such as dyes and fertilizers. Inventors designed new products that aided not only industry, but society as a whole. One of the most famous of these nineteenth-century inventors was **Thomas Alva Edison,** an American genius whose inventions included the light bulb and the phonograph.

Business Finance

When historians speak of industrial expansion before 1860, they refer to the increase in the number of small business partnerships. After 1860 large corporations began to replace the small businesses that found it difficult to meet the high cost of machinery, factories, and workers' wages. As corporations became more common, banks and other financial institutions became more important. These institutions not only helped to organize and finance new corporations, but they also controlled many of them.

Consequences of Industrialism

British society changed dramatically during the age of industrialism. Some of the changes were for the good, and others for the bad. This age saw sharp contrasts of prosperity and poverty, opportunity and oppression, morality and immorality, hope and despair.

Thomas Alva Edison in his laboratory

Poor Living and Working Conditions

In the early stages of the Industrial Revolution, living and working conditions were wretched. The cities were ill-equipped to meet the needs of the great number of rural unemployed that flocked to the industrial centers. Housing sprang up quickly to meet the heavy demand—so quickly that little thought was given to the comfort and health of the occupants. As a result, some families lived in cellars, while others had to share a one-room dwelling. Crowded slums soon appeared in almost every factory town, and people lived in the midst of disease and filth.

The working day in most factories was exhausting, and working conditions were often dangerous. It was not uncommon for men, women, and even children to work fourteen to sixteen hours a day. Greedy mill owners often took advantage of their workers. One owner who employed children told parliamentary investigators that during busy times of the year, he expected the children to work from

3:00 A.M. to 10:00 P.M. (They regularly worked from 6:00 A.M. to 8:30 P.M.) Conditions in the mines and factories in which they worked were unpleasant and dangerous. Coal mines, for example, were poorly ventilated, and factory machinery had few if any safety features. If a worker suffered serious injury on the job, the employer simply hired another worker to fill his place.

Increased Population and Productivity

There were, however, many positive contributions of the Industrial Age. People were better nourished, enjoyed a higher standard of living, and had a longer life span than people of the previous century. It is estimated that the population of Europe increased from 190,000,000 in 1800 to 460,000,000 in 1900. The growth in population was especially noticeable in the cities. Prior to 1840, England had only two cities with more than 100,000 people. But by 1910 there were forty-eight English cities with more than 100,000 residents.

The increase in population was accompanied by an increase in the food supply and in industrial production. Greater efficiency and productivity reduced the prices of many goods, and as a result more people of the nineteenth century had a greater abundance of material possessions than those of any previous century.

Evaluation of the Industrial Age

Some today see nothing but evil in the Industrial Revolution. They condemn capitalism, which made possible the industrial growth, for producing the poor living and working conditions. They blame the free enterprise system for allowing a few to get rich while the many remained poor. But this view overlooks the fact that conditions in the rural areas were often no better than those in the crowded cities. Farm workers had to work as long and under as many adverse conditions as did the factory workers. Also, it must be remembered that industrialism provided jobs for the increasing number of unemployed farm workers. It is a distortion to say that no one was concerned about the conditions in which the workers lived and worked. The moral and social conscience of the Victorian Age initiated many reforms.

On the other hand, some are too enthusiastic about the growth of industrialism. While the Industrial Revolution created new opportunities and provided a greater abundance for more people, it also led to a growing emphasis upon material goods and a decrease in spiritual concern. People tend to forget God when they seek material gain. The Apostle Paul warns against false teachers that promote the idea that "gain is godliness." "From such," he says, "withdraw thyself" (I Tim. 6:5).

> But godliness with contentment is great gain. For we brought nothing into this world, and it is certain we can carry nothing out. And having food and raiment let us be therewith content. But they that will be rich fall into temptation and a snare, and into many foolish and hurtful lusts, which drown men in destruction and perdition. For the love of money is the root of all evil: which while some coveted after, they have erred from the faith, and pierced themselves through with many sorrows.
> —I Timothy 6:6-10

We must remember that the problems in any society—both individual and collective—are the result of sin. In the Industrial Age, as in any other, greed and cruelty, discontent and immorality were to blame for poor conditions.

Section Review

1. In what country did the Industrial Revolution begin? In what industry did the Industrial Age make its real breakthrough?
2. List four inventions that aided the development of the textile industry. Identify the inventor of each.
3. What is the name of the system in which workers labored at home, using their own tools and determining how much they wanted to work and produce?
4. Name four new methods of transportation that aided the progress of the Industrial Revolution.
5. List the four new production methods that helped manufacturers produce more goods at cheaper prices.

Responses to the Industrial Revolution

Response of Government

Great Britain was the leader not only in industrial production but also in attempts to remedy the social and political problems created by the rapid industrial expansion. During the 1830s and 1840s the British Parliament passed the first significant social reforms. The members of Parliament who sponsored this legislation were sincere in their efforts to correct the abuses of industry and the accompanying problems in society. But they failed to realize that increased government involvement could easily lead to government control of industry and a decline in individual freedom.

Except for a few isolated incidents, Great Britain did not experience the violent uprisings that shook the European continent during the first half of the nineteenth century. The British people sought change through parliamentary reform, not through revolution. They sought to make Parliament represent the views of *all* the people. During this century, Parliament passed many political reform bills that broadened the electorate and enabled more people to have a voice in government.

Reform

The word *reform* implies a change for the better. During the Victorian Era, people from all walks of life worked to improve their society. Because of their zealous efforts, historians often call this period an age of reform. But in spite of their sincere attempts, not everything these people called reform was beneficial for society. Some reforms brought only change, and, as time proved, change for the worse. The value of any political, social, or economic reform should be measured only according to the standards of God's Word.

Social Reform

Among the earliest pieces of social legislation passed by Parliament were acts intended to curb abuses in the factories. Parliament enacted several bills to restrict the long hours and harsh conditions under which many women and children had to work. In 1833 it passed the first effective Factory Act to limit child labor. According to this law, no child under nine years of age was to work in a textile mill. Children from nine to thirteen years old could work, but no more than eight hours a day. In addition, they were to receive at least three hours of schooling daily. Those between the ages of thirteen and eighteen could work no more than twelve hours a day. To enforce the law, Parliament appointed government inspectors to make sure the mill owners obeyed it.

Other reforms soon followed the Factory Act of 1833. The Poor Law of 1834 placed the national government in charge of relief measures for those who were too old or too sick to work. The Mines Act (1842) barred all females, as well as males under ten years old, from the coal mines. In an effort to further regulate working hours, Parliament passed the Ten Hour Bill in 1847, which limited women and children in any industry to a ten-hour day.

Child working in a textile mill

Some social reforms grew out of the humanitarian efforts of the British people. One prominent example was the antislavery movement led by **William Wilberforce.** Motivated by his Christian faith and a sincere compassion for his fellow man, Wilberforce campaigned against the slave trade. His efforts were rewarded when in 1807 Parliament passed a law abolishing the slave trade in British territory. Another act in 1833 freed all the slaves in the British Empire.

Economic Reform

In 1846 Parliament repealed the **Corn Laws.** These laws had placed a high tariff on imported grain. Such tariffs limited foreign competition and allowed British landowners to sell their grain at higher prices. The repeal of these laws not only brought down the price of grain (relieving the bur-

den of workers, who had been forced to pay high prices), but it also signaled a shift in British economic policy toward free trade. Britain chose to become dependent on cheaply imported food while increasing her efforts toward industrialization.

Political Reform

Reform Bills—At the outset of the nineteenth century, the aristocrats and wealthy landowners controlled Parliament. Property qualifications kept most of the people from voting in parliamentary elections. In addition, voting districts called boroughs had not changed for almost 150 years. Thus the landholding class retained control of Parliament, denying fair representation to residents of the growing industrial centers. Members of the middle class, therefore, demanded change. By 1830 they persuaded the House of Commons to pass a

William Hogarth's Canvassing for Votes *illustrates the type of corruption the Reform Bill of 1832 sought to correct.*

William Wilberforce: "No Common Christian"

The leader of the fight against the British slave trade was the outstanding Christian statesman William Wilberforce (1759-1833). In 1785, five years after he entered Parliament, Wilberforce underwent a conversion that he later called "the great change." In his efforts to turn from his previously worldly lifestyle, he considered abandoning politics altogether. However, he heeded the advice of Anglican pastor John Newton to stay in Parliament. Newton said, "It is hoped and believed that the Lord has raised you up for the good of His church and for the good of the nation."

Wilberforce became a serious and fervent Christian. His pastor wrote, "He is no common Christian; his knowledge of divine things and his experience of the power of the Gospel are very extraordinary." Nor was he the kind of politician who makes a religious profession to sway voters but makes worldly wisdom his political philosophy. Wilberforce said, "A man who acts from the principles I profess reflects that he is to give an account of his political conduct at the Judgement seat of Christ."

Although he supported many worthy causes, Wilberforce pressed none so hard nor so consistently as the abolition of the British slave trade. He declared on one occasion, "If it please God to honor me so far, may I be the instrument of stopping such a course of wickedness and cruelty as never before disgraced a Christian country." He faced tremendous opposition to his efforts. The slave trade was profitable, and the planters in Britain's Caribbean possessions predicted economic disaster if the trade were abolished. The economic arguments swayed many politicians who were concerned about financial prosperity—and their re-election. Several times Wilberforce presented to the House of Commons a motion to abolish the trade. Sometimes he lost by wide margins, at other times by narrow ones. Even when he managed to get his bill through the House of Commons, the House of Lords rejected it.

Other Christians sought to encourage him. Isaac Milner, a clergyman and close friend, said, "If you carry this point in your whole life, that life will be far better spent than in being Prime Minister many years." John Wesley, shortly before his death, wrote to Wilberforce, "Unless God has raised you up for this very thing, you will be worn out by the opposition of men and devils. But if God be for you, who can be against you." Finally, in 1807, Wilberforce succeeded in guiding an abolition bill through both houses of Parliament. The slave trade was abolished.

Wilberforce was not finished. Although the trade was illegal, slavery continued to exist in British territories. The fight to abolish slavery, however, took more years than Wilberforce had left. Ill health forced him to retire from Parliament in 1825 and leave the battle to others. Only three days before his death in 1833, Wilberforce learned that the House of Commons had voted to abolish slavery completely.

While others praised him for his humanitarian activities, Wilberforce remained painfully aware of his human failings and frailties, saying, "The genuine Christian . . . humbles himself in the dust and acknowledges that he is not worthy of the least of all God's mercies." On another occasion he said, "I wish I had been as active as I ought about the poor slaves. However, the Blood of Jesus Christ cleanses from all sin and there is the comfort which combines the deepest Humiliation with the firmest Hope."

Queen Victoria
Queen Victoria (1837-1901) has become the symbol of nineteenth-century Britain. Her sixty-three-and-a-half-year reign was the longest in British history. Her moral standards and her political ideas exemplified the attitudes of many Britons.

In 1840 Victoria married Albert, a German prince of strong character. During their twenty-one years of marriage, Victoria and Albert did much to restore respect for the British monarchy. Not only did they lessen court expenditures, but they also set an example of moral uprightness. The relationship between the queen and the prince was a happy one. When Albert died of typhoid fever in 1861, Victoria was heartbroken. For the next thirty-nine years she lived in relative seclusion, doing everything in her power to perpetuate the memory of her beloved Albert.

Because many of her nine children and thirty-four grandchildren married into other royal families, Victoria has been called the "grandmother of Europe." One of her grandsons was Kaiser William II of Germany, and one of her granddaughters was the wife of Nicholas II, the last of the Russian czars. Other of her children and grandchildren married into the royal lines of Sweden, Norway, Spain, and Rumania. Three monarchs during World War I—Kaiser William II, Alexandra (wife of Nicholas II), and King George V of Britain—were cousins.

reform bill, but the House of Lords vetoed it. When the king threatened to create new lords to ensure that there would be a majority to pass the bill, the House of Lords backed down, and the **Reform Bill of 1832** became law.

The Reform Bill lowered property qualifications for voting, increasing the electorate by an estimated fifty per cent. It also reorganized the voting districts, giving representation to middle class citizens in the new industrial cities. Merchants, bankers, and factory owners now had a voice in government. But the Reform Bill had not extended the voting privilege to the workers. As a result, dissatisfied workers supported a new movement called **Chartism.** The Chartists advocated universal manhood suffrage, the secret ballot, equal electoral districts, pay for members of Parliament, no property qualifications for members of Parliament, and annual elections to Parliament. The Chartists presented several petitions, but each time Parliament refused to act. The Chartist movement failed, but all of its demands—except annual elections to Parliament—eventually became law.

In 1867 Parliament passed a second major reform bill, which again reduced property qualifications for voting. This action nearly doubled the electorate and shifted additional political power to Britain's industrial centers.

Disraeli and Gladstone—Reforms continued throughout the remainder of the century as two dominant political figures, **Benjamin Disraeli** (dihz RAY lee; 1804-81) and **William Gladstone** (1809-98), alternated as prime minister of the British Parliament. Benjamin Disraeli began his political career as a liberal but later became the colorful and witty leader of the Tory, or Conservative, party. It was through his efforts that Parliament passed the Reform Bill of 1867. While he was prime minister, Parliament passed several bills related to public health and housing. But Disraeli was primarily involved in foreign affairs. Perhaps his greatest success occurred when on behalf of the British government he bought forty-four per cent of the shares in the Suez Canal from the ruler of Egypt. This purchase enhanced British dominance in the Mediterranean region and greatly aided British trade.

Disraeli's political opponent was William Gladstone, the leader of the new Liberal party. Gladstone, the son of a wealthy Scottish businessman, was a man of strong character. As a statesman he placed his moral convictions above political expediency and earned the respect of both friends and enemies. As a man of strong religious faith, he diligently studied the Scriptures and regularly gathered his family for prayer. He also wrote several works on theology. It was undoubtedly his religious beliefs that shaped his political outlook and made him a man of compassion toward those less fortunate than he.

During his four terms as prime minister (1868-74, 1880-85, 1886, and 1892-94), he emphasized domestic reforms that established a single national court system, instituted voting by secret ballot, and in 1884 extended the voting privilege to rural communities. Gladstone also supported several education bills, believing that better education would promote wiser voting.

One particularly pressing problem during Gladstone's ministry was the matter of British rule of Ireland. Under James I (1603-25), Protestants had begun settling in Northern Ireland. The rest of the island was primarily Roman Catholic. Southern, Catholic Ireland became increasingly restless under British rule and began demanding "home rule." "My mission is to pacify Ireland," Gladstone had said as he took office for the first time. But in spite of diligent effort, he never achieved his goal. The "Irish Question" was not settled until after World War I. (See pp. 525-26.)

The Parliament Bill of 1911—The capstone of Britain's political development came in 1911 with the passage of the **Parliament Bill.** After much heated debate and political maneuvering, the House of Commons managed to wrest some power from the House of Lords and assert itself as the supreme governing body in Britain. As a result of this bill, the House of Lords could only temporarily

The two dominant figures in British politics in the late nineteenth century: Benjamin Disraeli (left) and William Gladstone (right)

delay legislation passed by the House of Commons, not absolutely veto it, as before. Also, in 1911 the House of Commons for the first time voted a salary for its members, making it financially possible for poorer citizens to become members of Parliament.

As Britain's government came to represent more of the people, their attitude toward the role of government began to change. Many people began to expect the government to be directly involved in establishing and funding various social programs. Britain began to develop into a **welfare state** (a state in which the government assumes the responsibility for the material and social well-being of every individual "from the cradle to the grave"). Within just a few years, Parliament passed bills providing for unemployment insurance, health protection, workman's compensation, and old-age pensions. In addition, it placed secondary education under state control.

Ideas of the Socialists

Man has responsibilities both to God and to society. Christ makes it clear that man's first responsibility is to God and his second is to his fellow man: "Thou shalt love the Lord thy God with all thy heart, and with all thy soul, and with all thy mind. This is the first and great commandment. And the second is like unto it, Thou shalt love thy neighbour as thyself" (Matt. 22:37-39). But too often ungodly man has rejected his obligation to God and sought by his own efforts to correct the ills of society.

Many people during the nineteenth century sought to remedy the evils around them by changing society. These people believed that man is basically good, failing to realize that *sin* is at the root of all social evils. This mistaken attitude, which assumes the perfectibility of man and society, found its clearest expression in socialism.

Most people today assume that **socialism** is only an economic term. It is defined as government ownership of the means of production and the distribution of goods for the presumed welfare of society. This definition is correct, but it is important to realize that belief in socialism, like a belief in any other philosophy, affects every area of life. For example, since socialism emphasizes the group rather than the individual, many socialists advocate establishing an international government to replace independent national states. The influence of socialism in religious circles has promoted the desire to break down all denominational and religious barriers and unite all religions—regardless of their beliefs—into one. Socialism rejects individual responsibility, limits individual choice, and replaces individual initiative with collectivism (rule by the group).

Four major types of socialism developed in the nineteenth century. Although each form sought to achieve the perfect society through different means, each was built on the same set of false ideas: (1) man is by nature good—it is society that has corrupted him; and (2) if society can be improved, then man will be improved, and all injustice and cruelty will cease.

Adam Smith

One of the most influential books on political economics is Adam Smith's *Wealth of Nations*. Published in 1776, this book attacks mercantilism, the prevailing economic system of most European nations during the eighteenth century. Smith defined national wealth not by how much gold or silver a nation possesses, but by how many goods it can produce and sell. In other words, wealth depends on productivity.

Smith proposed a policy of "free trade" among nations. A nation, he believed, should manufacture what it can best and most efficiently produce. What other goods it needed it should purchase from other countries. If each nation were driven by "self-interest," all countries would do their best to produce superior products that others would want to buy. With increased demand, production would improve and all would benefit.

Smith attacked the economic policies of the British government as restrictive of free trade. He advocated a "hands-off" policy known as laissez faire. According to this policy, government is not to interfere in business and trade, but it is to provide a favorable climate for business activity. Smith believed that the role of government, apart from maintaining law and order, is to provide an adequate education system, road system, and defense.

Utopian Socialism

Utopian socialism was a direct result of the French Enlightenment. Like many of the eighteenth-century *philosophes,* the utopian socialists believed that if the inequities in society could be abolished, man's natural goodness could be perfected. These socialists considered the profit motive of capitalism to be the basic source of evil. They believed it stimulated greed and hatred.

Because they assumed that one's environment produced social evil, the utopians believed that proper surroundings and a good education would solve all problems. To test these ideas, several men in Europe and America formed socialist communities that they hoped would set the example for sweeping changes in society. **Robert Owen** (1771-1858), a textile manufacturer, established one such community for his workers at his textile mill in Scotland. He later established an agricultural community at New Harmony, Indiana. But both his "utopias" failed after only a short time—people were not as unselfish and reasonable as he and others assumed.

Marxism

Another form of socialism was advanced by **Karl Marx** (1818-83), the son of a prominent Ger-

Karl Marx

man lawyer. Marx abandoned the study of law in order to study philosophy and history. At the age of twenty-three he received a doctor of philosophy degree, but no German university would hire him because of his radical political views. The Prussian government forced him to leave the country. Marx then fled to Paris, where he met **Friedrich Engels** (1820-95). The two men became lifelong friends. Working together, they produced the *Communist Manifesto,* which appeared during the revolutionary year of 1848. This book called upon the workers of the world to unite in opposition to capitalism.

From Paris, Marx went to England, where he spent the last thirty-three years of his life. There he wrote his most famous work, *Das Kapital,* in which he explains in detail his socialist ideas. Marx thought the utopian socialists (a term that he and Engels coined) were impractical; he considered them idle dreamers. He believed that his ideas, which he called "scientific socialism," were based on provable economic principles. Yet actually his views were anything but scientific.

Marx believed that economic forces determine the course of history. To him, every social, political, or religious movement springs from a desire by one group of people to take economic advantage of another group. According to this view of history, even the Protestant Reformation was not primarily a religious movement; religion was simply a veil that obscured the real economic issues.

Marx also believed that history would naturally progress toward perfection. During this process, conflicts between various social, political, or religious movements would be inevitable. Each conflict, however, would somehow be successfully resolved, enabling man to "progress" to a higher stage of development. These conflicts are an essential feature of history, Marx said, and they will continue until man finally reaches the perfect society—a society where everyone is equal and gladly shares the fruit of his labor with others. This perfect condition is what Marx called *communism.*

According to Marx, all of history is dominated by class struggle. From earliest times, the oppressed have fought their oppressors, Marx said. During the Roman Republic the plebeians struggled against the patricians; during the Middle Ages the serfs struggled against their lords; and during Marx's time the **proletariat** (workers) struggled against the industrialists (factory owners). Marx believed that under communism such struggles would cease, since all class distinctions would be eliminated.

Marx taught that one of the ways in which the industrialists exploited, or took advantage of, the workers was by paying them less than they deserved. According to Marx, it is the workers who create wealth, and the value of a product is the amount of labor it takes to produce it. Yet the wages that the workers receive are always less than the value of the products they produce. Therefore, said Marx, the capitalist is robbing the workers and unjustly living off the labor of others. (Marx ignored the fact that the capitalist invests great funds in building the factories and in buying machines and raw materials—without these, industrial goods could not be produced.)

How would communism end such "injustices" and achieve the perfect society? Marx said the answer lay in revolution. He believed that communist revolutions were a necessary and inevitable part of communist development and that they would begin in industrialized nations, where there was a large, class-conscious proletariat. The proletariat would overthrow the capitalist bourgeoisie (middle class) and establish their own rule, called the "dictatorship of the proletariat." Once in power, the proletariat would begin to systematically eliminate anything that opposed the ideals of communism, such as private ownership of property and private business. In addition, they would destroy Christianity, for, according to Marx, religion is a "drug" used by the ruling class to keep the workers in subjection. Once the last remnant of capitalism had been eliminated, the dictatorship of the proletariat would disappear. Thus, Marx believed, man would become a perfect being in a perfect society and would no longer need a state to govern him.

Fabian Socialism

British socialists who sought to achieve a socialist society without revolution called themselves **Fabians.** They took their name from Quintus Fa-

bius Maximus, a cautious Roman general who tried to wear down his opponent Hannibal little by little instead of engaging him in open battle. The Fabian socialists believed that the best way to destroy capitalism was to gradually undermine it rather than seeking to suddenly overthrow it. The Fabians and similar groups throughout Europe and America worked to bring about gradual change by urging the passage of welfare legislation.

Christian Socialism

The Christian socialists were theological liberals who believed that Christianity and capitalism were incompatible. They believed that unregenerate society could and should live according to the Sermon on the Mount (Matt. 5-7). They sought to establish an earthly millennium where peace and justice would reign. Because many people opposed socialism in any form, the Christian socialists tried to portray it in a positive manner. Socialism is nothing more than "the embodiment of Christianity in our industrial system," they said. In fact, according to an early Christian socialist paper, "Christianity and Socialism are almost interchangeable terms." These men, although claiming to be Christian, failed to see that the very basis of socialism, the perfectibility of man by man, is contrary to the teaching of Scripture.

Concern of Christians

Following the admonition of the Apostle Paul, who said, "As we have therefore opportunity, let us do good unto all men, especially unto them who are of the household of faith" (Gal. 6:10), Christians were among the first to respond to the needs and problems of an industrialized society. These Christians were not simply social reformers hoping to improve living conditions, help the poor, and reduce crime. They realized that sin lies at the root of all social ills. As William Booth, the founder of the Salvation Army, said, "My only hope for the permanent deliverance of mankind from misery, either in this world or the next, is the regeneration or remaking of the individual by the power of the Holy Ghost through Jesus Christ."

One of the earliest movements founded to minister to the laboring classes in the cities was the

Spurgeon: "The Prince of Preachers"

During the Industrial Age, England benefited from the ministry of one of her greatest preachers since Wesley, Charles Haddon Spurgeon (1834-92). Born in the home of a minister, Spurgeon had a godly upbringing and was converted at the age of fifteen. In 1854 he became pastor of the New Park Street Chapel, a Baptist church in London. His congregation grew so large that he had to construct a new building. In 1861 Spurgeon opened the London Metropolitan Tabernacle, seating five thousand people. In 1857 he even preached in the Crystal Palace to a crowd of more than twenty-three thousand. His earnest delivery, wonderful oratory, and searching style earned him the title "the Prince of Preachers."

Spurgeon oversaw numerous other ministries as well. He operated a college for preachers, an orphanage, and a tract society for the sale and free distribution of books and pamphlets. He published a magazine, *The Sword and the Trowel*, and wrote several works, the most famous of which is his commentary on the book of Psalms, *The Treasury of David*.

Near the end of his life, Spurgeon became concerned about the growth of theological liberalism within the Baptist denomination. *The Sword and the Trowel* began publishing articles attacking the "downgrading" of Scripture by those who denied its inerrancy and authority. Called the "Downgrade Controversy," this conflict led Spurgeon to withdraw from the Baptist Union (an organization of English Baptist churches). Members of the Union attacked and rebuked Spurgeon for his stand, and voted overwhelmingly to condemn him.

Spurgeon's importance today does not lie in the size of his ministry, the number of converts he won to Christ, or even his unmatched eloquence. Spurgeon is still remembered because of the doctrinal solidity of his message and his refusal to sacrifice principle for popularity. Other popular ministers of the era (who are now little remembered) preached on sentimental or moralistic topics. Spurgeon offered his congregation sound teaching regardless of the controversy it might arouse. To the end of his life, Spurgeon did not yield to the opposition but remained faithfully obedient to the Word of God.

Sunday school. Sunday schools, first begun in England in the late eighteenth century by **Robert Raikes,** sought to reach the poor, illiterate, working-class children. The Sunday schools not only taught the children about Jesus Christ but also instructed them in reading and writing. Many churches made Sunday school a part of their regular ministry to reach underprivileged children for Christ and to provide further instruction in God's Word for the members of the church. Since most of the Sunday school teachers were laymen, Bible institutes were founded to train laymen to be more effective Christian workers. In addition to the Sunday schools, concerned Christians established homes for juvenile delinquents as well as orphans. Perhaps the best-known orphanages were founded by **George Mueller** in Bristol, England.

In 1844 twenty-two-year-old George Williams established in London the Young Men's Christian Association, commonly called the **YMCA.** The purpose of this organization was to minister to young men who worked in the city and to win them to

Christ. Although the primary purpose of the YMCA was spiritual, Williams also emphasized educational, social, and athletic development. The YMCA soon became a worldwide organization, and before long others established a women's organization, the YWCA. Sadly, these organizations no longer have the spiritual concern of their founders.

Another ministry of worldwide impact was the Salvation Army. This organization was founded by **William Booth** (1829-1912). Booth began working in the London slums in 1865, preaching the gospel and seeking to meet the physical needs of those around him. Throughout his ministry, Booth tried to counteract the apathy of some Christians toward the plight of the poor. He wrote, "Why all this apparatus of temples and meeting-houses to save men from perdition in a world which is to come, while never a helping hand is stretched out to save them from the inferno of their present life?" Booth believed that an unconverted individual needs to see that a Christian has a genuine concern for him, just as Christ showed compassion for people during His earthly ministry by healing them and feeding them.

The outpouring of Christian charity during the nineteenth century was due in large part to great revivals that swept across Great Britain and the United States. In the eighteenth century the Wesleyan revivals prompted the first surge of Christian activity; in the nineteenth century the revivals of **Dwight L. Moody** (1837-99) and other evangelists brought about a second. Moody and his partner, Ira Sankey (1840-1908), believed that conditions in society would improve only when those who live in that society have experienced true conversion. Beginning in 1873, Moody and Sankey held evangelistic campaigns in the large industrial cities of Britain and America, bringing thousands of people to Christ. Many of their converts became soulwinners, and some of them devoted themselves to various Christian ministries designed to win those in the inner cities to Christ.

How many thousands or even millions of souls were snatched from eternal hell by Christ through the efforts of Raikes, Mueller, Williams, Booth, Moody, and others may never be known. While their methods were inventive and unique, their message was the same: "Believe on the Lord Jesus Christ, and thou shalt be saved" (Acts 16:31).

Section Review

1. List the six goals of the chartist movement.
2. Name the two dominant prime ministers of Britain during the latter part of the nineteenth century. Give the political party of each.
3. Define a "welfare state."
4. What force did Karl Marx believe determined the course of history? In what famous work did he explain his socialist ideas?
5. Match each of the following men with the ministry below with which he was associated: Robert Raikes, George Mueller, George Williams, William Booth, Dwight L. Moody, Charles H. Spurgeon.
   a. Salvation Army
   b. YMCA
   c. orphanages
   d. evangelistic meetings
   e. pastor of the London Metropolitan Tabernacle
   f. Sunday schools

Dwight L. Moody

Changing Outlooks in European Society

Faith in Scientific Progress

During the second half of the nineteenth century, Europe experienced a rapid expansion in scientific knowledge and technology. Practical inventions provided material comforts that previous ages had not known. The telegraph and telephone, for example, made possible rapid communication. Improved methods of transportation made travel easier. Better nutrition and methods of diagnosing and treating disease increased the average lifespan. Greater industrial output raised the material standard of living for most Europeans. To many people, science became the source of hope for the future. They believed that there was nothing that mankind could not achieve if given the chance. The impact of science on this age greatly influenced man's perception of himself and the world.

Evolutionary Outlook

Scientists during the Age of Reason viewed the world of nature much like a machine that operates according to "fixed," unchanging laws. To them the order reflected by nature demonstrated the existence of God and His creative power. But in the second half of the nineteenth century, scientists began to look upon man and nature as the products of an evolutionary process. The man who laid the basis for the modern theories of biological evolution was **Charles Darwin** (1809-82).

In his famous work *Origin of Species* (1859), Darwin tried to prove that organisms developed from simple to complex structures through natural causes. No species is fixed and changeless, said Darwin; it is gradually shaped by its environment over countless ages. Those creatures best able to adapt to their environment survive; those with inferior characteristics perish. This theory is called the "survival of the fittest."

In 1871 Darwin published a book entitled *The Descent of Man,* which was even more shocking than the previous work. In this book Darwin applied his evolutionary theory to man himself. Darwin observed that man resembles other creatures. Instead of recognizing the hand of a common Creator, he taught that man developed from animals. His theory opposed the biblical doctrine of the special, direct creation of man by God. Scripture, however, says that God made each different animal group to reproduce "after his kind" (Gen. 1:24).

Revolution in the Physical Sciences

During the 1800s and early 1900s significant developments in the physical sciences greatly expanded man's understanding of matter and energy, the components of the physical universe. Scientists of this period discovered that matter was made up of distinct units called chemical elements. An English Quaker named **John Dalton** (1766-1844) proposed that all chemical elements were composed of unique particles called atoms. His ideas helped to explain the distinct characteristics of various substances. Today he is recognized as the formulator of the atomic theory.

Later scientists sought to identify and classify the chemical elements. Knowing that certain elements shared similar characteristics, the Russian chemist **Dmitri Mendeleev** (MEN duh LAY yef; 1834-1907) organized the chemical elements in a chart according to their atomic masses. His system of classification is called the periodic table.

As scientists continued to investigate, they found more characteristics that distinguished the chemical elements as unique particles. Aiding them in their discoveries was the X-ray tube. The German physicist **William Roentgen** (RUNT gun; 1845-1923) accidentally discovered X-rays while working with vacuum tubes. He called these *x-rays* because he did not fully understand the energies he had discovered. His device was used by a young British scientist named **Henry Moseley** (1887-1915) to discover more about atoms. The more scientists found out about the properties of elements, the better able they were to organize and revise Mendeleev's chart.

The discovery of radioactive matter added new elements to the chart. The husband-and-wife team of **Pierre** (1859-1906) and **Marie** (1867-1934) **Curie** found two new elements in a uranium ore called

Marie Curie

ments of time, mass, and length did not vary. According to Einstein's theory, however, moving objects increase in mass as they decrease in length. The amount of increase or decrease depends on the speed of the object.

Albert Einstein

pitchblende. These radioactive elements would naturally break down into simpler elements, indicating that all atoms, and thus all matter, were made up of even smaller particles. Such an idea was advanced by the British physicist **Ernest Rutherford** (1871-1937). He stated that the atom was composed of at least two distinct parts—a positively charged nucleus surrounded by negatively charged electrons. The Danish physicist **Niels Bohr** (1885-1962) built on Rutherford's theory. Bohr's model of the atom shows a nucleus composed of two kinds of particles—positive protons and neutral neutrons. Around this nucleus the electrons moved in orbits much like planets revolving around the sun.

It was the work of perhaps the greatest scientific thinker of the twentieth century, **Albert Einstein** (EYN stine; 1879-1955), that showed the relationship between matter and energy. This he demonstrated through the equation $E = mc^2$ (energy equals mass times the speed of light squared). Another of his contributions to science was his theory of relativity. Scientists in the past believed that measure-

Impact of Science on Society

The advances in science caused many people to look upon science as the means of progress. People began to apply scientific theories of the physical world to the study of man and society. "Scientific" became a new standard by which society's institutions and values were measured. To many people, science became a new religion. They rejected the authority of God's Word for the authority of scientific theory. Often something done in the name of science was judged true and worthy regardless of whether there was evidence to support it. For example, many people praised Darwin's theory of evolution as scientific while dismissing the biblical account of creation as mythical. In rejecting the Genesis record, they also rejected their responsibility to God as their Creator. Others incorrectly applied scientific theory to society. Modern philosophers, for example, embraced Einstein's theory of relativity as the guide for the study of ethics (questions of right and wrong). They claimed that since all things in the universe are relative, moral principles are relative too. Moral principles simply evolved as man has evolved, so they believed. Through such belief and teaching, sinful men demonstrated their rebellion against God and His Word.

Challenges to Christianity

Although the nineteenth century was a time of great revivals and missionary activity, the Christian church, as we have seen, was besieged by many foes. Even many religious leaders departed from the Faith. They no longer accepted the inspiration and inerrancy (freedom from error) of the Scriptures. Instead they tried to "scientifically" discern what portions of God's Word are true and what portions are false. Basing their theories upon the evolutionary ideas of Darwin, these men claimed that Judaism and Christianity slowly developed out of the Near Eastern civilization. They rejected the fact that God revealed His truth directly to "holy men of God" (II Pet. 1:21). Many liberal theologians claimed that Moses did not write the first five books of the Bible. They also rejected the miracles mentioned in the Bible. They invented their own natural explanations for these supernatural events. Likewise, because they did not believe in prophecy, they said that the Old Testament writers wrote down their "prophecies" after the events had happened.

The purpose and mission of the church also came under attack. Those who promoted the "social gospel" believed that the major purpose of Christianity is to change society, and that by changing society individuals will be made better. They rejected the New Testament teaching that the only gospel is the story of the death, burial, and resurrection of Jesus Christ (I Cor. 15:1-4). They preached a gospel of social improvement instead. The Apostle Paul warns against such in Galatians 1:7-8—

> But there be some that trouble you, and would pervert [change] the gospel of Christ. But though we, or an angel from heaven, preach any other gospel unto you than that which we have preached unto you, let him be accursed.

The work of Christ was also challenged by a growing materialism and secularization of society. Many people began to concentrate on the things of this world and to neglect spiritual things. The number of church members, especially in Europe, remained high, but the number of people who actually attended church was very small. In addition, a small but increasing number of people began breaking with centuries-old traditions and leaving the church entirely. Weakened by worldly members, the Christian church as an institution lost much of its influence on the lives of Europeans.

Common to all the foes of Christianity was a spirit of humanism—the exaltation of man above God. Modern humanists accepted the evolutionary theories and the social gospel, which taught that man was neither created by nor responsible to God. Instead, man was responsible to himself and to society. They did not believe in heaven and hell but rather believed that whatever fulfillment man was going to receive would come through his own efforts in this life.

In the late nineteenth century, these humanists were a small minority, consisting primarily of infidel religious leaders and theologians as well as godless intellectuals. But the growing secularization of society and the spread of this humanistic spirit increased rapidly and pervaded all areas of society during the twentieth century.

New Trends in the Arts

Realism

By the 1850s a new form of artistic expression known as **realism** had become widespread in Europe. Realists had a growing awareness of the world around them. They rejected the idealist emotion of romanticism, as well as its fascination with exotic themes and faraway places. Realists believed that life should be portrayed as it really is. Although they did not abandon emotion, they sought to give expression to those feelings that touched their everyday life. They were conscious of the social problems around them and sought with "scientific" objectivity to represent reality. They tended, however, to highlight the darker side of European society: poverty, injustice, and immorality.

Charles Dickens

Other writers wrote about man's struggles in this life. The British novelist and poet **Thomas Hardy** (1840-1928) portrayed man as engaged in a hopeless struggle against impersonal forces beyond his control. The American **Samuel Clemens,** better known as Mark Twain (1835-1910), viewed life as did Hardy; unlike Hardy, however, he used humor to convey his ideas. The famous Russian novelist **Leo Tolstoy** (1828-1910) realistically described life in Russia during the Napoleonic Wars.

In reaction to the romantic artists, many of whom painted faraway places, realist painters concentrated on observable, commonplace subjects. They tried to portray life as they saw it, not as they imagined it to be. According to **Gustave Courbet** (KOOR BEH; 1819-77), a famous realist painter, "an abstract object, invisible or nonexistent, does not belong to the domain of painting." "Show me an angel," he said, "and I'll paint one." Instead of painting angels, he and his fellow realists painted such works as *The Stone Breakers* and *The Third Class Carriage*.

Gustave Courbet, Beach in Normandy, *National Gallery of Art, Washington, D.C.*

Impressionism

Near the end of the nineteenth century, French artists created a new style of painting known as **impressionism.** The impressionists turned away from photographic realism in their painting. Instead they made light and color their chief concerns. The

One of the earliest realist writers was the English novelist **Charles Dickens** (1812-70). Dickens was a social critic who attacked injustice in society through his vivid portrayals of such places as industrial slums and debtors' prisons. In his famous novel *Hard Times,* he depicted living conditions in industrial cities by describing the imaginary city of Coketown:

> It was a town of red brick, or brick that would have been red if the smoke and ashes had allowed it; but as matters stood it was a town of unnatural red and black like the painted face of a savage. It was a town of machinery and tall chimneys, out of which interminable serpents of smoke trailed themselves for ever and ever, and never got uncoiled. It had a black canal in it, and a river that ran purple with ill-smelling dye, and vast piles of buildings full of windows where there was a rattling and a trembling all day long.

Two works by Claude Monet: The Bridge at Argenteuil, *National Gallery of Art, Washington, D.C. (above) and* Bazille and Camille, *National Gallery of Art, Washington, D.C. (right)*

impressionists did not clearly outline their figures, but used short, choppy brush strokes to capture the vibrating nature of light. To the impressionists, light was all-important; what the light revealed did not matter. The most famous of the French impressionists are **Auguste Renoir** (REN wahr; 1841-1919) and **Claude Monet** (moh NAY; 1840-1926).

Another Frenchman, **Auguste Rodin** (roh DAN; 1840-1917), was one of the foremost sculptors of the nineteenth century. It is difficult, however, to place him within a particular style; for though his subject matter is romantic, his technique is often impressionistic. Like the impressionistic painters, Rodin did not make his art photographically exact. As a result, many of his works are not finely polished and have an "unfinished" look. Perhaps his best-known sculpture is "The Thinker."

Still another Frenchman, **Claude Debussy** (DEB yoo SEE; 1862-1918), was largely respon-

Left: Auguste Renoir, Two Young Girls at the Piano, *Metropolitan Museum of Art, New York*
Below: Paul Cézanne, House of Père Lacroix, *National Gallery of Art, Washington, D.C.*

sible for the impressionistic style in music. Debussy used unique chord structures in an attempt to express musically what the impressionistic painters were portraying visually—the shimmering effects of light. As a result he only vaguely outlined the melody and harmony in his works. The impressionistic movement that Debussy championed, however, quickly died out as composers searched for new forms of musical expression.

Post-Impressionism

Not all artists agreed that color and light should be the ultimate objects of painting. **Paul Cézanne** (say ZAN; 1839-1906), a Frenchman, and **Vincent van Gogh** (van GOH; 1853-90), a Dutchman, believed that impressionism rejected too many traditional artistic concepts and advocated a style that became known as **post-impressionism.** Among other things, Cézanne and van Gogh tried to em-

phasize universal themes and to outline more clearly the figures in their paintings. For example, Cézanne believed that the artist can reduce everything in nature to basic geometric shapes. He urged his fellow artists to "treat nature in terms of the cylinder, and the sphere and the cone" in order to make the outlines of various objects clearer. This geometric emphasis in his art made Cézanne a forerunner of cubism (see p. 543). Van Gogh, on the other hand, often distorted the figures in his paintings in an effort to portray the intense emotions he felt toward his subjects. For this reason he was a forerunner of expressionism (see p. 543).

Section Review

1. What man laid the foundation for the modern theories of biological evolution? In what book did he set forth his theory of "survival of the fittest"?

2. Identify the contribution to science of each of the following men: John Dalton, Dmitri Mendeleev, William Roentgen, Niels Bohr, and Albert Einstein.

3. What did advocates of the "social gospel" movement believe was the major purpose of Christianity?

4. What was the new form of artistic expression in the latter half of the nineteenth century that sought to portray life as it really is?

5. Identify the occupation and artistic style of each of the following: Charles Dickens, Gustave Courbet, Auguste Renoir, Claude Debussy, and Vincent van Gogh.

A Glimpse Behind and a Glimpse Ahead

European society was transformed during the nineteenth century. This was an age of machines, an age of science, an age of hope. People of this century enjoyed more material comforts and brighter prospects for the future than had people of previous centuries. But this age also witnessed the devastating consequences of human pride. People rejected the Bible as their source of truth and their guide for life. Instead they placed their faith in human ingenuity. Some people looked to the social theories of intellectuals who promised a perfect society; others trusted in the "cult of science," hoping to find the solutions to all of life's problems. Some religious leaders and theologians departed from the "old-time religion." They claimed that while the Bible contained the Word of God, it also included the mistakes of human writers. Denying the inspiration and authority of Scripture, they interpreted God's Word according to their preconceived ideas.

Despite the challenges that undermined the Christian faith, adversity brought renewed zeal to the church. Christians increased their efforts to combat religious infidelity and the growing secular attitude of society. At the same time they were motivated by Christian compassion to help the downtrodden and needy. Industrialism and technology provided greater opportunities for Christian outreach and service. Dedicated, creative Christians answered the challenge by developing effective methods to reach the lost with the gospel of Christ.

Chapter Review

Can You Explain?

Industrial Revolution	interchangeable parts	socialism	Christian socialism
enclosure movement	division of labor	utopian socialism	realism
domestic system	assembly line	Marxism	impressionism
factory system	Chartism	proletariat	post-impressionism
automation	welfare state	Fabian socialism	

Can You Identify?

Jethro Tull	Robert Fulton	Friedrich Engels	Niels Bohr
Charles Townshend	Orville and Wilbur	Robert Raikes	Albert Einstein
Robert Bakewell	Wright	George Mueller	Charles Dickens
John Kay	Henry Ford	YMCA	Thomas Hardy
James Hargreaves	Thomas Alva Edison	William Booth	Samuel Clemens
Richard Arkwright	William Wilberforce	Dwight L. Moody	Leo Tolstoy
Samuel Crompton	Corn Laws	Charles Darwin	Gustave Courbet
Eli Whitney	Reform Bill (1832)	John Dalton	Auguste Renoir
Henry Cort	Benjamin Disraeli	Dmitri Mendeleev	Claude Monet
Henry Bessemer	William Gladstone	William Roentgen	Auguste Rodin
John McAdam	Parliament Bill (1911)	Henry Moseley	Claude Debussy
Richard Trevithick	Robert Owen	Pierre and Marie Curie	Paul Cézanne
George Stephenson	Karl Marx	Ernest Rutherford	Vincent van Gogh

How Much Do You Remember?

1. List three factors that made the Industrial Revolution possible.
2. In addition to the above factors, list three reasons the Industrial Revolution began specifically in Great Britain.
3. What changes took place in the lives of workers because of the factory system?
4. How did the British government attempt to correct the social and political abuses in British society during the nineteenth century?
5. List the four major types of nineteenth-century socialism and briefly explain the main idea of each.

What Do You Think?

1. In what ways was nineteenth-century Europe the "best of times" and the "worst of times"?
2. How did new inventions and scientific research contribute to the Industrial Revolution?
3. What standard should be used to determine whether a "reform" is truly a "change for the better" or simply a "change" that might be for the worse?
4. Explain the dangers of socialism.

Expansion and Evangelism

The early explorers who traveled around the world opened the door to a great flood of European migration. During the seventeenth and eighteenth centuries, thousands of Europeans crossed the oceans in search of fortune, adventure, or religious freedom in these new lands of opportunity. Although they left their homelands, they did not leave behind their European heritage or culture. They established new settlements that were like "little Europes" overseas. Despite strong cultural and economic ties to Europe, many of these settlements gained political independence in the late eighteenth and early nineteenth centuries and began developing as new nations.

The period of European expansion was renewed during the nineteenth century. Industrialized nations sought new overseas territories as sources of raw materials for their factories and as markets for their industrial goods. Later in the century, nationalistic pride prompted other countries to seek to build overseas empires to symbolize their power and glory. As a result, European nations competed for control of much of the world—especially Africa and Asia. This new scramble for territory came to be known as imperialism.

Although imperialism was an economic and political movement, it provided the opportunity for missionary outreach. The nineteenth century was the greatest period of missionary activity since the first three centuries of the Christian era. Godly men and women dedicated their lives to carrying out the Great Commission: "Go ye into all the world, and preach the gospel to every creature" (Mark 16:15).

Extension of European Culture

After the Age of Exploration, European civilization was carried to all parts of the globe as Europeans settled in the newly discovered regions of the world. For the most part, the early settlers went to isolated lands—the Americas, Australia, New Zealand, and South Africa—where there was no dominant culture among the native people. Overcoming the dangers and obstacles of frontier life, transplanted Europeans built thriving colonies. As these colonies grew and prospered, they attracted more European emigrants. At the same time they became more and more independent of their homelands.

The following section will survey the settlement, development, and independence of the British colonies of Canada, Australia, New Zealand, and South Africa and the Spanish colonies in Latin America. In a previous chapter we traced the American struggle for independence. Since the United States was considered a model for developing colonies, let us begin by examining the growth of this young nation.

Growth of the United States Following Independence
Geographic and Political Expansion

In the years following independence, the American nation rapidly expanded westward. From the very outset of her nationhood, pioneers pushed westward across the Allegheny Mountains, laying claim to vast tracts of land. In 1803 President Thomas Jefferson purchased over eight hundred thousand square miles of French territory west of the Mississippi River from Napoleon for $15 million. Known as the **Louisiana Purchase,** this land almost doubled the size of the United States. Much of the territory that makes up the southwestern portion of the United States today was acquired after a war with Mexico (1846-48). In 1849 the discovery of gold in

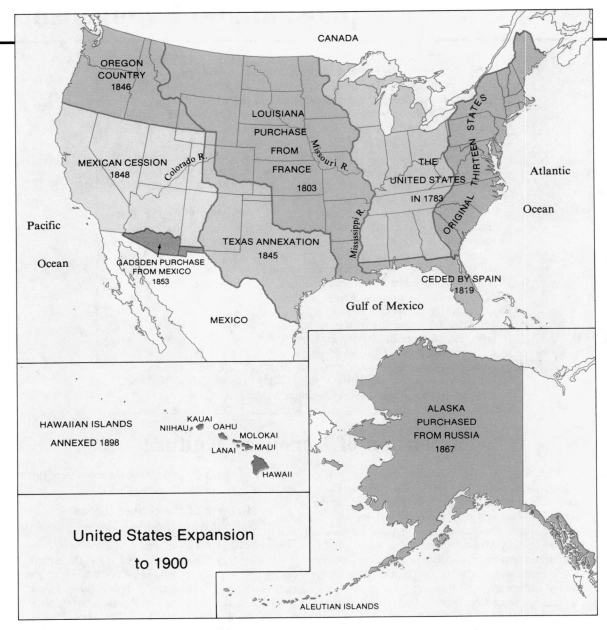

OREGON
COUNTRY
1846

CANADA

LOUISIANA
PURCHASE
FROM
FRANCE
1803

Missouri R.

THE
UNITED STATES
IN 1783

Atlantic

ORIGINAL THIRTEEN STATES

Ocean

MEXICAN CESSION
1848

Colorado R.

Pacific

Mississippi R.

Ocean

GADSDEN PURCHASE
FROM MEXICO
1853

TEXAS ANNEXATION
1845

CEDED BY SPAIN
1819

Gulf of Mexico

MEXICO

HAWAIIAN ISLANDS

ANNEXED 1898

KAUAI
NIIHAU   OAHU
MOLOKAI
LANAI   MAUI

HAWAII

ALASKA
PURCHASED
FROM RUSSIA
1867

United States Expansion

to 1900

ALEUTIAN ISLANDS

California prompted a great rush to the far West. In this manner—through settlement, purchase, and war—the United States expanded her borders from the Atlantic to the Pacific. Further territory was added in 1867 when the United States purchased Alaska from the Russians. By the end of the cen-

tury, the government also controlled Hawaii, Cuba, Puerto Rico, and the Philippines.

Paralleling the expansion of American territory was an expansion in the number who had the right to vote and hold office. Early in the nation's history, laws restricted widespread participation in government. But westward expansion encouraged a more democratic spirit. Frontier conditions broke down social and economic barriers. Men were judged by their character and ability rather than by their social class or their financial status. As a result, many of the western states were among the first to adopt universal manhood suffrage. Gradually other states adopted this democratic practice. In similar fashion, Americans living in the territories were given the opportunity to be represented in the United States government. New states were allowed to join the Union on an equal basis with the original thirteen.

Sectional Differences

Despite the early growth and prosperity of the United States, rival sectional loyalties, especially between the North and the South, divided the young nation. Each section had a different way of life, different values, and different interests. Northern society was primarily urban, built around industry. Southern society was predominantly rural and aristocratic, revolving around the cotton plantations. The North wanted high tariffs on imported goods to protect her industry from more cheaply produced foreign goods. The South, on the other hand, did not want to pay more for manufactured goods just to help Northern industry. The South wanted to buy the cheaper, imported goods from Great Britain in hopes that she would buy more of the South's cotton. Finally, the Northern states had prohibited slavery while the Southern states permitted it.

As pressing issues came before the United States Congress, it became clear that sectional interests overshadowed national unity. During the first half of the nineteenth century, united action on national issues was possible only through political compromise. Crucial to the interests of both sides was the expanding influence of the West. As western territories asked for admission into the Union, there was much debate in Congress over whether they should enter as slave states or as free states. After the election of Abraham Lincoln in 1860, eleven Southern states seceded from the Union. The bloody Civil War that followed (1861-65) ended with the defeat of the Southern forces. The Union was preserved, but the wounds of war were slow to heal.

Growth in Industry and Population

As peace was restored, the nation entered a period of rapid industrial expansion. A number of factors made possible this growth: the hardworking American spirit, an abundance of raw materials, new inventions, and the expansion of the railroads. But this prosperity resulted primarily from God's blessing and provision. Throughout the nineteenth century—even during the Civil War—the American nation experienced great spiritual revivals. God allowed this young country to enjoy material prosperity and to become a major world power.

A growing population provided industry with a large labor force. During the nineteenth century, the population of the United States rose from 4 million in 1790 to 99 million in 1910. Over one-third of that increase came from immigrants who each year entered this land of opportunity by the thousands. From 1821 to 1910 about 34 million immigrants from all over Europe came to the United States. Many of them remained in the cities, providing the backbone of America's rapidly developing industries.

Isolation in Foreign Affairs

The United States was not always as involved in world affairs as she is today. From the presidency of George Washington, the government had maintained a policy of neutrality and isolation from European politics. Americans were more interested in national security and trade than in becoming involved in "entangling alliances." In a message to Congress in 1823, President James Monroe enunciated what has come to be called the **Monroe Doctrine.** He told Europe that North and South America, "by the free and independent condition which they have assumed and maintain, are henceforth not to be considered as subjects for future colonization by any European powers." Monroe went on to say that the United States would regard "any attempt" by Europe to extend her control "to any portion of this hemisphere as dangerous to our peace and safety." In return, Monroe promised that the United States would not interfere in European affairs.

Although the United States avoided making foreign alliances, she could not remain isolated from world affairs. The first challenge to her isolation came as American merchants and businessmen expanded their foreign trade and investments. To protect and help Americans in their overseas business ventures, the United States government signed trade agreements with several European nations. Later in the century, the United States competed with European nations for trade opportunities in new markets such as China and Japan.

Another challenge came from the French emperor Napoleon III, who was eager to build an empire in the New World. He sent French troops into Mexico and placed an Austrian archduke named **Maximilian** in charge of the country. This action was a clear infringement of the Monroe Doctrine, but the United States was embroiled in the Civil War and took no immediate action. When the war was over, however, an American army gathered on the Mexican border and forced Napoleon III to withdraw his troops. Mexican forces captured and executed Maximilian in 1867.

Late in the nineteenth century, additional problems in Latin America drew the United States out of her isolationist position. During the 1890s, reports of Spain's mistreatment of her colony of Cuba roused American sympathy for Cuban independence. In 1898 the United States battleship *Maine* was sent to Havana Harbor to protect American interests during a series of uprisings in Cuba.

On February 15, the battleship exploded, killing 260 American sailors. Although mystery surrounded the explosion, Spain was blamed. The United States Congress declared war, and troops were sent to Cuba. After brief fighting, the Spanish forces on the island surrendered. As part of the treaty ending the Spanish-American War, Spain ceded to the United States the territories of Guam, Puerto Rico, and the Philippines.

Further problems arose when some Latin American countries that had borrowed funds from European banks did not or could not repay their loans. In response, European governments threatened to intervene in those countries if necessary to force them to meet their obligations. The American president Theodore Roosevelt, however, refused to permit European intervention in Latin America, even for legitimate reasons. Instead, Roosevelt proclaimed what is known as the **Roosevelt Corollary** to the Monroe Doctrine. In case of wrongdoing on the part of any Latin American state, the United States claimed the right to intervene in that country and set its affairs in order.

By World War I the United States had definitely moved away from the longstanding policy of isolation. But it was not until after World War II that the United States became heavily involved in world politics.

British Colonies Granted Independence

At the outset of the nineteenth century, Spain lost most of her colonial possessions. During this same period, Great Britain was acquiring new territory. By the end of the nineteenth century, Britain boasted that the sun never set on her empire. British emigrants transplanted British culture into many lands, among which were Canada, Australia, New Zealand, and South Africa. They carried with them the British tradition of self-government. As these colonies developed, Britain allowed them greater self-government—she had learned from her experience with the American colonies. As a result, the British colonies eventually gained national independence without experiencing widespread revolts.

Canada

Unlike other British possessions, Canada was originally a French colony. From the beginning of

The U.S.S. Maine rests at anchor in Havana Harbor on the afternoon of February 15, 1898. That night a mysterious explosion sank the ship and helped touch off a war between the United States and Spain.

European settlement in North America, relations between the French Canadians and the British colonists were unfriendly. The national rivalry between Great Britain and France in Europe often spilled over into the colonies, bringing war and unrest. When the Seven Years' War (known in North America as the French and Indian War) came to an end in 1763 (see Chapter 13), Britain emerged victorious. As part of the peace settlement, France ceded Canada to Great Britain.

In order to keep the French Canadians loyal to British rule, the British Parliament passed the **Quebec Act** in 1774. This act permitted the French Canadians the right to retain their language, law, and customs, and to freely practice their Roman Catholic religion. Although the act angered the predominantly Protestant American colonies, its concessions pleased the French Canadians.

During the American War for Independence, thousands of British Loyalists fled to Canada. The French Canadians felt threatened by the growing British population. At the same time, the British colonists did not want to live under the long-established French customs and law. To end the friction, the British Parliament divided Canada into two provinces: Upper Canada (now Ontario), where most of the Loyalists lived; and Lower Canada (now Quebec), where most of the French lived. Each province was granted its own governor, legislative council, and elected assembly. Nevertheless, discontent continued.

The British government sent to Canada a new governor general, Lord Durham, to study problems in the colonies. He recommended that Britain grant Canada self-government in domestic matters while retaining control of foreign affairs. At the same time he called for a united Canada. Parliament adopted this latter recommendation and combined Lower and Upper Canada by an Act of Union in 1840. In 1867 the government was reorganized again by the **British North America Act.** This act

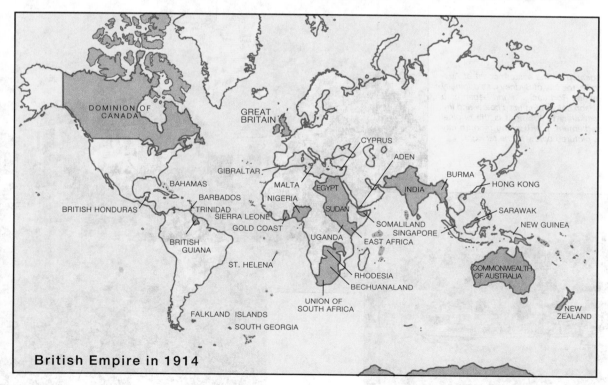

British Empire in 1914

created the Dominion of Canada, a federation of four provinces—Quebec, Ontario, Nova Scotia, and New Brunswick. (It also provided for new territories to be added to the union.) Canada still remained a part of the British Empire, but she had a much greater degree of self-government than before.

Australia and New Zealand

Australia is an island continent located in the South Pacific. It is nearly as large as the continental United States. Despite its size, it remained virtually unknown prior to the seventeenth century. Dutch explorers discovered this land in the early 1600s, but they did not establish a colony there. More than a century later (1770), an Englishman, Captain **James Cook,** explored the eastern coast of Australia. His exploration laid the basis for British claims to the area.

With the outbreak of the American War for Independence in 1775, Britain no longer had a place to send criminals from her overcrowded prisons. (Prior to the war, Britain had transported convicts to penal colonies in Georgia.) It was this situation that led to the founding of the British settlement at Port Jackson (now Sydney), Australia, in 1788. The first ''settlers'' were mostly convicts from British jails and soldiers sent to supervise them. Most of the convicts were not dangerous criminals but had been imprisoned for minor crimes or for debt.

During the nineteenth century, the Australian settlements grew economically and politically. Free settlers were attracted to Australia by the abundance of cheap land and the discovery of gold. By the end of the century, Australia became a world producer of wool and meat. In 1901 the independent

Located on the eastern coast of Australia, the city of Sydney was originally named Port Jackson and began as a prison colony. Pictured below and immediately to the right is the original settlement. The bustling modern city is pictured below to the far right.

Australian colonies, with the approval of the British Parliament, united into a federal union, forming the Commonwealth of Australia.

Located about a thousand miles southeast of Australia, the islands of New Zealand were first sighted by the Dutch. Captain Cook later made five visits to the islands, exploring them and mapping their coastlines. Among the first European settlers in New Zealand were escaped convicts from the penal colonies in Australia and seamen who had deserted their ships. In addition, the islands were inhabited by native New Zealanders, the **Maoris,** who enjoyed a better situation than many colonized peoples. Through two wars with the Europeans, the Maoris won representation in the government. In 1907 New Zealand became a self-governing dominion in the British Empire.

South Africa

The Dutch were the first Europeans to settle South Africa. In 1652 they established the Cape Colony on the southern tip of Africa. During the Napoleonic Wars, Britain seized the colony and encouraged British people to settle at the Cape. The Dutch colonists, called **Boers** (Dutch for "farmers"), resented British rule. Beginning in 1836, hundreds of them began a migration, called the **Great Trek,** northward into the interior. There they founded the republics of the Transvaal and the Orange Free State. In the 1850s Britain granted these republics their independence.

For several decades the Boers lived in relative isolation from the British settlers along the coast. But in 1867 diamonds were discovered in the Orange Free State, and in 1886 gold was discovered in the Transvaal. Before long thousands of miners—mostly British—poured into the region. Growing tension between the Boers and the British led to the **Boer War** (1899-1902). The British won the war and extended their control over these republics. They were lenient with the Boers, however, providing them with financial help to recover from the war and allowing them to use their own language in schools and courts. In 1910 the British colonies at the Cape and the old Boer republics combined to form the Union of South Africa, joining the British Empire as a dominion.

Latin America Gains Independence

Latin America covers almost eight million square miles and is larger than the United States and Canada combined. It stretches from the northern border of Mexico to the tip of South America. These lands were the homes of the major Amerindian civilizations—the Maya, the Aztec, and the Inca. But by 1500 the Spanish and Portuguese had claimed most of this vast region. Because of the strong influence of Spanish and Portuguese customs and languages, which derived from the "Latin" culture of ancient Rome, this region is known as Latin America.

Struggle for Independence

Unlike the English colonies in North America, which experienced a large measure of self-government, the Latin American colonies were tightly controlled by Spain and Portugal. Officials appointed by the crown directed colonial affairs. In the Spanish possessions, most of these civil officials were *peninsulares,* Spaniards born and reared in Spain. They controlled the government and economic wealth of the colonies. Often they selfishly used their positions to amass personal fortunes with which they returned to Spain to live lives of ease. Their arrogant attitude angered the *criollos* (Spaniards born in the New World). There was also dissatisfaction among the rest of the people—Indians, *mestizos* (those of mixed Spanish and Indian blood), and blacks—who were held in low esteem and used by the other two groups to achieve their own ends.

Over the years, growing discontent with the economic restrictions and political corruption of Spanish rule gave rise to independence movements. These movements found support among many of the educated people in Latin America, who were influenced by the works of Locke, Rousseau, and Voltaire. They were also encouraged by the example of the American War for Independence. As a result, isolated uprisings broke out. But it was not until the early nineteenth century that widespread revolution swept across Latin America.

The Napoleonic Wars in Europe stirred these revolts. Napoleon removed the Spanish king and placed his brother Joseph Bonaparte on the Spanish

Simón Bolívar (in the center on the white horse) leads his forces to victory against the Spanish in *La Batalla de Araure ("The Battle of Araure")* by Tito Salas.

throne. The colonists, though dissatisfied with Spanish rule, would not tolerate French rule. Two men, **Simón Bolívar** (boh LEE vahr; 1783-1830) and **José de San Martín** (SAHN mahr-TEEN; 1778-1850), dreamed of a Spanish South America free from outside control. They raised troops to fight "wars of liberation." Bolívar, called "the Liberator," led the struggle for freedom in the north. His troops crushed the Spanish forces and secured the independence of Gran Colombia (comprising what are now the countries of Colombia, Venezuela, Panama, and Ecuador). To the south, San Martín, backed by Argentina (which had already gained its independence), led an army over the Andes Mountains and freed Chile and then Peru from Spanish domination.

The Portuguese colony of Brazil experienced a more peaceful transition to independence. In 1807 French troops invaded Portugal, forcing the royal family to flee to Brazil. From his new capital in Rio de Janeiro, the king ruled the Portuguese empire. Brazil prospered during this period as trade and industry flourished. In 1821 the king returned to Portugal. He left behind his son **Dom Pedro** as his regent. But when the Portuguese legislature attempted to reduce Brazil to its former colonial status, Dom Pedro declared Brazil independent and became the emperor of Brazil. Under his rule and that of his son Dom Pedro II, Brazil became a thriving nation. But eventually, growing sectional differ-

ences in the large country and discontent among Brazil's military leaders forced Dom Pedro II to abdicate. In 1889 Brazil was proclaimed a republic. In the years that followed, however, the military dominated the government.

Problems of Self-government

From the time of independence through the rest of the nineteenth century, the histories of the new Latin American nations shared similar characteristics. The following generalizations, however, may not fully apply to every Latin American country.

1. *Political instability.* After gaining their independence, most Latin American countries followed the example of the United States and established republics. But unlike the United States, they had little experience in self-rule. Ambitious military leaders called *caudillos* often seized power. They ruled as dictators, satisfying their own desires at the expense of their countries. Military uprisings were frequent, as rival generals competed for power. As a result, Latin American countries experienced constant changes in government as one military dictator was overthrown and another took his place.

2. *Monopoly of land and wealth by a few.* From early colonial days, Latin America was dominated by a wealthy, powerful upper class. Though a small minority, this social class owned most of the land, controlled the wealth, and manipulated the government in many Latin American countries. The vast majority of the people remained poor and had little voice in the everyday workings of the government. Without a large middle class to provide stability, Latin American countries suffered from the effects of political favoritism and class conflict.

3. *Powerful influence of the Roman Catholic church.* As the Spanish and Portuguese came to the New World, they firmly established Roman Catholicism in Latin America. This religious system became a dominant influence on Latin American culture. The Roman Catholic church controlled large amounts of land as well as the educational system. As a result, church leaders heavily influenced the political process.

4. *Racial disunity.* In addition to blacks, Indians, and inhabitants of European descent, a large number of Latin Americans were of mixed ancestry. Hatred, jealousy, and conflicts of interest often existed among the racial groups.

5. *Problems among Latin American countries.* Unlike the United States, the Latin American colonies did not form one nation after gaining their independence. Soon after the wars of liberation, the Latin American people divided up into a number of small countries rather than into several larger ones. This condition in Latin America led to several border wars among the nations.

6. *Economic weakness.* During the nineteenth century, Latin America had virtually no industry. (Foreign investment from the United States and Europe accounted for what little industry there was.) In most countries the economy was built around only a few products, such as bananas, coffee, rubber, or wood. A poor growing season or a bad world market could bring economic disaster to a country.

7. *European and United States involvement.* Political and economic problems within the Latin American countries prompted European nations to interfere in their domestic affairs. The Europeans wanted to protect their foreign investments and to ensure that loans made to these countries would be repaid. The actions of the European nations in Latin America brought concern to the United States. Because the United States opposed European intervention, she assumed a greater responsibility for policing Latin American affairs. But with the increased dominance of the United States in the affairs of the Western Hemisphere came a

Latin America After Independence
□ Formerly Portuguese
■ Formerly Spanish

growing fear of the United States on the part of the Latin American countries.

Section Review

1. List four possessions outside the North American continent that the United States controlled by the end of the nineteenth century.
2. What man's exploration laid the basis for the English claim on Australia? What was unusual about the first "settlers" there?
3. What were Dutch colonists in South Africa called? What people did they fight for control of the mineral resources found in Transvaal and the Orange Free State?
4. Explain the differences between the *peninsulares,* the *criollos,* and the *mestizos.*
5. Who were the two leaders of South America's struggle for independence?

Extension of European Power

The quest for colonies in the sixteenth and seventeenth centuries was motivated primarily by the economic policy of mercantilism. (See Chapter 12.) European countries looked upon their colonial possessions as a source of wealth. But by the late eighteenth century, European countries found it financially draining to maintain and protect their colonies, many of which were now seeking independence. Likewise, a free trade policy was slowly replacing the one-sided trade of mercantilism. Revolts in Europe during the early nineteenth century further diminished the interest in overseas colonies.

But during the years 1870-1914, the race for overseas possessions revived. European nations competed in a new form of empire-building known as **imperialism,** the extension of power by one people or country over another country. During the late nineteenth century, European nations eagerly sought to extend their spheres of influence over most of the world. Empire-building became increasingly important to the foreign policy of many European nations, resulting in fierce rivalry that would eventually lead to World War I.

Reasons for Imperialism

The motives behind imperialism were as diverse as the nations that practiced it. In fact, the motives of any particular nation often differed from one overseas possession to another or from one time to another.

First, the expansion of industrialism in the late nineteenth century increased the demand for raw materials and new markets. Industrialized nations did not want to be dependent on other nations for their industrial supplies. They sought to control areas of the world that would meet their industrial needs. In addition, tariffs among Western nations were so restrictive that many believed the acquisition of colonies would provide an outlet for manufactured goods.

Second, imperialism was also strongly motivated by the intense nationalism that characterized Europe from 1870-1914. An overseas empire brought national honor and prestige. It provided the newly formed nations of Germany and Italy the opportunity to display their national strength and maturity. The race for new colonies provided Western nations an outlet for their competitive energies. They were quick to seize control of strategic locations in order to establish military bases to protect their worldwide interests.

Third, another motive for imperial expansion was humanitarianism. The British poet Rudyard Kipling expressed this popular nineteenth-century thought as he urged his contemporaries to "take up the white man's burden." Many Europeans viewed their society as superior to the "backward" civilizations of Asia and Africa. They felt it their responsibility to share the fruit of Western culture— education, medical care, industry, and technology. They launched sincere efforts to improve educa-

tion, abolish slavery, and stamp out disease and famine in colonial territories. Although many native peoples profited from Western aid, they objected to the "superior" attitude held by most Westerners. They often considered these "humanitarian" concerns as an excuse to exploit the wealth of their countries.

Fourth, a dominant feature of Europe's worldwide expansion was the dramatic spread of Christian missions. The nineteenth century was the "great century" of missionary activity. As European countries built overseas empires, Christians became acquainted with the spiritual needs of people in distant lands. In many lands, Western political and economic control opened the doors for missionary activity. Yet, although imperialism aided the spread of missions, Christian missionaries were not motivated by a desire to exploit or subject foreign peoples. They had a sincere desire to tell the good news of the Savior who died for the sins of the world. In some parts of Africa, missionaries preceded the coming of traders and government officials. Missionaries such as David Livingstone opened up the interior of Africa as they preached Christ in thousands of villages.

Regions of Imperialism

Asia

When Europeans sailed to the New World, they found a sparsely populated land with no dominant culture. Thus they were able to transplant European culture into these lands with little opposition. But the situation in Asia was different. This densely populated continent was the home of strong and ancient cultures. While the industrial and military might of Western nations successfully opened many Asian lands to Western trade, it was difficult to establish Western culture.

India—After Vasco da Gama's discovery of an all-water route to India, European nations set up trading posts along the Indian coast. By the eighteenth century, French and British trade companies had established thriving bases in India. But early in the 1700s, the security of these bases was threatened by the collapse of the Mughul Empire (see p. 166), which left India once again divided into small rival

"Unto the Uttermost Part of the Earth": William Carey in India

Young **William Carey** (1761-1834) gave little indication of the great things God was going to accomplish through his life. At school he liked history, science, and mathematics. But he had little interest in the Bible. He went to church because he had to, not because he wanted to. As a boy he mastered Latin, then Greek, and later Hebrew. As a young man he taught himself French and Dutch. It may have seemed odd that Carey, a cobbler's apprentice, had such a talent for learning languages. Time would show that God was preparing him for the great work He had for him in India.

For many years Carey had been interested in foreign lands. Next to his workbench he had a crude hand-drawn map of the world on which he wrote geographic and religious facts about each country. When he tried to get others interested in sending missionaries to these countries, they told him that the injunction "Go ye into all the world,

and preach the gospel" was given only to the apostles. Later, at a meeting of Baptist ministers, Carey made his plea for missions: "Expect great things from God; attempt great things for God." As a result of this sermon, others joined with Carey in establishing the Baptist Missionary Society. Carey, the first appointed missionary, took his family to India in 1794.

When the Careys landed in India, they were faced with many hardships. But William Carey was well established in his faith, competent in linguistics, and firmly resolved to do God's will. He quickly went about establishing the work under two principles: (1) the missionary must be a companion to and an equal with the native peoples; and (2) the missionary must, as soon as possible, become self-supporting. While on the mission field, Carey worked both as an indigo planter and as a horticulturist. He established his first church by preaching to plantation workers. He also worked on a translation of the Bible into the native Bengali languages.

In order to be able to master the various Indian dialects, Carey set about learning Sanskrit. He translated the Bible into Bengali in 1798. He went on to translate the Bible into twenty Indian dialects and supervised its translation into twenty more. In 1798 a printer joined Carey in his work. Together they set up a printing press and produced the first Bible and tracts in the Indian dialects.

Carey never returned to England. Having once settled in India, he devoted his life to bringing the gospel to the Indian people. By his pioneering accomplishments in mission work, he earned the title "the Father of Modern Missions." Yet once when someone was talking about his remarkable accomplishments, Carey replied, "Do not talk about Dr. Carey's this or Dr. Carey's that. Talk about Dr. Carey's Saviour." He lived by the verse "He must increase, but I must decrease" (John 3:30).

states. The British and French used this political unrest for their economic advantage. They extended their control in India by making alliances with local rulers or by outright conquest of territory.

The strong British-French rivalry that dominated European affairs during the eighteenth cen-

tury extended to India. During the Seven Years' War (1756-63), an Indian ruler who sided with the French attacked the British settlement at Calcutta. In the decisive **Battle of Plassey** (1757), the British forces led by **Robert Clive** defeated the Indian ruler. Three years later he defeated the French as well. The victories made the British East India Company the dominant authority in India. None of the small Indian states were strong enough to challenge its power.

For the next hundred years, the British East India Company governed much of India. The British government supervised the company's affairs but did not exercise any direct rule over the country. Because the East India Company was primarily a commercial organization, financial considerations played an important role in determining its political policies. For example, the company tried to keep William Carey and other missionaries from preaching the gospel in India. They believed that such preaching might cause unrest among the Hindu and Muslim populations and thus hurt their business interests. Yet, it was the expansion of the company's authority as well as the growing efforts by the British to impose Western ways on Indian society that led to unrest.

In 1857 *sepoys,* the native Indian troops employed by the East India Company, revolted. The immediate cause of the **Sepoy Mutiny** was the introduction of new rifle cartridges. These cartridges—the ends of which had to be bitten off—were greased with sheep fat to keep the powder dry. It was rumored that the grease used was cow and pig fat. (The Hindus consider the cow sacred, and the Muslims consider the pig unclean.) Although the revolt symbolized the nation's dissatisfaction with

The Mughul emperor Shah Jahan (1628-58) built this beautiful mausoleum as a memorial to his favorite wife. It is called the Taj Mahal and stands at Agra, India.

Western rule, the sepoys received little support from the rest of the Indian people. British troops were called in, and after several months of bloody fighting, the mutiny was suppressed.

As a result of the mutiny, the British government assumed control of Indian political affairs. It appointed a viceroy to govern India, and in 1877 Prime Minister Disraeli conferred the title of empress of India upon Queen Victoria. The British government also assumed the responsibility of providing for the welfare of the Indian people. Sanitation and medical care were improved, roads and railroads were built, and factories were constructed. New schools teaching Western thought and culture were also established. But as many young Indians studied the political ideas of the eighteenth century, they became even more desirous of self-government. A movement for self-rule began to build by the end of the nineteenth century.

China—Despite China's vast territory and her large population, the Chinese were not able to fully withstand European imperialism during the nineteenth century. The **Manchu dynasty,** which had ruled China since 1644, had closed all Chinese ports except Canton to foreign merchants. By the nineteenth century internal problems had crippled Manchu leadership. China's growing weakness prompted Western nations to seek greater trade privileges.

Chinese attempts to restrict foreign trade led to war between China and Great Britain. For years Chinese rulers had done nothing to stop British traders who smuggled opium (a dangerous drug) into China in return for tea and silks. When Chinese officials finally sought to put a stop to this drug trade, British merchants objected. Tension over the opium trade, and over foreign trade in general, sparked the **Opium Wars.** In 1842 the British forced China to sign the Treaty of Nanking, which opened four more trade ports and gave Britain the island of Hong Kong. A second war (lasting from 1856-60) further weakened China, as French and British forces joined to win additional trade concessions.

Although China never officially lost her independence, other nations heavily influenced her policies and forced her to bend to their will. By the end of the century, many Western countries had secured treaties forcing China to open her ports to

"Unto the Uttermost Part of the Earth": J. Hudson Taylor in China

J. Hudson Taylor (1832-1905) was a man who set himself to do God's will and would not allow anything to stop him. At the age of five, after hearing his father talk about the need of taking the gospel to China, he declared that one "day he would go to that country." In 1849, at the age of seventeen, he dedicated himself to the Lord's service. It was then that he knew that God was calling him to China. After receiving a medical degree, he set sail for China in 1853.

In those days missionaries were allowed to labor only in the coastal regions of China, near the treaty ports. Soon after he landed, however, Taylor became deeply burdened for the people living inland. During the next seven years he made many inland trips. With each visit, his burden increased for the millions who had not heard the gospel. In 1860 poor health forced him to return to England. Yet his concern for the Chinese did not diminish. While in England, he revised the Chinese New Testament.

Five years went by and his health did not improve. It appeared that he would never be able to return to China. But one weekend in the summer of 1865, while resting in Dover, he prayed that God would send twenty-four skilled and willing workers to the inland areas of China. After he prayed he experienced a calmness of heart and body. When he returned to London, his wife remarked that Dover seemed to have been good for him. He told her of his request and about the renewed strength that the Lord had given him. Two days later, with less than £10, he opened a bank account in the name of the China Inland Mission, an organization dedicated to enlisting people and funds for missionary work in China. On May 26, 1866, Taylor, his family, and twenty-four others set sail for China.

Missionary work in inland China was difficult. The Chinese were reluctant to welcome the missionaries, even though Taylor and the others adopted Chinese dress. But Taylor's faith was unwavering. He knew that he was doing God's work and that God would protect and prosper the work. God did exactly that. New areas in China opened up to the mission. More missionaries joined in the task of reaching the Chinese for Christ. Taylor, who had once asked the Lord for twenty-four colaborers, now prayed for one thousand; God answered his request.

their trade. Two demands found in many of these treaties especially angered the Chinese: the right of Western nations to station their warships in China's waters, and the right of Westerners to **extraterritoriality.** According to the principle of extraterritoriality, Westerners who broke Chinese law had the right to be tried in their own national courts rather than in Chinese courts.

Particularly embarrassing to China was her loss to Japan in the **Sino-Japanese War** (1894-95). China had always thought of Japan as an inferior nation. After this humiliating defeat, Western nations increased their demands for more trade concessions, and China had little choice but to grant them.

Angered by Western actions, some Chinese organized secret societies, pledging to rid China of Western influences. In 1899 members of these societies began to terrorize Westerners as well as Chinese Christians. (The Chinese considered Christianity a Western religion.) Throughout the country, rebels destroyed railroads and bridges and tortured or murdered Western diplomats, missionaries, and merchants. This uprising, known as the **Boxer Rebellion** (named after a leading society called the "Righteous and Harmonious Fists"), became so serious that European and American troops intervened. The rebellion failed, and with it came the collapse of the Manchu dynasty.

American, Japanese, and British forces storm the palace in Beijing. About twenty thousand foreign troops helped suppress the Boxer Rebellion.

Japan—Japan entered the nineteenth century with a feudal society dominated by the warrior class. Shoguns of the **Tokugawa** family ruled Japan as they had done since the beginning of the seventeenth century. Like China's rulers, Japan's rulers intended to exclude all Western influence and to maintain the country's traditions. But in July of 1853 **Matthew Perry,** a United States naval commander, sailed into Edo Bay (later called Tokyo Bay) with a small fleet of ships. His mission was to persuade the Japanese to allow trade between the United States and Japan. After presenting the American request, Perry sailed away, telling the Japanese that he would return later for their answer. In February of 1854 Perry returned with even more warships. The shogun realized Japan's weak position and reluctantly agreed to open trade. Both nations signed the **Treaty of Kanagawa,** the first treaty Japan ever signed with a Western nation.

The period of Japan's isolation had now ended. But how were the Japanese going to respond to Western influences? Would they resist like the Chinese, or would they adopt some Western ways? It took a civil war to settle the issue. The struggle overthrew the shogun and restored the Japanese emperor to his position of authority. The emperor, who adopted the name Meiji (MAY jee; "enlightened rule") for his reign, declared, "The uncivilized customs of former years shall be abandoned."

During the **Meiji Period** (1867-1912), Japan was transformed from a feudal society to a major industrial power. Japanese commissions were sent to Western nations to study their governments, industries, schools, and militaries. The Japanese copied what they considered to be the best methods and institutions. Within a relatively short period, Japan became the first industrial nation of Asia. The Japanese government abolished feudalism and adopted a Western constitution. It also established new edu-

Admiral Perry delivers presents at Yokohama, Japan. Today, Kanagawa (where the Treaty of Kanagawa was signed) is part of the city of Yokohoma.

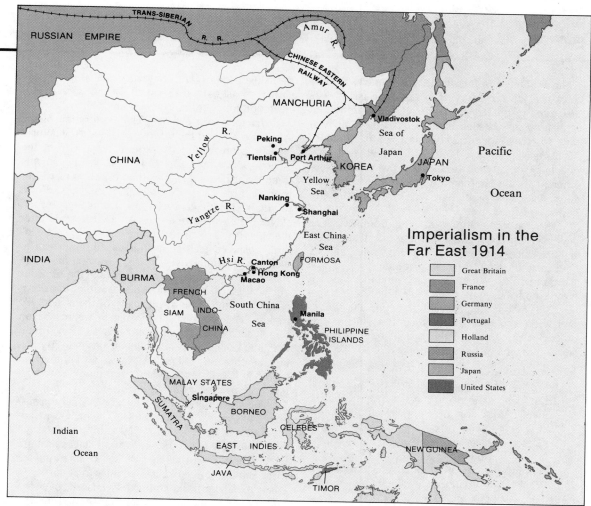

Imperialism in the Far East 1914

Great Britain
France
Germany
Portugal
Holland
Russia
Japan
United States

cational and judicial systems and reorganized the military forces according to Western models.

By adopting some Western ways, Japan was able to resist Western imperialism. Her new industrial and military might enabled her to compete with Western nations for territory and influence in Asia. Japanese expansionism led to war, first with China (1894-95), a conflict that exposed the weakness of the Chinese state. In the **Russo-Japanese War** (1904-5), Japan stunned the Western powers by defeating the supposedly mightier Russians on both the sea and the land (see p. 530). The tiny island nation, by thrashing her much larger opponents, proved herself to be a major world power. During the first half of the twentieth century, Japan continued her expansionist policies. Her aggression would contribute to the outbreak of World War II.

Southeast Asia—Southeast Asia includes the territory east of India and south of China, as well as many of the islands in the Pacific and Indian oceans. Prior to the nineteenth century, several parts of Southeast Asia had come under European control. But during the nineteenth century the Europeans seized virtually the entire area. The only major territory that remained independent was Siam (today called Thailand), which became a buffer state between British and French possessions. (See the map above.)

One of the most valuable British possessions was Ceylon (modern Sri Lanka), an island taken from the Dutch in the eighteenth century. Rubber trees and tea grew well there, and the island was also a source of lead and sapphires. Other important British possessions in Southeast Asia included Malaya (part of modern Malaysia), Burma (modern Myanmar), and Singapore. The French had only one large colony in Southeast Asia, called Indochina. This land bordered on the South China Sea and included the modern nations of Vietnam, Cambodia, and Laos.

The major Dutch possession in Southeast Asia was a group of islands known as the Dutch East Indies—modern Indonesia. The East Indies include over three thousand islands spread out over several thousand miles. When the Dutch took these islands they established what they called a "culture system." They required the natives to use one-fifth of their land and one-fifth of their time in growing crops for the Dutch. This system, reminiscent of some elements of feudalism, ended about 1900.

Section Review

1. During what time period was the race among European nations for overseas possessions revived? What was this empire-building called in which one country sought to extend its influence over another country?
2. In what region of the world was it difficult for Western nations to establish Western culture? What form of control were they able to establish over this region?
3. What was the immediate cause of the Sepoy Mutiny?
4. What is the name of the Chinese uprising that sought to rid China of Western influences?
5. During what period of Japanese history was Japan transformed from an isolated, feudalistic society to a major industrial world power?

Africa

As we learned in Chapter 6 (pp. 167-71), Africa was the home of several thriving civilizations before 1500. A profitable trade existed between the African kingdoms on the one hand and the Arabs, Asians, and Europeans on the other. European expansion, however, changed the African people from trading partners to subjects. Imperialism in Africa was a mixture of exploitation (as shown by the slave trade) and humanitarian impulse (as shown by Christian missions). In either case, African culture could not remain unaffected.

African Slave Trade—The exploration of the African coast and the discovery of the New World by Europeans indirectly prompted the rise of the African slave trade. In 1441 Portugal began this trade by bringing a small group of Africans to Europe. Yet until the opening up of the New World in the sixteenth century, few Europeans owned slaves. They were first used on a large scale after the Spanish arrived in Latin America. The Spaniards enslaved the native Indians, forcing them to work in the mines or on large plantations. The Indians, however, could not withstand the rigorous physical labor, nor the new diseases that the Europeans brought. As a result many of them died. To replenish their labor supply, the Spaniards began importing black slaves from Africa. They found that blacks had a better rate of survival. By the eighteenth century, black slavery was common in the New World, and traders from many European nations participated in it.

The slave trade proved to be extremely profitable and thus expanded rapidly. The heaviest trading occurred from 1700 to 1850, during which time approximately eighty per cent of all slaves brought to the New World arrived. It has been estimated that from the early sixteenth century to about 1870, when the slave trade completely ceased, over 9.5 million African slaves were transported to the Americas and Europe. Most of the slaves came from western Africa.

The European slave traders did not usually capture the slaves themselves. Instead they bought them from other blacks on the African coast. Often victorious African chiefs sold the prisoners they captured during tribal warfare. Sometimes certain tribes or villages had to pay tribute to their rulers by turning over a specific number of slaves. Some bands of Africans even launched slave raids on unsuspecting villages, capturing the inhabitants and selling them into bondage.

Before purchasing a boatload of slaves, the white slave trader had his surgeon examine the captives to determine their physical condition. He then selected only those slaves who seemed to be

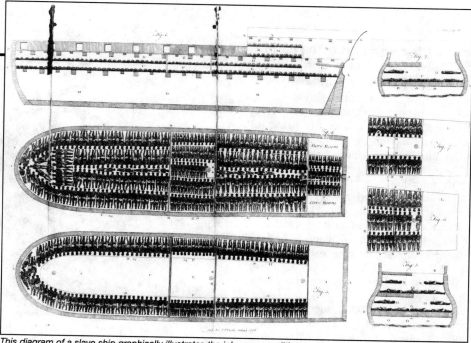

This diagram of a slave ship graphically illustrates the inhuman conditions under which Africans were forcibly taken from their homeland.

in good physical condition, since weak or sickly slaves cut down on his profits. He wanted slaves who could withstand the voyage across the Atlantic and bring a good price at the end. After paying for the slaves with such things as guns, gunpowder, liquor, tobacco, trinkets, cloth, iron, or copper, the trader had the slaves branded with a red-hot iron. The brand insured that the slaves he purchased would not be confused with those purchased by other slave traders.

Not all the slaves put on ships lived to see the New World. About one-fourth of all those who left Africa died during the long voyage across the Atlantic. Crowded conditions on board allowed disease to spread rapidly. Lack of exercise and contaminated food and water supplies contributed to illness and death.

Opening up the Interior—Prior to the nineteenth century, few white men had ever set foot in the interior of Africa. It was an unknown land, often called the "Dark Continent." Among the first European explorers to travel inland was **David Livingstone** (1813-73). Livingstone had planned to be a medical missionary to China, but was prevented from going there by the outbreak of the Opium War. He went to Africa instead, motivated by reports of people who had seen the "smoke of a thousand villages" in the interior, where the gospel had never been heard.

Enduring great physical hardship, Livingstone journeyed into the African interior. He was devoted to opening up Africa to the gospel and in the process bringing an end to the slave trade. While on one of his lengthy expeditions, he remained away from civilization for so long that people wondered whether he were still alive. As part of a publicity campaign, a New York newspaper hired the British explorer **Henry Stanley** to find Livingstone. In 1871 Stanley found him at Lake Tanganyika and casually greeted him with the now-famous line "Dr. Livingstone, I presume." After this meeting Livingstone continued to travel and preach but died in his beloved Africa two years later.

Word of his endeavors created great enthusiasm for missions in Britain and the United States. His journeys, as well as those of other missionaries and explorers, opened the door for European trade and imperialism in the areas he had explored.

The Partitioning of Africa—Prior to 1880, Europe controlled only about ten per cent of the African continent. From 1880 to 1914, however, the race for territory in Africa became so intense

"Unto the Uttermost Part of the Earth": David Livingstone and Mary Slessor in Africa

On his fifty-ninth birthday David Livingstone wrote in his journal: "My Jesus, my King, my Life, my All; I again dedicate my whole self to Thee. Accept me, and grant me, O gracious Father, that ere this year is gone I may finish my task." These words were penned two years before the death of this faithful missionary. David Livingstone had dedicated his life to reaching Africa for Christ. In his last days he was often too sick to walk; yet borne on the shoulders of faithful natives, he continued to go to villages where the gospel had never been preached. Finally, on May 4, 1873, his task on earth was ended. While on his knees in prayer, he went to be with his Lord.

Livingstone's body was transported to the coast and sent back to England. His heart, however, was left behind in Africa, buried by natives at the foot of a mvula tree. Today his earthly remains lie near the central nave in Westminster Abbey in London. The black slab that marks his resting place bears this inscription:

Brought by faithful hands
Over land and sea,
Here rests
DAVID LIVINGSTONE
Missionary, Traveler, Philanthropist
Born March 18, 1813
At Blantyre, Lanarkshire
Died May 4, 1873,
At Chitambo's Village, Llala

The slab also bears his favorite missionary text: "Other sheep I have, which are not of this fold: them also I must bring, and they shall hear my voice" (John 10:16).

Livingstone's life affected many; his death affected one woman in particular. **Mary Slessor**

(1848-1915) was a petite Scottish girl with brilliant blue eyes and curly red hair. She was born into a poor family; her father was a drunkard, but she had a godly mother. At the age of eleven, Mary went to work at a spinning mill. She worked twelve hours a day, six days a week, in order to help with the family's finances. In her heart, however, she dreamed of going to Africa as a missionary. When she heard the news of David Livingstone's death, she asked her mother if she could offer herself for missionary service. Her mother gave her permission. Learning of the heathen customs and poor living conditions in Calabar, West Africa, Mary believed that was the place God would have her labor.

In September 1876 she sailed for Calabar. She began her work with youthful impatience, wanting to see immediate results. But she was reminded to wait patiently on God. Among the many heathen practices which she found among the people, perhaps the most appalling was the

that by World War I only Ethiopia and Liberia remained independent.

Britain was interested in the entire continent of Africa. In the north, she secured controlling interest in the newly built Suez Canal (1869). To protect this life line of British trade with India and the Far East, the British government assumed control of the Egyptian economy and government. In southern Africa, British imperialism was directed by **Cecil John Rhodes** (1853-1902), called "the empire-builder." As a young man, Rhodes went to southern Africa and made a fortune in diamonds. He became a firm supporter of British imperialism, working tirelessly to advance British interests (as well as his own) in

custom of killing newborn twins. The natives believed that twins were the children of demons. Mary was able to rescue some of these children, whom she raised as her own. As the years went by, these children became teachers and missionaries to their own people.

After spending a few years at the mission station on the coast, Mary felt the call of God to go upriver to witness to several cannibal tribes. At first the mission was opposed to the idea, but finally she was allowed to go. Taking her children with her, she settled in one of the cannibal villages. Her love for the people was clearly shown: she tended their sick and cared for their unwanted. They returned her love by giving her the honored title of *Ma* ("mother"). Later they came to consider her as their queen. When Calabar was taken over by the British government in 1889, she was made vice consul for the interior of the Niger Coast Protectorate. She was responsible for establishing law and order among the wild and savage people. Nonetheless, she remained true to her primary task of winning people to the Lord. She faithfully gave out God's Word, trusting that it would enlighten their hearts. When she moved to another area some fifteen years later, she left behind a thriving Christian community.

After thirty-nine years of self-sacrificing service, her frail body could take no more; she went to be with her Lord on January 13, 1915. What was the secret to her successful labor for the Lord? In her own words, "I have no idea how and why God has carried me over so many hard places, and made these hordes submit to me . . . except in answer to prayer at home for me. It is all beyond my comprehension. The only way I can explain it is on the ground that I have been prayed for more than most. Pray on—power lies that way."

Africa. He dreamed of an uninterrupted line of British territory stretching from Egypt in northern Africa to the Cape Colony in southern Africa. Although his goal "from Cape to Cairo" was only partially realized, he helped Britain acquire additional territory in Africa, including Rhodesia (modern Zambia and Zimbabwe), which was named after him. His name now lives on in the Rhodes Scholarships which provide funds for students from the British Commonwealth, South Africa, and the United States to study at Oxford University.

While Britain acquired African territory in the southern and northeastern parts of the continent, France acquired most of the northern and much of western Africa. In 1830 France slowly began to build her African empire by sending troops into Algeria. The following year Louis Philippe established an elite army group that would figure prominently in the history of French imperialism—the famous **Foreign Legion.** By the end of the century, France had extended her hold over most of West Africa, building the largest land empire in Africa (though it was mostly desert).

Belgium's African possessions consisted of one large mass of land in central Africa called the Congo. Between 1878 and 1884 King **Leopold II** of Belgium hired Henry Stanley as well as other explorers to acquire as much of the region as possible. As a result of this activity, Leopold soon personally controlled the nine-hundred-thousand-square-mile Congo Free State, a land area over seventy-five times larger than Belgium. Unlike the British and the French, Leopold's agents severely mistreated the natives. When the news of their atrocities reached Europe, there was such an outcry that the Belgian parliament forced Leopold II to turn over the administration of the Congo to the Belgian government, which renamed it the Belgian Congo (modern Zaire).

Germany was slow in entering the race for colonies. The effort toward German unification kept German attention focused on domestic matters rather than imperial concerns. In addition, Bismarck was never very enthusiastic about acquiring overseas territories because he believed that they would dilute Germany's strength. After German unification had been achieved, however, Germany wished to prove her strength as a new nation. In the 1880s she claimed her first African colony—German Southwest Africa (modern Namibia). Of all Germany's African possessions, her most valuable from a geographic standpoint was German East Africa (modern Tanzania). The German explorer Dr. **Karl Peters** secured this area, prevent-

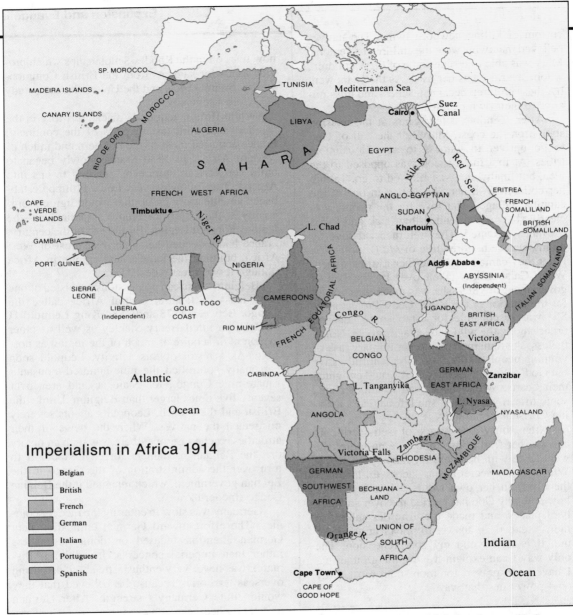

Imperialism in Africa 1914

- Belgian
- British
- French
- German
- Italian
- Portuguese
- Spanish

ing the British from acquiring an unbroken stretch of territory from the Cape to Cairo.

The Balkans and the Near East

For centuries the Turks had controlled the Balkans and the Near East. But with the decline of the Ottoman Empire in the nineteenth century, European nations began to extend their spheres of influence into this region. The most aggressive nation was Russia. Russian imperialism was different from that of other European nations. Whereas Britain and France, for example, sought territory overseas in Africa and Asia, Russia sought to gain additional territory by simply expanding her borders.

The Suez Canal

In ancient times the Egyptian pharaohs directed the construction of a canal linking the Red Sea and the Nile River. Drifting sand, however, closed the canal several times. In later centuries the Persians and the Romans reopened the canal, but in the eighth century the Arabs closed it. Over one thousand years later, Napoleon invaded Egypt. Part of his plan included the construction of a new canal that would directly link the Mediterranean Sea with the Red Sea. His defeat by the British forced him to abandon this idea.

But interest in the canal did not die. A Frenchman, Ferdinand de Lesseps (1805-94), secured permission from the Egyptian ruler and organized an international company to finance and build the waterway. Under de Lesseps's direction, the company sold four hundred thousand shares of stock and began construction in 1859. Costs were much higher than anticipated, but the hundred-mile-long canal was opened in 1869.

Great Britain at first opposed the building of the Suez Canal, thinking that it would threaten her trade with Asia. She refused to purchase any of the original shares of stock, and thus had no say in how the canal was operated. Yet as time went on she became increasingly aware of the canal's strategic importance. So when the ruler of Egypt offered to sell his 176,602 shares in the canal (he was in debt and needed the money), Prime Minister Benjamin Disraeli seized the opportunity. He borrowed £4 million and bought the shares for the British government. Over the next several years, Britain became the canal's strongest defender, and the canal became the life line of British trade with the Orient.

One of Russia's major territorial objectives was to control the straits leading from the Black Sea to the Mediterranean. But Russian expansion in the Balkans threatened to upset the balance of power in Europe. Such concerns had led to the Crimean War in 1854-56. In 1877 Russia renewed her efforts to extend her influence into this region by initiating war with the Turks. After suffering disastrous defeats, the Turks surrendered and signed the Treaty of San Stefano. This war strengthened Russia's position in the Balkans while virtually pushing the Ottomans out of Europe. But once again the European nations stepped in. At the Congress of Berlin (1878) they forced Russia to back down from some of her gains won from the Turks.

Russia continued her expansionistic designs, however. She made a concerted effort to push southward through Afghanistan and Persia towards

the Persian Gulf. The British feared that such expansion would imperil both their prize possessions of India, and the Suez Canal, which was their life line to India and the East. The rivalry between the two was temporarily settled in 1907 by the **Anglo-Russian Entente.** This agreement divided Persia (Iran) into three zones: the British dominated the southern zone, the Russians dominated the northern zone, and the middle zone remained neutral. In Afghanistan, the Russians recognized British influence and agreed not to interfere in Afghanistan's internal affairs.

Results of Imperialsm

Negative Results

The military and industrial might of European nations enabled the Europeans to exploit the people and wealth in their overseas empires. Occasionally, greedy territorial officials and foreign merchants amassed personal fortunes at the expense of the native populations. Some Europeans even abused the native peoples. When dividing up African territory, for example, imperial powers often ignored ancient tribal boundaries. This action produced strife as opposing tribes were grouped together or as tribes were split and ruled by different European countries. Similarly, Westerners tended to downgrade native cultures. Many of the Africans and Asians resented having Western culture imposed upon them.

Positive Results

Though much wrong was wrought by imperialism, much good was accomplished also. The most outstanding benefit to the native populations was the missionary outreach. God used the imperialistic movement to open foreign lands to the gospel. In many territories, missionaries helped to establish a written language for the native people so that the Bible could be translated for their use. Westerners also built schools, hospitals, and public buildings, and introduced railroads, industry, and modern technology. They did their best to abolish the remnants of the slave trade.

The concern shown by United States President William McKinley sums up many of the motives for western imperialism. When the United States acquired control of the Philippines following the Spanish-American War, President McKinley said:

When next I realized that the Philippines had dropped into our laps I confess I did not know what to do with them. . . . I walked the floor of the White House night after night until midnight; and I am not ashamed to tell you, gentlemen, that I went down on my knees and prayed Almighty God for light and guidance more than one night. And one night late it came to me . . . (1) That we could not give them back to Spain—that would be cowardly and dishonorable; (2) that we could not turn them over to France or Germany—our commercial rivals in the Orient—that would be bad business and discreditable; (3) that we could not leave them to themselves—they were unfit for self-government—and they would soon have anarchy and misrule over there worse than Spain's was; and (4) that there was nothing left for us to do but to take them all, and to educate the Filipinos, and uplift and civilize and Christianize them, and by God's grace do the very best we could for them, as our fellow-men for whom Christ died.

Section Review

1. Who was the famous missionary that opened up the interior of Africa to the gospel message?
2. What canal did Britain secure control of in order to protect her trade with India and the Far East?
3. What man directed Britain's imperialistic efforts in southern Africa, becoming known as the ''empire-builder''? What was his goal for British imperialism in Africa?
4. What European king personally controlled an area in Africa seventy-five times the size of his own country? What was this area in Africa called?
5. What congress of European nations in 1878 forced Russia to give up territorial gains in the Balkan region?

A Glimpse Behind and a Glimpse Ahead

In their quest for overseas empires, some Western nations were motivated by an extreme nationalism. They looked upon overseas possessions as an opportunity to prove their national might and glory. But this competitive rivalry produced an increased tension among the European nations and would become a major factor in leading to the outbreak of World War I.

Chapter Review

Can You Explain?

Boers	*criollos*	*caudillos*	extraterritoriality
peninsulares	*mestizos*	imperialism	

Can You Identify?

Louisiana Purchase	Great Trek	Manchu dynasty	culture system
Monroe Doctrine	Boer War (1899-1902)	Opium Wars	David Livingstone
Maximilian	Simón Bolívar	Sino-Japanese War	Mary Slessor
Roosevelt Corollary	José de San Martín	Boxer Rebellion	Henry Stanley
Quebec Act (1774)	Dom Pedro	J. Hudson Taylor	Cecil John Rhodes
British North America Act	Battle of Plassey	Tokugawa	Foreign Legion
James Cook	Robert Clive	Matthew Perry	Leopold II
Maoris	Sepoy Mutiny	Treaty of Kanagawa	Karl Peters
	William Carey	Meiji Period	Anglo-Russian Entente

Can You Locate?

Louisiana Purchase	Venezuela	Siam	Suez Canal
Cuba	Panama	Ceylon	Rhodesia
Puerto Rico	Ecuador	Malaya	Algeria
Philippines	Argentina	Burma	Belgian Congo
Canada	Chile	Singapore	German Southwest Africa
Australia	Peru	Indochina	German East Africa
New Zealand	Brazil	Dutch East Indies	Libya
Cape Colony	Canton	Ethiopia	Afghanistan
Colombia	Hong Kong	Liberia	

How Much Do You Remember?

1. What were the major differences between the Northern and Southern states that led to the Civil War?
2. List six problems that Latin American countries experienced after gaining their independence.
3. List four motives that prompted European nations to build overseas empires.
4. How did the Russian method of imperialism differ from that of France and Britain?
5. List two negative and two positive consequences associated with the imperialistic movement.

What Do You Think?

1. In what way did the independence movement in the British colonies and in the Latin American colonies differ?
2. In what ways did imperialism in Africa differ from that in Asia?
3. What factors aided the worldwide spread of the gospel during the nineteenth century?
4. Is it right for one country to extend its control—whether politically or economically—over another country?

UNIT VII

The bright promise of the nineteenth century collapsed in the disasters of the twentieth. Two global wars destroyed the myth that man is constantly progressing and improving. The totalitarian dictatorships of the Nazis and Communists mocked the earlier cries of "liberty and justice for all." The democratic nations seemed at times weak and tired. After World War II the world lived for nearly fifty years in a balance of terror between two great nuclear superpowers and their allies. The order of the nineteenth century is far removed from the relativism and chaos of the twentieth. Rarely has an age so aptly illustrated Paul's statement to Timothy: "In the last days perilous times shall come" (II Tim. 3:1).

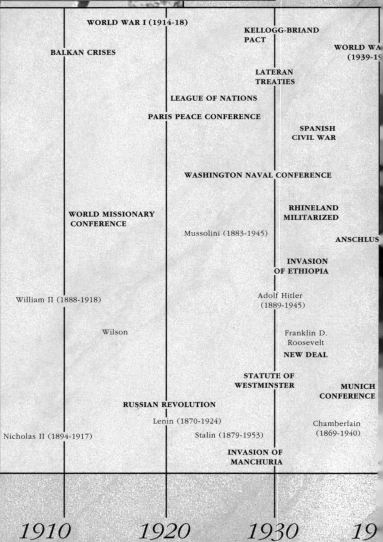

WORLD WAR I (1914-18)

KELLOGG-BRIAND PACT

BALKAN CRISES

WORLD WAR (1939-19

LATERAN TREATIES

LEAGUE OF NATIONS

PARIS PEACE CONFERENCE

SPANISH CIVIL WAR

WASHINGTON NAVAL CONFERENCE

WORLD MISSIONARY CONFERENCE

RHINELAND MILITARIZED

Mussolini (1883-1945)

ANSCHLUS

INVASION OF ETHIOPIA

William II (1888-1918)

Adolf Hitler (1889-1945)

Wilson

Franklin D. Roosevelt

NEW DEAL

STATUTE OF WESTMINSTER

MUNICH CONFERENCE

RUSSIAN REVOLUTION

Lenin (1870-1924)

Chamberlain (1869-1940)

Nicholas II (1894-1917)

Stalin (1879-1953)

INVASION OF MANCHURIA

1910   *1920*   *1930*   *19*

THE MODERN WORLD

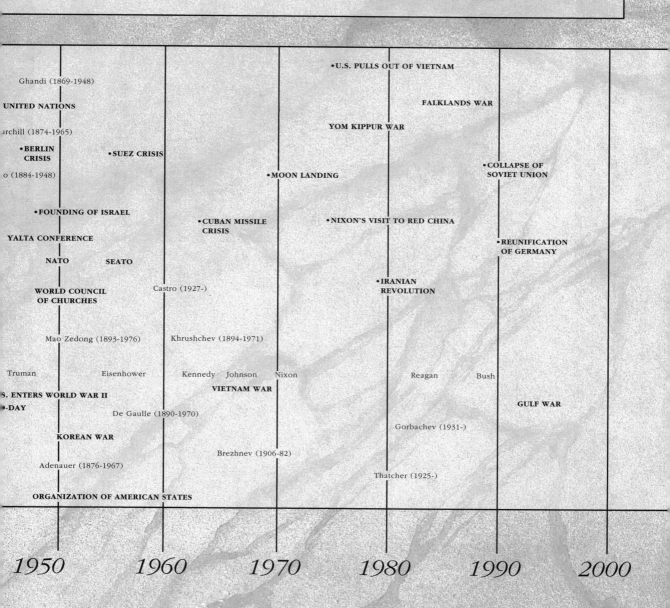

Ghandi (1869-1948)

UNITED NATIONS

urchill (1874-1965)

•BERLIN CRISIS   **•SUEZ CRISIS**

o (1884-1948)

•FOUNDING OF ISRAEL

YALTA CONFERENCE

NATO   **SEATO**

WORLD COUNCIL OF CHURCHES

Castro (1927-)

Mao Zedong (1893-1976)   Khrushchev (1894-1971)

Truman   Eisenhower   Kennedy   Johnson   Nixon

•U.S. PULLS OUT OF VIETNAM

FALKLANDS WAR

YOM KIPPUR WAR

•COLLAPSE OF SOVIET UNION

•MOON LANDING

•NIXON'S VISIT TO RED CHINA

•CUBAN MISSILE CRISIS

•REUNIFICATION OF GERMANY

•IRANIAN REVOLUTION

Reagan   Bush

VIETNAM WAR

S. ENTERS WORLD WAR II

•-DAY

De Gaulle (1890-1970)

GULF WAR

KOREAN WAR

Gorbachev (1931-)

Adenauer (1876-1967)

Brezhnev (1906-82)

Thatcher (1925-)

ORGANIZATION OF AMERICAN STATES

1950   1960   1970   1980   1990   2000

"The lamps are going out."

A psychologist of the early twentieth century taught his patients to say to themselves, "Every day in every way, I'm getting better and better." Many people in the nineteenth and early twentieth centuries thought the same of the world. The future seemed bright and full of promise. But alongside man's pride in his own accomplishments was the reality of his sinfulness. In 1914, a great war shattered the dreams of the optimists. Tension and discord confronted hope and enthusiasm. Peril replaced promise as nations rushed headlong into the catastrophe now known as World War I.

Promise and Peril

Reasons for Hope

Winston Churchill, a leading statesman of the twentieth century, described the nineteenth century as a time when the "accumulation of health and wealth had been practically unchecked." The rise of industrialism made possible a higher standard of living for more people than ever before. Science seemed to be eradicating disease; efforts at peace and international cooperation increased as the century continued. Because of this apparent progress most people were optimistic about the future.

International Cooperation

The late nineteenth century saw the rise of organizations to promote international cooperation. In 1864 Jean Henri Dunant, a Frenchman who believed that "all men are brothers," founded the Red Cross. This international organization seeks to help those who suffer from natural disaster or war. International cooperation also improved as communications improved. In 1868 the International Telegraph Union was founded, followed by the Universal Postal Union in 1875. In addition, many countries standardized their systems of weights and measures. In 1889 the Pan-American Union was established to promote trade and peace among the countries in the Western Hemisphere. In 1896, in a symbolic gesture of cooperation, a number of countries organized a revival of the Greek Olympic games.

International Efforts at Peace

With the breakdown of the Concert of Europe (see p. 420), various individuals and organizations tried to maintain world peace. One individual who became famous for his promotion of international

peace was the wealthy Swedish chemist **Alfred Nobel** (1833-96). In his will he established the Nobel Peace Prize to recognize men and women whose accomplishments furthered the cause of peace. Nobel had gained his fortune through the invention of dynamite. Misgivings about his invention's great destructive potential had prompted him to set aside funds for the cause of peace.

Nobel was not alone in his efforts; another philanthropist was **Andrew Carnegie** (1835-1919), an American steel manufacturer. Carnegie donated funds to build the Peace Palace at The Hague (the

Andrew Carnegie

Opposite Page: World War I British tank

seat of government in the Netherlands). He intended that The Hague be a place where international disputes could be settled through peaceful means. Ironically, the Palace was completed just as World War I began. By 1910 about 160 peace organizations were in existence; between 1800 and 1914, 250 international disputes had been arbitrated (settled by a third party).

Reasons for Fear

Neither scientific progress nor attempts at international cooperation could prevent dark clouds of suspicion and hatred from forming on the European horizon. As the nineteenth century drew to a close, several developments made war an increasing possibility, despite continued talk of cooperation and peace. From the earliest chapters in this book we have seen that in spite of man's efforts to maintain peace, "wars and rumours of war" (Matt. 24:6) persist. In his epistle, James asks the question, "From whence come wars and fightings among you?" They come, he says, from "your lusts that war in your members" (James 4:1). This principle helps us to understand the real source of tension that produces war. The following are the outward, historical expressions of the pride, fear, and greed of men and nations that led to the Great War.

Extreme Nationalism

Although patriotic love for one's country is not wrong, Europeans during the late 1800s carried patriotism too far. They began to consider other races and nations inferior. Unbridled nationalism, or **chauvinism**, caused many people to desire war so that they could prove their superiority over other nations. As one German put it, war "is not only a necessary element in the life of a people, but also an indispensable factor in culture, indeed the highest expression of the strength and life of a truly cultured people."

Militarism

Many European nations during this time increased their military might far beyond what was necessary for a strong national defense. The primary purpose for such military build-up was national glory. A large standing army became a symbol of power. In several countries—Germany, for

example—the military dominated the civil government. When disputes broke out among nations, it became very easy for a government to immediately resort to the use of force. Compounding the problem was the fact that many citizens glorified war, believing that war was the noblest task in which any nation could engage. These militaristic attitudes in Europe helped foster the full-scale war that lay ahead.

Imperialism

Another cause of antagonism among countries was competition for colonies. Many European nations, jealous of Britain's colonial empire and industrial strength, desired colonies of their own. Germany and Italy, which had recently become unified nations, were especially eager to prove their new national strength by acquiring territory in Africa and Asia. Since colonies provided economic benefits for their growing industrial might, European nations sought those territories that were the richest in natural resources. Conflicting claims nearly led to war on several occasions. Usually the nations involved worked out peaceful solutions, but they were not always satisfied with the results. As competitions increased, so did jealously, hatred, and suspicion.

Rival Alliances

Deep-seated fear and distrust among European nations led to the formation of protective alliances. Two nations, or sometimes several nations, made agreements (often in secret) promising to come to one another's aid in the event of a foreign attack.

Rival Alliances 1914

▢ Triple Alliance 1882
▢ Triple Entente 1904-7

By the late nineteenth and early twentieth centuries, Europe was divided into rival alliances. It was this alliance system that helped to drag most of Europe into war.

Steps Toward War

The Building of Bismarck's System

Germany became a unified nation after her victory over France in the Franco-Prussian War (1870). Bismarck, who continued as chancellor of the new German state, feared that France would seek revenge for her humiliating loss. He therefore set out to create a system of alliances among the major nations of Europe to prevent France from finding a strong ally to help her. By keeping France diplomatically isolated, Bismarck believed that Germany would be safe from French attack and that the political balance of power could be maintained. This system of alliances that Bismarck created is often called **Bismarck's System.**

The first alliance that Bismarck established was the **Three Emperors' League** (1873). It included Germany, Austria-Hungary, and Russia. These nations made vague promises of mutual aid in the event that war broke out with France or the Ottoman Empire. But despite its promising beginning, the league fell apart. Conflict broke out between Russia and Austria-Hungary over the Balkans. Both countries wanted to extend their influence over this region in place of the weakening Ottoman Empire. Since Austria-Hungary and Russia would not cooperate, Bismarck realized that he would have to cultivate closer ties with one or the other. Fearing the growing power of Russia, he chose Austria-Hungary. In 1879 Germany joined with Austria-Hungary, pledging mutual aid if one or the other was attacked by Russia. This alliance, sometimes called the Dual Alliance, soon became the foundation of German foreign policy.

Bismarck continued his efforts to prevent France from finding a strong ally. In 1882 the **Triple Alliance** brought Germany, Austria-Hungary, and Italy together in an anti-French coalition. But Bismarck still was not satisfied. He wanted to bring Russia back into the circle of German allies. Through skillful diplomacy, he negotiated a secret alliance with

Russia, known as the **Reinsurance Treaty** (1887). In addition, he worked to bring England into the Triple Alliance. But England continued her long-standing policy of isolation, not wishing to get involved in European rivalries. Bismarck did not despair over the failure to create an Anglo-German alliance: Britain was such a determined foe of France and Russia that it seemed unlikely that she would unite with either nation. In effect, France was now diplomatically isolated.

The Breakdown of Bismarck's System

In July of 1888, a young, impulsive **William II** (1888-1918) became kaiser (emperor) of Germany. William, not yet thirty years old, was a proud and

After William II dismissed Bismarck as chancellor of Germany, this cartoon, "Dropping the Pilot," appeared in the British magazine Punch in 1890. William II, determined to run the ship of state by himself, watches as the former "pilot" (Bismarck) leaves the vessel.

arrogant man who resented the domination of Bismarck in German affairs. He determined that as kaiser he would be the real leader of Germany and that no one would overshadow him. Therefore, in 1890, he forced Bismarck to resign as chancellor. William assumed control of Germany's foreign policies, but he was not Bismarck's equal. His words and ill-advised actions served to heighten European tensions.

One of William's first mistakes was to allow the Reinsurance Treaty with Russia to expire. France quickly capitalized on this error and approached Russia with offers of an alliance. Fearing a possible alliance between Germany and Britain (which never took place), Russia joined France in a defensive alliance (also called the Dual Alliance) in 1894. According to this treaty,

> if France is attacked by Germany, or by Italy supported by Germany, Russia shall employ all her available forces to attack Germany. If Russia is attacked by Germany or by Austria supported by Germany, France shall employ all her available forces to fight Germany.... These forces will engage with all their might, so that Germany has to fight both on the East and West.

A second major mistake made by William was to antagonize Britain. Germany began a massive shipbuilding program that threatened British naval domination. British people became alarmed; Britain traditionally had to rely on her fleet to maintain her empire and to protect her homeland. In addition, Germany began to interfere with British affairs in Africa. Germany was late entering the race for colonies, but William was determined to build an overseas empire in one generation, although it had taken other nations many generations. As a result of these developments, Britain's fear of Germany soon became stronger than her fear of France. In 1904, contrary to every German hope or expectation, Britain and France put aside their differences and came to a "friendly understanding" in what is called the *Entente Cordiale.*

That same fear of Germany impelled Britain to patch up her differences with Russia. For some time Russia had been trying to expand into eastern Europe in order to acquire an outlet to the Mediterranean Sea. She had also attempted to expand into the Persian Gulf region. The British feared that such expansion would imperil both their prize possession of India and the commercial trade going through the Suez Canal. But in spite of their deep-seated rivalry, these two countries signed the Anglo-Russian Entente in 1907. This agreement, like the *Entente Cordiale,* tended only to lessen tension and promote cooperation between the two nations. Since Britain had previously formed a friendly understanding with France, her agreement with Russia paved the way for the **Triple Entente** between Britain, France, and Russia.

The Testing of the Alliance System

By 1907 secret agreements, friendly understandings, and formal alliances had divided Europe into two rival sides. Yet many questions remained unanswered: How strong were these alliances? How long would they last? Would a nation who promised to come to another's aid in the event of war actually fulfill its promise? During the early years of the twentieth century, Europe went through a series of crises that answered many of these questions. These crises solidified the newly made alliances but at the same time increased international tension and fear.

Twice, in 1905 and 1911, Germany interfered with French plans to control Morocco (a country in northwest Africa). Not only did Germany hope to block France's attempt to take Morocco as a colony, but she also hoped to break up the entente between Britain and France. Yet Germany's actions had just the opposite effect. Britain gave France her firm support, and France succeeded in gaining Morocco. As a result, bad feelings between Germany and France mounted; they were becoming too intense to be settled peacefully.

Another series of crises occurred in the Balkans. Here small national groups were struggling for their independence from Turkish control. By 1900 several Balkan nations had won their independence from the Ottoman Empire. In 1912 they joined together to drive the Turks out of the Balkans. In short order, the Balkan nations smashed Turkish resistance and gained the victory. But less than a month later, a new war broke out as the Balkan nations fought among themselves to decide who would control the remaining Balkan territory.

Ottoman Empire in 1913

Lost by Ottoman Empire between 1683 and 1913

Lost by Ottoman Empire in 1913

RUSSIA

Danube R.
Vienna
Budapest

BOSNIA
Belgrade
ROMANIA
HERZEGOVINA
SERBIA
Bucharest

MONTENEGRO
BULGARIA
Black Sea
ALBANIA
Sofia

ITALY
Constantinople

GREECE
OTTOMAN EMPIRE
Athens

RHODES
CRETE
To Italy
(1912)
CYPRUS
To Gr. Br.
(1878)

Mediterranean
Sea

The Balkans 1914

The weakness of the Ottoman Empire and the instability of the Balkans encouraged the interven- tion of major European nations—especially Austria-Hungary and Russia. Austria-Hungary disliked hav- ing such unrest on her southeastern border; she also hoped to extend her borders farther into the Balkans. The Russians were of the same ethnic background (Slavic) as most of the peoples of the Balkans. By posing as the defender of her ''brother Slavs,'' Rus- sia, too, hoped to extend her influence in this region. While the major powers sought to keep the crisis in the Balkans a local war, their selfish interests and deep-seated hatred for one another only hastened the coming of widespread war. The Balkans were rightly called the ''powder keg of Europe.''

Section Review

1. Describe the efforts of Alfred Nobel and An- drew Carnegie to maintain world peace.
2. What two countries were eager to prove their new national strength by acquiring territory in Africa and Asia?
3. Who was the architect of a system of alliances designed to isolate France diplomatically?
4. What country claimed to be the defender of ''brother Slavs''?
5. What area was called the ''powder keg of Europe''?

The Pressing Conflict

The Commencement of War

The spark that set off World War I ignited in the Balkans. On June 28, 1914, Archduke **Francis Ferdinand,** the heir to the throne of Austria-Hungary, was assassinated while on a visit to Sarajevo, the cap- ital of Bosnia. (Austria had annexed this Balkan prov- ince in 1908 over the opposition of the Slavic nations.) A Bosnian revolutionary, acting on behalf of an anti-Austrian terrorist organization based in Ser- bia, shot and killed the archduke and his wife. Austria accused the Serbian government of knowing about the plot and failing to inform Austria. Meanwhile, Kaiser William of Germany promised Austria full support for any action she might take. Austria de- cided to crush Serbia once and for all, and on July 23 sent an **ultimatum** (a list of demands with threats) to the Serbian government. The ultimatum not only demanded an explanation and an apology for the assassination but also demanded that Serbia undertake a thorough investigation of the crime. It further demanded that Serbia suppress all anti-Aus- trian publications and organizations.

Austria did not want, or expect, Serbia to meet her demands. As it turned out, Serbia rejected out- right only one demand. Nonetheless, Austria pro- ceeded to use the assassination as an excuse to attack, and on July 28, 1914, declared war on Ser- bia. Two days later Russia began to **mobilize** (make ready) her troops to come to Serbia's de- fense. Germany, realizing that full-scale war was imminent, warned Russia to cease mobilization within twelve hours. When Russia did not heed her warning, Germany came to the aid of Austria by declaring war on Russia on August 1. Likewise,

Archduke Francis Ferdinand (left) with Austrian Emperor Franz Joseph (right)

when France refused to give the Germans solid assurances of French neutrality, Germany declared war on France as well. Thus the alliance system had effectively drawn the great powers into open conflict with one another. On one side were the **Central Powers** (Germany and Austria-Hungary), and on the other side were the Allies (Russia, Serbia, and France).

Much of Europe greeted the declaration of war with joy. As the troops marched to the front, people cheered and threw flowers. In the following weeks, thousands of young men rushed to enlist in the army, eager to win glory on the field of battle. Since both sides expected that a few short campaigns would end the war (as had been the case in the wars of the 1860s and 1870s), neither side prepared for, nor anticipated, the four terrible years of war that were to come.

Not everyone, however, cheered the outbreak of war. Sir Edward Grey, the British foreign secretary, uttered prophetic words when he said, ''The lamps are going out all over Europe; we shall not see them lit again in our lifetime.'' For him, as well as for many others, the apparent progress of the nineteenth century, with all of its aspirations and dreams, was soon to end on the fields of France and the plains of western Russia.

War in the West

With the outbreak of war, Germany found herself in a precarious position. She had an enemy on two fronts: Russia on her eastern front (or border), and France on her western front. But the Germans had prepared for such a situation. Several years before the war a German general named Schlieffen had devised a plan to be used in such an emergency. Acting upon this **Schlieffen Plan,** the German generals decided to put most of their forces in the west and attack France first. It would take Russia longer, they believed, to organize for war because her territory was more extensive than France's. The Germans planned to surprise the French by marching through the flat plains of neutral Belgium and attacking France from the north. The German generals believed that within six weeks Paris could be encircled and defeated. The victorious German armies could then be quickly sent to the east to meet the advancing Russians.

Austrian troops pose for a picture; European leaders confidently expected their armies to be absent for only a few weeks. Instead, the war lasted over four years.

The Germans had demanded that the Belgians allow the German army to pass through their country

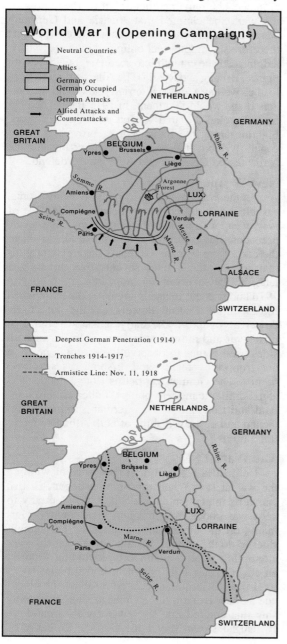

on the way to France. The Belgians refused. On August 4, the German army crossed into Belgium, breaking a seventy-five-year-old treaty that guaranteed Belgian neutrality. "Necessity knows no law," the German chancellor said; "we shall try to make good the wrong we have thus committed as soon as we have reached our military goal." The British, angered over Germany's disregard of this treaty, joined with the Allies and declared war on Germany. The Germans soon pushed on into France and within a month were outside of Paris. But at the Marne River, the French (with reinforcements brought to the front in Paris taxicabs) stopped the German advance. By the end of the year, both sides solidified their positions by constructing a long series of trenches that stretched from Switzerland to the English Channel.

War in the East

In the east, the Russians had been able to mobilize their forces more quickly than the Germans expected. As a result, the Russian armies achieved several initial victories against the Austrians and the Germans. In the battles of Tannenberg and the Masurian Lakes, however, the German armies under the leadership of General **Paul von Hindenburg** (1847-1934) defeated the Russians. They captured over 200,000 prisoners and began to push the demoralized Russian troops back toward Russia. Although they continued to fight for several more years, the Russians did not threaten German borders again during the war.

The inadequacy of Russian factories to produce the needed supplies fatally weakened the Russian war effort. Few supplies were available even from her allies, for German warships had closed the Baltic Sea. In addition, Russia's northern ports were frozen for many months of the year. To remedy this desperate situation, the British decided to force open a sea route to Russia via the Black Sea by taking control of the Dardanelles.

The Ottoman Empire, which had entered the war in 1914 on the side of the Central Powers, controlled the straits between the Black Sea and the Aegean Sea. In 1915 Britain made an attempt to gain control of that strategic waterway by launching a naval attack and then landing Allied troops on the Gallipoli

Peninsula. Poor planning coupled with strong Turkish resistance, however, doomed the invasion to failure. After months of inconclusive fighting and over one hundred thousand casualties, public opinion at home forced the British to withdraw their troops and abandon the project. Meanwhile, the Bulgarians had joined the Central Powers and helped to conquer Serbia by the end of 1915.

The Course of the War

During most of the war, the situation on the western front was a **stalemate** (a situation in which both sides were at a standstill). While in the east armies shifted back and forth across miles of open territory, in the west neither side could break through the intricate system of trenches that both had dug. During each year of the war, both sides conducted major offensives that cost thousands of lives but produced few gains. For example, in 1916 the British conducted an offensive along the Somme River in France. After four months of fighting, the Allies gained only 125 miles of mud, while losing six hundred thousand men. On one day of this campaign, the British alone lost sixty thousand men. Earlier in 1916, the Germans had tried to break through the French lines at the fortress of Verdun. After six months of heavy bombardment and fierce battles, the French held firm. The conflict in France became a deadly war of **attrition** in which one side tried to gradually wear the other down.

Italy Joins the Allies

Although Italy had been a member of the Triple Alliance, she remained neutral at the beginning of the war. She claimed that Austria and Germany were conducting an offensive, not a defensive, war; therefore she did not feel obligated to come to their aid. Instead she entered into secret negotiations with France, Britain, and Russia. The Allies promised her a loan as well as additional territory adjoining her borders if she would join them. In 1915 Italy ended her neutrality and declared war on the Central Powers. Fighting along the Italian border proved to be inconclusive, but it became yet another line for the hard-pressed Germans and Austrians to defend.

New Weapons of War

As the war continued to rage on many fronts, casualties multiplied, partly because of the use of new weapons. Infantrymen used machine guns, grenades, flame throwers, and mustard gas. Near the end of the war the Germans began using guns that lobbed shells over seventy-five miles. The tank, a British invention, appeared in combat in 1916 and was put to use in breaking the entrenched forces of the Central Powers. (While potentially powerful weapons, the early tanks were hard to maneuver and moved very slowly.) In the air both sides used planes to observe the enemy's position and troop movements, and in some cases to drop bombs. The German **zeppelins** (long, slender airships similar to modern blimps) raided eastern England and London. At sea, German submarines attacked and destroyed ships of both Allied and neutral nations.

The War at Sea

Both sides realized the importance of winning the war at sea. When the fighting began, British warships implemented a blockade of Germany to keep war goods from reaching that country. Germany, on the other hand, counted on her submarines to do the same to Britain. Soon each side was attempting to stop all imports, including food, in an effort to starve its opponent into submission.

In 1915 Germany declared a submarine blockade against Britain, threatening to sink any enemy ship that entered into the ''war zone'' around the British Isles. On May 1 the German Embassy is-

The Lusitania *leaving New York for England;* **Inset:** *The warning that appeared in New York newspapers prior to the ship's departure*

sued a warning to passengers planning to leave New York for Liverpool, England, aboard the British liner *Lusitania*.

On May 7, a German submarine sank the *Lusitania* off the coast of Ireland. The attack claimed 1,198 lives, including 128 Americans. This incident, as well as the sinking of various merchant ships, touched off a storm of protest in America and forced the Germans to temporarily curtail their sinking of unarmed merchant and passenger ships.

By 1916 the British had not only chased down and destroyed isolated German warships at sea, but they had also effectively maintained their blockade of the German coastline. Facing shortages of supplies at home, the Germans decided to send their navy out to break the blockade. The fleets met in the Battle of Jutland, off the coast of Denmark. Although the British suffered more damage than the Germans, the blockade remained intact and the German fleet returned to port, where it stayed for the duration of the war.

The German generals persuaded Kaiser William that an all-out submarine campaign would quickly win the war for Germany. When William and others voiced the fear that such a campaign might bring the Americans into the war, the chief of German naval operations told the kaiser, "I give Your Majesty my word as an officer that not one American will land on the continent." In February of 1917, the Germans resumed **unrestricted submarine warfare**—the sinking of all ships, whether armed or not, that carried supplies to the Allies. By the end of the year, the Germans had sunk nearly three thousand ships. But the Allies overcame these losses by improving their methods of antisubmarine warfare.

War on the Home Front

In warfare prior to the twentieth century, civilians in the battle zones suffered, but those behind the lines went about their business relatively unaffected. In World War I, however, what became known as **total war** affected the civilian population in several ways. First, political control became more centralized. In most of the warring nations a group of generals or a small, tightly knit cabinet made

The Red Baron

World War I was the first war in which airplanes were used as weapons. In addition to such activities as reconnaissance (inspection to gain military information) and bombing, opposing planes often tangled in "dogfights" (air battles). Pilots who shot down at least five enemy airplanes were called "aces."

The most successful ace was a German nobleman, Baron Manfred von Richthofen (1892-1918), better known as the "Red Baron." Early in the war Richthofen transferred from the cavalry to the air service. His first efforts proved less than impressive. He crash-landed on his first solo flight and failed his first pilot's exam. Once he had developed his skill, however, Richthofen proved a deadly foe to Allied fliers. He shot down eighty enemy planes during the war, more than any other pilot on either side.

Because he flew a scarlet red airplane, the Allies called Richthofen the "Red Devil," "Red Knight," and, of course, the "Red Baron."

Richthofen became a national hero in wartime Germany. He formed a special fighter squadron of aces, nicknamed the "Flying Circus" because all the pilots flew colorfully-painted planes and because they used tents as hangars (so they could move their base of operations quickly).

On April 21, 1918, the Flying Circus encountered a squadron of Allied fighters. A Canadian pilot, Captain A. Roy Brown, fired at a German plane that was chasing a friend of his. Although Brown did not know it at the time, he had shot the Red Baron. Wounded, Richthofen managed to land his plane behind enemy lines, but died in the cockpit. Although Richthofen was an enemy pilot, the British buried him with full military honors in recognition of his bravery and gallantry.

decisions and implemented policies. Second, the governments rigidly controlled the economic life of their countries. At the outset of the war, many saw no need for such control. For example, when someone approached the German chief of staff about the need for economic planning, the general replied, "Don't bother me with economics. I am busy conducting war." But as the war dragged on, the tremendous cost was felt at home. Morale began to decline. Strikes and food riots plagued Germany, famine swept through the Balkans, and in Russia, civilian miseries culminated in revolution.

Collapse of Russia

Russia was totally unprepared to fight a lengthy war. Her economy and government were inefficient and corrupt, and as casualties and shortages increased, the people's anger and frustration led to strikes and violence. An unplanned, popular uprising that began in the Russian capital of St. Petersburg

soon spread to other cities. Czar **Nicholas II** abdicated his throne on March 15, 1917. For several months a provisional government under Alexander Kerensky attempted to restore order as well as to continue the war against Germany. But in November of 1917 a second revolution occurred, bringing the Communists to power. In 1918 Nikolai Lenin, the new Russian leader, signed a peace treaty with the Germans. The **Treaty of Brest-Litovsk** effectively took Russia out of the war and gave Lenin time to consolidate his power. Russia gave up 1.3 million square miles of land that was inhabited by over sixty million people (approximately one-third of her population). In addition, she lost nearly ninety per cent of her coal mines and over fifty per cent of her industry. As a result, Germany gained access to badly needed raw materials; more importantly, Germany could now concentrate her troops in the west against France and Britain and possibly win the war.

German U-Boats

In 1870 Jules Verne's novel *Twenty Thousand Leagues Under the Sea* was published. In this novel, Verne describes the fictitious adventures of the mad Captain Nemo, who sails beneath the ocean surface in his submarine, the *Nautilus*. At the time this novel was published, it was considered a fantasy and was received with great skepticism (despite the fact that a few primitive submarines had been invented before Verne's time). Just forty-four years later, however, the *Nautilus* became a devastating reality in the form of the German **U-boat**—short for *unterseeboot* ("undersea boat").

During World War I, the Germans launched an all-out attack on British shipping in order to stop the flow of war supplies into Britain. The Germans found that their surface ships were no match for the large British fleet. Instead, they relied on their U-boats to enforce the blockade around the British Isles. The men on the U-boats realized that their task was of the utmost importance to the German war effort. They were willing, therefore, to endure appalling conditions onboard these submarines.

In the early years of the war, the German U-boats badly mauled British shipping. The British were hard pressed to stop this deadly menace. They used merchant ships equipped with guns to combat these submarines. These ships, called Q-ships, could quickly alter their appearance from a British freighter to one of another country. (Early in the war, the German U-boats sank only British ships.) By posing as a merchant ship of a neutral nation, the Q-ships hoped to lure unsuspecting U-boats in close and then open fire. Sometimes, however, the British ships were unsuccessful in fooling the captains of the U-boats and were sunk themselves. As one of the most courageous of the Q-ships captains said, "It was no use pretending to be something you were not unless you attended to every detail."

Later in the war the Allies enjoyed much better success in defending against U-boat attacks. Allied ships traveled in large convoys and used blimps to spot U-boats. With the invention of depth charges, Allied surface ships had an effective means to destroy U-boats lurking beneath the ocean surface. Even so, German U-boats, during the course of the war, sank over six thousand Allied ships.

"On long patrols . . . crews lived in an atmosphere of increasing squalor. The heat was oppressive, the air stale and foul and reeking of bilge water [water that collects in a ship's hull], wet oilskins, rubber boots, sweat, and diesel fumes so thick that a man's hair became pitchy mire. The U-boat grew steadily damper from the intense condensation and the frequent leakage of water through the hatch of the conning tower. Bunks smelled moldy and charts began to rot. A gray-green film of mildew coated shoes and shirt."[1]

The United States Enters the War

When war broke out in 1914, the United States remained neutral. At that time, most American citizens probably agreed with the statement of President **Woodrow Wilson:** "The United States must be neutral in fact as well as in name. . . . We must be impartial in thought as well as in action, [we] must put a curb upon our sentiments." Yet only a few years later, President Wilson addressed Congress and called for a declaration of war against Germany. In his speech he stated that Americans would "fight for the ultimate peace of the world, and for the liberation of its people. . . . The world must be made safe for democracy."

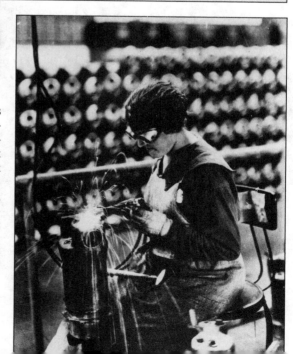

Women such as this welder helped in the war effort on the home front.

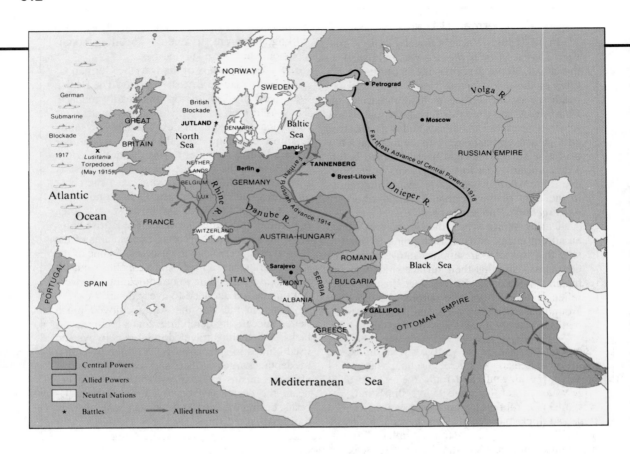

World War I

ALLIES

Serbia (July 28, 1914)
Russia (August 1, 1914)
France (August 3, 1914)
British Empire (August 4, 1914)
Montenegro (August 5, 1914)
Japan (August 23, 1914)
Italy (May 23, 1915)
San Marino (June 3, 1915)
Portugal (March 9, 1916)
Rumania (August 27, 1916)
United States (April 6, 1917)

Panama (April 7, 1917)
Greece (June 27, 1917)
Siam (July 22, 1917)
Liberia (August 4, 1917)
China (August 14, 1917)
Brazil (October 26, 1917)
Guatemala (April 23, 1918)
Nicaragua (May 8, 1918)
Costa Rica (May 23, 1918)
Haiti (July 12, 1918)
Honduras (July 19, 1918)

British

French

German

Austrian

CENTRAL POWERS

Austria-Hungary (July 28, 1914)
German Empire (August 1, 1914)

Ottoman Empire (November 2, 1914)
Bulgaria (October 14, 1915)

What caused this shift in American sentiment? Why did Wilson, who in 1916 won re-election to the presidency with the slogan "He kept us out of war," ask for a declaration of war five months later? The following reasons provide some of the answers to these questions.

1. Many Americans were angered by the loss of life and property resulting from Germany's submarine campaign, which reached its height in 1917. They regarded the sinking of unarmed merchant ships without warning as immoral conduct and a violation of international law.

2. The United States had close ties with France and Britain. The United States enjoyed bonds of language and cultural heritage with England. She felt she had a debt to repay to the French, who helped the American colonies in their War for Independence. Furthermore, the United States had been on friendly terms with France and Britain throughout much of the preceding century.

3. Great Britain uncovered a German plot to bring Mexico into the war against the United States. The Germans planned to offer the Mexicans financial aid and the promise of territory in southwestern New Mexico and Arizona (territories that the United States had gained from Mexico in 1848) if Mexico would declare war on the United States.

4. Allied propaganda helped turn American opinion against the Germans. American newspapers received nearly all of their war news from the British, and the British often exaggerated stories and incidents to stir up anti-German sentiments.

5. The United States had close monetary ties to the Allies. American businessmen and farmers profited from British and French purchases of American goods. In addition, American bankers had lent large sums of money to the French and British governments. These Americans did not want to lose either their markets or their investments.

6. The United States also wanted to maintain the balance of power in Europe. She feared what would happen if a victorious Germany with her strong militaristic ways were to dominate Europe.

For these reasons, and at the request of the president, the United States Congress declared war on Germany on April 6, 1917. Since the United States did not have a large, well-trained army, American soldiers provided little help to the struggling Allies until 1918. In the last months of the war, however, over 250,000 American troops landed in France every month. Under the leadership of General **John J. Pershing,** the American Expeditionary Force (AEF) provided the necessary edge to finally defeat the Germans.

18th U.S. Infantry 1st Division near Exermont, Ardennes, France, during the Argonne offensive

Conclusion of the War

Germany made a last attempt to win the war before American forces could turn the tide against them. With Russia out of the war, Germany was able to send her veterans from the eastern front into France for a final series of offensives that began in March of 1918. At first the German attacks were successful; the weary French and British soldiers were on the verge of collapse. However, under General **Ferdinand Foch** (who had just been named commander in chief of the Allied armies in France), the Allies stopped the German advance.

American forces in France advancing during the final months of fighting

Then, with reinforcements from the United States, they mounted a counterattack.

While the Allies were slowly pushing the Germans out of France, Germany's allies collapsed. Revolts of subject nationalities under Turkish and Austrian control had weakened an already faltering war effort and hastened their defeat. In September Bulgaria surrendered, and by the beginning of November, the Ottoman Empire and Austria-Hungary had surrendered. Germany saw the end coming and appealed to President Wilson for an **armistice** (a temporary cessation of fighting) based on his proposed Fourteen Points (discussed later). Wilson, however, refused to negotiate with a government that he believed did not truly represent the German people. In the meantime, mutinies and revolts broke out across Germany. The kaiser fled to Holland, and a German republic replaced the Second German Reich. Leaders of the new government agreed to an armistice. On November 11, 1918, at 11:00 A.M., German and Allied officials met in a railroad car in the Compiègne Forest in France and signed the armistice that ended World War I.

Although the armistice brought an end to the fighting, it could in no way repair the damage that the war had done. The cost of the war in terms of human lives was staggering. Out of the approximately 64 million men who were mobilized, 10 million died, approximately 20 million were wounded, and about 6 million were missing or unaccounted for. Civilian deaths through starvation, disease, massacres, submarine attacks, and so on

The Lost Battalion

During the Meuse-Argonne offensive in October 1918, the Americans of the 308th Infantry Battalion under the leadership of Major Charles Whittlesey advanced unknowingly through a hole in the German line. Not aware that they were ahead of their own lines, they suddenly found themselves surrounded by the enemy. Quickly, they dug in and tried to defend their position until help came.

But in the days that followed, all attempts to notify the division headquarters of their position ended in failure. The men that Major Whittlesey sent out to take word of their situation back to the Allied lines were either captured or killed. The Germans sent back one of the captured soldiers to Major Whittlesey with the message that the Americans should surrender. To make matters worse, Allied artillery began shelling the "lost" battalion's position.

Desperate, they decided to see if the last of their carrier pigeons could get through with a message. To the leg of a pigeon named Cher Ami, they attached the following message: "We are along the road parallel 276.4. Our own artillery is dropping a barrage directly on us. For heaven's sake, stop it!" When released, the pigeon just perched on a tree and preened himself. But after the men yelled and threw rocks at him, he flew away.

At four o'clock that afternoon, Cher Ami flew into the pigeon loft at the division headquarters with one eye gone, his breastbone smashed, and one leg shot off. Soon the artillery barrage stopped, and within a day the lost battalion was rescued.

Major Whittlesey received the Congressional Medal of Honor, and Cher Ami was later stuffed and placed in the Smithsonian Museum in Washington, D.C.

probably equalled the deaths on the battlefield. All told, the average loss of life for each day of the war was approximately fifteen thousand. In terms of money, the total direct cost of the war neared $200 billion, while indirect costs totalled over $151 billion. Directly and indirectly, the war cost approximately $9 million an hour.

While these figures give a somewhat cold and approximate account of the cost of the war in lives and dollars, there is really no way to measure the total effect that this war had on the world—especially Europe. How do you measure personal suffering or the loss of a generation of young men? How do you measure the devastation to industry, countryside, and economy? This war, like all other wars in history, demonstrated the fact that "whatsoever a man [or nation] soweth, that shall he also reap" (Gal. 6:7). The only difference between this war and previous wars was that new technology increased man's destructive power.

Section Review

1. What occurred on June 28, 1914? Why is this date significant?
2. What country's neutrality did the Germans violate as they made their way to France? What European country declared war on Germany as a result of this attack of a neutral country?
3. What was the German policy which called for the sinking of all ships, whether armed or not, that carried supplies to the Allies?
4. What country left the struggle against Germany in 1918? What country joined the struggle against Germany in 1917?
5. Define *armistice*. Give the hour, day, month, and year for the armistice ending World War I.

The Pursuit of Peace

The Paris Peace Conference

In January of 1919 the **Paris Peace Conference** opened. Seventy delegates representing thirty-two nations met to negotiate the peace settlement for World War I. Unlike the victorious nations at the Congress of Vienna, which had allowed France (the defeated nation) to participate in the negotiations (see p. 436), the Allies excluded the defeated Central Powers from the conference. Russia also was not invited, since she had withdrawn from the war in 1918 after the Communist revolution.

The dominant leaders at the conference were Woodrow Wilson, the president of the United States; Georges Clemenceau, the premier of France; and David Lloyd George, the prime minister of Great Britain. These men largely determined the character and content of the peace treaties.

When the Germans signed the armistice ending World War I, they did so with the understanding that Wilson's peace program would be the basis of the peace treaty. Wilson had advocated a moderate settlement, known as the **Fourteen Points,** which would not seek revenge upon the defeated powers.

Woodrow Wilson in France

When he arrived in Europe, enthusiastic crowds welcomed him wherever he went; he did not receive such a hearty welcome by all the diplomats at the conference, however. Many considered him to be an idealist; they found him stubborn and preachy.

Wilson's Fourteen Points

In a speech made to the United States Congress on January 8, 1918, President Wilson outlined his "fourteen-point" peace plan:

1. "Open covenants of peace; openly arrived at."
2. "Absolute freedom of navigation upon the seas, outside territorial water."
3. "The removal . . . of all economic barriers."
4. Armament reduction.
5. "Adjustment of all colonial claims," keeping the interests of the native peoples in mind.
6. "The evacuation of all Russian territory" and a fair "settlement of all questions affecting Russia."
7. "Belgium . . . must be evacuated and restored."
8. "All French territory should be freed and the invaded portions restored." Germany must also return Alsace and Lorraine to France.
9. Italy's borders should be readjusted "along clearly recognizable lines of nationality."
10. "The people of Austria-Hungary . . . should be accorded the freest opportunity of autonomous development."
11. The independence of the Balkan states must be maintained. Serbia must be given an outlet to the sea.
12. Non-Turkish peoples under Turkish control should be given the "opportunity of autonomous development." The Dardanelles should be open to all ships.
13. "An independent Polish state should be erected" with "free and secure access to the sea."
14. "A general association of nations must be formed under specific covenants for the purpose of affording mutual guarantees of political independence and territorial integrity to the great and small states alike."

The leader of the French delegation, **Georges Clemenceau,** was known as the "Old Tiger." He was a cynical and crafty politician who had no use for the idealism of Wilson. He once commented that "even God was satisfied with Ten Commandments, but Wilson insists on fourteen." Clemenceau's main concern was the security of France. He desired to keep Germany militarily weak; in addition, he wanted Germany to pay for the war damages inflicted on France.

The third of these men, **David Lloyd George,** wanted to see Germany punished, but his treaty proposals were not so severe as Clemenceau's. He hoped that German industry could soon be revived, since the staggering British economy desperately needed as many markets as possible. At the same time he wanted to protect British colonial and naval interests.

The Treaty of Versailles

Of the five major treaties drawn up by the Allied delegates in Paris, the most important was the **Treaty of Versailles**—the treaty between the Allies and Germany. The Germans had expected the treaty to be in accord with Wilson's moderate proposals. Instead its provisions were very harsh.

Territorial Provisions—According to the treaty, Germany had to return Alsace and Lorraine to France and grant smaller amounts of land to Belgium and Denmark. Clemenceau had originally demanded that all German territory west of the Rhine River come under French control, but the United States and Britain would not agree to such a demand. So the Allies worked out a compromise whereby they would jointly occupy the Rhineland for fifteen years. During this time the French would be allowed to control the rich Saar coal field located in the Rhineland.

In the east, the treaty reestablished an independent Polish nation. East Prussia was detached from the rest of Germany in order to give Poland an outlet to the Baltic Sea. The land separating East Prussia from Germany became known as the Polish Corridor. It included the port city of Danzig (Gdańsk), which came under the control of the League of Nations. A portion of the coal-rich province of Silesia went to Poland, and Lithuania received the German port of Memel. In addition, Germany lost all of her Asian and African colonies.

The signing of the peace treaty at the Palace of Versailles

Altogether the Germans lost twenty-five thousand square miles of territory inhabited by six million people. (See map on p. 518.)

Economic Provisions—The Treaty of Versailles also specified that large amounts of coal from German mines had to be sent to several of the Allied nations for a period of ten years. It required the Germans to turn over many of their merchant ships and fishing vessels to the Allies, in addition to building new ships for them. But the most damaging economic provision of the treaty was the Allied demand that Germany pay **reparations** (payment for war damages). In spite of the fact that the Allies could not agree on the amount of the war damages, the treaty demanded an immediate payment of $5 billion. The delegates established a special commission to decide later on the final amount.

Military Provisions—The Versailles Treaty restricted the German army to one hundred thousand men. It also established a thirty-mile-wide zone east of the Rhine River that was to remain **demilitarized.** The army could have no tanks and no large guns, and the navy could have no submarines and only six warships. All military aircraft had to be destroyed, and no new ones could be built.

The "War Guilt" Clause—The basis for all of these repressive provisions was Article 231 of the treaty, which stated, "The Allied and Associated Governments affirm and Germany accepts the responsibility of Germany and her allies for causing all the loss and damage to which the Allied and Associated Governments and their nationals have been subjected as a consequence of the war imposed upon them by the aggression of Germany and her allies." This so-called **war guilt clause** placed the entire blame for the war upon Germany and her allies. Germany at first refused to sign the treaty. While she was willing to accept some blame for the war, she believed it unjust that she should have to shoulder all the blame. But when the Allies threatened to continue the war if the Germans would not cooperate, a German delegation at Versailles signed under protest. In the years following Versailles, German resentment and anger at this unjust provision soon changed to hatred, and thoughts of revenge began to mount. Before long many Germans began to listen seriously to Adolf Hitler as he fiercely condemned the treaty and advocated the building of a new Germany that would right the "wrongs" of Versailles. (See Chapters 20 and 21.)

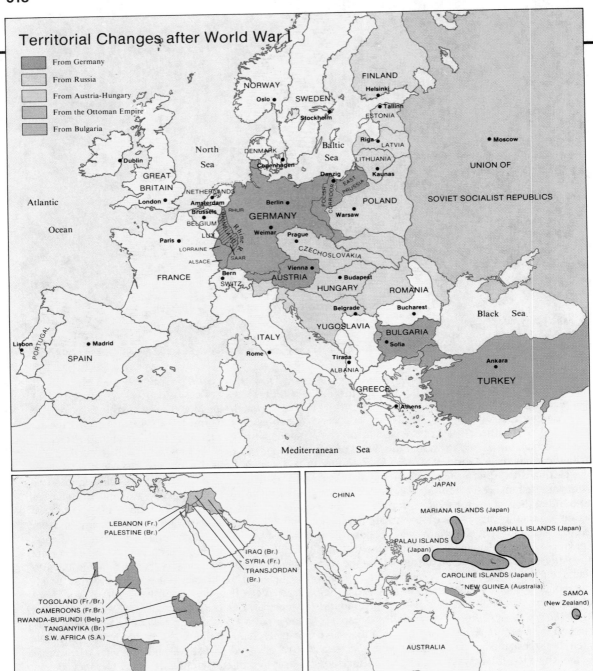

Territorial Changes after World War 1

- From Germany
- From Russia
- From Austria-Hungary
- From the Ottoman Empire
- From Bulgaria

NORWAY

SWEDEN

FINLAND
Helsinki

Oslo
Stockholm

Moscow

Baltic
Sea

Riga
LATVIA

ESTONIA
Tallinn

North
Sea

DENMARK
Copenhagen

LITHUANIA
Kaunas

UNION OF

Dublin

GREAT
BRITAIN

NETHERLANDS

Danzig
POLISH
CORRIDOR
EAST
PRUSSIA

POLAND

SOVIET SOCIALIST REPUBLICS

Atlantic

Ocean

London
Amsterdam
Brussels
BELGIUM
LUX

Berlin

GERMANY

Warsaw

RHUR
Rhine R.

Weimar

Paris

LORRAINE
ALSACE

SAAR

Prague

CZECHOSLOVAKIA

Bern
SWITZ.

Vienna
AUSTRIA

Budapest

HUNGARY

ROMANIA

Bucharest

Black Sea

FRANCE

Belgrade

YUGOSLAVIA

Lisbon

PORTUGAL

Madrid

SPAIN

ITALY

Rome

Tirana
ALBANIA

BULGARIA
Sofia

GREECE

Athens

Ankara

TURKEY

Mediterranean Sea

Africa

LEBANON (Fr.)
PALESTINE (Br.)

IRAQ (Br.)
SYRIA (Fr.)
TRANSJORDAN (Br.)

TOGOLAND (Fr./Br.)
CAMEROONS (Fr.Br.)
RWANDA-BURUNDI (Belg.)
TANGANYIKA (Br.)
S.W. AFRICA (S.A.)

Pacific Ocean

CHINA

JAPAN

MARIANA ISLANDS (Japan)

MARSHALL ISLANDS (Japan)

PALAU ISLANDS
(Japan)

CAROLINE ISLANDS (Japan)

NEW GUINEA (Australia)

SAMOA
(New Zealand)

AUSTRALIA

NEW
ZEALAND

Other Peace Treaties

The Paris Peace Conference drew up treaties with the other defeated Central Powers as well. Austria signed the **Treaty of St. Germain,** in which she turned over territory to Italy and recognized the independence of Czechoslovakia, Hungary, Poland, and Yugoslavia. (Yugoslavia was composed in part of Serbia and several other Slavic territories in the Balkan region.) Altogether, Austria lost about three-fourths of her territory and population. She also had to pay reparations, limit the size of her army, and agree not to seek *Anschluss* (political unification) with Germany. Both Hungary and Bulgaria signed similar treaties as well.

The **Treaty of Sèvres** dismantled the Ottoman Empire. The Turks retained Asia Minor (modern Turkey), where they constituted the majority of the population. Their Arabian territories, however, such as Syria, Palestine, and Iraq, came under British and French control. These territories, as well as the former German colonies, were called **mandates,** territories technically under the control of the League of Nations, but administered by various Allied countries. Turkey retained control of the straits between the Black Sea and the Aegean Sea, but surrounding territory had to be demilitarized and the straits opened to ships of all nations.

World War I cemetery at Verdun, a fortress which was the site of some of the fiercest fighting of the war

Attempts to Maintain the Peace

The League of Nations

Woodrow Wilson was the one person most responsible for the creation of the **League of Nations.** He was convinced that future war could be avoided by creating an international organization in which nations could discuss their differences instead of fighting about them. Therefore he was willing to compromise many of his other proposals at the Paris Conference in order to enlist support for a league of nations.

The purpose of the League of Nations was "to guarantee international cooperation and to achieve international peace and security." After its establishment in 1920, the League sought to maintain peace by seeking arms reductions and by settling disputes through arbitration. Various commissions tried to make sure that Germany and her former allies carried out the provisions of the peace treaties. In addition, the League sought to promote the rights of colonial peoples and to improve economic and social conditions around the world through groups such as the International Labor Organization.

> The members of the League undertake to respect and preserve . . . against external aggression the territorial integrity and existing political independence of all Members of the League. . . . In case of any such aggression or in case of any threat or danger of such aggression the Council shall advise upon the means by which this obligation shall be fulfilled.
>
> —League Covenant, Article X

Despite the League's success in settling minor disputes among weaker nations, it lacked the authority to settle major crises among powerful nations. Strong nations simply ignored or defied the League, and later some of them even withdrew their membership from the organization.

Historians list many reasons for the failure of the League.

1. The United States did not join the League of Nations. Despite the fact that President Wilson was the chief proponent of the League, the United States Senate would not ratify the treaty. The mood in the United States after the war was one of isolation from foreign involvement. Thus the nation that emerged from the war as the strongest nation did not become a member of the League. Many historians have blamed the United States for the League's failure to maintain world peace. But it must be remembered that United States membership in the League's modern counterpart, the United Nations, has not prevented the outbreak of a number of wars since World War II.

2. The League had the power only to recommend action on the part of its members. It could not require them to take action.

3. Important decisions required a unanimous approval on the part of every member nation.

4. The League had no armed forces of its own to police troubled areas.

5. Members of the League were hesitant about using force, which might lead to another war.

Although these factors hampered the League's effectiveness, the League was actually doomed to failure from the start. Those who refuse to recognize the sinfulness and selfishness of men and nations and who reject the true peace that comes from God cannot hope to establish lasting peace on earth.

Reparation Revisions

The Paris Peace Conference set up a special commission to determine how much Germany owed in reparations. In addition to the $5 billion that the Allies originally demanded, the reparations commission finally settled on an additional sum of $32 billion. Germany made several payments but soon stopped because her economy was not strong enough to bear the burden. When payments did not resume, France retaliated (see p. 540) by invading the Ruhr Valley (an industrial district in Germany). British and American opposition finally forced France to withdraw.

Realizing Germany's financial problems, an American banker, **Charles Dawes,** formed a committee in 1924 to find a solution. Taking as their slogan "Business, not politics," the committee decided to lend Germany money and allow her to spread the reparation payments out over a longer period. In 1929 **Owen Young,** an American lawyer, devised another plan that lessened the amount of reparations and gave Germany until 1988 to complete

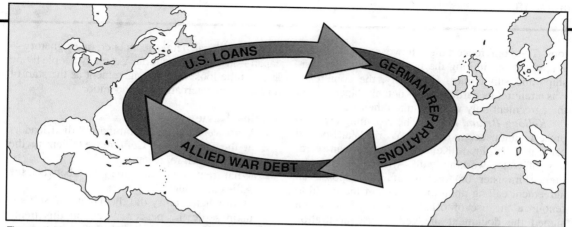

The war debts–reparations payment cycle created an unhealthy flow of money between Europe and the United States.

her payments. When economic problems continued, President Herbert Hoover in 1931 advocated a one-year **moratorium** (suspension) on all reparations payments. After this moratorium, however, Germany never resumed making payments.

Closely associated with the German failure to pay reparations was the failure of Britain and France to pay their **war debts** to the United States. During the war, Britain, France, and other countries had borrowed huge amounts of money from the United States. The Allies had planned to use some of the money Germany paid them in reparations to repay their war debt. But when Germany could not meet the reparation payments, the Allies in turn could not repay their creditors. Intending to lessen the problem, American and British bankers made loans to Germany, hoping that she would invest that money in her economy. As her economy became stronger, she would better be able to meet the reparation payments. But instead of investing the money, Germany immediately used most of it for reparation payments to Britain and France. Britain and France in turn used the money to pay off their war debts to the United States, and again Germany needed another loan. The Allies found this reparations/war-debt cycle impossible to break, and before long all war-debt and reparation payments ceased. This cycle contributed to the world-wide depression of the 1930s.

Disarmament and Nonaggression Pacts

The Locarno Pact—To a Europe apprehensive about the possibility of another war, the Locarno Conference seemed to offer hope. In the fall of 1925, several European nations met in Locarno, Switzerland. At this conference, Germany signed a treaty with France and Belgium in which she agreed to recognize her present borders with those two nations as being permanent. In addition, all three nations promised not to go to war with one another except in self-defense. Although Germany did not recognize her eastern borders as permanent, she did agree not to seek any change in them through war. This **Locarno Pact,** which involved other agreements as well, seemed to hold the promise of peace in Europe. Nations that hated each other now, at least on the surface, appeared to be friends. European tensions relaxed somewhat, and for several years this ''spirit of Locarno'' gave Europeans a false sense of security.

Washington Naval Conference—Men who refuse to believe that wars result from the natural sinfulness of man will sometimes conclude that wars are caused by weapons. They believe that if they eliminate weapons, they can eliminate war. This elimination of weapons or arms is called **disarmament.** The best example of an attempt at disarmament in the 1920s was the **Washington Naval Conference** (1921-22). The great naval powers—Britain, the United States, Japan, and others—agreed to limit the number of warships each could build. They also established a ratio by which to limit the build-up of large warships. They decided, for example, that for every five tons of American shipping, Britain could have five tons, and Japan three tons. The conference failed, however, to reach any agreement on limiting the number of smaller warships and submarines. Ultimately, the conference was a failure; its participants—notably Japan—kept the agreement only when it suited their purposes.

Kellogg-Briand Pact—The crowning effort to preserve the peace in the post–World War I period came in 1928. Frank Kellogg, the American secretary of state, working with Aristide Briand, the French minister of foreign affairs, proposed an agreement calling upon the nations of the world to renounce the use of offensive war. Nations that signed the document pledged to use arbitration rather than force to settle their disputes. In short, this document, known as the **Kellogg-Briand Pact,** sought to unite ''the civilized nations of the world in a common renunciation of war as an instrument of their national policy.'' Sixty-two nations eventually signed this idealistic agreement, which simply made war illegal. Three years later, one signatory—Japan—invaded Manchuria. Yet many people living at that time looked to this agreement as the start of a new era of international cooperation.

Section Review

1. Who were the three dominant Allied leaders at the Paris Peace Conference? Identify the country each represented.
2. What treaty concluded the peace between the Allies and Germany?
3. With what country did the Treaty of St. Germain settle the peace? What did this treaty forbid this country from doing?
4. What major Allied nation did not join the League of Nations? Why not?
5. What agreement called upon the nations of the world to renounce the use of offensive war and seek arbitration to settle international disputes?

A Glimpse Behind and a Glimpse Ahead

At the outset of the twentieth century, feelings of optimism and progress abounded. Yet the illusion of promise was shattered by perhaps the most destructive war the world had seen up to that time. The nations of Europe entered the war with deep-seated hatred for and suspicion of one another; they ended the war in the same manner. Nevertheless, they sought to establish lasting peace without really getting to the root of their problems. They placed their hope for peace in international agreements and cooperation. But their attempts at maintaining peace proved to be miserable failures. They simply sowed more seeds of discontent and discord, which would eventually lead to World War II. Lasting peace on earth will be possible only when the Lord Jesus Christ returns and establishes the day when men ''shall beat their swords into plowshares, and their spears into pruninghooks: nation shall not lift up sword against nation, neither shall they learn war any more'' (Isa. 2:4).

Chapter Review

Can You Explain?

chauvinism
Bismarck's System
ultimatum
mobilize
Schlieffen Plan

stalemate
attrition
zeppelins
unrestricted submarine
   warfare

total war
armistice
reparations
demilitarized
war guilt clause

Anschluss
mandates
moratorium
war debts
disarmament

Can You Identify?

Alfred Nobel
Andrew Carnegie
Three Emperors'
   League
Triple Alliance
Reinsurance Treaty
William II
Entente Cordiale
Triple Entente

June 28, 1914
Francis Ferdinand
Central Powers
Paul von Hindenburg
Lusitania
Nicholas II
Treaty of Brest-Litovsk
U-boat
Woodrow Wilson

John J. Pershing
Ferdinand Foch
November 11, 1918
Paris Peace Conference
Fourteen Points
Georges Clemenceau
David Lloyd George
Treaty of Versailles
Treaty of St. Germain

Treaty of Sèvres
League of Nations
Charles Dawes
Owen Young
Locarno Pact
Washington Naval
   Conference
Kellogg-Briand Pact

Can You Locate?

Morocco
Sarajevo
Bosnia
Serbia
Marne River

Tannenberg
Masurian Lakes
Gallipoli
Somme River
Verdun

St. Petersburg
Bulgaria
Rhineland
Polish Corridor
Danzig

Yugoslavia
Syria
Palestine
Iraq
Ruhr

How Much Do You Remember?

1. List four underlying causes of World War I.
2. Identify the countries that belonged to each of the following alliances and ententes formed prior to World War I: the Three Emperors' League, the Triple Alliance, the Reinsurance Treaty, the Dual Alliance of 1894, the *Entente Cordiale,* and the Triple Entente.
3. List five new weapons of warfare used in World War I.
4. List six reasons explaining why the United States entered the war on the side of the Allies.
5. What were five weaknesses of the League of Nations?

What Do You Think?

1. It has been said that every nation in Europe can be blamed for the outbreak of World War I. List the major European nations and briefly describe how each contributed to the coming of war.
2. How was World War I different from previous wars?
3. What do you believe was the major difference between the Treaty of Versailles and the Fourteen Points?
4. How did the peace settlements of World War I increase the likelihood of another war?
5. Can peace be achieved through military disarmament?

Notes

1. Douglas Botting, *The U-Boats* (Alexandria, Va.: Time-Life Books, 1979), p. 17.

CHAPTER 20

"Evil triumphs when good men do nothing."

Discontent and Experimentation

For a world that was tired and disillusioned from four years of bloodshed, the transition from war to peace proved difficult. Economic weakness, political instability, and changing moral values multiplied in the years following World War I. During the 1920s world leaders attempted to solve these problems through peace treaties and economic agreements. By the 1930s, however, it was apparent to all that their efforts had failed. The Great Depression brought worldwide economic chaos. The rise of new dictators shattered President Wilson's idealistic promise of a world "safe for democracy." Standards of morality declined, and moral decay increased as a growing number of people abandoned belief in the authority of God's Word.

Edmund Burke, an eighteenth-century British statesman, wrote: "The only thing necessary for the triumph of evil is for good men to do nothing." The two decades following World War I were marked by widespread apathy—especially among the victorious Allied nations. Individual citizens and national governments allowed evil to multiply. Socialist ideas crept into the economy of many countries. Self-serving dictators captured control of the governments of both small and large countries. Religious liberals infiltrated the churches, turning many away from the truth of God's Word. The attitude of indifference that allowed these forces of evil to triumph eventually led to the outbreak of World War II.

Weakness Within the Democracies

One of the most serious problems facing Europe and America after World War I was the change from a wartime to a peacetime economy. Once the fighting stopped, governments relaxed their economic controls. But as inflation and then depression struck, many governments reestablished those controls.

Great Britain

As veterans returned home from the war, the British Prime Minister Lloyd George promised that Britain would be a land "fit for heroes." The two decades between the world wars, however, did not match his optimistic promise. Britons witnessed the steady decline of their empire. In addition, the British economy suffered greatly; the war had seriously hurt her trade, and her burden of debt was ten times greater than it had been in 1914. Hardest hit was the coal-mining industry. Strong foreign competition and increased use of other energy sources resulted in diminished demands for coal. Layoffs and miners' strikes resulted. Unemployment in all industries increased so dramatically that by 1932 almost one Briton in four was out of work. Many were on the **dole** (government relief for the unemployed). In that same year Britain abandoned her policy of free trade and initiated protective tariffs (taxes on imported goods).

As economic problems deepened, Britain gradually developed into a welfare state. Parliamentary appropriations for social welfare programs dramatically increased during the 1920s and 1930s. Another indication of the trend toward socialism was the rise of the Labour party led by **Ramsay MacDonald** (1866-1937). In 1924 MacDonald became the first Labour party prime minister of Britain. Although he held the office for less than a year, the Labour party established itself as a major force in British politics.

Not only had the war increased Britain's economic woes, but it also stimulated demands for home rule, or complete independence, on the part of several British possessions. After several years of fierce fighting, Britain finally gave in to Irish demands for independence and created the Irish

Free State in 1921. (Northern Ireland—Ulster—remained under British control.) In Egypt strong nationalism forced the British to recognize that country's independence, although Britain still maintained a naval base there to protect the Suez Canal. Nationalists in India continued clamoring for independence. In 1935 the British Parliament passed the Government of India Act, which granted the Indians greater self-government. In the **Statute of Westminster** (1931), Britain approved a 1926 report that had declared Canada, Australia, New Zealand, and South Africa to be ''autonomous communities within the British Empire, equal in status, in no way subordinate one to another in any aspect of their domestic or external affairs, though united by common allegiance to the crown and freely associated as members of the British Commonwealth of Nations.''

France

During World War I France suffered heavier losses in life and property than Great Britain did; yet she achieved greater economic recovery. New factories replaced those destroyed during the war. The recently returned territories of Alsace and Lorraine provided rich mineral deposits as well as important industrial plants. Even in the face of worldwide economic problems, unemployment never became as severe in France as it was in Britain. Most of the French people were small businessmen or farmers, and although violent strikes did occur, France weathered the economic storms better than much of Europe.

Nevertheless, France remained politically unstable. The Third French Republic (established after the French defeat in the Franco-Prussian War) was plagued by so many political parties that no one was able to gain a majority. As a result, the government was established on shaky coalitions of several political parties. Between 1920 and 1940, France changed prime ministers some forty times. As successive governments failed to solve France's domestic problems, discontented radical groups, which threatened the republic, became increasingly popular. During this same period various Socialist and Communist political parties became stronger. In

The Maginot Line

After World War I, the French were determined to protect their border with Germany. They wanted to be ready for a future German attack. In 1929, under the leadership of André Maginot, the French began building a line of fortifications stretching from Switzerland to the Belgian border. Below the fortifications was a network of underground chambers containing power stations, ammunition supplies, hospitals, recreation halls, theaters, and living quarters. Each fortification was joined to the others by an underground subway, which made possible quick and safe transportation of troops anywhere along the line.

Many Frenchmen confidently believed that the Maginot line would stop any German attack. During World War II, however, the Germans simply by-passed those fortifications, rendering them completely useless. Like so many other people throughout history, the French relied on human devices for their security. The psalmist wrote, ''Some trust in chariots, and some in horses: but we will remember the name of the Lord our God. They are brought down and fallen: but we are risen, and stand upright'' (Ps. 20:7-8).

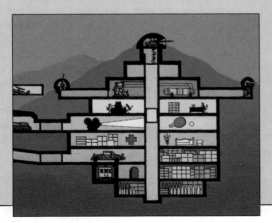

1936 these parties, calling themselves the Popular Front, managed to gain control of the government, naming **Léon Blum** (1872-1950) as prime minister. This coalition soon fell apart, however, and France returned to more conservative control.

In foreign affairs, the French remained wary of Germany. They questioned the League's ability to provide protection in case of another war. Furthermore, Britain and the United States refused to guarantee aid to France in the event of renewed German aggression. In response to this situation, France formed defensive alliances with some of the smaller European nations. Between 1924 and 1927, for example, France signed agreements with Czechoslovakia, Rumania, and Yugoslavia. In addition, she began building a series of fortifications, called the **Maginot Line,** along her border with Germany. These fortifications became France's main line of defense against any future German attack.

The United States

World War I had thrust the United States into a strong leadership role in world affairs. After the war, however, many Americans wanted to return to a policy of isolationism. Although Wilson advocated United States participation in world affairs through the League of Nations, the United States Senate twice refused to ratify the Versailles Treaty, which contained the League provisions. In 1920 Americans turned away from the idealism and internationalism of Wilson. They elected as president Warren G. Harding, who promised them a "return to normalcy." Harding's successor, Calvin Coolidge, continued to emphasize domestic well-being over foreign involvement. (This is what Harding meant by "normalcy.") Coolidge declared, "The business of the United States is business." By the end of the 1920s, conditions seemed to be so favorable that President Herbert Hoover stated in his inaugural speech in 1929, "I have no fears for the future of our country. It is bright with hope."

The Great Depression

On the surface, all seemed to be going well in the United States. New technology enabled factories to mass-produce large amounts of consumer goods. People were enjoying more leisure time. But under the surface of this period known as the "Roaring Twenties," there was great decay in the moral life of the nation. By the end of the decade, this was readily apparent. One of the characters in John Steinbeck's novel *The Grapes of Wrath* summed up the popular moral attitude of the day:

> There ain't no sin and there ain't no virtue, there's just stuff people do. . . . Some of the things folks do is nice and some ain't nice, but that's as far as any man got a right to say.

Heavy advertising as well as credit purchases helped to weaken old ideas about thrift. America was fast becoming a nation in which the rush for wealth and pleasure was the most important pursuit in life. In 1929 the seeming prosperity of the 1920s came to a sudden end. The collapse of the stock market in October triggered a drop in prices, a decline in foreign trade, the closing of factories, the failure of banks, and a dramatic rise in unemployment. Unemployed workers receiving food in bread lines and soup lines became a common sight in many American cities. It is estimated that by the winter of 1932-33, thirteen to seventeen million people were unemployed (approximately one-third of the work force). Though the crash occurred only a few months into his presidency, Herbert Hoover received most of the blame for America's economic woes. Looking for a solution to their problems, the American people elected **Franklin D. Roosevelt** (1882-1945) to the presidency in 1932.

The New Deal

After his inauguration, Roosevelt immediately began to promote his program of relief, recovery, and reform under the name of the **New Deal.** Job programs such as those connected with the Works Progress Administration sought to provide immediate relief for the millions of unemployed. Other organizations, such as the Agricultural Adjustment Administration, were designed to meet long-term goals. Roosevelt promoted many changes, hoping to end the threat of another depression and at the same time provide financial security for Americans. The Securities and Exchange Commission was established to regulate stock exchanges, and Congress passed the Social Security Act (1935).

Relief, Recovery, and Reform

Roosevelt's New Deal included programs designed to provide relief, stimulate recovery, and institute reforms. Listed below are several of the organizations that came into existence as part of the New Deal.

Relief

(1) Civilian Conservation Corps (CCC)—provided employment for young men in the field of conservation (for example, tree planting and dam building).

(2) Home Owners Loan Corporation (HOLC)—provided money at low interest rates in an effort to help people continue paying on their mortgages.

(3) Works Progress Administration (WPA)—participants built or remodeled buildings such as hospitals and schools. The program provided funds for cultural activities as well as for financial aid to students.

Recovery

(1) Agricultural Adjustment Administration (AAA)—urged farmers to cut production in order to raise the price of farm products. The government provided subsidies to those farmers who participated in the program.

(2) National Recovery Administration (NRA)—set guidelines for wages, prices, and production in various industries.

Franklin Roosevelt and his wife, Eleanor

(3) Public Works Administration (PWA)—provided work building such things as courthouses, sewage plants, and bridges.

Reform

(1) Federal Deposit Insurance Corporation (FDIC)—insured bank deposits.

(2) Securities and Exchange Commission (SEC)—provided the means by which the government regulated stock exchanges.

Historians, economists, and politicians have debated the value of the programs of the New Deal. No one doubts that Roosevelt's policies dramatically affected the United States. The key question is whether the effect has been positive or negative. In retrospect, the New Deal may have done more harm than good. It provided temporary relief for many Americans but failed to end the depression and provide any real economic recovery. In addition, Roosevelt's policies, which were often ill-planned and experimental, increased government spending and the power of the federal **bureaucracy** (the nonelected officials who handle government affairs). This led to increased government involvement in economic and social matters, accelerating the trend in the United States toward a welfare state.

Section Review

1. List six possessions of Great Britain that were given self-rule or complete independence after World War I.

2. What factor contributed to the political instability within the Third French Republic following the war?

3. What was the name of the French line of defense that protected her border from Switzerland to Belgium?

4. Who was the president of the U.S. who sought to promote relief, recovery, and reform to get the country out of the Great Depression? What was the name given to his programs?

5. What are the nonelected officials who handle government affairs called?

Rise of Totalitarian Dictatorships

In times of hardship and unrest, people often rely on strong leaders to solve their problems. The psalmist warns against such folly: "It is better to trust in the Lord than to put confidence in man" (Ps. 118:8). Nevertheless, as Europe struggled to overcome the postwar problems, dictatorial governments became more and more common. Many Europeans supported ambitious men in their quest for power. They hoped that these men would bring economic and political stability to their countries. But they soon realized that "confidence in an unfaithful [deceitful] man in time of trouble is like a broken tooth, and a foot out of joint" (Prov. 25:19).

Once in power, these dictators established **totalitarian states**. Although no two totalitarian states were exactly alike, they did share several general characteristics:

1. The use of propaganda to promote the ideas and programs of the state.
2. The use of an efficient secret police to arrest or assassinate those who opposed the state and its policies.
3. Emphasis upon the goals of the state rather than upon individual rights or concerns.
4. State control of every aspect of life—political, economic, cultural, educational, and religious.
5. A government maintained by force and not accountable to the people for its actions.
6. A one-party political system led by a powerful dictator.

All across Europe, in both old established countries and newly created nations, dictators came to power. In Portugal, for example, Antonio de Oliveira Salazar became dictator, and in Spain following a bloody civil war, Francisco Franco gained control of the government. In Turkey, Mustafha Kemal (keh MAHL), a champion of Turkish nationalism, established himself as dictator. But it was under dictators in Russia, Italy, and Germany that totalitarianism assumed its most terrible forms between the world wars.

Communism in Russia

Collapse of Czarist Russia

The reforms of Czar Alexander II came to an end with his assassination in 1881 (see p. 434). His successor, **Alexander III** (1881-94), attempted to suppress revolutionary ideas and activities. He ordered the state police and courts to intensify their efforts and demanded a strict censorship of the press. In addition, he persecuted various minority national groups such as the Poles and the Finns. He wanted to force them to become "Russian" in language, religion, and attitude. He also supported organized government massacres called **pogroms,** which killed thousands of Jews living in Russia.

The harsh policies of Alexander III were continued under his son **Nicholas II** (1894-1917). During his reign popular discontent burst into revolutionary activity. Radicals and liberals of all kinds organized themselves into political parties; one of the most radical was the Social Democratic party (1898). To escape arrest and imprisonment, some of its members fled to Switzerland. There they carried

Nicholas II

on their work, awaiting an opportunity to return to Russia. But philosophical differences within the party caused a small group called the **Bolsheviks** to break away from the larger, more moderate group known as the **Mensheviks.** The Bolsheviks advocated change through violence; the Mensheviks desired change through more peaceful measures.

Prelude to Revolution—For a while Nicholas II was able to maintain the authority and stability of the government. But disasters in the **Russo-Japanese War** (1904-5) brought popular discontent to the surface. Russian expansion in the Far East during the late nineteenth century had clashed with Japanese expansionist interest, leading to open hostility. Fighting broke out, but the war was rather short— poor organization, incompetence, and low morale among the Russian troops helped Japan gain several important victories. At the urging of American President Theodore Roosevelt, a humiliated and shaken Russian government met with Japanese leaders and signed the Treaty of Portsmouth. Russia surrendered both territory and economic advantages in the Far East to Japan.

The most dramatic illustration of popular discontent during the war was a workers' march to the czar's winter palace in St. Petersburg. On January 22, 1905, a peaceful procession of two hundred thousand singing men, women, and children moved toward the palace. They carried a petition calling upon Nicholas II to improve the lot of the workers, convene a National Assembly, and order elections in which all the people could vote. But the marchers never saw the czar; instead, government soldiers met the unarmed marchers and opened fire, killing scores of people and wounding many more. The horrifying events of this day, known as **Bloody Sunday,** turned the loyalty of many Russians away from the czar. They began to look elsewhere for an answer to their suffering.

In the following months, unrest and disorder increased as peasant uprisings, strikes in the factories, and mutinies among the armed forces spread throughout the country. In October a strike that began among railway workers triggered strikes in all areas of the economy. In order to better direct and maintain the general strike, the workers in St. Petersburg organized themselves into a **soviet** (council). Groups of workers

in other cities soon followed their example. After a few days, the czar's government yielded to the strikers. Nicholas issued the October Manifesto, promising a constitutional government with free speech as well as a national assembly, called the **Duma,** to be elected by the people.

St. Petersburg

Like some other cities, the city of St. Petersburg has had more than one name during its history. The city was founded in 1703 when Peter the Great built the Fortress of St. Peter and St. Paul to protect his newly conquered Baltic territories. The city itself was called St. Petersburg because it was a German name which reflected Peter the Great's interest in the West. When war broke out with the Germans in 1914, the Russians renamed the city Petrograd—the Russian equivalent of Petersburg. After Lenin's death in 1924, the Communists renamed it Leningrad in his honor. But with the breakup of the former Soviet Union, the people of the city once again named it St. Petersburg.

Outbreak of Revolution—In the next several years, however, the czar sought to restrict the powers of the Duma. At the same time he promoted various social reforms. Economic expansion and industrialism resumed, but local strikes and other symptoms of unrest continued. Dissatisfaction with the czar's government remained strong, and the hardships and suffering of World War I stirred that discontent into revolutionary action.

The Russian people at first seemed to support the war. But early disastrous defeats (see p. 507) caused serious morale problems. Poor planning created food shortages in the cities, and heavy casualties among the soldiers weakened Russia's ability to continue fighting. To try to save the military situation, Nicholas II personally took command of the troops, leaving the empress at home under the evil influence of the monk **Rasputin.** Rasputin was a religious fraud who won the favor of the empress when it appeared that he had healed her son of a blood disorder. He became an adviser to the royal family, but his greedy desires and corrupt influence only further weakened the czar's government. With

Nicholas gone from the capital, the political situation rapidly deteriorated. Several Russian nobles murdered Rasputin, hoping that their action would restore public confidence in the government; but even this did not accomplish their purpose.

On March 8, 1917, the people's anger and frustration could be contained no longer. Strikes and riots broke out in the capital of St. Petersburg. As chaos gripped the city, the troops which had been ordered to quell the disturbances joined with the strikers. News of the uprisings quickly spread throughout the country, and in city after city, workers overthrew local authorities and organized revolutionary soviets. In St. Petersburg, Nicholas disbanded the Duma, but its members ignored his order and established a provisional government. Four days later on March 15, Nicholas II abdicated, bringing to an end over three hundred years of Romanov rule.

In the months following the fall of the czar, a provisional government headed by the moderate (Menshevik) **Alexander Kerensky** tried its best to restore order. But the more radical Bolsheviks organized workers in opposition to this government. They sought an immediate end to the war and the implementation of radical social reforms. Worker opposition at home and the war abroad made the situation very difficult.

To make matters worse, the Germans, eager to knock the Russians out of the war, helped exiled Bolshevik leaders return to their homeland. The Germans hoped that these radical leaders would further disrupt Russia's internal affairs and thus disrupt Russia's war effort. Their plan succeeded.

Founding of the USSR

Bolsheviks Seize the Revolution—The leader of the Bolsheviks was **Nikolai Lenin** (1870-1924). Lenin was a brilliant young man who became involved in revolutionary activities while attending a Russian university. Through his study of Karl Marx, he became a dedicated member of the Social Democratic party and later assumed the leadership of the Bolshevik wing of that organization. Although a follower of Marxist teaching, Lenin differed from Marx on several points. Whereas Marx saw some possibility of a peaceful change from

Nikolai Lenin

capitalism to communism, Lenin believed in the absolute necessity of violent revolution. Marx believed that Communist revolution would occur in developed capitalist states from the spontaneous uprisings of the proletariat—the working class. Lenin, on the other hand, believed that a revolution would not occur unless directed by strong, determined leadership. Marx had also advocated the "dictatorship of the proletariat," the wide distribution of political power through a massive worker's organization. Lenin, however, limited real power to a small, dedicated band of revolutionaries, who would wield great power, supposedly in the public interest.

Assisted by the Germans in his return to Russia from Switzerland in April of 1917, Lenin rallied his followers in opposition to the provisional government. They championed such slogans as "All power to the soviets" and "Peace, land, and bread." For the downtrodden Russian people, the Bolsheviks seemed to offer hope for a brighter future. Urban labor organizations, which were more radical and better organized than any other group in Russian society, proved to be most susceptible to Bolshevik propaganda.

On the morning of November 7, 1917, Lenin's followers seized the government offices in St. Petersburg and arrested many of the leaders of the provisional government. With very little bloodshed, the Bolsheviks came to power, with Lenin as a virtual dictator.

There are several reasons for Lenin's success. The Russian people had not wholeheartedly supported the provisional government. This government wanted to continue the war against Germany. But most of the Russian people, including the soldiers, desired an immediate end to the fighting. Discipline was so low among the armed forces that those officers who might have opposed the Bolshevik takeover did not have the support of their troops. (In 1917 over two million soldiers deserted the army.) Besides wanting an end to the war, the peasants and industrial workers expected the provisional government to provide immediate solutions to Russia's economic problems. When the government failed to do so, many Russians turned to Lenin and the Bolsheviks.

Civil War Breaks Out—Once the Bolsheviks seized power, they faced serious problems of their own—the most serious of which was the war with Germany. Lenin realized that the Communists (the name Bolsheviks had adopted in 1918) could not consolidate their power and fight a war at the same time. Therefore, in 1918 they signed the Treaty of Brest-Litovsk, exchanging large amounts of Russian territory for peace. The Allies were angered that Russia had deserted the war effort and were disheartened by the radical change that had swept over Russia. They sent troops to several Russian ports in an effort to aid anti-Bolshevik groups in Russia.

For the next several years Russia suffered through a bloody civil war (1918-21) which raged throughout the entire country. Initially, the Communists seemed to be at a disadvantage; they lacked a strong, well-trained army. But through the efforts of **Leon Trotsky,** the Communists organized the so-called Red Army. Their opponents, known as the Whites, had the support of the Allies. Although the Whites won some notable victories, they were never able to coordinate their efforts. Also, many Russians feared that the Whites wished to restore the old order of the czar. In the end, the Communists retained their power.

Russia Becomes a Communist State—Within the first years of its existence, the new Communist state underwent several official changes. For example, in 1918 Lenin moved the Russian capital from St. Petersburg (or Petrograd) to Moscow because of the threat of advancing German armies. After the war Moscow remained the new capital and became the center of what was called the Russian

The Allied nations of World War I intervened in the Russian civil war to help the anti-Communist forces. Pictured here are Japanese troops in Vladivostok in 1921.

Union of Soviet Socialist Republics

Soviet Federated Socialist Republic (RSFSR). After the death of Lenin in 1924, the official name of the country became the Union of Soviet Socialist Republics **(USSR).** This new country was composed of fifteen republics. But the central government controlled virtually every aspect of the country, dominating the individual republics and leaving the people with no real voice in their government.

During the violent days of civil war, Lenin instituted a tightly regulated system of economic controls which he called **war communism.** In Lenin's words, it was "a frontal attack" on "the citadel of capitalism" designed to implement pure Marxist economic principles. Among other things, the government nationalized Russian industry (placed it under state ownership) and demanded that the peasants turn over all their surplus crops to the state for a set price. Forced labor and lack of incentives brought an already ailing economy to the point of collapse. For example, by 1920 the production of iron ore had dropped 98.4 per cent from its 1913 level; the manufacture of cotton goods had fallen 95 per cent. Overall, industrial production was only 13 per cent of what it had been in 1913. As signs

of deep resentment against the Communist system began mounting, the government abandoned its policy of war communism and in 1921 instituted the **New Economic Policy** (NEP).

The NEP, which lasted from 1921 to 1928, was nothing new at all. It was simply a temporary retreat from communism in order to rescue the Russian economy and to quiet growing anti-Communist sentiment within the country. Various aspects of capitalism, such as private trade and profit-making, became legal once again. By the time the program was ended, the Russian economy had significantly improved. Ironically, the capitalistic principles that Lenin vowed to destroy were used to save the Communist government and economy.

Strengthening of the USSR

When Lenin died in 1924 a power struggle developed between Leon Trotsky and **Joseph Stalin** (1879-1953). Trotsky was a brilliant and egotistical man known for his fiery speeches. Stalin, on the other hand, was a quiet, dependable yet ruthless, party man, little known outside the Soviet Union. By 1927 Stalin had established himself as the new dictator of the USSR. In the years before Lenin's death, Stalin had appointed many of his supporters to high government positions. After Lenin's death, he used his influence to force Trotsky and his supporters from the government.

Five-Year Plans—In 1928 Stalin ended the NEP and embarked on a series of programs called the **Five-Year Plans.** These programs, designed to build up industrial production and **collectivize** agriculture (bring under central government control), turned the country back toward socialism. The government established production goals for each industry. Although some of the heavy industries met the government's demands, many other industries did not. Manufactured products were always in short supply. Inefficient, bureaucratic mismanagement further illustrated the serious weaknesses in Communist economic theory.

Stalin's program to collectivize agriculture met with hostile resistance on the part of many peasants. The secret police and the army used whatever means were necessary—execution, deportation, or burning peasant homes—to force the peasants to comply with government demands. In desperation, peasants fought back; they burnt their crops and killed their livestock. Yet in the end, their resistance was crushed. The struggle was so severe that between 1928 and 1933 over half the homes in the Soviet Union had been destroyed. In addition, a severe famine struck the country during 1932 and 1933. This, along with the struggle over collectivization, led to the deaths of over five million people.

Stalin's Five-Year Plans had several other significant results. First, as economic depression hit the Western democratic countries in the 1930s, many of them followed the example of Stalin and turned to a planned economy. Many naive Western leaders, unaware of the failures of Stalin's program and the terrible cost in human life, marveled that a backward nation like Russia could make such apparent industrial progress. Second, the most significant result of what has been called Russia's Second Revolution was the ever-tightening grip of the state over the people. What little liberty the people may have had under Lenin rapidly disappeared under Stalin.

Reign of Terror—As we have seen, Stalin often resorted to violence and terror to force his will upon the Russian people. During the years 1936 to 1938, he turned upon his own Communist party. He was determined to wipe out anyone who might prove disloyal to his regime. To accomplish his goal, Stalin instituted a system of **purges** in which eight hundred thousand Communist party members were murdered, including many of the ruling elite. Even the military suffered, as Stalin ordered the execution of most of the army's top leaders as well as many of the lesser officers. These events created such fear in the Soviet Union that Stalin's power became more secure than it had ever been.

Because communism seeks to control every aspect of life, the Soviet state under both Lenin and Stalin made a strong effort to wipe out any form of Christianity within its territory. Within twenty years, the government had forced thousands of churches and schools to close and had killed many pastors and priests. The reason for such cruelty was the Soviet government's realization that Christian virtues were completely contrary to Communist ideas and goals. Their hatred for Christianity is well illustrated by these words of Lenin:

> Every religious idea, every idea of God, even flirting with the idea of God, is unutterable vileness . . . vileness of the most dangerous kind, "contagion" of the most abominable kind. Millions of sins, filthy deeds, acts of violence and physical contagions . . . are far less dangerous than the subtle, spiritual idea of a God decked out in the smartest "ideological" costumes.[1]

Lenin and Stalin

The Soviet Union's first two Communist dictators—Nikolai Lenin and Joseph Stalin—were not actually named Lenin and Stalin. In 1901 Vladimir Ilyich Ulyanov took the name Lenin in an effort to confuse the Russian police. (The name may come from the Lena River in Siberia.) Joseph Stalin, Russia's next dictator, was really named Iosif Vissarionovich Dzhugashvili. In his early writings he used several pseudonyms, but his favorite was Stalin ("man of steel"). After 1913 he called himself Stalin on a regular basis.

Peter Vins: "Choosing Rather to Suffer Affliction"

The suffering of Soviet Christians at the hands of their Communist government is well illustrated by the life of Russian Baptist pastor Peter Vins. He was born in 1898 into the family of Jacob Vins (or Wiens), a pastor among the Mennonites and Baptists in Russia. Persecuted by the czarist government, Jacob went into voluntary exile in North America in 1911, and his family joined him the following year. In 1919, after the Bolshevik Revolution, Jacob Vins returned to his homeland. Peter remained in the United States to attend seminary and prepare for the ministry. In 1926 he joined his father as an "American missionary" holding American citizenship.

In the years immediately following the Bolshevik Revolution, there was a surprisingly large amount of religious freedom in Russia (or the Soviet Union, as it came to be called). Different factions were fighting for control of the country, and even the Communists allowed some liberty in order to win supporters to their side. Jacob Vins began his ministry in 1919, for example, in a section of eastern Russia that was temporarily occupied by the Japanese.

Lenin had written, "We require that religion should be a private matter as far as the state is concerned. The state must have nothing to do with religion. . . . Religious and church societies must be completely free unions of like-minded citizens independent of the authorities."[2] Al-

though the atheistic Lenin found it convenient to accommodate religion for a while, his successor Joseph Stalin moved ruthlessly to transform the Soviet Union into a religionless state. When persecution broke out, Christians with foreign citizenship had the choice of leaving or becoming Soviet citizens. Peter, now with a wife and son, chose to give up his American citizenship and remain.

Peter Vins was able to minister to the Russian people only two years before he was arrested and sentenced to three years in a labor camp. After his release in 1933, he moved to the city of Omsk. With meetings for worship forbidden, he sought to encourage believers privately in their homes. He knew it was only a matter of time before he was arrested again. He and his wife sewed parts of the Bible into his clothing so that he would have the Scriptures with him when he returned to prison.

In 1936 Peter Vins was arrested, served ten months, was released, and then arrested again in 1937. This time he received a ten-year sentence for "anti-Soviet" views. He was denied visitors. Instead, his wife and young son would come to the street outside the prison, where they could look at him through the barred windows. The prison authorities, disliking even this distant contact between prisoners and their families, began building boxes around the windows. These boxes allowed light in from the top but did not permit anyone to see in or out. Each time Peter's family visited, they saw the boxes getting closer to his window. Finally, his window was covered. Only years later did his wife learn that he had been sent to a prison camp, where he died in 1943.

Appropriately, Peter Vins's favorite passage from Scripture was Hebrews 11:24-26—"By faith Moses, when he was come to years, refused to be called the son of Pharaoh's daughter; choosing rather to suffer affliction with the people of God, than to enjoy the pleasures of sin for a season; esteeming the reproach of Christ greater riches than the treasures in Egypt." As Vins's son later wrote, "He had a profound understanding of the Biblical truth that it is better to suffer with God's people, to bear the vilification of Christ, than to have transient sinful enjoyment and earthly treasures."[3]

Foreign Policy—After the Bolshevik revolution, Lenin believed that Communist revolutions would soon sweep across Europe. To further his goal, he established the "Communist International," commonly called the **Comintern.** Its purpose was to found Communist parties in other countries and to take an active role in stirring up discontent in hopes of producing revolution.

Under Stalin, Soviet foreign policy shifted away from the open radicalism of its early years. Stalin, like Lenin, hoped to see communism spread throughout the world; unlike Lenin, however, he believed that the most important thing for the Soviet Union was first to build up communism at home. Once that was accomplished, the USSR could then take a more active role in promoting world revolution. Despite the fact that the Soviet Union had openly declared its intention to destroy Western democratic governments, many Western nations gave diplomatic recognition to the Soviet government. By the end of 1924, Britain, France, and Italy, among others, had granted such recognition. In 1933 the United States followed their example, officially recognizing the Soviet Union as well as establishing trade relations.

Joseph Stalin

Fascism in Italy and Germany

After the rise of communism in Russia, a new type of totalitarian government called **fascism** (FASH IZ um) came to power in Italy and Germany. (German fascism is usually called **nazism.**) Many of the citizens in those countries had grown discouraged with representative government; yet they feared communism. Fascism seemed to provide an attractive alternative because it promised stability and security.

In theory communism and fascism differ:
1. Under fascism businesses are privately owned but rigorously controlled by the government. (A fascist economy is often referred to as a corporate economy.) Under communism, the government both owns and controls business.
2. Fascism is highly nationalistic; communism ideally seeks a classless, international society.
3. A military dictatorship usually openly governs a fascist state; communism deceptively emphasizes the "dictatorship of the proletariat."
4. Fascism glorifies the state; communism teaches that the state will gradually wither away.

Despite the theoretical differences between communism and fascism, there is little difference in the everyday life of people living under these forms of governments. Both firmly control the people and greatly restrict their liberty.

Mussolini in Italy

Italy entered the postwar era a disappointed and dispirited nation. In spite of her sacrifices in the Great War—including the loss of five hundred thousand men—she gained very little in return except additional problems. While Britain and France received former German and Turkish territory as mandates, Italy received none. Furthermore, Italy's borders were not expanded as she believed they should be (because of her support for the Allies). On the economic front, strikes, inflation, and debt plagued the Italian economy. In the political arena small party factions created disunity and hindered government action.

In the midst of this turmoil and confusion, the Italian people became increasingly disenchanted with the direction in which Italy was heading. Wealthy landowners and industrialists, fearful of a

Communist revolution, wanted protection for their businesses and property. Returning war veterans found that jobs were in short supply and that few Italians appreciated their wartime services. Strong nationalists wanted Italy to become a great military power, to expand her borders, and to acquire additional colonies. The man who seemed to draw these groups together was **Benito Mussolini** (1883-1945).

Mussolini and the Fascist Party—Mussolini, the son of a blacksmith, became a well-known Socialist while still in his twenties. He wrote for several Socialist newspapers. But his violent articles incurred the wrath of the authorities, and on several occasions he was thrown into jail. He soon fell out of favor with the Socialists because he supported Italy's entrance into World War I. His political career, however, did not end. In 1921 Mussolini

ssolini addressing a rally of his followers

helped to organize the Fascist party. This party took as its emblem the symbol of authority in ancient Rome called the *fasces;* hence the name *Fascists.*

Most Italians were not Fascists, but they were tired of the unrest and trouble caused by labor unions and Socialist political groups. Mussolini seemed to offer some promise of stability and order. He decided that the time was ripe to seize power. In October 1922 thousands of his followers marched on Rome and demanded that King Victor Emmanuel III appoint Mussolini premier of Italy. The king, believing he had no other choice, agreed to the Fascists' demands, and Mussolini became the new leader of Italy.

Mussolini and the Fascist State—Once in power, Mussolini slowly turned Italy into a totalitarian state. He established his authority by appointing Fascists to numerous government posts. By the end of 1925, he had manipulated the political process so completely that he had a firm grasp on the affairs of the state. Mussolini was now a dictator, but he maintained the appearance of a representative government just as Octavian had done almost two thousand years earlier (see pp. 95-96).

In Fascist Italy, as in Communist Russia, the party was the real source of political power. Fascist political organizations began on the local level and provided the basis for a highly structured organization that culminated in the Fascist Grand Council. In theory this group of approximately twenty individuals ran the Italian government. The final authority, however, lay in the hands of *Il Duce* ("leader" or "commander")—a title Mussolini used for himself.

One of Mussolini's major goals was to make Italy economically self-sufficient. He wanted Italy to be able to produce everything she needed, including manufactured goods and foodstuffs. In order to achieve this program of **autarky,** as it was called, he organized Italy's entire work force into thirteen groups or **syndicates.** Each syndicate represented a different division of the work force. Under the watchful eye of the government, these syndicates established business policies, wages, prices, and working conditions.

Unlike Stalin or Hitler, Mussolini had no clearly defined political program. As did most dictators, he suppressed freedom of speech, freedom of the press, and opposing political parties. Nevertheless, Mussolini's own political philosophy was rather vague. A member of his government gave this explanation of fascism:

> We all participate in a sort of mystic sentiment, [in which] we do not form clear and distinct ideas, nor can we put into precise words the things we believe in. . . . The Fascist spirit is will, not intellect.[4]

As dictator, Mussolini enacted a popular series of agreements known as the **Lateran Treaties** with the Roman Catholic church. Since 1870 relations between the Roman church and the Italian state had been strained. The state had taken territory that for centuries had belonged to the papacy. With the unification of Italy, that territory became part of the Italian state. In retaliation, the Roman church had refused to recognize or cooperate with the new state. For nearly sixty years successive popes remained isolated in the Vatican. In 1929, after lengthy negotiations, Mussolini and the Roman Catholic church finally reached an agreement. The pope agreed to recognize the Italian government and renounce all territorial claims. In return the government granted the pope a large sum of money. In addition, they established a small independent state known as Vatican City and placed it under the pope's control. The provisions of this treaty remain in effect today.

Hitler in Germany

As World War I was coming to an end, the German kaiser, William II, abdicated his throne. Spontaneous revolutions had broken out throughout the country, forcing him to flee to Holland. In place of the vacated monarchy, the German people organized a republic. In 1919 delegates from around Germany assembled in the town of Weimar and drew up a constitution for the young republic. Among other things, the new constitution granted the German people the right to freely elect representatives to the **Reichstag** and to elect a president to a seven-year term. The president appointed a chancellor from the strongest political party in the Reichstag. In turn the chancellor selected people to fill the

Adolf Hitler

various cabinet posts of the government. In addition, the constitution guaranteed the German people a number of basic freedoms, including the freedom of speech, press, and religion.

In spite of its promising start, the **Weimar Republic** had serious weaknesses. Many Germans did not support the republic; they were apathetic toward government in general. In addition, the German people had no experience in running a republic, nor did they have a strong traditional attachment to its ideals. Furthermore, numerous political parties made it difficult for the government to function effectively because no party ever won a majority in the national elections. These weaknesses helped prepare the way for the rise to power of one of the most murderous and tyrannical dictators of modern history, **Adolf Hitler** (1889-1945).

Hitler and the Nazi Party—As a young man Adolf Hitler had shown little promise of ever succeeding at anything. When his hopes of becoming an artist or architect ended in failure, he wandered about the city of Vienna, barely making a living. At the outbreak of World War I, however, he entered the German army and served honorably. After the war Hitler came in contact with a small political organization that soon became known as the National Socialist German Workers' party, or Nazi party. Finding many of its ideas to his liking, he promptly joined the group in 1920; a year later, he became its leader.

In 1923 Hitler led an uprising in the city of Munich, attempting to overthrow the government. Popular support was not behind him, however, and the revolt quickly subsided. The government arrested the leaders of the revolt, and the courts sentenced Hitler and several others to prison. Hitler, who served less than a year of his five-year sentence, did not remain idle while in prison. He wrote a book entitled *Mein Kampf* ("My Struggle"). In this work he attacked the Weimar Republic, blamed the Jews for Germany's problems, and demanded the renunciation of the Versailles Treaty. He also proclaimed that the Germanic peoples were a "master race" called the Aryans. Once out of prison, Hitler continued to spread these ideas in public speeches, and before long, large numbers of Germans began to listen to him.

Hitler's Rise to Power—The reasons for Hitler's amazing rise to power are varied. First, as we have seen, the Weimar Republic was rather weak and inefficient. The Nazis realized this fact and exploited the political weakness for their own purposes. Second, the Nazis seized upon the anger that many Germans felt toward the "war guilt" clause of the Versailles Treaty; they used every opportunity to condemn this agreement. Third, economic problems, especially inflation and unemployment, caused many to listen to the Nazi promises of economic recovery. Fourth, Hitler and the Nazis were violently anti-Communist, a position which pleased those Germans worried about their wealth. Finally,

German troops use a borrowed British tank to put down a Communist uprising in Berlin (January 1919).

The Collapse of the German Mark

After World War I Germany had severe economic problems. Not only were government expenditures high, but Germany also had a huge debt resulting from the war. One indication of the country's plight was the high rate of inflation. During World War I prices had risen about 100 per cent, but in the early 1920s inflation increased at an even more alarming rate.

When French troops invaded the Ruhr Valley in 1923, many Germans in that region went on strike. In an effort to support the strikers while they were unemployed, the government began printing large amounts of paper money. Consequently, inflation skyrocketed, bringing about the collapse of the German mark (the German monetary unit similar to the American dollar).

As inflation climbed in 1923, over three hundred paper mills and two thousand printing establishments worked twenty-four hours a day to supply the necessary paper money. By August of 1923 the government was printing 46 billion marks per day. In light of the worsening conditions, employers began paying their employees twice a day and allowing them time off from work to rush to the stores and buy what they needed before prices rose again. Restaurants did not even price items on their menus. The restaurant figured a customer's bill when he was ready to leave, since the value of the mark might have declined from the time he had sat down at a table.

The following example may help illustrate the devastating nature of German inflation. In 1914 if someone possessed 100,000 marks, he could have exchanged them for nearly 24,000 American dollars. In November of 1923 that same 100,000 marks would have been worth only a minute fraction of a cent—$.00000024.

Finally, the German government abolished the old currency and instituted a new mark—the Rentenmark. People with the old currency could trade in one trillion of their old marks for the new Rentenmark. As a result of such terrible inflation, many Germans lost their savings and their confidence in the Weimar Republic. As they searched for answers to their country's problems, many people began to listen to a man by the name of Adolf Hitler, who promised a new and better Germany.

Date		Number of marks equal to one dollar (monthly average)
July	1914	4.2
Jan.	1919	8.9
Jan.	1921	64.9
Jan.	1922	191.8
July	1922	493.2
Jan.	1923	17,972
July	1923	353,412
Aug.	1923	4,620,455
Sept.	1923	98,860,000
Oct.	1923	25,260,208,000
Nov.	15, 1923	4,200,000,000,000

Hitler's personal leadership and his brilliant use of propaganda techniques drew people to the Nazi party who otherwise would have had little use for the organization.

As economic problems became more severe after 1930 because of worldwide depression, the Nazis steadily increased in strength and numbers. After each election, the number of Nazis in the Reichstag grew, until by July of 1932 they were the largest party in the German republic (although not a majority). Since they had won such a large number of seats, the president of the republic, **Paul von Hindenburg,** asked Hitler to join in a coalition government as vice-chancellor, but Hitler refused.

Since no party held a majority of seats, this refusal made it difficult to form a government. New elections had to be held in November. When the results were in, the Nazis received two million fewer votes than they had received in the July elections. In addition, they lost thirty-four seats in the Reichstag. In spite of the apparent decline in Nazi strength, Hitler demanded the position of chancellor. Hindenburg, who saw no other way out of the political impasse, appointed Adolf Hitler chancellor of Germany on January 30, 1933.

Hitler now realized that the power he craved was within reach. New elections would be held in

Paul von Hindenburg

lished the so-called Third Reich—an empire that he said would last for a thousand years.

Germany Under Nazi Rule—Once in power, Hitler began to manifest clearly the racist beliefs of Nazi ideology. In his work, *Mein Kampf*, Hitler had violently blamed the Jews for causing Germany's defeat in the First World War. He accused them of corrupting the pure Aryan race and plotting to rule the world. ''The wretched Jew,'' said Hitler, is the ''enemy of the human race'' and the ''cause of all our miseries.'' Within months after coming to power, the Nazis turned this hatred of Jews into action. Jews were deprived of citizenship and were forbidden to marry other Germans. Many of their businesses were destroyed and before long many were sent to concentration camps and ruthlessly exterminated.

Other groups also came under Nazi persecution. Hitler attempted to close all church-run schools. The secret police, known as the **Gestapo,** arrested pastors who opposed the state. To the Nazis, Christian virtues such as humility and gentleness encouraged a slave mentality and needed to be eliminated. Some German Protestants supported Hitler, however, and under Nazi sponsorship they organized what they called the German Christians. Their motto was ''The Swastika on our breasts, the Cross in our hearts.'' This group discarded most of the Bible since it was written by Jews. They allowed only Aryans to be members of their churches. They claimed that Christ was not really a Jew and that through His

March. In an effort to win a majority of the votes, the Nazis used propaganda, violence, and threats. The culmination of the entire election campaign occurred six days before the voting took place. A fire broke out in the Reichstag building, partially destroying it. The Nazis blamed the Communists and tried to whip up mass hysteria. (There was strong suspicion that the Nazis may have set the fire themselves.) When the election results came in, the Nazis found they had won only 44 per cent of the vote. Although they lacked a majority, the Nazis persuaded enough Reichstag members to pass the Enabling Act, which suspended the republic and made Hitler dictator of Germany. He estab-

Hitler was a powerful orator. To increase his effectiveness, he studied photographs of himself experimenting with various gestures. Hitler selected the most dramatic gestures for use in his speeches.

death He had preserved the world from Jewish domination. To them, Hitler was a second messiah destined to perfect the work that Jesus had begun. One German pastor said, "Christ has come to us through Adolf Hitler. . . . We know today the Saviour has come. . . . We have only one task, be German, not be Christian." As if the blasphemy of these so-called German Christians was not enough, some Nazis even abandoned all pretense of Christianity and openly promoted a return to the pagan idols of the ancient Germanic tribes.

A German honor guard at a Nazi rally in Nuremberg

Within the Nazi movement were two major organizations: the Storm Troopers (S.A.), or "Brown Shirts," and the Defense Detachments (S.S.), or "Black Shirts." The Storm Troopers, organized in the early days of the Nazi movement, fought against Communists and other opponents of the Nazi party in bloody street brawls. They staged massive propaganda demonstrations and guarded Nazi meetings. Through their strong-arm tactics they helped the Nazis acquire power, but their very strength made them a threat to Hitler. Therefore, in 1934, he ordered a party purge in which the

leaders of this group were killed and the organization itself was drastically reduced in power. The S.S., on the other hand, was an elite organization whose original function was to protect Hitler. Under Heinrich Himmler the organization grew in importance, especially after Hitler suppressed the Storm Troopers. The S.S. ran both the Gestapo and the concentration camps, and during World War II even organized itself into military units.

In the economic realm, Hitler advanced his Four-Year Plans. The first one, begun in 1933, sought to end unemployment through a massive rearmament program and the building of public works such as the famous *Autobahnen* (super highways). The *Autobahnen* was to provide a military highway through Germany in case it became necessary to fight another two-front war. The second Four-Year Plan attempted to make Germany economically self-sufficient so that in the event of war, Germany could not be hurt by a blockade. To accomplish these goals, the government outlawed strikes. In addition, all workers and employers came under the direction of the German Labor Front, which had the power to determine wages and settle labor disputes. To gain the cooperation of labor, the Nazis established the "Strength through Joy" movement, which provided vacations and entertainment at low cost. In these ways, Hitler successfully brought Germany under Nazi control, establishing a strong totalitarian state. It would not be long before he would attempt to expand the territory of his Third Reich (see the next chapter).

Section Review

1. Who was the last czar of Russia? In what year was his government overthrown?
2. What Communist leader instituted war communism? What Communist leader instituted a system of purges, eliminating all who were disloyal to his regime?
3. Who was the leader of the Fascist party in Italy? In what year did he come to power?
4. What was the name of the fascist party in Germany? Who became its leader?
5. Whom did Hitler call the "master race"? What people did Hitler blame for Germany's problems?

Era of Disillusionment

During the latter half of the nineteenth century, many artists and writers reacted against the impact of industrialism on society. They rejected conventional art forms and embraced new, experimental techniques. This reaction continued in the early twentieth century as the arts reflected the death and destruction of the war period. The devastation of war, economic depression, and moral decay led to feelings of despair. As this mood affected modern art and literature, artists and writers portrayed a pessimistic and disjointed view of man, his world, and the future.

Painting

Expressionism

In art, two of the better-known twentieth-century movements (or schools) are expressionism and cubism. In **expressionism** the artist tries to paint how he feels about his subject rather than trying to reproduce realistically what he sees. **Henri Matisse** (1869-1954), the best representative of this school, explained it this way: "What I am after,

above all, is expression. . . . I am unable to distinguish between the feeling I have for life and my way of expressing it."[5] Figures in expressionistic paintings are of secondary importance. Color is the real subject; it is through this medium that the artist can most graphically express his emotions. Bright colors, simplified designs, and clearly outlined figures are characteristic of Matisse's work.

Cubism

The second major artistic movement of this century is **cubism**. Its best representative is the Spanish-born **Pablo Picasso** (1881-1973). To a much greater degree than Matisse, Picasso abandoned the Renaissance ideal that what a painter sees in nature he should portray upon the canvas. Picasso believed that what we see may not be final reality; therefore, he contended that art that simply copied the visible world was useless. Instead, he often reduced his figures to various geometric shapes (hence the name cubism), which he portrayed from several different perspectives at once. His technique distorted the figures in his paintings.

Pablo Picasso, Still Life, *National Gallery of Art, Washington, D.C.*

His approach, however, was not as radical as that of a fellow cubist who said, "My aim is to create new objects which cannot be compared to any object in actuality." Picasso, as well as many other twentieth-century artists, deliberately tried to shock the viewer and challenge his perception of the world.

Architecture

During the twentieth century, architecture has undergone a drastic change. New building materials—concrete, glass, and steel—have revolutionized architectural design. In large cities, soaring steel and glass skyscrapers dominate the skyline. Since steel eliminates the need for heavy stone or brick walls to support a building, most architects try to convey a sense of openness through the extensive use of glass. In many ways modern architecture reflects the mechanized and urban society of the twentieth century.

Of the men who helped establish these modern architectural trends, three are especially noteworthy. **Louis Sullivan** (1856-1924) was an American architect who is credited with developing the skyscraper. His motto was "form ever follows function"; that is, the design of a building should match the purpose for which it is built. Excessive decoration is eliminated in order to achieve a clean, simple appearance. **Walter Gropius** (1883-1969), also a functionalist, helped to popularize this style in Europe. The American architect **Frank Lloyd Wright** (1868-1959) followed a variation on the functionalist approach. He believed that in order for form to follow function, he should design a building in a manner that would allow it to blend with its surroundings. One art historian comments that "Wright's dwellings . . . hug and adjust to the landscape, almost as if they were meant to be part of it and concealed by it."[6]

Music

Music in the twentieth century is extremely varied, encompassing everything from jazz (which reached its peak of popularity in the 1920s) to electronic music. As in all the art forms, radical experimentation increased after World War I as many composers abandoned traditional musical concepts. The Russian composer **Igor Stravinsky** (struh VIN skee; 1882-1971) and the Austrian **Arnold Schönberg** (SHURN behrg; 1874-1952) influenced modern musical trends. Stravinsky is sometimes considered the father of modern music. He developed a new musical theory known as **polytonality,** which he first put into practice in his famous orchestral work *The Rite of Spring*. In the past, composers had used only one musical key at a time; Stravinsky used several keys simultaneously. Arnold Schönberg, on the other hand, entirely abandoned all fixed tone patterns or keys and created what is called **atonal music.** Instead of using one

The Kaufmann House, located at Mill Run, Pennsylvania, is an example of Frank Lloyd Wright's architectural philosophy of blending structures with their surroundings. Called "Falling Water," the house sits perched over a waterfall and seems to be almost a natural feature of the landscape.

of the common eight-tone scales, Schönberg based his compositions on a twelve-tone scale, giving no special emphasis to any one tone.

In spite of several technical differences among modern composers, their music exhibits certain common characteristics—which also contrast markedly with the music of earlier eras. For example, the melody line often contains unusual intervals (jumps in pitch), and musical phrases are often nonsymmetrical (lacking balanced proportions). Odd and complex meters (the number of beats to a musical measure) become increasingly common and often change constantly throughout a musical composition. Likewise modern rhythms are often jarring and violent. In contrast to the harmony of earlier periods, modern music

T. S. Eliot

makes much greater use of dissonance (clashing tones). Composers during the twentieth century have also experimented with widely divergent musical styles, such as jazz and rock.

Literature

Like music, literature reflected the attitudes prevalent between the wars. For example, **T. S. Eliot** (1888-1965), in his complex poem "The Waste Land," tries to portray the desolation and meaninglessness of modern life. In his poem "The Hollow Men," Eliot replaces the cataclysmic view of the end of the world taught in Scripture (II Pet. 3:10, 12-13) with a bleak, feeble one: *"This is the way the world ends / Not with a bang but a whimper."* Another author, the German novelist **Thomas Mann** (1875-1955), presents his central characters as passive figures, victimized by the uncontrollable forces that surround them. Much of the literature of the first half of the twentieth century is filled with hopelessness, pessimism, and pacifism. Many writers rejected the concept that literature should teach moral lessons. The techniques they used also dem-

Igor Stravinsky

onstrated a break with the past. Modern poetry, for example, often lacks a rhyme scheme and a regular rhythm pattern. In addition, some prose writers and poets tend to be deliberately obscure. This is illustrated by the work of the novelist **James Joyce** (1882-1941), who developed the so-called stream-of-consciousness technique in which the reader is forced to decipher the fragmented and often rambling thoughts of the major character. Despite their diverse forms and styles, all of the artists—painters, composers, and writers—united in portraying a world that was hopeless, barren, and dehumanizing.

Section Review

1. What are two well-known movements, or schools, of painting in the twentieth century?
2. Identify three noteworthy architects who helped establish modern architectural trends.
3. What is the name for the musical theory that uses several keys simultaneously? Who developed this modern musical style?
4. What poet sought to describe the desolation and meaninglessness of life prevalent between the world wars? What was the name of his major work?

A Glimpse Behind and a Glimpse Ahead

Many people during the post–World War I era realized the vanity of life. They had sought security by trusting in human leaders, but many of these leaders became great oppressors, depriving them of their security. Some sought satisfaction through material prosperity, but the Great Depression demonstrated the fleeting nature of this world's riches. Still others sought enjoyment from earthly pleasures but found that sinful pleasure cannot satisfy the longing for peace in their souls. As a result, feelings of discontent, despair, and pessimism abounded. Many people regarded life as vain. They could readily agree with the writer of Ecclesiastes that "all is vanity." "So I returned," wrote King Solomon, "and considered all the oppressions that are done under the sun: and behold the tears of such as were oppressed, and they had no comforter; and on the side of their oppressors there was power; but they had no comforter" (Eccles. 4:1). God's Word aptly describes the plight of modern man, but it also has the answer to man's hopelessness and disillusionment:

Behold, thou hast made my days as an handbreadth; and mine age is as nothing before thee: verily every man at his best state is altogether vanity. Surely every man walketh in a vain shew: surely they are disquieted in vain: he heapeth up riches, and knoweth not who shall gather them. And now, Lord, what wait I for? *my hope is in thee.*

—Psalm 39:5-7

Chapter Review

Can You Explain?

dole
bureaucracy
totalitarian states
pogroms
soviet
Duma

war communism
New Economic Policy
collectivize
purges
fascism
nazism

Il Duce
autarky
syndicates
Reichstag
Autobahnen
expressionism

cubism
polytonality
atonal music

Can You Identify?

Ramsay MacDonald
Statute of Westminster
Léon Blum
Maginot Line
October 1929
Franklin D. Roosevelt
New Deal
Alexander III
Nicholas II
Bolsheviks

Mensheviks
Russo-Japanese War
Bloody Sunday
Rasputin
Alexander Kerensky
Nikolai Lenin
Leon Trotsky
USSR
Joseph Stalin
Five-Year Plans

Comintern
Benito Mussolini
Lateran Treaties
Weimar Republic
Adolf Hitler
Mein Kampf
Paul von Hindenburg
Gestapo
Henri Matisse
Pablo Picasso

Louis Sullivan
Walter Gropius
Frank Lloyd Wright
Igor Stravinsky
Arnold Schönberg
T. S. Eliot
Thomas Mann
James Joyce

How Much Do You Remember?

1. How did Britain, France, and the United States cope with their economic problems after World War I?
2. List six characteristics shared by totalitarian states.
3. List four ways in which communism and fascism differ—at least in theory.
4. List five factors that assisted Hitler's amazing rise to power in Germany.
5. How was the Era of Disillusionment reflected in the arts?

What Do You Think?

1. "The only thing necessary for the triumph of evil is for good men to do nothing." How does Matthew 5:13-16 relate to this statement?
2. What are the dangers of a welfare state?
3. During difficult times, people want immediate solutions to their problems. Such "solutions," however, often bring harm rather than good. What situations among the leading democratic nations following the war illustrate this principle?
4. How did Lenin's economic policy of war communism affect Russia? Why do you think it was a failure?

Notes

1. Robert Conquest, ed., *Religion in the U.S.S.R.* (New York: Praeger, 1968), p. 7.
2. Georgi Vins, *Testament from Prison*, trans. Jane Ellis (Elgin, Ill.: David C. Cook Publishing Co., 1975), p. 7.
3. Ibid., pp. 33-34.
4. Gordon A. Craig, *Europe Since 1914*, 3rd ed. (Hinsdale, Ill.: Dryden Press, 1972), p. 550.
5. Robert Goldwater and Marco Treves, ed., *Artists on Art* (New York: Pantheon, 1945), p. 409.
6. Helen Gardner, et al., *Art Through the Ages*, 5th ed. (New York: Harcourt, Brace & World, 1970), pp. 740-41.

The Second World War

Despite the fact that World War I was called "the war to end war," it was not long before the nations of the world faced an even more devastating conflict—World War II. For two decades people had relied on the vague promises of peace made by world leaders. They had trusted in ineffective treaties and organizations. But as in the days of the prophet Jeremiah, people were crying, "Peace, peace; when there [was] no peace" (Jer. 6:14). Had they been alert, they could have seen the signs of approaching war. Power-thirsty dictators were on the march, building large armies and stockpiling weapons. By the time the rest of the world realized the danger, it was too late to avert the outbreak of a war that was truly a "world war."

Global Tension

Dictators Defy the League of Nations

After World War I, world leaders met to organize the League of Nations. They hoped that this organization would thwart any new military aggression and thus maintain world peace and security. But during the 1930s the military-minded governments of Italy, Germany, and Japan began to threaten world peace. For Mussolini in Italy, Hitler in Germany, and the military rulers of Japan, war became an accepted and legitimate means of achieving their personal and national goals. Although the League of Nations made several feeble attempts to stop their military aggression, its system of collective security was a complete failure.

Japanese Expansion in Asia

Japan entered the twentieth century as a greatly transformed country. During the Meiji Period (see p. 486), Japan had thrown off centuries-old feudalistic customs and had adopted many modern ways. Her new industrial and military might enabled her to win decisive victories over the much larger countries of China and Russia. In the years prior to World War I, Japan continued to develop her industry and modernize her military forces. When World War I broke out, Japan joined the side of the Allies. In spite of her limited role, she emerged from the war as a major world power.

After World War I, civilian officials controlled the Japanese government. They followed a more restrained and conciliatory policy than Japan was accustomed to. In 1922 the Japanese leaders signed the Nine Power Treaty, agreeing with other major powers to respect the sovereignty and territory of China. Japan also joined and participated in the activities of the League of Nations. But by the end of the decade, a spirit of militarism had gripped the country. Japanese military leaders believed that Japan should take advantage of her position of strength and extend her influence in the Pacific. They sought to use Japan's military might to create a "new order" in Asia. When Japan's civilian government collapsed in the 1930s, a military **clique** (an exclusive, elite group) assumed control of the government. Under this military leadership, Japan actively embarked on a program of territorial expansion.

Chinese Weakness—Japan carried out her expansionist policy at the expense of China. China lacked a strong central government and was seething with internal political turmoil. In 1911 there had been a revolt against the ruling Manchu dynasty. Within four months the Manchu had fallen from power and a Chinese republic was proclaimed. **Sun Yat-sen** the organizer of the Kuomintang (KWOH min TAHNG), or Nationalist party, led the revolt. In order to give direction to this new party, Sun enunciated what he called the Three Principles of the People: nationalism, democracy, and social progress. But Sun never gained the support he needed to establish a stable government. Years of anarchy ensued as local leaders known as warlords fought one another for political power.

After the death of Sun Yat-sen, **Chiang Kai-shek** (CHANG KYE-SHEK; 1887-1975) took control of

Opposite Page: American dive bombers attack the Japanese fleet during the Battle of Midway

Chiang Kai-shek

troops seized the entire province of Manchuria, which had been under nominal Chinese control. The Chinese government protested the Japanese action to the League of Nations. But the League did little except to pass several resolutions urging Japan and China to settle their differences through negotiations. In the end, Japan refused to withdraw from Manchuria but withdrew from the League of Nations instead.

Realizing that Japan was a continuing threat to China, the Communists under Mao and the Nationalists under Chiang called a truce to their civil war and united their efforts to defeat the Japanese. But even a united Chinese front could not withstand Japan's full-scale invasion of China, which began in 1937. The Japanese captured several major Chinese cities as well as most of China's valuable economic resources. Although the League of Nations condemned Japan's actions, no country was willing to go to war to halt Japanese aggression.

Italian Revenge in Africa

Italy was the second major nation to successfully defy the League of Nations. Mussolini sought to recreate the grandeur of the Roman Empire by building a new Italian empire. In doing so, he hoped also to illustrate the vitality of fascism. His first target was the country of Ethiopia—an independent African nation that had defeated an invading Italian army in the late nineteenth century. In 1935 a large, well-equipped Italian army invaded Ethiopia. The Ethiopians, who fought with primitive weapons such as bows and arrows, were no match for the Italians. Using a combination of air power, tanks, and poison gas, the Italians easily conquered the country.

The League of Nations was unwilling to use military force against Mussolini because its most important members, Britain and France, wanted to stay on good terms with Italy in order to isolate Hitler's Germany. Instead the League decided to impose economic **sanctions**—forbidding the sale of certain materials to Italy. These sanctions did not really hinder Italy's war effort because they did not include oil, which fueled Mussolini's tanks, planes, and other motorized vehicles. Mussolini defied every effort the League made to halt his invasion.

the Kuomintang. He began a military campaign to reunite China under a national government. But in 1927 rival factions within the Kuomintang caused a split in the party. Civil war broke out between Chiang's conservative forces and the radical Communist forces led by **Mao Zedong** (MOU DZUH-DONG; 1893-1976). By stirring up peasant uprisings, Mao hoped to bring about a Communist revolution. Chiang countered by launching an all-out effort to drive the Communists from their strongholds in southern China. But the Communist forces slipped past Chiang's lines, and in their famous Long March they traveled some six thousand miles to northwestern China. Further attempts by Chiang to drive the Communists out of the country failed because of Japanese aggression during the 1930s.

Japanese Invasion—Japan's easy defeat of China in the Sino-Japanese War (1894-95) had revealed just how weak and vulnerable China was. When the military clique gained control of the Japanese government, the Japanese launched their daring program of territorial expansion. In 1931 Japanese

In the end he made Ethiopia a part of his growing empire. In addition, he seized the small Balkan nation of Albania in April of 1939.

German Rearmament in Europe

Like Mussolini, Hitler also sought to build a new empire. Once he had firmly established himself in power, he began laying the foundation for a new German empire—the **Third Reich.** Hitler wished to provide the German people with additional *lebensraum* (LAY bens ROWM; "living space"). To accomplish this goal, he knew that he would need to rearm Germany. In 1933 Hitler ended German participation in the Geneva Disarmament Conference (1932-33). He also pulled Germany out of the League of Nations. Two years later, in violation of the Versailles Treaty, Hitler reestablished the German General Staff and reintroduced a military draft.

Only one task now remained before Hitler could actively begin building his empire—he had to fortify the Rhineland. According to the Treaty of Versailles and the Locarno Treaties, German territory west of the Rhine River had to be demilitarized (free from troops and military equipment). But Hitler had no intention of abiding by these treaty provisions. On March 7, 1936, he ordered German troops to march into the Rhineland. France reacted angrily to Hitler's conduct but took no action against Germany. Furthermore, the League once again proved itself unable to prevent or solve an international crisis. No significant check was placed upon Hitler's action.

The Third Reich

There have been three *reichs* (empires or kingdoms) in German history. Otto the Great established the first one in 962, when he became the first Holy Roman Emperor. This first *reich* lasted until 1806, when Napoleon abolished it. Later Otto von Bismarck helped unify Germany, creating a second German empire. This *reich* lasted from 1871 to 1918. Adolf Hitler created what he called the Third Reich. Although he declared that it would last for a thousand years, it lasted for only twelve (1933-45).

Hitler Challenges European Security

Germany Forms Alliances

Until 1935 Germany was diplomatically isolated in Europe; even Italy sided with Britain and France in verbal opposition to Hitler. European displeasure with Italy's conquest of Ethiopia, however, drove Mussolini closer to Hitler. In 1936 Germany and Italy formed an alliance. This alliance became known as the **Rome-Berlin Axis,** taking its name from a speech made by Mussolini. Mussolini had described a "line" running between Berlin and Rome, a line that was "not a partition but rather an axis round which all European states animated by the will to collaboration and peace can

Hitler and Mussolini formed the Rome-Berlin Axis in 1936.

also collaborate." That same year Germany and Japan signed the **Anti-Comintern Pact,** which on the surface was an agreement directed against communism in general, but in reality was aimed specifically at Russia. The following year, Italy and Japan signed a similar agreement, bringing together the three major nations that would constitute the Axis powers in World War II. Their opponents would come to be known as the Allies.

The Spanish Civil War

The event that brought Germany and Italy together was the outbreak in 1936 of civil war in Spain. In that year, the Fascist followers of General **Francisco Franco** (1892-1975) revolted against Spain's republican government. Recognizing that Franco had a political philosophy similar to theirs, Mussolini and Hitler supported his war effort with men and materiel. The Germans primarily provided planes and tanks; Italy supplied Franco with fifty to seventy thousand troops as well as one thousand

planes. Russia offered some material assistance to the Loyalists (supporters of the Spanish government), but France and Britain followed a policy of nonintervention in Spain's affairs. Lacking supplies and foreign support, the Loyalists resisted stubbornly; but when Madrid fell to the rebel forces in early 1939, the war came to an end. The victorious Franco became dictator of Spain.

In addition to the tremendous significance this civil war had for the history of Spain, it also proved to be a "dress rehearsal" for World War II. By assisting Franco, Germany and Italy gained the opportunity to try out new weapons under actual battle conditions and to learn how to use them effectively. When World War II broke out in Europe, these nations—Germany in particular—had an initial advantage over their opponents.

Hitler Takes Austria

According to a post–World War I treaty, Austria was forbidden to join with Germany in a political union. Yet Austria was the first area of Europe that Hitler sought to add to his Reich. Located directly south of Germany, Austria had a population composed primarily of Germans. (Other nationalities formerly under her control had been separated from her after World War I.) During the

Hitler and some of his associates at a Nazi rally in Nuremberg. Those standing with Hitler include Heinrich Himmler (second from the left), head of the S.S. and the Gestapo, and Hermann Göring (far right), head of the German air force, the Luftwaffe.

interwar years, economic and political weakness hindered the growth of a stable economy and threatened to undermine the new republic.

In 1934 Hitler had attempted to seize Austria, but his effort had failed, partly because of Mussolini's opposition. To soothe Austria's fear, Hitler promised to respect Austrian independence. This promise, however, was only one of many that he did not intend to keep. In 1938 Hitler was ready to try again. Taking advantage of political turmoil in Austria, Hitler demanded that a Nazi be installed as chancellor of the country. Mussolini, now on friendlier terms with Hitler, was heavily involved in the Spanish Civil War and did not give the Austrian government his support as he had in 1934. Austria was too weak to resist Hitler's demands. When the new Nazi chancellor was installed, he "requested" Hitler to send troops into Austria and reestablish order. As Europe stood by, Hitler seized the entire country.

Allies Trust in Appeasement

Sudetenland Sacrificed at Munich—Encouraged by his success in Austria, Hitler next turned his attention to Czechoslovakia—a nation where 3.5 million of the inhabitants were German. Most of these Germans lived near the border of Germany and Austria in an area known as the Sudetenland (named after the Sudeten Mountains). Unlike Austria, Czechoslovakia had a strong economy and a stable, republican form of government. Nevertheless, Hitler's agents stirred up discontent among the German inhabitants of the country. Hitler openly demanded that the Sudetenland become a part of the German Reich.

As tension between Czechoslovakia and Germany increased, **Neville Chamberlain** (1869-1940), prime minister of Great Britain, met several times with Hitler to seek a solution to the Czech crisis. Convinced that Hitler was willing to go to war over the Sudetenland, Chamberlain—with the support of the French government—put pressure on Czechoslovakia, urging her to capitulate to Hitler's demands. In his efforts to avoid war, Chamberlain foolishly believed Hitler's promise that "after the Sudeten German question is regulated, we have no further territorial claims to make in Europe."

Although surrounded by German territory on three sides, Czechoslovakia refused to surrender to Hitler's wishes. War seemed imminent. At the last minute, Hitler, at Mussolini's urging, invited Chamberlain and **Édouard Daladier** (the prime minister of France) to meet in Munich and settle the crisis. On September 29, 1938, after hours of negotiations, the other leaders gave Hitler the Sudetenland. Incredibly, representatives from Czechoslovakia had not even been allowed to participate in the **Munich Conference.**

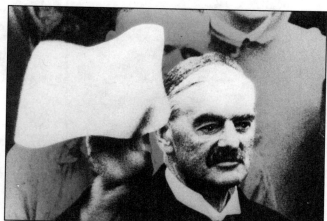

British prime minister Neville Chamberlain returned from the Munich Conference proclaiming "peace for our time." Less than a year later, World War II began.

When Chamberlain returned to Britain, he told an enthusiastic crowd, "I return from Germany bringing peace with honor." However, Chamberlain sought to halt Hitler's expansionistic plans through a policy of **appeasement** (buying off an aggressor by territorial concession). Chamberlain believed that he had helped to establish "peace for our time"; but within a year Europe had plunged into World War II.

Czechoslovakia Falls to the Germans—On October 3, 1938, Chamberlain stood in the House of Commons and spoke in defense of his appeasement policy. He claimed that the "great and imminent menace" of war had been removed, and that "the new Czechoslovakia [would] find a greater security than she [had] ever enjoyed in the past."

German and Italian
Expansion 1935-39

☐ Axis Powers

■ Axis-controlled lands. Sept. 1, 1939

TAKE ME TO CZECHOSLOVAKIA, DRIVER

YES SIR!

Although the road to peace might be difficult, he said, "I believe that there is sincerity and good will on both sides." Two days later **Winston Churchill,** (1874-1965), a member of the House of Commons, stood in the same place and denounced appeasement. "We have sustained a total and unmitigated defeat." he declared. He predicted that all of eastern Europe would be subjected to Nazi tyranny. Furthermore, he concluded with a somber warning and challenge:

A grim political cartoon from the Chicago Daily News *(September 8, 1938) condemns German aggression.*

And do not suppose that this is the end. This is only the beginning of the reckoning. This is only the first sip, the first foretaste of a bitter cup which will be proffered to us year by year unless by a supreme recovery of moral health and martial vigor, we arise again and take our stand for freedom as in the olden time.

Time was to prove Churchill right. On March 15, 1939, German troops marched into Prague (the capital of Czechoslovakia) and brought most of the country under Nazi rule. Poland and Hungary occupied the rest of Czechoslovakia.

In the past Hitler had claimed that all he wanted to do was to bring all Germans in Europe under one rule. Several European nations, particularly Britain, felt that Germany had been treated unfairly in the Versailles Treaty. Many leaders regarded Hitler's seizure of "German" territory as a means of correcting that injustice. In addition, the people of Europe remembered the last great war. They wanted to avoid renewed bloodshed at all costs.

As it turned out, however, the policy of appeasement only made war certain. Following Hitler's seizure of Czechoslovakia, even the most naive of political leaders (including Chamberlain) realized that appeasement had failed. Hitler did not intend to confine his territorial demands as they had blindly believed. Instead, he sought to incorporate as much territory into his empire as possible with little regard for national or political boundaries. Afraid for their own safety, Britain and France now determined to use force if necessary to oppose any further Nazi aggression.

Stage Set for War

Hitler's next target was Poland. Within a week after taking Czechoslovakia, he demanded that Poland cede to Germany a strip of territory known as the "Polish Corridor," which would connect East Prussia with the remainder of Germany. This time, however, France and Britain decided to defend Poland's independence regardless of the cost. Chamberlain, in a complete reversal of his earlier appeasement policy, stated that in the event "of any action which clearly threatened Polish independence, and which the Polish government accordingly considered it vital to resist with their national

forces, His Majesty's Government would feel themselves bound at once to lend the Polish government all the support in their power."

To increase their effectiveness against Hitler, Britain and France tried to reach a military agreement with the Soviet Union. They ran into diffi-

Hitler addressing the Reichstag

culty, however. Not only had the Soviet Union been ignored in the crisis over Czechoslovakia, but Stalin also felt that the Soviets had been snubbed by Chamberlain all along. He was not about to meekly cooperate with Britain now.

While Britain attempted to negotiate with the Soviet government in Moscow, Hitler was not idle. In May, he and Mussolini finalized a military alliance known as the **Pact of Steel.** Furthermore, Hitler shocked the world by announcing on August 23 that Germany and the Soviet Union had signed a nonaggression pact known as the Nazi-Soviet Pact. Both sides agreed that for ten years they would "refrain from any violence, from any aggressive action, and any attack against each other, individually or jointly with other powers." Two nations that had been sworn enemies now appeared to be on friendly terms. But as William Shakespeare once wrote, "'Tis time to fear when tyrants seem to kiss."

With this agreement, Hitler confidently believed that Britain and France would not try to stop him if he invaded Poland. He had seen them weakly give in to his demands in the past. He had no doubt that in spite of their promise to defend Poland they would back down once again. Hitler miscalculated this time, however, and Europe was plunged into another war.

Section Review

1. What territories did Japan invade in 1931 and 1937?
2. What country did the Italians invade in 1935? What did the League of Nations impose as a result of this invasion?
3. What country experienced a civil war in which other nations—especially Germany and Italy—took part in shaping the outcome?
4. Where did European leaders meet in 1938 to settle the question of the Sudetenland? To what country did the Sudetenland belong?
5. With what country did Hitler sign a nonaggression pact prior to his invasion of Poland?

Global Conflict

Axis Successes

Sweep Into Poland

On September 1, 1939, German forces numbering 1.7 million men suddenly attacked Poland and rapidly advanced across the country. Contrary to Hitler's expectations, Britain and France immediately demanded that Germany cease hostilities. When the German government did not respond, Britain and France declared war on Germany. It was now too late for Hitler to turn back—World War II had officially begun. In less than four weeks Germany, utilizing her powerful armored, or *panzer,* divisions and superior air force—the *Luftwaffe*—defeated Poland. This fast-moving attack, which sought to penetrate enemy lines, is known as *blitzkrieg* ("lightning war").

Meanwhile, as the Germans were invading Poland from the west, the Soviets invaded Poland from the east. According to the Nazi-Soviet Pact, the two countries divided Polish territory between themselves. In addition, Hitler agreed to recognize the Soviet claim to the small Baltic nations of Estonia, Latvia, and Lithuania. The Soviets forced these nations to allow the establishment of Soviet military bases within their countries. The Soviets then demanded that Finland grant them the same military concessions. When Finland refused, fighting broke out in late 1939. Although outnumbered five to one, the Finns held off the Russians for a while and won several victories. In the end, the Soviets broke the Finnish resistance and forced the Finns to give up territory. The conflict, however, cast grave doubts on Russia's ability to wage war.

Invasion of Scandinavia

While all this military activity was occurring in eastern Europe, little was happening in western Europe. The Allies, unprepared for a full-scale war, decided that a blockade of Germany would be the most effective strategy while they waited for the next German move. On the German side, Hitler wanted to attack in the west, but bad winter weather hampered his plans. For seven months this "phony war," or *sitzkrieg* (literally, "sitting war"), continued without either side launching a major offensive.

In April of 1940 Germany ended the military inactivity on the western front by attacking Denmark and Norway. Hitler feared that the Allies intended to establish military bases in Norway. He therefore attacked and seized the country for the Axis powers. Both Norway and Denmark were caught by surprise and were easily conquered. Denmark, in fact, surrendered after only a few hours of fighting.

One factor that particularly aided the German conquest of Norway was the presence within the country of traitors known as **fifth columnists.** The term *fifth columnist* was coined during the Spanish Civil War. It refers to individuals within a country who secretly aid the enemy by spying, spreading enemy propaganda, carrying out acts of sabotage, or other similar activities. In Norway, **Vidkun Quisling** was the most notorious of these fifth columnists. His subversive activities helped the Germans conquer his country. Today his name is a synonym of *traitor.*

The Fall of France

After the conquest of Norway and Denmark, Hitler turned to his long-awaited offensive in the west. Although the Low Countries (Belgium, the Netherlands, and Luxembourg) could provide little resistance, most observers thought that France would prove much more formidable than had Germany's other foes. The French and the British had several thousand troops on the French-Belgian border to protect against a German attack across the flatlands of central Belgium. Also, along the French-German border, the French had established a strong line of fortifications known as the Maginot Line (see pp. 526, 527). No one expected a stunning *blitzkrieg* like the one in Poland.

The attack came on May 10, 1940. The German forces easily crushed the Low Countries; Holland and Luxembourg fell in less than a week, and the Belgians held out for only two weeks. The Allies, in the meantime, swept into Belgium to meet the Germans. Britain and France had made a serious error, however. While they strongly defended most of the French border, the Allies stationed very few troops in the Ardennes region by southern Belgium. The Allies thought that the heavy forests there would be enough to stop any German attack through the Ardennes. Hitler thought otherwise, and sent a large armored force through the forests, bypassing the heavy fortifications of the Maginot Line along the French-German border and the massive buildup of Allied troops along the French-Belgian border. The heavy tanks pushed through the Ardennes with only minor difficulty and attacked a small and very surprised Allied force near the city of Sedan.

The German forces broke through the Allied lines and soon had a large Allied army encircled in northwestern France. The Allies had their backs to the English Channel and seemed doomed as the Germans relentlessly pushed them toward the coast. Before long the French and the British found themselves on the beaches at the port city of Dunkirk. Surprisingly, the Germans halted their advance. This pause gave the British time to send out a call for help. From all along the British coastline, sailors and civilians came in barges, tugboats, private yachts—more than eight hundred boats of all types and sizes—and ferried the Allied soldiers across the channel to Britain. Thus an entire army of over 350,000 men was saved from almost certain destruction. Churchill, however, told the House of Commons, "We must be very careful not to assign

The German Offensive (May 1940)

The Miracle of Dunkirk

In May of 1940, news reached Britain that Hitler's *panzer* divisions had pushed through the Ardennes Forest into France. The surprised British Expeditionary Force and thousands of other Allied troops were forced to retreat to the port city of Dunkirk. Over 350,000 Allied soldiers faced almost certain capture or death. When the peril of the British army became known, Christians throughout the British Empire prayed for God to deliver them. A close examination of the events of the rescue of Dunkirk shows how God granted deliverance in the midst of seemingly hopeless circumstances.

When the commander of the British forces realized that his army could not withstand the waves of German troops and tanks, he ordered the retreat to Dunkirk. Although this action was contrary to orders from Britain, he reasoned that at Dunkirk there would be a chance of escaping by sea. Had he remained in his present position, he would have been surrounded, with no means of escape.

To the surprise of the Allies, the advancing German *panzer* divisions stopped twelve miles short of Dunkirk. Hitler, thinking that there was little hope of the Allies escaping, ordered this halt. He agreed with many of his top aides that the annihilation of the trapped Allied army should be left to the *Luftwaffe*. The *panzers* could be better used in the invasion of France. Hitler had been assured that within three days the *Luftwaffe* could annihilate the British army.

But the *Luftwaffe* bombers were thwarted by bad weather. Pouring rain, fog, and low cloud cover hindered their efforts. The British seized the opportunity to send for help. A call went out for boats of any size or kind to come to the rescue

Evacuated British soldiers look back at the port of Dunkirk.

of the beleaguered troops at Dunkirk. A flotilla of more than eight hundred vessels, manned by British soldiers and private citizens, crossed the channel to ferry the men back to England.

The notoriously treacherous channel weather was unusually cooperative. Prevailing winds were light and westerly—had they been strong and northerly, which is often the case, the rescue would have been much more difficult. In addition, wave heights were lower than normal. Above the rescue operation, haze and dense fog obscured the beaches from the *Luftwaffe* pilots. *Luftwaffe* records state that wave after wave of bombers reported "lack of good bombing conditions" and as a result returned to base.

For nine days, from May 26 to June 4, 1940, the rescue operation went on. In the end, more than 350,000 soldiers were rescued, two-thirds of whom were British. In that day, as well as today, this amazing evacuation was known as the "miracle at Dunkirk." God used human instruments as well as the forces of nature to answer the prayers of concerned, but trusting, British Christians. Truly, "the effectual fervent prayer of a righteous man availeth much" (James 5:16).

to this deliverance the attributes of a victory. Wars are not won by evacuation."

Meanwhile, another German force pushed southward into France. As a French defeat became more and more certain, Italy, hoping to gain more territory, declared war on France and Great Britain.

"I need a few thousand dead," said Mussolini, "so that I can attend the peace conference as a belligerent [one who engaged in warfare]." The French government, which had already fled from Paris, rejected Britain's plea that the French army withdraw to North Africa and continue fighting. Instead, the political parties appointed Marshal **Henri Pétain** (1856-1951), a hero of World War I, to head a new French government. Pétain immediately asked the Germans for an armistice. On June 22, 1940, the French signed the surrender documents in the same railroad car in which the Germans had surrendered to the Allies in World War I. France had fallen in just forty-two days.

According to the agreement with France, the Germans would occupy over half of France, including Paris, the entire Atlantic coastline, and the northern section of the country. The rest of France would remain unoccupied, and a government under Marshal Pétain would rule for the Germans. Since the city of Vichy became the new seat of government, the entire region under Pétain's rule became known as Vichy France. Many of the Frenchmen who had escaped to Britain refused to recognize the leadership of the Vichy government. Instead they joined the Free French movement led by **Charles de Gaulle** (1890-1970). These Frenchmen continued to wage war against the Axis powers.

Invasion of North Africa

Inspired by Hitler's impressive victories in Europe, Mussolini attempted to duplicate them in North Africa. He knew that Britain was facing terrific pressure from Hitler in Europe and that she would not be able to send many additional troops to Africa. Consequently, Mussolini launched an invasion of Egypt. Such an invasion, he hoped, would not only seriously weaken Britain's position in the Mediterranean but also provide an access to the oil fields of the Middle East. But Mussolini had underestimated the British, and his invasion proved a disaster. The British pushed the Italian invaders out of Egypt and back into Libya. In addition, they captured over one hundred thousand prisoners as well as much valuable war materiel.

To prevent a total Italian collapse, Hitler intervened. In the spring of 1941 a brilliant German commander, General **Erwin Rommel,** arrived in North Africa with specially trained German forces. Rommel, known as the ''Desert Fox,'' often displayed his tactical ability but was unable to win a crushing victory; he lacked sufficient supplies and reinforcements. By 1942 his forces had advanced

into Egypt, coming within seventy miles of the British naval base at Alexandria. Both sides were exhausted, however, and for four months there was a lull in the fighting.

Axis Blunders

At the beginning of Hitler's rule, many of his generals did not trust his military judgment or strategy. After the fall of France, however, his military prestige increased to the point that his ideas were rarely challenged. But Hitler's military success did not continue. We can now look back and see that many of his decisions proved to be military blunders.

The Battle of Britain

Although France was defeated, Hitler could not immediately direct his attention toward Britain. German troops first had to consolidate their position in the newly conquered territories. The British knew that the lull in the fighting was only temporary and that soon they too would experience the fierceness of Hitler's attack. Like France, they were in a precarious position, having already suffered several military setbacks and having little with which to defend themselves.

Although the future seemed dark, the British found hope in the courageous and energetic leadership of Winston Churchill, who had replaced Neville Chamberlain as prime minister. Churchill encouraged the British people with these words:

> We shall not flag or fail. We shall go on to the end. We shall fight in France, we shall fight on the seas and oceans, we shall fight with growing confidence and growing strength in the air. We shall defend our island, whatever the cost may be. We shall fight on the beaches, we shall fight in the fields and in the streets, we shall fight in the hills. We shall never surrender.

The will of the British people to withstand the Nazis was soon tested. Hitler not only ordered a complete air and submarine blockade around Great Britain, but he also ordered the *Luftwaffe* to begin bombing the island in preparation for an invasion. While the *Luftwaffe* bombed British airfields and radar installations, Hitler's generals began gathering a fleet of barges and training their troops for

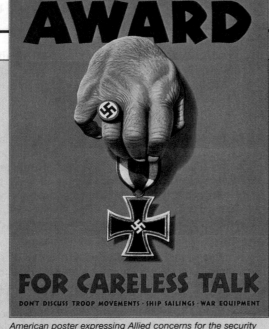

AWARD

FOR CARELESS TALK

DON'T DISCUSS TROOP MOVEMENTS · SHIP SAILINGS · WAR EQUIPMENT

American poster expressing Allied concerns for the security of their armed forces

Britain Prepares For Invasion

Soon after the fall of France, the British people were keenly aware of the threat of a German invasion. They began making careful preparations. In a radio address, Anthony Eden, the secretary of war, said, "Those of you who are not in the Forces: Stay where you are! Refugees on roads and railways hamstring those upon whom your defense depends. . . . The mass of refugees helped to lose the battle of France; they will not lose the battle of Britain."

All across Britain, obstacles were placed on roads and in fields to prevent the enemy from landing planes. People were instructed to immobilize their cars and trucks by removing and hiding vital engine parts, thus denying the invading enemy an additional means of transportation. Public information leaflets further instructed the British people: "Do not give any German anything. Do not tell him anything. Hide your food and your bicycles. Hide your maps. . . . Think always of your country before you think of yourself." School children were taught that if German soldiers asked them for directions they should answer only, "I can't say."

To further confuse the Germans in the event of an invasion, the government ordered that "no person should display or cause or permit to be displayed any sign which furnishes any indication of the name of, or the situation or the direction of, or the distance to any place." Consequently, all signposts were removed from the roads; wherever the name of a town was written, it was painted over. As it turned out, however, the invasion did not come, and the British people did not have to test their precautionary measures.

an **amphibious** (land and sea) assault. He believed that once the Nazis had control of the skies over Britain, Operation Sea Lion (the code name for the invasion plans) could proceed.

The German attacks against the British airfields seemed to be succeeding. In early September, however, the *Luftwaffe* changed targets. German bombers now dropped their loads on British cities. At the height of the bombing three to six hundred Londoners were killed each day. Hitler hoped that bombing civilian targets would destroy the British people's morale and thus break their will. But British morale did not weaken. In the end, German bombing became more sporadic; having failed to win the air war over Britain, Hitler now directed his energies toward an invasion of Russia.

The blunder of the Battle of Britain was Hitler's underestimation of the spirit of the British people. Their determined effort to resist the Nazis was demonstrated by the heroism of the British **RAF** (Royal Air Force). The *Luftwaffe* outnumbered the British fighters, but the British had better planes and the advantage of the newly invented radar. Before the war, Britain had begun to build an air defense system that allowed them to track enemy planes and then direct their own planes to meet the attackers. Time and time again, the RAF met the oncoming waves of bombers and inflicted heavy losses. Between August 8 and October 31 of 1940, official government estimates placed the number of German planes shot down at nearly 1,400, compared to 800 British planes lost. The German air force never recovered from these terrific losses. With each passing week Hitler's invasion plans became less and less likely to succeed. Summing up the work of the British pilots, Winston Churchill said, "Never in the field of human conflict was so much owed by so many to so few."

Although the United States was not yet at war with the Axis powers, America clearly indicated her support for the Allied cause. First, the United States gave Britain fifty World War I destroyers in return for a ninety-nine-year lease on eight British military bases in the Western Hemisphere. Second, the United States Congress passed the **Lend-Lease Act** in 1941, authorizing the president to "sell,

HOLDING THE LINE!

A British poster combines a picture of Churchill with the bulldog and the British flag, both symbols of British patriotism.

transfer title to, exchange, lease, lend, or otherwise dispose of" military supplies to any country whose security was important to the United States. Third, Winston Churchill and Franklin Roosevelt drew up and signed the **Atlantic Charter.** This eight-point document set forth the "common principles" on which both countries "base[d] their hopes for a better future for the world." The charter provided that after the "final destruction of the Nazi tyranny" the signatories would seek such things as the disarmament of aggressor nations, freedom of the seas, and equal economic opportunities.

The Invasion of Russia

Late in 1940 Hitler issued an order directing his generals to begin "preparation to crush Soviet Russia in a lightning campaign even before the termination of hostilities with Great Britain." Under the code name of Operation Barbarossa, plans went forward in the spring of 1941 for an invasion of Russia. Although Stalin and Hitler had signed a nonaggression pact in 1939 (the Nazi-Soviet pact), Hitler decided to attack Russia in order to secure both *lebensraum* and needed natural resources such as oil. (The British naval blockade was preventing the German importation of needed raw materials.) In addition, Hitler hoped that a Russian surrender would put increased pressure on Britain by removing her last hope of finding a European ally.

But the attack on Russia proved to be a serious blunder. The Nazis underestimated not only the Soviet industrial capacity but also the length of time necessary to win a victory. Although some Russians welcomed the Germans as liberators from the cruel Stalin regime, the harshness of the German conquerors soon united the Russian people to fight for "Mother Russia." Like Napoleon in 1812, the Nazis made no provision for the severe Russian winters, and like Napoleon, they found that in the end the weather helped defeat them.

The invasion was delayed one month while the Germans established Nazi control over Greece and Yugoslavia, but Hitler finally launched his attack on June 22, 1941. With thousands of planes and tanks and over 600,000 other motor vehicles, 3 million Nazi soldiers advanced into Russia along a front 1,800 miles long. For the first several months the

Nazi forces advanced rapidly, capturing thousands of prisoners and miles of territory (over 500,000 square miles). As the Russians retreated, however, they carried out a scorched-earth policy, just as they had done when Napoleon invaded in 1812. They destroyed or removed anything that might have been used as supplies by the invading Germans.

By December 1, the Russian armed forces had suffered 4 to 5 million casualties, including over 1 million prisoners of war. German forces had besieged Leningrad (St. Petersburg) and had nearly reached Moscow. But the coming of winter ended their advance. Temperatures in early December fell to -40° F, bringing in the earliest and coldest winter of the century. Machinery would not function, and soldiers suffered from lack of winter clothing. Hitler's campaign failed to quickly knock Russia out of the war. Now he had to wait until spring to try again.

In the spring Nazi troops pushed farther into southern Russia, toward the oil fields. At the same time they attacked the city of Stalingrad. Not only was Stalingrad a strategic transportation center, but it also carried Stalin's name. Hitler was therefore determined to capture the city at all costs. For months German troops shelled Stalingrad, but the Soviets refused to surrender. As the Nazis advanced slowly into the city, they found that the Russians were using the rubble of the destroyed buildings as fortresses. For several more months desperate hand-to-hand fighting raged in the city. Neither side was able to defeat the other. Finally the Russians managed to surround the Germans, and what was left of the German army surrendered in February of 1943. Several days earlier the Russians had also broken the German siege of Leningrad.

Up to this point Russia had received only a limited amount of aid from the West. In a speech broadcast at the start of the German invasion of Russia, Churchill had promised that

> any man or state who fights against Nazidom will have our aid. . . . We shall give whatever help we can to Russia and to the Russian people. . . . We have offered to the government of Soviet Russia any technical or economic assistance which is in our power.

Yet supply routes were few. British and American supply ships regularly sailed around Norway to the

The Holocaust

In *Mein Kampf* and in his many speeches, Hitler said that the Jews were "culture destroyers" and had to be annihilated to save the "master race" (the Germans) from contamination. However, even though the Jews were horribly mistreated and frequently placed in concentration camps, few people outside of Germany (and only a few in Germany) believed that Hitler really meant what he said.

When the German invasion of Russia began, Hitler instructed the S.S. to eliminate all Soviet Jews. In town after town and village after village, the Nazis systematically rounded up the Jews and shot them. In Kiev, for example, they herded the Jews to the cemetery, forced them to dig a large communal grave, undress, and then in groups climb into the grave. Each group was machine-gunned and covered with a layer of dirt.

In January 1942 Hitler called for a meeting of his top advisers to devise a way to annihilate the entire European Jewish community as quickly as possible. They rejected starvation and

Concentration camp at Dachau, Bavaria

shooting; the first was too slow and the second too costly. The Nazis decided that the most economical and efficient method was to build large gas chambers at the existing concentration camp sites. In these chambers hundreds could be gassed at once. The disposal of the bodies, however, was a problem. In one camp they were just stacked and allowed to decay, and in another they were placed in huge graves. But in most of the other camps, the Nazis built large crematoriums (furnaces for cremating bodies).

The largest "disposal" center was in the Polish village of Oswiecim (in German, *Auschwitz*). There three camps were built to receive thousands of Jews from all over eastern Europe. They were brought to the camps in closed railroad cars made to accommodate forty people. One hundred fifty people were crammed into each car. With little food or water and no toilet facilities, they traveled for days before reaching the camp. Usually by the time the train reached its destination, scores of people in each car were dead. Upon arrival at the camp, the Nazis divided the victims into two groups: those who were fit to work and those who were not (the old, sick, or very young). The Nazis took this second group to the "showers," as the gas chambers were called, and disposed of them. They put the rest to work until they were no longer useful, and then they sent them to the "showers" as well.

Toward the end of the war, as the Germans grew desperate, most incoming victims were sent directly to the gas chambers. The slaughter was so immense that the crematoriums could not keep up with the demand.

Millions of Europeans died in the Nazi concentration camps from the awful brutality of the S.S. But this pales when one thinks of the millions of Jews (two and a half million at Auschwitz alone) who were methodically murdered supposedly to save the "master race" from destruction.

northern Russian port of Murmansk and Archangel, but the ships were in danger from Nazi submarine and air attacks. Consequently, the Allies opened up an alternative supply route into southern Russia through Iran. By 1943 supplies began to pour into Russia. By the end of the war the United States alone had supplied the Soviets with $11 billion in Lend-Lease aid.

Attack on Pearl Harbor

Japan was already at war in Asia before World War II officially began. In September of 1939, when war broke out in Europe, Japan took advantage of the situation and moved into Southeast Asia. The free nations of Europe were struggling against Hitler for their very survival and could do little to halt Japanese aggression. Japan needed only to neutralize the military power of the USSR and the United States to proceed with her plans of conquest in the Pacific. In April of 1941 Japan and Russia signed a nonaggression pact. Only the United States remained an obstacle.

Although U.S.-Japan relations had become increasingly strained because of Japanese aggression, the United States remained officially neutral. However, in the fall of 1941, a fanatical militarist named

A Japanese poster uses a samurai warrior to symbolize the power of the Axis alliance.

Hideki Tojo (1885-1948) became the virtual dictator of Japan. He and his fellow generals decided that if the American fleet stationed at Pearl Harbor, Hawaii, were destroyed, there would be no power strong enough to stop Japanese expansion into Southeast Asia. Such expansion was necessary, they believed, if Japan were to become economically self-sufficient.

Just before 8:00 A.M. on Sunday morning, December 7, 1941, nearly four hundred Japanese planes descended on Pearl Harbor. In a well-coordinated attack, the Japanese knocked out American airfields and seriously crippled the United States Pacific Fleet, which was anchored in the harbor. Through a combination of carelessness and miscalculation—some historians even claim a deliberate government conspiracy—the Americans at Pearl Harbor were caught by surprise. The Japanese attack destroyed two-thirds of the American aircraft, sank or seriously damaged five battleships and three cruisers, and killed more than two thousand Americans.

In a day when a nation's naval strength rested on its battleships, the American losses seemed insurmountable. But absent from Pearl Harbor were the American aircraft carriers, which were out on maneuvers. They escaped the devastation of the Japanese attack and would eventually play a leading role in defeating the Japanese in the Pacific.

Although the Japanese considered their attack on Pearl Harbor a resounding success, it stirred the

...we here highly resolve that these dead shall not have died in vain...

REMEMBER DEC. 7th!

American people to action. President Roosevelt declared the unprovoked attack a "day that will live in infamy." On December 8, the United States Congress declared war on Japan. Three days later, Germany and Italy declared war on the United States. The entrance of the United States into the war brought renewed vigor to the Allies in Europe. Soon the United States Navy—led by her aircraft carriers—began to turn back Japanese expansion in the Pacific. The fears of the Japanese Admiral Yamamoto had come true: the attack on Pearl Harbor had awakened a "sleeping giant."

Section Review

1. The German invasion of what country led to the official beginning of World War II? When did this invasion—and thus the war—begin?
2. At what port city were more than 350,000 Allied soldiers rescued from almost certain destruction?
3. What prime minister of Great Britain encouraged the British people never to surrender despite the gloomy prospects?
4. What people whose systematic extermination he ordered did Hitler label as "culture destroyers"?
5. Give the month, day, and year for the Japanese attack on Pearl Harbor.

Allied Advances

From North Africa to Italy

The year 1942 witnessed the halt of the Axis advance and proved to be the turning point for the Allies. In spite of Rommel's brilliant leadership in North Africa, the Germans were defeated by the British commander General **Bernard L. Montgomery** at the battle of El Alamein. At the same time, an American invasion force under General **Dwight D. Eisenhower** landed on the Algerian coast. By May of 1943 the outnumbered Axis troops in Africa had surrendered.

Two months later a force of 160,000 men under Eisenhower landed in Sicily, bringing the war directly to the Italian people. This invasion not only cost Mussolini what little popular support he still had, but it even turned some of the top-ranking members of his own Fascist party against him. Hav-

British tanks cross the North African desert.

ing no alternative, Mussolini resigned his position and was quickly imprisoned. A new Italian government headed by one of his former associates immediately began secret negotiations with the Allies about terms of surrender. As Allied troops landed on the Italian peninsula itself, Italy unconditionally surrendered in September of 1943. Nevertheless, hundreds of thousands of German troops continued fighting in Italy until the surrender of Germany.

Mussolini himself met a violent end. German troops rescued him from prison and established him as a puppet ruler in the German-controlled areas of Italy. As the Axis collapsed, Mussolini, his mistress, and some friends attempted to escape to Switzerland. But Italian **partisans** (fighters who harass an enemy occupying their territory) captured them. They shot both Mussolini and his mistress, took their bodies to Milan, and hung them upside down in front of a gas station.

From Britain to Normandy

Allied Summit Conferences—In 1943 the Allies held two conferences that greatly influenced the outcome of the war. In January, Churchill and Roosevelt met for ten days at Casablanca, Morocco, where they declared that nothing less than the "unconditional surrender" of the Axis would be acceptable to them. The reason for such a declaration was that after World War I many Germans began to believe the myth that they had not really been defeated; Churchill and Roosevelt wanted to make sure

Opposite Page: A World War II poster uses the Pearl Harbor attack as a rallying point (top), and smoke billows from the U.S.S. West Virginia after the Japanese attack on Pearl Harbor (bottom).

that this time Germany would know she had been beaten. But by establishing the principle of unconditional surrender, the Allies unintentionally lengthened the war, uniting the Germans more firmly behind their government.

In late 1943 the so-called **Big Three** (Churchill, Roosevelt, and Stalin) held a major **summit** (conference of high-level officials) at Teheran, Iran. The topic of their talks was military strategy. Churchill wanted the Western Allies to concentrate their military efforts in the Mediterranean to check Soviet expansion there and in Eastern Europe. Stalin, on the other hand, wanted to control Eastern Europe. He therefore opposed any plans that would call for American and British troops in Eastern Europe. Since Roosevelt sided with Stalin, Churchill had to abandon his ideas and agree to an invasion of France instead.

The Normandy Invasion—After the Teheran Conference, the United States and Britain began planning an invasion of France under the code name of **Operation Overlord.** Since it would be impossible to conceal from the Germans the fact that countless tons of supplies as well as thousands of aircraft and motor vehicles were being stockpiled in Britain, the Allies attempted to mislead the Germans as to the time and place of the invasion. To accomplish that deception, work crews built fake military installations in southeastern England across from Calais in France. They even constructed rows of dummy tanks that appeared real to German airmen flying over the island. The military then created a nonexistent invasion force complete with its own commander, sent false messages which they allowed the Germans to intercept, and even conducted naval movements off that section of the French coast. All of this activity was designed to make the Germans believe that an attack was coming near the French-Belgian border. The plan succeeded, for when the real Allied attack came, the Germans had amassed their best troops in the area of France where they expected the invasion to come.

Left: Supplies pour onto the beaches of Normandy after the successful D-day invasion.
Right: General George Marshall greets American troops in France shortly after the Normandy landings.

The Allies actually planned to invade Europe by way of Normandy. Dwight Eisenhower, now the supreme Allied commander, decided to plan **D-day** (in military terminology, the day when an attack is to be launched) for the month of June. Everything had to be just right for the attack, including the weather, the tides, and the amount of moonlight. Finally, on June 6, 1944, in spite of threatening weather, Eisenhower ordered the attack to proceed on five different Normandy beaches. This assault, which was the greatest amphibious operation in history, had been thoroughly rehearsed in order to insure its success. Over ten thousand planes bombed coastal targets and provided aerial cover for the invasion forces. Five thousand large ships, as well as four thousand smaller landing craft, followed minesweepers across the English Channel to the designated landing spots. Paratroopers landed behind the German lines and secured important objectives.

In the end D-day succeeded, in spite of underwater barriers, explosive mines, and stiff German resistance at several of the beaches. Within three weeks of the invasion, the Allies had landed nearly 1 million men, 500,000 tons of supplies, and 177,000 vehicles in France. Germany's defeat was assured; it was only a matter of time before she surrendered.

If defeat seemed so certain, why did the Germans continue fighting for another year? First, Hitler and his staff believed that new "miracle weapons" would turn the tide and save Germany from defeat. For example, in 1944 the Nazis began launching rocket bombs (the British called them "buzz bombs") against the Allies. These V-1 rockets (short for *Vergeltungswaffe,* "retaliatory weapons"), the more sophisticated V-2 rockets, and the newly developed jet aircraft all came too late to save the Nazis from defeat. Had German scientists succeeded in their efforts to develop the atomic bomb before the end of the war, the outcome might have been different.

A second reason that the Nazis prolonged the war is that Hitler expected the United States and Britain to fall into serious disagreement with Russia and split their alliance. He and his staff did not believe that the Western democracies would allow the Soviet Union to conquer Germany.

Third, the Nazis stirred up a fear of Russian communism among the German people. Nazi propaganda began to emphasize the importance of Fortress Europe *(Festung Europa)* rather than the concept of *lebensraum,* which had been so prominent in their ideology a few years earlier. With the cry of "Victory or Bolshevism" ringing in their ears, many Germans wearily tried to do their part in salvaging the collapsing Third Reich.

From Island to Island

The Fall of the Philippines—After the attack on Pearl Harbor, the Japanese military command ordered attacks throughout the Pacific. One of these attacks struck the Philippines. American defenders on the islands had too few aircraft and too few men to defend the entire territory, so they decided to concentrate on defending the largest and most important of the islands, Luzon. American and Filipino forces held out for several months. But with the surrender of the fort at Corregidor in May of 1942, all organized resistance in the Philippines ceased. The American commander, General **Douglas MacArthur,** escaped, but he vowed, "I shall return."

Elsewhere in the Pacific, Japanese troops overran the British colonies of Hong Kong, Malaya, Singapore, and Burma, as well as the Dutch East

General Douglas MacArthur wades ashore at Lingayen Gulf in the Philippines, fulfilling his vow to return to the islands.

Breaking the Japanese Codes

Because radio transmissions can be easily intercepted by the enemy, both the Allies and Axis Powers took pains to maintain the secrecy of their communications. Most often they employed ciphers and codes in transmitting their radio messages. In a cipher, the letters and numbers in a message are exchanged for different letters and numbers. In a code, a word, phrase, or sentence is replaced by one letter or several letters or numbers. Most messages are sent in both cipher and code.

By World War II Americans had broken many of the Japanese military ciphers and codes. This knowledge became a vital help to the Allied war effort—especially after the devastating American losses at Pearl Harbor. The significance of such code breaking is illustrated by the Battle of Midway.

Having cracked a new Japanese code, the Americans learned of a planned Japanese attack on an undisclosed target coded "AF." Though they had a hunch that "AF" referred to Midway Island, naval intelligence was not certain. They had to be sure if they were to stop the Japanese invasion. In order to confirm their suspicions, naval intelligence had Midway send an uncoded message to naval headquarters at Pearl Harbor stating that the freshwater distilling plant was broken. Pearl Harbor radioed back that they would send a barge with fresh water. Knowing that the Japanese monitored such messages and reported such routine matters to Tokyo, the Americans waited for the Japanese transmission. Not long afterwards, the Americans intercepted a Japanese message that said that "AF" was short of fresh water. Now they knew for sure that the target was Midway.

Because of this advance warning, the American fleet—led by three aircraft carriers—was able to catch the Japanese invasion fleet off guard. In the ensuing battle, airplanes launched from these aircraft carriers severely crippled the Japanese fleet. Midway was saved, and the tide of Japanese expansion was stopped.

Indies (Indonesia). Other nations were also unprepared for war, and Japan won a series of relatively easy victories. Yet she overextended herself. Her resources were no match for America's industrial potential. Before long, American war production surpassed that of the Japanese. By the end of 1942, only one year after the attack, most of the ships that had been damaged at Pearl Harbor were repaired or replaced. The Allies had suffered serious reverses, but under the leadership of General MacArthur, who became the supreme commander of all Allied forces in the southwest Pacific, the tide turned against Japan.

Island-Hopping Campaign—In 1942 the United States defeated Japan in two major naval battles, halting further Japanese expansion. In the first battle, the Battle of the Coral Sea, American planes launched from aircraft carriers sank 100,000 tons of Japanese shipping. These losses prevented the Japanese from launching a full-scale invasion of Australia. One month later a Japanese force of eighty ships converged on Midway Island, an American naval base 1,300 miles northwest of Honolulu, Hawaii. Although seriously outnumbered, the Americans struck first, sinking several Japanese aircraft carriers and turning back the Japanese attack. After this defeat, Japan was placed on the defensive for the rest of the war.

American forces soon began an island-hopping campaign; that is, they began recapturing strategic Japanese-held islands in the Pacific. Instead of conquering every island in their path, the Americans seized only those that offered good sites for air bases. They simply by-passed Japanese troops on other islands. Fighting was often difficult and bloody because very few Japanese troops surrendered. Most chose to die in battle or to commit suicide rather than face the dishonor of surrender.

As American forces moved closer and closer to the home islands of Japan, some of the Japanese soldiers engaged in fanatical suicide efforts against the enemy. For example, American forces sometimes faced ***banzai*** charges (so named because of the war cry shouted by the Japanese troops). Waves of Japanese soldiers, some without weapons, would charge American infantry positions only to be slaughtered.

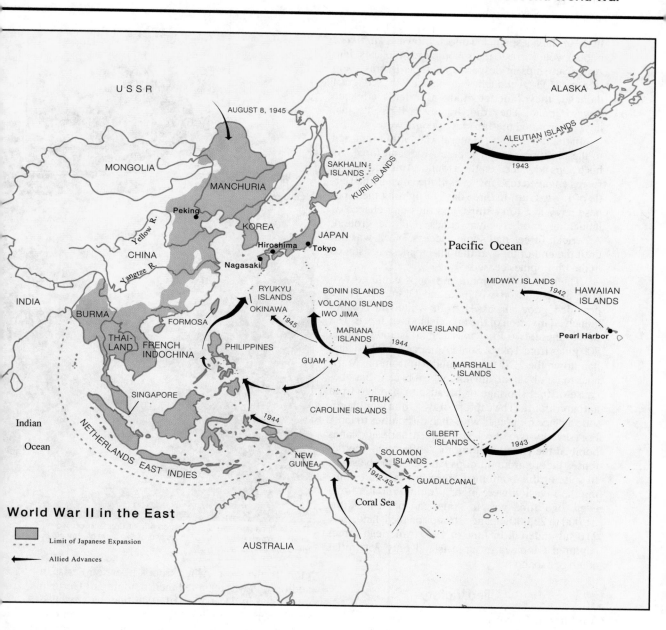

World War II in the East

Limit of Japanese Expansion

Allied Advances

In the air Japanese suicide pilots, known as *kamikaze* pilots, would crash their bomb-laden planes into American ships in desperate attempts to sink them (see p. 161). Although such attacks caused great damage, they failed to halt America's advance toward Japan. They did, however, illustrate just how determined the Japanese people were.

In the fall of 1944, General MacArthur returned to the Philippines with a large American force. As his troops advanced on the ground, American naval forces engaged the Japanese off the coast in the Battle of Leyte Gulf. In three days of fighting the Japanese navy lost forty ships, and thus any chance of launching another naval attack. On the ground, American forces had some success, but it was not until the end of the war that all Japanese resistance in the Philippines ceased.

Then, in 1945, American troops captured two strategic islands—Iwo Jima and Okinawa. These provided good air bases from which they could launch an invasion of the main islands of Japan. The first of these, Iwo Jima, was a small island less than 700 miles from Tokyo. Some American B-29s, which had flown the 2,700-mile round trip from the Marianas to bomb Japan, did not make it back to base because of fuel shortage or because of damage from antiaircraft fire. The capture of Iwo Jima would provide a place for planes with such difficulties to land. For seventy-two days straight, American planes bombed the island, hoping to "soften up" the defenses before ground troops landed on the beaches. In spite of this bombing, American casualties during the invasion were high. Within a month, however, Iwo Jima was in American hands. Of the 21,000 to 23,000 Japanese troops on the island, only 216 surrendered. In June of 1945 American forces captured Okinawa, a large island only 350 miles south of Japan.

Top: Marines raise the U.S. flag atop Mount Suribachi on Iwo Jima; Bottom: Aerial view of the island of Iwo Jima shortly after the U.S. Marines landed

Allied Victory

Victory in Europe

Throughout 1943 and 1944 Soviet troops, well-supplied by the West, relentlessly pushed the German troops back toward Germany. They struck into eastern Europe and drove out the Nazis, establishing their own form of totalitarianism over that region. In the west, Allied troops liberated Paris. In addition, they intensified their bombing of German cities, and by December of 1944 they had reached the border of Germany. Hitler decided to order one final effort to shatter the Allied advance. In December, German armored troops suddenly attacked a weakly held section of the Allied line and pushed back the American forces in that area. Despite some initial success, the German drive halted as the Allies

World War II in the West

- ▨ Major Axis Powers
- ▨ Maximum Areas of Axis Control
- ☐ Neutral Nations
- ••••••• Maginot Line
- ------- Siegfried Line
- ➡ Allied Advances

forced the Germans back to their original position. The **Battle of the Bulge** (as it came to be known) wasted much of Germany's remaining strength and probably hastened the end of the war in Europe.

In February of 1945, as Allied victory seemed certain, Churchill, Roosevelt, and Stalin met in the Russian city of Yalta in the Crimea to determine what policies they would follow in the months ahead. "We have considered and determined the military plans for the final defeat of the common enemy," they proclaimed. They went on to say that although they had agreed on surrender terms, "these

The "Big Three" (Churchill, Roosevelt, and Stalin) meet at Yalta.

terms [would] not be made known until the defeat of Germany has been accomplished.'' Although they avoided specific public statements, the Allies did make certain general principles clear to the public. Germany would have to pay reparations; German war criminals would be brought to trial; all German forces would be disarmed and disbanded; and Germany would be divided into zones of occupation. In addition, Stalin secretly promised America and Britain that he would go to war against Japan within three months after the war ended in Europe.

The **Yalta Conference** recognized Soviet control of eastern Europe. In fact, at the time of the conference, Russian troops already controlled large portions of eastern Europe. Unless the United States and Great Britain wanted war with Russia, Stalin intended to maintain Russian control over the area. Roosevelt and Churchill were eager to gain Soviet aid in the war against Japan; therefore they made a conscious effort at Yalta not to antagonize Stalin. Stalin promised Churchill and Roosevelt that he would allow free elections in eastern Europe following the war, but within a few years even the most naive Western observers realized that Stalin did not intend to keep his word.

Advance to Berlin—Although American forces could easily have taken Berlin, Eisenhower ordered American troops to halt on the Elbe River to allow the Russians to close in on the city. (The agreement to do so had been made at Yalta.) Before Russian troops ar-

rived, on April 30, 1945, Adolf Hitler committed suicide in his underground bunker in Berlin. His aides then burned his body with gasoline. The next day, however, German radio announced that Hitler had died at the head of his troops, fighting to his last breath against bolshevism. On May 7, the Germans unconditionally surrendered, and the Allies declared May 8, 1945, ''V-E'' Day (''Victory in Europe''). The war in Europe was over.

Two months later the leaders of the three victorious powers met at Potsdam, Germany, where they drew up a declaration charting the future course of Germany according to the decisions reached at Yalta. Since Roosevelt had died in April of 1945, President **Harry Truman** represented the United States. Near the end of the conference, **Clement Atlee,** who had been elected the new British prime minister, replaced Churchill at Potsdam. In addition to discussing Germany, the United States and Britain issued an ultimatum to Japan. They warned her that unless she surrendered, she would face serious consequences: the United States had developed the atomic bomb.

Victory in the Pacific

After the surrender of Germany, war continued in the Pacific. American planes using incendiary bombs (bombs designed to start fires) leveled whole sections of Japanese cities. In a one-night raid against Tokyo, for example, fire destroyed nearly sixteen square miles of the city, and more than eighty thousand people died. Although many Japanese people wanted to see the war brought to an end, Japan's military leaders refused to surrender. Instead they gathered together as much war materiel as they could, including a force of eight thousand planes, which they intended to use against the Americans should they attempt to invade Japan.

American and British troops steadily advanced toward Japan. Allied leaders, however, dreaded the long and bloody struggle that lay ahead of them. President Truman and his military staff believed that Japanese and American casualties would reach into the hundreds of thousands should American troops actually invade the home islands of Japan. In an effort to shorten the war and save lives, Truman ordered an atomic bomb to be dropped on the Japanese city of Hiroshima. On August 6, 1945, the bomb was dropped. Its blast wiped out 4.7 square miles of the city and killed an estimated seventy thousand people; another seventy thousand were injured. When Truman announced the dropping of the bomb to the American people, he issued another stern warning to Japan. ''We are now prepared to obliterate more rapidly and completely every productive enterprise the Japanese have above ground in any city.'' If the Japanese leaders did not accept Allied terms of surrender, said Truman, they could ''expect a rain of ruin from the air, the like of which has never been seen on this earth.''

Realizing that the war against Japan would end quickly, the Soviets finally declared war on Japan on August 8 for the sole purpose of gaining territory in the peace negotiations. On August 9 the United States dropped a second atomic bomb on the city of Nagasaki. On August 14 Japan surrendered with the condition that their emperor, Hirohito, would be allowed to remain on his throne. On September 2, 1945 (''V-J'' Day), hostilities formally ended as Japanese and Allied representatives signed the surrender document on board the USS *Missouri* anchored in Tokyo Bay.

Left: An atomic bomb explodes at Nagasaki. **Top Right:** The Japanese foreign minister signs the surrender document.
Bottom Right: Admiral Chester Nimitz signs the document as other Allied commanders look on.

Section Review

1. Who were the "Big Three" Allied leaders who met at Teheran in 1943? Where did these leaders decide to invade Europe to get a foothold on the Continent?
2. Who was the Allied leader of the Normandy Invasion? Give the date for D-day.
3. What strategy did American forces employ as they began to recapture strategic Japanese-held islands in the Pacific?
4. What new weapon did the U.S. use against two Japanese cities in August of 1945?
5. On what ship and on what day did the Japanese sign the surrender documents ending the war in the Pacific?

A Glimpse Behind and a Glimpse Ahead

In a sense, the consequences of World War II have affected the course of history ever since that time. First, World War II proved to be the most costly war in history; costly in the number of lives lost and the amount of money lost. Over forty million people (military and civilian) died—more than double the number of the First World War. The cost reached approximately $1.5 trillion—four times the cost of World War I.

Second, the war transformed the political, social, and economic situation in Europe. The totalitarian governments of Germany and Italy fell, and both countries experienced physical devastation, shattered morale, and financial collapse. The victors were only slightly better off. Neither Britain nor France could any longer claim to be world powers, for the same destruction, financial weakness, and sense of despair hampered their recovery. Britain and France also lost income and prestige through the breakup of their overseas empires. In addition to these problems in Western Europe, the peace of May 1945 left all of Eastern Europe (including the eastern half of Germany) under the control of the Soviet Union. Western Europe was exhausted, and Eastern Europe was enslaved.

Third, the world divided into two groups, each led by a "superpower." In the West the United States became the predominant world power, dedicated to preserving peace and freedom. In the East the USSR became the leader, seeking to expand its totalitarian influence and stir up revolution around the world. These two rival camps entered a period of tension known as the "Cold War."

Finally, one of the most visible results of World War II was the creation of the United Nations organization. The Allies had used the term *United Nations* during the war to signify their unity in opposition to the Axis powers. At the Yalta Conference the Big Three announced that a conference of the United Nations would meet in San Francisco in 1945. In June of that year, fifty nations signed a charter that established the United Nations as a permanent organization. Like the League of Nations, the UN idealistically hoped "to save succeeding generations from the scourge of war." But also like the League, the UN soon demonstrated the inability of man to establish lasting peace through his own efforts.

Chapter Review

Can You Explain?

clique   appeasement   fifth columnists   summit
sanctions   *blitzkrieg*   amphibious   *banzai*
lebensraum   *sitzkrieg*   partisans   *kamikaze*

Can You Identify?

Sun Yat-sen   Munich Conference   Erwin Rommel   Operation Overlord
Chiang Kai-shek   Winston Churchill   RAF   D-day (June 6, 1944)
Mao Zedong   Pact of Steel   Lend-Lease Act   Douglas MacArthur
Third Reich   September 1, 1939   Atlantic Charter   Battle of the Bulge
Rome-Berlin Axis   *panzer*   Hideki Tojo   Yalta Conference
Anti-Comintern Pact   *Luftwaffe*   December 7, 1941   May 8, 1945
Francisco Franco   Vidkun Quisling   Bernard Montgomery   Harry Truman
Neville Chamberlain   Henri Pétain   Dwight D. Eisenhower   Clement Atlee
Édouard Daladier   Charles de Gaulle   "Big Three"   September 2, 1945

Can You Locate?

Manchuria   Leningrad   Hong Kong   Iwo Jima
Ethiopia   Stalingrad   Malaya   Okinawa
Albania   Pearl Harbor   Singapore   Yalta
Sudetenland   El Alamein   Burma   Potsdam
Polish Corridor   Casablanca   Indonesia   Tokyo
Ardennes   Teheran   Coral Sea   Hiroshima
Dunkirk   Normandy   Midway Island   Nagasaki
Vichy France   Philippines

How Much Do You Remember?

1. Outline the steps of Japanese aggression in the Pacific.
2. List major steps that led to war in Europe.
3. Define the following German words: *panzer, Luftwaffe, blitzkrieg, sitzkrieg.*
4. What important decisions did the Allied leaders make at each of the following conferences: Casablanca, Teheran, Yalta, and Potsdam?
5. List four consequences of World War II.

What Do You Think?

1. Why do you think Hitler was surprised when France and Britain declared war after his invasion of Poland?
2. Did the policy of appeasement decrease or increase the likelihood of war?
3. How would you account for Hitler's amazing success during the early years of the war?
4. Were the Allies justified in dropping the atomic bomb?

Less than a year after the Allied victory in World War II, the British statesman and wartime hero Winston Churchill traveled to the United States on a speaking tour. At a stop in Fulton, Missouri, he addressed a gathering at Westminster College on March 5, 1946. "Time may be short," he said. "A shadow has fallen upon the scenes so lately lighted by the Allied victory." His words expressed concern that the Allied victory over the totalitarian states of Germany, Italy, and Japan was being undermined by what could prove to be an even more dangerous foe, the Soviet Union—a former ally.

During the months following the war, Soviet expansion threatened to enslave the Europe that the Allies had so recently freed from the grip of Hitler and Mussolini. "Nobody knows what Soviet Russia and its Communist international organization intends to do in the immediate future, or what are the limits, if any, to their expansive and proselytizing tendencies." But what was already too apparent to Churchill was that much of Europe had fallen under Soviet domination. "From Stettin in the Baltic to Trieste in the Adriatic," Churchill observed, "an iron curtain has descended across the Continent."

This **"iron curtain"** of barbed wire divided Europe, separating Communist Eastern Europe from Western Europe. It was not long before this so-called iron curtain came to symbolize an even greater division. The world that emerged from World War II became divided into two competing camps—the Communist world dominated by the Soviet Union and the Free World led by the United States. Decades of apprehension, hostility, and competition between the Soviet Union and the United States followed. Since this conflict was not an actual "hot war" of the major powers in open combat, as World War II had been, people referred to it as the **Cold War.**

From Europe to Asia, from Africa to Central America, the ambitions of the Communists replaced those of the defeated Axis powers. In response to the growing danger posed by Communist aggression, the United States, who emerged from the war as *the* superpower, took steps to contain and stop further acts of Communist expansion. At the same time, world leaders sought to lessen this tension through peace efforts, international cooperation and agreements, and disarmament treaties. In the end communism would prove a failure and the Soviet Union would break apart, but only after more than forty-five years of costly struggle during the Cold War era.

Postwar Confrontation

Background of the Cold War

After World War II, the United States and the Soviet Union emerged as the two greatest military powers in the world. During the Cold War period, neither country engaged directly in military conflict with the other. Nevertheless, both waged diplomatic and propaganda "wars" and occasionally through their allies fought "hot" wars. The constant struggle between the two did not suddenly emerge after World War II. Decades of mistrust had clouded relations between the two sides.

Opposite Page: *East German border guards carry away the body of eighteen-year-old construction worker Peter Fechter, shot trying to escape over the Berlin Wall on August 18, 1962.*

A Heritage of Mistrust

Since the Bolshevik Revolution of 1917, relations between the Soviet Union and the West had been characterized by suspicion and mistrust. Lenin created ill will among the Allies when he took his country out of World War I and made a separate peace with Germany. Furthermore, the West was appalled at how ruthlessly the Communists slaughtered their opponents in order to establish their dictatorship. During the Russian civil war that followed the revolution, the Allies assisted the non-Communist forces with supplies and a limited number of troops in an unsuccessful attempt to rid Russia and the world of Bolshevism. In addition, the United States withheld diplomatic recognition from the Communist government of the Soviet Union. Not until 1933 did President Franklin Roosevelt—out of a desire to increase trade during the Great Depression—end this period of diplomatic and commercial isolation between the two countries.

Relations between the Soviets and the West worsened when the Soviets signed a nonaggression pact with Nazi Germany in 1939. In June of 1941, however, when Hitler cynically disregarded the nonaggression pact and invaded the Soviet Union, Britain, and later the United States, joined with the Communists to fight the common threat of Nazism. Throughout the remainder of the war, the Soviets were allied with the Americans and the British in the war against the Third Reich. As the war progressed, though, it became clear that the alliance between the Soviets and the West was more a "marriage of convenience" to defeat the Nazis than an alliance based on mutual trust. After the war ended, naked Soviet aggression put an end to the shaky alliance.

Communist Motives

Three motivations fueled Soviet expansion: fear of the West, zeal for their ideology, and desire for power. The Soviet Union remained suspicious of the Western world, an attitude resulting in part from centuries of Russian isolation but even more from the nature of the totalitarian Communist system. Since their own rule was built on fear and repression, the Soviets always assumed the worst motives of their opponents. Stalin during World War II, for instance, believed that the United States and Britain delayed opening another front in France just to increase Soviet losses on the battlefield. During the Cold War, Soviet leaders reinforced this fear and suspicion by painting a threatening picture of the United States. By inventing an America allegedly intent on destroying the Soviet Union, the Communist dictators diverted attention from communism's domestic woes and preserved discipline and loyalty. The threat of another foreign invasion made economic hardship and political oppression more tolerable for the Soviet people. Territorial expansion was one means of "protecting" the Soviet Union from its enemies—real and imaginary.

A second factor was Communist ideology. The basic philosophy of communism called for expansion of its system around the world. In fact, as mentioned in Chapter 20, one of Lenin's greatest "contributions" to Communist thought was his conviction that violence was the primary means of spreading the Communist revolution. (Marx had taught that the revolution would emerge spontaneously in the industrialized nations.) If the workers of the Free World would not overthrow their governments, then the Communist powers would use force to spread their system.

Finally, a simple desire for power motivated the Communists. Like the Nazis, the Communists wanted to add other territories to their empire in order to increase the wealth, power, and prestige of their state. Although they constantly criticized Western imperialism, the Communists built a worldwide empire that dwarfed the ancient empires of Persia and Rome.

Soviet Expansionist Policies

The Soviet Union had a special interest in Eastern Europe. Twice in the twentieth century, would-be conquerors had invaded Russia; Soviet leaders wanted to make sure that it would not happen again. The Soviet Union sought to extend her sphere of influence over the bordering territories in Eastern Europe, creating a buffer zone between the Soviet Union and the West. In addition to providing a buffer, Soviet control over this territory would help provide badly needed raw materials to help rebuild the Soviet economy. Truly, World War II had devastated the Soviet Union. The Russian

Winston Churchill delivering the "Iron Curtain" speech at Westminster College

The Iron Curtain

Beware, I say, time may be short. . . . A shadow has fallen upon the scenes so lately lighted by the Allied victory. Nobody knows what Soviet Russia and its Communist international organization intends to do in the immediate future, or what are the limits, if any, to their expansive and proselytizing tendencies. . . .

From Stettin in the Baltic to Trieste in the Adriatic, an iron curtain has descended across the Continent. Behind that line lie all the capitals of the ancient states of central and eastern Europe. Warsaw, Berlin, Prague, Vienna, Budapest, Belgrade, Bucharest, and Sofia, all these famous cities and the populations around them lie in what I must call the Soviet sphere, and all are subject, in one form or another, not only to Soviet influence but to a very high and, in many cases, increasing measure of control from Moscow. . . .

In a great number of countries, far from the Russian frontiers and throughout the world, Communist fifth columns are established and work in complete unity and absolute obedience to the directions they receive from the Communist center. Except in the British Commonwealth and in the United States, where communism is in its infancy, the Communist parties, or fifth columns, constitute a growing challenge and peril to Christian civilization. These are sober facts for anyone to have to recite on the morrow of a victory gained by so much splendid comradeship in arms and in the cause of freedom and democracy. But we should be most unwise not to face them squarely while time remains. . . . What the Russians desire is the fruits of war and the indefinite expansion of their power and doctrines.

—Winston Churchill, March 5, 1946

Europe and the Cold War

- NATO (includes Canada and the U.S.)
- Warsaw Pact Countries
- Other Communist Countries

ICELAND

NORWAY
SWEDEN
FINLAND
Helsinki
Oslo
Stockholm

North Sea
DENMARK
Copenhagen
Baltic Sea
Moscow

GREAT BRITAIN
Dublin
IRELAND
London
NETH.
Amsterdam
Berlin
EAST GERMANY
POLAND
Warsaw
U.S.S.R.

Brussels
BELG.
Bonn
Prague
CZECHOSLOVAKIA

Atlantic
Ocean
Paris
LUX.
WEST GERMANY
Vienna
AUSTRIA
Budapest
HUNGARY

FRANCE
Bern
SWITZ.
ROMANIA

Belgrade
YUGOSLAVIA
Bucharest

BULGARIA
Sofia
Black Sea

ITALY
Rome
Tirane

PORTUGAL
Madrid
SPAIN
ALBANIA
GREECE
Athens
Ankara
TURKEY

Lisbon

Mediterranean Sea

countryside and cities suffered enormously from the prolonged attack of Nazi Germany. Estimates of Soviet casualties range from 15 to 20 million, a figure that far outnumbers the total American war dead of 389,000. What the Soviets conveniently ignored, of course, was that they were trampling on the rights of those people in Eastern Europe whom they conquered. The Western Allies had fought World War II to free Eastern Europe from Nazi tyranny. Now, that region suffered under a totalitarian regime just as oppressive.

In the wartime conferences at Teheran, Yalta, and Potsdam, the Allied leaders had wrestled with the difficult question of what to do with Germany and her former empire. They agreed that Germany should be divided and occupied by Western and

Marshal Tito

Stalin, Truman, and Churchill meet at the Potsdam Conference in Germany.

Soviet forces. The Allies could not agree, however, on the issue of Eastern Europe. Great Britain and the United States favored the establishment of democratic republics. But the Soviet Union, with its Red Army already in this region, insisted on regimes friendly to Soviet interests. To Stalin, the prospect of democratic, pro-Western governments on the Soviet western border was intolerable. At the end of the war, the Allies recognized special Soviet territorial gains in Eastern Europe with the understanding that free elections would ultimately resolve that area's fate.

The Soviet Red Army, however, refused to leave Eastern Europe. The Soviets managed to place Communists in power in several countries in this region. In 1945 both Poland and Rumania fell under Communist control. Soviet puppet governments were established the following year in Bulgaria and Albania. In 1947 Hungary succumbed to Soviet domination, and in 1948 Czechoslovakia did also. In Yugoslavia, Josip Broz, better known as **Marshal Tito,** came to power. Tito established a Communist government, but he dismayed Stalin by insisting on a greater degree of independence from Moscow than did other East European countries. Since Stalin had no common border with Yugoslavia, he could not send in his army to enforce his will. The Soviet dictator could only fume and denounce Tito.

Elsewhere in Eastern Europe, though, for nearly fifty years, the Soviet Union exercised virtual colonial control over the Communist-bloc countries. Kremlin leaders dictated the political, economic, and social affairs of their satellite states. When any Soviet-dominated country in Eastern Europe attempted to overthrow this imperialistic yoke, Soviet tanks and troops moved in swiftly and brutally to crush the revolts. Such was the case in Hungary in 1956 and in Czechoslovakia in 1968. In Eastern Europe, the Soviets built an empire founded on fear and maintained by force.

American Containment Policies

American Ideals

When World War II ended, the United States was undoubtedly the most powerful nation in the world. Her economic and military might were without equal. The only nation with the atomic bomb, the United States could not retreat to its traditional prewar isolationism. In another break with tradition, America began a peacetime defense build-up.

The United States at this time enjoyed an enormous amount of prestige, as well as good will, from those nations who benefited from her assistance during the war. America entered the postwar period with a clear sense of superiority and mission. Her goal was to spread democracy and to promote free trade throughout the world.

Containment

Americans became alarmed, however, at the spread of communism beyond the borders of the Soviet Union. They denounced Soviet aggression and the occupation of Eastern Europe. When President Harry S. Truman sternly lectured the Soviet foreign minister about the issue, the Soviet official indignantly replied that he had never been talked to like that in his life. Truman shot back, "Carry out your agreements and you won't get talked to like that." But little changed. With a dwindling Allied presence in Eastern Europe and the continued influence of the Soviet armed forces, one country after another fell into Communist hands. In response, Truman implemented a foreign policy designed to contain the spread of communism.

By 1946 it became obvious that the Soviet Union intended to expand beyond Eastern Europe. The Soviets supported Communist guerrillas in Greece and made territorial demands upon Turkey. President Truman could not let this intervention in the eastern Mediterranean go unchecked. In 1947 he announced that the United States would support any country threatened by Communist aggression. This principle of assisting countries in a struggle against communism became known appropriately as the **Truman Doctrine.** To implement the Truman Doctrine, the president secured economic and military aid from the United States Congress for Greece and Turkey. United States aid helped turn back the Communist challenge in both lands.

The Truman Doctrine underscored the major objective of American foreign policy during the Cold War—**containment.** In July of 1947, a little-known State Department official, George Kennan, stated that the best strategy against Soviet power would be "long term, patient but firm . . . containment of Russian expansive tendencies." Kennan, who helped devise the plan of containment, also noted prophetically that Soviet power possibly bore within itself the seeds of its own destruction. Containment as set forth by the Truman administration would not mean the use of military force to remove communism where it currently existed, but it would mean the use of military, economic, diplomatic, and psychological means to curtail its further advance. Truman believed that the American public would not support a war to remove the Soviet influence from Eastern Europe.

The Marshall Plan

The United States also worried about Western Europe. War had wrecked the economies in the region, and economic chaos immediately after the war encouraged the growth of Communist parties in Italy and France. In June of 1947, one month after Truman signed the bill of aid to Greece and Turkey, the United States secretary of state George Marshall announced plans for massive economic assistance to war-ravaged Europe. In April of 1948 Truman signed the European Recovery Act, or **Marshall Plan,** as it was popularly called, which provided $5.3 billion for the program. Western European countries eagerly accepted the funds, and over the next four years the aid brought dramatic improvement to their faltering economies.

The long-term purpose of the Marshall Plan was to rebuild Western Europe economically and thereby thwart any advance of communism in that area of the Continent. It not only reduced the appeal of communism in Western Europe but, by rebuilding and strengthening Western economies, the United States also helped create strong trade partners. Not surprisingly, this act further intensified the Cold War. The Soviet Union and her East European subjects rejected the American offer of economic assistance, fearing a scheme that meant greater American influence. Acceptance or rejection of the aid divided Europe into pro-American and pro-Soviet sides.

U.S./Soviet Confrontation

Germany

After World War II Germany was divided into four zones, each occupied by a major Allied country—France, Great Britain, the United States, and the Soviet Union. The German capital of Berlin was also divided: the Western Allies occupied West Berlin, and the Soviets occupied East Berlin. The Western Allies organized the Federal Republic of Germany, which included West Germany and West Berlin. (The city of Bonn became the capital.) The Soviet Union responded by establishing the German Democratic Republic, composed of East Germany and East Berlin. Unfortunately West Berlin lay deep inside hostile East Germany.

In 1948 Berlin became a test for the policy of containment. The Soviets, upset with the Marshall Plan and unification of West Germany, cut off all highway and rail contact between West Berlin and Western Europe. This action brought the Communist-bloc nations and the Free World very close to war. With President Truman providing the leader-

Occupation of Germany After World War II

Children in Berlin stand on piles of rubble during the Berlin Airlift and cheer the arrival of American planes loaded with food.

ship, the American and British authorities ordered an airlift to provide the people of West Berlin with vital supplies. For more than a year, the West flew in fuel and food to the besieged city. At the height of the airlift, planes were landing every three minutes, twenty-four hours a day. So successful was the airlift that the Soviet Union lifted the blockade. The West had scored a major victory in the Cold War without becoming involved in an actual conflict.

NATO

Containment took a more militaristic turn in 1949. Tensions were high over the Berlin crisis and the inability of the United Nations, the international body formed at the end of World War II, to provide peace and security. The West sought a more effective means of insuring its defense against Soviet expansion. The solution was a regional military alliance called the North Atlantic Treaty Organization, or **NATO.** Organized in 1949, NATO orig-

inally included nations in the geographical area of the North Atlantic, principally the United States, Canada, Great Britain, France, and Italy, along with less powerful nations. In 1952, during the Korean War, NATO expanded to include the eastern Mediterranean countries of Greece and Turkey. In 1955 West Germany joined the mutual alliance system. The Soviet Union responded by creating its own regional military alliance, the **Warsaw Pact,** which included its Eastern European satellite states.

Arms Race

Also in 1949 the Soviet Union exploded its first atomic bomb, ending the American atomic monopoly. This development brought more uncertainty to the Cold War. The West wondered how this achievement would affect Soviet behavior. Since 1945 the United States had exercised restraint with its exclusive control of atomic weapons. Americans feared that the Communists would use their nuclear capa-

A U.S. NATO fighter undergoes maintenance in England. The Cold War necessitated a large American military presence in Europe.

duction of the hydrogen bomb, or "super" bomb. This new "H-bomb" was hundreds of times more powerful than the atomic weapons dropped on Japan by the United States in World War II. Over the next three decades both the Soviets and the Americans increased their peacetime production of nuclear and conventional weapons. Both sides wanted to maintain a position of strength; both wanted to prevent the other side from gaining a military edge.

Section Review

1. Define the term *Cold War*.
2. List the three major motivations for Soviet expansion after World War II.
3. What was the purpose of the Truman Doctrine?
4. What city, divided after the war into Soviet and Western sectors, was the focus of a blockade and airlift?
5. What is the name of the major Western regional military alliance organized in 1949? What was the name of its Soviet counterpart?

bility to blackmail and intimidate their foes. The Soviet production of the atomic bomb also marked the beginning of the postwar East-West **arms race.** In January of 1950, President Truman ordered the pro-

Spread of Communism

Eastern Europe was not the only critical region of the Cold War era. Bolstered by the Soviet Union, the unrelenting march of communism continued around the world. From the Orient, through the Middle East, in Africa, to Latin America, country after country fell under the yoke of communism. The Soviet empire alone encompassed one-fourth of the world's land surface and one-third of its population. During the postwar period, tension between the Free World and the Communist bloc flared several times into wars limited to specific geographic areas, often called contained or **limited wars.** Instead of directly confronting each other in these military actions, the United States and the Soviet Union indirectly supported other nations in these limited wars in order to protect and maintain their sphere of influence around the world. The Soviets supported North Vietnam against the United States in the 1960s and early 1970s, for example, and the U.S. gave aid to Afghan forces against the Soviet forces in the 1980s.

Fall of China

One of the first areas outside Europe to face the threat of communism was China. After the defeat of Japan in World War II, civil war once again resumed in China between the Nationalist forces of Chiang Kai-shek and the Communist forces of Mao Zedong. (See page 550.) The conflict continued from 1945 to 1949. In spite of more than $2 billion in American aid, the Nationalist forces could not defeat the Communists. As that aid was reduced, the leaders of China, who had relied on American help to defeat the Communists, found themselves militarily and economically vulnerable. By 1949 Mao's forces had captured the major cities of China, sealing the defeat of Chiang. The Communist forces drove the Nationalist armies off the mainland; Chiang and his Nationalist followers fled to the nearby island of Formosa (Taiwan).

Chiang's collapse was a major blow to American interests in Asia. America fought World War II,

As dictator of the world's most populous nation, Mao Zedong (left) was able to forge a position of leadership in world affairs despite his repressive policies in China. Here he is pictured with American secretary of state Henry Kissinger. In the background is Zhou Enlai, Chinese premier (1949-76) and diplomat.

in part, to secure the freedom of China from Japanese militarism; yet in the years following 1945, the country fell to the Communists. For the next thirty years the United States recognized Taiwan as the "real" China and cut off diplomatic ties with the Communist government in Beijing. A huge land mass encompassing the Soviet Union and China now under Communist rule posed a serious problem for the West during the Cold War era.

The Korean War (1950-53)

Invasion and Reaction

In 1950 Asia was again a "hot spot" in the East-West confrontation when Communist North Korea invaded South Korea and sparked the **Korean War.** At the close of World War II Korea had been divided, like Germany, into Communist and non-Communist occupation zones. North Korean forces, trained and financed by the Soviet Union, now sought to unite all of Korea under Communist rule. In June of 1950 North Korean forces invaded South Korea, confirming the worst fears of the West—the Communists intended once again to expand their influence.

President Truman viewed this invasion as another example of Soviet expansion; such aggression, he believed, had to be stopped. Therefore Truman called upon the Free World, led by the United States, to halt the Communist conquest of South Korea. Rather than appealing to Congress for a declaration of war, President Truman sought action by the United Nations. Although other nations joined the fight against the North Koreans, the war was primarily an American effort.

Success and Defeat

The initial North Korean advance had overrun most of the Korean peninsula. But under the command of General **Douglas MacArthur,** UN forces, composed primarily of American and South Korean troops, mounted a daring counteroffensive. Following an amphibious assault at Inchon, UN forces secured South Korea, driving the enemy across the **38th parallel** (the border between North and South Korea). They pursued the North Koreans deep into North Korea, pushing all the way to the Yalu River (the border between North Korea and Communist China). Just as the UN forces seemed on the verge of victory, waves of Communist Chinese troops swept across the China-Korea border. The Communist forces overwhelmed MacArthur's army and sent it reeling back to the 38th parallel.

General MacArthur, wanting to gain a military victory, proposed a major assault on North Korea combined with the bombing of Chinese bases in Manchuria. Such action would bring an escalation to the conflict but would be necessary for ultimate victory. But the risk of widening the war in Asia, possibly involving both China and the Soviet Union, led Truman to prefer a limited war with a negotiated settlement. Truman's chairman of the Joint Chiefs of Staff, General Omar Bradley, expressed the administration's sentiment that MacArthur's plan would provoke "the wrong war, at the wrong place, at the wrong time, and with the wrong enemy." The frustrated MacArthur bypassed regular channels for expressing his views to the government and made his views public. In response, on April 11, 1951, an angry Truman relieved General MacArthur of his duties as UN commander. That same year negotiations to end the war began.

The Korean War

CHINA

MANCHURIA

USSR

Yalu R.

Farthest
Advance of
U.N. Forces.
November 1950

NORTH
KOREA

★ Pyongyang

Armistice Line
July 1953

38th Parallel

★ Seoul
Inchon

SOUTH
KOREA

● Pusan

Elements of the 1st Marine Division during their heroic retreat from Chosin in North Korea

Stalemate and Exhaustion

For two years both hostilities and peace negotiations continued. Finally in July of 1953 an armistice was signed ending the war. It provided for a demilitarized zone between North and South Korea. It also called for a conference to settle questions about Korea's future, but the conference was never held. The years of bloodshed had ended in a stalemate with the Korean peninsula returning to its prewar divided state. Communism had been "contained"—not defeated—but at a great price. More than a million Koreans and Chinese lay dead from the conflict; about 54,000 Americans would not return home. These died fighting a "limited" war to safeguard against another global war. But the indecisive conclusion to the Korean conflict and the failure of the Free World to secure a military victory served only to encourage Communist aggression in other areas of the world.

The War in Vietnam

The French Phase

Another significant challenge to the containment of communism during the Cold War era came in the Southeast Asian country of Vietnam. French Indochina, which included Vietnam, passed into the hands of the Japanese during World War II. After the war, the French wanted to recover their colony. But Vietnamese nationalist **Ho Chi Minh,** who was also a Communist, declared his country's independence and a struggle ensued with the French. This Indochinese war increased in significance after China's fall to communism in 1949 and the beginning of the Korean War the next year.

The year after the Korean armistice, the Vietnamese Communists scored a major victory over the French in the **Battle of Dien Bien Phu,** anni-

The Cold War

Truman

Stalin

Yalta Conference condemns Eastern Europe to Communist domination	1945	1945
		Soviets take over Poland and Rumania
		Tito establishes Communist regime in Yugoslavia
Soviets take over Hungary	1947	1947 U.S. announces Truman Doctrine
Soviets take over Czechoslovakia Truman signs European Recovery Act ("Marshall Plan")	1948	1948 Organization of Federal Republic of Germany (West Germany) Berlin Airlift Yugoslavia expelled from Soviet bloc; remains Communist

Organization of NATO — 1949
Fall of China to communism

1949 USSR explodes its first atomic bomb
Communist guerrillas put down in Greece

Eisenhower

Korean War — 1950-53

1952 U.S. explodes H-bomb

Battle of Dien Bien Phu — 1954

1954 Organization of SEATO

1955 Organization of Warsaw Pact

Soviets crush uprising in Hungary — 1956

1957 USSR launches *Sputnik*

Mao Zedong launches Great Leap Forward in China — 1958

1959 Cuba falls to communism

U-2 Incident — 1960

1961 Erection of Berlin Wall

Khrushchev

Cuban Missile Crisis — 1962

1964 Gulf of Tonkin Resolution

Kennedy

U.S. steps up involvement in Vietnam War — 1965

1965 U.S. forestalls Communist takeover in Dominican Republic

1966 Mao Zedong launches Cultural Revolution in China

Tet offensive — 1968

1968 Soviets crush uprising in Czechoslovakia

Nixon visits Communist China — 1972

1972 U.S. and USSR sign SALT treaty

U.S. forces end involvement in Vietnam — 1973

Johnson

1975 South Vietnam falls to communism

USSR invades Afghanistan — 1979

1979 Sandinistas take power in Nicaragua

Brezhnev

1981 Communists suppress Solidarity labor union in Poland

Soviets shoot down Korean airliner — 1983

1983 U.S. topples Marxist regime in Grenada

Communist Chinese government cracks down on prodemocracy students in Tiananmen Square
Poland elects non-Communist government — 1989

1989 Berlin Wall torn down; government of East Germany collapses
End of Communist governments in Hungary and Czechoslovakia
Anti-Communist revolution in Rumania

Nixon

End of Communist government in Yugoslavia; country fragments — 1990

1990 Germany reunited

Communist regime in Albania collapses
Baltic States declare independence from Soviet Union — 1991

1991 Hard-line Communists in USSR fail in attempt at coup
Soviet Union dissolves into Commonwealth of Independent States

Reagan

Gorbachev

U.S. Marines are pinned down by enemy fire in a rice paddy in South Vietnam.

hilating a major French army. The French, no longer able or willing to reclaim their former colony, sought a negotiated settlement. At the Geneva Conference of 1954, the Communists won a diplomatic victory: Vietnam was divided into two parts—the Communist north and the non-Communist south. Almost immediately, Communist guerrillas, known as the **Viet Cong,** began subversive activity in the south. Their goal was to weaken the South Vietnamese government so that they could unite Vietnam under their Communist leader, Ho Chi Minh.

In order to keep South Vietnam and other Asian nations free from communism, the United States, Great Britain, France, and several non-Communist Asian nations formed the Southeast Asia Treaty Organization (**SEATO**) in 1954. In theory, the member nations agreed to "consult" each other concerning any Communist aggression in that part of the world. In practice, they were pledging each other military assistance against the Communist menace.

As the chief member of SEATO, the United States began supporting the non-Communist government in South Vietnam with economic and military assistance. Behind America's foreign policy lay what U.S. president Dwight Eisenhower called the **domino theory.** According to this theory, once Vietnam fell to communism, then other countries of Asia would fall like dominos toppling against one another. The United States was determined that Vietnam would not be that first "domino." Although presidents Eisenhower and Kennedy sent only a limited number of American military advisers to help South Vietnam, their aid marked the beginning of a major military commitment. American leaders had decided to settle the conflict through direct military involvement.

The American Phase

In 1964 three North Vietnamese torpedo boats attacked American destroyers that were in international waters in the Gulf of Tonkin. Through the **Gulf of Tonkin Resolution,** the American Congress authorized President Lyndon Johnson to "take all necessary measures to repel any armed attack against forces of the United States and to prevent further aggression." Congress also authorized the president to take "all necessary steps, including the use of armed force, to assist any member . . . of the Southeast Asia Collective Defense Treaty requesting assistance in defense of its freedom." The number of American military personnel in Vietnam climbed from 23,000 in 1964 to a high of 542,000 in 1969. In 1965 the United States also began air bombing Communist supply routes and bases in North Vietnam.

The year 1968 proved to be a pivotal year in American involvement in the Vietnam War. Military officials believed that they were making progress against the Communist enemy. But the Viet Cong demonstrated surprising strength in their **Tet** (New Year) **offensive** on South Vietnamese cities. In this attack, the Communists temporarily occupied many major cities of South Vietnam and even briefly captured part of the American embassy. In purely military terms, the offensive was a failure. American and South Vietnamese forces drove the Communists back and inflicted heavy casualties. Its propaganda value was enormous, however. Tet showed that the war was not almost won, as the American government was claiming. For many Americans, frustration increased, and victory seemed even further away. President Johnson, faced with growing popular dissatisfaction with American involvement in the war, saw no likely prospect of military success through limited war. He decided not to seek re-election, halted the bombing of North Vietnam, and initiated peace talks with the Communists.

Richard Nixon, who won the 1968 presidential election, began a negotiated American withdrawal from Vietnam. He sought to turn the burden of the fighting gradually over to the South Vietnamese in a program he called **Vietnamization.** However, to keep pressure on the North, he continued heavy bombing in that region and in the spring of 1970 ordered an invasion of Cambodia to cut Communist supply routes. Nixon finally achieved what he called "peace with honor" by negotiating a peace settlement with the North Vietnamese in January of 1973. According to this agreement, U.S. troops evacuated South Vietnam. However, without American troops, the South Vietnamese could not defeat the Communists nor hold on to their own country. In 1975 the war ended with the achievement of Ho Chi Minh's goal: a unified Vietnam under Communist control. In addition, the Communists also took over the neighboring countries of Laos and Cambodia. The "domino theory" was holding true.

Vietnam would prove to be one of America's biggest failures during the Cold War era. Communism had not been contained; in fact, it had been completely victorious. In addition, the United States had engaged in its longest war and had suffered its first military defeat. The war cost far more than the 50,000 American dead and the $146 billion spent. It provoked a new spirit of isolation in America, as the public expressed opposition to any American military intervention in the world, no matter what the cause. This overreaction only encouraged Communist aggression around the world. The loss in Vietnam marked the end of an era for the United States. In the 1940s America had enjoyed enormous power and prestige. By the 1970s the United States recognized that its power was limited by the strength of the Soviet Union and Communist China, by the increasing threat of nuclear weapons, and by the lack of resolve of the American people.

American soliders engaged in a fire fight with Vietnamese Communist guerrillas

Communism in Africa and Latin America

Africa

As in Asia, Moscow had an opportunity in Africa to extend its influence in the wake of the disintegration of European colonial empires. (See pp. 618-21.) Following World War II, one African country after another gained its independence from European colonial rule. Many countries turned to the Soviets for assistance in their nationalistic struggle against the "imperialistic" forces of the West. In other countries, Communist forces took advantage of the turmoil and discontent by encouraging revolution. Communist regimes enjoyed some success in Ethiopia, Mozambique, and Angola. Newly independent countries sought financial and military assistance from the Soviet Union and her Communist allies. Many African countries soon began to realize that their pro-Soviet alliances came with strings attached. These countries fell under a new form of colonial control as Soviet, Cuban, and Chinese Communists preyed upon the instability of the continent to extend the Communist ideology and control.

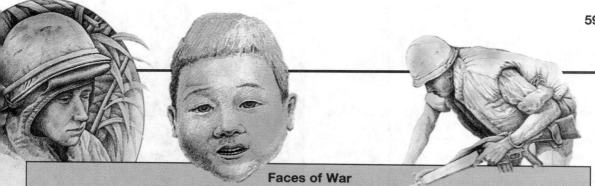

Faces of War

The Vietnam War divided the American public more than any other conflict of the twentieth century. The lack of dramatic battlefield victories and the lengthy casualty lists created a weariness among segments of the American people. The government of South Vietnam was so corrupt that it was easy to lose sight of the overall American goal of containing Communist expansion.

However, many thousands of American soldiers served loyally in Vietnam, including many Christians. Among them was Steve Crain, who served as an illustrator for the Information Office of the United States Army in the Republic of Vietnam. During his tour of duty, Crain drew the faces of war—his interpretation of the war as seen in the faces of the people. Some of his drawings are reproduced on this page.

Concerning the war itself, Crain wrote, "I have met several Christian friends from all parts of the United States. . . . Being here has strengthened my faith in Christ. I find that the biggest 'hang-up' with most GI's is the excuse, 'everything will be different when I get out of Vietnam; I will think about God then.'

"It is a very strange war. There is much corruption; the issues are not as clear-cut as some Americans think. There are over-generalizations from both liberals and conservatives. I have spent most of my time in support areas which are fairly secure. Therefore, I have seen other enemies besides the Viet Cong or the North Vietnamese—alcohol, drugs, prostitution, boredom, racial tensions, greed, and disillusionment. If I did not know that my sins were forgiven and that Christ lives in my heart, I would also be an easy victim for the 'enemy.' But Christ does live in my heart and He is the answer regardless of where in the world you are."

The West did not respond to the Communist infiltration of Africa with the same resolve as she did in Eastern Europe and Asia. Many Western countries no longer felt compelled to assist their former colonies in resisting the advances of communism, especially in the wake of recent revolts against colonial rule. The West denounced what they viewed as "unwarranted interference" on the part of the Soviet Union, Cuba, and China in Africa. Yet the Western powers did not take an aggressive stand to contain the spread of communism on the continent. Even after Soviet communism collapsed and much of the economic assistance from Moscow stopped flowing to Africa, many African countries continued to be plagued by the revolutionary, socialist legacy of communism.

Latin America

The cause of "containing" the spread of communism moved closer to home for the United States as communism gained a foothold in Latin America. In the decades following World War II, Latin American countries were faced with such problems as social and political inequality, poverty, poor education, and dictatorial governments. As the Communists began to exploit the unsettled conditions in the region, Americans became more and more alarmed. Some Latin American countries looked to the Soviets, instead of the United States, for economic assistance in reaction to what they called "Yankee imperialism."

In 1959 the Communist dictator **Fidel Castro** seized power in Cuba and allied his country with the Soviet Union. Cuban-backed guerrilla groups

American Marines patrol the streets of Grenville, Grenada, after American intervention in 1983.

Fidel Castro

began stirring up revolutionary activity throughout the region. Communism threatened Central American countries such as Nicaragua, El Salvador, and Panama. In Nicaragua, the Sandinistas, a left-wing group, captured power in 1979 and ruled the country for ten years. No longer was the Communist threat halfway around the world; it was being nurtured in the United States' back yard. At the same time, many Americans were hesitant about becoming involved in the struggle for Latin America out

of fear that intervention in that region might become another Vietnam experience.

Nonetheless, the U.S. showed stronger resolve in dealing with communism in Latin America than it did in Africa. In 1965 President Johnson sent American Marines into the Dominican Republic to halt a Communist takeover. The American CIA supported the overthrow of a Marxist government in Chile in 1973. In the 1980s, President Ronald Reagan responded to the Communist threat in Latin America by encouraging free and democratic elections, providing economic assistance to faltering economies, and offering military assistance to countries threatened by Communist aggression. In 1983, for example, Reagan sent American troops to the Caribbean island of Grenada to topple a Marxist regime that had seized power and endangered its neighbors. This firm stand ultimately began to pay dividends in the collapse of Marxist regimes south of the U.S. border.

Section Review

1. To where did the Nationalist forces of Chiang Kai-shek flee at the end of the Chinese civil war?
2. What country provided a large number of troops to aid the North Koreans during the Korean War?
3. What is the name of the theory that maintains that if one country is allowed to fall to communism, then soon others near it will also topple?
4. What resolution authorized the American president to take whatever steps necessary to stop further acts of aggression by the Viet Cong?
5. What Latin American country allied itself to the Soviet Union in the 1950s and stirred up revolutionary activity throughout the region?

Showdown Between the Superpowers

"Coexistence" and Tension

Despite the ongoing struggle between the Free and Communist worlds over the spread of communism, relations between the United States and the Soviet Union improved during the 1950s. In 1953 Stalin died and **Nikita Khrushchev** (KROOSH chef) emerged as the new leader of the Soviet Union. He

Nikita Khrushchev

and the new American president, Dwight Eisenhower, pursued a course of **"peaceful coexistence."** According to Khrushchev, "The main thing is to keep to the positions of ideological struggle without resorting to arms to prove that one is right."

The prospect for peaceful coexistence was short-lived, however. By the late 1950s East-West relations once again were stormy. In 1957, the Russians launched *Sputnik,* the first manmade satellite. This unexpected Soviet breakthrough caused great alarm for the people of the United States. Americans looked upon their country as the world leader in science and technology; they now found themselves in second place in the race for space. They particularly feared that the Soviets would use this new capability for a possible nuclear missile strike.

America responded with a renewed resolve to strengthen education (especially in scientific fields) and an intense speeding up of its own space program. President John Kennedy pledged to put a man on the moon by the end of the 1960s—a promise that the government kept. In addition, the United

The "space race" between the U.S. and the USSR had profound military implications. This American Titan missile carries military communications satellites into orbit.

States sought to strengthen its defense while keeping a closer eye on the Soviet military build-up.

In an attempt to keep track of what the Soviets were up to, the United States suffered an embarrassing setback in May of 1960. An American U-2 reconnaissance (spy) plane was shot down over the Soviet Union. Washington at first denied responsibility but was later forced to acknowledge the spy mission. The Soviet defense minister announced that in the event of any further flights over the USSR, the Soviets would fire rockets on the base from which the plane took off.

The **"U-2 incident"** was only a mild prelude to clashes of the Free World with Soviet totalitarianism in the early 1960s. The first center of tension was Berlin. The constant flow of refugees from Communist East Germany into Western Europe was a living testimony to the failures of communism. Irked and embarrassed, in August of 1961 the Soviets built a concrete and barbed wire wall physically separating East and West Berlin. The **Berlin Wall** became the most recognizable symbol of the Cold War struggle between the Free and Communist worlds. The wall was in a sense an admission of failure by the Communists, but it kept their most productive citizens within the Communist bloc.

The superpowers nearly heated the Cold War into a world war over Cuba. The United States discovered that the Soviets were installing offensive missiles and air bases in Fidel Castro's Cuba.

An East German border guard opposed to the building of the Berlin Wall leaps over barbed wire to freedom in West Berlin in 1961.

In what has been called the **Cuban Missile Crisis,** President John Kennedy insisted that the Soviets remove the missiles. To enforce his demand, he ordered a blockade of the island. Faced with the ultimatum and a possible invasion of Cuba by the United States, Khrushchev backed down and had the missiles removed. The United States had achieved a major victory without resorting to full-scale war.

"Thaws" in the Cold War

In the early 1970s, President Richard Nixon took dramatic steps to end the Cold War. In 1972 he

Aleksandr Solzhenitsyn: Out of the Dragon's Belly

"I have been in the dragon's belly, in its red-hot innards. It was unable to digest me and threw me up. I have come to you as a witness to what it is like there, in the dragon's belly," said Russian writer Aleksandr Solzhenitsyn (SOLE zhuh NEE tsin). As a victim of Soviet oppression and an eventual exile from his homeland, Solzhenitsyn gave a ringing testimony to the true nature of the Communist state.

Born in 1918, Solzhenitsyn grew up a dedicated Communist. He studied science, history, and literature and served briefly as a teacher. With the Nazi invasion of 1941, Solzhenitsyn entered the army. He eventually rose to the rank of captain and twice received medals for his service. Then in February of 1945, he was arrested. The Soviet secret police found a passage in one of the soldier's private letters which seemed to criticize the Soviet dictator Stalin.

What followed was an eight-year ordeal that revealed the real character of communism. Solzhenitsyn spent three years in prison and five years in Communist labor camps. Released after Stalin's death in 1953, Solzhenitsyn returned to teaching mathematics and physics. But he also began to indulge a lifelong love for writing. He did not expect his work to be published. He observed simply, "When you've been pitched headfirst into hell you just write about it."

His work might have remained unknown, but Soviet leaders in the late 1950s and early 1960s inaugurated a period of "openness." Communist authorities sought to improve relations with the West by criticizing the Stalin regime, implying that things were now much better in the Soviet Union. In 1962 Solzhenitsyn published *One Day in the Life of Ivan Denisovich,* a painful, masterful portrayal of a single day in the life of a prisoner in a Soviet labor camp. Other works followed, and Solzhenitsyn's fame became international. When the Soviet government decided in the mid-1960s that "openness" had gone too far, it was unable

to crack down on the author as it would have liked. He was too famous to be safely silenced.

Nevertheless, a struggle ensued between Solzhenitsyn and the Communist government. The Russian author refused to knuckle under to the pressure to conform. Then in 1973, the first part of Solzhenitsyn's *Gulag Archipelago* was published in Paris. *Gulag* was the name for the system of Soviet labor camps. Solzhenitsyn unsparingly portrayed the dehumanizing cruelty of the Gulag, providing a full history of its brutal policies. He described, for example, the method of interrogation known as "bridling": "A long piece of rough toweling was inserted between the prisoner's jaws like a bridle; the ends were then pulled back over his shoulders and tied to his heels. Just try lying on your stomach like a wheel, with your spine breaking—and without water and food for two days!" Angered at the publication of the book, the Soviet government expelled Solzhenitsyn from the country in 1974.

When he came to the West, Solzhenitsyn faced a world which was not eager to hear his message. Years of struggle in the Cold War had wearied the Free World. Voices in the media and the academic world declared that communism had reformed. Even if the Communists had not changed, they argued, the threat of nuclear war made it necessary for the West to accept Communist domination where it already existed and to be cautious about opposing its further expansion. President Gerald Ford of the United States refused to invite Solzhenitsyn to the White House, fearing that such an act would anger the Soviets.

Solzhenitsyn replied by warning the West about the realities of life behind the iron curtain. He said that the Soviet system was "a system without an independent press; a system without an independent judiciary; where the people have no influence either on external or internal policy; where any thought which is different from what the state thinks is crushed." The exile chided those who thought that communism could reform. In 1975 he said, "Recently, the leader of the Swedish socialists . . . said that the only way that Communism can survive is by adopting the principles of democracy. That is the same thing as saying that the only way in which a wolf can survive is to stop eating meat and become a lamb." He pleaded with the West not to passively accept a situation that left millions in the bondage of totalitarian slavery: "You cannot love freedom for yourselves alone and quietly agree to a situation where the majority of humanity, spread over the greater part of the globe, is subjected to violence and oppression." He reasoned, "Whenever you help the persons persecuted in the Soviet Union, you not only display magnanimity and nobility, you're defending not only them but yourselves as well. You're defending your own future."

Some Americans listened to the Russian exile and heeded him. Others scorned him. Whatever the reaction to his words, Solzhenitsyn refused to be silent. As he said in accepting the Nobel Prize for Literature (quoting a Russian proverb), "One word of truth shall outweigh the whole world."

Richard Nixon visits the Great Wall during his historic trip to China in 1972.

became the first American president to visit mainland China, even though the United States at that time did not recognize the Communist Chinese government. Furthermore, his secretary of state, Henry Kissinger, worked toward a policy of **détente** (relaxation of tensions) with the Soviet Union. Cooperation and summit meetings replaced the harsh language and hostile positions of the superpowers. In 1972 Nixon visited the Soviet Union and signed the **SALT** (Strategic Arms Limitations Talks) treaty with the Soviets, which limited the number of nuclear weapons that each superpower could possess. Additional SALT talks continued throughout the decade.

But by the end of the 1970s, it was all too apparent that the Soviets were violating the arms treaties and were still intent on military aggression. In December of 1979, Soviet troops invaded neighboring Afghanistan. The Free World was alarmed, not only over Soviet occupation of Afghanistan but also over the looming Soviet threat to the world's oil supplies in the Persian Gulf region.

The United States, the leader of the Free World, entered the 1980s in a weakened position. Economically, recession gripped the country. Militarily, years of disarmament talks and unkept agreements left the United States in a precarious position of having to catch up to the military production of her Soviet counterpart. But the American resolve to stand against the threat of communism found a champion in President **Ronald Reagan,** elected in 1980. He was determined to restore America's prestige in the world; at the same time he denounced the evils of communism. Wanting to deal with the Soviets from a position of strength, he gained support for a build-up of America's military. He initiated a new weapons system, the Strategic Defense Initiative (**SDI**), commonly called "Star Wars." This defense program was designed to use American space, laser, and satellite technology to provide a shield in space against incoming Soviet missiles.

Although there was skepticism in the United States about the SDI project, the Soviets were alarmed. The arms race which had been imbalanced in their favor was now tipping toward the United States. They withdrew from arms-control negotiations, insisting they would not return until the U.S. was willing to stop work on SDI. Relations between the two superpowers further deteriorated when in 1983 the Soviets shot down a Korean passenger plane, claiming they thought it was a spy plane. A total of 269 people, a number of whom were Americans, including an American congressman, died in the incident. Horrified by this action, Reagan denounced the Soviet Union as an "evil empire" in a televised address.

Collapse of the Soviet Empire

Reasons for Decline

In the midst of this renewed confrontation between the superpowers, the relationship between the Soviet Union and the Free World began to change. Several factors made this dramatic development possible. One was the growing unrest of the people of Eastern Europe who suffered under the yoke of Soviet rule. They expressed their opposition to Soviet control through demonstrations and uprisings. The Soviets responded by suppressing such nationalistic or democratic movements—often by force. But during the 1980s the rising discontent among the Soviet-bloc countries and internal weakness within the Soviet state made it increasingly difficult for the Soviets to deal with new waves of protest in Eastern Europe.

Another factor contributing to change was the leadership of the Soviet Union. In the first six and a half decades following the creation of Communist Russia, the leadership of the Soviet government had been vested mainly in the hands of four men: Lenin, Stalin, Khrushchev, and Leonid Brezhnev. But the continuity and longevity of leadership were broken in 1982 with the death of Brezhnev. Over the next three years three different men headed the Soviet state. This rapid change in Soviet leadership was partially the result of the advancing age of the elite within the Communist party. A battle began to emerge between the younger, more progressive leaders and the aging "hard-liners" tied to Communist ideology.

The economic woes so prevalent under the Communist system caused many younger Soviets to recognize the need for reform. Communism had built basic industries in Russia early in the century but could not match the material abundance of the West's consumer society. Soviet farms consistently performed poorly. Central planning rather than market forces guided the economy, and the lack of incentives for the Soviet workers meant low productivity. In the high-technology scientific world of the 1980s, the Soviets were lagging far behind the West.

Contributing to the Soviet economic decline was the enormous drain of national wealth spent on defense. The arms race during the Cold War ultimately bankrupted the Soviet Union, especially in the 1980s after President Reagan increased the pressure with America's defensive build-up. In addition, the cost of maintaining control over its "empire" in Eastern Europe and assisting Communist insurgents in Africa and Latin America became too expensive for the beleaguered Soviet economy. When the war in Afghanistan bogged down, it too proved costly in terms of both lives and resources.

Perestroika **and** *Glasnost*

By the 1980s the defects in the Soviet political and economic system could no longer be covered up. The new Soviet premier, **Mikhail Gorbachev,** called for a wide range of social, political, and economic reforms called *perestroika,* or "restructuring." Through *perestroika,* he sought to increase industrial productivity, stimulate technological development, restructure the stagnant and inefficient bureaucracy, decentralize management of the economy, and experiment with a free-market system.

Gorbachev knew that his quest for reform would be in vain unless he could gain public support to put pressure on the "Old Guard" in the Communist party. In addition, he desperately needed financial assistance from the West to implement his programs. Thus he linked to *perestroika* the concept of *glasnost,* or "openness." Gorbachev hoped to create a more democratic atmosphere where the Soviet government would be more forthright and accountable to the people. He encouraged open discussions of the problems facing the country and a self-examination of the Soviet state. Under *glasnost,* the Soviet people were encouraged to evaluate and even to criticize their leaders in order to promote better government. But given an opportunity they had not experienced for more than seventy years, the Soviet people voiced opposition to the very foundation of the Soviet state—communism. They did not want to reform this corrupt system; they wanted to abolish it.

In a speech to the United Nations in December of 1988, Gorbachev said, "It is evident that force or the threat of force neither can nor should be instruments of foreign policy." He further remarked, "The principle of freedom of choice is mandatory. Refusal to recognize this principle will have serious consequences for world peace. To deny a nation the freedom of choice, regardless of the pretext or the verbal guise in which it is cloaked, is to upset the unstable balance that has been achieved. . . . Freedom of choice is a universal principle. It knows no exceptions." Whether purposefully or inadvertently, Gorbachev set in motion forces that led to the undoing of the Soviet state and the repudiation of communism. As a former White House official said, "Gorbachev has let the genie out of the bottle and his successors will not be able to stuff it back in."

Mikhail Gorbachev

Unrest in Eastern Europe

As the 1980s drew to a close, the Soviet state and empire began unraveling with amazing speed. Gorbachev's internal reforms encouraged new waves of protest against the Soviet Union in Soviet-dominated Eastern Europe. In Poland resistance to the Communist government had been kept up by **Solidarity,** a powerful labor union. In 1989 Solidarity-led forces secured the election of the first non-Communist prime minister in Poland since World War II. In 1990 **Lech Walesa,** the head of Solidarity and leader of the movement for reform and resistance, was elected president. Hungary and Czechoslovakia, nations in which the Soviets had crushed democratic movements in 1956 and 1968 respectively, began distancing themselves from the Soviets and repudiated communism.

One of the liberalizing acts of Hungary and Czechoslovakia was to open their borders to the West. This action had an unexpected effect on East Germany, supposedly one of the most prosperous Soviet-bloc countries. Discontent with the Communist regime took the form of a new exodus. By hundreds, and then thousands, East Germans went around the Berlin Wall, escaping to the West through Hungary and Czechoslovakia. By the time the Communist government tried to act, it was too late. The momentum of protest was out of hand and would not be satisfied until communism and Soviet control were overthrown.

In November of 1989 East German protesters attacked the symbol of Communist isolationism and totalitarianism—the Berlin Wall. They began hammering away at the concrete structure; soon even the guards who had once shot people for getting too close to the wall joined the protesters in tearing it down. Through its breaches, East Germans poured into West Berlin; many were reunited with family members, while others experienced the Free World for the first time. The government of East Germany collapsed, and in 1990 the two Germanies reunited into one nation.

The astonishing events were repeated throughout Eastern Europe. In one country after another, Communist governments were toppled—some, such as Rumania, through bloody conflict; others with the help of weary Communist leaders. The

Above: The Reichstag's flag flies over a united Germany for the first time since the Soviet army tore the swastika from its smoldering battlements in 1945.
Right: German border guards chat with each other as hundreds of Germans line the formerly forbidden area atop the Berlin Wall in 1989.

newly democratic states began the difficult transition from communism to free-market economics; from one-party rule to free and open elections; and from Soviet interference and control to independent, nationalistic rule.

Unrest in the USSR

While Soviet leaders witnessed the disintegration of their domination over Eastern Europe, they were struggling to maintain control over things at home. Many internal challenges threatened to tear the country apart. Ethnic unrest in the Soviet republics of Armenia and Azerbaijan led to widespread violence. The Baltic republics of Estonia, Latvia, and Lithuania moved toward separating from the Soviet Union. Reformers, upset at the slow pace of Gorbachev's reforms, called for his resignation. They supported decentralization of government, the independence movements of the republics, a speedier transition toward a free-market economy, and more freedom of expression. Leading the

opposition to Gorbachev was **Boris Yeltsin,** an ex-Communist whose support of reform helped him be elected president of the Russian republic, the largest of the Soviet republics.

In August of 1991, the hard-line Communists made a last stand. Soviet Communist leaders detained Gorbachev and announced he was ''ill.'' Furthermore, the Communist party ordered a six-month ''state of emergency.'' Led by Yeltsin, the Soviet citizens resisted. They launched a general strike as Yeltsin denounced the action of the hardliners. The army refused to obey orders to fire on

The River of Time

In 1992 Mikhail Gorbachev spoke at Westminster College in Fulton, Missouri, where Churchill had given his "iron curtain" speech in 1946. For many, Gorbachev's speech marked the conclusion of the Cold War. Entitled "The River of Time and the Imperative of Action," the address was not always accurate. Gorbachev tried, for example, to assign as much blame to the United States for causing the Cold War as he did to the Soviet Union. He also showed

an unrealistic faith in the United Nations to achieve progress toward world peace. Some of his comments, however, were an appropriate epilogue to the Cold War.

More than 46 years ago Winston Churchill spoke in Fulton and in my country this speech was singled out as the formal declaration of the "Cold War." This was indeed the first time the words, "Iron Curtain," were pronounced, and the whole Western world was challenged to close ranks against the threat of tyranny in the form of the Soviet Union and Communist expansion. . . .

Since that time the world in which we live has undergone tremendous changes. Even so, however paradoxical it may sound, there is a certain similarity between the situation then and today. Then, the prewar structure of international relations had virtually collapsed, a new pattern of forces had emerged along with a new set of interests and claims. . . .

What are the characteristics of the world situation today? In thinking over the processes which we ourselves have witnessed, we are forced to conclude that humanity is at a major turning-point. Not only the peoples of the former USSR, but the whole world is living through this watershed situation. This is not just some ordinary stage of development, like many others in world history. This is a turning-point on a historic and worldwide scale and signifies the incipient substitution of one paradigm of civilization by another.

the crowds, and the coup collapsed. Communism was now completely discredited. In December of 1991, eleven of the Soviet republics declared their independence from the Soviet Union. Following the leadership of Russia, they formed the Commonwealth of Independent States (CIS). Gorbachev was now a ruler without a country. On December 25, with little fanfare, he resigned. The Soviet Union dissolved into independent republics and with its demise, communism in the Russian sphere was repudiated.

Section Review

1. What did Khrushchev mean by "peaceful coexistence"?
2. The invasion of what country by the Soviet Union in 1979 potentially threatened the world's oil supplies in the Persian Gulf region?
3. What crisis over missiles being deployed close to the U.S. border almost led to war between the United States and the Soviet Union?
4. Define *perestroika* and *glasnost*.
5. Who was the last leader of the Soviet Union?

Aftermath of the Cold War

The collapse of the Soviet Union signaled "a new birth of freedom" for many oppressed peoples. With that freedom, however, came many problems. And for some, there was little difference; the change in governments was more like the changing of jailers in a prison than the opening of the prison doors. In some cases, not even the jailers changed.

The Former Soviet Union

The events within the former Soviet Union illustrated the blessings and difficulties of the Communist collapse. Some former republics of the USSR—notably the Baltic states of Estonia, Latvia, and Lithuania—wanted little to do with their former overlords. Some of the newly independent republics merely maintained repressive rule under another name. Three republics in particular dominated the

new Commonwealth of Independent States. Ukraine and Belarus, located the farthest west, are among the most populous, most prosperous, and most industrialized of the new republics. Their transition to independence, therefore, was a little easier. The most important of the new republics, however, is Russia. With over half of the population and over three-fourths of the land mass of the former Soviet Union, Russia is a notable world power on its own. The United Nations recognized this fact by granting Russia the Soviet Union's seat on the UN Security Council.

The Russians now enjoyed greater freedom than they had at any other time in their history—freedoms of religion, of speech, and of the press. But the drastic change from communism to a free-market economy created inflation and unemploy-

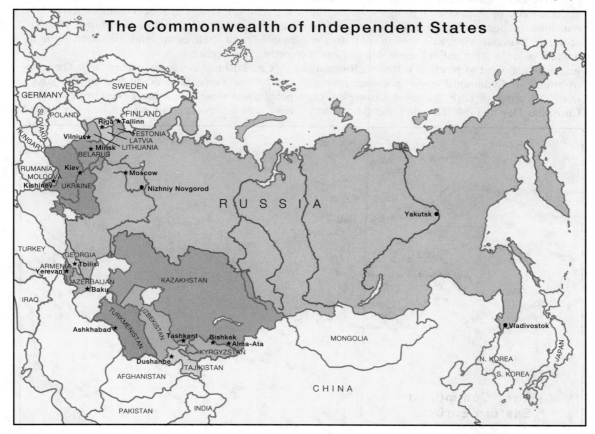

The Commonwealth of Independent States

ment. The troubles of the Soviet economy, which had sparked the drastic political changes in the first place, did not disappear with the overthrow of communism. With its antiquated technology, inefficient management policies, poor system of transportation, and nearly worthless currency, Russia had to begin almost from scratch to rebuild its economy. Furthermore, some of the richer republics were no longer willing to sell their goods to other republics when higher prices were to be found abroad. President Boris Yeltsin, who had been praised for standing up to the Communist coup in August 1991, found himself roundly criticized for problems that he could do little to solve. Shortages and unrest marked the difficult transition from tyranny to freedom.

Boris Yeltsin

Eastern Europe

The former Soviet ''empire'' in Eastern Europe likewise endured a difficult transition. Some nations, such as Poland and Hungary, made the transition to democratic government and a free economy without violence, though not always without pain. In other nations, economic suffering was overshadowed by physical suffering. Rumania overthrew its Communist leader in violent revolution, executing dictator Nicholas Ceausescu on Christmas Day in 1989. The violence did not stop

with that act, however. Riots continued to rend the nation after the Communist overthrow, and Rumania found itself exchanging one form of dictatorship for another.

Czechoslovakia was an unusual case. The western half of the nation, dominated by the Czech people, was eager to embrace a Western-style economy. The less prosperous eastern half, dominated

Post-Communist Eastern Europe

by the Slovak people, preferred a slow transition from a Communist, controlled economy. Faced with an irreconcilable conflict, the two halves decided peacefully to pursue separate paths. On January 1, 1993, Czechoslovakia became two nations: the Czech Republic and Slovakia.

The division of Czechoslovakia was peaceful; the same cannot be said of Yugoslavia. Ever since its creation after World War I, Yugoslavia has been an uneasy mixture of different ethnic groups (including Serbs, Croats, Slovenes) and religious groups (Eastern Orthodox, Catholic, Muslim). Without the unifying force of the Communist regime, the different regions of that nation began to pursue independence. Slovenia, Croatia, Bosnia and Herzegovina, and Macedonia all claimed independence in 1991. Only Serbia and Montenegro remained together under the name "Federal Republic of Yugoslavia."

Violence marred the breakup of Yugoslavia. The Serbs particularly resented the reduction of their power and feared for the fate of Serbs who were now minorities in the other former Yugoslav republics. The result was bloody civil war. Thousands of civilians died, particularly in Bosnia, where the Serbs sent arms and troops to "protect" Serb minorities—and carve out more territory for the Serb-dominated government of Yugoslavia. To help knit the acquired regions to Yugoslavia, the Serbs began "cleansing" these areas of non-Serbs, particularly Muslims. By *cleansing* they meant the forced removal—or even killing—of non-Serbs in the conquered regions. Anarchy reigned, as the UN tried to find a peaceful solution. Described as the "powder keg of Europe" before World War I, the Balkans had again become a center of terror and violence by the end of the twentieth century. Years of Communist rule had done little to bring a sense of unity to that troubled region.

China

In a speech given in 1990 after he had left office, former president Ronald Reagan reviewed the collapse of communism. "Communist dominoes are falling over the world," he said. But he added, "There are still those that must fall—China, North Korea, North Vietnam, North Yemen, and . . . Cuba."

China was a special reminder that the collapse of the Soviet Union did not mean the end of totalitarian communism. After taking over the mainland from the Nationalist government in 1949, Mao Zedong and his Communist forces established a cruel dictatorship in China. Thousands of people considered "dangers" to the Communist state—former Nationalists, intellectuals, businessmen, Christians—were sent to prison camps. Like the Soviet Communists in the 1920s, the Chinese sought to establish an atheistic state through force and repression.

Seeing the need to compete with the Free World and the Soviet Union, Mao launched great crusades to modernize and thoroughly revolutionize China. With the **"Great Leap Forward"** of the late 1950s, Mao sought to improve Chinese agriculture and bring industry up to Western standards. Instead, his ill-planned Communist reforms wrecked the Chinese steel industry and caused a famine. In the late 1960s, Mao launched the **"Cultural Revolution,"** an attempt to stir up zeal for radical communism. Young Communists, called the Red Guards, held rallies and indulged in acts of violence designed to promote revolutionary fervor. They disrupted the Chinese educational system until it could be "purified" in an acceptably radical manner. The result of the Cultural Revolution was civil chaos and economic decline. Mao abandoned it after only a few years, and he allowed his former radical supporters to be suppressed.

Western leaders were somewhat relieved when Mao died in 1976. It appeared that the Communist leaders who succeeded him were more "realistic" in their rule. China's Communist overlords allowed limited free-market reforms and scaled back some of Mao's more repressive measures. The true nature of the Communist state had not changed, however, as was shown tragically in 1989.

In a year when communism seemed to be collapsing around the world, a reform movement sprang up among Chinese students. They called for the reform of the Chinese state, particularly the granting of greater political freedom. In April 1989 a group of students took over **Tiananmen Square** in the Chinese capital of Beijing. As people around the world watched on television, the students rallied and protested against repressive rule. Then the Communist authorities cracked down. In early June,

A portrait of Mao Zedong looks down on Tiananmen Square, the scene of 1989's prodemocracy demonstrations, from the walls of the Forbidden City (former palaces of the Chinese emperors).

tanks rolled into Tiananmen Square. Over two thousand people were killed as the government quashed the student movement and reestablished its authority. There was no rebirth of freedom in China, as there had been elsewhere in the former Communist bloc. The students, though, had demonstrated that strong dissent still existed within Communist China despite forty years of oppression.

The students also revealed the inspiration and model for their call for freedom; as a symbol of their movement, they created a thirty-foot replica of the Statue of Liberty in the center of Beijing. As Ronald Reagan said less than a year later, "We should not be timid in our embrace of democracy. We should be as bold and brash in our democratic ideals as ever in our history. The Golden Age of Freedom is near because America has remained true to her ideals." Whatever else the Cold War might have demonstrated, it showed the inherent strength of the spirit of freedom against the fiercest totalitarian oppression.

Section Review

1. Which of the former Soviet republics became the most important in world politics? Who was its first president?
2. After the collapse of Soviet communism in Eastern Europe, what former Communist nation broke into several smaller republics and engaged in ethnic civil war?
3. Who was the major leader of Communist China? With what program did he attempt to improve Chinese agriculture and industry in the 1950s?
4. What location in the city of Beijing was the site of a student rally for reform? How did the Chinese Communist rulers respond?

A Glimpse Behind and a Glimpse Ahead

In the spring of 1992, the former Soviet president Mikhail Gorbachev made a visit to the United States. He spoke at Westminster College in Fulton, Missouri, where forty-six years earlier Winston Churchill had given his famous "iron curtain" speech. Unlike Churchill's historic address, Gorbachev's speech drew little attention. Yet his presence at the college was historic in that it symbolized the end of the Cold War. The iron curtain which Churchill said had descended across the Continent had been torn down. The Communist state that built that curtain no longer existed. The state of tension and hostility between the two superpowers was no more. There remained but one military superpower in the world—the United States. The West had triumphed against Communist Russia, and the ideal Communist state had proved a failure. The world that emerged from the Cold War era was no longer divided into two camps, and world leaders talked of a "new world order."

Chapter Review

Can You Explain?

Cold War	limited wars	détente
containment	domino theory	*perestroika*
arms race	Vietnamization	*glasnost*

Can You Identify?

iron curtain	38th parallel	Tet offensive	Ronald Reagan
Marshal Tito	Vietnam War	Fidel Castro	SDI
Truman Doctrine	Ho Chi Minh	Nikita Krushchev	Mikhail Gorbachev
Marshall Plan	Battle of Dien Bien	"peaceful coexistence"	Solidarity
NATO	Phu	*Sputnik*	Lech Walesa
Warsaw Pact	Viet Cong	U-2 incident	Boris Yeltsin
Korean War	SEATO	Berlin Wall	Great Leap Forward
(1950-53)	Gulf of Tonkin	Cuban Missile Crisis	Cultural Revolution
Douglas MacArthur	Resolution	SALT	Tiananmen Square

Can you Locate?

Eastern Europe	North and South	Vietnam	Afghanistan
Berlin	Korea	Gulf of Tonkin	Commonwealth of
Bonn	Inchon	Cambodia	Independent States
Taiwan (Formosa)	Yalu River	Laos	Beijing
	Manchuria	Cuba	

How Much Do You Remember?

1. List five examples from the Cold War period that illustrated that a state of hostility and tension existed between the United States and the Soviet Union.
2. Define "limited wars" and list two examples during the Cold War era.
3. Identify the opposing leaders in the Chinese civil war. Which one led the Communist forces? Which side won the civil war?
4. List three factors that contributed to the dramatic change in superpower relations in the mid- to late 1980s.

What Do You Think?

1. Do you think President Truman was justified in relieving General MacArthur of his command during the Korean War? Why or why not?
2. Compare and contrast the United States' involvement in Vietnam with the Soviet involvement in Afghanistan.
3. Which policy do you think would have been the most effective for the Western world to pursue against communism in the Cold War era: appeasement, containment, "peaceful coexistence," or confrontation?

CHAPTER 23

"Wars and rumours of war"

American soldiers pose by an Iraqi T-72 tank destroyed by American forces during the Gulf War (1991).

World War II ended the European phase of world history and ushered in a new era. European politics no longer dominated international events as they had for the previous two centuries. The most important major clash in the postwar world—the Cold War—was a worldwide conflict pitting the United States and the Soviet Union against each other and involving Europe only as a potential battleground. Nor was the Cold War the only theme of world history since 1945. The underdeveloped and overpopulated "Third World" countries of Africa, Asia, and Latin America have challenged the East-West dominance of the globe. In the strife-torn Middle East, war has erupted several times between Arab and Jew, between Arab and Westerner, and between Arab and Arab. Europe, in contrast to its earlier leadership in world affairs, found itself following the lead of one of the superpowers and struggling to compete in an increasingly competitive world economy.

Throughout the postwar era, leaders sought peace and unity. Idealistic institutions such as the United Nations and more practical organizations such as the European Common Market sought to achieve peace through human planning and organization. The industrialized nations were able to produce enough wealth and material goods theoretically to abolish poverty and want. This progress combined with the collapse of Soviet communism caused international leaders to dream of a "new world order." But despite attempts at international cooperation and the advance of peace and freedom in some regions, the postwar era witnessed the same "wars and rumours of wars" that have always pockmarked world history.

Attempts at Unity

The United Nations

Organization of the United Nations

Prior to the conclusion of World War II, world leaders sought to revive the concept of an organization similar to the League of Nations that they believed would ensure a lasting peace in the war's aftermath. In April of 1945, representatives of fifty governments met in San Francisco to formally organize the **United Nations** (UN). The purpose of this organization, as defined by its charter, is the maintenance of international peace and security. In addition, the UN seeks to foster cooperation among nations in solving worldwide economic, social, and humanitarian problems. Usually, the UN respects the sovereignty of member nations, although in extreme cases it can directly intervene. When the central government of the African nation of Somalia collapsed and mass starvation threatened the people, the United Nations—without invitation—sent in relief forces in 1992 to stabilize the country and bring in food and medical supplies.

To accomplish their idealistic goals, member nations created three major bodies: the Secretariat, the General Assembly, and the Security Council. The **Secretariat,** with the Secretary General at its head, serves as the administrative organ of the UN. All member nations are represented in the **General Assembly,** where they debate world issues in regular annual sessions. The **Security Council** embodies the executive or enforcement power of the UN. Five permanent members—the United States, Russia (formerly the Soviet Union), China, Great Britain, and France—along with ten nonpermanent members elected for two-year terms by the General Assembly—compose the council.

In addition to these bodies, there are special agencies that make up the UN bureaucracy. For example, the Economic and Social Council pro-

This 1943 war poster anticipated the formation of the United Nations after the war.

The United Nations Building stands by the East River against the New York skyline.

motes better living standards and human rights throughout the world; the Trusteeship Council assists colonial peoples; the International Court of Justice is the judicial arm of the UN for resolving disputes among nations. Other specialized agencies include the International Labor Organization; the World Health Organization; and the UN Educational, Scientific, and Cultural Organization (UNESCO). The United States, which earlier had shunned the League of Nations, not only joined the UN but also became its host. New York City serves as the headquarters of the international body.

Activity of the UN

The UN displays the shortcomings that often characterize international organizations. As with the earlier League of Nations, its primary weakness has been its lack of authority. As a voluntary international organization, it has lacked the power to enforce its actions, even upon member nations. Furthermore, each of the five permanent members of the Security Council has veto power over any council decision. In the first ten years, the veto right was used seventy-eight times, seventy-five of which were by the Soviet Union. During the Cold War era, the superpowers clearly dominated the world organization; their competing differences rendered the Security Council ineffective. The threat of nuclear war, and not the UN, prevented the outbreak of another world war.

Despite its weaknesses, the United Nations has enjoyed some limited success in the years follow-ing World War II. The UN administered the partitioning of Palestine between Arabs and Jews after World War II and the withdrawal of the Dutch from Indonesia. Twice the United Nations has served as the vehicle for organizing an international army to halt aggression. First, in the Korean War in the 1950s, UN forces repelled the Communist invasion of South Korea. Then, in the 1990s, a UN coalition forced Iraq out of neighboring Kuwait in the Gulf War. (See p. 632.) In both cases, though, the United States took upon itself most of the burden of the fighting. The UN also has served occasionally as an effective peace-keeping force in Africa and the Middle East.

During the 1960s the character of the UN changed dramatically as new nations from Africa and Asia joined and gained a majority of seats in the General Assembly. Western dominance of the UN ended as these "Third World" nations (discussed later in the chapter) became the dominant force in the organization. With the new African and Asian majority, the UN has expanded its role in economic and technological development in the developing regions of the world. In 1945 the United Nations had fifty members; by 1992, with 178 members, it had become truly a world organization.

The European Community

The United Nations has had mixed results in its efforts to promote unity. Somewhat more effective has been the European Community. After World War II, many Europeans felt that in order to prevent future wars, the European nations should form a federation called the United States of Europe. Although most European governments resisted such a political union, they did like the idea of an economic union. In 1951 Belgium, France, Italy, Luxembourg, the Netherlands, and West Germany signed a treaty establishing the European Coal and Steel Community (ECSC). They combined their coal and steel industries to eliminate waste and inefficiency. As a result, the nations of the ECSC were able to produce heavy industrial products more cheaply and easily.

Because the ECSC proved so successful, in 1957 these same nations formed the European Economic Community (EEC), popularly known as the

"Common Market." The EEC extended the idea of the ECSC to include the entire economies of the member nations. Now not only steel and coal but also other products could be sold without trade barriers. Citizens of the Common Market countries found that they could buy a wider array of goods—televisions, cars, stereos—at lower prices. Other nations eventually joined the Common Market: Great Britain, Denmark, and Ireland (all joining in 1973), Greece (1981), Spain, and Portugal (both 1985). In 1967 the ECSC, EEC, and European Atomic Energy (Euratom) joined under a single umbrella—the **European Community** (EC). The European Parliament administers the EC.

The European Community has succeeded in becoming a major force in the world economy. The road to achieving its goal of complete European unity has been bumpier. The EC has faced opposition from members who understandably want to guard their national interests. In 1991, for instance, the EC drafted a treaty to strengthen the organization's power to shape the social, political, and economic policies of its member nations. The citizens of Denmark, however, first voted to reject the treaty and those of France approved it only narrowly. (The Danes later approved it.) Likewise when the EC desired to establish a common currency for all of Europe, opposition from Britain and Denmark forced the organization to give those nations the option of not participating. The idea of a "United

The Uniting Church stands in the city square of Brisbane, Australia. The Uniting Church in Australia was formed in 1977 as a union of Australian Congregationalists, Methodists, and Presbyterians. The word uniting in its name refers to the group's claim that it is but one step in the unification of all Christian churches.

States of Europe" was a feasible dream as the twentieth century drew to a close, but it nonetheless remained a loose economic federation.

The Ecumenical Movement

Paralleling the political movements toward world unity was a religious effort at unity known as the **ecumenical movement.** The word *ecumenical* means "universal" or "worldwide." In the twentieth century, religious leaders used the phrase "ecumenical movement" to refer to various activities aimed at uniting churches and denominations. The ultimate goal was the union of all professing Christians in the world. Some proponents even call for the union of *all* religions, Christian and non-Christian.

Sometimes this union involved merging two or more religious groups into a single body. Usually

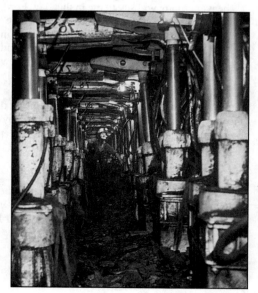

Coal mine in Lancashire, England

such unions joined different bodies of the same denomination. The Methodist Episcopal Church in the United States, for example, merged with the Evangelical United Brethren in 1968 to form the United Methodist Church, one of the largest Protestant bodies in America. Sometimes the union took place across denominational lines. A good example is the United Church of Canada, formed in 1925. Nearly all of Canada's Methodists and Congregationalists and most of that nation's Presbyterians participated in the merger.

At other times proponents of the ecumenical movement have supported the idea of religious federations. Unlike unions, bodies in a federation keep their distinct identity and independence but work with other like-minded groups in an organization. The most significant force in the ecumenical movement is a federation, the **World Council of Churches** (WCC). In fact, the origin of the modern ecumenical movement lies in the history of the WCC. The "birth" of the ecumenical movement was the World Missionary Conference held in Edinburgh, Scotland, in 1910. This was a large gathering of over a thousand delegates representing nations and major denominations around the world. By its apparent success in bringing together Christians of diverse theological views, the Edinburgh Council spurred the creation of other organizations devoted to Christian unity. In 1937 two organizations that had arisen from the Edinburgh conference offered proposals for forming a world council of churches. Finally, in 1948 the World Council of Churches was officially formed in Amsterdam.

The Roman Catholic church at first stood apart from the ecumenical movement. Then the Second Vatican Council (1962-65), commonly called **"Vatican II,"** seemed to herald a new era of openness in the church. For the first time, observers from the Eastern Orthodox churches and Protestant bodies were allowed to watch some of the sessions of a Catholic council. Furthermore, the council referred to Protestants and the Eastern Orthodox as "separated brethren" and advocated freedom of worship around the world. In its Decree on Ecumenism, the council actively encouraged Catholics to participate in ecumenical discussions.

Troubling questions have surrounded the ecumenical movement, however. Even non-Christians criticized the WCC for its support of radical social causes. For example, the WCC's "Program to Combat Racism," founded in 1969, funneled funds to radical groups in Africa and Latin America that were involved in bloody military and revolutionary activities. As offensive as these political activities may be to the Christian, they are only a symptom of the real problem with the ecumenical movement. The movement is eager to unite all groups that call themselves "Christian" (and even some that are non-Christian) regardless of any false doctrines those groups may hold. Vatican II, for instance, changed only some *practices* of the Roman Catholic church and attempted to restate traditional Catholic teaching in modern language. It did not really settle the serious *doctrinal* questions that have divided Catholicism and Protestantism since the Reformation. Unsurprisingly, the ecumenical movement has had its strongest appeal among liberal Protestants who do not affirm many biblical teachings such as justification by faith alone, the deity of Christ, and the inspiration of the Bible.

The ecumenical movement attempts to unite people who simply claim to worship Christ. But Jesus said,

> Not every one that saith unto me, Lord, Lord, shall enter into the kingdom of heaven; but he that doeth the will of my Father which is in heaven. Many will say to me in that day, Lord, Lord, have we not prophesied in thy name? and in thy name have cast out devils? and in thy name done many wonderful works? And then will I profess unto them, I never knew you: depart from me, ye that work iniquity (Matt. 7:21-23).

Genuine Christian unity can exist only among those who are saved by faith in Christ and kept by His power. True Christian union is union in the truth of God (John 17:11, 17).

A New World Order?

The collapse of the Soviet Union and the diminishing threat of communism spurred a new optimism in the late 1980s and 1990s. In 1990 U.S.

D. Martyn Lloyd-Jones

As the ecumenical movement grew in size and popularity, many concerned Christians sounded warnings concerning its teachings and practices. In Great Britain one of the leading critics of ecumenism was D. Martyn Lloyd-Jones. Born in Wales in 1899, Lloyd-Jones studied medicine and became a respected physician. He was converted in the 1920s and surrendered to God's call to become a minister. After a rich twelve-year ministry in Wales, Lloyd-Jones accepted a call in 1938 to the Westminster Chapel in London. He served there as co-pastor with and later successor to famed Bible commentator G. Campbell Morgan.

For twenty-five years (1943-68) Lloyd-Jones served as sole pastor of Westminster Chapel. Like Spurgeon in the nineteenth century, Lloyd-Jones centered his ministry on the preaching of the Word of God. He delivered tightly constructed sermons that carefully laid out the plain teaching of the Bible and applied it pointedly to the life of the individual. When he collected his sermons into books, such as his *Studies in the Sermon on the Mount,* they became devotional favorites of both pastors and laymen. A deep lover of Puritan writings, Lloyd-Jones also supported the re-publication of many classic Puritan works.

In the late 1950s and early 1960s, Lloyd-Jones and other conservatives agreed to attend a series of private meetings with liberal leaders of the ecumenical movement. The two sides discussed the major doctrines of Scripture, including inspiration, the deity of Christ, and the nature of His atonement for sin. In one session, Lloyd-Jones told the liberals, ''I don't think we agree about *any* of the cardinal doctrines.'' Afterwards he observed, ''We had demonstrated that no cooperation was possible.'' In 1966 Lloyd-Jones went even further. He called for all Bible-believing Christians in Britain to leave denominations which were supporting religious liberalism and ecumenism and to form a new, biblically sound

denomination. Few heeded his call, but Lloyd-Jones led his own church out of the Congregational Union when it decided to join a new ecumenical denomination.

In 1962 Lloyd-Jones gave two addresses on John 17 and Ephesians 4, passages that supporters of the ecumenical movement liked to quote in defense of their movement. These were later published in a short but weighty book entitled *The Basis of Christian Unity.* In the conclusion of this book, Lloyd-Jones criticized as unscriptural ecumenism's overriding stress on Christian unity. He wrote, ''It is . . . clear that the question of unity must never be put first. We must never start with it, but always remember the order stated so clearly in Acts 2:42, where fellowship follows doctrine. . . . The present tendency to discount and to depreciate doctrine in the interests of unity is simply a denial and a violation of plain New Testament teaching.''

D. Martyn Lloyd-Jones died in 1981, true to the end to the Lord whose Word he had so faithfully proclaimed.

president George Bush spoke before a joint session of Congress concerning the recent Iraqi invasion of Kuwait. After listing four American objectives in the clash with Iraq, Bush said,

> We stand today at a unique and extraordinary movement. . . . Out of these troubled times, our fifth objective—a new world order—can emerge: a new era, freer from the threat of terror, stronger in the pursuit of justice, and more secure in the quest for peace. . . .
>
> A hundred generations have searched for this elusive path to peace, while a thousand wars raged across the span of human endeavor. Today that new world is struggling to be born.

This idealistic call for a "new world order" expressed the same kind of optimism that characterized the founders of the League of Nations and the United Nations—the sincere desire for world peace. On the UN Building in New York appear the words of Isaiah 2:4,

> They shall beat their swords into plowshares, and their spears into pruninghooks: nation shall not lift up sword against nation, neither shall they learn war any more.

Yet such optimism ignores the biblical teaching that wars spring from the root of human sinfulness (James 4:1). It also ignores the deep divisions in the modern world. Although the gulf between the Free World and the Communist world has diminished, there are still differences between East and West, between the industrialized nations and the developing nations, between adherents of different religions. Each region and group has its own spe-cial interests and concerns. But this fact has not stopped world leaders from vainly seeking global unity. Throughout history man has unsuccessfully striven for a manmade, one-world government. The fall of many empires over the centuries illustrates that any human unity which denies God cannot succeed. Mankind should remember the lesson of the Tower of Babel:

> And they said, Go to, let us build us a city and a tower, whose top may reach unto heaven; and let us make us a name, lest we be scattered abroad upon the face of the whole earth. . . . And the Lord said, Behold, the people is one, and they have all one language; and this they begin to do: and now nothing will be restrained from them, which they have imagined to do. . . . So the Lord scattered them abroad from thence upon the face of all the earth: and they left off to build the city.
> Genesis 11:4, 6, 8

Section Review

1. What are the three major bodies of the United Nations?
2. In what two crises did the United Nations succeed in organizing an international army to halt aggression?
3. What is the purpose of the European Coal and Steel Community?
4. What is the leading example of a denominational merger across denominational lines?
5. What event marks the birth of the modern ecumenical movement?

The Industrialized Nations

Among the divisions in the postwar world was an important distinction among the democratic Western powers, the Communist world, and the developing Third World. The countries of North America, Western Europe, and Japan compose the "industrialized nations" that have combined democratic government with capitalistic economies to become the economic leaders of the world.

United States

Many experts predicted economic decline in the United States after World War II, perhaps even a return to the Great Depression. What followed instead was an economic boom with low unemployment, increased income, and large-scale consumer spending. One writer nicknamed American culture "the affluent society" because of its enormous

Images of postwar America: civil rights leader Martin Luther King, Jr. (top left); American astronauts on the surface of the moon (top right); Lyndon Johnson, whose presidency was torn by war and internal dissension (bottom left); and Ronald Reagan (bottom right, pictured with his wife), who sought to restore the United States to the international dominance it had enjoyed immediately after World War II

wealth and productivity. Along with this economic prosperity was a continuation of the "big government" policies of Franklin Roosevelt. The climax of this trend was Lyndon Johnson's **"Great Society"** in the 1960s. Like previous government leaders, Johnson assumed that American wealth and government action could solve the nation's problems. He spent billions of dollars on federal health, housing, and education programs to build the ideal welfare state. American technology outstripped that of all other nations, symbolized by America's successful landing on the moon in 1969. As the mightiest economic and military superpower on the planet, the United States stood as the leader among nations in the first twenty years following the war.

Nonetheless, internal difficulties troubled the nation. Black Americans did not believe that they were receiving fair and equal treatment. Launching what was called the **civil rights movement,** African-Americans made enormous gains in politics and society. The U.S. Supreme Court declared segregation of public schools by race to be unconstitutional. Martin Luther King, Jr., the movement's most visible spokesman, emerged in the 1950s and 1960s to lead a nonviolent crusade for voting rights and equal access to public facilities for blacks. Congress passed the 1964 Civil Rights Act and the 1965 Voting Rights Act. But violence also erupted as whites and blacks clashed during civil rights protests. Riots tore apart black sections of large American cities such as Los Angeles and Detroit.

In addition to this racial conflict, there was a generational one. In the 1960s many young people revolted against authority—parental, educational, and governmental. Long hair, rock music, drugs, and sexual immorality symbolized the revolt of youth. The Vietnam War particularly divided the older and younger generations. Demonstrations against the war sometimes even ended in bloodshed, and large numbers of young men refused to serve in the armed forces.

Vietnam did more than divide Americans; it destroyed their prosperity. President Johnson attempted to pay for the war without cutting the massive spending needed to build his Great Society. Eventually economic stagnation set in, and the United States suffered high unemployment and high inflation in the 1970s. There was a national drift in leadership as well. Faced with growing unpopularity, President Johnson did not run for re-election in 1968. His successor, Richard Nixon, was forced to resign the presidency in 1974 amid charges of political corruption. His successors, Gerald Ford and Jimmy Carter, proved to be uninspiring leaders and were repudiated by the American voters. The apparently growing military strength of the Soviet Union seemed only to heighten the perception that the United States was on the decline.

A change occurred, however, with the election of **Ronald Reagan** as president in 1980. Reagan was the first president since the 1930s to question the premise of the welfare state. He sought less government regulation and lower taxes, and Congress obliged with huge tax cuts. Reagan also enjoyed the support of religious and social conservatives offended by the radicalism of the 1960s. He supported issues important to such conservatives, notably an end to legalized abortion and the restoration of prayer and Bible reading in schools, outlawed by the Supreme Court in the 1960s.

Under Reagan's presidency in the 1980s, an increase in defense spending combined with tax cuts created a huge budget deficit. But the economy continued to grow, as inflation and interest rates were dramatically reduced, and the United States again clearly became the leading military superpower. A strong economy and revived military strength caused Americans to view the Reagan tenure as the restoration of the United States to world leadership. Under Reagan's successor, George Bush, the collapse of Soviet communism and a successful war against Iraqi dictator Saddam Hussein (see p. 632) seemed a fitting climax to Reagan's call for America to "stand tall" again in world affairs.

Yet in 1992, a sluggish economy caused voters to reject Bush and return the Democratic party to power. Furthermore, the Reagan-Bush years had not seen a remarkable improvement in American morals. Abortion continued to be widely practiced, and groups such as homosexuals pushed successfully for legal recognition of their sinful lifestyles. As the 1990s unfolded, it was difficult to see what would be the lasting effect of the Reagan legacy on American society.

Europe

The postwar era saw the decline of the remaining dictatorships in Western Europe. In Spain, dictator Francisco Franco had seized power in the Spanish Civil War in the 1930s. (See Chapter 21.) When he died in 1975, though, Spain restored the monarchy under King Juan Carlos. The new king in turn restored democratic government to the nation, paving the way for Spain to join the European Community in 1985.

The end of the dictators did not mean the end of strong rulers in Europe. Within the democracies, leaders with strong views and even stronger character dominated the politics both of their countries and the Continent. Three are of particular importance: Konrad Adenauer of West Germany, Charles de Gaulle of France, and Margaret Thatcher of Great Britain.

Germany

Germany traveled a remarkable road after war—from a ruined, wrecked shell of a nation to a world economic giant. The Cold War divided Germany into Communist East Germany and democratic West Germany. West Germany had the fastest growing economy in Europe by the 1950s, due in large part to the polices of Chancellor **Konrad Adenauer.** The mayor

Konrad Adenauer

of Cologne from 1917, Adenauer had been dismissed from his office by the Nazis in 1933. In 1944 the Gestapo put him in prison, where the warden told him, "Now, please do not commit suicide. You would cause me no end of trouble. You're sixty-eight years old, and your life is over anyway."

Adenauer's life was far from over, however. In 1949 he became the first chancellor of West Germany, an office he held for fourteen years. The chancellor fashioned what was called the *Wirtschaftswunder* ("economic miracle"). Rejecting socialism and following free-market principles, Adenauer rebuilt German industry and revived the German economy. Income tripled while he was chancellor, and by 1955 the nation was producing more goods than it had before the war, despite the fact that West Germany was only about half the size of prewar Germany. Although not a military power, West Germany became an economic superpower in Europe.

Adenauer also followed a strong pro-West policy. When West Germany was allowed to begin rebuilding its army in the face of the Communist threat, the chancellor did not hesitate to commit his country to NATO. He used trade as a means of tying West Germany more closely to the West and sought the friendship of the other great power of the Continent, France. Adenauer's policies became the accepted practices of West German government. Even when more leftist parties led the government in the 1960s and 1970s, they did not interfere with West Germany's booming capitalist economy or seriously contemplate abandoning their Western allies. The freedom and prosperity of West Germany was a constant allure to the oppressed Germans of Communist East Germany. In the late 1980s, during the collapse of the Soviet empire in Eastern Europe, the flow of refugees from East Germany to the West and the unrest in East Germany itself toppled the Communist regime. In 1990 Germany became unified once more, and it remains the leading economic power in Europe. Adenauer's legacy lives on.

France

France experienced two new governments in the decades after World War II. After the liberation of the French from the Nazis in 1944, **Charles de Gaulle,** leader of the Free French during the war, led a provisional government until 1946. He angrily rejected the new constitution for the Fourth Republic, however, because it did not give sufficient power to the president. De Gaulle retired, and his predictions about the weaknesses of the Fourth Republic proved true. Multiple parties dominated the powerful legislative branch and a succession of cabinets made it difficult to solve major problems. The French army, humiliated by the Germans in 1940, sought to restore its honor by holding on to the empire. Instead, the army endured bitter defeat at the hands of Vietnamese Communists and had to pull out of Indochina in 1954. In 1956 the French joined the British and the Israelis in an attempt to recapture the Suez Canal from Egypt. (See p. 628.) International opposition forced France and Britain to relinquish their gains, though, humiliating the French even more.

Most serious was the Algerian crisis. In 1956 nationalists in France's North African colony of Algeria sought independence, but the issue was complicated by the presence of about a million Europeans in the colony who wanted to remain tied to France. Furthermore, the army, having lost in Indochina, was determined to win in Algeria at any cost. Radical Algerians resorted to violence against Europeans and moderate Arabs; the French resorted to torture against the radicals. French citizens were bitterly divided over the war and a civil war in France seemed possible. But in 1958 the crisis ebbed when the army forced the recall of de Gaulle to lead France out of the dilemma.

De Gaulle replaced the Fourth Republic with the **Fifth Republic,** a government with a constitution that provided for a strong president. De Gaulle shocked the army in 1962, however, by agreeing to Algerian independence. Surviving three assassination attempts by opponents of Algerian independence, de Gaulle brought stability and order to France. It became the leading military power of the Continent and was surpassed only by West Germany in economic might. After de Gaulle's retirement in 1969, his system endured. Even the election of François Mitterand in 1981, the first socialist president of the Fifth Republic, did not shake the

Charles de Gaulle

nation. Since the French Revolution in 1789, the Third Republic (1870-1940) is the only government to have lasted longer than the Fifth Republic.

Great Britain

The postwar era was a major period of transition and decline for Great Britain. The sun finally set on the British Empire as her once glorious holdings began to slip away. India, Pakistan, and Burma gained independence in the late 1940s, and by the 1960s few territories remained under British rule. Economic and military weakness at home meant that the British no longer had the means nor the spirit to maintain their empire. Great Britain, at one time one of the "great powers," began to play a supporting role in world affairs to the United States during the Cold War. Her humiliation in the Suez crisis (see p. 628) reinforced the perception of the decline of British power. Her weak economy was not helped when the Labour party took power after World War II and began to pursue socialist policies to build a welfare state. The result was greater personal security through reforms such as a national health insurance plan but also higher taxes and stifling government regulation. Labour "nationalized" (took control of) many major industries such as coal and the railways and made them government agencies. These inefficient nationalized industries made Britain less competitive economically with the rest of the capitalist West.

At first Britain's Conservative party went along with Labour ideas, trying only to modify them or soften their impact. Then in 1975 **Margaret Thatcher** became leader of the Conservatives. A staunch opponent of Labour policies, she campaigned against Great Britain's "slither and slide toward socialism." In 1979 she and the Conservatives swept into power. Her election as prime minister marked a sense of renewal in Great Britain. She

Margaret Thatcher being greeted by President Ronald Reagan

sold many of the nationalized industries back to private investors and slashed the nation's tax rates to spur economic growth. She confronted the powerful labor unions that stifled the British coal and newspaper industries and broke their power. Thatcher appropriately became known as the "Iron Lady."

Thatcher displayed the same kind of iron in foreign affairs. She strongly supported the anti-Communist actions of the United States under President Reagan. She also led Britain to military victory over Argentina in the South Atlantic. Britain and Argentina had long feuded over possession of the Falkland Islands. In 1982 the military dictatorship of Argentina tried to prop up its shaky rule by seizing the islands and their British inhabitants, gambling that the British would not respond. Instead,

Thatcher fought back. Warned of the difficulties of fighting a war eight thousand miles from Britain's coasts, she responded defiantly, "Defeat—I do not recognize the meaning of the word." She launched a military armada that routed the Argentines and recaptured the islands. Likewise when Iraq invaded Kuwait in 1991, Thatcher provided the iron backbone behind the Western resistance to the aggression. Winner of three elections and holding office from 1979 to 1990, Thatcher served longer than any other British prime minister since the early nineteenth century. Next to Winston Churchill, she is, in the opinion of many, the most important British political leader of the twentieth century.

Japan

Like West Germany, Japan made great strides politically and economically after World War II. General Douglas MacArthur headed the occupation government that oversaw the rebuilding of the devastated nation. When the emperor Hirohito publicly repudiated his claims to deity, MacArthur stepped in and became the real leader of the Japanese nation. Launching a massive reform movement, the general called for women's suffrage, promoted the formation of labor unions, and, ultimately, imposed a new constitution on Japan. The result was a stable democracy, a remarkable achievement given Japan's recent militaristic tradition. With the removal of the occupation government, Japan proved competent to rule herself. The Liberal-Democratic party took power in 1955 and held it continuously until 1993.

A key factor in Japan's remarkable economic recovery has been its international dominance in automobile production.

The party drew support from a broad spectrum of Japanese citizens, including the agricultural workers and the middle class.

Political stability contributed to striking economic growth, and the United States played a key role in this area as well. In addition to billions of dollars in financial aid, America supplied Japan with technology, markets, and raw materials for her to build a strong industrial base. The military protection by the Western powers allowed Japan to pour its wealth into industrial development with little spent on national defense. (MacArthur's new constitution, in fact, forbade Japan from having an army.) In addition, their own hard work and a superior educational system pushed the Japanese to the economic forefront of the world. The Japanese excelled in heavy industry. In automobile manufacturing, their well-built, fuel-efficient cars allowed the nation to displace the United States as the world's leader in auto production. The Japanese pioneered in the development of electronics by stressing the use of transistors and other technological innovations. In the 1950s critics joked that "Made in Japan" was a synonym for cheap, shoddy products. Yet by the 1980s Japan was cornering the world market in televisions, stereos, radios, and other electronic equipment. Japanese companies such as Mitsubishi, Toyota, Sony, and Nintendo became household words around the world.

Japan still faced problems, though. The dominance of the Liberal Democrats brought not only stability but also corruption. Scandals rocked Japan as it became known that government officials had been taking bribes. Finally, in 1993 angry Japanese voters turned the Liberal Democrats out of power and elected a reform coalition. Foreign nations also resented the fact that the Japanese government set high tariffs and trade restrictions to protect Japanese industries from competition. Although these actions did protect Japan, they prompted Japanese trading partners to retaliate with their own trade barriers. Still, the rise of a prosperous, democratic Japan from the rubble of totalitarianism and military defeat was one of the great success stories of the postwar era.

Section Review

1. Who was the most important leader of the American civil rights movement?
2. What was the *Wirtschaftswunder* of West Germany?
3. What new French government arose out of the Algerian crisis? Who was its first president?
4. What does it mean when a government "nationalizes" an industry?
5. Who headed the occupation government of postwar Japan?
6. What political party dominated Japanese politics after World War II?

The Third World

During the Cold War, nations that were not part either of the "first world" of the capitalistic industrialized bloc or the "second world" of the Communist Soviet bloc (discussed in the previous chapter) were named the **"Third World."** The emergence of these developing nations in Asia, Africa, and Latin America has been a major theme of twentieth-century history. The first step in the formation of the Third World was **decolonization,** the winning of independence by colonies in Asia and Africa from Western imperial nations. The native peoples in colonial lands demanded self-rule, and many citizens of the Allied powers thought that holding colonial empires seemed hypocritical after their nations had fought for the freedom of lands dominated by the Axis. Furthermore, the European nations, weakened economically and militarily by the world war, found it beneficial to grant freedom to their expensive and unprofitable colonies.

In a remarkably peaceful process, eventually 120 nations emerged from the old European empires after World War II. These newly independent countries, however, faced many obstacles. Many suffered from overpopulation and a lack of industrial and agricultural production. Also contributing to their problems were the threat of communism and a

Poverty and even the threat of starvation afflicts regions of the Third World, such as Africa.

general political instability caused by a lack of experience with self-rule. With the removal of European control, divisions along tribal, religious, racial, or linguistic lines created friction—the same factors that had divided them before Western powers brought order. The Western powers only aggravated the divisions by drawing new national boundaries that ignored these differences.

The greatest problem for Third World countries has been poverty, and the reasons for this poverty are numerous. Large populations and high illiteracy rates limit economic improvement in Third World nations. A major reason is the failure to industrialize. Defenders of the Third World point out that such nations lack the natural resources and investment capital usually needed for industrialization. But some nations that lack natural resources, such as Japan, still managed to industrialize. Likewise large amounts of capital from rich nations have not always transformed the economies of Third World nations that have received such aid. The money often ends up in the hands of the government and bureaucracy, not the people or businessmen. Income from the oil exports of certain Middle East nations, for example, goes to wealthy elites.

Some critics blame continued "exploitation" by the West for the Third World poverty. They charge that huge multinational corporations practice "economic imperialism" by removing wealth from the Third World to enrich themselves. But Third World nations that are most closely tied to the industrialized West develop the fastest. Countries such as Indonesia, Malaysia, Brazil, and especially South Korea, Taiwan, Hong Kong, and Singapore have made dramatic economic gains. In the end, Third World economic problems arise from within—from their traditions and government policies—not from outside.

Asia

The Indian Subcontinent

The first major Third World country to gain its independence was India, the "Jewel in the Crown" of the British Empire. The leader of the Indian nationalists was **Mohandas Gandhi** (GAHN dee). He mounted a campaign of **passive resistance,** a nonviolent program designed to defy British rule through strikes (including hunger strikes and sit-down strikes), mass demonstrations, and refusal to pay taxes. Between the world wars, the British government granted the Indian people more political power; but it was not until 1947 that India achieved full independence. Gandhi enjoyed little of the fruits of victory; he was assassinated by a Hindu extremist in 1948.

Because of the sharp division between Hindu and Muslim factions, the British divided India into two sovereign nations: India and Pakistan. War followed between the two new nations, leaving over half a million dead. Predominantly Hindu India became a federal republic in 1949 under the leadership of **Jawaharlal Nehru** (NEH roo), a close associate of Gandhi and one of the organizers of the Third World bloc in the 1950s. Pakistan, with its Muslim majority and military government, was separated geographically into East and West Pakistan on opposite sides of India. In 1971 East Pakistan, believing itself mistreated by the government in West Pakistan, rebelled. With Indian aid, the region fought for and won independence as the nation of Bangladesh, only to emerge as one of the poorest nations in the world.

Mohandas Gandhi (center), leader of the Indian independence movement

Muslim Pakistan and Hindu India have constantly clashed over dominance in the Indian subcontinent. The military, with a few exceptions, has ruled Pakistan since its independence. India has been called "the world's largest democracy," but it has struggled to establish a democratic tradition. The family of Nehru has dominated Indian politics. After his death, Nehru's daughter **Indira Gandhi** (not related to Mohandas Gandhi) was the major leader of India. She served as prime minister for most of the period stretching from 1966 to 1984. Although she received international recognition from other nations (particularly those with Communist and leftist governments), she had difficulty dealing with India's enormous problems of overpopulation, hunger, and poverty. At one point, Mrs. Gandhi even suspended the constitution and ruled on her own authority. She proved unable to solve India's ethnic, social, and religious divisions. In fact she was assassinated in 1984 by two of her own bodyguards who opposed her treatment of the Sikhs, an Indian religious sect. Her son, Rajiv Gandhi, replaced her, but he was voted out of office in 1989 over charges of corruption. He was likewise assassinated in 1991 while campaigning to recapture his office. Independence has not brought stability or prosperity to India.

Southeast Asia

Nationalist movements also grew stronger in Southeast Asia. Since the late 1930s, this region had been under Japanese domination, and its people did not want to return to the colonial rule of Western nations after World War II. In 1946 the United States granted independence to the Philippines. In 1949 Indonesia, the largest nation in Southeast Asia, won its independence from the Dutch. With India no longer a colony, Britain had no need to retain control of nearby Burma and Ceylon; in 1948 both became independent. In 1957 Malaya and Singapore left British control, and in 1963 Borneo followed. In Indochina, the Vietnamese defeated the French and prevented them from reasserting colonial rule. But as seen in the last chapter, in the years following independence, all of Vietnam, as well as Laos and Cambodia, became Communist.

Africa

Africa also witnessed a rapid series of independence movements in the postwar period. In 1950 there were only four free states on the continent; by the 1990s there were over fifty. In the year 1960 alone, eighteen former colonies became independent nations. In their rush for independence, though, the African states encountered many problems.

Opposite Page: *African herdsmen watering their cattle*

Tribal Conflict

A major problem for the emerging African nations has been tribal rivalry. When Western colonial powers divided Africa in the late nineteenth century, many tribes were split or moved from their homelands. European rule held the tribes together, but as African countries began to gain their independence, tribal loyalties superseded national unity. In one African country after another, tribal jealousy led to civil war. In Kenya and the Congo (later renamed Zaire), for example, bloody wars raged between opposing tribes.

A terrible example of tribal conflict occurred in Nigeria in the 1960s. Three leading tribal groups—the Ibo, the Yoruba, and the Hausa—all competed for dominance in that nation. Finally, the Ibo attempted to secede from Nigeria and form the state of Biafra in 1967. The rest of Nigeria refused to recognize the secession, and the **Biafran War** resulted. Three years of fighting followed. The Nigerian forces pushed back the Ibo, reducing their territory from 44,000 square miles at the beginning of the war to a crowded area of about 2,500 square miles. In this overcrowded territory, starvation became a deadlier weapon than guns or tanks. Thousands died in the fighting, but starvation raised the final total to perhaps as many as one million dead.

Political Instability

Widespread political instability is another problem. Most African nations emerged from coloni-

alism possessing carefully crafted democratic constitutions prepared by their former colonial rulers. Yet with few exceptions, many African nations fell prey to military dictatorships or authoritarian one-party states. This instability provided a fertile field for Communist activity during the Cold War. Both the United States and the Soviet Union provided military and economic assistance to African nations to win their support. The Soviets were also quick to encourage rebellion and violence in order to establish Marxist states.

One of the cruelest of the postwar African dictatorships was that of Idi Amin Dada in Uganda. Amin, a military officer, seized power in 1971 and unleashed terror and bloodshed on the nation for eight years. A Muslim, Amin persecuted the nominally Christian majority of Uganda. A Marxist, he sought close relations with pro-Communist nations such as Libya. He expelled all Asians from the country and established secret police forces to eliminate his opponents. Amin even practiced cannibalism and murdered members of his own family. As many as two hundred thousand Ugandans may have died in Amin's massacres. He was finally ousted in 1979 by a combined force of exiled Ugandans and troops from neighboring Tanzania, which Amin had invaded a few months before.

Racial Conflict

Racial conflict is another source of tension in Africa. During the colonial period, a white Euro-

pean minority dominated the black African majority. In many countries the whites held special privileges and rights. After independence, the whites in some nations sought to maintain their position of dominance. There was bloodshed in some countries as black majority leaders sought to gain political power. In the years since independence, white rule in Africa has ended—except in the country of South Africa. There the white minority continues to rule. In many ways, South Africa embodies the problems and tensions of postcolonial Africa: the question of white dominance, the violent activities of Marxist rebels, and intense tribal rivalry. In one respect, though, South Africa differs from most African nations. With its European economic system and its enormous wealth in gold, diamonds, and chromium, South Africa is a prosperous nation. Its wealth has helped the nation withstand external and internal pressures to change its system of government.

South Africa has a larger white population than other sub-Saharan nations; about 18 per cent of South Africans are white, with 68 per cent black and 10 per cent "coloured" (those of mixed white, black, and Asian descent). The whites are split into English-speaking descendants of the British, and descendants of the Dutch, who speak a language called Afrikaans.

The policy of apartheid involved the resettlement of blacks in impoverished, allegedly semi-independent "homelands" within South Africa, such as this village in the homeland of Natal.

Chapter 18 (p. 479) described the original settlement of the South African cape by the Dutch, the entry of the British, and the formation of the Union of South Africa after the Boer War. The British originally dominated the government of the Union of South Africa, but after World War II the Afrikaner population became a majority of the whites. The new Afrikaner government instituted a policy called **apartheid** (uh PART HITE; from an Afrikaans word meaning "separate"), an elaborate system of racial separation and white supremacy. In theory, apartheid provided for separate development of the racial groups in South Africa. It also, however, preserved white political control of the nation. To support this policy, the government instituted repressive policies regulating contact between the races and limiting the types of jobs and rates of pay that blacks and coloureds could have.

Black resentment of apartheid led to protests and riots. Drawing on this discontent, Marxist groups drew support among black South Africans. On the other hand, some tribal groups in that nation, notably the Zulus, formed groups to protect their own interests. The result was conflict, not only between blacks and whites but also among the blacks themselves. Meanwhile, international pressure grew on South Africa. Other Third World nations condemned the government's policies as racist and a holdover of imperialism. International pressure from the United Nations and other countries pushed the South Africans toward reform. For a time, South Africa was able to win some Western support by its fiercely anti-Communist stance. The winding down of the Cold War, however, removed that prop and left the nation increasingly isolated. Finally, in the 1980s, the white minority government began dismantling most of the apartheid laws and taking hesitant steps toward sharing political power with the black majority and nonwhite minorities. The last bastion of colonialism began to fall.

Africa's Future

There are hopeful signs for Africa's future. The more capitalistic countries like the Côte d'Ivoire (Ivory Coast) and Kenya are faring better than their neighbors and thereby encouraging other nations to adopt free-market policies. Long plagued by dicta-

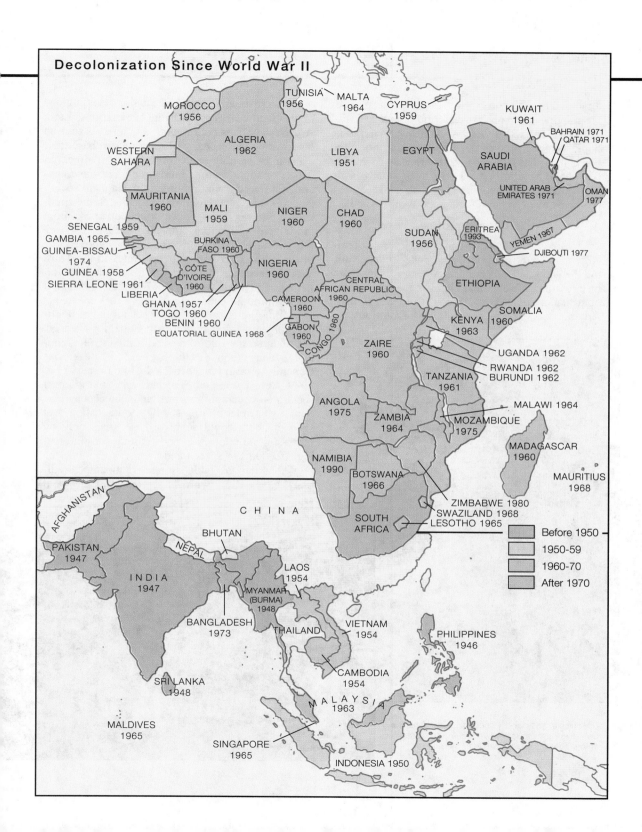

Decolonization Since World War II

MOROCCO 1956
TUNISIA 1956
MALTA 1964
CYPRUS 1959
KUWAIT 1961
BAHRAIN 1971
QATAR 1971

WESTERN SAHARA
ALGERIA 1962
LIBYA 1951
EGYPT
SAUDI ARABIA

MAURITANIA 1960
MALI 1959
NIGER 1960
CHAD 1960
SUDAN 1956
ERITREA 1993
UNITED ARAB EMIRATES 1971
OMAN 1977
YEMEN 1967
DJIBOUTI 1977

SENEGAL 1959
GAMBIA 1965
GUINEA-BISSAU 1974
GUINEA 1958
SIERRA LEONE 1961
LIBERIA
BURKINA FASO 1960
NIGERIA 1960
CÔTE D'IVOIRE 1960
GHANA 1957
TOGO 1960
BENIN 1960
EQUATORIAL GUINEA 1968
CAMEROON 1960
CENTRAL AFRICAN REPUBLIC 1960
ETHIOPIA
SOMALIA 1960
KENYA 1963
UGANDA 1962
RWANDA 1962
BURUNDI 1962

GABON 1960
CONGO 1960
ZAIRE 1960
TANZANIA 1961

ANGOLA 1975
ZAMBIA 1964
MALAWI 1964
MOZAMBIQUE 1975
MADAGASCAR 1960
MAURITIUS 1968

NAMIBIA 1990
BOTSWANA 1966
ZIMBABWE 1980
SWAZILAND 1968
LESOTHO 1965
SOUTH AFRICA

Before 1950
1950-59
1960-70
After 1970

AFGHANISTAN
CHINA
BHUTAN
NEPAL
PAKISTAN 1947
INDIA 1947
LAOS 1954
MYANMAR (BURMA) 1948
BANGLADESH 1973
THAILAND
VIETNAM 1954
PHILIPPINES 1946
SRI LANKA 1948
CAMBODIA 1954
MALAYSIA 1963
MALDIVES 1965
SINGAPORE 1965
INDONESIA 1950

torships and one-party rule, several African states are moving to democracy and multiparty systems. The situation in South Africa seems to hold out some hope of racial progress, with white minorities and black majorities learning to accommodate each other for mutual benefit. Perhaps Africa can finally begin to overcome the economic, social, and political problems that have emerged since World War II.

Latin America

Unlike Asian and African countries, most Latin American countries gained their independence during the early 1800s. Yet Latin America shares many of the same problems that confront the other developing nations of the world. Since World War II, Latin America has experienced political revolutions, ec-

onomic crises, and social upheaval. Possessing one of the world's fastest-growing populations, Latin America contains poor masses and a small but rich landowning class. Many of its countries base their economies on only one export, such as coffee, bananas, or sugar. Latin American nations have generally suffered from high inflation, stagnant socialist economies, and large foreign debts. Some countries, however, have developing industries, more productive agriculture, and an increasingly large middle class. Brazil, for example, has enjoyed one of the highest economic growth rates in the Third World, despite a huge foreign debt. Likewise, oil has helped enrich Mexico and Ecuador, although it has not brought economic recovery to Venezuela.

Military dictatorships have been a major political problem for this region. Argentina, for instance, has endured the rule of several military rulers, notably Juan Perón (1946-55, 1973-74). Likewise General Augusto Pinochet ruled Chile from 1973 to 1989. Both Peron and Pinochet were able to enact social and economic reforms, and Pinochet in particular was able to bring stability to his nation. But such dictators could achieve these goals only by repressing all opposition and limiting (or eliminating) freedoms of speech and the press.

Other nations built stronger democratic traditions. Costa Rica, with its stable democracy and

Both wealth and poverty abound in Latin America. On the left is a modern city scene from Colombia; on the right is a shantytown in El Salvador.

relatively high standard of living, is a shining example of democracy in Central America. Mexico endured a series of revolutions and dictatorships in the first hundred years of its independence. Then during World War I, the nation adopted a new constitution which has provided relatively stable government to the present day. Furthermore, the 1980s saw the replacement of many Latin American military dictatorships with civilian governments. Argentina's military rulers fell from power in 1982, when Great Britain decisively defeated the Argentinians in the Falklands War. (See p. 617.) A freely elected civilian government came to power the next year. In 1989 Pinochet allowed free elections in Chile, which put an end to his rule.

Communism and Marxism have also threatened Latin America. In 1948 the countries of Latin America and the United States formed the **Organization of American States** (OAS), a regional organization designed to prevent Communist expansion in the Western Hemisphere. The OAS did not stop Fidel Castro from coming to power in Cuba in 1959, though, and that island nation became a seedbed for Communist revolution in Latin America and around the world. Rebels in Nicaragua toppled a military dictatorship in 1979 and established the Marxist Sandinista regime. The United States gave massive aid to several nations, notably El Salvador, to help them combat Communist rebels. President Alberto Fujimori suspended constitutional government in Peru in 1992 in part to deal more firmly with a deadly Communist guerrilla force in that nation.

Although the Communist threat did not disappear in the late 1980s and early 1990s, it did diminish. The end of Soviet subsidies gravely weakened the economy of Communist Cuba. The Sandinistas lost power in Nicaragua when they held free elections in 1990. The decline of communism and the growth of democratic government have enabled Latin America to shift its focus to pressing economic and environmental problems, such as the challenge of massive foreign debt and the delicate problem of developing ecosystems (the Amazonian rain forest, for example) without destroying them. Latin America's future offers both trials and opportunities.

Section Review

1. Into what two nations did Great Britain divide colonial India? What third country emerged from one of these two nations in 1971?
2. What three major problems did the new African states face in postcolonial Africa?
3. What group came to dominate South Africa politically after World War II? What social/economic policy did it establish?
4. How do the nations of Latin America differ significantly from the Third World nations of Asia and Africa?
5. What Caribbean nation became a center of communism in the late 1950s?

The Middle East

The Middle East is part of the Third World, just like Asia, Africa, and Latin America. The region has held a special importance in the postwar era, however, as a strategic source of wealth and a troubled center of conflict. Located where Europe, Asia, and Africa converge, the Middle East has assumed great significance for the western industrial nations because of its vast oil supply—the world's largest oil reserves.

From ancient to modern times but especially since World War II, this region of the world has been the scene of turmoil. The causes of this turmoil lie in the region's internal divisions. Traditional monarchs, or sheiks, rule some countries, such as Saudi Arabia and Kuwait. Others, such as Egypt and Iraq, are secular states that are controlled by the military. Iran has an "Islamic Republic" in which Muslim holy men rule the nation. The Jewish state of Israel has the oldest and best established democracy in the region. Middle East nations also divide along economic lines. Those with abundant oil—such as Saudi Arabia, Kuwait, and the Gulf states—possess great wealth, while other desert nations in the region struggle with extreme poverty.

The most disruptive elements in the Middle East are ethnic and religious. Most countries in the area are Arab, except for Iran and Turkey; Israel, of course, is predominantly Jewish. Islam is the pervasive religion of that part of the world, although pockets of Jews and nominal Christians exist. All of these elements—political, economic, ethnic, and religious—contribute to making the Middle East a potentially explosive region.

The Arab-Israeli Conflict

Much of the postwar tension in the Middle East has resulted from the return of the Jewish people to Palestine and the creation of the national state of Israel. The history of Israel and its neighbors has been one of armed truces punctuated with open warfare. In each conflict Israel showed amazing strength and strategic military cunning to overcome its more numerous foes. But military victory has yet to bring peace.

Founding of Israel

Early in the twentieth century, the **Zionist movement** arose in Europe. This movement was dedicated to securing a national home for the Jews in Palestine. During World War I, the Zionist movement gained the support of the British government, which in 1917 issued the famous **Balfour Declaration.** The British promised to "view with favour the establishment in Palestine of a national home for the Jewish people, and [to] use their best endeavours to facilitate the achievement of this object." The declaration also provided that the rights of the non-Jewish community already in Palestine should be safeguarded.

At the end of World War I, Palestine was predominantly an Arab land with only a small Jewish population. Britain received the area as a mandate. (See p. 519.) Under British administration, Jews began returning to the land of God's promise. When the Nazis began persecuting European Jews, larger numbers began to emigrate to Palestine. When the British mandate came to an end after World War II, the Jewish provisional government proclaimed the independent state of Israel in 1948.

Arab-Israeli Wars

The nation of Israel was literally born out of war in 1948. The United Nations attempted to di-

Jews gather daily to pray at the "Wailing Wall" in Jerusalem, the only remaining section of the Jewish temple.

vide Palestine peacefully between the Jews and the Arabs. Instead, war followed as Arab forces from Egypt, Jordan, Syria, Lebanon, and Iraq tried to drive the Jews from Palestine. Against great odds the Israelis defeated their opponents and won their war for independence. The uneasy peace provided no final settlement, though. The Arab states refused to recognize the existence of Israel and resented the Jewish presence in Palestine. The tension between Israel and the Arab community led to war again in 1956 in the **Suez crisis.** Fearing Egyptian moves against their nation, the Israelis gladly agreed to aid Britain and France by moving into the Sinai Peninsula, thereby giving those nations an excuse to take control of the Suez Canal. The Israeli army conquered Sinai with surprising ease, but it had to withdraw when international pressure forced Britain and France to back down. (See p. 628.)

Left: Israelis fighting in the Sinai during the Six-Day War (1967);
Right: Israelis planting their flag on Mt. Hermon, which they
captured during the Yom Kippur War (1973-74)

A UN peace-keeping force remained in Sinai until 1967. In that year the Egyptian government, wanting to launch a new attack on Israel, asked the UN forces to leave. When Israel realized that Egypt, Syria, and Jordan were preparing to attack her, she launched a pre-emptive strike. The Israeli air force caught the Egyptian planes on the ground and destroyed them, and then turned on Syria and Jordan. In the **Six-Day War,** the Israelis again routed a larger foe. It also resulted in the capture of the Sinai Peninsula, the West Bank (Arab territory on the western bank of the Jordan River, including Jerusalem), the Gaza Strip along the Mediterranean coast, and the Golan Heights along the Israeli-Syrian border.

Victory still did not bring peace. In 1973 Egypt and Syria attacked again, launching their assault on October 6, Yom Kippur (the Jewish Day of Atonement). In the **Yom Kippur War,** as it became known, the Arab allies enjoyed initial success. The Israelis recovered and won a narrow victory but at great cost. Twenty-five years of conflict had not succeeded in settling the difficult situation.

Search for Peace

Surprisingly, the long-term outcome of the somewhat inconclusive 1973 war was more positive than the earlier one-sided Israeli victories. Egypt, weary of war, presented a peace overture to Israel. The leaders of the two nations joined in peace talks at Camp David, Maryland (a presidential retreat just

outside Washington, D.C.), with the American president Jimmy Carter as mediator. The resulting agreement, known as the **Camp David Accords,** became the basis for an Israeli-Egyptian peace treaty, signed in 1979. Despite many unresolved problems, Israel returned the Sinai Peninsula to Egypt, and Egypt recognized Israel's right to exist, renouncing years of Egyptian military hostility.

Many other Arab countries, however, condemned the treaty and maintained hostility toward Israel. The Israeli government continued to suffer from raids based in Arab lands. In 1983 Israel even

U.S. president Jimmy Carter with Egyptian president Anwar el-Sadat and Israeli prime minister Menachem Begin at the signing of the historic Camp David Accords between Egypt and Israel

The Suez Crisis

One of the most serious international crises of the postwar era centered in the Middle East. It involved not only Egypt and Israel but also the superpowers (the U.S. and the USSR), and the two leading military powers of Europe (Great Britain and France). The Suez crisis blended the nationalism of the emerging states, the violent Arab-Israeli conflict, and one of the last gasps of colonialism.

British control of Egypt ended completely after World War II. The government remained pro-West, however, and Britain still maintained a presence in Egypt through the Suez Canal Company, which operated the canal. Then in the 1950s, the Egyptian military overthrew the pro-West king, and Colonel Gamal Nasser eventually became head of the government. Like many Third World rulers, Nasser attempted to play the Free World and the Communist bloc off each other for his own advantage. When the West refused to help Nasser pay for the Aswan High Dam (see p. 31) because of his overtures to the Communist nations, Nasser welcomed Soviet help to build it. Furthermore, the Communists began arming Nasser to prepare for another war against Israel. He used bases in the Sinai Peninsula to attempt to close the Red Sea to Israeli shipping. Then, in what was the last straw for the West, Nasser seized control of the Suez Canal in 1956.

The British and the French were infuriated by Nasser's action and feared for free international use of the canal. When they realized that Israel was endangered by the Egyptian military build-up, the British and French proposed a deal. The Israelis would strike the Egyptian forces in the Sinai Peninsula and drive toward the canal. Then the European nations, acting in accordance with a previous agreement with Egypt to safeguard the canal, would intervene militarily to "protect" the canal.

The Israeli part of the plan began with impressive smoothness on October 29, 1956. Four Israeli planes cut Egyptian communications by flying twelve feet off the ground and snapping telephone lines in the Sinai Peninsula with their wings and propellers. Israeli paratroopers dropped behind the Egyptian forces while Israeli armor pierced the front-line Egyptian defenses. Within a hundred hours, the Israelis had gained control of nearly the entire Sinai Peninsula.

The European powers moved more slowly—too slowly. While the Anglo-French task force moved lethargically across the Mediterranean, international observers easily guessed what the force had in mind and roundly condemned it. U.S. president Dwight Eisenhower, in the middle of a re-election campaign, angrily denounced the action. The Soviet Union, eager to distract attention from her bloody repression of an anti-Soviet uprising in Hungary, joined the chorus of condemnation and even hinted at military intervention. Shortly after the British and French forces landed successfully in the canal zone, their governments backed down. The Israelis too were forced to withdraw from Sinai.

For the European powers, the Suez crisis was a humiliating fiasco. Not only did the action fail to gain control of the canal but it also confirmed the popularity of the anti-Western Nasser in Egypt. The Israelis came out somewhat better. They demonstrated their military prowess in convincing fashion, and they forced the Egyptians to stop interfering with Israeli shipping in the Red Sea. Unfortunately, the crisis left Nasser festering with rage against Israel. In 1967 another conflict—the Six-Day War—resulted from the inconclusive result of the Suez crisis.

invaded southern Lebanon in an attempt to destroy enemy bases there. Furthermore, the "occupied territories" of the Gaza Strip, the West Bank, and the Golan Heights contain Arab majorities who resent Israeli rule. Riots and violent uprisings often rend these areas. Diplomats continue to search for a means of bringing Jew and Arab together and finding a formula for lasting peace.

Sources of Tension in the Middle East

Oil

In 1945 several Arab states formed the Arab League to strengthen the ties among the participating states. The league sought to coordinate the members' political programs while preserving their independence and sovereignty. The league has been less than successful politically because of competing national interests and hostility among the rival Arab countries. The Arab world has had much greater success, though, with economic cooperation over its greatest resource—oil.

In 1960 many oil-producing nations in the Middle East joined with other oil-producing nations to form the Organization of Petroleum Exporting Countries, or **OPEC,** as it is more commonly known. Through collective action, these nations have sought to control the production and price of petroleum around the world. In the 1970s, for example, OPEC dramatically raised oil prices four hundred per cent and placed an oil embargo against the United States for helping Israel in the 1973 Yom Kippur War. This incident illustrates how the OPEC countries—especially those in the Middle East—have tried to increase their political and economic influence by manipulating the flow of oil to industrial nations. The need of the industrialized West for oil has given the Arab nations political and economic clout far beyond their size.

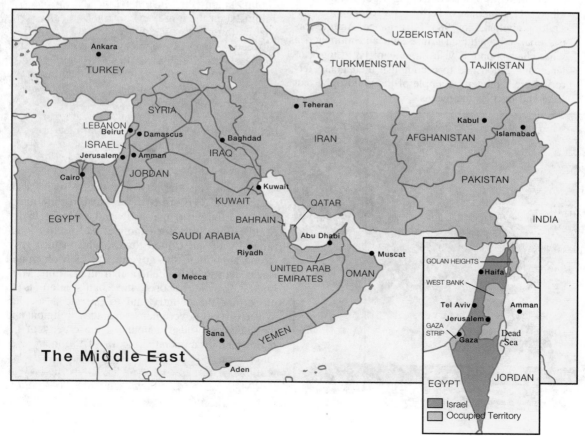

The Middle East

Terrorism

The Arab failure to destroy Israel as well as economic and religious differences among the Arab nations created frustration and tension in the Middle East. These conditions gave rise to extremist Arab groups, the most famous of which is the **Palestine Liberation Organization** (PLO). The PLO claims to represent the Muslim Arabs living in Israeli-occupied areas, such as the West Bank and the Gaza Strip, and calls for the destruction of the Jewish state and the establishment of a Palestinian state. To advance their causes, groups such as the PLO turned to **terrorism,** the use of terror and violence to achieve a goal. Encouraged by media attention from the West, terrorist groups hijacked airplanes and ships, bombed buildings, and took hostages. In 1983 Muslim extremists in Beirut, Lebanon, rammed a truck filled with explosives into the quarters of American Marines stationed there as a peace-keeping force. The attack killed 241 Americans. Terrorists also delight in assaulting civilians. In 1985, for instance, Arab terrorists hijacked an Italian cruise ship and murdered a wheelchair-bound Jewish American. By using violence and bloodshed to accomplish their goals, terrorists are a modern example of the philosophy that "the end justifies the means."

The Ayatollah Ruholla Khomeini

Radical Islam

One would expect that Islam would be a source of unity among the Muslim people and nations. But within Islam there are several rival branches. The Islamic faith of the Middle East is divided mainly between the majority Sunni and the minority Shiite factions. The division of these two groups goes back to the death of the prophet Muhammad. The Sunnites are followers of the *caliphs,* the chosen "successors to the prophet." (See pp. 139-40.) Shiites, however, believe that only Muhammad's son-in-law and those descended from him are true successors to the prophet. Iran and Iraq are mostly Shiite, whereas Sunnites are the majority in most other Middle East countries.

Beginning in the 1970s, radical Muslim sects began to stir up hostility in the Muslim community and contributed to the strife and violence in the Middle East. Iran, for example, had been a longtime ally of the United States, who in turn gave strong support to the government of Mohammed Reza Shah Pahlavi. Fanatical Iranian Shiite Muslims, however, opposed the shah's attempts to modernize the country and to operate a secular, Western-style government separating religion and the state. They also denounced the cruelty of his regime and his autocratic rule. In 1979 Iranian revolutionaries, led by the religious leader **Ayatollah Ruholla Khomeini** (EYE-uh-TOH-luh rue-HO-lah koh-MAY-nee), overthrew the shah. (*Ayatollah,*

Fires touched off in Kuwaiti oil fields by Iraqi dictator Saddam Hussein during the Gulf War (1991)

Mausoleum in Isfahan, Iran; members of the Qajar dynasty (1795-1925) are buried here.

Persian for "reflection, or sign, of Allah," is the highest title of honor that a Shiite Muslim can hold.)

The Iranian Shiites instituted an "Islamic Republic" in which Muslim religious law was to guide the state. A startling example of the fanatical extremes of these Muslims occurred in 1989. British ex-Muslim Salman Rushdie wrote a novel called *The Satanic Verses,* which contained passages that Muslims considered blasphemous. Khomeini did not simply condemn the book; he pronounced a death sentence on the author—who quickly went into hiding. The Iranians viewed their revolution as but a first step in worldwide change. Khomeini said, "We will export our revolution to the four corners of the world because our revolution is Islamic; and the struggle will continue until the cry of 'There's no god but Allah, and Muhammad is the messenger of Allah' prevails throughout the world."

Iran's extremists were the most visible expression of a movement that affected many Muslim nations. Other groups echoed the Iranian call for "pure" Islamic states untainted by contacts with the "corrupt" ways of the West. In no other country did these radicals seize power, although the Algerian government canceled elections in 1992 that likely would have given radicals control of the legislature. Numerous smaller groups nonetheless committed acts of terrorism to undermine secular Muslim regimes. With the decline of communism, many observers concluded that Islamic extremism might become the new ideological threat to international peace and stability.

Strife in the Middle East

Lebanon

Since World War II, the Middle East has often suffered the ravages of war. In addition to the Arab-Israeli conflicts, war has plagued other Middle Eastern countries. During the 1970s and early 1980s, the tiny country of Lebanon was besieged by civil war between Muslim and nominally Christian factions. This war became more complex when Israeli and Syrian forces moved into the country—the Israelis to reduce terrorist activity based in Lebanon, and Syria in an attempt to extend her own authority. In 1983 four nations (the United States, France, Italy, and Britain) sent peace-keeping forces to Beirut, the capital, but this force could not bring an end to the fighting.

Iran-Iraq War

In 1980 a serious conflict broke out between Iran and Iraq. These two nations had had a long history of dispute, dating back to troubles between Persia and the Ottoman Empire. After the Iranian revolution in 1979, the Iraqi dictator **Saddam Hussein** feared the spread of Iran's radical Islamic revolution into his own country. He also saw the disorder in Iran as an opportunity to seize some of her oil-rich territories for Iraq. Therefore, he launched a massive attack across the border. Saddam expected the war to be

Saddam Hussein

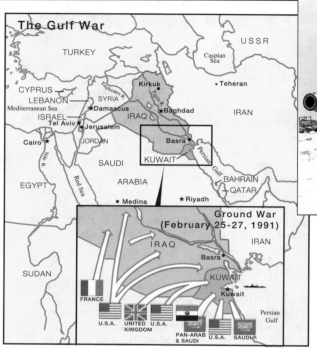

The Gulf War

Ground War
(February 25-27, 1991)

American Marines clamber over an Iraqi tank captured in Kuwait during the brief but decisive Gulf War. The ground campaign that devastated the Iraqis took only about one hundred hours.

over in three weeks; instead, the **Iran-Iraq War** lasted eight years. After initial Iraqi successes, the Iranians united behind their revolutionary government and threw the invaders back. A deadly war of attrition set in, resembling in some ways the trench warfare of World War I. Saddam resorted to chemical warfare and the bombing of Iranian cities to try to break the stalemate. The Iranians sought to topple Saddam's government and establish a radical Muslim state in Iraq. Eventually, economic hardship, diplomatic pressure from the West and the Soviet Union, and sheer exhaustion drove the two sides to halt the conflict. Over three hundred thousand people died in the fighting—for no purpose. Neither country made any important gains from the war.

The Gulf War

Frustrated by the failure of his war on Iran, Saddam Hussein sought a weaker—but still potentially profitable—victim. In August of 1990 Saddam's forces invaded the neighboring country of Kuwait. By doing so, Saddam not only seized con-

trol of the huge oil reserves of tiny Kuwait but also threatened the safety of Saudi Arabia. Western powers such as the United States and Great Britain determined to turn back this aggression and protect Saudi Arabia. Instead of taking independent action, the Western powers worked through the Security Council of the United Nations. The UN authorized a multinational force led by the United States to use "all necessary means" to liberate Kuwait. President Bush of the United States condemned Iraq's action and vowed, "This will not stand." Other Arab states lined up with the Western powers against Iraq.

On January 16, 1991, the allies launched the **Gulf War** with a massive air strike against Iraqi forces. For five weeks, the American-led coalition pounded Iraqi forces in Kuwait and struck targets in Iraq itself with bombs and missiles. After the air attacks had softened enemy positions, ground forces struck the Iraqis on February 24. In only a hundred hours, the coalition of American, British, French, and Arab forces outflanked and surrounded the Iraqi forces in Kuwait. Saddam's dispirited soldiers surrendered. Iraqi losses numbered in the tens of thousands; the coalition forces lost fewer than two hundred.

The remarkably swift and sweeping victory over Iraq sent a surge of joy and optimism through the Western world. The United Nations had proved to be unusually successful in uniting its member

U.S. Marines provide covering fire during a raid on a weapons cache in Somalia in 1993. What had begun as a relief mission to that African nation quickly bogged down into a conflict between U.N. forces and native warring factions. The "New World Order" proclaimed by politicians in the wake of the Gulf War proved to be short-lived.

nations against aggression. President Bush spoke glowingly of the "new world order" that he expected to arise from the war. Reality soon set in, though. Saddam was defeated in Kuwait, but he still held power in Iraq and threatened the stability of the Middle East. Islamic extremism continued to thrive. Countries that had been allied while at war began again to argue and compete when at peace. Bush himself was voted out of office less than two years later. No matter how many problems a decisive military victory eliminates, it still creates new ones.

Section Review

1. What is the Middle East's most valuable natural resource?
2. Name the nation in the Middle East that has the oldest and best established democracy.
3. Whom does the Palestine Liberation Organization claim to represent?
4. What nation was the site of a radical Islamic revolution in 1979? Who was its leader?
5. What two nations did Saddam Hussein invade in two different wars? What were the results of each invasion?

Toward the Future

The opening of the twentieth century was characterized by buoyant hope. International cooperation—seen in organizations such as the International Red Cross and activities such as the Olympic games—reached unprecedented heights. A widespread peace movement, encouraged by a lack of major multinational conflict for nearly a hundred years, predicted the complete abolition of war. In religious circles there was the mood that man was going to bring in the millennial kingdom prior to the return of Christ. But these hopes were dashed by the two world wars followed by a tense era of "cold" war.

As the twentieth century drew to a close, there was a similar mood of optimism. The menace of global destruction by the two superpowers diminished with the breakup of the Soviet empire. International efforts at keeping the peace were stimulated by the apparently effective work of the United Nations. World leaders used phrases like the "new world order." Teachers encouraged students to think of themselves as citizens of the world instead of holding to the "provincialism" of national cultures.

But while there is seeming progress toward building a more secure world where nations are working to create a new world order, the Christian must keep in mind the lesson of the dawn of the twentieth century: rosy dreams of future progress will encounter the harsh reality of human sinfulness. Prospects for peace and unity while left in man's hands will ultimately fail because of the sinful nature of fallen man. Human efforts at international cooperation, even when promoted for good reasons, cannot permanently succeed.

Men have attached many labels to the postwar era—the "space age," the "nuclear age," and, of special concern to Christians, the "secular age." As people have reaped the benefits of technological advances, they have adopted worldly and temporal standards and values. As a result, modern society has little concern for God or spiritual matters. People strive for material gain and a life of affluence. They follow the religion of humanism, making themselves the ultimate authority. They reject belief in God, scoff at the Bible, and ridicule Christians.

Despite technological marvels and modern man's self-reliant spirit, the world is full of problems that man cannot solve. The threat of war is ever present. Crime continues to increase at staggering rates. The murder of unborn children through abortion has become socially acceptable. Homosexuals and lesbians miltantly seek respectability. Many people seek to escape from their own problems and the problems of society around them by using alcohol and drugs. But God's standards do not change. As in every other age, modern man must face the consequence of his sin.

> This know also, that in the last days perilous times shall come. For men shall be lovers of their own selves, covetous, boasters, proud, blasphemers, disobedient to parents, unthankful, unholy, without natural affection, trucebreakers, false accusers, incontinent [without self-control], fierce, despisers of those that are good, traitors, heady [reckless], highminded, lovers of pleasures more than lovers of God; having a form of godliness, but denying the power thereof: from such turn away.
>
> —II Timothy 3:1-5

Chapter Review

Can You Explain?

ecumenical movement	decolonization	Zionist movement
civil rights movement	passive resistance	terrorism
Third World	apartheid	

Can You Identify?

United Nations	Ronald Reagan	Biafran War	OPEC
Secretariat	Konrad Adenauer	Organization of	Palestine Liberation
General Assembly	Charles de Gaulle	American States	Organization
Security Council	Fifth Republic	Balfour Declaration	Ayatollah Ruholla
European Community	Margaret Thatcher	Suez crisis	Khomeini
World Council of	Mohandas Gandhi	Six-Day War	Saddam Hussein
Churches	Jawaharlal Nehru	Yom Kippur War	Iran-Iraq War
Vatican II	Indira Gandhi	Camp David Accords	Gulf War
Great Society			

Can You Locate?

India	Israel	Suez Canal	Lebanon
Pakistan	Jordan	West Bank	Iran
Bangladesh	Syria	Gaza Strip	Iraq
Nigeria	Sinai Peninsula	Saudi Arabia	Kuwait
South Africa			

How Much Do You Remember?

1. What countries are the five permanent members of the UN Security Council?
2. What organizations comprise the European Community? What body administers the EC?
3. What body is the most significant force in the modern ecumenical movement?
4. In what ways was the presidency of Ronald Reagan considered a change from previous administrations?
5. What European nation was reunited in 1990?
6. With what nation did Great Britain fight a war in the 1980s? Over what territory was it fought?
7. List at least three reasons for Japan's remarkable economic recovery after World War II.
8. List at least five problems confronting most nations of the Third World.
9. List the four major Arab-Israeli wars (1948, 1956, 1967, 1973) and briefly note the results of each.
10. What are the two major divisions within Islam in the Middle East? To which of these did the leaders of the 1979 Iranian Revolution belong?

What Do You Think?

1. What should be the Christian's attitude toward the ecumenical movement? Use scriptural evidence to support your answer.
2. How much do you think the Western imperialistic powers are to blame for the problems of the Third World?
3. Is the goal of a "new world order" a proper one for a Christian to pursue?

EPILOGUE

"What manner of persons ought ye to be?"

Epilogue

> But the day of the Lord will come as a thief in the night; in the which the heavens shall pass away with a great noise, and the elements shall melt with fervent heat, the earth also and the works that are therein shall be burned up. Seeing then that all these things shall be dissolved, *what manner of persons ought ye to be* in all holy conversation and godliness, looking for and hasting unto the coming of the day of God, wherein the heavens being on fire shall be dissolved, and the elements shall melt with fervent heat? Nevertheless we, according to his promise, look for new heavens and a new earth, wherein dwelleth righteousness. Wherefore, beloved, seeing that ye look for such things, be diligent that ye may be found of him in peace, without spot, and blameless.
>
> II Peter 3:10-14

Our survey of world history from creation to the present is now complete. Our study has taken us to many different lands, where we have examined many different peoples. We have considered both the successes and the failures of bygone generations. Students of history should not be concerned solely with the past, however. We can look with certainty to the prophecies in God's Word, knowing that what the Bible predicts will come to pass. Of primary importance to the study of world history and to every individual are the return of Jesus Christ to the earth and the coming day of God's judgment. The Bible teaches that every person will one day stand before God and give an account of his life. In light of the knowledge of these coming events, the Apostle Peter asks the sobering question, "What manner of persons ought ye to be in all holy conversation and godliness?" (II Pet. 3:11).

Lessons of History

The American philosopher George Santayana once said, "Those who cannot remember the past are condemned to repeat it." History is full of examples of men repeating the sins and failures of the past, and as a result suffering similar consequences. This truth prompted the German philosopher Georg Hegel to remark, "What experience and history teach is this—that people and governments never have learned anything from history, or acted on principles deduced from it."

Your study of world history would be without profit if you did not learn any lessons from the past—lessons that would help you understand the present or that would help you in life. Below is a list of a few principles or lessons derived from our study. What other lessons can you add to this list?

God fulfills His promises. He has done what He said He would do. Since God is all truth, not one of His promises has ever failed; therefore, we can confidently expect Him to bring to pass those promises that are yet in the future.

Sin is the source of the world's problems. Many people mistakenly believe that war, hunger, crime, and other social ills are the cause of man's problems rather than the result of his sinfulness.

Our current problems and evils are nothing new. The writer of Ecclesiastes tells us that "there is no new thing under the sun" (1:9). Man's nature has remained the same since the fall of Adam. Although men have made technological advances in society, they are still faced with the consequences of their sin: poverty, crime, greed, and war.

War has been a common theme of our survey of world history. God has given man the duty to rule (exercise dominion) in the earth. He has allowed him to have dominion over the earth itself

Opposite Page: *The Mount of Olives, seen here from Jerusalem's Golden Gate, was the place to which the glory of God departed from Jerusalem in Ezekiel's vision (Ezek. 11:23). Many Bible scholars believe that the mount will be the site to which Christ shall return at His Second Coming (Zech. 14:4).*

(its land, seas, and natural resources) and over all the animals of the earth. But because of the depravity of the human heart, men and nations have abused the authority God granted them. Repeatedly, men have sought to assert their rule over other men—and the result has been war.

Many different factors have led to war. Weakness on the part of one nation encourages a stronger nation to attack. Fear of a country's growing power, the desire to possess another's resources, or anger and hostility among nations cause war. In addition, war results when one nation tries to force its convictions and beliefs on another nation. While these as well as other external factors may lead to armed conflict, Scripture teaches that the primary cause of war is the sinful lust of the human heart (James 4:1).

Understanding the causes of war may help a people to deter war or to be better prepared in the event of war. But it is folly to believe that sinful man will ever achieve lasting peace by his own efforts. Many will demand and predict peace, but there will continue to be wars and rumors of war until the Prince of Peace establishes His reign on the earth.

Life is uncertain. History illustrates the biblical truth given in Proverbs 27:1: ''Boast not thyself of to morrow; for thou knowest not what a day may bring forth.'' Like the rich fool, many have planned for lives of luxury and ease only to find themselves facing death instead (Luke 12:19-20). In spite of the uncertainty of this temporal life, the Christian can have confidence in the Lord. In the words of the psalmist, ''The Lord is my rock, and my fortress, and my deliverer; my God, my strength, in whom I will trust; my buckler, and the horn of my salvation, and my high tower'' (Ps. 18:2).

God's people are in the minority. This has been true since the first day of the Christian church. In certain lands at particular times in history, Christians have exercised a strong influence on society and have made up a large percentage of the population. Nevertheless, the ungodly will always outnumber God's people: ''For wide is the gate, and broad is the way, that leadeth to destruction, and many there be which go in thereat: Because strait is

Albrecht Dürer, The Four Horsemen of the Apocalypse, *National Gallery of Art, Washington, D.C.*

the gate, and narrow is the way, which leadeth unto life, and few there be that find it'' (Matt. 7:13-14).

God never leaves Himself without a witness. In each generation, He raises up individuals to proclaim His word. The ancient world, for example, had Abraham and Moses, while more recent centuries have heard the voices of Martin Luther and John Wesley. God uses people who have different personalities and who are from different lands and backgrounds. In every age, He expects those who have experienced His grace to make Him known to others.

O God, Our Help in Ages Past

O God, our help in ages past,
    Our hope for years to come,
Our shelter from the stormy blast,
    And our eternal home!

Under the shadow of thy throne
    Still may we dwell secure;
Sufficient is thine arm alone,
    And our defense is sure.

Before the hills in order stood,
    Or earth received her frame,
From everlasting thou art God,
    To endless years the same.

A thousand ages, in thy sight,
    Are like an evening gone;
Short as the watch that ends the night,
    Before the rising sun.

Time, like an ever rolling stream,
    Bears all its sons away;
They fly forgotten, as a dream
    Dies at the opening day.

O God, our help in ages past,
    Our hope for years to come;
Be thou our guide while life shall last,
    And our eternal home!

—Isaac Watts

National repentance must start with the people of God. Second Chronicles 7:14 tells us that if God's people will humbly seek Him in prayer and turn from their wicked ways, God will hear them. He will first forgive their sin and then heal their land.

The prosperity of the wicked and the suffering of the righteous are only temporary. As a Christian looks at history, he may despair. He may ask himself the question, "Why do the wicked prosper while the people of God suffer persecution?" But the psalmist reminds us that the Lord does not forget His people:

Fret not thyself because of evildoers, neither be thou envious against the workers of iniquity. For they shall soon be cut down like the grass, and wither as the green herb. Trust in the Lord, and do good; so shalt thou dwell in the land, and verily thou shalt be fed. Delight thyself also in the Lord; and he shall give thee the desires of thine heart. Commit thy way unto the Lord; trust also in him; and he shall bring it to pass. And he shall bring forth thy righteousness as the light, and thy judgment as the noonday. Rest in the Lord, and wait patiently for him: fret not thyself because of him who prospereth in his way, because of the man who bringeth wicked devices to pass.

—Psalm 37:1-7

Likewise, Habakkuk wrote that a believer's trust should be in the unchanging care of his God:

Although the fig tree shall not blossom, neither shall fruit be in the vines; the labour of the olive shall fail, and the fields shall yield no meat; the flock shall be cut off from the fold, and there shall be no herd in the stalls: *yet I will rejoice in the Lord, I will joy in the God of my salvation.*

—Habukkuk 3:17-18

Our life on earth is brief. The Bible says, "For what is your life? It is even a vapour, that appeareth for a little time, and then vanisheth away" (James 4:14). What is seventy years, for example, when compared to several thousand years of human history? Because our earthly life is so short, how much better it is for us to live with eternal values and goals in mind.

A single individual can have a significant influence on the course of history. For example, energetic leaders such as Alexander the Great and Napoleon Bonaparte used their military genius to build large empires. Stirred by creative curiosity, men such as Eli Whitney and Thomas Edison made numerous inventions that have dramatically altered daily life. Consider also the influence of John Bunyan, whose *Pilgrim's Progress* has inspired Christians for over three hundred years. Although history books record the names and deeds of only a relatively few people, everyone has some influence, whether for good or evil, on his own age. What impact are you having on your family, among your friends, and in your neighborhood and city?

History's Last Chapter

Jesus Christ is at the center of human history. Ancient history culminated with His death on the cross; subsequent history moves toward its climax with His glorious return. Christ will soon come again in power and majesty to reign over the earth. In that day, every person will bow his knee and confess that Jesus is Lord.

God has demonstrated His holiness and justice in human history. At the fall (Gen. 3), man began to learn the awful consequences of his sin. Adam's

Gustave Doré, The Ascension, Bob Jones University Collection of Sacred Art; Acts 1:11 says that Jesus will return in the same way that He went up into heaven.

sin brought physical and spiritual death to the entire race. The earth, man's dominion, was placed under a curse. At the time of the Flood and at the Tower of Babel, God judged man's wickedness. These judgments and all those that have been made throughout the world's history have been sent from a loving God. He has constantly reminded man of his sin—of the failure and vanity of all human endeavor apart from God. From the beginning, God's desire has been that men should see the misery they have brought upon themselves, repent, and trust in God's gracious provision for their salvation.

Even so, the tragic tale of man's persistence in sin and rebellion continues. His refusal to accept God will not go unpunished. The horrors and suffering of centuries gone by cannot compare with that which is to come in the final judgment. "But the heavens and the earth, which are now, by the same word are kept in store, reserved unto fire against the day of judgment and perdition of ungodly men" (II Pet. 3:7).

God will one day separate those who have trusted in Him from those who have not. The saved shall enjoy eternal life with Him and blessings beyond human imagination. The unsaved shall suffer in the lake of fire forever.

God is "not willing that any should perish, but that all should come to repentance" (II Pet. 3:9). Have you repented of your sin or persisted in it? When the book is closed on the history of the world, where will you be?

Late afternoon on the Dead Sea

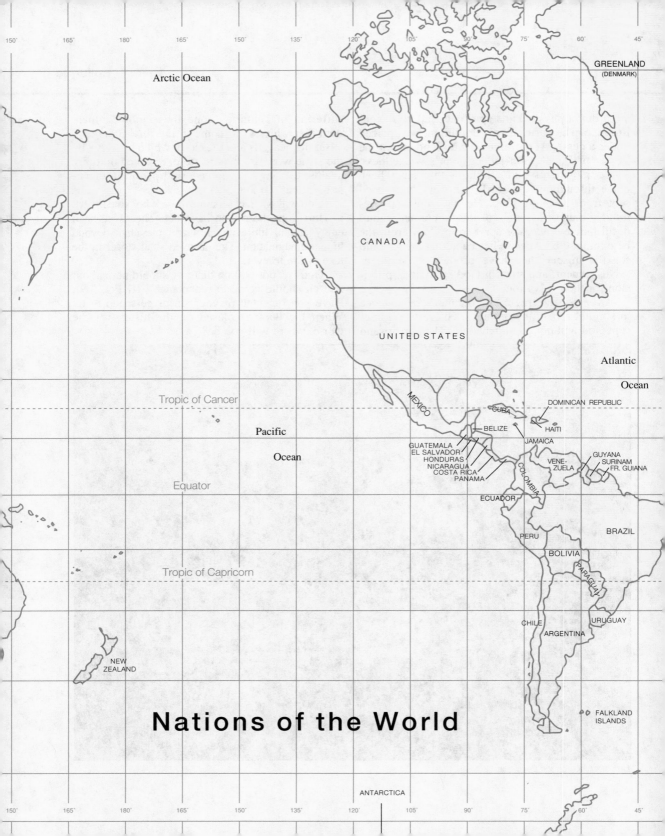

Nations of the World

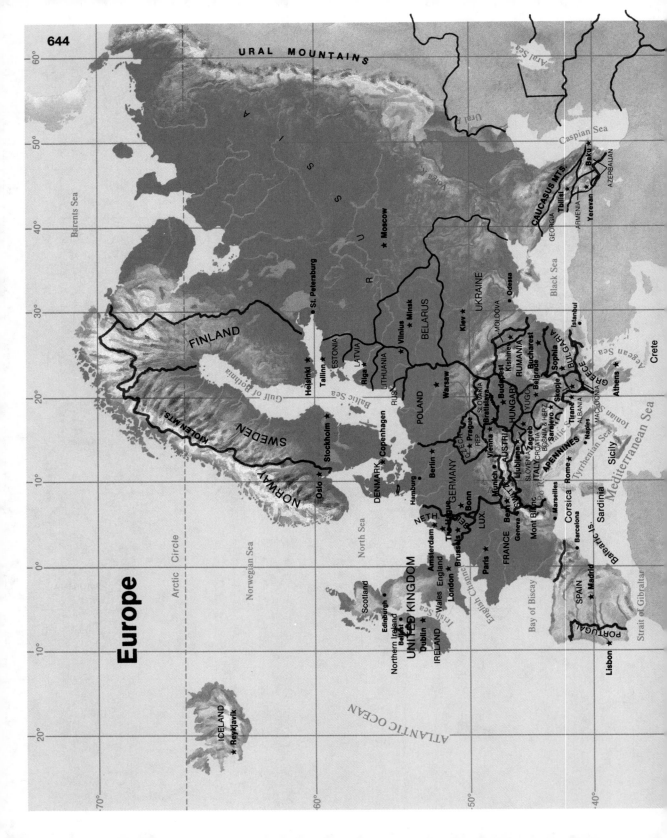

Europe

URAL MOUNTAINS

Barents Sea

Caspian Sea

CAUCASUS MTS.

AZERBAIJAN

Baku ★

GEORGIA   Tbilisi ★

ARMENIA   Yerevan ★

Moscow ★

St. Petersburg ●

UKRAINE

MOLDOVA

Black Sea

Odessa ●

Kiev ★

BELARUS

Minsk ★

Vilnius ★

Istanbul ●

Bucharest ★

Kishinev ★

RUMANIA

SERBIA

BULGARIA

Sophia ★

FINLAND

ESTONIA

LATVIA

Tallinn ★

Riga ★

Helsinki ★

LITHUANIA

RUS.

POLAND

Warsaw ★

SLOVAKIA

Budapest ★

HUNGARY

Belgrade ★

YUGO.

Skople ★

GREECE

Aegean Sea

Crete

Bratislava ★

CZECH REP.

Prague ★

AUSTRIA

Zagreb ★

CROATIA

BOSNIA & HERZ.

Sarajevo ★

Titane ★

ALBANIA

MACEDONIA

Athens ★

Ionian Sea

Gulf of Bothnia

Baltic Sea

SWEDEN

Stockholm ★

KJOLEN MTS.

NORWAY

Oslo ★

DENMARK

Copenhagen ★

Berlin ★

Hamburg ●

GERMANY

Vienna ★

Ljubljana ★

SLOVENIA

ITALY

APENNINES

Rome ★

Naples ●

Tyrrhenian Sea

Sicily

Mediterranean Sea

Sardinia

Mont Blanc ▲

SWITZ.

Bern ★

Munich ★

Bonn ●

Geneva ●

Marseilles ●

Corsica

Adriatic Sea

NETH.

Amsterdam ★

The Hague ★

BEL.

Brussels ★

LUX.

FRANCE

Paris ★

London ★

England

Wales

UNITED KINGDOM

Scotland

Edinburgh ●

Northern Ireland

Belfast ●

IRELAND

Dublin ★

Irish Sea

English Channel

North Sea

Norwegian Sea

Bay of Biscay

Barcelona ●

Balearic IS.

SPAIN

Madrid ★

PORTUGAL

Lisbon ★

Strait of Gibraltar

ICELAND

Reykjavik ★

Arctic Circle

ATLANTIC OCEAN

60°

50°

40°

30°

20°

10°

0°

10°

20°

70°

60°

50°

40°

Aral Sea

Ural R.

Volga R.

Po R.

Rhone R.

Asia

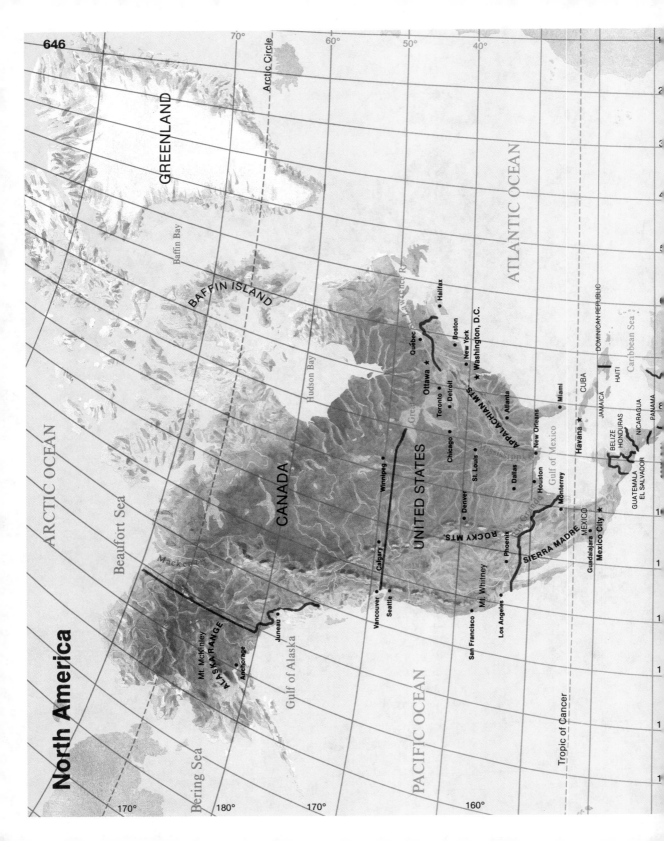

North America

GREENLAND

Baffin Bay

BAFFIN ISLAND

ARCTIC OCEAN

Beaufort Sea

Hudson Bay

CANADA

Mackenzie

Bering Sea

Gulf of Alaska

Mt. McKinley • ALASKA RANGE
Anchorage •
Juneau •

PACIFIC OCEAN

Vancouver •
Seattle •

San Francisco •
Los Angeles •

Mt. Whitney •

Phoenix •

Calgary •

Winnipeg •

Denver •

ROCKY MTS.

UNITED STATES

St. Louis •

Dallas •

Chicago •

Detroit •
Toronto •

Ottawa ★

Québec •

St. Lawrence R.

Halifax •

Boston •
New York •
Washington, D.C. ★

APPALACHIAN MTS.

Atlanta •

New Orleans •

Houston •
Monterrey •

Miami •

Gulf of Mexico

Rio Grande

SIERRA MADRE

MEXICO

Guadalajara •
Mexico City ★

ATLANTIC OCEAN

Havana ★
CUBA

DOMINICAN REPUBLIC

HAITI

Caribbean Sea

JAMAICA

BELIZE
GUATEMALA
EL SALVADOR
HONDURAS
NICARAGUA
PANAMA

Tropic of Cancer

70°
60°
50°
40°

Arctic Circle

170°
180°
170°
160°

South America

PACIFIC OCEAN

ATLANTIC OCEAN

VENEZUELA
Caracas ★
L. Maracaibo

Georgetown ★
Paramaribo
GUYANA
SURINAM
FRENCH GUIANA
Cayenne ★

Guiana Highlands

Bogotá ★

COLOMBIA

Quito ★
ECUADOR
Guayaquil ●

● Manaus

● Belém

Amazon Basin

PERU

BRAZIL

● Recife

Lima ★

Cuzco ●

BOLIVIA

L. Titicaca

La Paz ★

Paraguay R.

★ Brasilia

Sucre ★

Brazilian Highlands

ATACAMA DESERT

PARAGUAY

Gran Chaco

Paraná R.

● Concepción

São Paulo ●

● Rio de Janeiro

★ Asunción

ARGENTINA

Mt. Aconcagua

URUGUAY

Santiago ★

Buenos Aires ★

★ Montevideo
Río de la Plata

CHILE

Pampas

Patagonia

FALKLAND ISLANDS
★ Stanley

Strait of Magellan

Tierra del Fuego

10°
0°
10°
20°
30°
40°
50°

90°   80°   60°   50°   40°   30°

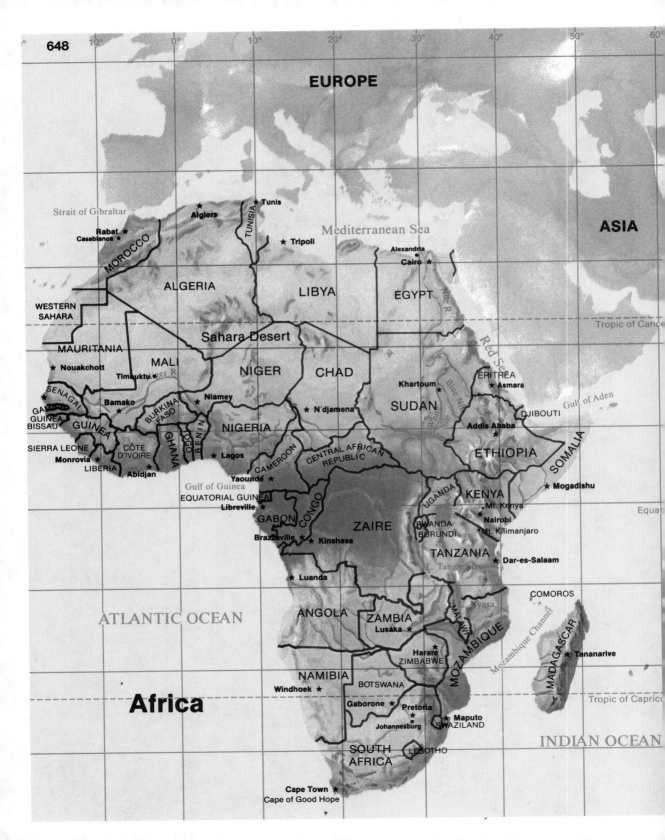

EUROPE

ASIA

Strait of Gibraltar

Mediterranean Sea

★ Tunis

Algiers ★

TUNISIA

Rabat ★

Casablanca ●

MOROCCO

★ Tripoli

Alexandria ●

Cairo ★

WESTERN
SAHARA

ALGERIA

LIBYA

EGYPT

Nile R.

Tropic of Canc

Sahara Desert

Red Sea

Gulf of Aden

MAURITANIA

MALI

★ Nouakchott

Timbuktu ★

Niger R.

NIGER

CHAD

Khartoum ★

ERITREA

★ Asmara

SENEGAL

★ Niamey

SUDAN

Blue Nile

DJIBOUTI

GAM.

Bamako ★

BURKINA
FASO

★ N'djamena

White Nile

Addis Ababa ★

GUINEA
BISSAU

GUINEA

TOGO

NIGERIA

CENTRAL AFRICAN
REPUBLIC

ETHIOPIA

SOMALIA

SIERRA LEONE

CÔTE
D'IVOIRE

GHANA

BENIN

★ Lagos

CAMEROON

Monrovia ●

LIBERIA

Abidjan ●

Yaoundé ★

UGANDA

KENYA

★ Mogadishu

Gulf of Guinea

EQUATORIAL GUINEA

Libreville ★

Mt. Kenya

Equat

GABON

CONGO

ZAIRE

RWANDA
BURUNDI

Nairobi ★

Mt. Kilimanjaro

Brazzaville ★

★ Kinshasa

TANZANIA

★ Dar-es-Salaam

L. Tanganyi

★ Luanda

COMOROS

ATLANTIC OCEAN

ANGOLA

ZAMBIA

MALAWI

Nyasa

Mozambique Channel

MADAGASCAR

★ Tananarive

Lusaka ★

Harare ★

ZIMBABWE

MOZAMBIQUE

Africa

NAMIBIA

BOTSWANA

Windhoek ★

Tropic of Capric

Gaborone ★

Pretoria ★

Maputo ★

Johannesburg ●

SWAZILAND

INDIAN OCEAN

SOUTH
AFRICA

LESOTHO

Cape Town ★

Cape of Good Hope

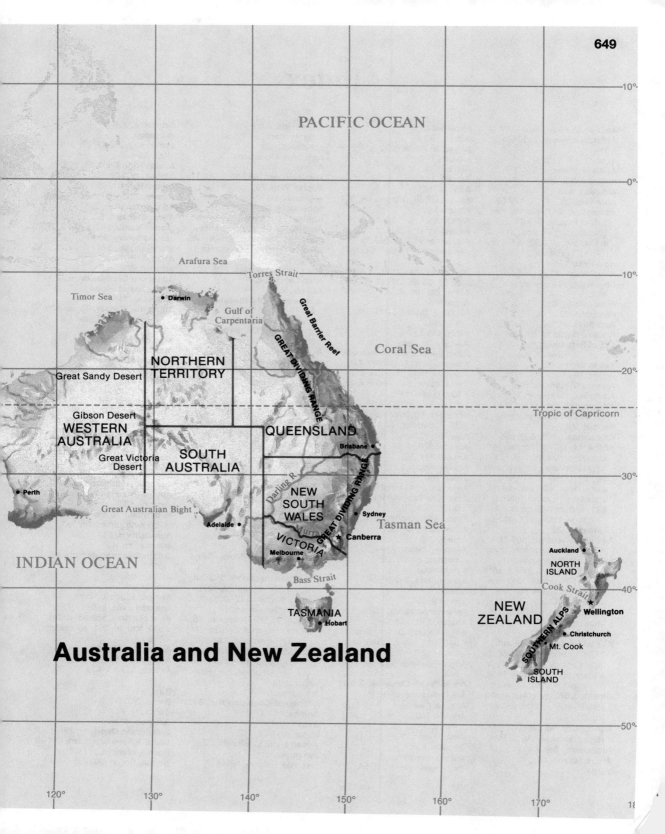

PACIFIC OCEAN

Arafura Sea

Torres Strait

Timor Sea

• Darwin

Gulf of
Carpentaria

Great Barrier Reef

Coral Sea

Great Sandy Desert

NORTHERN
TERRITORY

GREAT DIVIDING RANGE

Gibson Desert

Tropic of Capricorn

WESTERN
AUSTRALIA

SOUTH
AUSTRALIA

QUEENSLAND

Great Victoria
Desert

Brisbane •

• Perth

Darling R.

NEW
SOUTH
WALES

GREAT DIVIDING RANGE

Great Australian Bight

• Sydney

Tasman Sea

Adelaide •

Murray R.

★ Canberra

VICTORIA

INDIAN OCEAN

Melbourne •

Auckland •   •

NORTH
ISLAND

Bass Strait

Cook Strait

NEW
ZEALAND

TASMANIA

SOUTHERN ALPS

★ Wellington

• Hobart

• Christchurch

Mt. Cook •

Australia and New Zealand

SOUTH
ISLAND

120°   130°   140°   150°   160°   170°   18

10°

0°

10°

20°

30°

40°

50°

Index

652

Index

Index

Index

Index

Index

Photograph Credits

The following agencies and individuals have furnished materials to meet the photographic needs of this textbook. We wish to express our gratitude to them for their important contribution.

Aramco
Art Institute of Chicago
Association Frédéric et Iréne Joliot-Curie
Austrian Press and Information Service
Gary Balius
Banner of Truth
Bob Jones University Bible Lands Museum
Bob Jones University Collection of Sacred Art
British Library
British Museum
Churchill Memorial Library, Westminster College
George R. Collins
Grace Collins
Columbus Memorial Library
Steve Crain
Creation Research Society
Stewart Custer
Evan Drake
Egyptian Tourist Authority
David Fisher
Gene Fisher
Fisher Scientific Company
Folger Shakespeare Library
French Embassy Press and Information Division
French Government Tourist Office
German Information Center
Greenville Public Library

Dwight Gustafson
Jim Hargis
Imperial War Museum
Information Service, Rome
Consulate General of Israel
Embassy of Israel
Italian Cultural Institute, N.Y.
Italian Government Travel Office
Italian Tourist Agency
Paul Jantz
Craig Jennings
Lyndon Baines Johnson Library
Tim Keesee
Library of Congress
Edith Long
Maureen McGregor
Metropolitan Museum of Art, N.Y.
National Aeronautics and Space Administration (NASA)
National Archives
National Gallery, London
National Gallery of Art, Washington, D.C.
National Museum of American Art, Washington, D.C.
National Portrait Gallery, Washington, D.C.
Marshall Neal
Nelson-Atkins Museum of Art
Robert Nestor
New York Public Library
Overseas Missionary Fellowship

Parke-Davis, Division of Warner-Lambert Company
Wade Ramsey
Réunion des Musées Nationaux
Ed Richards
Tim Rogers
Russian Federation
Russian Gospel Ministries
Scala Institute
Mark Sidwell
Sword of the Lord
Thyssen-Bornemisza Collection, Switzerland
Turkish Embassy
Turkish Ministry of Tourism
United Nations
United States Air Force
United States Department of State
United States Marine Corps
United States Navy
Unusual Films
Sue Vanderbilt
Venezia
Harry Ward
Western Pennsylvania Conservancy/ Harold Corsini
White House/David Johnson
John Wolsieffer
World Bank
Xinhua News Agency

Title pages

Unusual Films, Wade Ramsey ii-iii; Bob Jones University Bible Lands Museum 1; Aramco 2 (top left), 3 (bottom), 2-3 (background), 4-5 (all); Unusual Films 2 (middle left), 3 (middle); National Archives 2 (middle right); New York Public Library 2 (bottom left)

Introduction

Bob Jones University Collection of Sacred Art 6-7; Unusual Films, Wade Ramsey 9, 10 (both); NASA 12; Unusual Films 13

Unit I Opener

Unusual Films, Wade Ramsey 14-15, 16

Chapter 1

Unusual Films, Wade Ramsey 18, 23, 33 (top), 36, 41, 45 (all); Bob Jones University Collection of Sacred Art 21, 38; Metropolitan Museum of Art, N.Y. 22, 29; Gene Fisher 26; Egyptian Tourist Authority 30-31 (all); British Museum 32; Courtesy of Gene Fisher 27, 33 (bottom), 39; Turkish Ministry of Tourism 35

Chapter 2

Unusual Films, Wade Ramsey 48, 61 (all), 68; Gene Fisher 50; Stewart Custer 52 (both); Courtesy BJU Press Files 56; Bob Jones University Collection of Sacred Art 59; Italian Tourist Agency 62; Metropolitan Museum of Art, N.Y. 65

Chapter 3

Unusual Films, Wade Ramsey 72; Metropolitan Museum of Art, N.Y. 75, 86; Information Service, Rome 76; George R. Collins 79; Italian Cultural Institute, N.Y. 91

Chapter 4

Bob Jones University Collection of Sacred Art 94, 107, 108, 117; Stewart Custer 101, 110; Unusual Films, Wade Ramsey 102; George R. Collins 104 (top); Grace Collins 104 (bottom); French Government Tourist Office 105; Unusual Films 116

Unit II Opener

Unusual Films, Wade Ramsey 120-21; New York Public Library 122

Chapter 5

Unusual Films, Wade Ramsey 124, 128, 142; Turkish Ministry of Tourism 125, 130, 132; Bob Jones University Collection of Sacred Art 131; Tim Keesee 134; Aramco 136-37 (all), 141

Photograph Credits

Chapter 6

Robert Nestor 144; Nelson-Atkins Museum of Art 148; Courtesy of Gene Fisher 149; Greenville County Library 150; Metropolitan Museum of Art, N.Y. 156-57 (both), 161, 171 (all); Xinhua News Agency 158; Aramco 166-67 (both); British Library 170

Unit III Opener

Paul Jantz 174-75, 176

Chapter 7

Bob Jones University Collection of Sacred Art 180, 183, 185; Turkish Embassy 184; Library of Congress 189; Metropolitan Museum of Art, N.Y. 190, 194, 197; Gene Fisher 193

Chapter 8

Evan Drake 200; Bob Jones University Collection of Sacred Art 203, 205; French Embassy Press and Information Division 204, 212, 222; Library of Congress 207, 216; Austrian Press and Information Service, N.Y. 209; Harry Ward 210; BJU Press Files 214; Unusual Films, Wade Ramsey 220

Chapter 9

French Embassy Press and Information Division 224, 248; National Gallery of Art, Washington, D.C. 227; Louvre, Réunion des Musées Nationaux 228; Paul Jantz 229; Dwight Gustafson 231; German Information Center 232; Maureen McGregor 233; Bob Jones University Collection of Sacred Art 237; Reproduced by permission of The Huntington Library, San Marino, California 239; Evan Drake 240 (top left); Ed Richards 240 (bottom left, top right, bottom right); Library of Congress 243; Courtesy of Maureen McGregor 244

Unit IV Opener

Bob Jones University Collection of Sacred Art 252-53, 254

Chapter 10

Italian Tourist Agency 256, 274; National Gallery of Art, Washington, D.C. 259, 260, 266 (bottom right); Italian Government Travel Office 260 (top); Library of Congress 263, 268; Folger Shakespeare Library 264; Venezia 266 (top left); French Embassy Press and Information Division 269; Italian Tourist Agency 271; Bob Jones University Collection of Sacred Art 272, 277; The National Gallery, London 273; BJU Press Files 275

Chapter 11

Bob Jones University Collection of Sacred Art 280, 303; Library of Congress 281, 293, 299; Craig Jennings 284 (both); Scala Institute 285; Unusual Films, Wade Ramsey 286; German Information Center 288-89 (all); Thyssen-Bornemisza Collection, Switzerland 294; National Gallery of Art, Washington, D.C. 295; Courtesy of Gene Fisher 296; Folger Shakespeare Library 298; Jim Hargis 300 (top); George R. Collins 300 (inset)

Chapter 12

Maureen McGregor 311; Library of Congress 312; 320, 321; National Museum of American Art, Washington, D.C./Art Resource, N.Y. 316, 317; John Wolsieffer 319 (all); National Portrait Gallery, Washington, D.C. 324; Metropolitan Museum of Art, N.Y. 325; Courtesy of Gene Fisher 327

Unit V Opener

Réunion des Musées Nationaux 331-32, 333

Chapter 13

Library of Congress 334, 339, 345 (both), 347, 355; Bob Jones University Collection of Sacred Art 336, 349, 351; National Gallery, London 337; Dwight Gustafson 340; German Information Center 342; Ed Richards 343; Austrian Press and Information Service 344, 354

Chapter 14

NASA 363 (top); Maureen McGregor 363 (bottom); Library of Congress 364, 370, 373 (bottom), 375 (Susanna Wesley), 382, 383; Fisher Scientific Company 365; Courtesy of Parke-Davis, Division of Warner-Lambert Company 366; National Gallery of Art, Washington, D.C. 368, 378 (left), 379 (top); German Information Center 373 (top); Ed Richards 378 (bottom right, inset); Bob Jones University Collection of Sacred Art 379 (bottom); George R. Collins 380

Chapter 15

George R. Collins 388, 390, 391 (both), 393; Library of Congress 386, 400, 407, 408; Metropolitan Museum of Art, N.Y. 392; French Embassy Press and Information Division 395, 396, 398, 399, 406; National Gallery of Art, Washington, D.C. 405

Unit VI Opener

George R. Collins 412-13, 414

Chapter 16

Austrian Press and Information Division 418; Edith Long 420; French Embassy Press and Information Division 424; Library of Congress 425, 426, 427, 438 (top); Courtesy of Mark Sidwell 428, 429, 430 (right), 432, 434, 436, 438 (right), 439 (both); Marshall Neal 430 (left); Tim Keesee 433; Maureen McGregor 435; Greenville County Library 437; The Art Institute of Chicago 440; National Gallery of Art, Washington, D.C. 441

Chapter 17

Unusual Films, Tim Rogers 444; Library of Congress 447 (both), 451, 454, 455, 457, 459, 460 (right), 463, 465 (right); General Electric Company 452; Courtesy of Mark Sidwell 458 (left), 467 (left); Sword of the Lord 462; Association Frédéric et Irène Joliot-Curie 465 (left); National Gallery of Art, Washington, D.C. 467 (right), 468 (both), 469 (right); Metropolitan Museum of Art, N.Y. 469 (left)

Chapter 18

National Portrait Gallery, Washington, D.C. 472; National Archives 476, 486 (bottom); Creation Research Society 478; Columbus Memorial Library 480; Greenville County Library 484; Overseas Missionary Fellowship 485; Library of Congress 486 (top), 489, 490; World Bank 493

Unit VII Opener

NASA 496-97, 498

Chapter 19

George R. Collins 500; Library of Congress 501, 515; National Archives 506, 509, 511, 513, 514, 517; Imperial War Museum 508; Ed Richards 519

Chapter 20

National Archives 524, 528, 532, 538, 541 (bottom), 542, 545 (right); Library of Congress 529, 531, 536, 537, 539, 541 (top), 545 (left); Russian Gospel Ministries 535; National Gallery of Art, Washington, D.C. 543; The Western Pennsylvania Conservancy/Harold Corsini 544

Chapter 21

National Archives 548, 550, 551, 552 (top), 553, 555, 564 (bottom), 566 (both), 567, 570 (both), 573 (top right, bottom right); Library of Congress 552 (bottom), 554, 572; Imperial War Museum 558, 565; BJU Press Files 560, 561, 563, 564 (inset); Ed Richards 562; U.S. Air Force 573 (left)

Chapter 22

German Information Center 576, 584, 594, 599 (bottom); Churchill Memorial Library, Westminster College 579; National Archives 581 (left), 587, 589, 590, 596; Library of Congress 581 (right), 583, 592 (left); U.S. Air Force 585, 593; U.S. Department of State 586; Courtesy of Steve Crain 591; U.S. Navy 592 (right); Russian Federation 593 (left), 598, 602; Tim Keesee 599 (top); Sue Vanderbilt 600; Gary Balius 604

Chapter 23

U.S. Marine Corps 606, 630, 632, 633; BJU Press Files 607; United Nations 608, 609 (bottom), 622; Creation Research Society 609 (top); Banner of Truth 611; Library of Congress 613 (top inset), 620; NASA 613 (top left); Lyndon Baines Johnson Library 613 (bottom left); White House 613 (bottom right); German Information Center 615; White House, David Johnson 617 (left); George R. Collins 617 (right); World Bank 619, 621, 624 (both); Unusual Films, Wade Ramsey 626, 631; Consulate General of Israel 627 (top left, top right); Embassy of Israel 628

Epilogue

Unusual Films, Wade Ramsey 636, 641; National Gallery of Art, Washington, D.C. 638; Bob Jones University Collection of Sacred Art 640